LAW AS RELIGION, RELIGION AS LAW

The conventional approach to law and religion assumes that these are competing domains, which raises questions about the freedom of, and from, religion; alternate commitments of religion and human rights; and respective jurisdictions of civil and religious courts. This volume moves beyond this competitive paradigm to consider law and religion as overlapping and interrelated frameworks that structure the social order, arguing that law and religion share similar properties and have a symbiotic relationship. Moreover, many legal systems exhibit religious characteristics, informing their notions of authority, precedent, rituals and canonical texts, and most religions invoke legal concepts or terminology. The contributors address this blurring of law and religion in the contexts of political theology, secularism, church-state conflicts, and the foundational idea of divine law. This title is also available as Open Access on Cambridge Core.

David C. Flatto is Professor of Law and Jewish philosophy at The Hebrew University of Jerusalem. His most recent book is The Crown and the Courts: Separation of Powers in the Early Imagination (Harvard University Press, 2020).

Benjamin Porat is Professor of Law, Vice-Dean of the Faculty of Law, and the Director of the Matz Institute for Research in Jewish Law, at The Hebrew University of Jerusalem. He is the author of The Principles of Welfare Regulations: From Biblical Law to Rabbinic Literature (2019).

Law As Religion, Religion As Law

Edited by

DAVID C. FLATTO

The Hebrew University of Jerusalem

BENJAMIN PORAT

The Hebrew University of Jerusalem

CAMBRIDGE
UNIVERSITY PRESS

CAMBRIDGE
UNIVERSITY PRESS

Shaftesbury Road, Cambridge CB2 8EA, United Kingdom

One Liberty Plaza, 20th Floor, New York, NY 10006, USA

477 Williamstown Road, Port Melbourne, VIC 3207, Australia

314–321, 3rd Floor, Plot 3, Splendor Forum, Jasola District Centre, New Delhi – 110025, India

103 Penang Road, #05–06/07, Visioncrest Commercial, Singapore 238467

Cambridge University Press is part of Cambridge University Press & Assessment, a department of the University of Cambridge.

We share the University's mission to contribute to society through the pursuit of education, learning and research at the highest international levels of excellence.

www.cambridge.org
Information on this title: www.cambridge.org/9781108707923

DOI : 10.1017/9781108760997

First published 2022
First paperback edition 2025

A catalogue record for this publication is available from the British Library

Library of Congress Cataloging-in-Publication data
NAMES: Porat, Benny, editor. | Flatto, David C., editor.
TITLE: Law as religion, religion as law / edited by Benjamin Porat, Hebrew University of Jerusalem; David C. Flatto, Hebrew University of Jerusalem.
DESCRIPTION: Cambridge, United Kingdom ; New York, NY : Cambridge University Press, 2022. | Includes bibliographical references and index.
IDENTIFIERS: LCCN 2021051470 (print) | LCCN 2021051471 (ebook) | ISBN 9781108486538 (hardback) | ISBN 9781108707923 (paperback) | ISBN 9781108760997 (ebook)
SUBJECTS: LCSH: Religious law and legislation. | Jewish law. | Canon law. | Religion and law.
CLASSIFICATION: LCC KB270 .L39 2022 (print) | LCC KB270 (ebook) | DDC 208/.4–dc23/eng/20220128
LC record available at https://lccn.loc.gov/2021051470
LC ebook record available at https://lccn.loc.gov/2021051471

ISBN 978-1-108-48653-8 Hardback
ISBN 978-1-108-70792-3 Paperback

Contents

List of Contributors *page* vii

Introduction 1
David C. Flatto and Benjamin Porat

A SANCTIFICATION AND SECULARIZATION 5

1 **Desanctification of Law and the Problem of Absolutes** 7
Jeremy Waldron

2 **The Paradox of Human Rights Discourse and the Jewish Legal Tradition** 29
Suzanne Last Stone

3 **Sovereign Imaginaries**
Visualizing the Sacred Foundation of Law's Authority 53
Richard K. Sherwin

B LEGAL-RELIGIOUS LANGUAGE 81

4 ***Dat*: From Law to Religion**
The Transformation of a Formative Term in Modern Times 83
Abraham Melamed

5 **Law As Religion, Religion As Law**
Halakhah from a Semiotic Point of View 113
Bernard S. Jackson

6 **Canonicity As a Defining Feature of Legal and Religious Discourse**
A Programmatic Essay 151
Daniel Reifman

C LEGAL-THEOLOGICAL ROOTS 171

7 **Exceptional Grace**
Religion As the Sovereign Suspension of Law 173
Robert A. Yelle

8 **A Bad Man Theory of Religious Law (Numbers 15:30–31 and Its Afterlife)** 197
David C. Flatto

9 **Soviet Law and Political Religion** 225
Dmytro Vovk

10 **International Law as Evangelism** 248
Kevin Crow

D RELIGIOUS CONCEPTIONS OF LAW 271

11 **"Enjoin Them upon Your Children to Keep" (Deuteronomy 32:46)**
Law as Commandment and Legacy, or, Robert Cover Meets Midrash 273
Steven D. Fraade

12 **"Between Man and God" and "Between Man and His Fellow"**
Categories in Polemical Context 291
Itzhak Brand

13 **Christian Feasts and Administration of Roman Justice in Late Antiquity** 314
Silvia Schiavo

E LAW IN FORMATION: RELIGIOUS PERSPECTIVES 341

14 **Law as a Problematic Aspect of Religion**
Paul's Skepticism in a Broader Jewish Context 343
Serge Ruzer

15 **When Law Meets Theology**
Legality and Revelation in the Jewish, Islamic, and Zoroastrian Traditions in the Abbasid Period 362
Yishai Kiel

Contributors

Itzhak Brand, Bar-Ilan University

Kevin Crow, Asia School of Business and MIT Sloan School of Management

David C. Flatto, The Hebrew University of Jerusalem

Steven D. Fraade, Yale University

Bernard S. Jackson, University of Manchester

Yishai Kiel, The Hebrew University of Jerusalem

Suzanne Last Stone, Cardozo School of Law, Yeshiva University

Abraham Melamed, University of Haifa

Benjamin Porat, The Hebrew University of Jerusalem

Daniel Reifman, Institute for Advanced Torah Studies, Bar Ilan University

Serge Ruzer, The Hebrew University of Jerusalem

Silvia Schiavo, University of Ferrara

Richard K. Sherwin, New York Law School

Dmytro Vovk, Yaroslav Mudryi National Law University

Jeremy Waldron, New York University School of Law

Robert A. Yelle, Ludwig Maximilian University, Munich

Introduction

David C. Flatto and Benjamin Porat

The conventional approach to evaluating the relationship between law and religion operates on the assumption that these are discrete domains that often compete, and at times even clash, with one another. This orientation animates scholarship and public discourse on such salient topics as mediating between church and state; balancing freedom of religion and freedom from religion; weighing the alternate commitments of religion and human rights; and delimiting the respective jurisdictions of civil and religious courts.

A dichotomous paradigm, however, is not the only way to conceptualize the intersection between law and religion. The "Law As Religion, Religion As Law" volume explores a different perspective that has emerged in recent scholarship which regards law and religion as overlapping frameworks that structure the lives of individuals as well as the social order. From this vantage point, law and religion arguably share similar properties, and may even have a symbiotic relationship. Moreover, many legal systems exhibit religious characteristics, informing their notions of authority, precedent, ritual and canonical texts, and most religions invoke legal concepts or terminology (this phenomenon is especially evident in the thick normative traditions of the Abrahamic religions). This suggestive blurring of categories pervades the wide-ranging chapters that comprise this volume.

By exploring manifold interconnections between religion and law, the chapters of the "Law As Religion, Religion As Law" volume participate in, and contribute to, several influential discourses that are ongoing in the academy and the public square.

One is the surge of interest in political theology, a mode of inquiry that critiques secular liberal political theory and posits that certain modern sovereign powers and principles derive from, or replace, theological institutions or doctrines. Recent studies by Paul Kahn, Mark Lilla, and Seyla Benhabib have evaluated this claim in the political domain,[1] and Harold Berman, Steven Smith, and Jeremy Waldron

[1] Paul W. Kahn, Political Theology: Four New Chapters on the Concept of Sovereignty (2011); Mark Lilla, The Stillborn God (2007); Seyla Benhabib, Dignity in Adversity (2011).

have focused on analogous themes in the legal sphere.[2] In a critical essay surveying this growing field, Cecile Laborde argues persuasively that political theology forces commentators to think harder about the category of religion.[3] This volume contains penetrating studies that honor this call by reevaluating the nexus between religion, law, and politics from a plurality of perspectives that lend new depth to this inquiry.

A second, related, scholarly discourse on secularism has challenged the Weberian account of modernity as a period of growing disenchantment. Indeed, political and empirical developments of the past decades have further unsettled long-held predictions about the waning of religion. Employing the lenses of anthropology, philosophy, sociology, and history, scholars have instead considered the manner in which secularism is itself a constructed category (see, e.g., the works of Asad, Taylor, Berger, Cavanaugh, as well as the more recent studies of Copson and Crane).[4] By revisiting and complicating the categories of "law" and "religion," and their presumptive connotations in a "secular age," from an analogously broad range of disciplines, this volume adds critical texture to these arguments.

A third relevant discourse relates to contemporary approaches to church and state. Certain scholars have presented trenchant criticisms of traditional paradigms (Laborde, Shakman Hurd, Mahmood)[5] or called for important revisions of leading church-state doctrines (Eisgruber and Sager, Greenawalt).[6] Some have promoted greater integration of religious minorities into the public square, but this has also evoked concerns about the vexing social challenges that this would precipitate. For instance, Michael Ignatieff has expressed skepticism about whether liberal polities can find ways to accommodate religious legal traditions within the larger normative order.[7] Not discounting the formidable hurdles that may be encountered, such a rejoinder presupposes certain narrow or rigid definitions of law and religion. The studies in this volume thus suggest significant modifications worth considering in this regard.

Finally, a number of recent pioneering works in the field of religious studies have addressed the foundational theme of divine law. In a sweeping study that relates to

2 Harold Berman, Faith and Order: The Reconciliation of Law and Religion (1993); Steven D. Smith, The Disenchantment of Secular Discourse (2010); Jeremy Waldron, God, Locke, and Equality: Christian Foundations of Locke's Political Thought (2002).

3 Cecile Laborde, *Three Theses about Political Theology: Some Comments on Seyla Benhabib's 'Return of Political Theology'* 17 Crit. Rev. Int. Soc. Political Philos. 689–96 (2014).

4 Talal Asad, Formations of the Secular (2003); Charles Taylor, A Secular Age (2007); Peter L. Berger, The Desecularization of the World: Resurgent Religion and World Politics (1999); William T. Cavanaugh, Theopolitical Imagination (2003); Andrew Copson, Secularism: Politics, Religion and Freedom (2017); Tim Crane, The Meaning of Belief: Religion from an Atheist's Point of View (2017).

5 Cecile Laborde, Liberalism's Religion (2017); Elizabeth Shakman Hurd, Beyond Religious Freedom: The New Global Politics of Religion (2015); Saba Mahmood, Religious Difference in a Secular Age: A Minority Report (2015).

6 Christopher L. Eisgruber and Lawrence G. Sager, Religious Freedom and the Constitution (2007); Kent Greenawalt, Religion and the Constitution (2006–08).

7 Michael Ignatieff, *Making Room for God*, The New York Review of Books, June 28, 2018.

facets of medieval Judaism, Christianity, and Islam, Remi Brague presents a religious-philosophical analysis of the idea that norms which guide human actions are ultimately rooted in the divine realm.[8] A subsequent work by Christine Hayes returns to antiquity, where conceptions of divine law were first formulated and proved to be highly consequential.[9] Surveying a substantial body of early Greco-Roman and Jewish-Christian literature, Hayes identifies two contrasting paradigms of divine law. Both of these works, which are panoramic in scope, invite subsequent research into particular aspects of religious legal traditions, and the ways they navigate the tension between religion and law. In this vein, this volume offers discrete studies that add greater resolution and important nuance to these broader accounts.

The numerous chapters that comprise this volume implicate all of these discourses, either directly or indirectly, and advance them forward by employing multidisciplinary perspectives, evaluating specific case studies and engaging in analyses that straddle the ancient and modern periods.

This volume represents the culmination of a two-year research project that was convened at the Hebrew University dedicated to exploring new perspectives on law and religion, which included numerous workshops and an international conference. Leading scholars who participated in this project have contributed original chapters to this volume exploring "Law As Religion, Religion As Law" from a range of perspectives, religions and cultures, time periods, and subject matters.

This book benefited from the continual guidance of the outstanding editorial team at Cambridge University Press, led by Matt Gallaway, as well as Jane Bowbrick, Cameron Daddis, Akash Datchinamurthy, Jadyn Fauconier-Herry and Helen Kitto. We also wish to thank Gadi Haber, Rotem Sapir-Jacobs, and Elisheva Finkelman for their excellent assistance in preparing the manuscript for publication. Finally, we wish to thank the Aharon Barak Center for Interdisciplinary Legal Research for its generous financial support of our research project and the production of this volume.

8 Remi Brague, The Law of God: The Philosophical History of an Idea (2007).

9 Christine Hayes, What's Divine about Divine Law? Early Perspectives (2015).

A

Sanctification and Secularization

1

Desanctification of Law and the Problem of Absolutes

Jeremy Waldron

I INTRODUCTION

Desanctification of law? – we never even knew it was holy! Sure, centuries or millennia ago, positive law was bound up with religion. Trial was by combat or ordeal, so that God could render a verdict. The boundaries of cities and private property were consecrated by religious processions. Treaties were deposited in temples so the deities could supervise their implementation.[1] Contracts were spoken of as sacred. Writs and processes sounded in liturgy and magic as much as in rational inquiry.[2] The sovereign conceived as the fount of justice was anointed "with the oil of gladness at the hands of priests and prophets."[3] A great philosopher writing thousands of years ago about the rule of law could say, "He who bids the law rule may be deemed to bid God and Reason alone rule, but he who bids man rule adds an element of the beast," and expect to be understood.[4] Certain laws were revered as untouchable by human rulers because they dwelt in justice with the gods: "their life is not of to-day or yesterday, but from all time, and no man knows when they were first put forth."[5] And the sanction of divine authority, not to mention the threat of divine punishment, was taken for granted as key to the viability of any legal system.

But that was then. A few relics of this sanctity remain – some incantations ("God save this honorable court"), oaths taken on Bibles still, bishops as legislators (in the United Kingdom), and chaplains at executions. But nothing that would warrant excitement or hysteria or even a hesitant lecture about "desanctification."

The desanctification that I want to talk about in this chapter is not just the disentanglement of religion from law. It is also not just the separation of church and state, the sort of thing that prohibits the privileging of any particular religion, let

[1] See Delbert R. Hillers, Covenant: The History of a Biblical Idea 6 (1969).

[2] See Aldo Schiavone, The Invention of Law in the West Ch. 1 (2012).

[3] From the English Coronation Rite: see David Baldwin, Royal Prayer: A Surprising History vii (2009).

[4] The Politics of Aristotle Book III, Ch. xvi, 1287a, at 146 (Ernest Barker ed., 1958).

[5] Sophocles, Antigone 38, l. 455 (Ruby Blundell ed., 1998).

alone establishment or dominionism.[6] Nor is desanctification the sort of thing that is compromised just because law continues to respect the place of religion in people's lives through principles of religious liberty, for example, and techniques of accommodation.[7] All that is quite compatible with desanctification. Desanctification certainly doesn't just mean pulling down tablets with the Ten Commandments inscribed on them from the walls of American courtrooms.

I am thinking of it instead as a process whereby certain kinds of meaning and value are drained from legal norms and institutions. It is a process described by the early twentieth-century sociologist Max Weber in his late writings about the rationalization of law and the general disenchantment of the world.[8] I'll say more about Weber in a moment, but in this context desanctification involves the withering away of a spirit of transcendent normativity, a spirit that has in the past sustained certain legal absolutes and encouraged (indeed, required) us to press the hardest questions we can about the justice of our legal arrangements, but which now seems to be at odds with the rational spirit of the age.

Understood in this way, desanctification is not necessarily about religion at all. True, the transcendent normativity that has withered away is something that might once upon a time have been associated naturally with religion. It was not inappropriate to use words like "sacred" to refer to it. But it need not be understood in formally religious terms – though, as we shall see, participants in law's desanctification are still haunted by the specter of the divine. That's what frightens them; that's what they want to extirpate. (Some Weberian discussions even talk of "the disenchantment of religion" as well as the desanctification of law.)[9]

Anyway, religious or not, a dimension of transcendent normativity is supposed to have gone from law and from the evaluation of law. Blinking clear-eyed in the hard light of day, we can no longer apprehend certain kinds of deontic requirements that legal provisions used to embody or certain kinds of deontic principles that law used to respond to. This is what I would like to discuss.

6 Dominionism is a conservative doctrine that identifies the United States as a Christian nation and looks forward to the establishment there of a theocratic form of government that will rule on the basis of Biblical law. See BRUCE BARRON, HEAVEN ON EARTH? THE SOCIAL AND POLITICAL AGENDAS OF DOMINION THEOLOGY (1992).

7 See, e.g., Burwell v. Hobby Lobby Stores 573 U.S. 682 (2014). See also the discussion of religious accommodations in Jeremy Waldron, *One Law for All? The Logic of Cultural Accommodation*, 59 WASH. & LEE L. REV. 3 (2002).

8 My reference to Weber's late writings means works produced by him around the time of his death in 1919.

9 Michael Löwy, *Anticapitalist Readings of Weber's* Protestant Ethic: *Ernst Bloch, Walter Benjamin, György Lukacs, Erich Fromm*, 9 LOGOS 1 (2010): "Max Weber admired the protestant ethic as one of the great moments in the disenchantment of religion, and its transformation from magic rituals into an ethical life-conduct." See also MARCEL GAUCHET, THE DISENCHANTMENT OF THE WORLD: A POLITICAL HISTORY OF RELIGION (Oscar Burge trans., 1997).

II MAX WEBER

A body of practical reason can be desanctified as to its form or desanctified as to its content. Or both. I am going to begin with desanctification of the *form* of law – a process described by Max Weber in his late work, particularly in the second volume of his unwieldy and unfinished *Economy and Society*.[10] As we shall see, Jürgen Habermas provides a useful gloss on Weber's account, though Habermas also engages with it critically; he has his own agenda to pursue, which is to show that despite what Weber says, his (Habermas's) moral method is still available for use in evaluating modern law.[11] I won't say much about this rather self-serving critique, but since Habermas has a good understanding of what Weber meant, I shall from time to time draw on his words as a gloss on Weber's.

In *Economy and Society*, Weber describes what he calls the rationalization and formalization of law, a process that develops alongside the growth of an increasingly complex economic system. Legal machinery is needed to resolve "increasingly complex conflicts of interests."[12] Modern markets and large-scale capitalist industry require the commodification of almost all goods and the development of more and more complex instruments of exchange.

"[T]he calculability of the functioning of the coercive machinery" of government is the "technical prerequisite" of "development of a market economy," says Weber.[13] But that calculability comes at a cost. Law in the modern world has such complex tasks to perform and so many technical conceptions to relate to one another that it has to develop a conceptual apparatus of its own. Ordinary language categories will not do; nor will those that are made available in classic natural law theory. Law has to produce calculability but it cannot produce intuitive calculability. Instead, in order to guarantee its consistency and systematicity, events and transactions have to be characterized in law's own terms, which are no longer intuitive categories. Intuitive understanding is lost, but there is a corresponding gain in deductive rigor.

So, for example, a legal description of a transaction or event together with a set of accompanying conditions will generate more or less deductively a legal description of consequences. But the transactions, events, conditions, and consequences have to be classified in the conceptual matrix of legal logic, which has been established precisely to make these inferences work. As Weber put it, "facts of life are juridically construed in order to make them fit the abstract propositions of law and in accordance with the maxim that nothing can exist in the realm of law unless it can be

10 Cite to MAX WEBER, ECONOMY AND SOCIETY, two volumes (Guenther Roth & Claus Wittich eds., 1978) – hereinafter "WEBER, E&S." I also make use of MAX WEBER ON LAW IN ECONOMY AND SOCIETY (Max Rheinstein ed., 1954) – hereinafter "WEBER in Rheinstein."

11 See JÜRGEN HABERMAS, THE THEORY OF COMMUNICATIVE ACTION: VOL. 1: REASON AND RATIONALIZATION OF SOCIETY (Thomas McCarthy trans., 1981) – hereinafter "HABERMAS, TCA." Habermas points out that even after we turn law into a mere instrumentality, we can still deliberate argumentatively about the values and social purposes it should serve (HABERMAS, TCA, at 224).

12 WEBER in Rheinstein, *supra* note 10, at 61.

13 *Id.*, at 72.

'conceived' by the jurist in conformity with those 'principles' which are revealed to him by legal science."[14] The whole thing must constitute a formal system,[15] involving what Habermas calls "the systematization of legal propositions, the coherence of legal doctrine, that is to say, the rationalization of law according to internal, purely formal criteria of analytic conceptual structure, deductive rigor, principled explanation and justification, and the like."[16]

The result is technical law, increasingly distant from the comprehension of the layman – "continuous growth of the technical elements in the law and hence of its character as a specialist's domain."[17] A legal specialist is no longer a specialist in the interplay of law and justice; instead he is someone who has gained the ability to manipulate and apply these specifically legal concepts but lost any inclination to associate with them intuitive or ordinary-language meaning or with the meanings we might find in ordinary moral expressions.

All of this is part and parcel of what Weber calls "the overall disenchantment of the world, a process of intellectualization and rationalization that has been at work in Western culture for thousands of years."[18] Our ability to control everything by means of technology and calculation seems to require that "the ultimate and most sublime values have withdrawn from public life. They have retreated either into the abstract realm of mystical life or into the fraternal feelings of personal relations between individuals."[19] Everything is detail; everything is means–end rationality. Ultimate values no longer frame any "big picture." At any rate, they are no longer part of the lawyer's public world. As Habermas glosses Weber's view, "The disenchantment of the religious worldview and the decentration of world understanding are the presuppositions for a transformation of sacred legal concepts."[20] Law no longer presents its norms and concepts for evaluation as moral principles. Instead it presents an interlocking array of technical elements for holistic evaluation in terms of the contribution made by the array to the efficient organization of market relations.

14 WEBER, E&S, *supra* note 10, at ii, 885.

15 WEBER in Rheinstein, *supra* note 10, at 64, states the conditions of formalization as follows: "[F]irst, . . . every concrete legal decision be the 'application' of an abstract legal proposition to a concrete 'fact situation'; second, that it must be possible in every concrete case to derive the decision from abstract legal propositions by means of a legal logic; third, that the law must . . . constitute a 'gapless' system of legal propositions, or must, at least, be treated as if it were such a system; fourth that whatever cannot be 'construed' legally in rational terms is also legally irrelevant; and fifth, that every social action of human beings must always be visualized as either an 'application' or 'execution' of legal propositions, or as an infringement thereof."

16 HABERMAS, TCA, *supra* note 11, at 256.

17 WEBER, E&S, *supra* note 10, at ii, 895.

18 Max Weber, *Science As a Vocation*, in MAX WEBER, THE VOCATION LECTURES, 13 (David Owen & Tracy Strong eds., 2004).

19 *Id.*, at 30.

20 HABERMAS, TCA, *supra* note 11, at 257.

III UNEVENNESS AND RESISTANCE

So far as legal developments are concerned, Habermas notes that, according to Weber, the process we have been describing "appears very unevenly in the legal developments of different nations [and] more pronouncedly in countries within a tradition of Roman law."[21] At the end of the nineteenth century, the rationalization of law is associated with codification and with law in Continental Europe. In Anglo-American law, by contrast, there was – certainly in Weber's day – not so much codification; the Common Law and its methods (which Weber disparaged as "inductive case-to-case methodology" and "charismatic judging and law-finding") continued to be dominant. There was less in the way of legal science, as Weber understood it.[22] And yet capitalism flourished.[23]

In *Economy and Society*, Weber also discussed various forms of push-back against this formalization of law where it did happen – pushback motivated by status concerns on the part of lawyers and judges who felt demeaned by the "mechanical jurisprudence" of law's formalism.[24] But it wasn't just the technicians who protested. The sentiments of some laymen also demanded a more intuitive (perhaps even moralized) body of law.[25] They thought law should have continued to have recourse to a "metapositive" objective natural law with an emphasis on ideas like justice and dignity.[26]

But this was futile, according to Weber. "The reproduction of social life was . . . far too complex to be comprehended in the meager normative motifs of natural law."[27] Once the process of rationalization was underway, "questions concerning the institutional embodiment of moral-practical rationality are not only shoved aside . . . : they now appear to be the source of irrationality," at any rate "of motives that weaken the formal rationalism of law."[28] According to Weber, "the role played in the development of the law by purely 'emotional' factors, such as the so-called 'sense of justice'"[29] represented a "flight into the irrational."[30]

Even so, it wasn't just moralists who pushed back in this way. The formal rationalization of law was also challenged from a point of view that emphasized

21 *Id.*, at 256.

22 WEBER E&S, *supra* note 10, at ii, 890–91.

23 AS MARK KELMAN, A GUIDE TO CRITICAL LEGAL STUDIES 245–46 (1987), puts it, the "powerful Weberian claim that developing capitalism requires a high degree of rule-bound-formality to increase certainty in planning is undercut by Weber's own comparative observations (England, for instance, industrialized without a highly predictable legal code)."

24 WEBER E&S, *supra* note 10, at ii, 886.

25 *Id.*, at 892.

26 *Id.*, at 885–88.

27 JÜRGEN HABERMAS, BETWEEN FACTS AND NORMS: CONTRIBUTIONS TO AN DISCOURSE THEORY OF LAW AND DEMOCRACY 45 (William Rehg trans., 1996), 45.

28 HABERMAS, TCA, *supra* note 11, at 267.

29 WEBER in Rheinstein, *supra* note 10, at 75.

30 WEBER E&S, *supra* note 10, at ii, 888–89.

the expectations of business people and the interpretation of legal propositions in terms of the meaning they would have in ordinary commerce.[31]

Max Rheinstein in his introduction to *Max Weber on Law in Economy and Society* presents this as being like the debate between formalists and realists in the early twentieth-century United States, with the realist side represented for example in Felix Cohen's critique of formalist jargon in "Transcendental Nonsense and the Functional Approach."[32] Cohen thought it was still possible to move away from the technical vocabulary of legal science to the sociologically and economically more realistic terms of public policy discourse for the formulation and elaboration of law. To a certain extent this succeeded, in American jurisprudence at least, with formalism being regarded these days by most American lawyers as a fatuous aberration. (We will come back to this – at length – in Section V of the chapter.)

But Weber's conclusion was different. He thought Common Law and Common Law jurisprudence was declining, even in its strongholds. He thought the increasingly technical character of law was irreversible, and notwithstanding all the pushback, the legal ignorance of the layman was bound to increase. Modern law could not now be regarded as anything other than "a rational technical apparatus which is continually transformable in the light of expediential considerations and devoid of all sacredness of content."[33]

IV NO ROOM FOR ABSOLUTES

To summarize then: the Weberian rationalization of law that I am associating with its desanctification combined a number of trends. The normativity of law was now systemic, rather than characteristic of any proposition in particular. No particular provision carried any categorical normativity considered as detached; its normativity was always relative to the system of deductively interconnected propositions of which it was a part. So far as justification is concerned, it was the whole system that was answerable to the demands of what Weber referred to as "expediential considerations" – that is, to ongoing experience of how the system worked for industry, commerce, and markets.

At the same time, the language of the law tended to become more technical, distancing it from the ordinary vocabulary in which moral demands were expressed, not to mention the vocabulary that characterized the more powerful demands of natural law. The process was confusing, however, since the technical language used in legal formalization often involved adding layers of systemically determined meaning to ordinary-language terms, rather than the invention of a whole new technical jargon.

31 *Id.*, at 885.

32 See Rheinstein's introduction, *supra* note 10, at xlvii–lxvii. See also Felix Cohen, *Transcendental Nonsense and the Functional Approach*, 35 COLUM. L. REV. 809 (1935).

33 WEBER E&S, *supra* note 10, at ii, 895.

This created the impression that legal formalization refuted – rather than just stood aloof from – classical natural law norms of property, contract, etc.

True, inasmuch as this whole process was uneven and incomplete, occasionally the ordinary-language meaning of legal propositions would erupt into view and be accorded substantive importance by a judge or a party. But there was no telling when this would happen, and the haphazardness of its occurrence and the attempts to deal with it under the auspices of formalized law created an additional layer of technical challenge to those who were trying to approach the law in ordinary-language terms.[34]

These developments made it harder overall to approach private law in moral terms. Certainly, it was not easy to sustain positions associated with the sanctity of property rights and contracts. One could hardly think of *pacta sunt servanda* or the inviolability of property rights as having sacred status now that "contract" and "property" had become in effect technical terms, whose normativity was determined systemically rather than by reference to some story we might tell – a Lockean story, for example – about the essential importance of the substantive content of any particular norm. In any case, it was harder to sustain a consistent sense of the importance of these concepts, when they surfaced only haphazardly in formal legal discourse. There came to seem something quaint and old-fashioned about regarding them as anything like absolutes.

Even the idea of *legal obligation* became problematic and remains so, as evidenced by the struggle of some modern American jurists to try to retrieve a sense in which contract law and tort law, for example, express categorical as opposed to negotiable obligations. (Here I have in mind the work of people like John Macpherson and Ben Zipursky in tort law and Peter Linzer in contract law pushing back against doctrines of "efficient breach.")[35] The doctrine of the "efficient breach" of ordinary civil obligations has meant their reconception as something more like options than like deontic requirements. We used to talk of the sanctity of contracts, but now we just balance different positions in a matrix of costs and benefits. Or that's the way it sometimes seems.

V LEGAL REALISM

I mentioned earlier that Max Rheinstein, one of Max Weber's American editors, presented Weber's account of technical rationalization as the victory of a certain sort of legal formalism.[36] We saw Weber talking too of the irrationality of any attempt to

34 Duncan Kennedy, *Form and Substance in Private Law Adjudication*, 89 HARV. L. REV. 1685, 1776 (1976): "[T]he acknowledgement of contradiction makes it easier to understand judicial behavior that offends the ideal of the judge as a supremely rational being. The judge cannot, any more than the analyst, avoid the moment of truth in which one simply shifts modes."

35 See, e.g., John Goldberg & Ben Zipursky, *Torts As Wrongs*, 88 TEX. L. REV. 917 (2010); and Peter Linzer, *On the Amorality of Contract Remedies – Efficiency, Equity, and the Second Restatement*, 81 COLUM. L. REV. 111 (1981).

36 See *supra* note 33 and accompanying text.

reconcile the technical vocabulary of formalized law with the professional expectations of business people, except insofar as they were legally trained, let alone the normative expectations of the ordinary citizen. But there is more to say about the fate of formalism in the American context, and, as Rheinstein acknowledged, a different story to be told in the USA about the processes of pushback against formalization.

Today, in American legal theory, it is legal formalism that is seen as irrational or, even worse, as sinister – for a lot of the legal realist critique was against the class interests being covertly promoted under cover of formalism's "transcendental nonsense."[37] At any rate, it is seen as largely a defeated movement, considered as a jurisprudential and educational theory. In large part, it is the legacy of the realists that has endured, not just in the modern cult of the personality of judges, but also in the openness of legal reasoning and law's elaboration to policy ideas, like law and economics.

But it is open only to a particular sort of policy discourse, with a momentum of its own; and that policy discourse also challenges the possibility of legal absolutes. It by no means represents a return to anything like natural law ideas. It is the language of economics – either cost–benefit analysis or the wealth-maximization approach of the formal economic analysis of law. Defenders of those approaches will no doubt complain that this process is incomplete; they may call for it to be taken further, to extirpate the last vestiges of old-fashioned morality from our legal thinking. My point is that, despite it being a more realistic as opposed to formalistic framework, it is no more hospitable to older deontic principles or to considerations of justice or human dignity than was the case with the older formalist discourse.

The problem of justice is particularly acute. Despite having seen a resurgence in moral and political philosophy,[38] considerations of justice continue to be excluded or at best represented in distorted fashion in modern policy calculations. There is the clumsy ineptness of viewing distributive justice as just one benefit among others in cost–benefit analysis. Some people have a taste for equity, we are told, so the equitable character of any legal provision generates at least that degree of benefit to be weighed in a consequentialist calculus alongside whatever other benefits or costs it involves. And the extent of the benefit should be determined by what the individuals in question – the ones who value justice – are prepared to pay or forgo for its sake. We may denounce these maneuvers as ethically tone-deaf, but it is less clear how we are actually to account for such values in cost–benefit analysis or in the business of wealth-maximization.[39]

[37] Cohen, *supra* note 32, at 820: "[O]ne may suspect that a court would not consistently hide behind a barrage of transcendental nonsense if the grounds of its decisions were such as could be presented without shame to the public."

[38] A resurgence heralded in the work of Rawls. See, e.g., John Rawls, A Theory of Justice (revised edition, 1999).

[39] There is also a similar process in trying to account for *dignity*: see, e.g., Jeremy Waldron, *It's All for Your Own Good*, N.Y. Rev. of Books, October 9, 2014, reviewing Cass R. Sunstein, Why Nudge? The Politics of Libertarian Paternalism (2008).

All this represents an aspect of desanctification that is no longer a simple function of the operation of a technically designed formal code. In some ways it is the emergence of exactly the realistic policy science that the realists called for in opposition to formalism. Its failure to accommodate ethical absolutes is no longer a matter of legal form, though it is, in a sense, a matter of the form and formalization of the modern science of policy.

VI FROM PRIVATE LAW TO PUBLIC LAW

A Mala in Se

Max Weber's account of formalization applied mainly to private law and certainly, in the American battle between formalists and realists, private law was the main battleground. Admittedly, the realists were skeptical of the public law/private law distinction. Weber also entertained doubts about the distinction.[40] If public law was understood as instructions to officials, private law could be viewed as instructions to officials to do something about private disputes.[41]

In any case, though the processes just described are processes involving private law formalism, we also find as great a normative loss in public law. Although, as we have seen, there has been a decline of belief in the "sanctity" of contracts and the "sacredness" of private property rights,[42] the problem of legal absolutes arises acutely in the realm of public law as well. Here, we have to think about ways in which the development of law and modern morality puts in question what used to be thought of as absolute prohibitions in criminal law, for example, and in the law of human rights. Weber is less directly helpful here, although we follow his insight that the desanctification of law can happen in several different ways, "depending on which of several possible courses legal thinking takes towards rationalization."[43] The process whereby erstwhile absolutes were drained of their deontic normativity certainly followed a different path in areas of avowedly public law. Weber's account offers a starting point, but we need to fill out the characterization of the whole process.

Let us begin with those criminal law prohibitions that used to be seen as representatives of ancient *mala in se* – "Thou shalt not kill" etc.[44] Even they are no longer conceived – or certainly no longer presented – in directly deontological

40 See, e.g., WEBER, E&S, *supra* note 10, at the start of vol. 2 and WEBER in Rheinstein, *supra* note 10, at 41 ff.

41 Robert Hale, *Coercion and Distribution in a Supposedly Noncoercive State*, 38 POLITICAL SCI. Q. 470 (1923).

42 WEBER in Rheinstein, *supra* note 10, at 39.

43 *Id.*, at 61.

44 1 WILLIAM BLACKSTONE, COMMENTARIES *40 (1765): "[C]rimes and misdemeanors, that are forbidden by the superior laws, and therefore stiled mala in se, such as murder, theft, and perjury … contract no additional turpitude from being declared unlawful by the inferior legislature. For that legislature in all these cases acts only … in subordination to the great lawgiver, transcribing and publishing his precepts!

terms. They are technical in their presentation: there is no categorical norm addressed directly to the populace. Instead, the style of modern criminal law formulations is to address just the decisions and problems that officials face in regard to killings by citizens: offenses are defined in elaborate terms and distinguished from one another, and punishments are specified (though this itself is often indirect too, referring to classes of felony, provision for the punishment of which is made elsewhere in the code.)[45]

Hans Kelsen was convinced that this was an important feature of modern law, that it mostly addressed itself to the officials of the state. "For Kelsen, a law consists exclusively of an instruction . . . for a government agent to apply a punishment under a set of defined circumstances."[46] He said that if we infer a duty upon the subject to avoid the conduct to which the punishment is attached, "this 'ought' is, so to speak, an epiphenomenon of the 'ought' of the sanction." We "overhear" the instruction to apply a sanction and figure out from that what we are not supposed to do.[47] We may find it stylistically pleasing to refer to this inference as the norm. But according to Kelsen, the only true "ought" in the situation is the "ought" addressed to the official.[48] H. L. A. Hart insisted, in response to Kelsen's characterization, that it is the function of such laws, nevertheless, to guide the conduct of citizens.[49] But his insistence on this is simply dogmatic – rooted in an "old-fashioned" sense of what it is that law *must* do. It is certainly not grounded in any of the ways in which modern legislation is expressed.

If, as Blackstone thought, "the very essence of right and wrong depends upon the direction of the laws to do or to omit them,"[50] then our laws no longer try to get at the essence. Despite containing what ought to be thought of as *mala in se*, our laws formulate them in precisely the style that Blackstone specified for *mala prohibita*.[51] *Mala in se* are supposed to be binding in conscience so that positive law adds little or nothing to the prohibition and penalties applied by divine law. But as for *mala prohibita*, "[t]hese become either right or wrong, just or unjust, duties or misdemeanors, according as the municipal legislator sees proper, for promoting the welfare of the society, and more effectually carrying on the purposes of civil life." Such offenses "have no foundation in nature, but are merely created by the law, for the purposes of civil society."[52] All there is to their proscription is a definition and

45 The logic of the formulation is: "First degree murder is X, Y, and Z. The punishment for first degree murder is A or B."

46 This characterization of Kelsen's view is from Edward Rubin, *Law and Legislation in the Administrative State*, 89 Colum. L. Rev. 369, 374 (1989).

47 Cf. the discussion of "acoustic separation" in Meir Dan Cohen, *Decision Rules and Conduct Rules: On Acoustic Separation in Criminal Law*, 97 Harv. L. Rev. 625 (1983).

48 Hans Kelsen, General Theory of Law and State, 60–61 (1945).

49 H. L. A. Hart, The Concept of Law 38–42 (1961).

50 Blackstone, *supra* note 44, *41.

51 *Mala prohibita* are things that are offenses simply because they are prohibited by public policy, not on account of any intrinsic moral character of their own. Over-parking, for example, is a *malum prohibitum*.

52 Blackstone, *supra* note 44, *41.

the specification of a penalty.[53] My point is that *mala in se* – of which we are supposed to have an independent moral understanding – are now expressed in this *mala prohibita* form also. It is as though the only important thing about them is how they are officially defined and what penalty they are associated with.

One might say that this is just a matter of draftsman's technique.[54] Perhaps we were never going to find "Thou shalt not kill" written in the books of positive law. Positive law is never *just* an application of moral ideas; it involves specification, or as the natural lawyers call it *determinatio*.[55] Moral ideas do not initially present themselves in law-like form, if what we mean by law-like is something that can work in the real world like a law. Real-life laws are complex bodies of articulate doctrine and ordered criteria. The layman sometimes complains that cases in law are won or lost on "technicalities." But lawmaking is largely a technical matter, with all sorts of devices that look counterintuitive to the sensitive conscience but which are required to ensure administrability (e.g. in the particular and themselves highly regulated circumstances of a court), to take into account other moral needs that may be relevant to administration (procedural fairness, for example), and to allow a given provision to take its place in a coherent and complex corpus juris.[56]

These technical aspects of positivization would have to apply even if the legal norm in question purported to be just an embodiment of a moral norm. So even in the case of rules which undoubtedly are not conventions – for example the rule against killing – John Finnis observes that "it is the business of the draftsman to specify, precisely, into which of these costumes and relationships an act of killing-under-such-and-such-a-circumstance fits. That is why 'No one may kill . . . ' is legally so defective a formulation."[57] Details have to be settled; rules of evidence, presumptions, and burdens of proof laid down; bright lines drawn; operationalized criteria established; and so on. All of this can be acknowledged. Still it makes it harder for law to function as any sort of great public morality, embodying officially endorsed moral absolutes.

B FUNDAMENTAL RIGHTS

The other category of what might have been thought of as transcendent absolutes arises in human rights law. Some have argued that human rights can't properly be

53 *Id.*, *43.

54 The two paragraphs that follow are adapted from the essay *Civilians, Terrorism and Deadly Serious Conventions, in* Jeremy Waldron , Torture, Terror, and Trade-offs: Philosophy for the White House 80, 95 (2010).

55 See Thomas Aquinas, *Summa Theologiae*, I-II, Q. 95, a. 2, in Aquinas: On Law, Morality, and Politics 54 (Richard Regan trans., 2002).

56 The best modern account of this is John Finnis, Natural Law and Natural Rights Ch. 10 (1980).

57 *Id.*, at 283.

understood except in religious terms.[58] There is no doubt that the dignitarian terms in which they are presented are open to that interpretation, even if they do not compel it. Certainly human rights are expressed in deontic terms, at least in the great charters and covenants. Those documents are unabashed about referencing the supra-positive inspiration of these rights;[59] their formulation in the texts of these covenants is explicitly presented as the positivization of what are supposed to be morally compelling ideas. So, for example, Article 7 of the International Covenant on Civil and Political Rights (ICCPR) makes the following no-nonsense claim: "No one shall be subjected to torture . . . ." Not only that, but the Article 7 provision is explicitly insulated from any consideration of emergency conditions. Article 4 (1) of the ICCPR says that "[i]n time of public emergency which threatens the life of the nation . . . the States Parties to the present Covenant may take measures derogating from their obligations under the present Covenant to the extent strictly required by the exigencies of the situation." But then it is quick to add in subsection (2) that "[n]o derogation from article[] . . . 7 . . . may be made under this provision."[60]

However, as they work their way into a municipal legal system, the deontic character of their formulation is diluted. Human rights provisions are often doubly or multiply positivized – for example, in national as well as in international human rights law.[61] And the second positivization of the torture provision in American law is much more technical than its positivization in the ICCPR. There is nothing equivalent to the deontic formula "No one shall be subjected to torture . . . ." Instead there is a reversion to the Kelsenian directive form. Our torture statute[62] contains an elaborate definition of the offense:

> As used in this chapter—(1) "torture" means an act committed by a person acting under the color of law specifically intended to inflict severe physical or mental pain or suffering (other than pain or suffering incidental to lawful sanctions) upon another person within his custody or physical control; . . . .

And then that is followed by an (admittedly quite draconian) provision for punishment.

> Whoever outside the United States commits or attempts to commit torture shall be fined under this title or imprisoned not more than 20 years, or both, and if death

58 See, e.g., Michael Perry, *Is the Idea of Human Rights Ineliminably Religious?*, *in* Legal Rights: Historical and Philosophical Perspectives 205 (Austin Sarat & Thomas R. Kearns, eds., 1996).

59 See Gerald Neuman, *Human Rights and Constitutional Rights*, 55 Stan. L. Rev. 1863 (2003), for this term. It means that they are "conceived as reflections of nonlegal principles that have normative force independent of their embodiment in law, or even superior to the positive legal system."

60 See also the Convention against Torture and Other Cruel, Inhuman or Degrading Treatment or Punishment, Art. 2(2), Dec. 10, 1984: "No exceptional circumstances whatsoever, whether a state of war or a threat or war, internal political instability or any other public emergency, may be invoked as a justification of torture."

61 See Neuman, *Human Rights and Constitutional Rights*, *supra* note 59, 1868, for the idea of dual positivization.

62 18 U.S.C. §§ 2340 and 2340A.

> results to any person from conduct prohibited by this subsection, shall be punished by death or imprisoned for any term of years or for life.

The punishments threatened are fierce. But "Thou shalt not torture" does not get a look in. There is not a lot of normativity in §2340.

Again we could dismiss this as just a matter of drafting technique. But when the United States was actually faced with a years-long crisis about official use of torture in our black prisons overseas in the first decade of the war on terror, all sorts of maneuvers were adopted to reinterpret §2340 or to find indeterminacy in its formulations that could be exploited to make room for "coercive interrogation." Boalt Hall Professor John Yoo's and Judge Jay Bybee's technique of "reading down" the statutory definition, in a memo from the Office of Legal Counsel, became notorious.[63]

The Bybee memo also raised the possibility of a necessity defense against any allegation of a violation of the anti-torture statute:

> As it has been described in the case law and literature, the purpose behind necessity is one of public policy ... "the law ought to promote the achievement of higher values at the expense of lesser values, and sometimes the greater good for society will be accomplished by violating the literal language of the criminal law." [T]he more likely it appears to be that a terrorist attack is likely to occur, and the greater the amount of damage expected from such an attack, the more that an interrogation to get information would become necessary.[64]

63 Jay Bybee, *Standards of Conduct for Interrogation under 18 U.S.C. 2340–2340A*, Memorandum from the Justice Department's Office of Legal Counsel for Alberto R. Gonzalez, counsel to President Bush (August 1, 2002). (This memorandum is also available in THE TORTURE PAPERS: THE ROAD TO ABU GHRAIB (Karen J. Greenberg and Joshua Dratel eds., 2005), 172.) The approach in the memo involved drawing on statutes governing medical administration, where, it was said, attempts to define the phrase "severe pain" had already been made.

> [T]he phrase "severe pain" appears in statutes defining an emergency medical condition for the purpose of providing health benefits. ... These statutes define an emergency condition as one "manifesting itself by acute symptoms of sufficient severity (including severe pain) such that a prudent lay person, who possesses an average knowledge of health and medicine) could reasonably expect the absence of immediate medical attention to result in – placing the health of the individual ... (i) in serious jeopardy, (ii) serious impairment to bodily functions, or (iii) serious dysfunction of any bodily organ or part." ... Although these statutes address a substantially different subject from §2340, they are nonetheless helpful for understanding what constitutes severe pain.

From this, the Bybee memo concluded that "physical pain amounting to torture must be equivalent in intensity to the pain accompanying serious physical injury, such as organ failure, impairment of body function, or even death." It is hard to know where to start in criticizing this "analysis." The statutory provision that was quoted uses conditions (i) through (iii) to define the phrase "emergency condition," not to define "severe pain." The medical administration statute says that severe symptoms (including severe pain) add up to an emergency condition if conditions (i), (ii), or (iii) are satisfied. But since the anti-torture statute does not use the term "emergency condition," conditions (i) to (iii) are irrelevant to its interpretation.

64 *Id.*, at 41.

A similar argument was made, and conceded in principle, in the Israeli High Court's torture decision of 1994. The court said that it was "prepared to accept that in the appropriate circumstances, GSS investigators may avail themselves of the 'necessity' defence, if criminally indicted." (The court did however go on to insist that no ex ante authorization could possibly be inferred from this.)

The absolutism of individual rights is often taken as the *leit-motif* of American jurisprudence.[65] In fact, although rights are spoken of as absolutes, time and again courts prove themselves ready to balance them and trade them off against one another – and not only against one another but against various considerations of the general interest, whenever it seems appropriate to invoke that. As Mark Tushnet puts it, "Rights become indeterminate as first one side and then the other attaches new long term consequences to recognition or denial of particular claims of right."[66] These are Critical Legal Studies claims and none the less insightful for that.

We need to look at rather than fantasize about the commitment to rights in American law. As Duncan Kennedy has observed, there is in real-life American jurisprudence a sort of flattening out of the distinction between rights-arguments and policy arguments. Talk of constitutional rights does not preclude "open-textured arguments from morality, social welfare, expectations and institutional competence and administrability. . . . The rights are just legal rules, more or less abstract, more or less easy to administer, that we are trying to interpret along with all the other legal materials to justify our outcomes."[67] In other words, our actual experience with rights in law is far from the sort of reverence for them and paramount enforcement of them that rights-rhetoric would suggest. The use of balancing and proportionality as characteristic of the actual administration of most rights (i.e., rights set out in the Constitution and in international covenants, as well as ordinary rights in statute and common law). One or two philosophers may conceive of rights as trumps;[68] but in law they are just cards – and pretty low cards at that – played in the ordinary suits or currency of political compromise.[69] In other words, what we see in all of this is the erasure of any uncompromising deontology. Rights no longer present themselves as the legal embodiment of absolutes. Like everything else in law, they have been made tractable, negotiable – *reasonable*.

VII THE DESANCTIFICATION OF MORALITY

So what? Even if law itself is developing and changing in these various ways, still are we not able to deploy whatever moral standards we like to evaluate the law as it is,

65 See MARY ANN GLENDON , RIGHTS TALK: THE IMPOVERISHMENT OF POLITICAL DISCOURSE (1993).

66 Mark Tushnet, *An Essay on Rights*, 62 TEX. L. REV. 1364 (1984).

67 Duncan Kennedy, *The Critique of Rights in Critical Legal Studies, in* LEFT LEGALISM/LEFT CRITIQUE 195–96 (Janet Halley & Wendy Brown eds., 2002).

68 RONALD DWORKIN, TAKING RIGHTS SERIOUSLY 6 (1977).

69 See Tushnet, *supra* note 66, at 1373.

and if need be to denounce it? If existing legal practice appears to countenance something that ordinary language would call "torture" or if it doesn't seem hospitable to an absolute prohibition of the practice, can we – who are disturbed by this – not use traditional deontological prohibitions to condemn this? John Yoo once said to me in a debate in 2005, "I think it would be very difficult to be a Kantian and have any responsibility in the government."[70] But surely from outside government, we critics can say anything we like. We might even use religious arguments against torture, as I tried to do in 2006 in an article in *Theology Today*,[71] or as David Gushee and others did in 2007 in *An Evangelical Declaration against Torture*.[72]

This is fine, up to a point. As critics, we *can* do what we like and judge the laws that apply to us by whatever standards seem appropriate, irrespective of the processes that modernism dictates and Max Weber describes. And if moral evaluation of law were a purely personal matter, that would be a reasonable response. If it were purely a matter of determining one's conscientious stance as a citizen toward a given law or one's own compliance, in circumstances where cooperation in evil was called for, one could deploy any moral standards that seemed right or true.

But in social and political life, we mobilize shared standards to evaluate the law *together*; in criticizing a law for failing to meet a given standard, one offers that criticism to one's fellow citizens and one expects what one is saying to make sense to them. I am not distinguishing here between critical and positive morality (though the latter category is woefully under-explored in political and legal philosophy).[73] I am talking about modes of critical moralizing that seem natural, appropriate, and familiar to those with whom one shares the enterprise of evaluating positive law. And the worry is that, at this level, the shared standards that make social sense – that seem appropriately put forward – as a reasonable basis for the moral evaluation of law also seem to be losing the deontic dimension of their meaning. One says something – something deontological as it might be – and one receives a sort of blank stare from one's audience. (I remember such a blank stare in a faculty seminar once at Columbia Law School when I suggested that the design of bankruptcy law was a problem in distributive justice rather than economic efficiency.)[74]

What I am suggesting here is that the desanctification of law is not a matter of detaching it as an autonomous discipline from its erstwhile moral

70 See *Waldron-Yoo Debate on Torture*, COLUM. L. SCH.: FEDERALIST SOC'Y BLOG! (April 21, 2005), http://expost.blogspot.com/2005/04/waldron-yoo-debate-on-torture.html.

71 Jeremy Waldron, *What Can Christian Teaching Add to the Debate about Torture?* 63 THEOLOGY TODAY 330 (2006), reprinted in WALDRON, TORTURE, TERROR AND TRADE-OFFS, *supra* note 54.

72 Evangelicals for Human Rights, *An Evangelical Declaration against Torture: Protecting Human Rights in an Age of Terror*, published by National Association of Evangelicals (March 2007), available at www.nae.net/an-evangelical-declaration-against-torture/, reprinted in DAVID GUSHEE , THE FUTURE OF FAITH IN AMERICAN POLITICS: THE PUBLIC WITNESS OF THE EVANGELICAL CENTER 253 (2008). The *Evangelical Declaration* is discussed extensively in Jeremy Waldron, *Two-way Translation: The Ethics of Engaging with Religious Contributions in Public Deliberation*, 63 MERCER L. REV. 845 (2012).

73 For the distinction, see HART, *supra* note 49, at 169.

74 For the distributive justice characterization of bankruptcy law, see FINNIS, *supra* note 56, 188–93.

underpinnings.[75] Maybe as law becomes more technical and harder to appreciate intuitively, it is correspondingly more difficult to apprehend as the embodiment of extralegal principles. But what is even more difficult is to relate law systematically to a set of, as it were, *old-fashioned* moral principles. New law has its own new morality to go along with it.

I say this to avoid the impression that desanctification is just legal positivism in another guise. Legal positivism is connected with desanctification. And legal positivism did try to drain law of its moral content and moral meaning – though not necessarily to discredit the moral enterprise as such. The idea was to separate law and morality, not to destroy the latter. One or two positivists might have inclined in a more destructive direction – Thomas Hobbes, for example, in his suggestion that law's function was to supersede morality,[76] and Hans Kelsen's corrosive moral relativism.[77] For most legal positivists, however, morality is kept separate from law and intact – first, so as to clarify one's sense of the objective legal situation without contamination from wishful thinking. Then, second, one keeps morality separate so that it can be brought back, in its uncontaminated character, to bear on the task of evaluating law and determining our (morally) appropriate attitude towards it. Or at least that is the official story.[78]

It does not follow, however, that the processes Weber and others described have no impact on morality, that is, that they only have impact on law. It is perfectly consistent with the positivist picture – crude and un-thought-through as it is in the hands of most modern legal philosophers – that those processes have an impact on the morality (that is reserved for the critical appraisal of law) which is quite like its impact on law itself. Put more simply, I am inviting us to consider the possibility that the social processes that change the character of law also change the character of morality concomitantly.[79] The process of the rationalization and desanctification of law may be matched by isomorphic processes of rationalization and desanctification of morality – at least of the morality that can plausibly be put in play where legal evaluation and legal change are at issue. The morality that results is not necessarily

[75] HABERMAS, *supra* note 11, at 243, paraphrases Weber's position as describing what he (Habermas) calls in a characteristic bit of jargon, "the detachment of subsystems of purposive-rational action from their moral-practical foundations." Habermas is responding to a familiar Weberian pessimism to the effect that under instrumental rationality we lose touch with ends and values.

[76] THOMAS HOBBES, LEVIATHAN 183 (Richard Tuck ed., 1988): "I define Civill Law in this manner. Civill Law, Is to every Subject, those Rules, which the Common-wealth hath Commanded him, by Word, Writing, or other sufficient Sign of the Will, *to make use of, for the Distinction of Right, and Wrong*" (my emphasis).

[77] HANS KELSEN, PURE THEORY OF LAW, 64 (1934). See also HANS KELSEN, WHAT IS JUSTICE? 141 and 179 (1960).

[78] HART, *supra* note 49, 210–12. See also the discussion in Liam Murphy, *Better to See Law this Way*, 83 N.Y.U. L. REV. 1088 (2008).

[79] The insight is from HABERMAS, *supra* note 27, at 105: "[A]t the postmetaphysical level of justification, legal and moral rules are simultaneously differentiated from traditional ethical life and appear side by side as two different but mutually complementary kinds of action norms."

tame or uncritical; but it subjects law only to certain kinds of critique and it makes other moral critiques seem odd or inappropriate.

So consider, for example, the transformation of "morality" contemplated as a realistic standard of evaluation by the American legal realists. Maybe the Langdellian formalists had their own vision of morality to map onto their legal logic.[80] Be that as it may, certainly some of the legal realists envisaged making law amenable to substantive evaluation. There would be a perspective from which law could be evaluated for the purposes of reform and to which it could be made accountable. But the realists thought it important to emphasize that it was going to be *a new sort of evaluation* and *a new sort of moral accountability*.

"[T]he man of the future," said Oliver Wendell Holmes, "is the man of statistics and the master of economics."[81] If there was to be morality in the work of legal scientists, it was not going to be a theological or deontic morality. Thirty years later, Felix Cohen put the point this way:

> What a judge ought to do in a given case is quite as much a moral issue as any of the traditional problems of Sunday School morality. It is difficult for those who still conceive of morality in otherworldly terms to recognize that every case presents a moral question to the court. But this notion has no terrors for those who think of morality in earthly terms. Morality, so conceived, is vitally concerned with such facts as human expectations based upon past decisions, the stability of economic transactions, and even the maintenance of order and simplicity in our legal system.[82]

The words "ethics" and "morality" mean a lot of different things, says Cohen, but "[t] he spontaneous outpourings of a sensitive conscience unfamiliar with the social context" are not what modern law needs.[83]

> If ethics is chiefly concerned with the problems that teachers of ethics have discussed during the past three or four hundred years, that is to say, with the conduct of a man towards his next door neighbor and towards his next-door neighbor's wife ... and, on the whole, with questions of *manners* rather than with basic questions of social values, then ethics has little to offer to those who practice or study law. ... [T]he basic problems of the law today involve social forms and patterns that cannot be compressed into the narrow confines of what may be called "Sunday School ethics." Only an ethics that squarely faces the problems which modern commerce and modern science have brought into our world can offer any worthwhile gifts to modern law.[84]

80 Opinions seem to have varied as between those who saw the formal logic of law as utterly autonomous and those who sought to map it on to the nostrums of laissez-faire economics. See Neil Duxbury, Patterns of American Jurisprudence 26 ff. (1997).

81 Oliver Wendell Holmes, *The Path of the Law* (Reprint), 78 B.U. L. Rev. 699, 708 (1998).

82 Cohen, *supra* note 32, at 840.

83 *Id.*

84 Felix Cohen, *Modern Ethics and the Law*, 4 Brook. L. Rev. 33, 36 (1934).

This is certainly a rejection of pure formalism; it involves a substantial rationalization of law. But the nature of the rationalization and the nature of the evaluations it contemplates make it harder to accommodate values like justice and dignity, and harder still to insist on moral absolutes.

All that is from the side of the lawyers. What about the philosophers? Well, it would be wrong to deny that modern moral philosophy is also complicit in this new understanding of social morality. Its main features are a pervasive consequentialism and a reliance on "reflective equilibrium" to avoid conclusions that sound dogmatic or unreasonable.[85]

For example, everyone makes fun of Kant's remark that lying is absolutely wrong: we just know that lying is sometimes right and, unlike the old Prussian dogmatist, we have the methodology to accommodate that conviction.[86] It just *can't* be right that there is a duty to tell the truth when better results will accrue from falsehood; any principles that seem to have that implication obviously require some adjustment. Or to take another example: I remember during the torture crisis of 2003–08 finding precious few moral philosophers who were prepared to stand for a moral absolute in that regard. I found both lawyers and moralists saying that there just could not *be* – they couldn't make sense of – an absolute prohibition on torture. There would always have to be some necessity one could appeal to in order to excuse if not justify torture, some technique of "reading down" the prohibition, or some indeterminacy in the legal meaning of words like "torture" that would make ostensibly implacable norms negotiable. The thought seemed to be that effective but coercive interrogation just *can't* be something whose use is simply foreclosed (as opposed to being rendered inadvisable in most circumstances). There were always ticking bomb hypotheticals to be manufactured[87] and residual doctrines of the avoidance of "catastrophic moral horror"[88] to mitigate the rigor of morality's strictures. Habermas talks of the erasure of "the deontological dimension of normative validity" within morality itself.[89] I fear he is right.

One or two philosophers, conscious of this transformation, have suggested that it is actually the loss of *the law's ability to sustain absolutes* that has led to a loss of faith in them in moral philosophy. If law has lost some of its moral bearings, morality too is losing some of the bearings that it took from a certain conception of law. Morality used to be structured partly in the way that law was once thought to be structured.[90] Now it

85 For reflective equilibrium, see RAWLS, *supra* note 38, 40–46 (revised edition, 1999).

86 Immanuel Kant, *On a Supposed Right to Lie from Philanthropy* (1797), *in* IMMANUEL KANT, PRACTICAL PHILOSOPHY 611 (Mary Gregor ed., 1996); Cf. Richard Epstein, *Smart Consequentialism: Kantian Moral Theory and the (Qualified) Defense of Capitalism*, NYU Law Faculty Lunch Presentation (Fall 2015): "It is hard to deny the simple proposition that lying in defense of self and third persons constitutes from the ex ante perspective a strong Pareto and Kaldor-Hicks improvement."

87 See Jeremy Waldron, *What are Moral Absolutes Like?* 18 HARV. REV. OF PHILOSOPHY 4 (2012).

88 The phrase has been taken up by philosophers from a throwaway line in ROBERT NOZICK, ANARCHY, STATE AND UTOPIA 30n (1974). See also Michael Moore, *Torture and the Balance of Evils*, 23 ISR. L. REV. 327 (1989).

89 HABERMAS, *supra* note 27, at 49.

90 HABERMAS, *supra* note 11, at 251 says that Weber "plays down the structural analogies that obtain between moral development and the rationalization of law."

is harder to see either enterprise as deontological. I know that when I wrote about moral absolutes a few years ago I said (rather over-confidently), "we know what legal absolutes look like" – categorical prohibitions stated starkly that do not seem to brook any justifying conditions – and I said it would do no harm to begin with them as our role models.[91] But now I think there are no such role models, and morality is impoverished because there is so much less to be learned from the law.

Almost sixty years ago, G. E. M. Anscombe was already venturing this diagnosis.[92] Concepts like moral obligation and moral duty and the moral sense of "ought" are nowadays quite mysterious, she said. "It is as if the notion 'criminal' were to remain when criminal law and criminal courts had been abolished and forgotten. . . . The situation, if I am right, [is] the interesting one of the survival of a concept outside the framework of thought that made it a really intelligible one."[93] Concepts like moral obligation and moral duty used to be intelligible within a framework of divine law; now they are so no longer, and the result is a complete transformation in our sense of what we ought to tolerate:

> Every one of the best known English academic moral philosophers has put out a philosophy according to which, e.g., it is not possible to hold that it cannot be right to kill the innocent as a means to any end whatsoever . . . . Now this is a significant thing: for it means that all these philosophies are quite incompatible with the Hebrew-Christian ethic. For it has been characteristic of that ethic to teach that there are certain things forbidden whatever consequences threaten, such as: choosing to kill the innocent for any purpose, however good.[94]

Anscombe believes that this failure to accommodate the possibility that certain things are prohibited "simply in virtue of their description as such-and-such identifiable kinds of action, regardless of any further consequences" is surely the most important fact about modern moral philosophy.[95]

It is not just a matter of convictions. It is also a matter of moral methodology. Since Anscombe's day, philosophers have become accustomed to the methodology of "reflective equilibrium," a process by which we bring our abstract and universal commitments into line with our considered judgments about particular matters by making adjustments at both ends – reconstructing our principles and abandoning or modifying a few of our considered judgments. The hope is that we will eventually be left with a set of considered judgments we can cling to, which is in rough equilibrium with a set of principles rigged to generate them.[96]

In this process, it seems, we think of the principles we are working on as "ours" – ours to change or modify as the exigencies of reflective equilibrium dictate. Can we still say

91 Waldron, *supra* note 87, at 8.
92 G. E. M. Anscombe, *Modern Moral Philosophy*, 33 PHILOSOPHY 1 (1958).
93 *Id.*, at 6.
94 *Id.*, at 10.
95 *Id.*, at 9–10.
96 For reflective equilibrium, see RAWLS, *supra* note 38, at 18–19 and 40–46.

of the result that it is objectively true? Maybe; but if so, objectivity is just a label we paste on to the product of our rethinking, the product of our drive to find a position we are comfortable with. A deeper sense of objectivity would cover principles that present themselves to us in a more uncompromising and non-negotiable way. These would not be treated as norms that *we* have control over; they would not be for us to tamper with.[97] Understanding such principles as divine commands or transcendent givens, we would understand ourselves as more passive in the recognition and construction of principles put forward for the evaluation of law than modern moral philosophers generally take themselves to be.

VIII ULTIMATE ENDS AND "POLITICS AS A VOCATION"

Some will say it is not an impoverishment to cut both law and public morality away from their more irrational and sectarian manifestations. We need a body of law that is apt for use in the modern world, they will say, and it needs to be matched by a morality that can be used rationally by the members of a political community, acting together, to evaluate law's serviceability for that purpose.

The idea of "public reason," introduced in John Rawls's later work, can be understood as a way of disciplining the moral evaluation of law along these lines.[98] Though in principle people might deploy all sorts of standards – some traditional, some religious, some deeply philosophical – to evaluate the laws we have, the idea is that we should limit the evaluative arguments that we introduce into the public realm to those we can reasonably expect all others to understand. Nothing can be regarded as an appropriate contribution to public deliberation unless it is phrased in terms that make sense to all the members of the society, in all their ethical, philosophical, and religious diversity. That means that we should be very wary of introducing religious conceptions into politics – since these are inherently divisive – and very wary of taking a public stand on moral absolutes if the grounding of these presupposes religious or philosophical commitments on which a large number of our fellow citizens have long since turned their backs. If I say that terrorists must be respected like everyone because they are created in the image of God,[99] or if I say that torture "is a sin against the Holy Ghost,"[100] I am not saying anything that my secular fellow citizens can get their minds around and I am myself committing the sin of incivility by simply giving voice to my own theological

97 This is adapted from Waldron, *supra* note 71, at 338.

98 See JOHN RAWLS, POLITICAL LIBERALISM 212 ff. (1996).

99 See HCJ 769/02 Public Committee against Torture in Israel and Palestinian Society for the Protection of Human Rights and the Environment v. Government of Israel and others §25 (2005) (Isr.): "Needless to say, unlawful combatants are not beyond the law. They are not 'outlaws.' God created them as well in his image; their human dignity as well is to be honored" (president Barak J.).

100 F. S. Cocks (United Kingdom delegate), as reported in 2 *Council of Europe, Collected Edition of the "Travaux Préparatoires" of the Eur. Conv. on H.R.* 40 (1975).

convictions instead of engaging with my fellow deliberators on terms we can all understand.

The Rawlsian idea of public reason remains controversial;[101] I mention it here simply as an instance of the way in which some philosophers think morality has to transform itself to match the needs of a desanctified body of law.

Finally and even more substantively, we may circle back round to one last thesis from Max Weber. As we saw in Section II of this chapter, Weber's account of the processes we have been describing is mainly formalistic: law has had to become formalized in a way that puts it beyond the reach of certain kinds of evaluation. But Weber matches that with a substantive thesis as well. In his great lecture from 1919, "Politics as a Vocation," he maintained that a responsible person with a vocation for politics must, in a sense, commit himself broadly speaking to a consequentialist ethics.

> [T]here is a profound abyss between acting in accordance with the maxim of an ethic governing an ethics of conviction and acting in tune with an ethics of responsibility. In the former case this means, to put it in religious terms, "A Christian does what is right and leaves the outcome to God," while in the latter you must answer for the foreseeable consequences of your actions.[102]

Sanctity and political responsibility stand on opposite sides of this abyss. Someone committed to an ethic of ultimate ends is admirable in a way, but with his repudiation of every action that makes use of morally suspect ends he must be kept away from politics.

> No ethic in the world can ignore the fact that in many cases the achievement of "good" ends is inseparable from the use of morally dubious or at least dangerous means ones and that we cannot escape the possibility or even probability of evil side effects. . . . [I]t is not true that nothing but good comes from good and nothing but evil from evil, but rather quite frequently the opposite is the case. Anyone who does not realize this is in fact a mere child in political matters.[103]

It is not just a point about consequentialism; it is a point about politics itself and its artifact, law. For, however elevated our jurisprudence may be, there is no getting away from the fact that "[i]n politics, the decisive means is the use of force" and that the making, changing, and evaluation of law is also about the way in which in the last resort force will be used in our society.[104] "Whoever makes a pact with the use of force, for whatever ends (and every politician does so), is at the mercy of its particular consequences."[105]

101 My own doubts about the public reason idea are voiced in Jeremy Waldron, *Public Reason and 'Justification' in the Courtroom*, 1 J.L. PHIL. & CULTURE 107 (2007).

102 Max Weber, *Politics as a Vocation*, *in* THE VOCATION LECTURES, *supra* note 18, at 83.

103 *Id.*, at 84 and 86.

104 *Id.*, at 84.

105 *Id.*, at 89.

Myself, I don't believe that this means that a responsible politician gives up on the very idea of certain actions – actions of certain kinds – being beyond the pale in politics. It is one thing to accept that politics will inevitably involve distasteful actions;[106] quite another to say that no action, however wrong or distasteful can ever be finally excluded. The trouble is that the denigration of those who renounce the merely distasteful in politics probably makes it much harder for us to sustain any sense that, nevertheless, there are some things that are forbidden.

IX CONCLUSION

It has been hard to know what tone to take in this chapter. The English satirical magazine *Private Eye* used to have an "old fogey" poet on its staff in the 1980s who would write doggerel beginning, "Oh, isn't everything awful / in this dreadful modern age." The tone of what I have written sounds, on rereading, like a litany of grumpiness or frustration or both, and that worries me. Obviously I regard some of the developments I have set out as deplorable. But the aim has been to describe and characterize desanctification – admittedly from the perspective of someone who cares about it – rather than to deplore it.

Also, it is easy to sound hysterical about all this, as though the processes described were univocal in their tendency and utterly out of our hands. But in exploring these developments, I do not want to commit myself to a hard-and-fast version of these processes. We are talking at most about tendencies – tendencies that have proceeded unevenly across legal systems and across areas of law for a century or more. The chapter tries to describe a reduction in the ease and naturalness – the increasing difficulty and a diminishing sense of the plausibility – of certain pathways of moral and legal thought.

Finally, the normative tenor of this piece is supposed to be diagnosis and vague lamentation; no recommendations are on offer. I do believe that we need some sense of absolute prohibitions in morality; we should not be turning our backs on a whole dimension of normativity. But the processes traced here – processes of desanctification identified by Weber and others – indicate how deep and difficult it may be to restore that normative dimension.

106 Cf. Bernard Williams, *Politics and Moral Character, in* PUBLIC AND PRIVATE MORALITY (Stuart Hampshire ed., 1978), arguing that things like "lying, or at least . . . the making of misleading statements; breaking promises; . . . sacrifice of the interest of worthy persons to those of unworthy persons; and . . . coercion up to blackmail" may all be required of a participant in ordinary politics, certainly a participant with any power in his hands, in order to have any chance of successfully promoting policies that he or she judges good and just."

2

The Paradox of Human Rights Discourse and the Jewish Legal Tradition

Suzanne Last Stone[*]

I INTRODUCTION

Nearly two decades ago, I was invited to contribute to a collection of essays convened to explore the possibility of "articulating a position of human rights on assumptions of humankind and of the cosmos other than those of Western liberal civilization."[1] The project was self-consciously constructive: to creatively mine potentialities within a given religious tradition that could support certain desirable insights of modernity while maintaining a commitment to tradition and religious identity. The hope of the project was that, with sufficient effort and creativity, religions, no matter how diverse, would discover that human rights were, in some fashion, always already there. After all, religions were each, in different ways, concerned with human worth and flourishing even if they did not ascribe to the politics or philosophical anthropology of Western modernity. In the case of Protestant Christianity and other reformed religions, the leap clearly would be short, for certain basic assumptions about religion (as primarily concerned with belief rather than law or public practice and with private conscience rather than group cohesion or institutional authority) are most congenial to the worldview that gave rise to Western rights discourse in the first place. With respect to non-Western or non-reformed religions, especially competing law-based religions, the hermeneutic project would be vastly more complex. Indeed, translation and reinterpretation are all the more difficult in a self-conscious age already suspicious of liberal or reformed religion. So other denominations and religions would simply have to work harder to remain reasonably faithful to their traditional texts, traditions, and internal viewpoints.

* An earlier version of this chapter appeared as "Religion and Human Rights: Conflict or Convergence, Babel or Translation?" in *The Discourse of Human Rights*, eds. Hanoch Dagan, Shahar Lifshitz and Yedidia Z. Stern (Jerusalem: The Israel Democracy Institute, 2014).

1 Adam B. Seligman, "Introduction," in *Religion and Human Rights: Conflict or Convergence*, ed. Adam Seligman (Hollis: Hollis Publishing Company, 2005), 11.

The conference also generated: Adam B. Seligman, ed., *Modest Claims: Dialogues on Toleration and Tradition* (Notre Dame: University of Notre Dame Press, 2004).

Suzanne Last Stone, "Tolerance versus Pluralism in Judaism," *Journal of Human Rights* 2 (1) (2003).

Projects such as these have only proliferated in recent years among human rights advocates, civil society groups, and theologians. In turn, scholars within the growing field of critical human rights, such as Sally Merry and Seyla Benhabib, have provided new theoretical frameworks for supporting them. While Merry emphasizes how the idea of human rights becomes meaningful only through translation in specific cultural contexts into a distinct vernacular,[2] Benhabib, drawing on Robert Cover's idea of law's jurisgenerativity, emphasizes the inevitably interpretive character of human rights.[3]

In this chapter, I want to suggest that such efforts to reconcile human rights and religion are at risk of foundering because of two category mistakes highlighted by this volume of essays: The first mistake is the assumption that the human rights project, as it has evolved, is primarily about law – that is, a modern normative and political project. The second mistake is the assumption that "religions" such as Judaism – especially its non-reformed versions – are not law. I am not the first to observe that human rights, in pursuing a politics of meaning rather than of exchange, increasingly has taken on a structure that could be fruitfully compared to religion. As Mark Goodale has pointed out, the study of human rights as discourse increasingly has revealed "the way in which actors embrace the idea of human rights in part because of its visionary capacity, the way in which it embraces the normative and the aspirational."[4] Far from providing a common ground with traditional religions, I contend that the contemporary emphasis on the philosophical underpinnings of human rights has been largely detrimental to the original normative and political project of human rights and to a possible convergence between the human rights tradition and many non-Christian, non-reformed religions. The incontrovertible or absolute character of human rights blurs the division between secular morality based on unaided reason and the realm of the sacrosanct, inviolable, or the sacred occupied by religion. While the intention may have been for the creation of a common language of natural morality, it has led instead to ever more divisiveness, as adherents of religions perceive human rights discourse as imputing sacredness, understood as ultimate meaning or concern, where it does not belong.

My second argument, in turn, is that the legal dimension of traditional religions such as Judaism has been vastly underexploited in these various projects of reconciliation. Legal traditions almost invariably contain a variety of doctrines that enable an exchange of norms and smooth out conflict of laws between legal regimes. Judaism is no exception. Commonplace legal arguments and legal sources, such as respect for conventions and for consensus such as the custom of the nations, offer a more useful framework for creating a rapprochement between human rights and

2 See Sally Engle Merry, "Transnational Human Rights and Local Activism: Mapping the Middle," *American Anthropologist* 108 (1) (2006): 38–51.

3 See Seyla Benhabib, "Claiming Rights Across Borders: International Human Rights and Democratic Sovereignty," *American Political Science Review* 103 (4) (2009): 691–794.

4 Mark Goodale, *Human Rights: An Anthropological Reader* (Oxford: Blackwell, 2009).

religion when dealing with legally based religions, such as traditional Judaism (and, by some accounts, Islam)[5] than appeals to biblical, religious imagery or an assumed common morality. Creating a rapprochement between human rights and traditional Judaism thus requires a double move: first, the retrieval of human rights as a lawyer's project – a normative project based on formal and informal conventions – and, second, the turn to legal doctrines and concepts within Judaism emphasizing the respect owed to international law and conventions, including informal law.

The chapter proceeds as follows: I will briefly survey what has happened in the discourse of human rights in the last several decades, focusing on developments that elide the difference between human rights as a modern secular political project (i.e., to extrapolate the concrete rights of citizens onto the international arena) and human rights as increasingly a quasi-religious project, or politics of meaning. I then offer a concrete example of the challenge of eliciting from Jewish sources, including from its most promising religious image – the creation of humans in the divine image – a common language of sanctity or a conception of rights equally held by all humans as such. That humans possess rights by virtue of being human alone detaches rights from the idea of desert, which I argue is central to the halakhic imagination. This does not mean that Judaism lacks a means of organizing life together with others, including on commonly recognized ethical notions, such as reciprocity. Reciprocity provides the crucial link to desert. Indeed, those thinkers within the halakhic tradition who have most advanced a discourse of human rights, such as Rabbi Hayyim David HaLevi, draw on a distinct tradition within Jewish legal thought that formulates duties owed to others around the ideas of reciprocity and recognition.

Finally, I will draw on Jewish legal sources to explore a different strategy of convergence between religion and human rights that emphasizes human rights as a purely political project revolving around consensus and convention. Indeed, there have been an increasing number of voices within the human rights tradition calling for a ratcheting down of the language of sacredness, of ethical universalism, of moral or ontological arguments, and a refocusing on human rights as a more limited international political project: a legal regime. Human rights, after all, as Adam Seligman writes, are a theory: "Though often treated as sacrosanct, they are but means to a further end ... They are one way to live together based on some commonly acceptable notions of fairness and justice."[6]

II HUMAN RIGHTS AS A SECULAR POLITICAL PROJECT?

The standard history of the rise of human rights as a modern Western political project goes as follows: Talk of rights can be linked historically to the decline of the feudal order, the emergence of national states and market economies, and to the

[5] See Sohail Hashmi, "Jihad and the Geneva Conventions: The Impact of International Law on Islamic Theory," in *Just Wars, Holy Wars, and Jihads*, ed. S. Hashmi (Oxford: Oxford University Press, 2000).

[6] Seligman, "Introduction," 12.

invention of the autonomous individual in the European imagination at the origins of modernity. From political rights of peoples and minority groups, political, civil, and social rights became extended to individuals as citizens in the state and eventually conceived as held by humans as such, inviolate and inalienable.[7] The discourse of human rights drew on diverse philosophic antecedents, from Locke and conscience to Kant and dignity and the reading of the self as a self-regulating agent. The common thread, however, was that identifying and securing human rights was a key political project of secular modernity and, as such, to be validated through public reason accessible to all.

What has changed? In order to make sense of the contemporary scene, it is useful to first distinguish between three expansive, modern visions of human rights that roughly correspond to three succeeding stages:[8] The first is human rights as a legal regime consisting of hard law such as binding conventions and bills of rights. The second is human rights as a set of universal moral standards that apply to all people in all places, irrespective of their beliefs. In this view, rights are rooted in fundamental values shared by all human beings by virtue of their being human. While it is common to suppose that the idea of human rights as moral rights has driven human rights law, the relationship is primarily the reverse. The intense preoccupation with substantive moral theories today generally grew out of what William Twining calls the misguided view that human rights as a legal regime "can and should be founded on a coherent philosophy or ideology" – on the straightforward embodiment of moral universalism. The fact, however, of diversity of beliefs on the ground led to the third vision: discourse ethics, which seeks to shift the conversation to "rights talk" as a form of discourse in public reasoned discussions that provides a framework for argument across societies.[9]

In all of these versions, however, the discourse is almost always centered on rights and the individual human being is viewed as the basic legal subject and unit of morality. This language of human rights has become the dominant mode of public moral discourse, replacing such discourses as distributive justice, the common good, and solidarity. Indeed, it has become something of a faith of its own. And in the course of constituting itself as a quasi-faith, certain intellectual trends within the discourse of human rights have become clearer or, at least, far more prominent. The most pertinent for my purposes is an increased blurring of the line between religion

7 I rely here primarily on John Clayton, "Human Rights and Religious Values," in *Religion and Human Rights: Conflict or Convergence*, ed. Adam B. Seligman (Hollis: Hollis Publishing Company, 2005). Other stories of origin have been told, some of which are discussed in the body of the chapter. See Nicholas Wolterstorff, *Justice: Rights and Wrongs* (Princeton: Princeton University Press, 2008); Max Stackhouse, "Why Human Rights Need God: A Christian Perspective" in *Does Human Rights Need God*, eds. Barbara Barnett and Elizabeth M. Bucar (Grand Rapids: Wm. B. Eerdmans Publishing Company, 2005).

8 See William Twining, *General Jurisprudence: Understanding Law from a Global Perspective* (Cambridge: Cambridge University Press, 2009).

9 *Id.*, 180.

and the secular and, in its wake, an increased confusion with respect to the question whether human rights is still a modern secular project or something else altogether.

Jurgen Habermas's "post-secular" turn was one step toward this blurring of boundaries.[10] In his 1981 *Theory of Communicative Action*, Habermas presented the modern disenchantment and disempowerment of the domain of the sacred as an unequivocal gain for humanity. Now, however, Habermas has called, among other things, for secularly minded citizens to engage critically, along with their religious compatriots, with the cognitive contents of religion.[11] More to the point, he calls on philosophy to open itself to – and utilize for its own projects – the power of religious imagery and narrative. Among Habermas's cited reasons for doing so is the developments in biotechnology, which threaten an instrumentalization of human nature that fundamentally endangers our understanding of ourselves as members of the human species. Resurgent religion and the events of the September 11 terror attacks also prompt the question whether modernization can be rescued by purely secular means. Critical engagement with religious content to produce images, intuitions, and insights are, of course, intended to enrich secular projects – not validate religious truth claims, or lead to greater convergence between religious traditions and modern projects. On this Habermas is clear. The salvaging of religious images, narrative, and moral intuitions occurs in the public sphere – the sphere of public opinion in the weak sense – and not in the strong arena of democratic politics.[12]

Yet, putting aside the questions whether the instrumental turn toward religion is good for religion[13] or coherent when shorn from any connection with metaphysical assumptions or beliefs,[14] in the context of human rights discourse, one could argue that there is already a deep – perhaps too deep – convergence between the modern secular project of universal human rights and religious images via Christianity. The recent revival of Paul as a political figure in European intellectual discourse in the wake of post-secular philosophy is telling. Consider Alain Badiou[15] and Slavoy Zizek's calls to the political left to discover the radical universalism of

10 This turn is analyzed in Maeve Cooke, "Salvaging and Secularizing the Semantic Contents of Religion: The Limitations of Habermas's Post-Metaphysical Proposal," *International Journal for Philosophy of Religion* 60 (2006): 187–207.

11 See, generally: Jürgen Habermas, *Between Naturalism and Religion: Philosophical Essays* (Cambridge: Polity, 2008); Jürgen Habermas, "'The Political': The Rational Meaning of a Questionable Inheritance of Political Theology," in *The Power of Religion in the Public Sphere*, eds. Eduardo Mendieta and Jonathan Vanantwerpen (New York: Columbia University Press, 2011).

12 Cooke, "Salvaging and Secularizing the Semantic Contents of Religion: The Limitations of Habermas's Post-Metaphysical Proposal," 187–207.

13 Charles Taylor, "Why We Need a Radical Redefinition of Secularism," in *The Power of Religion in the Public Sphere*, eds. Eduardo Mendieta and Jonathan VanAntwerpen (New York: Columbia University Press, 2011).

14 Cooke, "Salvaging and Secularizing the Semantic Contents of Religion: The Limitations of Habermas's Post-Metaphysical Proposal," 187–207.

15 Alain Badiou, *Saint Paul: The Foundation of Universalism*, trans. Ray Brassier (Stanford: Stanford University Press, 2003).

Paul[16] and Giorgio Agamben's project to restore Paul's letters to "the status of the fundamental messianic text for the Western tradition."[17] As Jose Mendonca writes, the reclamation of Paul is clearly caught up in "the current need to respond to the crisis of multiculturalism and the universal."[18] That crisis, at least in Europe, has taken the form of the demise of the multiculturalist paradigm in favor of a Christian, majority culture[19] and the post-political search for ever-increasing universal norms. In short, the specter of a new Christianized form of politics has haunted the human rights movement.

How indebted the human rights tradition is to Christianity has become a much-debated issue. In the West, the discourse of rights played out, of course, in a Christian context. It is not surprising that its suppositions would be congenial with Christianity. The claim increasingly is made, however, that it was impossible to think it without Christianity, whether due to the "hidden God of Locke," to the natural rights tradition developed by canon lawyers and theologians in the Middle Ages and inherited by the philosophers of the Enlightenment, or in the traditions of sectarian Protestantism (a very particular Christian tradition defined by beliefs in the inner light and the privatization of grace), and in the humanitarian concern with suffering, with its origins in Christian pity (along with Enlightenment sympathy). On the standard account, the human rights tradition borrowed from religion and then superseded it. From a system of politico-legal norms, it became the shared moral vocabulary of our time. Upendra Baxi puts it succinctly when she writes:

> Much of the twentieth century of the Christian Era (CE), especially its latter half, stands justly hailed as the Age of Human Rights. No preceding century in human history witnessed such a profusion of human rights enunciations on a global scale. Never before have the languages of human rights sought to supplant all other ethical languages. No previous century has witnessed the proliferation of human rights standards as a core aspect of intergovernmental desire . . . .constitut[ing] "a common language of humanity." Indeed, in some ways, human rights sociolect emerges, in this era of the end of ideology, as the only universal ideology in the making, enabling both the legitimation of power and praxes of emancipatory politics.[20]

And at the heart of the discursive tradition of human rights is the growing contention that its moral logic, and universalism, is ultimately conceptually incoherent apart

16 Slavoj Žižek, *The Fragile Absolute: Or, Why Is the Christian Legacy Worth Fighting For?* (London: Verso, 2000).

17 Jose Mendonca, "The Reactivation of Paul: A Critical Dialogue on Giogio Agamben," *Didaskalia* 41 (2) (2011): 2.

18 *Id.*

19 On the demise of the multiculturalist paradigm, see: Susanna Mancini, "To Be Or Not To Be Jewish: The UK Supreme Court Answers the Question," *European Constitutional Law Review* 6 (3) (2010): 481–502. For an analogous argument, see Christopher McCrudden, "Multiculturalism, Freedom of Religion, Equality, and the British Constitution: The JFS Case Considered," *International Journal of Constitutional Law* (I-CON) (2011) and *Oxford Legal Studies Research Paper* (2010): 72.

20 Upendra Baxi, *The Future of Human Rights* (Oxford: Oxford University Press, 2006), 1–2.

from the religious presuppositions. Thus, Michael Perry,[21] Max Stackhouse,[22] and Nicholas Wolterstorff[23] – drawing on diverse Christian themes and history in varying ways – all assert that the foundation of human rights is essentially theological. Certainly, the language of sacredness permeates the discourse; indeed, bare statements are common about the inviolate nature of humans and their sacredness, decoupled from secular justifications for treating humans as sacred (i.e., of ultimate value). Thus, the discourse has shifted from a Western political conception that flourished in a Christian setting; to a secular political and then moral tradition that claimed to have been made possible only by Christianity; and now to a discursive tradition whose key insights are validated by Christianity and by moral intuitions preserved primarily in Christianized readings of the Bible and other religious traditions and narratives.

The Christian reclamation of the human rights tradition has not gone unnoticed. The presumption is quickly vanishing that human rights are in some strong sense neutral, while competing religious claims are local and confined to the communities of interest embracing them.[24] But this leveling is only increasing the tension between religion and human rights. Within theory, this leveling and competition is addressed through the debate about public reasons. On the ground, however, it is often seen as a clash between religions.

In one sense, as Shmuel Trigano writes, the modern political always relied on a certain "immanent transcendence," as much as it may have also disavowed it. Both Spinoza and Rousseau recognized the need for religion – or religion under the guidance of the state – to bolster democracy.[25] In modern politics, nationalism, civic religion, and totalitarian political ideologies all took the structure of religion and contributed to a kind of re-enchantment.[26] Today it is the modern project of human rights that seeks, in Habermas's words, to salvage religion for modernity's purposes. As Sam Moyn argues in *The Last Utopia*, the birth of human rights on the heels of the death of prior political utopias, including communism, almost immediately led to the forgetting of the contingency of their emergence, especially among the philosophers. Whether this process is unconscious or a logical necessity, it is persistent and recurrent – and human rights discourse has followed this pattern.

In my view, the extreme tension today between resurgent religion and the liberal order seems less over secularism per se, but, rather, over this re-enchantment of the secular state. Whereas before, under thinner conceptions of liberalism, political and

21 Michael Perry, *Toward a Theory of Human Rights* (Cambridge: Cambridge University Press, 2007).

22 Max Stackhouse, "Why Human Rights Need God: A Christian Perspective," in *Does Human Rights Need God*, eds. Barbara Barnett and Elizabeth M. Bucar (Grand Rapids: Wm. B. Eerdmans Publishing Company, 2005).

23 Nicholas Wolterstorff, *Justice: Rights and Wrongs* (Princeton: Princeton University Press, 2008).

24 Clayton, "Human Rights and Religious Values."

25 Shmuel Trigano, "The Rediscovery of Biblical Politics," *Hebraic Political Studies* 4 (3) (2009): 306–07.

26 *Id.*, 204–318.

public space was secular in the strict sense – profane, or not holy – and holiness resided in the private sphere, increasingly, universal human rights, for better or worse presents itself – and is certainly perceived – as a competing transnational, universal, transcendent realm. Within the religious worldview, however, imputing sacredness to the wrong place is the equivalent of idolatry.

To be sure, philosophical writing about human rights is not the same as human rights as a discourse in public life. Indeed, the characterization of human rights as an absolute and transcendent discourse runs counter to many characteristics of human rights activism in sociological and anthropological scholarship.[27] That scholarship attempts to show that human rights discourse bears different meanings across cultural contexts and that it is constantly being translated and reformulated both at the periphery (at the grassroots level) and the center (UN Human Rights institutions), and, indeed, even has been forced to move from charisma to bureaucracy. Thus, Sally Engle Merry's concept of vernacularization, on which Seyla Benhabib builds, could be seen as congenial to my project here. All too often, in presenting this chapter to human rights activists, however, I have encountered a common objection resting on the continued assumption that the human rights project, in order to succeed, needs to retain its transcendent language and that, indeed, this is the best strategy in appealing to religious leaders.

III THE HUMAN AS SACRED: CREATION OF HUMANS IN THE IMAGE OF GOD

One can hardly imagine a more powerful religious image for philosophy to "salvage" from religion for its own political projects than the creation of humans in the image of God. Contemporary thinkers about human rights such as Michael Perry, Robert Dahl, Jeremy Waldron, and Max Stackhouse have all invoked the sacredness of humans, in different ways, to support human rights. In Stackhouse's succinct phrasing, human beings possess "a divinely endowed core that is the ultimate basis for the right to have rights."[28] The intuition that at the base of modern concepts of human equality and human rights is the sense of human sacredness is reflected in the invocation of creation in the image in the American Declaration of Independence and Lincoln's Gettysburg Address, of course, but even a self-conscious theorist such as Ronald Dworkin invokes this language – human life is sacred – without providing formal justification.[29] As George Fletcher argued, a coherent formal philosophical justification for equality has proved quite elusive

[27] See, e.g., Mark Goodale and Sally Engle Merry eds., *The Practice of Human Rights: Tracking Law between the Global and Local* (Cambridge: Cambridge University Press, 2008).

[28] Max Stackhouse, "The Sources of Human Rights: A Christian Perspective," in *Religion and Human Rights: Conflict or Convergence*, ed. Adam B. Seligman (Hollis: Hollis Publishing Company, 2005).

[29] Ronald Dworkin, *Life's Dominion: An Argument About Abortion, Euthanasia, and Individual Freedom* (New York: Alfred A. Knopf, 1993).

while holistic arguments (for him, Kant coupled with the Hebrew Bible) are far more successful.[30]

The translation of biblical themes through Christianity into political thought is a process that bypasses the rabbinic tradition in Judaism, however. And, within the rabbinic legal tradition, by contrast, creation in the image of God occupies a relatively negligible role. It is worth first understanding why this is so before taking up the question whether, freed from the diasporic setting of much of the rabbinic tradition, the principle could be more dynamically elaborated to meet present intuitions and the contemporary needs of a Jewish state.

Certainly, from the perspective of the rabbinic tradition, the creation of humans in God's image implies that humanity has special worth that distinguishes humanity from other creatures. Creation in the image may even embody an ethical ideal of social harmony between the diverse members of humankind – one that the prophets envision as the goal of the end of days. But, even in the biblical portrayal, humanity is not intended to be a universal human order, 'one fellowship and societie,' as Locke wrote.[31] The Tower of Babel, after all, is the closest analogue to a biblical image of world government. In his biblical commentary, the Netziv portrays it as the panopticon. The biblical remedy is the division of humanity into collectivities, each with their distinct language and identity.

Creation in the image of God is rather the beginning of the unfolding in biblical and especially rabbinic thought of a drama of hierarchy, distinction, and difference that moves from humanity to Noahide (i.e., civilized) society; to the political community of resident strangers and Jews; to the congregation of Israel charged with becoming "a holy nation of priests"; and, then, to the community of fellows, which at least in theory, excludes rebellious Jewish sinners.[32]

The rabbinic tradition reveals two opposing tendencies: one emphasizing the particular dimension of Judaism, and the other, the universal. The first tendency countenances discrimination against others by reserving thick obligations of social solidarity for fellow Jews. Confining obligations of social solidarity and even equal juridical rights to Jews can be understood from several perspectives. First, Jewish tradition draws a sharp line between monotheists and non-Jewish idolators. Jews are forbidden to associate with or extend civil rights to those who practice idolatry, which symbolizes in the Bible moral corruption. Second, from a communitarian standpoint, confining positive obligations of social solidarity and fellowship to Jews

30 George P. Fletcher, "In God's Image: The Religious Imperative of Equality Under Law," *Columbia Law Review* 99 (1999): 1608. Fletcher argues that the principle of equality is best grounded in a holistic view of human dignity, and he draws on the biblical ideal of creation in God's image as well as on Kant.

31 John Locke, "The Second Treatise of Civil Government," in John Locke, *Two Treatises of Government*, ed. Peter Laslett (Cambridge: Cambridge University Press, 1967), 401.

32 I address the rabbinic "ethical vision of social life" and its contemporary challenges at greater length in Suzanne Last Stone, "The Jewish Tradition and Civil Society," in *Alternative Conceptions of Civil Society*, ed. Will Kymlicka and Simone Chambers (Princeton: Princeton University Press, 2000), 208.

creates a strong sense of community and Jewish peoplehood. The more universal strain within rabbinic thought attempts to expand the circle of solidarity by imposing duties of fellowship based on factors other than Jewish membership, such as sharing political space or moral values.[33] The Talmudic rabbis mediated between these two poles essentially by upholding rules banning fellowship with idolators while also articulating certain principles, chief among them darkhei shalom, "pursuing paths of peace," which obligated Jews to extend social solidarity to idolatrous neighbors with whom they shared political space. It remained unclear, however, whether "pursuing paths of peace," was an ethical principle grounded in notions of equal human dignity or a pragmatic policy aimed at appeasing hostile neighbors, given the precarious situation of Jews as a minority within a larger pagan space. The protracted period of isolation, persecution, and disenfranchisement of Jews hardly created a context in which to develop the universalist strains within the tradition and even so potentially powerful a concept as creation in the image received scant attention.

As a halakhic category, man's creation in the divine image is invoked to justify the intrinsic equal value of human life,[34] the duty to procreate,[35] and the respect owed to the human body – even to the corpse of a killer. All these invocations are limited to physical matters, raising the question how the rabbis understood the similitude between man and God. Concentrating on the tannaite layer, Yair Lorberbaum has argued that a school of early rabbis understood the notion as expressing an iconic relationship between man and God.[36] In some sense, according to this school, man is an ontological extension of God – a view consonant with philosophical and ethical notions of the time. The consequences of this viewpoint, he argues, were played out primarily in the domain of criminal or judicial taking of life.

Ontological conceptions of creation in the image are hard to enlist in the service of ethical or moral theories about human rights; indeed, they can lead in quite the opposite direction, as evidenced by the persistent strain of rabbinic thought that often seeks to restrict the ambit of creation in the divine image to Jews.[37] This problem resurfaces in the contemporary application of creation in the divine image as a halakhic category in connection with the question whether autopsies done for the advancement of medicine are permissible. In contrast to Rabbi Uziel, who equates all humans in the matter of respect for the dead,[38] Rabbi Kook rules that such autopsies may be conducted only on non-Jews. He comments: "The

33 *Id.*

34 Genesis 9:6.

35 Tosefta, Yevamot 8:6.

36 Yair Lorberbaum, *Image of God* [Hebrew] (Tel-Aviv & Jerusalem: Schocken, 2004).

37 There is the view of Rabbi Shimon bar Yochai, which gave rise to the tosafists' question: "Are the gentiles called man (adam)?" (Tosafot, Bava Kamma 38a, s.v. "ela"). The tosafists seem to reject Bar Yochai's opinion, and Rabbenu Tam suggests that Scripture uses the term adam in different ways, some of which do include gentiles. But the Zohar and kabbalistic literature (although not halakhic sources) take up the view of bar Yochai in pursuing an ontological division between non-Jews and Jews.

38 Piskei Uziel, *Orah Hayyim*, 178–79. See also Rabbi Eliezer Waldenberg, *Tzitz Eliezer*, 4:14.

prohibition of desecrating a corpse is derived from the divine image in man, which is unique to Israel in its greater sharpness as a result of the sanctity demanded by the Torah."[39] Rabbi Kook's romantic and idealistic tendency, and the role played in his rulings of the concept of the special sanctity of the Jewish people, is well known.[40] In this ruling, Rabbi Kook notes the unique sanctity of the body of Jews who are charged with ritual commandments such as kashruth that fashion the body's sanctity.

It is an interesting question whether beneath the "conceptual and metaphysical garb" an "existential truth" regarding humans as sacred can still be rescued that is both consistent with the general rabbinic schema and does work in a larger secular context.[41] As Shlomo Fischer points out, an ontological conception also emphasizes "the external source of the sacred value of human beings. The concern is for a God who is 'present' in the human being, a Being who is totally outside the immanent human world." Even translated into the language of ethics, the perspective is distinctly heteronymous. "The value of humans lies in their subjection to commandments; it cannot anchor absolute human value in the immanent human being or in some human characteristic such as autonomy or the ability to self-legislate."[42] In short, the concept challenges, as much as it affirms, received notions of human rights.

Of course, the remarkable under-elaboration of this concept in halakhic thought also has much to do with lack of historical need or opportunity. The dynamic elaboration of principles such as creation in the image or the dignity principle, k'vod habriyyot, or pursuing paths of peace, darkehi shalom, and even the possibility of generating new norms from them, is precisely what this collection of chapters is in part designed to explore.[43] And it should be noted that Rabbi Kook does not, strictly speaking, limit the concept of creation in the image to Jews. Instead, he writes that

39 Rabbi Abraham Isaac Ha-Kohen Kook, *Da'at Kohen*, no. 199, 383.

40 Michael Z. Nehorai, "Halakhah, Metahalakhah, and the Redemption of Israel: Reflections on the Rabbinic Rulings of Rav Kook," in *Rabbi Abraham Isaac Kook and Jewish Spirituality*, eds. David Shatz and Lawrence J. Kaplan (New York: New York University Press, 1995), 120, 144–47.

41 Shlomo Fischer, "Kevod Ha'adam, Tzelem Elohim, and Kevod Habriot," in *Religion and Human Rights*, ed. Adam Seligman (Hollis: Hollis Publishing Company, 2004), 20.

42 *Id.*, at 21–22.

43 Gerald Blidstein, "Halakhah and Democracy," *Tradition* 32 (1) (1997): 29.

Blidstein argues that norms such as darkhei shalom, kiddush Ha-shem and hillul Ha-shem, which I term principles, have a dynamic quality, expanding and contracting "according to social realities and expectations." They "seem to respond to, and assimilate, the expectations and standards of their surroundings when these cohere with basic Jewish ethics." *Id.* at 29.

In his study of the principle Kevod Habriot (respect for human dignity), Shenaton Mishpat HaIvri, Blidstein suggests that, in the medieval period, this principle served to generate several new norms (See Gerald J. Blidstein, K'vod Habriyyot: Studies in the Development of Halakha [Hebrew], *Shenaton Ha-Mishpat Ha-Ivri* (1982–83): 9–10). This argument is not free from difficulty, however. Blidstein's own study of Kevod Habriot reveals that the range of halakhic application of this principle was severely circumscribed because of the principle's subjective, "aggadic," (narrative) character and its radical potential to supplant other halakhic norms.

Jews are, as it were, "more fully in the image" than non-Jews as a result of the sanctity bestowed by the Torah's ritual commandments. Although hardly promising at first blush, it is interesting that Kook treats creation in the divine image more as a comparative concept, a matter of degree. Jews are more fully in the image than non-Jews because they perform more commandments. In this view, the concept of creation in the image is a statement about the potential of humans to perfect themselves through observance of the law. It is a theory about human potentiality to become full moral and legal subjects through their actions.

The conceptual link between human creation in the divine image and human equality seems as follows: All humans are born equal in their capacity to become full moral and legal subjects and perfect themselves. When humans sufficiently realize their potential, they become rights holders under Jewish law. But when has this potential been sufficiently realized? Rabbi Kook, in emphasizing the ontological aspects of the ritual commandments, implies that only full observance of Torah suffices. But other stopping points short of conversion might be posited. The Me'iri ruled, for example, that juridical equality is owed to the non-Jews of his time, because they are members of nations under the rule of their religious law. According to the Me'iri, societies bound by religious law occupy an intermediate category between idolaters of old and Jews. Such societies have critically progressed toward perfection.[44] Their final perfection, he writes, is conversion. Yet, those within the intermediate category are entitled to juridical equality. The critical question, then, is what makes a person or a society ethical or just so as to merit juridical equality under Jewish law: observance of the entirety of Torah, observance of Noahide commandments, or the empirically observed creation of a just and decent society committed to the rule of law?

Thus, some concept of desert, and not the possession of rights by virtue of being a human as such, seems implicit in the traditional Jewish conception of the idea of creation in the image.

In one of the more creative contemporary rabbinic attempts to grapple with human rights, this comes to the fore. The specific problem that Rabbi Hayyim David HaLevi addresses – the rights of non-Jews in the Jewish State to enjoy equal citizenship rights and social solidarity within Israeli society – is all too topical. The issue is not about the content of Israeli (secular) law; rather, he is addressing whether obligations of social solidarity extend to all citizens within the state, pursuant to Jewish religious norms. HaLevi argues that the right of self-determination granted to Jews by the international community not only creates moral constraints on the exercise of Jewish majority rule; it triggers a new moral obligation of human solidarity only hinted at before in Jewish teachings.

Jewish sovereignty creates the condition for Rabbi HaLevi to develop this ethical universal strain. But how precisely does the fact of Jewish sovereignty create this

44 Rabbi Menahem Ha-Me'iri, Sanhedrin 59a.

perspectival switch? This question is all the more puzzling, given prevalent modern understandings of sovereignty. The Hobbesian conception of territorial sovereignty is concerned with legitimacy. Legitimate power over a defined territory is transformed into a centralized system of positive law. Morality and conscience may be equally obligatory domains, but they are political sovereignty's rivals. Thus, modern centralizing conceptions of sovereignty, coupled with the positivist separation of law and the legitimate exercise of power from morality, structures a certain relationship between sovereignty and ethics in which moral obligations arise from other domains of life but are not a consequence of sovereignty itself.

True, the social contract basis of democratic sovereignty is understood to create a political obligation on the part of the sovereign to treat all citizens equally. One could therefore easily understand Halevy as asserting that the constitution of Israel as a democratic state, and the new reality of Jews holding sovereign power over others, obligates the State to treat all its citizens equally. Halevy certainly so states. But this simple reading of the text still leaves unanswered, first, how the constitution of Israel as a democratic state is somehow halakhically obligating and, second, why individual Jews in civil society now owe a moral obligation of social solidarity to fellow non-Jewish citizens. The key to resolving this puzzle, in my view, lies in noting that Halevy offers a very different conception of Jewish sovereignty in the State of Israel than the one so prevalent in current statist, centralizing imaginations of sovereignty.

Because a variety of halakhic issues turn on the absence or presence of Jewish sovereignty, rabbinic jurists were forced to conceptualize whether the State of Israel was a manifestation of Jewish sovereignty *in the halakhic sense*. For in determining the applicability of various halakhic norms and the relevance of different possible analogies, halakhic decisors must first characterize the age or phenomenon under question. In the course of doing so, several rabbinic jurists, most prominently Halevy and also R. Herzog, proposed new conceptions of Jewish sovereignty.

The question arose primarily in the context of group relations – Jews and non-Jews – as a result of Maimonidean halakhic writings about the legal norms applicable when Jews have "the upper hand." As is well known, Maimonides held that the distinction between the unredeemed world and the messianic age is freedom from the subjugation of foreign sovereigns. Talmudic tradition bequeathed a binary model that distinguishes between the days when Israel holds sway over other nations, implying exclusive or absolute dominion, or alternatively when it is powerless and suffering. Various halakhic norms – conquest, conversion, group relations, etc., – theoretically turn on this distinction. Thus Maimonides seems to hold that there will be no converts in the messianic age of Jewish sovereignty because the motivation for conversion could be instrumental: the attraction to power. Therefore, "in these days" converts must be instructed that Jews have no political agency and are suffering.[45]

45 See Moshe Hellinger, "Religious Ideology that Attempts to Ease the Conflict between Religion and State," *Journal of Church and State* 51 (Winter 2009): 52–77.

The laws Maimonides codifies as part of his vision of the time of the upper hand are a vivid example of the ontology of sovereignty: the dedication of the king to the project of the perfection of the people. Maimonides repeatedly refers to the *ummah* or *am* and ascribes to the king the task of bringing the nation to political perfection. This requires purging the land of idolators and, read straightforwardly, drastically restricting the rights of non-Jewish residents.

Is Jewish sovereignty in the modern State of Israel equivalent to the Maimonidean age of the "upper hand" that is the condition precedent of the codified Maimonidean laws? Halevy and Herzog quickly dispel this illusion, each in subtly different ways, but there is one common thread: Jewish sovereignty in the State of Israel came into being through an act of recognition by the United Nations and therefore the State of Israel's sovereignty is not only limited, it is shared.

R. Herzog is most explicit on this point. His analogy of Israel to a corporation or business partnership between Jews and non-Jews seems, at first blush, comical but it reflects a conceptual commitment to thinking about sovereignty in terms of state interdependence. R. Halevy is even more explicit: Israel was recognized as a Western democratic country and so Jewish sovereign power is limited by that principle. Halevy writes: "In the Western democratic world, *to which we belong*, society is founded upon equal rights for every person; there is no place in a democratic state for religious discrimination. Even were we a superpower, we could not practice such [discrimination]."[46] Halevy is claiming that Israel "belongs" to the Western world because it was brought into being by the United Nations no less than by Jewish efforts. For Halevy and Herzog this is nonetheless a genuine form of *Jewish* sovereignty, sufficient to penetrate into the normative sphere of halakha. For example, it is sufficient to trigger a halakhic obligation to recite the Prayer of Thanksgiving on Independence Day. By contrast, R. Ovadiah Yosef, though he held by and large a positive view of the state, ruled against reciting that prayer because he did not recognize the state as falling within a halakhic category of *Jewish* sovereignty.

Both Halevy and Herzog seem to have been operating from within a larger cultural understanding of sovereignty in their time that still is attested to in Israel's Declaration of Independence. The shared assumption of the period was that the legitimacy of the state depended on recognition. Halevy goes a critical step further, however, in understanding recognition not merely as the ratification of an existing state of affairs but, instead, as constitutive of sovereignty. Recognition not only confers legitimacy on the state, it endows the state with its very identity.

This point warrants elaboration. There is a longstanding debate in international relations between the practice of recognition among states and the condition of statehood. While some theorists insist that states are states prior to their recognition

[46] Rabbi Hayyim David Halevy, "Ways of Peace in the Relations between Jews and Non-Jews," *Tehumin* 9 (1988): 71–78. Emphasis added.

as such, others argue that the recognition of a state is a constitutive act: it brings statehood into existence. The debate, as Patchen Markell has helpfully observed, captures the two senses of the term recognition. In the first, recognition is an awareness of a pre-existing state of affairs, of a status that already really exists. In the second view, recognition is an act that brings something new into being or transforms the world in some way.[47]

The different senses of recognition, Markell goes on to argue, trade on differing conceptions of self-determination and political agency. Zionism (and the view incorporated in Israel's Declaration of Independence), by and large, relies on the political imagination of the first sense of recognition. International acceptance ratified a pre-existing state of affairs: the national-collective will and identity of the Jewish people. But, pursuant to the constitutive sense of recognition, neither sovereignty nor political identity is the product of a singular will nor self-determination in its fullest sense.

It is this new relationship between Jews and the world that underlies Halevy's attempt to ground social solidarity in a principle "only hinted at before in Jewish teachings" – the creation of humans in the image of God. The "new reality of Israel," to which Halevy refers, is a new age of recognition by non-Jews of the humanity (and, hence, political agency) of Jews and not solely or even primarily the new reality that Jews are now a majority ruling over a minority. The question could have been framed within older talmudic paradigms addressing obligations of social solidarity in a mixed society – "pursuing paths of peace" could serve as a ready answer, for example. HaLevi refuses to follow this easy route. "Darkhei shalom," he insists, is a diasporic concept; it is only suitable to Jewish life as a minority population. Instead, Halevy insists that Jewish sovereignty demands a radical change in the mindset of Jews toward the world and that awareness of the new reality must penetrate the halakhic normative sphere. The exilic mindset requires alteration so that "we visit the gentile sick, bury their dead, and comfort their mourners out of a moral, human duty, not merely because of the 'ways of peace.'"

HaLevi insists that the source of this obligation is not contractual or conventional; it is a moral obligation rooted in the concept of a shared humanity. At the same time, HaLevi implies, one could not truly speak of a shared humanity before, given centuries of persecution and Jewish disenfranchisement. Now, with the recognition of Jewish sovereignty, HaLevi suggests, the immense distinction between Jew and non-Jew finally has been lessened. Consequently, Jews have a human moral duty to recognize the full humanity of others.

It is important to note the halakhic significance HaLevi assigns to the world's recognition of the political rights of Jews. It is equally important to note that this is the arena of reciprocity and exchange, not of transcendence, the moral absolute, or the sacred. The moral obligation Jews owe to the other – and to one another – is based on

47 See Patchen Markell, *Bound By Recognition* (Princeton: Princeton University Press, 2003).

ethical reciprocity, norms of mutuality, moral symmetry, and gratitude. In retrospect, it is the principle of reciprocity that may also underlie prior rulings extending solidarity beyond Jewish borders. HaMeiri, whom HaLevi cites, reinterpreted Talmudic rules permitting discrimination as confined to idolators who are not "restricted by the ways of religion." The nations who are under the sway of religion, Meiri implies, adhere to basic norms of morality that govern their behavior toward those with whom they share political space. Jews have a moral duty, in turn, to reciprocate.

The universal ideal of human solidarity that HaLevi draws out of Jewish teaching thus differs in an important respect from the core notion of Western human rights discourse: Rights are not absolute or inherent; they are not inviolable and they do not inhere in the human as such. Nor is HaLevi invoking sympathy, pity, or love for the other, irrespective of their actions or capacities for doing evil. A more fruitful comparison is to the political conceptions of rights and evocation of reciprocity made by John Rawls in his *Theory of Justice*. There, Rawls draws on principles of moral psychology, following Piaget, to argue that the sense of justice grows out of prior stages: first the morality of authority based on reciprocal love between parent and child and then the morality of association based on friendship.[48] "Because we recognize that they wish us well, we care for their well-being in return . . . The basic idea is one of reciprocity, a tendency to answer in kind."[49] Genuine other-regard depends on receiving benefits, inaugurating the play of gratitude and indebtedness. Rawls extends this to those who have only the potential to reciprocate; but there is a close connection between Rawls' invocation of a well-ordered society and the reasonableness of expecting benefits and therefore extending respect to those who only have the potential to reciprocate. HaLevi combines these notions: a well-ordered society is presupposed. "These are not the idolators of ancient times." Given tangible evidence of an ordered society – "they have wished us well" – a moral duty of equal concern and respect is created.

The line of thought HaLevi develops is a disavowal of any shared vision of the human as such as sacred but it captures the more modest notion of a regime of rights based on the play of recognition and exchange. As Adam Seligman writes:

> The world of the sacred and of religious authority is, by definition, a world marked off from the play of negotiation and exchange within which social order is defined. The

[48] While Rawls seemed to deny that the original position "explicitly" presupposed a principle of equal respect, Dworkin has claimed that this is the "deep theory" behind the original position. "This right, he says, is 'owed to human beings as moral persons', and follows from the moral personality that distinguishes humans from animals" (Ronald Dworkin, *Taking Rights Seriously* (Cambridge: Harvard University Press, 1978), 181.)

[49] John Rawls, *A Theory of Justice* (Cambridge: Harvard University Press, 1999), 433. By invoking Rawls here, I aim to elucidate my point in terms of modern political philosophy. I do not mean to suggest that HaLevi preempted Rawls' theory of justice, or that Rawls drew upon rabbinic literature. It would be a distraction to further discuss Rawls' relationship to Jewish thought in this essay. For an elaboration of Rawls and reciprocity, see: Thom Brooks, "Reciprocity as Mutual Recognition," *The Good Society* 21 (1) (2012): 57.

> sacred is that which is ineluctably Other, that which cannot be grasped, bartered, or exchanged. Its dictates impose obligations that are simply of a different order of experience, that involve totally different domain assumptions than those encompassed by the play of reciprocity and autonomy on which a regime of rights is based.[50]

IV FROM THE ABSOLUTE UNIVERSAL TO INTERNATIONAL CONVENTION AND TRANSNATIONAL CONSENSUS

Since Kant, we tend to reflexively endow the universal realm with transcendent status and grant priority to the universal over the particular. But the universal was once conceived as a common or shared realm, expressing a kind of *consensus gentium*. Recently, Jack Donnelly, among others, has urged a return to this more modest conception of human rights.[51]

If we were to approach human rights in this way, the question becomes whether Judaism gives weight, as a matter of the religion's internal viewpoint, to world consensus. In other words, would the Jewish tradition defer to the international legal regime of human rights or to an emerging translational understanding of global norms, including informal ones, just in virtue of consensus?[52]

This strategy of convergence between religion and human rights depends on retrieving the idea of human rights as a purely political discourse and emphasizing its legal forms by which immunities and liberties are inscribed as rights (e.g., the international legal regime of human rights), as well as "soft" or informal law, without recourse to the philosophy of the person and society with which human rights discourse has been entangled.[53] There need be no agreement between Judaism and human rights discourse on the content of the core principles of human rights – even a fine one. Deference, rather, would be based on second order reasons, such as tacit or hypothetical consent and possibly a certain moral – or religious – claim that consensus in itself makes on us.[54]

50 Seligman, "Introduction," 8.

51 Jack Donnelly, "The Relative Universality of Human Rights," *Human Rights Quarterly* 29/2 (2007): 281.

52 I do not mean to invoke a simple return to the classic conception of international law as the formal contracts made between sovereign states. On the contrary, the "soft" law character of international human rights law that Merry and others describe, need not be an impediment from the halakhic viewpoint. This needs further working out, but my initial reading of the halakhic material is that it is capacious enough to extend beyond formal norms and, indeed, writers such as Hirschenssohn were early advocates of what might now be deemed "grassroots" loci of norm creation. On the problems associated with consent (weak, formalist basis), see Marti Koskenniemmi, *From Apology to Utopia: The structure of international legal argument* (Cambridge: Cambridge University Press, 2015).

53 Charles Taylor urges the disentanglement of the human rights discourse as a set of legal forms by which immunities and liberties are inscribed as rights from human rights as a philosophy of the person and society. Either the form or the philosophy could then be adopted alone without the other. See Charles Taylor, "Conditions of an Unforced Consensus on Human Rights" (speech given at Bangkok Workshop, 1996).

54 See Clayton, "Human Rights and Religious Values," as to how this differs from Rawlsian overlapping consensus. Per Rawls, we would agree on the norms, while disagreeing on why they were the right norms.

These notions, it turns out, are quite deeply embedded in the Jewish tradition. I am now only beginning in a project of surveying halakhic attitudes to international law and global governance that will focus on the writings of R. Hayyim Hirschenssohn, who argued that the halakhic obligation of keeping "covenants" extends to international conventions and global agreements, whether formal or informal. These agreements need not be state-based; they can be embedded in global society and may even override halakha. The importance of consensus and custom also find expression in a variety of standard halakhic doctrines, such as *dina de-malkhuta dina* ("The law of the kingdom is the law"); *minhag Yisrael din hu* ("the custom of Israel is the law"), etc. Through these doctrines, contemporary practices of the people were incorporated into the halakhic system and translated into norms. These practices usually pertained to private law or fiscal matters, and parties are permitted to vary Jewish private law by contract, in any event. With the rise of the State of Israel, Jewish contemporary practice includes matters of public law, such as practices of war, statecraft, and the shaping of civil society. These practices pertaining to public law are absorbed from the larger environment: that is, the "family of nations." Recall HaLevi's statement: "In the Western democratic world, to which we (i.e., Jews in the State of Israel) belong, society is founded upon equal rights for every person." In other words, the environment of the State of Israel is the Western democratic world and its norms.

Still, incorporating norms generated from outside the halakhic world into the halakhic system raises a number of deep and complex issues, chief among them the question of limits. Contemporary responsa even in the area of private law well illustrate the dilemma. Thus, some rabbinic decisors have held that contemporary practices such as gender equality in splitting marital assets, meet the technical requirements of incorporation doctrines such as *dina de-malkhuta dina* and "customs of the people;"[55]while others contend that laws stemming from a "worldview" or a "religious or social ideology" cannot be incorporated because the "religious and social worldview of the Jewish people derives exclusively from the Torah."[56] To put it starkly, if the Declaration of Human Rights is absorbed into the halakhic system as the norm of the family of nations to which the State of Israel belongs, the halakhic tradition would no longer serve as a resource for contributing to a critique of contemporary politics, including human rights discourse itself. Instead, the halakha would be confined primarily to the ethico-spiritual realm; its political dimension would simply parallel that of the law of nations. What, then, is the role of the Jewish religion and the halakha in shaping a specifically Jewish politics as an expression of Jewish religious ideals and identity?

[55] See R. Shlomo Dichovsky, "The Shared Assets Rule – Is it Dina De-Malkhuta?" 29 (1997) *Techumin*: 18.

[56] See R. Avraham Sherman, "The 'Shared Assets' Rules in Light of the Laws of the Torah," 18 (1997) *Techumin*: 32.

I have dealt with these questions at length elsewhere and will only summarize here one fascinating line of thought supporting halakhic incorporation of the international legal regime of human rights in virtue of world consensus. Whether such deference to the international regime of human rights is halakhically permissible or even obligatory touches on a large and, at times, highly technical debate within Judaism concerning the status and contours of its doctrine of universal law, the Noahide Code. Put highly schematically, the claim is that international law and consensus are binding on Jews through the complex interaction of Noahide law with the Talmudic principle, "the law of the kingdom is the law." While Noahide law is ordinarily thought of as the universal moral law that God gave to humanity – superseded at Sinai for Jews – in fact, the relationship of Noahide law to Jewish obligations is far more complex. Noahide law can be seen, or so I have argued at length elsewhere, as an alternative source of norms even in a purely internal Jewish context, a form of fallback or residual law, which can be invoked when the particular law requires supplementation or functional adjustment.[57]

Paradoxically, although Noahide law is presented as a universal moral code given by God, the content of which is discerned and elaborated by Jewish tradition, it is sometimes the case that the content of Noahide law is essentially determined by the convention of the nations.

An analogous claim was, indeed, made by Rabbi Shaul Yisraeli, in a different – and highly politically charged – context when he ruled that the Jewish state was obligated by – and only by – international standards of war.[58] Rabbi Yisraeli based his view that the rules of war are those agreed to by the global community of nations on two legs. The first is that war is a part of statecraft – an activity committed to the Jewish king and its successor institutions such as the modern Jewish state. He cites Deuteronomy 17:14, in which the people ask for a king "like all the nations." And he couples this with the view, most clearly articulated by the Netziv in the nineteenth century, that war is a universal activity permitted to all societies and therefore should be waged by universal rules.

57 Suzanne Last Stone, "Sinaitic and Noahide Law: Legal Pluralism in Jewish Law," *Cardozo Law Review* 12 (3–4) (1991): 1157; Suzanne Last Stone, "Religion and the State: Models of Separation from Within Jewish Law," *International Journal of Constitutional Law*, 6 (3–4) (2008): 631–61; Suzanne Last Stone, "Law without Nation? The Ongoing Jewish Discussion," in *Law without Nations*, eds. Austin Sarat, Lawrence Douglas and Martha Umphrey (The Amherst Series in Law, Jurisprudence, and Social Thought, Stanford, Stanford University Press, 2010), 101–37. And now see the decision of the Jerusalem Rabbinical Court (R. Dikhovski, Sherman, Ben Shimon) #4276 (citing Zafnat Paneach for the proposition that Jews were given additional obligations at Sinai, including marriage and divorce laws, but were not relieved of their obligations imposed by Hebrew Law on Noahides), which function as fall-back law when the former are not applicable.

58 See Harav Shaul Yisraeli, *Amud Ha-Yemini*, 15:165–205. The ruling was a retrospective justification of the Kibiye massacre; however, as Gerald Blidstein commented, his innovative legal thinking would have traction, nonetheless. (Gerald Blidstein, "The Treatment of Hostile Civilian Populations: The Contemporary Halakhic Discussion in Israel," *Israel Studies* 1 (2) (1996): 27–45).

Deuteronomy 17:14 is ordinarily not viewed as a legal source. R. Yisraeli, it seems, is compressing a long tradition of legal and political discourse about Jewish kingship. To grasp both the inner logic at work here and the ethical and identity dilemmas they raise requires a bit of a detour through halakhic discourse about the status and validity of conventional government. I have dealt with this issue at length elsewhere and will only summarize the contours of the argument here.[59]

Within Judaism, there are a variety of doctrines that roughly correspond to a division between religious and political spheres. Several were developed in tandem with Islam and Christianity in the twelfth and thirteenth centuries along with the emergence of criminal law as public rather than religious law. Biblical evidentiary restrictions on conviction were jettisoned by all three religions, and various justifications emerged for the assignment of certain extralegal powers to political authorities who were not restrained by religious law. Far from positing a total society, unified under one sacral law, several medieval Jewish legal thinkers imagined the halakha as composed of different jurisdictions generating law in accordance with different principles. The political realm emerges in these writings as a space with its own distinct logic and laws.

The medieval Jewish discussion centers on the rights of monarchs, including the prerogatives of the "Jewish king," and is revived in modern halakhic discussions of the legitimacy of the law of the state, including a Jewish state. The Hebrew Bible sets up a tension between a model of kingship that is particular and culturally specific and one that is universal. That tension is fully exploited in the medieval discussion. Whether kingship is a realm of politics, discretion, and wisdom, or a realm of distinctive law, is a large and lingering question. Maimonides' codification of the laws of Jewish kings seems to transfer over to the Jewish king a separate body of Talmudic law about the universal "Noahide" laws that bind non-Jewish societies, from the Jewish perspective.[60] In addition to six substantive commands – exemplifying a civilized political community, such as prohibitions on murder, theft, and the like – Noahide law includes a seventh command of justice, *dinin*. For Maimonides, *dinin* is nothing but the requirement to establish governmental structures capable of preserving order by punishing violations of the other Noahide laws. As Gerald Blidstien noted, "Maimonides' entire edifice of monarchic powers identified Jewish and gentile governance as a single structure possessing similar goals and utilizing similar instruments."[61]

59 For further analysis, see Suzanne Last Stone, "The Jewish Law of War: The Turn to International Law and Ethics," in *Just Wars, Holy Wars, and Jihad*, ed. Sohail Hashmi (Oxford: Oxford University Press, 2012); see also Arye Edrei, "Law, Interpretation, and Ideology: The Renewal of the Jewish Laws of War in the State of Israel," *Cardozo Law Review* 28 (1) (2006): 187–228.

60 Gerald J. Blidstein, "'Ideal' and 'Real' in Classical Jewish Political Theory," *Jewish Political Studies Review* 2 (1–2) (1990): 58–60. Traditional jurists commenting on Maimonides note this connection. See Meir Simhah Cohen of Dvinsk, *Ohr Sameah*, Laws of Kings 3:1.

61 Blidstein, "'Ideal' and 'Real' in Classical Jewish Political Theory," 58.

The most far-reaching articulation of Jewish kingship as social order is that of Rabbi Nissim Gerondi who posits a central gap in the Halakha: the lack of conventional modes of governance able to preserve social order. Yet, the Torah itself provides the means for correcting this deficiency: monarchical powers. The monarch is merely the site of social order historically chosen by the people who may consent to another institutional form if they so desire. Although Gerondi is largely silent on whether this is a space of discretion or law and whether there are any inherent limits, I believe we can read him against the background of his predecessors and contemporaries as at the least implicitly incorporating the conventional rules of non-Jewish societies, insofar as they relate to matters of enforcing social order.

This underlying concept – that government, the task of which is the preservation of social order, is a universal Noahide norm incumbent on all societies, Jewish and non-Jewish alike and in more or less the same way – also underlies Rabbi Yisraeli's approach to war. Thus, Rabbi Yisraeli relies on prior precedent holding that war is not only permitted to non-Jewish societies but that it is a logical outgrowth of the Noahide command of *dinin*, because war in present times is a means to reduce social conflict and therefore to preserve social order. And the War Convention sets the limits of what is permissible. Thus, the link between Noahide law as a universal body of norms that was Jewishly discerned and elaborated and accordingly subject to internal standards of some sort – Judaism's contribution to discourse about human rights as a moral theory – becomes reversed. Now at least this one Noahide law is imagined as the tacitly agreed upon practices of conventional societies in pursuit of good governance.

The second leg of Rabbi Yisraeli's opinion relies on a more familiar halakhic principle: *dina de-malkhuta dina* (the law of the kingdom is the law, henceforward DDM), but he gave it a radically innovative meaning. Where formerly the dictum governed the obligations and privileges of individual Jews relative to their host states, in the elaboration by Yisraeli, it now governs the obligations and privileges of the Jewish nation acting in the international context. And where formerly, the dictum extended only to the laws of a sovereign ruler, such as king or state, here it extends to international law on the theory that the non-Jewish kingdom could be defined in global terms, as long as the collective will of the world's citizens ratified the global kingdom's law. (The perspective is quite similar to that of current United States Supreme Court jurisprudence holding that the convention and customs of the nations is incorporated into federal law.)

DDM is first articulated in the context of the power of foreign rulers to tax and expropriate land and eventually became a cornerstone for the successful integration of the formerly legally autonomous Jewish communities into the legal systems of the nation-state. Paradoxically, the principle originally served to make the halakha fully functional in exile but then the postulate took on a life of its own as the jurists began to theorize in the Middle Ages about its conceptual basis. The most prevalent conceptual base is one or another version of consent theory. Rashi, interestingly, connects the principle to Noahide law. He explains the Talmudic permission to Jewish litigants in an intra-Jewish dispute to take advantage of non-Jewish methods of validating deeds as resting on the notion that non-Jews are commanded to "institute justice" – citing the Noahide norm of *dinim*. Accordingly, they can be effective agents for all matters subsumed under that command. Recall that, from the internal perspective of rabbinic Judaism, this command obligates humanity to preserve social order by enacting systems of law. Accordingly, non-Jewish legal activity can serve here as an alternative norm even for Jews and even when it is at variance with Jewish law. The implication of Rashi's rationale is that large portions of the halakha are in fact replaceable by foreign law, thus shrinking the scope of halakha to matters of ritual and religious prohibition (including marriage and divorce).[62]

Yisraeli's opinion about the binding nature of international law seems to blend the underlying rationales of the consent school and of Rashi's turn to Noahide *dinim*. Jews can consent to be governed by international norms, just as they can consent to be governed by the civil laws of host states. Consent to laws pertaining to war is legitimate even though war involves the religious prohibition of bloodshed. War, however, is a chosen means to settle disputes in contemporary life and, as such, fulfills the goal of civilizing the world and securing social order, even if such wars are not undertaken for the sake of enforcing Noahide norms.

The laws of the Jewish king, the principle that the "the law of the kingdom is law," and the Noahide command of justice thus become all facets of a single concept. Still, the very existence of a "universal" code within a particular legal system has opened a deep fissure in Jewish thought. If Noahide law is God-sanctioned, what precisely is the point of the particular laws given later at Sinai? The various eighteenth- and nineteenth-century debates within Judaism about the modern state, from that of the Reformers to Mendelssohn, are in part attempts to answer that question.

Gerondi, too, anticipates this issue. For, in the course of outlining the Jewish king's powers, he addresses the purpose of the halakha's highly nonconventional system of order, as reflected in its criminal procedures. Certain biblical laws, such as judging in accordance with two witnesses, he argues, were never intended as a practical means to govern society. Rather, they are intended to bring on the divine effluence and to judge individuals in a manner exquisitely attuned to the rights of individual defendants without regard to social need. Gerondi is working off earlier rabbinic sources as well as extending the doctrine of Noahide law to one logical

[62] Jewish law maintains that with respect to financial matters, as opposed to religious matters, it is possible for parties to contract out of the law in any event, despite the fact that these norms originate in divine law. But the rationale which links the validity of Gentile law to the Noahide command of *dinim*, would suggest that it could extend to all laws subsumed under the Noahide command, including criminal law and punishment, traditionally categorized as "religious." Rashi's theory has very few internal limits, except that subjects unique to Jewish law cannot be displaced.

conclusion. He is following, as Blidstein pointed out, Yehuda Halevi, who wrote about "the social – ethical law given to humanity (i.e., Noahide law) to which the spiritual-ceremonial law is added at Sinai," and decisively splitting the two into the realm of the sacred and particular, where true justice is possible, as opposed to the realm of the profane and universal, where the needs of society are irreconcilable with the rights of individuals.

As we know from modern Jewish history, the coexistence of universal and particular elements in one tradition led to an internal splitting of the tradition along lines generally analogous to the modern differentiation of political and religious realms. Increasingly, the particular laws given exclusively for Jews at Sinai becomes seen as religion or ethics, even from an internal standpoint – and not only from the standpoint of the host nation-states in which Judaism later was set.

Modern separation or differentiation of realms not only allows different realms of human experience to proceed in accordance with different conceptual logics. It also provides a means for one realm or activity to critique the other. This is the most powerful claim of modern positivism's separation thesis: by differentiating between law and morality, strong moral critique of modern law is made possible. One of the more interesting questions for those observing the Jewish tradition today revolves around this issue of critique. What resources should or could the tradition use to critique the organization of the contemporary political sphere, including the discourse of human rights? Keen observers of the tradition will note that, outside the State of Israel (which presents a unique set of problems), the standards used to judge the political sphere are not, by and large, the particular religious or ethical aspirational norms of the Jewish tradition but, rather, they draw on the large body of Jewish sources which develop the universal Noahide Code. That body of law is in itself an ongoing project that develops in tandem with developments in the larger political sphere. For example, while the original markers of good government in the service of religion from the Talmudic period through the medieval period cite the Noahide ban on idolatry and blasphemy, over time, these criteria are reinterpreted to fit a secular age. Thus, the ban on idolatry is in the process of reinterpretation in terms of commitment to the rule of law. In short, the tradition continues to provide a standpoint from which to judge the very space it authorizes. In doing so, we can catch a glimpse of what – in the eyes of Judaism – is a well-ordered political space and what is, instead, seen as inimical to the common project of government.

It is here that Yisraeli's turn to the international legal regime is most vulnerable, for it entails abandonment of any standpoint from which criticism is possible. International codes of war, treaties, and so on, govern the state of Israel – from the halakhic perspective – and not indigenous, national-collective norms or particular, aspirational norms developed to govern relations of members within a covenantal community. In his analysis, Yisraeli makes clear that halakhic norms pertaining to use of force developed within the context of individual self-defense could not countenance the manner of conducting warfare acceptable within the international community. But rather than view halakha as a ground for ethical critique, he sees halakha as allowing the incorporation of looser standards of behavior when the nation acts beyond its borders. Should international society adopt more stringent norms than halakha, these too would be binding on the nation acting in the international arena. The Jewish nation-state is no longer modeled on a concept of exceptionalism; instead, it is merely a member of international society whose norms should converge.

Rabbi Yisraeli's position was re-examined recently in two American symposia on the topic of Jewish law and war. The responses it invoked are telling. Even those thinkers who are sympathetic to the idea that the laws of the Jewish king and Noahide law bear a "family resemblance" were deeply troubled both by the complete "surrender to comparative law" and by "the suspension of the normative ethics of Jewish law." The gist of both objections is that in turning to international law, Yisraeli left no standard for ethical critique or reason to contribute a distinctively Jewish ethical voice to society at large. What is at stake is both the role of the halakha as a resource for ethical thought (without necessarily a modifier) as well as the role of traditional Jewish sources, developed from within, in shaping a particular Jewish character and sensibility and providing an aspirational set of norms or set of superoragatories. In short, what is at stake is not only the status of halakha as an ethics, and not solely autonomous law, but also identity and exceptionalism, of carving out rules – even in heart of the political realm such as warfare – that reflect particularist ideals even if not adhered to by the rest of the world.

These internal debates about politics as a shared, universal realm of experience, about the Jewish tradition as a resource for ethical critique, and about Jewish identity, also shed light on the place of human rights discourse in contemporary Jewish Orthodox society. I do not need to belabor certain trends in the discourse of traditional Judaism, especially in Israel: increased ethnocentrism and the rise of romantic, utopian strains of religion emphasizing authenticity. Not that long ago, it was common to debate how coterminous halakha was with ethics and whether there was an equally obligatory ethic independent of halakha – and these debates were not confined to rarified academic or intellectual circles. Pursuant to that conception, human rights as an ethical theory need not always be elaborated from within; it could be obligatory independent of halakha. Now there is an increasing tendency to view halakha as comprehensive and all-encompassing, in which all rights and obligations, including political ones, must be generated exclusively from within a single sacral framework that emphasizes only one pole of biblical and rabbinic thought: the particular. At its most extreme, the sacred is perceived as the holy, in the face of which the norms of general society are irrelevant. The subject of religion and human rights is an occasion not only to resuscitate the question of the independence of ethics, but also to reflect on the reservoir of Jewish sources that speak to the other pole of biblical and rabbinic thought: the universal.

3

Sovereign Imaginaries

Visualizing the Sacred Foundation of Law's Authority

Richard K. Sherwin

But reason and science have always performed, and still perform, only an auxiliary function in the life of peoples, and it will be like that till the end of time. Nations are formed and moved by some other force whose origin is unknown and unaccountable . . . [1]

To be interested in thinking how we learn about thinking is a condition for politics (including ethics), theology, and metaphysics alike.[2]

I INTRODUCTION: SACRED FOUNDATIONS

If a world is to be lived in, it must be founded.[3] This foundational function belongs to the sovereign imagination. What a polity names as sovereign in the state of exception, when the sacred irrupts anew, is a matter of individual and collective responsibility. In this dispensation, law, politics, and religion become inescapably entangled in metaphysics. It behooves us to understand the nature and consequences of this state of affairs.

Throughout history the human mind has sought knowledge from the beginning of things. Mircea Eliade used the phrase "*Illud Tempus*," the beginning time, to describe "the stupendous instant in which a reality was created."[4] This is the moment at which foundational narratives call into being a *nomos*, a living legal reality, the emergence of a world. The beginning time marks the time of the sacred – that uncanny source of immeasurable abundance out of which a world of meaning emerges. Rudolf Otto called it the "numinous." Standing before the numinous as it shimmers in a place, a text, or an image, we sense a strange excess, the presence of something immanent, as yet unseen in the visible world. The numinous radiates an

[1] Fyodor Dostoevsky, *The Possessed*, trans. Andrew R MacAndrew (New York: Signet edition, 1962), Part II, Ch. 1, sec. vii, 236–37.

[2] Rowan D. Williams, "Between Politics and Metaphysics: Reflections in the Wake of Gillian Rose," *Modern Theology* 11: 1 (1995), 21.

[3] Mircea Eliade, *The Sacred and the Profane*, trans. Willard R. Frask (New York: Harcourt 1987 [1957]), 22.

[4] *Ibid.*, at 81.

inexpressible intensity. We shudder in wonder, or terror, at its absolute otherness.[5] The Event of the sacred calls out to us – for naming.

One senses in the sacred, for both law and religion, a curious bond between the bounded and the boundless. As the great American poet Wallace Stevens wrote: "A violent order is disorder; and a great disorder is an order. These two things are one."[6]

On the threshold of that impossible polarity, it is as if (to cite another of Stevens' lines) "an inhuman order" sounds on the evening air, as if a singer's song were "fluttering its empty sleeves," making a place for being – there, in the song the singer sings – even as the threshold on which we stand to hear it comes no closer to its source: for the song makes the sky "acutest at its vanishing."[7] That vanishing point marks the threshold of the sacred.

In law, the paradox of form and spirit, order and disorder, structure and anti-structure, arises under the rubric of sovereignty. Sovereignty directs us to an ultimate authority for law that lies outside law itself. As Harold Berman has written: "Law – in all societies – derives its authority from something outside itself."[8] Or as Jacques Derrida more recently put it: "The positing or establishing of law or right are exceptional and are in themselves neither legal nor properly juridical."[9]

As the concept of sovereignty emerged in the sixteenth century, it came to describe the absolute power of the ruler of the state. This power was generally thought to reside in the office of the king,[10] but it also could be held by the nobility, or the people.[11] Regardless of where its power lay, however, sovereignty was conceived as indivisible, absolute, unlimited. In this sense, it transcended positive (or written) law as such.[12] To command in the name of the state without the authority of the sovereign lacks legitimacy. If such a state of affairs were to persist, the rottenness at the core of things would fester and spread, and the state ultimately would most likely fail.[13]

To be sure, positive rules may generate and sustain valid legal systems. Rules demand obedience. To this extent, the power of the state is on their side. But extralegal values and beliefs aligned with a sovereign source of authority go beyond

5 Rudolf Otto, *The Idea of the Holy: An Inquiry into the Non-rational Factor in the Idea of the Divine and Its Relation to the Rational*, trans. John W. Harvey (New York: Oxford University Press, 1970 [1917]), 1–30.

6 Wallace Stevens, "Connoisseur of Chaos," in *Selected Poems* (ed. by John N. Serio) (New York: Alfred A. Knopf 2009), 124.

7 Wallace Stevens, "The Idea of Order at Key West," in *ibid.*, at 74.

8 Harold J. Berman, *Law and Revolution* (Cambridge: Harvard University Press 1983), 16.

9 Jacques Derrida, *The Beast & the Sovereign*, vol. 1, trans. Geoffrey Bennington (Chicago: University of Chicago Press 2009), 49.

10 See Debora Kuller Shuger, *Political Theologies in Shakespeare's England* (New York: Palgrave 2001), 72–101.

11 See Dieter Grimm, *Sovereignty: The Origin and Future of a Political and Legal Concept*, trans. Belinda Cooper (New York: Columbia University Press 2009), 21.

12 See Grimm, *ibid.*, at 22.

13 See Walter Benjamin, "Critique of Violence" in *Illuminations: Essays & Reflections*, trans. Edmund Jephcott (New York: Schocken Books 1968), 278–300.

formal validity. What is sovereign renders law legitimate. Higher values and beliefs inspire acceptance of the rules of law as "right" and "good." This sense of "rightness" goes beyond fear of disobedience as a basis for accepting law's commands. In this sense, the legitimacy that comes with higher values transmutes validity (based on fear of "the gunman writ large," as legal positivist H. L. A. Hart put it)[14] into moral significance (law's rightful authority as a warrant for respectful acceptance). In short, with legitimacy comes belief, and from belief comes fidelity to the rule of law.[15]

In a reflection on Kafka's modern parable, "Before the Law," Gershom Scholem once noted that under conditions of "validity without significance" legitimacy becomes but a rumor.[16] For Scholem, this encounter with the dead spirit of the law describes the nothingness of revelation, the zero point of law and politics, a legal space in which the Nothing appears. This begins to describe the metaphysics of nihilism, a topic to which we will return.

For now, let us take as our point of departure the irruption of the sacred, that numinous, irreducible excess – evident in Durkheim's "collective effervescence"[17] or Weber's "charisma"[18] – which animates and binds us to law beyond the merely formal claims of validity that a given legal system may demand. In the premodern era, one associates this excess with the divine right of kings. In the modern era, we associate it with the rise of popular sovereignty and the nation state.[19]

Carl Schmitt famously proclaimed, "Sovereign is he who decides on the exception."[20] Acting within a state of exception in the name of a sovereign authority, the sovereign – whether monarch, Parliament, or people – may choose to abandon constitutional law (the supreme law of the land). Contention over the rightful genealogy or nomenclature or interpretation of the decision that determines what is sovereign may significantly disrupt civil society, leading to political strife and perhaps ultimately civil war. In the state of exception, the history, form, and

14 H. L. A. Hart, *The Concept of Law* (Oxford: Clarendon Press 1979), 80.

15 See Richard K. Sherwin, "Opening Hart's Concept of Law," *Valparaiso Law Review* 20(1986), 385.

16 Scholem Gershom, *The Correspondence of Walter Benjamin and Gershom Scholem 1932–1940*, trans. Anson Rabinbach (Cambridge: Harvard University Press 1992), 142.

17 See Emile Durkheim, *The Elementary Forms of Religious Life*, trans. K. E. Fields (New York: Free Press, 1995), 212–13, 228; see also Victor Turner, *The Ritual Process: Structure and Anti-Structure* (Ithaca: Cornell University Press 1969), 132 ("[T]he spontaneity and immediacy of *communitas* – as opposed to the jural-political character of structure – can seldom be maintained for very long.").

18 See Max Weber, *On Charisma and Institution Building* (Chicago: University of Chicago Press 1968).

19 The vicissitudes of the sacred lie at the heart of Giambattisto Vico's *New Science*. In that masterwork, Vico sets out to trace the shifting, archetypal patterns of Providence in civil life – the languages, institutions and laws of humanity that arise and transform throughout history. Values give meaning to the trace of the sacred as it breaks into history. It is that meaning (for good or ill) which legitimates the exercise of state power. Following Vico, I believe it is possible to develop genealogies of the sacred in the history of human culture – in art, religion, and law. It is a matter of being guided by images marked by intense disruption. See Giambattista Vico, *The New Science of Giambattista Vico*, trans. Goddard Bergin and Max Harold Fisch (Ithaca: Cornell University Press 1968 [1744]).

20 Carl Schmitt, *Political Theology*, trans. George Schwab (Chicago: University of Chicago Press: 1985 [1922]), 5.

significance of sovereignty come into view. At such times, as history has shown, the people may repudiate a king's sovereign proclamation, just as the state may repudiate acclamations by the people – in blood, if need be.

Given the historic association of violence with the founding of political and legal systems, it should not prove surprising to witness the invisible ink of sovereignty materializing on the flesh of the body politic. As Thomas Jefferson famously wrote: "The tree of liberty must be refreshed from time to time with the blood of patriots & tyrants."[21] Or as Walter Benjamin observed: "Violence crowned by fate is the origin of law."[22] Jacques Derrida has followed suit: "Since the origin of authority, the foundation or ground, the position of law can't by definition rest on anything but themselves, they are themselves a violence without ground."[23] Or as Paul Kahn has more recently said: "The order of law begins in the exception of the Revolution."[24]

In its founding moment, law is neither legal nor illegal. Derrida calls this the absolute limit of the mystical foundation of law. We return here to Eliade's *Illud Tempus*, the beginning time, which signals an irruption of the sacred into the realm of the profane. The state of emergency or exception, the moment of the Schmittian decision, when sovereignty is named anew, is a time out of time, a Dionysian moment, a time of wonder or terror, often signed in blood.

How do we understand this recurrent, exceptional state of affairs out of which fundamental political and legal formations take shape? At the outset, it is important to recognize that this is a metaphysical question. To grapple with the sacred is to reckon with its nature and naming. This is simultaneously a matter of epistemology, ontology, poetics, affect, and history. Do we perceive the undifferentiated, as yet inchoate presence of the sacred, as a black hole, empty of content? Is this what Otto meant when he alluded to "the holy minus morality?"[25] Is this but another name for *Eros* – a formless intensity that shimmers beyond good and evil? Might this be the Nothing of revelation to which Scholem referred? Is this what Schmitt regarded as the modern secular version of the divine act of creation *ex nihilo*?

To feel appalled in the face of such a capricious nominalism, the Nothing of nihilism's empty, yet totalizing power, is already to identify a very different metaphysical origin.[26] But what if, rather than evoke the Nothing, one were to experience the original presence of the sacred as redolent with significance, rendering it inseparable from morality? What if, for example, at the heart of the numinous, one discerned the inexpressible abundance of love? An event such as this – simultaneously passing

21 Go to: http://tjrs.monticello.org/letter/100.

22 See Benjamin, note 13, at 286.

23 Jacques Derrida, "Force of Law: The Mystical Foundation of Authority," *Cardozo Law Review* 11:919 (1990), 943.

24 Paul W. Kahn, *Political Theology: Four New Chapters on the Concept of Sovereignty* (New York: Columbia University Press 2012), 11.

25 Otto, note 5.

26 Cf. Leo Strauss, *Natural Right and History* (Chicago: University of Chicago Press 1953).

human understanding, yet evoking "something understood"[27]– might conceivably identify the very source of our yearning for justice, a longing coupled with a hope to somehow complete in history what seems to arise outside it.[28] A metaphysic of love abhors exaltation of the Nothing. In Old Testament terms, to worship charisma or mystery or power for its own sake is the very definition of idolatry: the worship of a false god.[29] If love watches over justice,[30] the metaphysic of love cannot but condemn and repel a metaphysic of nihilism.

The question may come down to this: is the existence of the state, the autonomy of the political as such, the primary objective of politics and law, or does politics exist to serve a higher end?[31] The metaphysics of authority determines how we answer this question. But which metaphysic do we choose? For example, is it the one underlying Schmitt's political theology of executive decision as an act of creation *ex nihilo*, echoing the all-powerful will of a pre-Reformation deity unconstrained by natural law? Or does the sovereign acquire legitimate authority from a source extrinsic to his or her will, such as the scriptural promise of redemptive justice or love?

Let it suffice for now simply to say that the sacred presence in question points to an excess we can neither adequately measure or express. To encounter the sacred in the state of exception is to risk a suspension of familiar organizing structures and their respective norms, whether utility or right.[32] Therein lies both the danger and promise of the sacred. Disruption is its signature, yet it shimmers with possibility. When the sacred irrupts into profane time the flash of its presence, like an uncanny x-ray, momentarily captures the structures of order (of knowing and judging) that have been invisibly operating all along. It is as if to say, yes, this is the network of forms in which we have been living, thinking, feeling, judging. These are the codes, and this is the shared imaginary that has been organized around these largely hidden, unconsciously entangled, cognitive, epistemological, affective, and metaphysical components. These are the frames that have been constituting the form of life that normalizes (establishes and polices) law and politics as we have known them.

The irruption of the sacred provides potential liberation from pre-existing constraints, including laws and moral codes. This "anarchic breeze" (as Gershom

27 See George Herbert, *Prayer (I)*: go to www.poetryfoundation.org/poems/44371/prayer-i.

28 As Eliade writes, when the sacred breaks into profane time and space "something that does not belong to this world has manifested itself apodictically and in so doing has indicated an orientation or determined a course of conduct." Eliade, note 3, at 27.

29 See *Exodus* 32 (1): "And when the people saw that Moses delayed to come down out of the mount, the people gathered themselves together unto Aaron, and said unto him, Up, make us gods, which shall go before us ... " Go to: www.biblegateway.com/passage/?search=Exodus+32&version=KJV.

30 See Emmanuel Levinas, *Entre Nous: On Thinking-of-the-other*, trans. Michael B. Smith and Barbara Harhav (New York: Columbia University Press 1998), 108 ("Love must always watch over justice"); see also Regina Mara Schwartz, *Loving Justice, Living Shakespeare* (Oxford: Oxford University Press 2016), 97.

31 See David William Bates, *States of War: Enlightenment Origins of the Political* (New York: Columbia University Press 2012).

32 See Robert Yelle, *Sovereignty and the Sacred* (Chicago: University of Chicago Press 2018).

Scholem once put it),[33] akin to Benjamin's "divine violence,"[34] negates structure in order to permit what Smith has referred to as a "free response" to another order of being and knowing.[35] In this respect, the sacred is a highly charged state of affairs that offers a passage that may lead to a fundamental change in our state of mind, identity, heart, and tongue. The sacred shakes a polity to its foundation, reviving the violence of its origin. The emergence of the sacred coincides with a state of emergency in the life of the body politic, when basic norms are suspended. At such times, a particular form of life, a discrete way of knowing and being among others, may be either reaffirmed or given up for another. Dwelling within this paradoxical, disruptive, highly expectant state of knowing-unknowing, a sacred past may seem to merge anew with the present, or the present may seem to shimmer with the future perfect – the already now of a perennial, redemptive promise. Yet, the tenses remain asymptotic: the present is an imperfect meeting ground, a place of endless negotiation among others, for past and future only truly merge in messianic time.[36]

It is law, redolent of finitude, imperfection, and error,[37] like any other expressive form in profane time, that keeps messianic fulfillment at bay. Indeed, to presume messianic certainty in the state of exception is to risk totalizing both knowledge and will. This is the risk that would lead beyond good and evil, where power does what it will.[38] If justice, as I shall soon suggest, remains inextricably tied to the ever-present risk of error, then power, once totalized, remains forever estranged from justice. This threat, no less metaphysical than existential, waits upon naming what is sovereign. Whether such naming is an act of meaningful freedom or totalizing power takes us to the crux of the metaphysical dilemma that the sovereign imagination historically faces.

We hear this challenge resonate as far back as Plato in the course of his probing of the meaning of love: What god do you follow?[39] Which is to say, in the name of what

33 See Gersholm Scholem, *The Messianic Idea in Judaism and Other Essays on Jewish Spirituality* (New York: Schocken Books 1971), 2 1.

34 See Benjamin, note 13, at 297–300.

35 Ted A. Smith, *Weird John Brown: Divine Violence and the Limits of Ethics* (Stanford: Stanford University Press 2015), 117.

36 Compare Robert Cover, "The Supreme Court, 1982 Term – Foreword: *Nomos* and Narrative," *Harvard Law Review* 97:4 (1983), with " Bringing the Messiah Through the Law: A Case Study," in J. Pennock (ed.), *Nomos Vol. 30, Religion, Morality, and the Law* (New York: New York University Press 1988), 201–17; Richard K. Sherwin, "Illiberal Belief," *Georgetown Law Journal* 78 (1990), 1785.

37 The association of law and error has a long history. See, for example, Sir Philip Sidney's "The Countess of Pembroke's Arcadia" in Philip Sydney, *The Complete Works of Sir Philip Sidney*, Albert Feuillerat (ed.), Cambridge English classics, (Cambridge: Cambridge University Press 1926 [1593]).

38 The elevation of non-signifying material sensation might well augur a new de-humanism, a movement oddly averse to language and judgment itself. See Brian Massumi, *Politics of Affect* (Cambridge: Polity 2015), 99 ("Intensity is a value in itself."); Richard K. Sherwin, "Too Late for Thinking: The Curious Quest for Emancipatory Potential in Meaningless Affect and Some Jurisprudential Implications," *Law, Culture and the Humanities*, Vol. 15, Issue 1 (February 2019), 30–42.

39 Edith Hamilton (ed.), *The Collected Dialogues of Plato*, trans. Lane Cooper (Princeton: Princeton University Press: 1961) (see especially *The Symposium* [252-a-e, 255e2-b7]).

essence, if any at all, do you claim (or what god or essence claims through you) the meaning of your life among others? For to be in the image of God (or a god, or an essence) is to enact its reality, its being, its presence. One could say, in this sense, that political life, as well as life in the law, is rife with gods, or with none. What does the sacred call for? God's (or a god's) love of the beautiful and the just, or the impulse of terror in the face of death, or the ecstasy of a sovereign will that prompts us to divest all power from self to state sovereignty?

In short, naming promises (or threatens) to lead us from one state of knowing and being, one fundamental network or system of order, one polity or shared or individual identity to another. Knowing as a state of being means that we become what we come to know, the way coming to know love is to love and coming to know justice is to act justly. Knowledge in this sense is always a verb, a way of being in the world among others. The promise of naming lies in the hope of renewal, which is to say, transformation in the direction of some shared vision of flourishing. The threat of naming lies in not knowing, whilst in the grip of wonder or terror, what force one may be serving before the agony of naming and its consequences may be completed. Naming, in this sense, invites the kind of thinking that takes responsibility for thinking about thinking in the sudden freedom of choosing. Naming responds to what calls, bringing into being that which is named;[40] and yet, the danger of misnaming cannot be avoided. It is this inescapable risk of error that gives birth to the ethical: thinking with utmost care about thinking in the context of power and the negotiation of human needs.[41]

In the context of human affairs, when it comes to living in community among others, the foundational act (and constitutive offshoots) of naming operates within the realm of culture. As Castoriadis writes, "Culture is the domain of the imaginary . . . the domain of the *poietic*, of the element of society that goes beyond the merely instrumental."[42] The history of culture provides a vast panorama of the different ways in which the sacred irrupts into history – catalyzing the construction of "actual minds and possible worlds"[43] – entangling new esthetic and ethical forms, new epistemological and artistic registers, bound by the libidinal *conatus* of poetic imagination.[44] From Anaximander's *apeiron* (the boundless) to the hundred letter long thunderclap of Zeus accompanying the fall of Adam and Eve that irrupts on the first page of James Joyce's *Finnegan's Wake* ("*Bababadalgharaghtakamminarronnkonnbronntonnerronntuonnthunntrovarrhounawnskawntoohoohoordenenthurnuk*"): language harbors more than it can bare when it strives to elucidate the sacred. Similarly, foundational images also may shimmer

[40] See Jean-Louis Chretian, *The Call and the Response*, trans. Anne A Davenport (New York: Fordham University Press 2004).

[41] See Williams, note 2.

[42] Cornelius Castoriadis, *Figures of the Thinkable*, trans. Helen Arnold (Stanford: Stanford University Press 2007), 77.

[43] This is cognitive psychologist Jerome Bruner's phrase. See Jerome Bruner, *Actual Minds, Possible Worlds* (Cambridge: Harvard University Press 1986).

[44] Compare Giuseppe Mazzotta, *The New Map of the World: The Poetic Philosophy of Giambattista Vico* (Princeton: Princeton University Press 1999), 167 (on Vico's politics of the poetic sublime).

FIGURE 3.1 Vermeer's *Girl with a Red Hat* (1665)

with an irreducible excess.[45] Here as well a strange surplus pulses beneath the surface of form, sometimes marring the very form from which it seeks release.

We witness such radiance in early medieval times, for example, when viewers might gaze with the eyes of the spirit upon an image constituted not as a representation, but as a threshold. The icon thus becomes not simply a form or object, but an activity, a crossing over, a liturgical performance in which the flesh of the gaze meets with "the flesh of the resurrected," as Ivan Illich once put it.[46] Or, leaping forward in time by a millennium, consider Vermeer's *Girl with a Red Hat* (1665) where we witness another kind of uncanny visual excess (see Figure 3.1).

A *Vermeer's* Girl with a Red Hat *(1665)*

What is that looming vermillion field resting on top of this girl's head – that strange pictorial intensity that barely even pretends to be a hat? Its very presence seems to

45 See David MacDougal, *The Corporeal Image* (Princeton: Princeton University Press 2006); Jennifer Deger, *Shimmering Screens: Making Media in an Aboriginal Community* (Minneapolis: University of Minnesota Press 2006).

46 David Cayley, *The Rivers North of the Future: The Testament of Ivan Illich* (Toronto: House of Anasi Press 2005), 115; See also Marie-Jose Mondzain, *Image, Icon, Economy: The Byzantine Origins of the Contemporary Imaginary*, trans. Rico Franses (Stanford: Stanford University Press 2005).

FIGURE 3.2 *Four Darks in Red* (1958) Scala Archives
© Madrid, Museo Nacional del Prado

undermine the painting's representational coherence. We might say it is a kind of painterly disfigurement, an eruption that points toward an entirely different sort of aesthetic, as if another expressive code were breaking through. This esthetic disruption forces viewers to look differently. In the process, it also forces us to confront our assumptions about what painting is. Something is happening here. This isn't conventional mimesis as representation. It is as if something is bursting forth from the painter's unconscious – like a symptom.[47]

In mid-twentieth century abstract expressionist painting, we witness a further shift in representational authority – away from formal representation itself. In abstract expressionist works all representational form has been evacuated. Only a shimmering color field remains, as in Mark Rothko's *Four Darks in Red* (1958) (Figure 3.2).

B *Rothko's* Four Darks in Red *(1958)*

Without figures or representations of any kind to relate to, there are no stories to tell.

Words fall away, as will happen when one is immersed in music. All that remains is the slow dance of these shimmering color forms, and your own gaze feeling its way

[47] See Georges Didi-Hubermann, *Confronting Images* (University Park: Pennsylvania State University Press 2009).

across, around, and within the canvas. It is a strange visual dance, as if accompanied by an other-worldly score, watching subtle hues (black within black, red within red) separate out and move amongst themselves within each separate band, as each band oscillates against the unsettled borders of its neighbor, and the ensemble oscillates together as a unified whole within the larger luminous field of incandescent red. Without words, affect surges. An uncanny joy pierces the heart, a deathly despair, an insistent hope, as of daybreak…

By turns riddling, parabolic, discordant – the mystifying trace of the sacred is never fully at home in language or image. Ordinarily, the sacred remains immanent, latent in extant political, legal, and cultural structures. In times of crisis, however, when core beliefs are shaken and states "yet unborn"[48] may appear on the horizon, the polity undergoes an "ordeal of the undecidable."[49] It will ease once foundational cultural and cognitive sources of authority have been named anew.

One thing is certain: the sacred may be elusive, but it is not abstract. What we know of (or from) it is a *state* of knowing not a concept of one. One does not shudder from abstractions. We shudder in the grip of intense forces that threaten to destabilize all that we are and know. Forces on such a scale are sovereign: they go to the heart of the sovereign imaginaries that strive to contain them. Let us see, then, whether a bit more may be said about the historic nature and function of sovereign imaginaries.

II SOVEREIGN IMAGINARIES: ON THE THRESHOLD OF THE ABYSS

An imaginary is both a repository for and a discrete way of organizing sensory data as well as affective intensities, memories, beliefs, and other constituents of meaningful experience. Shared imaginaries generate common understandings that make possible common practices, expectations, and beliefs constituting a collective sense of political and legal legitimacy. The imaginary – or imaginaries – we inhabit are descriptive as well as normative: they tell us how things typically go, and how they ought to go. Since people ordinarily are not conscious of the constitutive elements of a given imaginary, conflicts or even contradictions that arise as we shift from one framework to another are usually not an issue. It's just "the way things are": the way events and others appear to us when a given set of cognitive routines, affects, and expectations are cued up by the particular set of circumstances we find ourselves in. As Jerome Bruner has noted, we inhabit different worlds when we shift from one way of knowing to another, shifting ways of minding self, others, and events around us.[50]

48 William Shakespeare, *Julius Caesar* (3.1. 111–16).

49 Jacques Derrida, "Force of Law: The 'Mystical Foundation of Authority,'" in Drucilla Cornell, Michel Rosenfeld, and David Gray Carlson (eds.) *Deconstruction and the Possibility of Justice* (New York: Routledge 1992).

50 See Bruner, note 43, at 67.

This understanding of sovereign imaginaries builds upon Charles Taylor's notion of the social imaginary, which is to say, the way people "imagine their social existence, how they fit together with others, how things go on between them and their fellows, the expectations which are normally met, and the deeper normative notions and images which underlie these expectations."[51] The social imaginary offers a common understanding which makes possible "common practices, and a widely shared sense of legitimacy."[52] Notably, Taylor also acknowledges that the social imaginary "can never be adequately expressed in the form of explicit doctrines, because of its very unlimited and indefinite nature."[53] In other words, the excess that it translates in coherent form carries an overarching authority that remains irreducible to any particular cultural (visual or textual) expression or repertoire of ceremonial or shared ritual practices. In short, the operative authority will never be fully theorized or modeled. A good deal of tacit understanding remains operative in the interpretive or adjudicative process. What may be experienced as an epiphany (a self-authenticating experience of the overpowering force of God's love, say, or existential anxiety before death in the midst of a Hobbesian state of nature) remains irreducible to the expressive forms that epiphany produces.[54]

What Taylor calls a sense of "fullness," what Durkheim calls "collective effervescence," and what I call the uncanny shimmer of the numinous in the presence of the sacred animates the sovereign authority that binds the community.[55] In this sense, one may say along with Santner that the libidinal investment of *Eros* in foundational rituals, texts and images provides the prime bonding energy that holds a community or polity together.[56] This includes the community of law. As Robert Cover famously wrote: "No set of legal institutions or prescriptions exist apart from the narratives that locate it and give it meaning. For every constitution there is an epic, for each Decalogue a scripture."[57] And whether in words or images (augmented perhaps by sound or the integration of multiple expressive media),[58] stories cannot be

51 Charles Taylor, *A Secular Age* (Cambridge: Harvard University Press 2007), 171; see generally Claudia Strauss, "The Imaginary," *Anthropological Theory* 6(3) (2006), 322–44.

52 Taylor, note 51, at 172.

53 *Ibid.*, at 173.

54 *Ibid.*, at 728–29.

55 In this context, cultural anthropologist Victor Turner uses the term *communitas*. See Victor Turner, *The Ritual Process: Structure and Anti-Structure* (New York: Routledge 1969), 94–130.

56 See Eric L. Santner, *The Royal Remains: The People's Two Bodies and the Endgames of Sovereignty* (Chicago: University of Chicago Press 2011), xiv–xvii, 45, 50.

57 See Martha Minow, Michael Ryan, and Austin Sarat (eds.) *Narrative, Violence, and the Law: The Essays of Robert Cover* (Ann Arbor: University of Michigan Press 1995), 95–96. As Hannah Arendt has written: "No philosophy, no analysis, no aphorism, be it ever so profound, can compare in intensity and richness of meaning with a properly narrated story." Hannah Arendt, *Men in Dark Times* (San Diego: Harvest Books 1970), 22.

58 See Richard K. Sherwin, "Performer la Loi. Présences et simulacres, sur scène et au tribunal," ["Law as Performance: Presence and Simulation Inside the Theater/Courtroom"] *Revue Communications*, Paris, No. 92 (2013).

adequately understood in isolation from the play of emotional, normative, and spiritual intensity. The same may be said in regard to the functional limits of abstract rules and concepts. They simply cannot be relied on to do the work of justice on their own. Narrative rises to the particular, as Jerome Bruner has said (citing Karl Marx).[59]

We find signs of such intensity in foundational representations of sovereignty as well as in sovereignty's nullification or absence. Here is where we encounter the disorder that lies at the heart of law's order. In this reckoning, sovereignty and the sacred occur together. While the anti-structural animus of the sacred disrupts conventional esthetic and ethical codes (like market economics and utility),[60] its incalculable excess offers a potentially revolutionary source of authority. Sovereignty arises out of the forge of these antiphonal forces. In the presence of such forces we shudder. That shudder, as we read in Plato's "Phaedrus,"[61] is the soul's signature: the mark of the sacred in the flesh.[62]

When law authorizes a particular world of meaning (along with a discrete set of meaning making practices) we may speak of a *sovereign* imaginary. It is sovereign because, like the one ring of power in J. R. R. Tolkien's great saga,[63] this one rules them all. If you operate in a knowledge system or use an expressive code unrecognized within law's sovereign imaginary you are off the power grid: your claims of right will remain unheard and unseen. This is why Aboriginal land claims in Australia, for example, based on alternative (non-logocentric) metaphysical assumptions (like the Ancestral Spirit), expressed in correspondingly alien codes, such as sacred songs and dances, fell upon deaf ears and blind eyes within the official Australian court system.[64] This is what it is like to lay claim to a metaphysical order that eludes conventional epistemologies.

If the operative code of a sovereign imaginary remains veiled or ill-understood, those who wield power in law's name remain unable to knowingly or intelligently justify the basis for law's authority – much less regulate the scope of its application in particular cases. Law's legitimation requires a knowing acceptance of the shared cultural resources for legal meaning and meaning making practices that constitute and codify the particular sovereign imaginary in which a given legal system operates.[65] By addressing this matter self-reflexively, cultural literacy informs critical judgment in

59 Jerome Bruner, *Acts of Meaning* (Cambridge: Harvard University Press 1990), 60.

60 See Yelle, note 32.

61 Plato, "The Phaedrus," note 39, supra at 497 ("But when one who is fresh from the mystery, and saw much of the vision, beholds a godlike face or bodily form that truly expresses beauty, first there come upon him a shuddering and a measure of that awe which the vision inspired. . .").

62 See Richard K. Sherwin, "Law in the Flesh: Tracing Legitimation to 'The Act of Killing'," *No Foundations: An Interdisciplinary Journal of Law and Justice* 11 (2014), at 44–46.

63 See J. R. R. Tolkien, *Lord of the Rings* (New York: Harper Collins 2005 [1968]).

64 See Craig Elliot, "Performance Evidence in Aboriginal Land Claims," in Richard K. Sherwin and Danielle Celermajer, *A Cultural History of Law in the Modern Age* (London: Bloomsbury 2021).

65 See Richard K. Sherwin, "Opening Hart's Concept of Law," *Valparaiso Law Review* 20(3) (1986), 385–411.

regard to a crucial task, namely: whether to affirm the legitimacy of a given sovereign imaginary – or perhaps imagine an alternative. Critical judgment embraces a process I shall describe shortly as "thinking about thinking." This kind of thinking may be seen as a prerequisite to the meaningful exercise of freedom in society.

Whether in politics or law, it matters not only in what values and beliefs we invest, but also where along a spectrum of possible affects and emotions we stake a shared public claim. For example, recently, in both the United States and England, voters faced a political landscape awash in the affective intensity of the friend/enemy polarity.[66] Rage against the alien Other was presented and widely accepted as the agency of a newly empowered nationalism. Nationalism of this sort typically operates within a localized affective bandwidth. Staking a claim within a dominant affect must be accounted for in cognitive as well as in esthetic and ethical terms.[67] Shifting interpretations of the sacred, including the manner in which authoritative interpretations are either justified or simply expressed, make genealogies of law's historic claims to sovereign authority both revealing and necessary. Each generation needs to recognize the actual and possible cultural, cognitive, affective, and metaphysical sources of authorized legal meanings and meaning making practices that originate within and operate alongside a given sovereign imaginary.

Charles Taylor has written that a salient feature of social imaginaries is their ability to help us recognize "ideal cases" and to discern the underlying moral or metaphysical assumptions that constitute the ideal. This is also the case in regard to sovereign imaginaries. For example, consider in this sense early modern legal emblems that visually depict the sovereign source of law's legitimacy. Ernst Kantorowitz famously coined the expression, the King's two bodies to describe the integration of the divine and the human in the symbol of royal authority.[68] This sovereign authority vividly appears in the legal emblem: "Wisdom dominates the stars" (1635) (Figure 3.3).

A Wisdom Dominates the Stars *(1635)*

Here the Sovereign stands between the globe and the heavens. As Peter Goodrich writes: "The celestial light rains down on the book of wisdom which as sovereign speech is the highest law."[69] In this image, the theological provenance of law's

66 See, for example, Paul D. Miller, "Trump's Nationalism Is Arbitrary, Dangerous, Incoherent, and Silly," *Foreign Policy*, January 3, 2018, http://foreignpolicy.com/2018/01/03/trumps-nationalism-is-arbitrary-dangerous-incoherent-and-silly/; Glyn Morgan, "Liberalism, Nationalism, and Post-Brexit Europe" (2016), www.centroeinaudi.it/images/abook_file/BDL_215_Morgan.pdf.

67 See, for example, Martha C. Nussbaum, *Political Emotions: Why Love Matters for Justice* (Cambridge: Harvard University Press 2015).

68 See Ernst Kantorowicz, *The King's Two Bodies* (Princeton: Princeton University Press 1957).

69 See Peter Goodrich, *Legal Emblems and the Art of Law: Obiter Depicta as the Vision of Governance* (Cambridge: Cambridge University Press 2013), 105; see also Peter Goodrich, "*Imago Decidendi*: On the Common Law of Images," *Brill Research Perspectives in Art and Law* 1(1) (2017), 22 (noting that the emblematic image is "the vision of power, the specular mode of subjective governance, and in the last

FIGURE 3.3 Wisdom dominates the stars (1635)

divine authorization is plain. The King's two bodies – human and divine – manifest the divine source of the law. As Louis XIV liked to say, "The King is like the Sun, holding everything together."

But something striking happened in the latter half of the seventeenth century. By 1656, eight years after the bloody, chaotic Thirty Years War in Europe (with its mind boggling eight million casualties), the divine authority of law's sovereignty seemed to be slipping away. We get a sense of this metaphysical shift in a famous, and very strange painting by Velazquez (Figure 3.4).

B *Velazquez,* Las Meninas *(1656)*

We stand before a painting of the king and queen of Spain. Except there's one problem: they're not really part of the picture. They are enigmatically present as absence – like ghosts, in the form of reflected images in a small mirror at the rear of the studio. They exist only as images within an image. Images without an original: how perfectly postmodern. King Philip IV and Queen Mariana are gazing out at us, the viewer. But there's something odd about this gaze. As our eyes (the gaze of the spectator) meet theirs (the royal gaze), together with the sovereign gaze of the painter, a sudden realization strikes. How uncanny! We can only meet the gaze of the king and queen from their mirrored image if we are standing in *the very place they themselves ought to be occupying*. How curious: we, the viewers, have taken over the space of the sovereign gaze. This is more than a little strange. Are we missing from the *mirror* where *our* image ought to be? Or are the king and queen missing from the external *reality* that their *image* mirrors? The image that is painted on the painting within the painting might tell us – if it weren't turned away from our eyes, as

instance the medium of the scopic regime of normative control. It is the exterior specter that enters and binds the juridical soul.").

FIGURE 3.4 Velasquez, *Las Meninas* (1656) Prado Meuseum
Museo Nacional del Prado Difusión

unknowable as its source. Dwelling on this paradox can trigger a sense of vertigo – like desire trying to grab hold of itself. In short, it's like standing on the threshold of an abyss – the province of the sacred.

In *Las Meninas* the vanishing point of perspective terminates in a vertiginous paradox. On the threshold of sovereignty we witness something phantasmal. The disruptive irruption of the sacred appears as an absconded authority, or perhaps as a subversive substitution. Is it royal or popular sovereignty that is angling for our gaze? Velazquez's vertiginous painting takes us beyond the conventional bounds of representable authority. It is as if the ground beneath our feet has opened. Somehow, we are falling while standing still, as if we've all suddenly been transported to some strange liminal no-man's-zone, like a dream from which it is difficult to awaken.[70]

[70] For an elaboration of this phenomenon, see Richard K. Sherwin, *Visualizing Law in the Age of the Digital Baroque: Arabesques & Entanglements* (New York: Routledge 2011).

This is what it's like when what is sovereign remains in suspension. Everything becomes phantasmal. As Foucault put it in his deft description of *Las Meninas*:

> All the interior lines of the painting, and above all those that come from the central reflection, point towards the very thing that is represented, but absent. At once object – since it is what the artist represented is copying onto his canvas – and subject – since what the painter had in front of his eyes, as he represented himself in the course of his work, was himself, since the gazes portrayed in the picture are all directed towards the fictitious position occupied by the royal personage, which is also the painter's real place, since the occupier of that ambiguous place in which the painter and the sovereign alternate, in a never- ending flicker, as it were, is the spectator, whose gaze transforms the painting into an object, the pure representation of that essential absence.[71]

The suspension of sovereignty activates the experience of vertigo that the state of exception triggers. We stand against a void. In the state of exception, the boundary condition for the bounded (naming what is sovereign) is the boundless. By reducing sovereignty to the vanishing point, Velazquez creates a startling, and perhaps dangerous tear in the fabric of authority. Nietzsche once wrote: "[M]an would rather will nothingness than not will."[72] The will to power, in this sense, seeks power in its naked intensity for the sake of life itself. But this kind of nihilism, the will to intensity in itself, independent of content, risks terror.[73]

These stakes are hardly abstract. By the eighteenth century, in post-revolutionary America, France, and England, popular sovereignty had become a *fait accompli*. The great French painter Jacques-Louis David captured the moment visually. David was a member of the extremist Jacobin group led by Robespierre. He was elected to the National Convention in 1792, and by 1793 he rose to a position of dominance in the art world in France. (His nickname was "Robespierre of the brush.") *The Death of Marat* (1793) (Figure 3.5) was one of David's masterworks. It invites us to visualize yet again the devolution of power that Velazquez dared to imagine in *Las Meninas*. Here we encounter in visceral terms the move away from the King's two bodies to what Eric Santner has called the People's two bodies.[74]

C *David's* The Death of Marat

Of particular interest in this image is the strange empty space that occupies nearly half of David's canvas. Art historian T. J. Clark has noted that in the cult of Marat,

71 Michel Foucault, *The Order of Things* (New York: Routledge 2001), 308; see also Anne Carson, *Eros The Bittersweet* (Princeton: Princeton University Press 1998), 72.

72 See Friedrich Nietzsche, *On the Genealogy of Morals; Ecce Homo*, trans. Walter Kauffman and R. J. Hollingdale (New York: Vintage Books 1969), 163.

73 See Richard K. Sherwin, "Law's Beatitude: A Post-Nietzschean Account of Legitimacy," *Cardozo Law Review* 24 (2002–03), 683.

74 See Santner, note 56. The phrase "the People's two bodies" occurs earlier in Edmund S. Morgan, *Inventing the People* (New York: W. W. Norton 1989), 78.

FIGURE 3.5 David, *Death of Marat* (1793) Royal Museum of Fine Arts, Belgium J. Geleyns – Art Photography © Royal Museums of Fine Arts of Belgium, Brussels

David saw the first forms of a liturgy and ritual in which "the truths of the revolution itself would be made flesh – People, Nation, Virtue, Reason, Liberty."[75] But how would such a "liturgy" find an appropriate form of expression? Santner discerns an aesthetic revolution at work in David's painting. It emerges as a new kind of abstraction. According to Santner (citing T. J. Clark), the painter "seems to make Marat much the same substance – the same abstract material – as the empty space above him."[76] Equating that enigmatic space with the King's sublime body ("the flesh"), this abstraction of sovereignty – its sudden vacancy – symbolizes "the

[75] T. J. Clark, *Farewell to an Idea: Episodes from a History of Modernism* (New Haven: Yale University Press 1999), 29.

[76] Santner, note 56, at 92.

impossible representation of the People." The provenance of popular sovereignty marks the revolutionary shift that is at work. No less is at stake here than the dissolution of the iconic representation of the incarnation of Christ, established for centuries, as the underlying model for the King's transcendental body. In this newly emergent sovereign imaginary, the people's transcendental body is animated by a libidinal excess, a somatic surplus of immanence, that we discern as a remnant of sacred violence.[77]

This uncanny *animus* is now viewed as something every citizen carries within his or her own flesh. *Eros*, the libidinal god translated as sovereign in the state of exception, bears the power of life and death, to declare who is worthy of life (*heimlich*) and who is not (*unheimlich*). Of course, as the ensuing Reign of Terror would all too vividly reveal, when popular sovereignty crowds out the self in favor of the "mass"[78] the risk of error is greatly ramified.

When we return to the beginning time of sovereign imaginaries we confront fundamental assumptions that constitute a given imaginary's founding vision. These assumptions are of metaphysical moment, which is to say, they address states of affairs not subject to human will.[79] It is at this juncture that we must return to a theme deferred: the difficult matter of clashing metaphysics. Naming what is sovereign in the state of exception poses a metaphysical dilemma. Is it the Nothing of revelation of which Scholem spoke, the naked power of deciding what is sovereign *ex nihilo*, which echoes in Carl Schmitt's executive decision in that state of exception? Or might we shift metaphysical registers from the nothingness of the *ex nihilo* to a sense of irrepressible abundance within an economy of excess wherein one might discern the shimmer of love watching over justice?[80]

III POISED BETWEEN POWER AND JUSTICE: IN THE PENUMBRA OF ERROR

In *Political Theology*, Carl Schmitt draws an analogy between the sovereign decision that declares a "state of exception" and the secular miracle of law that subsists beyond the will of the sovereign. Schmitt deems the decision that identifies the state of emergency as necessary in order to save the state from enemies within and without. There is no rule, no law, no institution that can constrain that decision. Both the Schmittian state of exception and the miracle signify a break with the

77 *Ibid.*, at 91–92.

78 *Ibid.*, at 96.

79 Williams, note 2, at 14.

80 Political and legal metaphysics may evoke aspirations of love or redemptive justice in sectarian terms of Christian love through divine sacrifice, or it may do so in secular terms of universal human rights and human dignity, or some other formulation. Though the terms may differ, they may yet express an overlapping consensus on the core values that legitimate the sovereign imaginary from which law and politics arise. The challenge is to negotiate a coherent master narrative that sustains the legitimacy of the system. See Levinas and Schwartz, both in note 30.

existing order of things; and both project a model of sovereignty that is based on absolute power. For Schmitt, this act models God's creation of the world out of nothing (*creatio ex nihilo*). As Schmitt writes: "the decision emanates from nothingness."[81]

Whether or not one accepts this interpretation of creation *ex nihilo* in the Old Testament, and the matter is controversial,[82] it is important to recognize the implications of doing so. If God remains unconstrained by nature, if his will alone is supreme, then (as Rudolf Otto puts it): "good is good because God wills it, instead of that God wills it because it is good."[83] If law's sovereignty follows this model then there can be no moral check on its power. No power exists to oppose the sovereign's "absolutely fortuitous will."[84] If the sacred is beyond good and evil, naming what emerges as sovereign from out of that numinous origin may proceed as an act of pure will unconstrained by moral considerations. Indeed, this is the divine command theory that Schmitt embraced. As Otto observed, the intensity of the numinous stands apart from any normative content.[85]

Whether the sacred gives rise to absolute sovereign power unconstrained by morality or remains bound to an essential claim (the unchanging natural law) of justice,[86] is a metaphysical question. As such it lies outside the realm of certainty. If uncertainty, then, is the one thing that is given, how might this point of departure shape and inform our approach to sovereignty and the sacred? In the dispensation proposed here, we need a metaphysic of freedom, based on the ineluctable risk of error, to guide thinking on the threshold of the abyss of the sacred. If power without moral content becomes the model for what is sovereign it is possible to exalt any value or none at all. This is nihilism.[87] In such a state, error in the grip of a totalized will to power risks becoming totalized. The safeguard against totalized error is thinking, or more particularly, what Rowan Williams (following Gillian Rose) calls "thinking about thinking."

If the intensity of the sacred rends structure and, in so doing, opens up the possibility of new political and legal forms, metaphysical reflection arises in the reflective moment of freedom that the possibility of error creates. As Williams writes: "Once we start creating a city in discourse, working at and testing the bonds that language requires and presupposes so as to rule out the arbitrary and the partial, the

[81] See Schmitt, note 20, at 31–32.

[82] See, for example, Robert McQueen Grant, *Miracle and Natural Law in Graeco-Roman and Early Christian Thought* (Eugene, OR: Wipf and Stock Publishers 1952), 136.

[83] See Otto, note 5, at 101. See generally Yelle, note 32.

[84] See Yelle, note 32.

[85] According to Otto, the numinous is "the 'holy' minus its moral factor." Otto, note 5.

[86] This is what the Deists believed. See Yelle, note 32.

[87] According to Michael Gillespie, nihilism arises out of the totalization of subjective will over reason and nature. It has its origin in medieval nominalism and finds its crucial moment in Fichte's rejection of the Enlightenment notion of reason in favor of an absolute subjectivism "that attempts to derive all reason from the infinite will of the absolute." Michael Allen Gillespie, *Nihilism Before Nietzsche* (Chicago: University of Chicago Press 1995), 99.

'passionate' in isolation, the task before us is finally 'metaphysical.'"[88] In Williams' terms, the primary metaphysical question from which the origin of law and politics arises is this: What name are we to assign to the "underlying intelligible structure" of "human bondedness and exchange?" This describes the shared responsibility of forging that brand of legal and political discourse in which particular ways of life may be negotiated, which is to say, articulated and defended among others.[89]

To the extent that metaphysics addresses the essence of what it is to be human, that state of affairs which remains exempt to willful or ideological forging, error and the sacred origin of sovereignty must walk hand in hand. Intensity requires the modulating effect of humility.[90] The inescapable prospect of error, getting the sacred wrong, argues for intelligible action, which is to say, "action that can be criticised and defended."[91] The alternative risks imposing erroneous names upon autonomous others. In short, it risks crushing actual minds and possible worlds by sheer force of will. The metaphysics of error tempers the metaphysics of power by interceding with self-doubt in naming what is sovereign. Williams aptly describes this as the way in which "properly political life is made functional to the economic exchanges in civil society."[92] By contrast, fiat, the totality of will evident in the Schmittian decision, cuts short the possibility of reflection (thinking about thinking) that meaningful freedom in the face of error requires.

The metaphysics of error and power are incessantly self-correcting in the face of the sacred. This elevates Keats's "negative capability," the ability to tolerate uncertainty as an inescapable condition of life among others, as the key to staving off the prospect of totalizing error.[93] Negative capability is the armor meaningful freedom dons against the tyranny of false certainty. This leaves us with the unending political and legal task of identifying and clarifying our individual and collective understanding of the source and authenticity of what we name as sovereign. In this sense, the task of legal and political thinking is inescapably metaphysical. Like theological thinking, legal and political thinking thinks what is difficult, which is to say, it holds fast to the prospect of error in naming what is sovereign. As Williams

88 Williams, note 2, at 6.

89 Williams calls this the understanding of a "vulnerable human group whose perception of their interest is as flawed and liable to violence as any other's, but who understand their fundamental task as embodying the 'non-interest' of God, the universal saving generosity of divine action." *Ibid.*, at 19.

90 Such is the Old Testament wisdom of Micah ("Walk humbly with thy God." Micah 6:8).

91 Williams, note 2, at 6.

92 *Ibid.*, at 13.

93 See *The Letters of John Keats*, ed. by H. E. Rollins, 2 vols. (Cambridge: Cambridge University Press, 1958), 193–94 ("[I]n my mind, & at once it struck me, what quality went to form a Man of Achievement especially in Literature & which Shakespeare possessed so enormously – I mean *Negative Capability*, that is when a man is capable of being in uncertainties, Mysteries, doubts, without any irritable reaching after fact & reason – Coleridge, for instance, would let go by a fine isolated verisimilitude caught from the Penetralium of mystery, from being incapable of remaining content with half knowledge.").

writes: "Thinking what is difficult, thinking in dispossession, is essential to a politics that is anything other than a programme for the alternation of tyrannies and the unthought conflict of unreflective interest; thinking what is difficult . . . insists on an ontology of some sort, capable of holding together the reality of difference and the imperative of work (i.e., reconciliation)."[94]

In an effort to anchor what has been said here to something firmer and closer by, I will close with a vivid, recent illustration of this kind of thinking in the act of naming what is sovereign on the threshold of the sacred. It is a story of political resistance and hope in the life of a teenager called by tragedy and love to political action. It narrates in brief how a young woman named Emma Gonzalez publicly assumed responsibility for naming what is sovereign.

IV THE SACRED NOW: HOLDING THE STILLNESS

Sovereign imaginaries arise, transform, and fall apart in a variety of ways. To trace this history in law and politics is to engage in a genealogy of the sacred in history. In early American history, for example, popular sovereignty emerged in public expressions of the people's will. At first, still parasitic upon the sovereign imaginary of the King's two bodies, the people or their representatives assumed responsibility for saying when the king's commands ran counter to the will of God.[95] Thereafter, public conventions of the people came to displace the royal will altogether.[96] Petitions and assemblies now became the source of a new sovereign authority: the people in the act of naming themselves as sovereign.[97] The American Declaration of Independence explicitly identifies that authority in its opening words: "We the People."

Over time, that sovereign authority has been reasserted in a variety of ways. For example, it has been identified in the form of labor's right to "the general strike" from which the right to overthrow the legal system may be inferred.[98] It also has been described as a "constitutional moment" in which the sovereign will of the people manifests itself by seizing control over all the branches of government. Starting with an appeal to "higher law," this kind of transformation culminates in the codification of novel claims of right ultimately sealed either by the combined authority of the legislature and the highest court in the land or by a super-majoritarian ratification of a proposed constitutional amendment.[99]

94 Williams, note 2, at 20. See also Gillian Rose, *The Broken Middle* (New York: Jon Wiley & Sons 1992) and Gillian Rose, *Love's Work* (New York: Schocken Books 1997).

95 Morgan, note 74, at 56.

96 *Ibid.*, at 118.

97 *Ibid.*, at 209, 230.

98 Benjamin, note 13, at 282.

99 Bruce Ackerman, *We the People: Foundations* vol. 1 (Cambridge: Harvard University Press 1991), 266–67.

At other times, the legal and political force of popular sovereignty irrupts in symbolic acts of organized violence. For example, in the years immediately preceding the American civil war, John Brown's raid on Harper's Ferry captured the imagination of the nation, and of opponents to slavery in particular. Brown's biblically based, righteous anger against the evil of slavery invoked a right to sovereign violence that made him a touchstone for justice in his time. While the action itself, in which Brown and twenty-one raiders seized arms from a federal arsenal with the intent of sparking a broad slave rebellion, was naïve and ineffective in practical terms, the spirit of the act far transcended its immediate outcome. When Brown was hanged for treason, Henry David Thoreau commented: "No man in America has ever stood up so persistently and effectively for the dignity of human nature, knowing himself for a man, and the equal of any and all governments."[100] When federal troops marched in the bloody civil war that put an end to slavery, singing "John Brown's body lay a mouldering in the grave, but his spirit goes marching on," they elevated his "body politic" over his natural body. As Smith writes, Brown "marched on as a figure for sovereignty."[101]

Non-violence has likewise captured the transcendent spirit of a popular, grass roots movement that sought to renew the meaning of justice in the people's name. Consider in this regard the American civil rights movement's quest for racial equality during the late 1950s and 1960s. It was a movement that forced into view the very foundation upon which the American republic was built. As Martin Luther King famously wrote from a Birmingham jail cell:

> An unjust law is a code that a majority inflicts on a minority that is not binding on itself. This is difference made legal. On the other hand, a just law is a code that a majority compels a minority to follow, and that it is willing to follow itself. This is sameness made legal ... One day the South will know that when these disinherited children of God sat down at [segregated] lunch counters they were in reality standing up for the best in the American dream and the most sacred values in our Judeo-Christian heritage.[102]

In the state of exception, the sacred irrupts anew. On such occasions new words come to frame foundational values as well as the emotional tone and texture of a community's or state's constitutive bond. Risks abound in the act of naming what is sovereign. As Judith Butler notes, "if and when political orders deemed democratic are brought into crisis by an assembled or orchestrated collective that claims to be the popular will, to represent the people along with a prospect of a more real and substantive democracy, then an open battle ensues on the meaning of democracy, one that does not always take the form of deliberation."[103] There is no predicting how the sacred will irrupt into

[100] Smith, note 35, at 18.

[101] *Ibid.*, at 20.

[102] Martin Luther King, *Letter from a Birmingham Jail* (New York: Penguin 2018).

[103] Judith Butler, *Notes Toward A Performative Theory of Assembly* (Cambridge: Harvard University Press 2015), 2.

history, whether with righteous violence or peaceful civil disobedience, whether in fiery words of retributive anger or the silent stillness of prayer.[104]

I want to pause for a moment over the latter possibility. Can silence make the sacred break into secular time, infusing words that ensue with the shimmer of sovereign authority? Let us consider one such moment in recent history – a moment in which a young student leader named Emma Gonzalez publicly held a fierce and sublime stillness in order to name justice anew.

Toward the end of the school day on February 14, 2018, nineteen-year-old Nikolas Cruz walked into Marjory Stoneman Douglas High School in Parkland, Florida, armed with an AR-15 military style semi-automatic rifle and multiple magazines. After firing indiscriminately at students and teachers, seventeen people lay dead, fourteen students and three teachers. Seventeen others were wounded. The carnage lasted a little over six minutes.

This was not an isolated event. In 2012, at Sandy Hook Elementary school in New Jersey, twenty children and six adults were shot dead. Since Sandy Hook, there have been 290 recorded shooting incidents at schools in the United States, ranging from mass killing and wounding to accidental gun discharges and suicides.[105] In the aftermath of the tragedy at Marjory Stoneman Douglas High School in Parkland, Florida, student survivors launched a high-profile campaign for tougher gun laws and safer schools. These efforts included the creation of a group called Never Again MSD through which student leaders organized public demonstrations around the country. The largest assembly was held in Washington, DC, on March 24, 2018.

Emma Gonzalez was one of those student leaders. Earlier on the day of the shooting at Parkland, in anticipation of Valentine's Day, Gonzalez had arranged a school event in which students inscribed and sent Valentine cards that expressed love to friends, acquaintances, and others known perhaps from afar. Some of the recipients of these love notes were killed or wounded later that day. Gonzalez's own brush with death was close. She and a friend had planned to be in one of the classrooms at a time when the gunfire there was most intense. If not for her assembly room teacher's unexpected insistence that students sign an attendance sheet Gonzalez herself might well have been among the casualties.[106]

Grieving for her lost friends, traumatized by her own proximity to death, and outraged by the unwillingness of elected officials to take action in support of safe schools and new gun control laws, Gonzalez took her place

[104] *Ibid.*, at 8 ("Silent gatherings, including vigils or funerals, often signify in excess of any particular written or vocalized account of what they are about. These forms of embodied and plural performativity are important components of any understanding of 'the people'. . .").

[105] Go to http://time.com/5168272/how-many-school-shootings/.

[106] Emma Gonzalez: "Fight For Your Lives, Before It's Someone Else's Job," interview broadcast on National Public Radio, Weekend Edition Sunday. Go to: www.npr.org/2018/03/25/596805330/emma-gonzalez-fight-for-your-lives-before-it-s-someone-else-s-job.

FIGURE 3.6 Marjory Stoneman Douglas student Emma Gonzalez at the 'March for Our Lives' demonstration for stricter gun control laws on March 24, 2018, in Washington, DC. (Mike Stocker/Sun Sentinel/Tribune News Service via Getty Images)

as the final speaker at the Washington rally on March 24, 2018 (see Figure 3.6). Gazing out at a crowd estimated at from 200,000 to as many as 800,000 people, Gonzalez began to speak: "Six minutes and about twenty seconds," she said. "In a little over six minutes, seventeen of our friends were taken from us, fifteen were injured, and everyone in the Douglas community was forever altered." She continued: "Everyone who has been touched by the cold grip of gun violence understands. No one understood the extent of what had happened. No one could believe that there were bodies in that building waiting to be identified for over a day. No one could comprehend the devastating aftermath or how far this would reach, or where this would go." She added: "For those who still can't comprehend because they refuse to, I'll tell you where it went: right into the ground, six feet deep."

Gonzalez went on next to name all the victims of the Parkland shooting. Then she stopped speaking altogether. She stood in silence, staring into the distance before her, tears streaming down her face, nearly immobile, audibly taking in great gulps of air, until a timer beeped. Six minutes and twenty seconds had elapsed: the time that it took, as she would tell the straining crowd before her, for Nikolas Cruz to kill and wound thirty-four teachers and students.

Gonzalez finished by speaking these words: "Fight for your lives before it's somebody else's job."

For six tense minutes Emma Gonzalez maintained a fierce, poignant, discomforting silence. Somehow, the focus and intensity of her passion proved strong enough to hold many thousands of people in a shared stillness.[107] It felt like the stillness of prayer.

Stillness and prayer are not strangers. As Rowan Williams has said: "You have to still your body and your imagination ... [P]rayer is communion, it's that allowing the depth within and the depth outside to come together."[108] Williams goes on to speak about the richness of silence:

> R. S. Thomas wrote a number of poems about prayer, and they're mostly to do with waiting and silence and a sense of the absence of God, and yet in the middle of that awareness of absence there is the realization that you have *arrived*: there is a reality and it's beyond the words you could find and you've got to wait, you've got to stay with it.[109]

According to this dispensation, prayer challenges us to hold that stillness. And it is in this sense, I submit, that Emma Gonzalez's embodiment of a fierce stillness invoked a state of exception in which naming what is sovereign emerged from an uncanny silence, a silence akin to a political and legal prayer.

Strange grace: the truth of tragic suffering and love that converged and filled Emma Gonzalez, distilling into a silent cry for justice. If, as Williams has put it, "the point of it all is that prayer is allowing truth and reality to flower in you, and therefore it's part of becoming more human and more yourself,"[110] then we may say that Emma Gonzalez's cry for justice radiated in those six tense minutes of silence the truth of her being. On the cusp of the sacred, knowing and being merged. It is the uncanny, shimmering grace of this uncontainable intensity that empowered Gonzalez to hold so many thousands of souls in a shared stillness. Thus empowered, Gonzalez sought to pry open the gates guarding state and federal houses of legislation in an effort to infuse life into the dead letter of gun control law.[111] In short, she dared to catalyze a state of exception in which tragic suffering, fused with love,

107 Rebecca Mead, writing for *The New Yorker,* compared Gonzalez to nineteen-year-old Renée Maria Falconetti who starred in Carl Theodor Dreyer's classic silent film, *The Passion of Joan of Arc* (1928). Mead described Gonzalez's Washington, DC speech this way: "Lifting her eyes and staring into the distance before her, González stood in silence. Inhaling and exhaling deeply – the microphone caught the susurration, like waves lapping a shoreline – González's face was stoic, tragic. Her expression shifted only minutely, but each shift – her nostrils flaring, or her eyelids batting tightly closed – registered vast emotion. Tears rolled down her cheeks; she did not wipe them away. Mostly, the crowd was silent, too, though waves of cheering support – "Go, Emma!" "We all love you!" – arose momentarily, then faded away. She stood in this articulate silence for more than twice as long as she had spoken." Rebecca Mead, "Joan of Arc and the Passion of Emma González," *The New Yorker* (March 26, 2018).

108 "The Archbishop Rowan Williams on Understanding Prayer," September 13, 2009: Mark Tully talks to the Archbishop of Canterbury about understanding Prayer for "Something Understood" on Radio 4. http://aoc2013.brix.fatbeehive.com/articles.php/660/the-archbishop-on-understanding-prayer.

109 *Ibid.*

110 *Ibid.*

111 New gun law legislation has followed the Parkland high school shooting and the ensuing student mobilization. See, for example, "Florida Governor Signs Gun Limits Into Law, Breaking with the N.R.A.," www.nytimes.com/2018/03/09/us/florida-governor-gun-limits.html (*The New York Times*, March 9, 2018) and "New York passes bill to strip all guns from domestic abusers,"

named anew what is sovereign. Taking public responsibility for naming what is sovereign, Emma Gonzalez called justice from a sacred, enfolding silence into impassioned speech, so that legal and political change might ensue.

This is how the sovereign imagination works. It is how the sacred bond that holds together a community, or a polity, may be woven anew – on the threshold of an abyss, in an exceptional moment, when the uncanny power of the sacred suddenly shines forth. When law and politics take flight in words that shimmer with an uncanny intensity, ensuing perhaps from the poetic stillness of a prayerful silence, justice may be named anew. Thus does the sovereign imagination expand and revitalize the constitutive bounds of legal and political discourse.

V CONCLUSION

The sacred radiates with an uncanny power, but lacks intrinsic content. Its nature is to disrupt, bringing structures of sovereign authority into question. On the threshold of the sacred, sources of legitimation, old and new, come into view. But judgments must be made reflecting the individual and collective responsibility for naming what is sovereign.

The sacred irrupts as a liberation from structure and utility, placing extant moral codes in suspense. In the state of exception we respond to a sacred call and a sacred calling. Akin to Scholem's "anarchic breeze"[112] and Walter Benjamin's concept (and John Brown's putative embodiment) of "divine violence," the sacred invites alternative ways of being and knowing. But is it the call of illimitable justice or naked power that invites this kind of free response? Following Schmitt, sovereignty invites us to name political and legal power *ex nihilo*, with no responsibility to others. Justice, on the other hand, invites us to name what is sovereign *in situ*, which is to say, in relation to others and the needs they exist in. The new names of justice that emerge out of the state of exception arise in response to those needs. They also arise against the ever-present specter of human error. To name what is sovereign absent self-reflexive awareness of error risks totalizing political and legal power on the basis of a false certainty. The competing metaphysics of justice and nihilism (the will to power *ex nihilo*) split around this pivot.

Thinking about thinking in the act of naming what is sovereign thinks about error. This is what safeguards thinking from injustice. Power gives birth to the ethical on

www.independent.co.uk/news/world/americas/gun-control-law-domestic-abuse-new-york-fire-arms-rifle-shotgun-trump-cuomo-parkland-a8283791.html (Independent, April 3, 2018). But signs of political entrenchment remain. See, for example, "Senate fails to pass new gun control restrictions in wake of Orlando shooting," www.theguardian.com/us-news/2016/jun/20/senate-gun-control-vote-orlando-shooting (The Guardian, June 20, 2016). There are also signs of shifts in the political and legal discourse. See, for example, "Ex-Justice Stevens's Call to Repeal the Second Amendment" (The New York Times, March 27, 2018) www.nytimes.com/2018/03/27/opinion/stevens-second-amendment-guns.html.

112 Scholem, note 33, at 21.

the back of the sacrificed other. Meaning is born in our attunement to need: the needs of self and the needs of others. This is the way love (self-love as well as love of others) watches over justice.[113]

Idolatry, according to the metaphysics of justice, is indifference to need. Justice, locked within the metaphysics of power, is the triumph of will. On the threshold of an abyss, when the sacred irrupts into presence, the sovereign imaginary prepares for grace or terror in the act of naming. Freedom gains or loses meaning in the choice of names we assign – which is to say, in the polities we enact and the identities we thereby assume – in the political and legal act of accepting (or rejecting) those names as our very own. In this sense, responsibility for freedom is metaphysical. And it is in freedom and wonder (or terror) that we name what is sovereign.

Sovereign imaginaries arise from states of exception in the course of which metaphysical truths about the way humans and things exist in the world come into play within history. The foundational narratives that constitute such imaginaries contain visions that are consonant with the metaphysical underpinnings of the narrative in question. Each narrative assumes certain constants about what it is to be human, what thinking and feeling are like, and how living within particular registers of thought and feeling gives rise to particular ways of being among others. This is what it means to speak of a sovereign imaginary as a constitutive *nomos*, a way of life – which includes discrete ways of being together in need and aspiration within a political and legal order.

The sacred may announce a new possibility, but how we construe that announcement remains crucial. The Schmittian decision in the state of exception totalizes will and occludes the interpretive and corrective power of thought and negotiated action. It refuses to acknowledge its totalitarian power is subject to error. Whether in the service of law or the political for its own sake,[114] the absolutized decision amplifies risk absolutely. By contrast, the constitutive metaphysical narrative of meaningful freedom under the rubric of error leaves uncertainty in place. In this view, interpretation and negotiated clarification of need and power are part and parcel of the dynamic of temporal fragmentation of the ideal. There is no release from the responsibility of thinking about thinking in the penumbra of error. That is our ethical calling.

On the threshold of a great abyss, we stand witness, bedeviled by the urgency of naming, as the sacred irrupts anew. When worlds of meaning are at stake, we can ill afford to disavow responsibility for the metaphysics of sovereign imaginaries.

[113] See Levinas, note 30.
[114] See Bates, note 31.

B

Legal-Religious Language

4

Dat: From Law to Religion

The Transformation of a Formative Term in Modern Times

Abraham Melamed

I FROM THE HEBREW BIBLE TO THE LATE MIDDLE AGES

The words we use in a given language change their meanings and contexts throughout the ages, being influenced by ever-changing social, cultural, and intellectual circumstances; some disappear, and are replaced by other words, which are better suited to transmit the meaning which the speaker and writer attempts to convey. One of the main methodological errors in reading texts from previous periods is the anachronistic assumption that the current usage is the only possible meaning of a given word. This meaning is superimposed on the reading of such texts, thus completely distorting their meaning. When reading a text from a given period, one should ask, first of all, what has been the specific meaning of a given word in the particular period when the text was written? We should also notice that some words are barely used in a given period, and become popular in other periods; this is also of importance, and has a meaning. Charting the changing meanings of key words in the history of a given culture is a useful means for the understanding of the intellectual transitions this culture went through.

Many key words in the long history of the Hebrew language, such as *ummah* (originally religious community, now nation), *goy* (originally people, now gentile), and *mofet* (in biblical Hebrew, miracle, in the middle ages, scientific proof, now model), for instance, changed their meaning throughout the ages. The history of the evolution of the meanings of the key word *dat*, throughout more than two millennia, is maybe the best, and most important, example of this phenomenon. It exemplifies, in a nutshell, the changes which the meaning of Judaism itself went through throughout the ages. This chapter will focus on this momentous change, as it evolved since early modern times, when the meaning of the term *dat* was transformed from law to religion, and Judaism became a religion.[1]

[1] This chapter is based on the findings of my book, *Dat: from Law to Religion, A History of a Formative Term* (Tel Aviv: Hakibbutz Hameuchad, 2014, Hebrew). See also Abraham Melamed, "De la loi a la

The term *dat* first appears in the *Scroll of Esther*, of the late biblical period. It is a Persian word, adopted by the Jews dwelling there. The original meaning of the Persian *datan* is to give, and by inference to decree a law.[2] Its original meaning is law, every law, mostly human law; not particularly divine law, or Jewish law. Every people has a particular *dat*, so do the Jews.[3] It is quite ironic that a Persian word which originally denotes pagan law, eventually came to designate Judaism, and it is used today more than in any other period, but now in a completely different meaning.

The Sages Judaized this term, mainly in the coinage concerning laws of matrimony: *ke-dat Moshe ve-Israel*, that is "In accordance with the laws of Moses and Israel." They however barely used this term; it appeared about twenty times only in the voluminous *Babylonian Talmud*.[4] To designate law in general, and divine law in particular, the Sages preferred to use biblical words such as *hukkim*, *torah*, and *mizvot*. They seemed to have managed very well without using the word *dat*. Today we cannot envision any talk about religious beliefs and practices in general, and Judaism in particular, without the ample usage of this particular term, but its meaning has dramatically changed.

While the sages barely used this term, it became popular from medieval Hebrew on, but its meaning varied. This was the result of the momentous encounter between the biblical and rabbinic traditions with the Muslim cultural environment in which the major Jewish cultural centers existed until about the early thirteenth century. Jewish scholars inherited the new meaning imbedded in the word *dat* in post-biblical Jewish literature, and connected it to the Muslim-Arabic terminology. The Muslim distinction between *din* – creed, faith, and *sharia* – religious law, was translated by some scholars into Hebrew as *dat* and *torah* or *mizvot*, respectively. The term *dat*, thus received, for the first time, a distinct theological meaning, and denoted belief, not law in particular. This development is mostly apparent in Maimonides' usage of this term, and was congruent with his revolutionary attempt to turn Judaism into a system based on true beliefs, first of all. Other Jewish scholars of this period, however, continued with the rabbinic usage of *dat* as law, thus equating it with *sharia*. Moreover, some, such as Judah ha-Levi and Abraham ibn Daud, did not hesitate to use it in the plain meaning of law in general, including human law, devoid of any theological connotations, as it originally appears in the *Scroll of Esther*.[5]

religion: metamorphoses du concept de dath dans a tradition politique juive," in *Entre ciel e terre, le judaisme*, ed. Sh. Trigano (Paris: Editions In press, 2009), 61–76.

[2] The Latin *mandare, datum*, and their derivations in modern European languages, *data*, come from the same source.

[3] For instance, *Esther* 1: 19: "and let it be written in the laws (*datei*) of Persia and Media"; 9: 14: "An edict (*dat*)was issued in Susa." Concerning the Jews in particular: 3: 8: "Their laws (*dateihem*) are different from those of all other people." See also in *Ezra* 8: 36 and *Daniel* 7: 25.

[4] I. Kosowsky, *Otzar Leshon ha-Talmud* (Jerusalem: Ministry of Education and Culture, 1961, Hebrew) vol. 9, 459.

[5] See the detailed discussion in Melamed, *Dat, supra* note 1, ch. 4.

This last meaning of the term became dominant in the philosophic-theological literature produced in Hebrew by Jewish scholars active in Christian Southern Europe in the late Middle Ages. Most scholars adopted the reading of *dat* as law, even human law. They rejected the Maimonidean usage, which will surface again only in early-modern times, due to completely different influences. The term *dat* became more and more synonymous to another popular term, *nimus*, an originally Greek word (*nomos*) which was transplanted into medieval Hebrew through its Arabic usage (*namus*). *Nimus* generally means strictly human law.[6] There are numerous examples of this usage of the term *dat* in late-medieval Hebrew literature. It climaxed with Joseph Albo's famous definition and classification of law at the beginning of his *Book of Roots* (*Sefer ha-Ikkarim*, Castile, mid-fifteenth century).[7]

Albo consistently used the term *dat* for every kind of law: from divine law, through natural law,[8] to human law. He was apparently already influenced here by Thomas Aquinas, who adopted the Latin *lex* to the Christian definition of Divine law (*lex divina*); Albo did the same with the Hebrew *dat*.[9] The Christian-Latin legal vocabulary started to influence the manner by which Jewish scholars read, interpreted, and used the word *dat*, a phenomenon which will increase in subsequent centuries.

Albo's new definition and classification of *dat* as law had a profound influence upon late medieval and early modern Jewish scholars. They started more and more to use this term to denote law, every kind of law, not specifically divine law or Jewish law, and often plain human law of every nation. We can find the influence of Albo's definition and classification among many Jewish scholars, up to the late Jewish Enlightenment in the nineteenth century.[10]

Moreover, various Jewish scholars systematically started to translate the Latin *lex*, and vernacular terms for law (such as *legge*, *loi*, *legal*) into the Hebrew *dat*; they preferred this term to other available Hebrew terms, which were often more appropriate, such as *hok*, *nimus*, and *din*. A later, fascinating example is the usage of this term in the Hebrew translation of the Declaration of Human Rights of the French Revolution, published in The Hague in 1794, after the French conquered the Netherlands and emancipated the Jews. Here the Hebrew *dat* was systematically used for the French *loi*. For instance, the famous sentence: "la loi est l'xpression de la

6 For the history of the term *nimus*, see in detail Melamed, *Dat*, *ibid.*, 21–28.

7 Joseph Albo, *Book of Roots*, 1:7. For the English translation see *Medieval Political Philosophy; A Sourcebook*, ed. R. Lerner and M, Mahdi (New: Free Press of Glencoe, 1967), 242–43.

8 Albo was the first one to introduce the theory of natural law to Jewish legal thought, see in detail Abraham Melamed, "Natural Law in Medieval and Renaissance Jewish Thought," *Da'at* 17 (1986), 49–66 (Hebrew). Abraham Melamed, Wisdom's Little Sister: Medieval Jewish Political Philosophy (Ra'anana: Open University, 2011), 207–26 (Hebrew).

9 See detailed discussion, Melamed, *Dat*, *supra* note 1, ch. 5. See also: Abraham Melamed, "Natural, Human, Divine: The Classification of the Law among Some Fifteenth and Sixteenth Century Jewish Thinkers," in Abraham Melamed, *Wisdom's Little Sister, Studies in Medieval and Renaissance Jewish Political Thought* (Boston, 2012), 244–71. See also, ibid., 180–226.

10 See detailed discussion, Melamed, *Dat*, *supra* note 1, ch. 6.

volunte general," was translated into: "The law (*ha-dat*) speaks for the whole people."[11]

Moreover, the term *dat* started more and more to specifically denote human law (*dat enoshit*) only. Quite a few scholars of this period refused to use it in any specific Jewish-theological context. They used it only to denote human and natural law. For divine law, they preferred to use terms such as *torah* and *mizvot*, but never *dat*. This was in order to sustain and amplify the inherent distinction between human and divine law. This shows that the usage of *dat* to denote only human law became commonplace in their environment, thus their refusal to use it for divine law.[12]

The main example for this phenomenon is Isaac Abravanel (Portugal-Spain-Italy, late fifteenth century), who not only, like others, systematically used this term only as human law, he also emphatically argued that only the Mosaic Law should be called *Torah*, while human law of the various nations should be called *dat* or *nimus*, never *torah*, otherwise the inherent difference between them might be blurred, thus undermine the pure divine essence of the Mosaic Law.[13]

II THE EARLY MODERN PERIOD

Particularly when the term *dat* was used as strictly law, mostly human law, devoid of any Jewish-theological contexts, the next revolutionary transformation of the meaning and usage of this term occurred. *Dat* started to acquire the meaning in which it is universally used today, as a religion, a set of theological beliefs and rituals, where the practical commandments are considered a derivation thereof. The legal components this term contains are weakened, and in any case, it started to relate to divine law only. While late medieval Jewish scholars used this term to denote human law, as distinct from divine law (*Torah*), in the modern usage it acquired a distinct theological meaning: *dat* became religion in its modern sense; nobody uses it to denote law anymore, definitively not human law. While Maimonides was quite unique among medieval Jewish scholars in his usage of this term as a set of theological beliefs, first of all, this particular meaning became ubiquitous in modern times. It is not translated any more into *lex*, *loi*, or law, but into religion, belief, creed, or confession, another term borrowed from Christianity. The evaluation of this momentous transformation is the focus of this chapter.

This revolutionary transformation of meaning and usage was directly influenced by the earlier transformation which occurred in early modern Christian thought, following the Reformation, in the meaning of the old Latin term *religio*. This term, which originally denoted God fearing, was used through the Middle Ages to describe strictly Christian worship. Now it was transformed into religion, a set of theological

11 *Ibid.*, 93–95.

12 See detailed discussion, *ibid.*, ch. 7.

13 Isaac Abravanel, *Commentary on Exodus*, ed. A. Shutland (Jerusalem: Horev, 1997), 283. See detailed discussion of Abravanel's stance, Melamed, *Dat*, *supra* note 1, 101–08.

beliefs, first of all, and was applied to every so-called religious phenomenon, Judaism included. Christian scholars started to identify Judaism as a religion, and applied Christian terms when describing Jewish beliefs and ritual.[14] See for instance the following classification of world religions by a Seventeenth Century English scholar, Richard Baxter, in his *The Reasons of the Christian Religion* (London, 1667):

> Four sorts of Religions I find only considerable upon earth: The meer Naturalists, called commonly Heathens and Idolaters; the Jews; the Mohametans; and the Christians. The Heathens by their Oracles, Augures and Auspices, confess necessity of some supernatural light; and the very Religion of all the rest consisteth of it.[15]

Judaism had become a religion, just like any other, seen and described from a Christian vantage point.

Jewish scholars, especially those who started to write in the vernacular since the seventeenth century, were influenced by this new trend. The changing terminology influenced their discussion of Jewish beliefs, rituals, and commandments. Consequently, they adopted the Protestant emphasis of religion as belief or creed, first of all. Later on, nineteenth-century Jewish scholars who wrote in Hebrew followed in their footsteps, and directly equated between the Hebrew *dat* and the vernacular "religion," and even used a transliterated form in Hebrew letters. The identification of *dat* and "religion" was finalized.

Judaism was traditionally identified as an unbreakable combination of three components: *Halacha* (Jewish Law), theological beliefs, and ethnic identity. Following early modern processes, such as the Reformation, the Enlightenment, secularization, the emergence of the modern nation-state, and emancipation, this combination started to disconnect, and the new religious aspect became more and more dominant. Some Jewish scholars, especially those who were more absorbed into early modern European culture, adopted the new Protestant vision of religion. They applied it to the Jewish context, and attempted to disconnect the new religious component from the old legal and ethnic components of Judaism, which they deemed to be less and less relevant to their modern existence and identity, and thereby purify it. They attempted to convert Judaism into a religion based on rational monotheism and universalistic ethics. More moderate scholars, and even those who apparently rejected this process, for halachic or national reasons, were also

[14] See W. C. Smith, *The Meaning and End of Religion* (New York: Harper & Row, 1964) chs. 2–3; J. Bossy, "Some Elementary Forms of Durkheim," *Past and Present* 95 (1982), 3–18; P. Biller, "Words and the Medieval Notion of 'Religion'," *Journal of Ecclesiastical History* 63 (1985), 351–69; J. Z. Smith, *Relating Religions: Essays on the Study of Religion* (Chicago: University of Chicago Press, 2004), 179–96; P. Harrison, *'Religion' and the Religions in the English Enlightenment* (Cambridge: Cambridge University Press, 1990); G. Stroumsa, *A New Science: The Discovery of Religion in the Age of Reason* (Cambridge, Mass: Harvard University Press, 2010).

[15] Quoted in D. A. Pailin, *Attitudes to Other Religions: Comparative religion in Seventeenth and Eighteenth-Century Britain* (Manchester: Manchester University Press, 1984), 154. See more examples for the identification of Judaism as a religion by contemporary scholars, *ibid.*, 156, 182, 184, 196: "The whole Jewish creed."

influenced by this transformation in due time, in various ways, albeit unconsciously; nobody could escape its powerful influence.

This process first started with Jewish scholars who dwelt in big urban centers, and were more integrated into the surrounding Christian-European culture, such as Simone Luzzatto in Venice, Manasseh ben Israel and Spinoza in Amsterdam, and Moses Mendelsohn in Berlin, and culminated with German-Jewish scholars of the nineteenth century.[16] The fact that some of these scholars, such as Manasseh ben Israel and Spinoza, came from a Maranno background, intensified this process. Marrano Jews rejected Christianity, but their religious mentality originated from it, thus their tendency to identify religion, Judaism included, with belief, not law. All the more so, since they were forced by circumstances to hide their Judaic tendencies, they turned the inner subjective religious experience in to a central component of their mentality. The emphasis on both theological beliefs and the inner subjective religious experience thus became the cornerstones of this new identification of Judaism as a religion. They took this mentality with them when they returned to Judaism. They were the first ones who redefined their Jewish identity, and they did it with Christian tools.[17]

In his *Discorso supra il state degli Ebrei in Venezia* (Venice, 1638), Luzzatto was the first Jew, known to me, who directly identified Judaism as religion (*religione* in Italian), just like any other:

> Although the Jews were different in their religion (*religione*) from any other people, they were not allowed to declare war on a neighboring people for religious purposes. . . . Religion is the strongest partnership which binds human society together . . .. This is why the Jews consider all those foreign to their religion (*loro religione*) to share in a common humanity, as long as they follow the rules of natural morality (*naturale moralita*) and have a certain understanding of the cause of causes.[18]

Luzzatto was the first Jew who used the phrase: "The Jewish religion" (*religione hebrea*).[19] He relates to the old Latin meaning of *religio*, as God fearing and Divine worship, but charged it with the new Christian meaning which evolved in Europe during his period, and superimposed it on his understanding of Judaism; *religio* was transformed into the Italian *religione*, and *religione* was now applied to Judaism.

16 See L. Batnizky, *How Judaism Became a Religion: An Introduction to Modern Jewish Thought* (Princeton, NJ: Princeton University Press, 2011), Introduction. Batnizky argues that this process originated with German-Jewish scholars since Mendelssohn. There is no doubt that this process culminated with them, but it started much earlier, already during the seventeenth century, as will be shown in the following.

17 See L. Strauss, *Spinoza's Critique of Religion*, trans. E. M. Sinclair (New York: Schocken Books, 1965), 53; Y. Kaplan, "The Sephardic Diaspora in Western Europe in Early Modern Times," in *Zionism and the Return to History: A Reevaluation*, eds. Sh. N. Eisenstaedt and M. Lisak (Jerusalem, 1999, in Hebrew), 195–210, esp. 200–01. See especially the illuminating paper by Y. Yovel, "The Jews in History: The Marrano in Early Modern Times," in *ibid.*, 211–48.

18 See Simone Luzzatto, *Scriti politici e filosofici*, ed. G. Veltri (Milan: Bompiani, 2013), 58: "Benche gli Hebrei erano differenti de religione dagli altri popoli, not gli era lectio mover Guerra a lor vicino per semplice cause di quella" (my translation).

19 See for instance *ibid.*, 59, 60, 62, 63.

The context of Luzzatto's discussion is clearly universalistic, not particular-Jewish. The term *religione* is used here for every faith, Judaism included. He argues that Judaism is the one and only true religion (*la vera religione*),[20] since more than any other religion it is based not only on the particular commandments (*riti*), which obligate Jews only, but also on universal moral laws (*legge*), which obligate all humanity (*li precetti della naturale moralita*), that is, natural law. The example he brings is that Jews are forbidden to wage war on other people not because of their particular commandments, but because of the moral universal laws which are imbedded in the Mosaic legal system (*legge Mosaica*). Judaism is described by him as the only religion which takes care of the well-being of the entirety of humanity.[21]

Luzzatto emphasizes that the Jews were commanded to teach the gentiles only the basic moral and monotheistic percepts, and forgo delivering them any knowledge of the particular divine revelation of their nation, and definitely nothing concerning their particular commandments.[22] The emphasis clearly shifts to a universal moral-theological worldview, which is typical of the modern understanding of religion. He empathetically uses for God the old Aristotelian term *una causa superiore* (cause of causes), a universal God, not the particular Jewish deity.

Moreover, he insists on the willingness of the Jews to fully obey the laws of the countries in which they dwell. This principle, of *Dina de-malchuta dina* (the law of the state is a [biding] law), is a well-ingrained ancient rabbinic dictum, and Luzzatto emphasizes it here in order to quell the suspicion of the Venetian authorities concerning the loyalty of its Jewish inhabitants to the republic. Still, it clearly shows that he embraces here the evolving concept of the modern state, that demands from its inhabitant's full public obedience to its laws, while religious commandments and beliefs became more and more a private matter of the believer, based upon internal persuasion. The judicial power of coercion gradually moved from the religious authorities to the secular state. This is another facet of the evolving modern definition of religion which Luzzatto adopted and applied to the Jewish context.

All the more so, Luzzatto adopted the revolutionary Machiavellian view which considered religious belief and ritual a useful means for the sustenance of an ordered political community. Religion was delegated from its lofty state of a spiritual end to a utilitarian means, in contradistinction with the traditional medieval view which considered temporal political life as subordinate to spiritual ends. This influence is apparent in Luzzatto's forceful refutation of Tacitus's vicious defamation of the Jews in the Fifteenth consideration of the *Discorso*.[23] Tacitus argued that the Jewish

[20] *Ibid.*, 76, 77.

[21] *Discorso*, Fifteenth consideration, in Veltri, *Scriti politici*, note 18, 58–65.

[22] *Ibid.*

[23] See on the whole issue, A. Melamed, "Simone Luzzatto on Tacitus: *Apologetica and Ragione di Stato*," in I. Twersky, ed., *Studies in Medieval Jewish History and Literature*, vol. 2 (Cambridge, MA: Harvard University Press, 1984), 143–70, reprinted in Melamed, *Wisdom's Little Sister, supra* note 9, 305–34; C. Hammill, *The Mosaic Constitution: Political Theology and Imagination from Machiavelli to Milton* (Chicago: University of Chicago Pres, 2012), 69–70.

religion caused the Jews to behave in an immoral and politically destructive manner, which brought upon the demise of their independent existence. Luzzatto refuted his accusations by arguing that the opposite is true; Judaism is the only true religion (*vera religione*) particularly because it is a rational religion, based on human initiative, and not on superstitions, which are contrary to natural laws and reason, and lead humans to lazy and passive existence, just as Machiavelli so boldly insisted, referring to the medieval Catholic experience. These are the ingredients he identified in the false religions; the Jewish *vera religione*, on the other hand, ensures the well-being of the people and the efficient functioning of the state. While Machiavelli complained that Catholicism created passive humans, detached from political reality, Luzzatto argues that the Mosaic law creates active and industrious people, who benefit the body politic.[24]

Luzzatto thus followed the Machiavellian revolution which rejected the medieval Catholic view that the state should be subordinated to religious authorities and purposes, and argued the contrary, that religion has to serve temporal political ends. Thus, Luzzatto first internalized the new Christian meaning of religion as faith. Still he continued to describe the Mosaic law as a religion of the law, but this time in its new Machiavellian transformation, as a utilitarian political means. From both vantage points, he embedded the Italian *religione*, as applied to Judaism, with a new modern meaning.[25]

What Luzzatto did in Italian, Manasseh ben Israel and Spinoza did in Amsterdam later in the century, both in Latin, Spanish, and English, and later on, in the late eighteenth century, Moses Mendelssohn in Berlin, writing in German. Luzzatto's influence upon Manasseh ben Israel is well known,[26] and he probably influenced him also here. There is a difference between the meaning in which the word *dat* appears in Manasseh ben Israel's Hebrew writings and the meaning in which the word "religion" appears in his non-Hebrew writings. In his Hebrew *Nishmat Hayyim*, he clearly distinguishes between the terms *torah* and *dat*. Like Abravanel, and many others previously, *torah* is specifically identified with Jewish law, while *dat* means human law, thus not associated with Judaism specifically.[27]

In his non-Hebrew writings, however, the word "religion" starts to appear in its new meaning. Manasseh ben Israel's *Esperanza de Israel* (*The Hope of Israel*), was

[24] *Scriti politici*, *supra* note 18, 58–83.

[25] Not coincidently, Luzzatto was also the first Jew to define the Jewish people as a nation (*nazione*), in the modern meaning of the term, also here directly influenced by Machiavelli. The whole *Discorso* begins with a proud reference to "The Hebrew Nation" ("*La nazione hebrea*," *Scriti politici*, *supra* note 18, 6). In this early stage, he defined Judaism both as a religion and a nation, later on these two definitions would go their separate ways, see in the following. See a detailed discussion in Melamed, *Dat*, *supra* note 1, 130–31.

[26] See B. Ravid, "'How Profitable the Nation of the Jews Are': The *Humble Addresses* of Menasseh ben Israel and the *Discorso* of Simone Luzzatto," in *Mystics, Philosophers and Politicians: Essays in Jewish Intellectual History on Honor of Alexander Altmann*, ed. J. Reinharz et. al (Durham, NC: Duke University Press, 1982), 159–80.

[27] Manasseh ben Israel, *Nishmat Hayyim* (Jerusalem: Yarid Hasfarim, 1995), 8.

originally published in Spanish (Amsterdam, 1650), and almost immediately appeared also in Latin and English editions. It discusses the then popular issue of the whereabouts of the lost ten tribes of Israel, and attempts to find them somewhere in America.[28] He based this hypothesis on the testimony of a Portuguese Jew who claimed to have encountered them (apparently some native-American tribes in whose traditions he fancied to find some resemblance to Jewish rituals), when visiting South America. This person is described as: "Portugues de nacion, Iudio de religion";[29] Portuguese by his nationality, a Jew by his religion. At such any early stage in the development of the modern nation-state, his national identity and his religious identity are already separated.[30] In another place, Manasseh ben Israel relates to a testimony on a meeting between a Jesuit and a Jew in China. The Jew confused between Judaism and Christianity, considering them to the same religions (*su misma religion*);[31] while a certain Spanish nobleman who converted into Judaism is described by Manasseh ben Israel as he "who adopted our religion" (*nuestra religion*).[32]

The same phenomenon can be found in Manasseh ben Israel's English writings. His *Vindiciae Judaeorum* (London, 1656) was published in an effort to persuade the English authorities to permit the resettlement of the Jews in England. Judaism is repeatedly described here as a "religion," just as Christianity and other religions.[33] The same goes for his famous letter to Cromwell, the *Humble Addresses*, where Manasseh ben Israel proudly calls Judaism "Our Religion," but, with the same pride, also: "The Nation of the Jews."[34] He makes a clear distinction between the religion of the Jews and their laws,[35] and uses the expression "Judaical laws" when referring to the permission the Jews received to live according their laws from the various governments in the countries in which they dwell.[36] The new distinction between religion and law was thus very clear in his mind.

Spinoza, Manasseh ben Israel's contemporary, and fellow resident of Amsterdam, continued this process. In his revolutionary *Theologico-Political Treatise* (*Tractatus Theologico Politicus*), written in Latin, he consistently distinguished between *religio*

28 On the whole issue see A. Melamed, "The Discovery of America in Sixteenth and Seventeenth Century Jewish Thought," in *Following Columbus: America 1492–1992* ed. M. Eliav-Feldon (Jerusalem: Zalman Shazar Center, 1997, in Hebrew), 443–64; A. Melamed, *The Image of the Black in Jewish Culture: A History of the Other* (London; New York: Routledge Curzon, 2003), 209–12.

29 Manasseh ben Israel, *Esperanza de Israel* (Madrid: Hiperión, 1881), 41.

30 Marrano Jews traditionally identified themselves as *nacion*, see Yovel, "The Jews in History," *supra* note 17, 229–33. Here a Jew is already described as Portuguese by nationality, in the modern sense of the term.

31 Manasseh ben Israel, *Esperanza*, *supra* note 29, 49.

32 *Ibid.*, 98.

33 Manasseh ben Israel, *Vindiciae Judaeorum* (London: Printed by R.D., 1656), on Judaism, 7, 30, 34; on Christianity, 21.

34 Manasseh ben Israel, *To his Highness the Lord Protector of the Commonwealth of England, Scotland and Ireland, The Humble Addresses* (Melbourne: Reprinted by H.T. Dwight, 1868), 4–5.

35 *Ibid.*, 19.

36 *Ibid.*, 4.

and *lex*; *religio* denotes beliefs, customs, and rites,[37] while *lex, legis*, denotes law, divine, natural, or human.[38] Only when he relates to the specific laws of the Biblical Hebrews (*Tractatus*, ch. 17), Spinoza connects between the two, but he makes it clear that in his view these laws are not applicable any more after the Hebrew state ceased to exist.

The last in this series of early modern Jewish scholars who adopted the new term religion and applied it to Judaism, is Moses Mendelssohn, already on the eve of the Jewish Enlightenment. In his *Jerusalem or on Religious Power and Judaism* (*Jerusalem oder uber religiose macht und Judentum*) (Berlin, 1783) he brought this process to fruition. At the very beginning of this treatise Mendelssohn boldly declares:

> State and religion – civil and ecclesiastical constitution – secular and churchly authority – how to oppose these pillars of social life to one another so that they are in balance and do not, instead, become burdens on social life, ... this is one of the most difficult tasks of politics.[39]

Mendelssohn uses the same German term (*verfassung*) for both civil and religious legislation, but it is clear that in his view they denote two entirely kinds of laws, thus cannot be in a state of competition, but should exist parallelly in peace:

> Here we already see an essential difference (*ein wesentlicher unterdhied*) between state and religion. The state gives orders and coerces, religion teaches and persuades. The state prescribes laws (*gesetze*), religion commandments (*gebote*). The state has physical power and uses it when necessary; the power of religion is love and beneficence.[40]

These are not just two sub-kinds of the law, but two completely different legal entities. For him the term *gesetze* (law) covers every kind of law, the law of reason (*gesetze der vernunft*), the law of nature (*gesetze der nature*), and human law. Religious commandments (*gebote*) are something else altogether; they are no law. Unlike state laws, they have no compulsory status; they should be followed only by voluntary choice. The emphasis that religion is a matter of love and beneficence, and not of binding laws, is of course Protestant in essence, and is now superimposed of his concept of Judaism. In the Medieval Jewish communal organization, the power to excommunicate (*herem*) was essential in order to force members to follow Jewish law and obey its official interpreters; the case of Spinoza is one late famous

37 Benedict Spinoza, *Works: Theological Political Treatise; Political Treatise*, trans. R. H. M. Elwes (New York: Dover Publications, 1951), the introduction, and many other instances along the text.

38 In many places, see for instance *Tractatus*, ch. 3, in Spinoza, *Works, ibid*. See the definition of law at the beginning of ch. 4. The same goes also for his *Political Treatise*, Spinoza, *Works, ibid*.

39 Moses Mendelssohn, *Jerusalem*, trans. A. Arkush, (Hanover and London: University Press of New England, 1983), 33. On the whole issue see recently M. Gottlieb, *Faith and Freedom: Moses Mendelssohn's Theological-Political Thought* (Oxford: Oxford University Press, 2011).

40 Mendelssohn, note 39, 45. See also towards the end of the whole treatise, were Mendelssohn implores the Jews: "Adapt yourselves to the morals and constitution of the land to which you have been removed, but hold fast to the religion of your fathers too." *Ibid.*, 133.

example, which did not work anymore. Now, when Mendelssohn rejects this coercive power as not relevant anymore, the traditional identification between law and religion in Judaism is eliminated.

Mendelssohn had to confront the Christian allegation that Judaism is an essentially political religion (*religioser regierung*), based on the duty to follow its biding laws, where religious authorities have the power to enforce obedience (*macht und recht der religion*).[41] Thus, they concluded, it competes with state laws, a situation the state cannot allow. Mendelssohn did agree that Judaism is essentially different from Christianity, being based on practical commandments and not on binding beliefs. However, he contended, following the commandments is essentially different from obeying state laws, since the former is based on voluntary choice and the power of loving persuasion, while the latter is based on coercion. Like Spinoza, he argues that the political nature of Judaism and the power of legal coercion were abolished long ago, in the early biblical period. When monarchy was established, the power of coercion was transferred from the religious authorities to the king, and they retained only the right to persuade by love and kindness. The traditional connection between Judaism and legal coercion is thus severed by Mendelssohn, enabling the Jew to become a true citizen in the modern state, where only one system of the law is binding. Judaism was transformed into a religion of universal monotheistic beliefs and ethical values, where obeying the commandment became a completely voluntary matter.

The distinction these early modern Jewish scholars made between law and religion, and the weakening of the connection between them, follows the Spinozian tendency to separate religion and the state. The Christian distinction between the spiritual and temporal authorities was secularized, and transmuted into the modern separation between religion and the state. Theological beliefs and rituals were now left to the realm of religion, while the laws, which regulate social life, fell under the authority of the state. Whatever religion represents became the matter of the religious community, while whatever the law represents became the matter of the state. While membership in a religious community and obedience to its rules became voluntary, the obedience to state law was now binding. Judaism, now a religion, like any other, was gradually dismantled from its abiding legal component, and became a matter of private voluntary beliefs and rituals.

III THE JEWISH ENLIGHTENMENT

The identification of Judaism as "religion," and consequently the radical change in the meaning of the Hebrew word *dat*, will fully ripen with scholars of the Jewish

[41] See for example Kant's famous assertion that Judaism is not really a religion, but a political organization, in his *Religion within the Limits of Reason Alone* Allen W. Wood and George di Giovanni, *Religion within the Boundaries of Mere Reason* (Cambridge: Cambridge University Press, 1998), with an Introduction by Robert Merrihew Adams. See recent discussion in S. Meld Shell, "Kant and the Jewish Question," *Hebraic Political Studies* 2 (2007), 101–36.

Enlightenment who wrote in Hebrew, all the more so those who wrote in other European languages, mainly German. This change is expressed on two levels: first, the final identification of the term *dat* as religion, in its new Protestant meaning; second, and following it, the usage of this Hebrew term became widespread, in dimensions unheard of hitherto, and gradually replaced traditional popular terms, such as *Torah*. These scholars not only purified Judaism from its strict halachic component, but also tended to reject its ethnic (now turned national) definition. They now tended to define it as a purely rational monotheistic religion, based on universal ethics. This tendency was later enhanced by Romantic Protestant influences which described religion as an amorphous feeling of awe and veneration of the sublime. All in order to enhance their own integration as equal citizens in the new nation-state, as German, French, or English citizens of the Jewish faith.

This can be clearly demonstrated by a series of new definitions of Judaism made by early nineteenth-century Jewish scholars. The very fact that they found it useful to make such new definitions, is clear proof of the need they found to redefine Judaism, under the pressure of their new circumstances. Most premodern Jewish scholars never bothered to define Judaism: its meaning was self-understood as far as they were concerned; now nothing was self-understood anymore. Let's look at a few typical examples. Gotthold Salomon, a German-Jewish scholar with reform tendencies, who was already influenced by the new romanticism, defined the Jewish religion in 1801 as follows:

> Religion means to us the holy owe and reverence with which the infinite fills us . . . . It means for us the conviction and that way of thinking with which the human being expresses his own relation . . . to the fullness of creation.[42]

In the opening statement of the new Jewish-German periodical *Sulamith* (1806), we read the following:

> Religion is the most essential intellectual and moral need of the cultured person. The purpose of *Sulamith* is to describe this religion in the most exalted manner. *Sulamith* strives to rouse the nation (*nazion*) to respect religion. This means those truths which alone are worthy to be called religion. It aspires to revive the urgent need for the religious feelings and concepts, but, at the very same time, it strives to pay attention to the truth – that the concepts and commandments which are included in the Jewish religion are not harmful in any way to the individual or to society at large.[43]

One of the radical Jewish *Maskilim*, Yehudah Leib Ben Ze'ev, published in 1811 a bilingual (Hebrew and German transliterated in Hebrew letters) Jewish catechism for youngsters. In the opening statement, he defined the term *dat* as follows: "What is

42 Quoted in M. A. Meyer, *The Origins of the Modern Jew* (Detroit: Wayne State University Press, 1967), 130–31.

43 Joseph Wolf, "Inhalt," *Sulamith*, vol. 1 (Leipzig, 1806), 9. The English translation appears in *The Jews in the Modern World*, eds. P. Mendes Flohr et. al., (New York: Oxford University Press, 2011), 85.

divine religion (*dat elohi, religion*)? It is the teaching of beliefs (*emunah, gloibens*) and the practical laws (*mishpat, gezetzen*), which God gave humans, according to which they should act during their lifetime in order to achieve eternal bliss."[44] In another Jewish catechism, *A Manual of Judaism* (London, 1835), this time in English, Joshua van Oven defined Judaism as follows: "Religion is an inward feeling of awe and veneration, induced by the knowledge of the existence of an omnipotent and eternal God, the creator, preserver, and regulator of the universal, whom we strongly feel bound to worship and adore."[45] All these definitions, something between pietist Protestantism and Enlighted Deism, are completely universal. The direct influence of the Protestant-originated German philosophy of the time – from Kant to Hegel – is strongly felt here. This influence caused the so-called "Protestantisation" of Judaism, from a religion of law into a religion of personal awe and veneration of an amorphous God. These tendencies strongly influenced the formation of Reform Judaism. With the Americanization of Judaism later in the Nineteenth century, it was even more emphasized. This process culminated with the Reform *Pittsburgh Platform* (1885), which proclaimed Judaism to be a pure universal religion, devoid of any ethnic component, and almost eradicated any legal-halachic component from it. Judaism is defined as "a progressive religion ever striving to be in accord with the postulates of reason."[46] Judaism was transformed into one of the legitimate American creeds.

Moreover, from now on, and practically until today, we can find an abundance of newly created hyphenated terms, which add a descriptive word to the vernacular "religion" or the Hebrew *dat*, in order to make clear the specific meaning that a given scholar ascribes to it, such as *Menschenreligion* (Human religion), *Religion des vernunft* (Religion of reason), *Religion der that* (Religion of actions), or *Religion des geistes* (Spiritual religion) in German, or *dat ivrit* (Hebrew religion), *dat ha-ruah* (spiritual religion) in Hebrew, and many more. The plain word *dat* was not sufficient anymore to express the new specific meaning now ascribed to religion or *dat*. Traditional terms such as *dat Israel* (the law – or religion – of Israel) or *dat ha-Torah* (the law – or religion – of the *Torah*), which served so well many generations of Jews, were not sufficient anymore to capture the many nuances the Jewish identity acquired in modern times. Franz Rosenzweig succinctly called this phenomenon: "Hyphenated Jews," a typical phenomenon of the so-called modern hyphenated identity: "This is a problem of one generation, mostly a century; there are Christian Jews, national Jews, religious Jews ... emotional Jews, traditional Jews. In short, various hyphenated Jews shaped by the nineteenth century."[47] Additional creative

44 Yehudah Leib Ben Ze'ev, *Yesodei ha-Dat* (Vienna: Anton von Schmid, 1811), 8–9. (My translation).

45 Quoted in D. Ruderman, *Jewish Enlightenment in an English Key* (Princeton and Oxford: Princeton University Press, 2000), 9.

46 See www.ccarnet.org/rabbis-speak/platforms/declaration-principles.

47 F. Rosenzweig, *Letters and Diary: A Collection*, ed. R. Horowitz (Jerusalem: Bialik Institute, 1987), 328 (Hebrew, my translation).

combinations, such as "religious beliefs," "religious experience," "religious meaning," "religious values," and so forth, continue to appear as time goes by. They are all created in order to suit the needs of the modern believer, who identifies *dat* as a set of theological beliefs or a vague religious experience, no more as strictly law. The traditional *dat Israel* is not sufficient anymore to capture such nuances.

Likewise, many of these scholars also rejected traditional terms for Jews and Judaism, which acquired a negative meaning in the surrounding Christian environment, and preferred to use other terms, neutral or positive in their view, which seemed to be more respectable, such as *Mosaische Religion* (the Mosaic religion), *Israelitische religion* (the religion of Israel), over such terms as *Judische religion* (Jewish religion). They preferred to call themselves *de confession Israelite* (of the Israelite confession) or *de confession mosaique* (of the Mosaic confession) instead of the negatively loaded *Jude* or *Juif*, while American Jews preferred to call themselves "Hebrews," instead of the loaded "Jews."[48]

By the early nineteenth century this new definition of Judaism and the Hebrew *dat* as "religion," started to influence also East European Jewish *maskilim*, such as the above mentioned Yehudah ben Ze'ev, maybe the first Jew to directly equate religion and *dat*. Appropriately, he clearly moved the emphasis of Judaism from obeying the practical commandments to theological beliefs:

> Even if a person will transgress any of the commandments by mistake, he will not cease to be a member of the religion (*dat*). However, if he will be ignorant of one of the principles of religion and mistakenly hold unto a false view, he will cease to be a member of the said religion. Whoever does not believe in the unity of God or will attribute corporality to his creator, will not be a member of the Hebrew religion (*dat Ivrit*), even if he will fulfill all the commandments of the Torah.[49]

ben Ze'ev strongly criticizes the abundance of commandments in Judaism and the severity of the halachic restrictions, which suffocate the believer. He insists that following the commandments automatically, without understanding them, and without the right intention, is futile. What is essential is the intention of the heart (*kavanat ha-lev*) and the understanding of the heart (*havanat ha-lev*).[50] This emphasis on right beliefs and the inner religious experience is clearly influenced by the new Protestant-Romantic views, now dressed in Jewish garb.

In his *Teudah be-Israel* (*The Mission of Israel*, Vilna, 1828), Isaac Ber Levinson makes ample use in the new term *dat Ivrit* (*Hebrew Religion*), coined by ben Ze'ev, and in addition uses traditional terms, such as *dat ha-Torah*, and *dat Yehudit*, in their new meaning, as religion. Levinson charged *dat Ivrit* with a broad national-cultural meaning, in his struggle to fulfill the aims of Jewish Enlightenment, especially the reform of Jewish education, to include also secular studies, the modernization of the

48 On the whole issue see details and many more examples in Melamed, *Dat*, *supra* note 1, 146–52.

49 *Yesodei ha-Dat*, *supra* note 44, First Introduction, unnumbered page (my translation).

50 *Ibid.*, Introduction, xii.

Hebrew language, and the productization of Jewish economic life. He distinguishes between *dat ha-Torah*, which is based on the authority of revelation, and *dat Ivrit*, which is based on what reason teaches us.[51] Judaism is transformed from a theological system into a broad national culture which combines the authority of the Torah with the teachings of reason. Influenced by the emerging national movements in Europe, he identifies Judaism not just as religion, but primarily as a national-cultural entity which contains a religious component.

This tendency is strengthened in Levinson's later *Beit Yehudah* (*House of Judah*, Vilna, 1839). In the very beginning of this treatise he directly equates the Hebrew *dat* with the vernacular "religion" (in Hebrew transliteration), and later on, he translates it into *dat toratit* (*dat of the Torah*) and *dat Elohit* (*Divine dat*) specifically.[52] From among the various kinds of *dat* (as law), this is the only kind which is directly equated with religion. Moreover, he even identified the Hebrew *emunah* (belief, equated with the German *glaube* in Hebrew transliteration), as specifically religion, and admits that this identification was influenced by Christianity.[53] Levinson concludes that the Mosaic religion is the only one which is a philosophical religion (*eine phlosofishe religion*, in Hebrew transliteration),[54] since it is the only one which combines all three kinds of law as classified long ago by Albo: human law (*dat nimusit*), natural law (*dat tiv'it*), and divine law (*dat elohit*).[55]

This attitude was typical of various Enlightenment and Reform Jewish scholars in Germany, and those East European scholars who were influenced by them.[56] An exceptional figure is Shmuel David Luzzatto who was active in Italy in the first half of the nineteenth century. He was a typical Italian rabbi, who easily combined strict orthodoxy with openness to the general culture. Luzzatto was unique in his critical attitude towards various facets of the Enlightenment, which German Jewish scholars so enthusiastically embraced. He rejected the anti-religious and anti-traditionalist tendencies of the radical Enlightenment, and what he viewed as its ultra-rationalist and individualistic tendencies. Following his pessimistic view on human life, Luzzatto was skeptical of the optimistic theory of human progress. He was strongly opposed to the effort to modernize Judaism, and argued that it would necessarily lead to assimilation. Luzzatto's emphasis on Jewish tradition over reason was clearly influenced by Romantic anti-Enlightenment tendencies of his period.

His religious views crystalized on the background of these influences. Although he was a strict orthodox Jew, and fiercely rejected reform tendencies, still also Luzzatto was influenced by the new Protestant concept of religion, albeit

51 Isaac Ber Levinson, *Teudah be-Israel* (Jerusalem: Zalman Shazar Center, 1977, reprint of the 1828 edition published in Vilna and Grodno), xvi.

52 Isaac Ber levinson, *Beit Yehudah* (Vilna: Menaḥem Man ben Barukh, 1839), 3, 5, 18.

53 *Ibid.*, 26.

54 *Ibid.*, 41.

55 *Ibid.*, 121. We can see here how he uses the term *dat* both in its old meaning as law and its new meaning as religion.

56 See more examples with detailed discussion, Melamed, *Dat, supra* note 1, 171–88.

unconsciously. This was the outcome of his imbedded ambivalence towards the Enlightenment project. Although he wrote in Hebrew, and did not have to use vernacular terms at all, still Luzzatto chose to consistently use the term "religion," in Hebrew transliteration, instead of using the Hebrew *dat*, which should have been his natural choice. Still, the Hebrew term does not appear even once in his *Yesodei ha-Torah* (*The Foundations of the Torah*), nor in his other Hebrew writings; It is consistently replaced by "religion." This only shows how deeply he internalized the Christian religious vocabulary.

Moreover, it was not only a matter of the term Luzzatto chose to use, this is also clear from the views which he expressed. The whole texts open with this term; It is anachronistically applied to Judaism from its very inception: "This religion was bequeathed to the people of Israel from their fathers Abraham, Isaac and Jacob."[57] And later on:

> This religion was sufficient for the people of Israel as long as they were only one family. However, when they became a people, and it was time to bring them to the land that God promised their fathers to give them, God decided that they need laws and ordinances to guide them in the right path, for the amelioration of their values, for the perfection of their society, and for the preservation of the religion. So that they will not leave it and follow the gentiles who surround them, and remain without a religion. This is why He gave them this *Torah* which Moses placed in front to the people of Israel.[58]

In doing so Luzzatto practically gave a traditionalistic justification for the usage of this originally Christian term, with all its Protestant connotations. It is clear from this that in his view, this religion was originally a matter of monotheistic belief. The need for laws came only later, when they became a people and settled in the promised land. The Mosaic laws are presented as a necessary means to sustain and preserve the religion itself. By doing this, Luzzatto practically adopted the Christian definition of religion as primarily belief, and superimposed it upon his image of traditional Judaism. Thus, not only Enlightenment Jews, but even so-called orthodox Jews started to internalize and use the Christian term "religion," with all the connotation attached to it, albeit unconsciously, and reinterpreted their image of Judaism thereby; the influence of the surrounding culture was so powerful. This phenomenon will only increase in the forthcoming generations, as we shall see in the following; nobody could escape modern religion.

IV EARLY TWENTIETH CENTURY

The last scholar who championed the definition of Judaism as rational monotheism, of the Kantian kind, was Hermann Cohen, who created the famous hyphenated

57 Shmuel David Luzzatto, *Collected Writings* (Warsaw: Ha-Tzeferah, 1913), 9 (my translation).

58 *Ibid.*, p. 11. The term "religion" always appears in Hebrew transliteration.

term "religion of reason" (*religion der vernunft*), in his great theological system, published already at the beginning of the twentieth century.[59] It was the epitome of the so-called "Protestant Judaism."[60] Scholars of the next generation, such as Franz Rosenzweig, Martin Buber, and Aharon David Gordon, will lead the concept of Judaism as religion to new and different directions: from reason to subjective personal experience, from religion to religiosity. They will continue with the criticism of halachic Judaism as oppressive, and identify the core of Judaism in the religious experience of the individual, but now this experience will no more be rational, Cohen style, but existential. As they rejected halachic orthodoxy, they also rejected the alternative of a rational religion; both were deemed to be oppressive and subjugate the creative spirit of the individual believer.

Franz Rosenzweig was strongly influenced by Cohen in his process of return to Judaism, but developed a system of existential Judaism, which was very remote from Cohen's rational Kantian views. He was the one who practically completed the process of the Protestantization of Judaism. Rosenzweig almost converted to Christianity in his youth, and considered it to be a true divine religion, alongside Judaism (so unlike his blatant negative view of Islam!). However, more than Judaizing Christianity, he Christianized Judaism. Due to his assimilatory education, he was better cognizant of Christianity than of Judaism. He read the Hebrew Bible from a distinct Christian point of view, and his knowledge of the rabbinic teachings was very limited at best. The very fact that he preferred the Bible over the oral *Torah* is in itself proof of a clear Christian orientation. His view of Judaism was anchored in a Christian vocabulary.[61] Rosenzwig's very ambivalent attitude towards Jewish law also fits very well into this description.

Rosenzweig rejected Zionism, and considered Judaism to be a religion, in the distinct meaning he applied to it, and not a nation. Turning Judaism from a revelation of the divine law or a revelation of reason – both of which reject Christianity, into a revelation of love, in a distinct Protestant-Pietist sense, is clear indication of this attitude. For Maimonides, the Knowledge of God was the first and most important commandment; for Rosenzweig it was the Love of God. While in the Jewish tradition revelation occurred foremostly at Sinai, for Rosenzwing it is exemplified in the dialogue of love in the *Song of Songs*, in its allegorical-Midrashic interpretation,

59 J. Rose, "Hermann Cohen: Kant among the Prophets," in G. Rose, *Judaism and Modernity* (Oxford: B. Blackwell, 1993), 111–25.

60 D. N. Myers, "Hermann Cohen and the Quest for Protestant Judaism," in *Leo Baeck Institute Year Book* 46 (2001), 195–214.

61 In an early letter from 1909 Rosenzweig indicated that: "We [=the Jews] turned into complete Christians; We live in a Christian state, study in Christian schools, read Christian books; In short, our entire culture in essentially Christian." F. Rosenzweig, *Briefe*, ed. E. Rosenzweig (Berlin: Schocken Verlag, 1935), 45 (my translation). See also G. Rose, "Franz Rosenzweig: From Hegel to Yom Kippur," in G. Rose, *Judaism and Modernity*, 128–29: "the work [=his *Star of Redemption*] retains a predominantly Christian orientation." Gershom Sholem, Rozenzweig's great adversary, wrote that he was most irritated by the fact that Rosenzweig turned Judaism into a kind of a Protestant-Pietist church, and his ongoing devotion to the so-called German-Jewish synthesis. See G. Sholem, *Devarum Bego* (Tel-Aviv: Oved Publishers, 1976, in Hebrew), 28.

which turned it into a tale on the love between humans and God. Loving God, the most significant religious duty, necessitates in his view also the love of our fellow humans, henceforth the connection to Buber's Dialogical philosophy which was taking shape at that very same time. His was a distinct existential tendency, which emphasized the inner experience of the individual and his relationships with others – human and divine, as he says in one of his letters: "Jews and Christians alike deny the basic ethical-religious idea (the love of God and the love of your friend), which is common to both."[62]

This tendency culminated with Martin Buber. Buber was the first one to introduce the term "religiosity" (*religiositate*, *datiyut* in Hebrew) to the Jewish context. This is yet another example of the need to create new conjugations and hyphenated terms in order to express the changing meaning of Judaism. Buber made a clear distinction between religion and religiosity:

> Religiosity (*religiositate*) is a human emotion, which is forever renewed. . . . The feeling of amazement and admiration in a person, which is beyond his ever-changing mode and dependence, there is something absolute . . . . Religion is the culmination of all customs and rules by which the religiosity of a specific period in the life of a people is expressed. It regulates the halachic rules and commandments given to all subsequent generations, as an ever-binding law, without any regard to religiosity, which is perpetually renewed. . . . Religiosity is the creative force; Religion is the organizing principle.[63]

Buber identified this religiosity with the perpetual renewal of the authentic inner feeling of awe for some absolute entity a person desires to connect with. This in contrast with "religion" (*dat*), which is identified by him as the external organizing facet of this religiosity, which tends to be fossilized in time; he identified this with Halachic Judaism. Buber transferred the focus of Judaism from religion, which he deemed to be its formal, external, and institutionalized manifestation, to religiosity, which is its inner, spontaneous, vital, and individualistic true expression. He identifies the new hyphenated term he created – Jewish religiosity – as "A pure divine feeling,"[64] and anachronistically reinterpreted the whole Jewish history on the basis of this idea, in order to legitimize it as an authentic Jewish creation, albeit its clear Protestant sources which he tended to overlook. In many respects, he adopted here Kierkegaard's religious-Christian existentialism, and dressed it in Jewish garb. Although he understood that this religiosity cannot be a matter of individualistic experience only, and needs some kind organized expression, still Buber was reluctant to make clear rules lest it would degrade into an oppressive system like rabbinic

62 F. Rosenzweig, *A Collection of Letters and Diary*, ed. R. Horowitz (Jerusalem: Bialik Institute, 1987), a Hebrew translation. See discussion in Rose, "From Hegel to Yom Kippur," *supra* note 61.

63 Martin Buber, *Teudah ve-Yeud; writings of Jewish Issues* (Jerusalem: Zionist Library, 1960, Hebrew), 70 (my translation). See on the whole issue: L. J. Silberstein, *Martin Buber's Social and Religious Thought: Alienation and the Quest for Meaning* (New York: New York University Press, 1989).

64 Buber, *Teudah ve-Yehod, ibid.*, 22.

Judaism. He was very conscious of the human need to live in an organized community, but instead of the oppressive rabbinic system, he preferred the new national Jewish entity which was developing in Palestine.

Religion as the spontaneous experience of the individual is also at the core of Aharon David Gordon's thought. It is ironic that the hyphenated term *Dat ha-avodah*, that is, "the religion of labor," which is so associated with him, never appears in Gordon's writings, and he himself rejected it. Yet, it well illustrates the centrality of human labor in his thought, and the strong relationship between his religious orientation and the concept of labor, especially working the land, as the supreme human value. Influenced by Romantic-Tolstoian ideas, he described labor, and through it the direct connection with nature, religiously, as the true worship of God. Tilling the Land of Israel became for him a substitute for the exilic-halachic existence. The *Kibbuz* movement adopted this religious interpretation of labor.[65]

The very fact that Gordon's views were defined as *dat* (despite his indignation), the fact that the hyphenated *dat ha-avodah* was quickly absorbed, and became popular among Hebrew speakers, well illustrate the amorphous, fluid nature the word *dat* acquired, so much that it became possible to use it in order to define and illustrate ideological tendencies which are very remote from its original meaning, even secular views which are completely detached from it. This tendency increased as time went by, as we shall see in the following.

Like Buber, Gordon also grew up in the Halachic world, but rejected it as an oppressive institution. Still, although he stopped following it, he was full of empathy to the world he left behind, and tried to inject religious components, a certain kind of religiosity, into the life of the *Haluzim* of the Second Aliyah. Like Willian James, he identified the powerfulness of the religious experience in the very fact that humans are never indifferent to it; they adopt it enthusiastically or reject it ferociously. Gordon defined it, however, in a distinct Deist-Pantheistic manner, which identifies God as a natural force. This is a subjective, authentic, and spontaneous personal experience; it is the direct instinctive bonding the individual and community with existence and nature, without the belief in divine providence, or obeying halachic norms:

> Religion (*ha-dat*) is the feeling of the full unity of the whole existence and its supreme and complete harmony. … Religion has no other basis, no other expression, and no other proof but emotions and their modes of expression. … Religion is completely subjective, but this is a unique subjectivism.[66]

While Buber made a distinction between religion and religiosity, Gordon distinguished between the form of religion and its content. The content is the inner

65 D. Can'ani, *The Second Aliyah and its Attitude Towards Religion* (Tel-Aviv Institute for Research of Workers and Society:, 1976, in Hebrew), 56–64; A. Shapirah, *Gordon's Thought and Its Sources in Kabbalah and Hasidism* (Tel-Aviv: Oved Publishers, 1996, in Hebrew).

66 Aharon David Gordon, *Writings*, vol. 2. (Tel-Aviv: Zionist Library, 1957, in Hebrew), 112–13 (my translation).

subjective experience, while the form is the external ritual expression of religion, which cannot follow the authentic flow of the experience, and tends to be fossilized and subjugate the soul:

> This is why the form of religion (*dat*) always stays behind the ongoing thinking and the purified spirit; It was always backward. There is no wonder then that it lately completely fossilized. ... until the content became completely superfluous. ... There is no wonder that lately the living thought, which seeks and surveys, in which the soul lives, which always seeks to be renewed, distanced itself from religion completely.[67]

In the formal religion, Gordon distinguishes between the historical religion and the philosophical religion; both were in his view a "dried-up abstraction."[68] As far as he was concerned, Jewish renewal meant both the rejection of the oppressive halachic religion, and the dry formal religion of reason, and their replacement with the living experience, which he, like Buber, identified in biblical prophecy. In his view, Judaism was closer than Christianity to this authentic religious experience, since it is by essence a national religion. In the national component, he identified not only an ethnic framework, but, more importantly, a vehicle which enables the mystical bonding with existence and nature in the Land of Israel. Both religion and nation are an expression of the human bonding with what he phrases as the "soul of the world," the unity of existence. He aspired Zionism to become a movement of religious renewal, in a Deistic-Pantheistic sense, which would enable the Jew to bond again with his land, thereby with nature and the wholeness of being.[69] Here is where *dat* and *avodah* (labor) coalesced, and enabled his followers to create the hyphenated *dat ha-avodah* (religion of labor), as the supreme expression of the revival of the nation in the Land of Israel. On this basis, they created an oxymoronic secular religiosity, so typical of the *Kibbuz* movement in its formative years.[70]

V THE ORTHODOX REACTION

So far, we have encountered the views of nineteenth- and early twentieth-century Jewish scholars who were influenced in various ways by the new meanings Judaism acquired in modern times, as a *dat* which is a religion. Whoever wrote in Hebrew continued to label Judaism as *dat*, but invested it with the new Protestant meaning of religion they acquired from the surrounding culture; all the more so those who wrote in various European languages, mainly German. However, other currents in Judaism and their scholars, who encountered the challenge of modernity, voiced

67 *Ibid.*, 125.
68 *Ibid.*, 127.
69 *Ibid.*, 120.
70 See many examples and discussion in Can'ani, *The Second Aliyah and its Attitude Towards Religion*, *supra* note 65; Melamed, *Dat*, *supra* note 1, 200–05.

strong reservations and rejected the process of turning Judaism into a religion, this from different and contrasting motives. Some acted from religious-orthodox motives, others on the basis of a secular, national, or cultural orientation. The very fact that such a fierce resistance evolved from so many different directions, only proves how deeply this new definition of religion penetrated the Jewish environment, and gradually dripped from Germanic Central Europe into Jewish centers in Eastern Europe. One never rejects, albeit so forcefully, a phenomenon which is nonexistent or is negligible; the powerfulness of rejection is a clear indication of how deeply this new concept of religion penetrated.

However, many among those who resisted were so deeply influenced by this modern concept of religion, and the Christian religious vocabulary which was used in the surrounding culture, that they imposed it on their reading of Judaism, even against their own will or unconsciously, so powerful was the influence of the new concept of religion.[71]

The Orthodox rejection of the identification of Judaism as religion, and the translation of the Hebrew *dat* into "religion," should be subdivided between Ultra-Orthodoxy (*Haredim*) and Neo-Orthodoxy. Paradoxically, the Ultra-Orthodox quest to freeze Judaism in its present condition (i.e. that of the early nineteenth century), as a means to combat modernism, created a new current in Judaism, just like the appearance of Reform Judaism. The creators of Ultra-Orthodoxy were unconscious of this fact, and in any case denied it vehemently.[72] Their contention that they are the one and only authentic inheritors of traditional Judaism is an invented tradition created to legitimize their claim. They were a new current in modern Judaism, just like any other, they were a response to modernity; the difference was in the nature of the response. Their response to the appearance of Reform Judaism was quite compatible, even in the terms used, to the reaction of the Catholic establishment to the Reformation. The irony is that the famous slogan of Hatam Sofer, the founder of Ultra-Orthodoxy, a freely interpreted Mishnaic dictum: "Anything new is strictly forbidden by the *Torah*," was in itself a major halachic innovation. Previous rabbinic authorities, who were not forced to confront the challenges of modernity and reform, had no need for such a radical theory about the unchangeability of the Halacha. Orthodoxy had to invent a tradition in order to defend its very existence.

Orthodox Jews continued to use traditional terms. This is clearly apparent from the collection of letters, known as *Eleh Divrei ha-Berit* (*These Are the Words of the Covenant*, 1818), a reaction to the formation of the first reform congregation in

71 See many examples in Melamed, *Dat*, *supra* note 1, 206–10.

72 Y. Katz, *Ha-Kerah Shelo Nitachah* (Jerusalem: Zalman Shazar Institute, 1995), 25–27; D. Ellenson, "Traditional Reactions to Modern Jewish Reform: The Paradigm of German Orthodoxy," in D. Ellenson, *After Emancipation: Jewish Religious Responses to Modernity* (Cincinnati: Hebrew Union College Press, 2004), 154–83; M. K. Silver, "The Emergence of Ultra-Orthodoxy: The Invention of Tradition," in *The Uses of Tradition*, ed. J. Wertheimer (New York: Jewish Theological Seminary of America; Cambridge, MA: Distributed by Harvard University Press, 1992), 23–84.

Hamburg.[73] The rabbis whose letters were published in this volume continued to use traditional terms, such as *dat Moshe ve-Israel* (*The law of Moses and Israel*), *dateno ha-kedosha* (*our holly law*), and so forth, all in the plain meaning of the commandments of the *Torah*. Judaism for them was *dat*, in the plain legal meaning, never a religion.

However, even here the new definition of *dat* as religion started to penetrate, albeit unconsciously. At the beginning of a letter by a rabbi from Alsace, a French seal appears, indicating that he was a member of the *consistoire*, the official organization of French rabbis established by Napoleon. At the center of this seal appear the French words: *Patrie-Religion* (*Homeland-Religion*).[74] This rabbi fiercely rejected religious reform, but ironically, his seal identifies Judaism as a religion, recognized by the secular state, which give it official status. Thus, also he had to practically accept the modern separation between state and religion, and recognize the fact that the power to enforce the law belongs to the state, and the religious establishment lost the right to enforce its rulings. This is a fascinating example of how even orthodox Jews were left with no other choice but to recognize the authority of the modern state, thereby practically adopting the identification of Judaism as religion, in the modern sense of the term.[75]

It is no coincidence that this appears in a letter by a French rabbi. Eastern European Orthodox Jews barely came in touch with these modern influences, and in any case, this happened much later. They were quite oblivious of the appearance of modern religion and its influence on the concept of Judaism. They will continue to use the Hebrew *dat*, in its traditional legal meaning, deep into the twentieth century, quite unconscious of the "Protestant" connotations it acquired. However, as already indicated, even they had with time to reconcile with the fact that the rabbinic authorities lost their autonomic judicial power, and were subjected now to the coercive authority of the modern state. They lost their most lethal tool, the right to impose a *herem* (excommunication) on a Jew; membership in a congregation and obedience to rabbinic authority became completely voluntary. As Hatam Sofer himself wrote in a famous conditional sentence, concerning the attitude towards reform Jews: "Had we had the legal authority, I would have decided to expel them from us."[76] The key phrase here is the conditional "Had we had;" he was already clearly conscious of the fact that this authority was taken away. Orthodox Jews thus attempted to leave the organized Jewish congregation whenever it became dominated by reform Jews, and form a separate congregation (*teilung*); they had to pressure the state to agree to such move. Thereby they practically accepted the new

73 *Eleh Divrei ha-Berit* (Altona, 1818). See D. Ellenson, *After Emancipation: Jewish Religious Responses to Modernity* (Cincinnati: Hebrew Union College Press, 2004), 156–59.

74 *Eleh Divrei ha-Berit*, *supra* note 73, 83.

75 See also Batnizky, *How Judaism Became a Religion*, *supra* note 16, in various places, especially 91.

76 Hatam Sofer, *Sefer Hatam Sofer* (Bratislava, 1840), section 89.

reality, in which Judaism became a religion, just another confession in the modern state.[77]

Neo-Orthodoxy, however, was already a conscious response to modernism and the reform tendencies, in Germany in particular. An acute observer already remarked that neo-orthodoxy pretended to be an authentic continuation of traditional Judaism (*Urjudentum*), but in reality, was nothing more than the Judaism of the hour (*uhrjudentum*).[78] It was described as "The Counter-Reform," just like the Catholic Counter-Reformation.[79]

Shimshon Raphael Hirsh, the founder of Neo-Orthodoxy, and the one who famously adopted the Mishnaic mantra: "*Torah* with *Derech Eretz* (*Derech Eretz* can mean both good manners and occupation)," illustrates his attitude very well. Like the Ultra-Orthodox, he rejected any changes in the *Halacha* (this is what *Torah* stands for in this equation), but unlike them, he added *Derech Eretz*, which means restricted openness to the general culture, both in education and occupation, and endeavored to find some delicate equilibrium between the two. Hirsh consciously avoided the usage of the term *dat*, this because of the strong association which already existed in his period, around the mid-nineteenth century, between the Hebrew *dat* and the Christian "religion." He insisted that Judaism is not a *dat*, but a *Torah*; the usage of the term *dat* distorts its meaning and practically Christianizes it. He criticized great Jewish philosophers – from Maimonides to Mendelssohn – of imposing alien concepts on Judaism, thereby distorting its very essence; while Maimonides imported Aristotle, Mendelsohn was influenced by Kant. Judaism should be defined only by its inner authentic criteria:[80] "Comparisons [=with Christianity] are useless. Judaism is not a religion, the synagogue is not a church, the rabbi is not a priest. Judaism is not some addition to life, it encompasses life."[81] Hirsh repeated this assertion in various places, and accused reform Jews of Christianizing Judaism by turning it into a religion.[82] However, even he was practically forced to identify Judaism as a confession, a religion based primarily on belief, just like the various Christian sects, and not as a separate ethnic component. Like emancipated Jews, also he wanted the Jews to become equal citizens in the German homeland. He refused to identify Judaism as *dat* (religion), and likewise rejected its identification as a separate ethnic group (*volk*), as German anti-Semites started to define it. Such Jews preferred to call themselves "German citizens of the

77 B. Brown, "The Two Faces of Religious Radicalism: Orthodox Zealotry and 'Holy Sinning' in Nineteenth-Century Hasidism in Hungary and Galicia," *The Journal of Religion* 93 (2013), 341–74. See also more examples and extended discussion in Melamed, *Dat, supra* note 1, 212–22.

78 M. Breuer, *Modernity within Tradition: The Social History of Orthodox Jewry in Imperial Germany*, trans. E. Petuchowski (New York: Columbia University Press, 1992), 23.

79 *Ibid.*, p. 19.

80 Shimshon Raphael Hirsh, *Igrot Zafon* (Jerusalem: Mosad Harav Kook, 1949), 75.

81 S. R. Hirsh, *Judaism Eternal: Selected Essays from the Writings of Rabbi Samson Raphael Hirsh*, trans. by I. Grunfeld, vol. 2 (London: Soncino Press, 1956), 237.

82 See more examples in Melamed, *Dat, supra* note 1, 222–26.

Jewish belief" (*deutche staatsburger Judichen glaubens*), like any other.[83] In order to make themselves indistinct they preferred to use the word *glaubens* (belief, faith), and not religion (or *dat*). This also concurred with their new concept of religion as belief, in the Protestant sense.

In the last count, even Hirsh has to accept in practice the designation of Judaism as religion, although the contents of this religion were of course quite different from the Reform view. In his view that Jews should participate in German society as equal citizens, he also practically accepted the fact that religious practice should be confined to the private sphere, and that practicing the *mizvot*, and membership in a Jewish congregation, became a voluntary matter. The emphasis moves to the private religious life of the individual in the congregation he chooses to become a member of. The emergence of the modern state necessitated this development.[84] This is the background of Hirsh's struggle to get permission from the German authorities to secede (*austritt*) from the Jewish congregation in Frankfurt, which was dominated then by reform followers. This also shows how reality forced him to identify Judaism as a confession, and the fact that Jews, just like Christians, split into different sects, recognized by the state. In his request to the government he used as arguments the precedent of the Christian schism, and the right to religious freedom. He apparently used these arguments in order to persuade the authorities, but there is no doubt that he also internalized them.[85]

Later orthodox scholars who followed in Hirsh's Neo-Orthodox path, rejected his refusal to identify Judaism as a *volk*, and adopted national-religious views (Religious Zionism), but continued to evolve the view of Judaism as a *dat* which is a religion. Rabbi Yehiel Michal Pines, one of the founders of Religious Zionism, rejected reform Judaism, but nevertheless expresses a religious sentiment that even radical reformers could identify with. Consequently, despite Hirsh's reservations, he did not hesitate to apply the loaded term "religion" to Judaism, and even used it in Hebrew transliteration. Since he wrote in Hebrew, Pines could just use the term *dat*, or its equivalencies, but he deliberately chose the use "religion," and this at the very beginning of his book:

> The *religia* (in Hebrew transliteration), has a secure place in the heart, and its roots are deeply planted in the essence of life. This is why it will never die .... This is a deep feeling among humans, which eternally whispers to them, and rings in their heart, just like a bell. There is a sublime and hidden force which cannot be seen; there is a cause for our existence and that of the universe, humans must give tanks to

83 M. A. Kaplan, *The Making of the Jewish Middle Class* (Oxford: Oxford University Press, 1991), 14. Also K. Koltun-Fromm, *Abraham Geiger's Liberal Judaism: Personal Meaning and Religious Authority* (Bloomington: Indiana University Press, 2006), 19: "Deutsche Glaubensbruder."

84 Batnizky, *How Judaism Became a Religion*, *supra* note 16, 40–43; M. Graupe, *The Creation of Modern Judaism* (Jerusalem: Shocken, 1990, in Hebrew), 195–97; E. Hammiel, *The Middle Course: The Beginnings of Modern Religiosity* (Jerusalem: Carmel, 2011, in Hebrew), 160–61.

85 Breuer, *Modernity within Tradition*, *supra* note 78, 295–96; Ellenson, *After Emancipation*, *supra* note 73, 76–77, 177–78, 242; J. Katz, *Ha-Halacha Be-Meizar* (Jerusalem: Magnes, 1991), 12–14.

> this force. . . . This feeling is common to all the children of Adam and Eve, and it is embedded in us as a natural orientation.[86]

This is a typical universalistic and Romantic, even Deistic, concept of religion that is no different from the list of such definitions we found above among early reformers. Pines distinguished among three kinds of religion (*dat*): "The positive civil *dat*" (*dat mehuievet ezrahit*), which is the application of the universal religious belief to the social distinction between good and evil, applied in different manners in different societies; "the positive *dat* of the individual" (*dat mehuievet l-adam ha-prati*), which is the individualistic bonding with the sublime. When this religious feeling goes through the prism of reason, the "*dat* of the philosophers" (*dat ha-filosofim*) evolves.

Here Pines finds the great advantage Judaism has over other religions, especially Christianity.[87] In Christianity, which is based primarily on a set of necessary beliefs, scientific discoveries undermine the foundation of religious beliefs, and cause a massive shift to secularism. Judaism, however, is essentially different, since it is not based on necessary beliefs, but on the obligation to follow the Halacha. This is the fourth kind of *dat*, "the Divine *dat*" (*dat Elohit*). Therefore, there is no danger, in his view, that Jews will abandon their religion. Here his national views come to the fore; the appearance of Zionism was for him a clear proof of the ongoing vitality of the Jewish people. Unlike Hirsh, Pines simultaneously defined the Jews as a *volk* and Judaism as a religion; these two ingredients coalesced in his view into one ever-lasting whole.

Pines' collaborator in the creation of religious Zionism, Rabbi Hayyim Hirshenzon, developed a system which tried to create a synthesis between Judaism and democracy, this under the influence of his encounter with the American political system in the long years he lived in the USA. Unlike Pines, Hirshenzon did make a clear distinction between the Jewish *dat* and the gentile "religion":

> *Dat Israel* is superior to the religions (*datei*) of other nations, which are called religion (in Hebrew transliteration). This is because they are obligated to a few practical commandments (*mizvot*) only, which are based on belief, while we received an abundance of commandments, which obligate us not by command, but through the tradition which we accepted upon ourselves, like any constitution (Hebrew transliterated), which was voluntarily accepted by a people. This is why our law (*dinenu*) is "A national *dat*" (*dat leumi*), while theirs is "A religious *dat*" (*dat religiosi*). The gentiles have a religion, while we, the Jews, have a *Torah*, and *dat*, just laws (*hukim*) and ordinances (*mishpatim*).[88]

86 Yehiel Michal Pines, *Yaldei Ruhi* (Mainz: Brill, 1872), 1–2. See I. Shalmon, "Yehiel Michal Pines: His Historical Image," in I. Shalmon, *Religion and Zionism: First Encounters* (Jerusalem: The World Zionist Organization, 1990, in Hebrew), 97–111.

87 *Yaldei Ruhi*, *supra* note 86, 3–4.

88 Hayyim Hirshenzon, *Sefer Berurei ha-Middot* (Jerusalem: The Hebrew Printing Press, 1929) vol. 1, 288–89. See E. Shweid, *Democracy and Halacha: The Thought of Rabbi Hayyim Hirshenzon* (Jerusalem: Magnes, 1978, in Hebrew).

In order to define the Christian's religion Hirshenzon created the oxymoronic combination: "religious *dat*." The difference between this *dat* and the Jewish *dat* is twofold: While the Christian religion is based on necessary beliefs, the Jewish one is based on the practical commandments. Second, while the Christian dogma is imposed upon the believers, the obedience to Jewish law is a voluntary matter. He defined the Halacha as a constitution which the people voluntarily agree to uphold, in the spirit of the American republican ethos.

While religious thinkers rejected the identification of Judaism as a "religion" from halachic reasons, secular Zionists rejected it from national reasons. Religious thinkers attempted to return to the original legal definition of Judaism, and eradicate the foreign influences, which have defined it as a "religion," thus practically Protestantized it. Secular Zionists, on the other hand, strived to belittle, even eradicate, the religious facets of Judaism, which they identified with the exilic existence, while emphasizing the national-cultural nature of Jewish existence. They also considered the modern definition of Judaism as religion to be a foreign influence, which should be abolished, but forgot to notice that the national idea itself was also a foreign import.

One of the first scholars to identify the Jews as a nation was the Historian Heinrich Zevi Graetz. Like Hirsh, his teacher, he also rejected the definition of Judaism as "religion," but this from a clear national-cultural point of view. He defined Judaism as a political entity, thus rejected its modern definition as religion. As he says:

> Even after the Talmud was closed, the national character remained embedded in the history of Israel, … It never became a sect or a religious church (*Kirchengeschichte*), since it is not based only on the *Torah*, the principles of faith and the moral values, but is a living people.[89]

Graetz's shift to Jewish nationalism was influenced by Moses Hess's famous *Rome and Jerusalem* (Leipzig, 1862), one of the first proto-Zionist treatises. Hess empathetically argued that "Judaism is a nation (*nationalitat*)."[90] He completely rejected the identification of Judaism as a religion (*religiose confession*), and argued that the reform movement endeavored to turn Judaism into a kind of rationalistic Christianity (*ein zweites Christentum*); he labeled the reform movement as "Our Jewish Protestants" (*unseren Judishen Protestanten*), who emphasize the salvation of the individual, Protestant style, at the expense of any congregational-national obligation.

Hess distinguished between two kinds of religions: "Natural Religion" (*Naturkultus*), which is the Greek religion, based on natural phenomena, and "Historical Religion" (*Geschiehtesreligion*), which is the Jewish religion, based on

89 Zvi Graetz, *Divrei Yemei Israel*, trans. sh. Rabinovitz (Warsaw: Ahisefer, 1893), vol. 3, 5.

90 Moses Hess, *Rome and Jerusalem*, trans. M. Waxman (New York: Bloch publishing company, 1918), 85–86. See in the German original, *Rom und Jerusalem* (Tel-Aviv: Hitachduth Olej Germania We Olej Austria, 1939), 50–51.

the appearance of God in nature and history. To these he added the Christian "Religion of Love" (*Religion der Liebe*), in its German variant. This is yet another manifestation of the abundance of new hyphenated terms which were coined in an effort to capture the ever-changing fluid meanings of modern Judaism.

Early Zionist thinkers, such as Judah Leib Pinsker and Theodor Herzel, both argued that Judaism is primarily a national entity, and de-emphasized its religious component. In their view, in the future Jewish state, religion should become the private matter of the individual, religious functionaries should serve the needs of the state, and have no independent power whatsoever. Ahad ha-Am strongly criticized Herzel's Political Zionism, which in his view diluted the Jewish cultural identity, but still argued that Judaism is a nation with a distinct culture, not a religion. He criticized Western-European Jews of Christianizing Judaism by turning it to nothing but a religious sect in the modern state. Religious Zionists (yet another newly coined hyphenated term), rejected secular-Zionism, and insisted on an integration between the national and religious facets of Judaism.

On the other hand, anti-Zionist Jews in Central and Western Europe, who endeavored to integrate in their respective countries as equal citizens – in the whole spectrum between Orthodox and liberal Jews – vehemently rejected the Zionist claims, and insisted that Judaism is nothing but a religion, like any other, in the modern sense of the term, of course. This debate was carried on in the twentieth century, both in Europe and the nascent Jewish entity in Palestine.[91]

VI CONTEMPORARY TRENDS: RELIGIOSITY AND SECULARIZATION

These trends are currently continuing at an accelerated rate. Modern religiosity – and Judaism is no exception – is a religious conversion of a secular cultural and political phenomenon, which in itself was a conversion of a Christian phenomenon. In its revolt against Papal coercion and corruption, Lutheranism emphasized the personal religious experience of the individual, his direct connection to his God, without the need for the mediation of any ecclesiastical authority. These concepts later went through a secular political conversion towards the principles of the centrality of individual, his rights and liberties in the modern state.[92] Now these secularized concepts are superimposed back onto the religious arena, and modern religions are going through a conversion to a religiosity based on the subjective spiritual experience of the individual in his private space, without the need for any binding authority and mediated interpretation of the Scriptures.

[91] See detailed discussion of these thinkers and others, in Melamed, *Dat*, *supra* note 1, 244–89.

[92] M. Walzer, *The Revolution of the Saints: A Study of the Origins of Radical Politics* (Cambridge, MA: Harvard University Press, 1965).

For Christianity, this was quite a natural process, since it was always based on the individual's duty to accept the right beliefs. In Judaism (and Islam) this conversion has a revolutionary impact. Traditional Judaism was always based on the duty to obey Halacha, first of all, and it has a strong ethnic and congregational component. The conversion from the emphasis on the duty to follow Halacha in an ethnic congregation, to the personal subjective religious experience in the private space, is revolutionary indeed. This process of diffusion, the privatization of religion, and the concentration on the individual believer, is nowadays moving from the level of the division of Judaism into different religious currents, which occurred since the early nineteenth century, to the division of these currents into endless voluntary congregations and individuals (the so called "sovereign self"), who adopt various shades, dosages, and combinations of beliefs, values, rituals, texts, and commandments, they choose from the enormous reservoir of the Jewish tradition, which they deem relevant and meaningful for themselves; these they constantly and creatively reinterpret to suit their liberal-pluralistic views, and the current gender attitudes.

Despite the myth that Orthodoxy is still trying to implement, Judaism was never a monolithic entity; it was always an evolving multi-lanyard culture, which went through endless theological and halachic disputes. Still, there was always a strong common denominator, created by the Sages, which lasted until the early nineteenth century approximately. This was the common obligation to follow the Halacha, at least in the public sphere. In premodern circumstances, halachic authorities had the power to enforce obedience. This power was eliminated with the advent of modernity. The majority of the Jews stopped following the Halacha, and the rabbis lost the power to enforce it. Judaism was divided into various currents, and now they are subdividing at an accelerated rate. One cannot speak of "Judaism" as one entity any more, there is an abundance of "Judaisms." Not only the word *dat* or "religion" is being hyphenated, Judaism itself is being hyphenated. We now have "Orthodox Judaism," "Haredi Judaism," "Conservative Judaism," "Reform Judaism," "Humanistic Judaism," "Secular Judaism," and so on. These processes are now accelerating in American Jewry with the appearance of the so-called "Post-Judaism," and its influence also reverberates among Israeli Jews, regardless of their religious orientation.[93]

As a consequence of these processes, the terms *dat* and "religion" became so amorphic, that today, any particular view, on any subject – religious or secular – which a person adopts is labeled "religion" (or *dat*). This labeling includes also completely secular phenomena, even belatedly anti-religious views.[94] Thus, we use today hyphenated terms such as "Humanistic Religion" (*dat humanistit*), or "Civil

[93] See detailed discussions in A. Eisen and S. Cohen, *The Jew Within: Self, Family, and Community in America* (Bloomington: Indiana University Press, 2000); Sh.Magid, *American Post-Judaism: Identity and Renewal in a Postethnic Society* (Bloomington: Indiana University Press, 2013).

[94] In a letter to the editors of the Israeli daily newspaper *Ha'aretz*, a reader recently stated that in his view: "Secularism (*hilloniut*) is a religion (*dat*)" ("Letters to the Editor," *Ha'aretz*, June 15, 2017, 13).

Religion" (*dat ezrahit*), which relate to the common rituals and norms of a given political culture.[95]

Radical ideologies are especially prone of semi-religious connotations, due to their totalitarian characteristics, their hero worship and tendency for indoctrination. Communism, a blatantly anti-religious ideology, used to be called a "religion," and now various extreme environmental and vegan ideologies are being labeled by the very same terms, such as: "The Dark Green Religion."[96] Psychoanalysis was called "a new religion" already in Freud's life.[97]

This usage proliferates now at an accelerated rate, as we can easily find in contemporary newspapers, which are a great source for detecting new meanings and usages of the terms and words we use. The belief that modern science replaced traditional religions as the source of all knowledge, is labeled as "the religion of science" (*dat ha-madah*), the religion of liberal secularism.[98] The enormous influence of the internet on our lives today is called: "the religion of information." In an article published a few years ago in the Israeli daily newspaper *Ha-Aretz* we find the following assessment: "We envision today the ascension (*aliyah*) of a new religion (*dat*), the religion of information (*dat ha-meidah*). The religion promises to improve our lives . . ., this under the condition that we will sanctify (*nekadesh*) the supreme value of the flow of information."[99] It is no incident that besides the repeated usage of the term *dat*, we find in these excerpts a collection of traditional religious components, now converted to a secular context: "Ascension" (*aliyah*), "improvement" (*shipur*), "sanctification" (*kidush*), "supreme value" (*erech elyon*), "the spirit of God" (*ruah Elohim*), "commandments" (*mitzvot*), and "holy war" (*milhemet kodesh*). Also, the manner by which we cope with the memory of the Holocaust, obsessive in the view of some, and the pilgrimage to Auschwitz, were recently labeled as: "the religion of the Holocaust": "This is a religion (*dat*), the religion of Holocaust (*dat ha-Shoah*), this is a symbolic and metaphysic act, in which the nation

95 Ch. S. Liebman and E. Don Yehiya, *Civil Religion in Israel: Traditional Judaism and Political Culture in the Jewish State* (Berkeley: University of California Press, 1983). The usage of *dat* or religion in this context is widespread. See for instance the Hebrew economic newspaper *Globs*, January 5, 2012: "The television program 'The Big Brother', has a status of a civil religion (*dat ezrahit*)." See also the remark of the American actress Robin Wright concerning award ceremonies. *New York Times*, February 5, 2014: "I don't get the award theory, rather I don't understand the religion of it . . . It's not my religion." Also, *New York Times*, June 2, 2017, concerning the new trend of tiny homes: "A tiny home is a state of mind, if not a religion."

96 B. Taylor, *Dark Green Religion* (Berkeley: University of California Press, 2010).

97 P. Ferris, *Dr. Freud*, trans. D. Levi (Tel Aviv: Books in the Attic, 2010), 360.

98 *Ha-Aretz Sefarim*, October 14, 2013, 10. See also in an article by Y. Caspi, *Ha-Aretz*, February 4, 2014: "Standing by itself, critical thinking erects a religion (*dat*) of its own."

99 Y. Harari, *Ha-Aretz*, February 23, 2013. See also in an article by B. Tsifer, *Ha-Aretz*, December 17, 2013: "We find recently more and more people that Facebook brought meaning to their life . . ., they found out that they have at last a function in a new militant religion (*dat hadashah*), which is being formed. The nature of this religion (*dat*) is not clear yet, but the spirit of God already hovers upon it; it is a militant spirit, and there are already commandments, or more precisely, one commandment: a holy war; let's call it a *Jihad*."

is united with the object of its belief (*emunatah*)."[100] The centrality of the army in Israeli life was recently labeled as: "the religion of the I.D.F." (*dat zahal*).[101] Likewise, the centrality of children in Israeli culture was recently labeled as: "the religion of the children" (*dat ha-yeladim*): "The child is holy, he is sublime, he is a little Buddha, he bestows you with a sense of meaning and purpose, you don't raise him, you worship him as if he was God. Secular people are looking for something to believe in. .... We are all devotees of the religion of the children."[102] Also here we find a collection of converted religious terms, even Buddhism, used to describe a secular sociological phenomenon.

Dat, a Hebrew term borrowed from the Persian, which originally denoted human law, was transformed to mean religion, creed, or fate. Now it has been re-secularized again, and acquired an elastic and amorphic meaning, which is being used to denote any social or intellectual trend in which people deeply believe in, with no necessary connection to religious beliefs anymore. This is alongside the traditional religious usages, which also acquire new meanings with the advent of modern religiosity. Thus, when we use this term now, it is essential to clarify which possible meaning of it is implied precisely; it does not stand by itself anymore. This is why we find so many hyphenated terms, in which an additional word is added to *dat* or "religion," in order to clarify the intended meaning, and various conjugations of this word, from *datiut* (religiosity) to *hadata* (to influence somebody to become religious). This is an ongoing process. What we call *dat* is going through a radical process of change in contemporary culture: secularization, on the one hand, and religiosity on the other. In any case, its original meaning as law has been eliminated altogether.

100 A. Misgav, "Auschwitz: We Came back to You Again," *Ha-Aretz*, January 25, 2014.

101 R. Alfer, "The Religion of the I.D.F.," *Ha-Aretz*, March 12, 2017.

102 N. Shore: "The Child is the New God," *Ha-Aretz*, July 8, 2016. See also: "The Man Who Turned the Stock Marker into the Religion (*dat*) of the Federal Bank," *The Marker Magazine*, May 15, 2017, 126; *The Marker*, July 11, 2017: "The Tycoons are the result of the religion of privatization (*dat ha-hafratah*)."

5

Law As Religion, Religion As Law

Halakhah *from a Semiotic Point of View*

Bernard S. Jackson

I INTRODUCTION

The title of this project, "Law As Religion, Religion As Law," no doubt deliberately begs several vitally important conceptual and methodological questions. Are the terms "law" and "religion" to be understood as conceptual absolutes, universally applicable to any culture, or are they to be regarded as themselves cultural constructs? My starting point will assume the latter. But then we are faced with further questions: From whose viewpoint may we debate whether, in any particular culture, "law" is to be regarded as a form, or an essential part, of "religion," and from whose viewpoint may we debate whether "religion" is to be regarded as a form, or an essential part, of "law"? And what is the relevant data? In the Jewish context, we may seek to explore what particular conceptions of "law" and "religion," and what type of interrelationships between them, we find in the whole range of traditional data of the *halakhah*.

But the issue turns out to be more complicated. The cultural world which we inhabit is not exclusively Jewish, nor should it be. *Ḥareidim* may give a different answer, and may even interpret differently the famous dictum of Ben Zoma in Pirke Avot 4:1: "Who is wise? He learns from all men" – stressing the proof-text which follows: "As it is written (Psalm 119:99) I have gained an understanding from all my teachers." But can we be sure that, even within Jewish discourse, the very concepts of law and religion are exclusively Jewish? I would argue not. It may, therefore, be necessary to distinguish between internal and external viewpoints on the matter, not only as an historical exercise, but also in order to clarify some of the conceptual issues involved. Yet even this, I would argue, will suffice only if we are not able to identify some neutral viewpoint from which to address the issues.

In this paper I argue for the use of a particular version of semiotics as providing such a neutral viewpoint. In Sections II–IV, I outline much of the work I have done over the years addressing these issues from more traditional internal and external (particularly jurisprudential) viewpoints, and the present chapter draws heavily on those earlier publications. Thereafter, I sketch both the general theoretical claims of the version of semiotics which I have used, and its applications to secular law, with a view to its use both in the context of *halakhah*, and more generally in discussing the relationship between law and religion.

This is an issue with which I have had to grapple for much of my career. My undergraduate degree was in secular (English) law; my doctorate was on early Jewish law, supervised by David Daube. Between 1968 and 1997, I taught in law faculties but with increasing opportunities to teach Jewish law, especially biblical law, for comparative purposes. From the early 1980s I began to explore interdisciplinary approaches to legal study, and quite quickly adopted the semiotic approach which I describe in this chapter. At that stage, I made little attempt to apply this to Jewish law, though I continued to research in Jewish law. I published four books on legal semiotics, the last being *Making Sense in Jurisprudence* of 1996.[1] At that stage, I felt that I had exhausted what I had to say in relation to secular law, and in 1997 I took up a chair in Jewish studies at the University of Manchester. I explained this to myself on the grounds that Jewish law was more central to teaching and research in Jewish studies (even in a theology department primarily oriented towards Christianity) than it was to any law faculty outside Israel. Increasingly, I applied semiotic approaches to biblical law.[2] I later became interested in the *agunah* problem (the "chained wife," whose divorce is blocked by her husband), and in 2004 established a research unit in Manchester in which I collaborated with four colleagues (including two PhD students). We worked together until 2009, and I have since published six books and over twenty working papers.[3] These publications adopted in part an analytical approach sufficiently "external" to disinterest the halakhic authorities, but they remained immune from semiotic analysis. Increasingly, however, I began to realise the relevance of semiotic analysis to some of the fundamentals of that research, and to Jewish law research more generally, and this is reflected in the present chapter.

II LAW

Despite the title of Hart's classical work, *The Concept of Law* (including the definite article), there is no such universal concept (unless, perhaps, we are Platonists), nor, indeed, is it clear that we need one. In fact, even Hart's book deals very little with

[1] Particularly: *Semiotics and Legal Theory* (London, Routledge & Kegan Paul, 1985; paperback ed. 1987, reprinted Liverpool: Deborah Charles Publications, 1997); *Law, Fact and Narrative Coherence* (Merseyside: Deborah Charles Publications, 1988); *Making Sense in Law* (Liverpool: Deborah Charles Publications, 1995); *Making Sense in Jurisprudence* (Liverpool: Deborah Charles Publications, 1996); later: *Studies in the Semiotics of Biblical Law* (Sheffield: Sheffield Academic Press, 2000; JSOT Supplement Series, 314), all here cited below by title and page. For a recent overview of my semiotic work, see: "A Journey into Legal Semiotics," *Actes Sémiotiques* 120 (2017), 1–43 (hereafter: Jackson, *Journey*), available at http://epublications.unilim.fr/revues/as/5669. Also frequently cited below is "Constructing a Theory of Halakhah" (2012), only available at http://jewishlawassociation.org/resources.htm (hereafter: Jackson, *Constructing*).

[2] Jackson, *Studies in the Semiotics of Biblical Law, supra* n.1.

[3] All available without charge at www.manchesterjewishstudies.org/publications/.

such a concept; rather, its concern is with legal rules and the legal system. Much the same could be said in the Jewish context. Amongst the plethora of terms used in the Bible and later, it is hard to identify one which uniquely denotes the concept of law. And when we speak of "the *halakhah*," we too have in mind a particular system of rules rather than an abstract concept.

In the secular context, the positivist paradigm[4] dominates our understanding of the legal system – arguably, for the citizen as much as the academic. This paradigm is often described as a "sources" theory: law is defined (or recognized) in terms of its sources, and these sources are human and political. While Austin and Bentham in the nineteenth century understood this primarily in terms of power (sovereignty and the imposition of sanctions), both Hart and Kelsen introduced the necessity of legitimacy, understood as sources of law defined by the legal system itself.[5] This movement on the part of Hart and Kelsen had a twofold purpose: on the one hand, to distinguish the rule of law from any illegitimate power source (a tyrant or gangster); on the other, to guard against abuse of power by legitimate political authorities and to ensure that citizens always had the capacity to choose their course of action in the light of its known legal consequences. This generated (for Hart, in particular) the "demonstrability" thesis: the ("secondary") rules of the system should be such as would enable "demonstrable" judgments to be made regarding the legitimacy (and, wherever possible, also the meaning) of any "primary" rule of the system.[6]

Such emphasis on the value of certainty is reflected in various ways in the methodology of reading legal texts in modern, positivist legal systems. Law is expressed in language and that language ought to be accessible to the citizen, albeit often advised by a professional. The starting point for interpretation is thus literalism: the law "covers" every situation within the syntax and semantics of the particular legal rule. Moreover, if the statute lays down conditions for any particular legal consequence, those conditions are regarded as not only sufficient but also necessary for that consequence. To put it differently, "If . . . " means "If and only if . . . ."[7]

The political ideology underlying the positivist paradigm entailed a negative view regarding the relationship between law and morality.[8] On the one hand, morality (whether from religious or other sources) did not count as an independent source of law; on the other, it did not count either as a criterion of the validity of law: an unjust law could not, on those grounds alone, be regarded as invalid, unless such criteria of

4 See Jackson, *Constructing*, *supra* n.1, s.2.1.

5 See further, including the approaches of Austin, Bentham, and Kelsen to "religious law": B. S. Jackson, "*Mishpat Ivri, Halakhah* and Legal Philosophy: *Agunah* and the Theory of 'Legal Sources', *JSIJ: Jewish Studies, an Internet Journal* 1 (2002), 69–107, available at www.biu.ac.il/JS/JSIJ/jsij1.html, ss.3.1–3.2.

6 See further, Jackson, *Constructing*, *supra* n.1, s.2.4; Bernard S. Jackson, "Literal Meaning: Semantics and Narrative in Biblical Law and Modern Jurisprudence," *International Journal for the Semiotics of Law / Revue Internationale de Sémiotique Juridique* [hereafter *IJSL/RISJ*] 13/4 (2000), 433–57, s.3.

7 See further, Jackson, *Constructing*, *supra* n.1, s.2.4; Jackson "Literal Meaning," *supra* n.6, at s.1.

8 See further, *Constructing*, *supra* n.1, ss.2.2, 3.4.

validity were explicitly adopted by the system of positive law itself. But this prompted attention to a more fundamental question: Does the law consist only of the rules themselves, or also the reasons for the rules? Kelsen took a very strong line on this: the law consisted only of the norms of the system, not the arguments for or against those norms.[9] Attention thus turned to the status and role of legal argument, and in particular "legal principles." Dworkin, in particular, argued that law consisted in both rules and principles; that the latter could be implicit in the system as a whole; and that they reflected the political morality implicit in that system.[10]

Important aspects of the positivist paradigm have been adopted by some Jewish law scholars, particularly those in the *mishpat ivri* movement, often for the pragmatic motive of advancing the adoption of Jewish law in the State of Israel.[11] Menachem Elon, in particular, adopted a version of the "sources" theory, and Lamm and Kirschenbaum followed the lead of Dworkin in stressing the role of principles in the *halakhah*.[12] Neither, of course, accepted the basic assumption of legal positivism that sources had to emanate from human, political institutions. We may note, however, that both Austin and Kelsen made some concessions to the idea of a system of religious law.[13]

There are, however, major conceptual problems involved in such a strategy of conceptualizing Jewish law. Radical change (from rules regarded as having "biblical" status) is virtually excluded in Jewish law: there can be no revolution against divine law; indeed in recent centuries (partly in reaction against progressive forms of Judaism), Orthodoxy has proved increasingly reluctant to make *any* changes in *halakhah*, as may be seen from a particular problem in the Jewish law of divorce.[14] Elon himself had to accept a significant qualification: in a religious system based on revelation, the Constitution is unamendable.[15] Moreover, there is an acute ideological problem at the very foundation of the application of Jewish religious law within the State of Israel. The State, whose own legal system is secular, in that ultimate authority belongs to a democratically elected legislature

9 See further Jackson, *Making Sense in Jurisprudence*, *supra* n.1, ch.4, esp. at 114–24.

10 R. Dworkin, *Taking Rights Seriously* (London: Duckworth, 1977), esp. chs. 2–4.

11 See further, Jackson, "*Mishpat Ivri*, . . . " *supra* n.5, at s.2; Jackson, *Journey*, *supra* n.1, 22f.

12 N. Lamm and A. Kirschenbaum, "Freedom and Constraint in the Jewish Juridical Process," *Cardozo Law Review* 1 (1979), 99–133. See also E. Dorff, "Judaism as a Religious Legal System," *Hastings Law Journal* 29 (1978), 1331–60, at 1339.

13 For Austin, it fell within his (semantic) understanding of the word "law" ("law properly so-called"), even though it was not within the phenomenon of positive law ("law strictly so-called"), the latter being the proper concern of jurisprudence. Kelsen was able to conceive of a "religious norm system" with a parallel (hierarchical) structure to that of a system of positive law. In fact, he defines the *Grundnorm* of such a system: "The basic norm of a religious norm system says that one ought to behave as God and the authorities instituted by Him command." For sources, see Jackson, "*Mishpat Ivri*, . . ., " *supra* n.5.

14 On the *agunah* problem, see text accompanying n.137.

15 For Elon, the constitution is the *Torah*, and the binding norm of the system is that "everything set forth in the Torah, *i.e.*, the written law, is binding on the Jewish legal system"; as for the source of its authority: "we leave jurisprudence and pass into the sphere of faith": Menachem Elon, *Jewish Law, History, Sources, Principles* (Philadelphia: Jewish Publication Society, 1994), I.232–233.

(the Knesset), may delegate certain powers to religious courts (Jewish, Muslim, and Christian), but that itself delegitimizes those courts in the eyes of some religious circles, who claim that the ultimate authority is divine, and therefore should operate solely through religious institutions rather than through the State. It is the religion, they would claim, which should define the powers of the State, rather than vice versa. This is a fundamental issue for "law and religion" issues everywhere, and may be regarded as defining the distinction between theocracy and democracy.

But this is not the only conceptual problem. The history of Jewish law shows that charismatic rather than rational sources have played an important role from biblical times. It is striking that a series of instructions to judges[16] fail to mention written sources of law: rather, they tell the judges to avoid partiality and corruption and apply their intuitive sense of justice (in the context, no doubt, of orally transmitted custom). Their authority was charismatic. Thus, the ninth century BCE King Jehoshaphat of Judah charges his judges to avoid partiality and corruption and assures them that "(God) is *with you* in giving judgement" (2 *Chronicles* 19:6), rather than their referring to written sources.[17] This survived in a residual power (explicit in talmudic sources but increasingly submerged since then) for the judge to depart from the strict law when intuitions of justice demanded it. Ben-Menahem has studied some thirty cases recorded in the Babylonian Talmud where it is said that the rabbinic judge decided the case "not in accordance with the *Halakhah*."[18] Indeed, the *halakhah* is regarded as a minimum standard, and the judges are expected to go beyond it, wherever possible, in pursuit of justice. Thus, the Talmud quotes R. Yoxanan as saying (*Baba Mezia* 30b): "'Jerusalem was destroyed only because they gave judgements therein accordance with Torah law . . .' Where they then to have judged in accordance with untrained arbitrators? – But say thus: because they based their judgements [strictly] upon Torah law, and did not go beyond the requirements of the law."

16 B. S. Jackson, *Wisdom-Laws: A Study of the Mishpatim of Exodus 21:1–22:16* (Oxford: Oxford University Press, 2006), 412–18. Perhaps the most famous is that of Deuteronomy 16:18, where the judges are commanded to pursue a "righteous judgment" (*tsedek tsedek tirdof*). On Deut. 16 and the (different) use of written law in Deut. 17, see Bernard S. Jackson, "Judaism as a Religious Legal System," in *Religion and Tradition. Comparative Studies in Religious Law*, ed. A. Huxley (London: Routledge Curzon, 2002), 34–48, at 37–38.

17 Jackson, *Wisdom-Laws, supra* n.16, at 412–14; further in Bernard S. Jackson, "Law in the 9th Century?: Jehoshaphat's Judicial Reform," in *Understanding the History of Ancient Israel*, ed. H. G. W. Williamson, *Proceedings of the British Academy* 143 (2007), 357–85. See further text accompanying n.40, below.

18 Hanina Ben-Menahem, *Judicial Deviation in Talmudic Law* (Chur etc.: Harwood Academic Publishers, 1991); see also, more broadly, his "The Judicial Process and the Nature of Jewish Law," in *An Introduction to the History and Sources of Jewish Law*, ed. N. Hecht, B. S. Jackson, D. Piattelli, S. M. Passamaneck and A. M. Rabello (Oxford: The Clarendon Press, 1996), 421–37, concluding, at 434f., that "we are justified in doubting the sufficiency of the modern, Western concept of law for the purposes of describing the *halakhah*."

III RELIGION

Much the same critique may be addressed to the concept of religion as to that of law. There is no single, universal concept and every reason to doubt whether we really need one.[19] Just as it may suffice to judge whether particular rules and courses of action are "legal," so too it may suffice to judge whether particular rules and courses of action are "religious." The sense of both the "legal" and the "religious" may be constructed without presupposing any metaphysical concepts of "law" or "religion."[20] And in both cases, the meanings of "legal" and "religious" are culturally contingent.

Equally variable is the role which any system of religious thought may attribute to law. In the Judeo-Christian tradition, this is discussed in the context of the divine-human relationship (covenant), including, but not restricted to, reward, punishment, and salvation both in this world and in the eschatological context.[21] Such matters are, indeed, much discussed in the context of Jewish theology, far less in the study of Jewish law (here too implicitly reflecting the positivist paradigm).

There has been much debate in academic departments of religion and theology as to the conceptualization and methodology of religion. "Religious Studies" are nowadays often presented as the study of "World Religions."[22] But does such a comparative approach imply a single, external criterion of religion, or admit the primacy of internal conceptions within any particular system?[23] The latter may appear the more authentic, but a neutral standpoint is required for comparison. Recourse is often made to social science approaches, or more philosophical approaches informed by phenomenology,[24] where much attention is paid to the

19 See the discussion in the Wikipedia article on "Religious Studies," including the observation that: "Conversely, other scholars of religious studies have argued that the discipline should reject the term 'religion' altogether and cease trying to define it" (citing Bradley L. Herling, *A Beginner's Guide to the Study of Religion* (London: Bloomsbury, 2016, 2nd sup. ed.), 36. In this perspective, "religion" is argued to be a Western concept that has been forced upon other cultures in an act of intellectual imperialism (citing John R. Hinnells, "Introduction," in *The Routledge Companion to the Study of Religion*, ed. John R. Hinnells (Abingdon: Routledge, 2005), 1–3. According to scholar of religion Russell T. McCutcheon, "many of the peoples that we study by means of this category have no equivalent term or concept whatsoever [citing his *Critics Not Caretakers: Redescribing the Public Study of Religion* (Albany: State University of New York Press, 2001), 10]. There is, for instance, no word for 'religion' in languages like Sanskrit."

20 See text following n.163, below.

21 See further, Jackson, *Constructing*, *supra* n.1. at ss.3.6.2–5.

22 See, e.g., Philip L. Tite, "Teaching Beyond the World Religions Paradigm?," *Religion Bulletin*, available at http://bulletin.equinoxpub.com/2015/08/teaching-beyond-the-world-religions-paradigm/.

23 See further B. S. Jackson, "Internal and External Comparisons of Religious Law: Reflections from Jewish Law," in *A Fresh Start for Comparative Legal Studies? A Collective Review of Patrick Glenn's Legal Traditions of the World, 2nd Edition*, N. H. D. Foster, ed. (London: Wildy, Simmons and Hill, 2005); *Journal of Comparative Law* 1/1 (2006), 177–99, on the comparative ("traditions" based) approach of Patrick Glenn.

24 On the Phenomenology of Religion, see the transcript of www.academia.edu/15646019/Podcast_with_James_L._Cox_on_The_Phenomenology_of_Religion_Religious_Studies_Project_14_January_2012. See also the Wikipedia article on "Religious Studies."

experiential dimension.[25] But can religious experience be isolated from the broader religious culture concerned?[26] In fact, some aspects of the phenomenological critique of the study of religions share points in common with the semiotic approach I elaborate below, while other aspects radically diverge.

The most explicit Jewish application of the phenomenological approach known to me is that of Rabbi Joseph Soloveitchik in his *Halakhic Man*, where his concern was to explore the *experience* of *Halakhah*, and this not from the ("public") vantage point of the judge but rather from the ("private") vantage point of the ordinary Orthodox Jew who is observant of the *Halakhah*.[27] Soloveitchik sought "to penetrate deep into the structure of halakhic man's consciousness" (p. 4). Halakhic man seeks to fashion mundane reality in accordance with the halakhic model, and this creative activity has an emotional (or spiritual) as well as a cognitive dimension: "Both the halakhist and the mathematician live in an ideal realm and enjoy the radiance of their own creations" (p. 25). Indeed, the mundane world of halakhic man is, from this vantage-point, even more desirable than is the world-to-come:

> The Halakhah is not at all concerned with a transcendent world. The world to come is a tranquil, quiet world that is wholly good, wholly everlasting, and wholly eternal, wherein a man will receive the reward for the commandments which he performed in this world. However, the receiving of a reward is not a religious act; therefore, halakhic man prefers the real world to a transcendent existence because here, in this world, man is given the opportunity to create, act, accomplish, while there, in the world to come, he is powerless to change anything at all. . . . When the righteous sit in the world to come, where there is neither eating nor drinking, with their crowns on their heads, and enjoy the radiance of the divine presence . . ., they [can only] occupy themselves with the study of the Torah, which treats of bodily life in our lowly world.[28]

Thus, the reward for observance of the *halakhah* is conceived by Soloveitchik as the capacity (merely) to *contemplate* the application (in the empirical world) of *halakhah* from the (nonempirical) domain of the world-to-come. The reward is thus less

[25] Thus, Tite, *supra* n.22, cites Warren Matthews, *World Religions* (Cengage Learning, 2010, 6th ed.): "Rather than authenticating this 'religion' via geo-political conflicts currently affecting public perceptions of Islam, Matthews exemplifies the very theoretical approach of the phenomenologist of religion, where sympathy with those being studied stands alongside giving interpretative force to the insider's private experiential truth claims (which also evoke the notion that religion is essentially a private, irreductive experience that the outsider can only approximate in his or her understanding of the insider's truth claims)."

[26] See further Ian G. Barbour, *Myths, Models and Paradigms: A Comparative Study in Science and Religion* (New York, Hagerstown, San Francisco, London: Harper & Row, 1976), ch.7.

[27] In Jackson, "Internal and External Comparisons of Religious Law: Reflections from Jewish Law," *supra* n.23, at 182–83, I question the extent to which the public and private spheres can be separated in studying the halakhah.

[28] J. B. Soloveitchik, *Halakhic Man*, transl. Lawrence Kaplan (Philadelphia: The Jewish Publication Society of America, 1983), 32, 38f.

satisfying than the act by which the reward is merited, for it is the latter which *transforms*, which is *creative*.

> The ideal of halakhic man is the redemption of the world not via a higher world but via the world itself, via the adaptation of empirical reality to the ideal patterns of Halakhah. If a Jew lives in accordance with the Halakhah … then he shall find redemption. A lowly world is elevated through the Halakhah to the level of a divine world.[29]

IV JEWISH LAW

In various respects, the practice of justice in Jewish law differs from that typical of secular law, in that (1) Jewish law functions through a system in which rationality is a function of revelation;[30] (2) its system of rule-making institutions exhibits a far less clear hierarchy, as indeed do its courts;[31] (3) adjudication functions in the private, rather than the public, domain, its operation not being, in principle, subject to public accountability;[32] (4) it frequently lacks enforcement powers in order to give effect to its decisions.[33]

In approaching these issues, it is important to address an underlying theoretical issue: In what sense is Jewish law to be regarded as a "religious system of law"?[34] For this purpose, I suggest, one may distinguish between "dualistic" and "monistic" models of Jewish law.[35] Is it conceived as a separate system from the direct operation of divine justice, operating under delegated authority from God in some semi-autonomous manner, and sharing significant elements in common with secular models of human justice (the "dualistic" model), or is it to be regarded as an integral part of a single system of divine justice (the "monistic" model)? I have argued that there is much biblical support for the monistic model, although rabbinic sources (increasingly) tend to follow the "dualistic" model, as does most modern scholarship on Jewish law. The *mishpat ivri* movement, which seeks the incorporation of Jewish law within the law of the State of Israel, strongly advocates it for ideological reasons. The two models, however, may not be mutually exclusive.

The Torah contains many rules, but it is far from clear that they were intended for judicial application in the manner of a modern statute in secular courts. Indeed, most of the pentateuchal sources which describe the judicial role make no reference

29 *Ibid.*, at 37f.

30 I have argued for a semiotically informed "Jurisprudence of Revelation" in Jackson, *Constructing*, *supra* n.1 at n.137.

31 See text accompanying n.42, below.

32 See further B. S. Jackson, "The Practice of Justice in Jewish Law," *Daimon* 4 (2004), 31–48, at 45f.

33 See further *ibid.*, at 41–45.

34 For a more thorough discussion of this issue, see Hanina Ben-Menahem, "Is Talmudic Law a Religious Legal System? A Provisional Analysis," *Journal of Law and Religion* 24 (2008–09), 379–401.

35 See further Jackson, "The Practice of Justice in Jewish Law," *supra* n.32, at 31f.; Jackson, *Constructing*, *supra* n.1, at s.3.0; and in greater detail Jackson, "Human Law and Divine Justice: Towards the Institutionalisation of *Halakhah*," *JSIJ* 9 (2010), 1–25, §§1.0, 1.3–4, 7.1, at pp.,1, 2–4, 23, available at www.biu.ac.il/JS/JSIJ/9-2010/Jackson.pdf or www.biu.ac.il/js/JSIJ/fa.htm.

to the application of written sources, but rather commit the resolution of disputes to the sense of justice of the judges, sometimes with a direct hint that their intuitive sense of justice will be divinely guided.[36] It is noticeable that two sources relating to the reign of the ninth-century Judaean King Jehoshaphat have him, on the one hand, appointing local judges to whom he says: "Consider what you do, for you judge not for men, but for the Lord; and he is with you in giving judgment" (*ve'imakhem bidvar mishpat*):[37] no mention here of recourse to any written law, nor is it clear that the Superior Court in Jerusalem (whether of Jehoshaphat or as conceived in other sources)[38] has such recourse either; on the other hand, the same king sends out a commission including princes, Levites, and priests to *teach* the people from the "book of the law of the Lord" (*sefer torat adonai*, 2 Chron. 17:7–9). The implication would appear to be that the first step in any dispute would be for the parties to try to resolve it themselves,[39] guided by torah laws, failing which they should have recourse to local judges applying a divinely guided sense of justice, and only thereafter should they refer to the central court in Jerusalem. In a study of the *mishpatim* of Exodus 21:1–22:16 which I published in 2006, I argued that there was considerable evidence from the substance of the rules that they were designed for "self-execution" rather than third-party adjudication.[40] I called them "wisdom-laws."

The situation becomes even more complicated in rabbinic law. On the one hand, the talmudic cases of adjudication "not in accordance with the halakhah"[41] may represent a survival of the divinely guided intuition of which we read in the bible. More generally, the "secondary rules" (Hart) allowing one to identify binding halakhah have many areas of doubt and controversy, as we found in the work of the Agunah Research Unit. Even such a basic rule as that of majority decision generated controversy as to whether it applies only to opinions expressed within the contemporary generation, or trans-generationally.[42] Indeed, the doctrines of *safeq* and *sfeq sfeiqa* ("doubt" and "double doubt") both attest to the significance of doubt within the halakhic system, and provide considerable discretion in dealing with such cases.[43]

36 This, indeed, is the original significance of *semikhah*.

37 2 Chron. 19:6, and see n.17 and the text accompanying it.

38 Jackson, *Wisdom-Laws*, *supra* n.16, at 418–25.

39 Prov. 25:7–9: "What your eyes have seen do not hastily bring into court (*lariv*). For what will you do in the end when your neighbour puts you to shame? Argue your case with your neighbour himself and do not disclose another's secret," discussed in *Wisdom-Laws*, *supra* n.16, at 30.

40 Jackson, *Wisdom-Laws*, *supra* n.16, at 29–35, 389–95 *et pass.*; Bernard S. Jackson, "Human Law and Divine Justice in the Methodological Maze of the *Mishpatim*," in *The Boston 2004 Conference Volume*, ed. E. Dorff, *Jewish Law Association Studies* XVI (2007), 101–22, at 109–10.

41 See *supra* n.18.

42 See Rabbi Dr. Yehudah Abel, "Halakhah – Majority, Seniority, Finality and Consensus," Section I (Working Papers of the Agunah Research Unit, June 2008, no.7, available at www.manchester jewishstudies.org/publications/); B. S. Jackson, *Agunah: The Manchester Analysis* (Liverpool: Deborah Charles Publications, 2011), pp. 49–50 (§2.8).

43 See further text accompanying n.139, below; Jackson, *Agunah*, *ibid.*, at 55–59; *Constructing*, *supra* n.1, at ss.3.1.2, 3.3, 3.5; Bernard S. Jackson, "Philosophy of Law: Secular and Religious (with some reference to Jewish family law)," in *Law In Society: Reflections on Children, Family, Culture and*

The orthodox understanding of revelation goes beyond the conferment of divine authority on that which is revealed. The medium itself is understood to have divine features. Thus, the bible is written in Hebrew, the *lashon hakodesh*,[44] the language of creation, which has special properties of multiple signification. Moreover, the torah is normally regarded as a single discursive whole, complete, consistent, and without redundancy – any apparent deviations from these standards being resolved in the oral law.[45] I have argued that the forms of analogy in Jewish law are distinctively religious rather and secular, insofar as they depend very often upon literary rather than substantive features of the biblical text.[46]

Does all this lead to the conclusion that we are able to reach (objective) truth via halakhic argumentation? Some halakhic authorities argue that we can.[47] I fear that they are unduly influenced by the modern secular model. There is much in the tradition which points in a different direction:[48] thus, famously, the Talmud records that a divine voice intervenes in a long-standing dispute between the Schools of Hillel and Shammai with the words: "These and these [contradictory opinions] are [both] the words of the living God" (*Erubin* 13b), but with an instruction to follow Beth Hillel on pragmatic grounds: pragmatic, both in the sense that we need such a decision for communal consistency, and in the sense that the grounds for preferring Beth Hillel are pragmatic in the linguistic sense: their speech behavior was respectful to the opinions of their opponents, and they took the views of the latter into account.[49] Indeed, the very concept of truth (and its

Philosophy. Essays in Honour of Michael Freeman, ed. Alison Diduck, Noam Peleg and Helen Reece (Leiden: Brill, 2015), 45–62, at 50–52.

44 On the rabbinic view of religious language, see Jackson, *Constructing*, *supra* n.1, at s.3.2; Jackson, "*Mishpat Ivri*, . . ., " *supra* n.5, at s.5.2; Jackson, *Journey*, *supra* n.1, at 26–27; and the recent Review by *Ben Rothke of Rabbi Reuven Chaim Klein, Lashon HaKodesh: History, Holiness & Hebrew* (Beth Shemesh: Mosaica Press, 2014) at http://blogs.timesofisrael.com/book-review-lashon-hakodesh-history-holiness-and-hebrew/.

45 See further Jackson, *Constructing*, *supra* n.1, s.3.2; Jackson, "*Mishpat Ivri*, . . ., " *supra* n.5, s.5.2.

46 See further Jackson, "A Semiotic Perspective on the Comparison of Analogical Reasoning in Secular and Religious Legal Systems," in *Pluralism in Law*, ed. A. Soeteman (Dordrecht: Kluwer Academic Publishers, 2001), 295–325.

47 Rabbi J. David Bleich, "Halakhah as an Absolute," *Judaism* (Winter 1980), 30–38, and see S. Resnicoff, "J. David Bleich: an Intellectual Portrait," in *J. David Bleich. Where Halakhah and Philosophy Meet*, ed. H. Tirosh-Samuelson and A. W. Hughes (Leiden and Boston: Brill, 2015), 1–22, esp. 2, 8, 13–14 (citing at 14 Bleich's comparison of halakhah and science in that "there is no room for subjectivity," in his *Contemporary Halakhic Problems IV* (Newark NJ; Ktav Publishing and Yeshiva University Press, 2011), xiii and at 30 of *Where Halakhah and Philosophy Meet*. See by contrast Rabbi Louis Jacobs, "Objectivity and Subjectivity in Jewish Legal Decisions: The Debate on AID," *Jewish law fellowship lecture* 3 (Yarnton: Oxford Centre for Postgraduate Studies, 1991), available at https://ochjs.eyedivision.com/wp-content/uploads/2011/09/3rd-Jewish-Law-Fellowship-Lecture-Objectivity-and-Subjectivity-in-Jewish-Decisions-The-Debate-on-Aid.pdf.

48 See H. Ben-Menahem, et al. eds., *Hamaxloket beHalakhah* (Jerusalem: Institute for Research in Jewish Law, 1991–2002, 3 vols.); H. Ben-Menahem et al. eds., *Controversy and Dialogue in the Jewish Tradition: a Reader* (London: Routledge, 2005).

49 See also text accompanying n.147 below, and further in Jackson, "Some Preliminary Observations on Truth and Argumentation in the Jewish Legal Tradition" (Heb.), *Moreshet Israel* 3 (2006), 22–33;

possible application to law)[50] is hotly debated in philosophy, and there is no reason to assume that its meaning is identical cross-culturally. As for early rabbinic sources, discussion must now commence with the remarkable chapter 5 of Christine Hayes' *What's Divine About Divine Law*,[51] in which she concludes that "divine law does not always align with formal logical proof"; that "the value placed on peace and mercy rather than truth . . . shows that divine law did not always promote judicial truth"; and that "divine law does not always align with mind-independent ontological reality" (p. 243). In short, the rabbis "did not embrace a broader conception of divine law that assumes the latter's verisimilitude and correspondence to some kind of objective truth" (pp. 243 f.). In Jewish philosophy, the relationship between *emet* and *emunah*, truth and trust (the latter understood in interpersonal terms) is often discussed.[52] One possible conclusion of our *agunah* study is that much depends on which contemporary authorities one chooses to trust (and what, in turn, are the sources of trust of those contemporary authorities themselves). I shall argue in the next section that there are strong semiotic reasons for such a conclusion (not only in religious, but also in secular law).

Finally, we may pose the question whether all rules of Jewish law are equally "religious." It is not difficult to make the case for the religious nature of the rules in the areas of ritual, life and death, and sexual relations, and the language of the biblical sources often reinforces this. But what of those "secular" rules which have direct counterparts in the civil law of other jurisdictions? I have addressed this question in relation to the *mishpatim* of Exodus 21–22.[53] Whatever the origins of the collection, we now find them incorporated into the Sinaitic covenant. But why, I asked, should God be interested in goring oxen (and many other aspects of the *mishpatim*)? I made some suggestions, but left the matter without any comprehensive substantive answer. Perhaps it represents an endorsement not merely of the necessity but also the value of negotiated settlement of civil disputes, on the basis of divinely endorsed wisdom-laws.[54] When we proceed beyond the biblical period, to a period when institutional adjudication has become available also for monetary matters (*dine mamonot*), we do find that they are treated, in significant respects, differently from the "more religious" categories of "prohibition and permission" (*issur veheter*). There is much more freedom to contract out of rules of *dine mamonot*,[55] to modify them by custom (*minhag*), and even to override them in favor of the law of the State (*dina demalkhuta*). Yet all these freedoms

English original in *Standing Tall: Hommages à Csaba Varga*, ed. Bjarne Melkevek (Budapest: Pázmány Press, 2012), 199–207, esp. at 205, 207.

50 See Anna Pintore, *Law without Truth* (Merseyside: Deborah Charles Publications, 2000), examining the respective claims of truth as correspondence, truth as coherence, truth as consensus and procedural truth.

51 Christine Hayes, *What's Divine About Divine Law? Early Perspectives* (Princeton and Oxford: Princeton University Press, 2015).

52 See further Jackson, *Journey*, *supra* n.1, s.4.7.

53 Jackson, "Human Law and Divine Justice," *supra* n.40, ss.1–2.

54 See text accompanying n.40, above.

55 See, e.g., E. Klingenberg, "Judgment and Settlement in Court in Jewish and Comparative Legal History," *The Jewish Law Annual* 8 (1989), 135–45, at 144.

may be taken to manifest the same value, that of human autonomy and responsibility, as was represented by the underlying values of the biblical wisdom-laws themselves.

A great deal of this section is in line with the argument of an article of Hanina Ben-Menahem, on Talmudic Law as a Religious Legal system[56] – in particular, his preliminary remarks under the headings: "The Notion of a 'Religious Legal System' Is Not Given in Nature, but Is a Product of Reflection";[57] "Religiosity is a Relative Concept: Whether a System is Religious is a Matter of Degree, as Opposed to an Either-Or Determination";[58] "A Legal System May Use Specialized Tools to Advance an Ideology";[59] and "Self-Reported Accounts of Legal Practice Are Not Necessarily Veridical,"[60] as well as his account of many of the features of a legal system which justify its designation as a religious legal system.[61] He concludes: "In my view, governance by judges rather than by rules is the primary feature of the talmudic legal system. Of the various elements of the judicial process that, as we have seen, may attest to the religious nature of a legal system, it is by far the strongest."[62] I shall argue, however, that adoption of a semiotic methodology in discussing these matters leads to an even more radical conclusion: it treats "the legal system" as a set of separate discursive practices rather than as a unified system in which one particular practice is dominant.[63]

V AN INTRODUCTION TO GREIMASIAN SEMIOTICS[64]

"Semiotics" is the name given to the research field which asks whether we can construct any *general* theory of sense construction: one which will not be confined to language or behavior, but which will both provide a common theoretical foundation

56 Hanina Ben-Menahem, "Is Talmudic Law a Religious Legal system? A Provisional Analysis," *Journal of Law and Religion* 24 (2008–09), 379–401.

57 *Ibid.*, at 380–81.

58 *Ibid.*, at 381–82.

59 *Ibid.*, at 382. In *Journey*, supra n.1 at 36, I wrote: "So how different (semiotically) is religious law from secular law? Some postmodernist thought has rejected any essential difference on theoretical grounds. Goodrich, for example, attributes a kind of legal theology to secular law, regarding the constitution as the locus of a (hidden) eternal presence: P. Goodrich, *Languages of Law: From Logics of Memory to Nomadic Masks* (London: Weidenfeld and Nicolson, 1990), 6."

60 Ben-Menahem, "Is Talmudic Law a Religious Legal System?" *supra* n.56, at 382–83.

61 Notably, "The Alleged Source of the System" (*ibid.*, 383–85); "The Areas Covered by the System's Rules" (385–87) and various aspects of the "The System's Mode of Operation" (388), especially whether judges are regarded as infallible (391–92); (Occasional) Reliance on Miracles in Decision-making (392); Modes of Punishment (393) and Atonement as an Objective of Punishment (393–94); "Formalistic Considerations v. Policy Considerations in Interpreting the Law" (395); and "Judicial Decisions are not Necessarily Reasoned, Based on a Pre-existing Set of Rules, Predictable, or Subject to Appeal" (397–401).

62 *Ibid.*, 401. He continues: "The conclusion that emerges from this analysis, namely, that talmudic law is a religious legal system because of the unlimited authority it delegates to human judges, may seem paradoxical. But we have to remember that the secularization process that legal culture has undergone was precisely the attempt to discipline the system's officials by imbuing in them a sense of accountability to the citizen. This was, in essence, the dawn of the notion of 'the rule of law'."

63 See further text accompanying n.136, below.

64 Abbreviated from my *Making Sense in Law*, *supra* n.1, 140–62, omitting most of the footnotes and other discussion of (sometimes critical) secondary literature on more technical points. For a more

for the different disciplines of sense-construction, and contribute to their hypotheses and methodologies. If so, it provides a neutral model for the comparison of sense construction in different areas and disciplines.[65]

Contemporary semiotics is dominated by the thought of two "schools," one inspired by the work of the American philosopher Charles Sanders Peirce (1839–1914), the other based upon the structural linguistics of Saussure, as most systematically developed in the work of Algirdas J. Greimas, the founder of the "Paris School" of semiotics. While the former remains philosophical in its orientation (Peirce was a leading logician, and this is reflected in his work on signs) and is concerned with the history, structure, and interrelations of concepts, the latter leans towards linguistics and to the analysis of empirical data. It is to this latter school of semiotics that my work in this area belongs.

The Saussurean basis of Greimasian semiotics, and particular its understanding of sense and reference,[66] has profound implications for ontology. Despite the claim that there exist universal processes of sense construction, Greimasian semiotics is fiercely empirical, in that it insists on starting with something accessible to our senses, such as a text (whether oral or written). While legal positivism also commences from an empirical claim – that there exists something that has been laid down ("posited") by a (normally human) authority – it goes on to assert the ontological existence (independent from any text) of laws and the legal system. The legal norm is claimed therefore to have an existence distinct from its linguistic expression.[67] This form of legal positivism thus makes ontological claims; semiotic positivism, on the other hand, seeks merely to explain how such ontological claims are constructed and make sense to those who accept them. It does not, and cannot, validate those claims; it can only show how, within legal discourse, such claims are validated through processes of recognition (an essential part of the "narrative syntagm").[68] This follows from the basics of Saussurean understanding of the relationship between sense and reference. The sense of terms used in language (its semantics) is not a function of its relationship (correspondence) to the empirical world outside, but rather its relationship to other terms within that linguistic system.[69] But when such language is used in the context of

detailed and technical discussion, with citation of sources, see my *Semiotics and Legal Theory*, *supra* n.1.

65 See further *Constructing*, *supra* n.1, last para.; *Journey*, *supra* n.1, in general.

66 See below, at n.69.

67 On the distinction between legal language and the logic of norms, see G. Kalinowski, *La logique des normes* (Paris: Presses Universitaires de France, 1972). I made extensive use of Kalinowski's work in *Semiotics and Legal Theory*, particularly in ch.3 on the semiotic square and its relation to the square of classical logic (as developed in modern times), and in ch.9, distinguishing the different paradigmatic structures in the different forms of legal discourse presupposed by Hart and Dworkin (on which see the paragraph commencing before n.96). See also the extensive bibliography of Kalinowski cited in *Semiotics and Legal Theory*, *supra* n.1, listed at 361–62.

68 See, text accompanying n.141, below.

69 F. de Saussure, *Course in Course in General Linguistics*, eds. C. Bally and A. Sechehaye, transl. W. Baskin (New York: McGraw-Hill, 1959); Jackson, *Semiotics and Legal Theory*, *supra* n.1, 32–33; *Making Sense in Law*, supra n.1, 23–31, 35–37; and as illustrated in the legal context by the "not guilty"

an assertion, a claim is thereby made that the language does indeed point to something in the outside world. This, however, is a speech act, and can itself be analyzed in terms of the narrative syntagm. It is, no more and no less, the performance of a speech act communicated by a sender to a receiver, in which the sender makes a claim about the outside world, to which the receiver accords some form of recognition. This referential skepticism entails the understanding that truth cannot be established merely within language; the recognition of truth claims, rather, most commonly depends upon interpersonal trust.[70]

My most recent work in this area has reinforced my view of the importance of a number of basic epistemological positions of Greimasian semiotics: its referential skepticism (better: its understanding of reference within pragmatics rather than semantics) and its methodology of approaching texts – these leading to what I would take to be its (universally relevant, if implicit) view of the relationship between truth and trust. All of this, in different ways, involves the relationships between syntactics, semantics and pragmatics.

For Greimasian semiotics, "is" and "ought" are simply different modalities applied to accounts of behaviour patterns (whose sense is constructed in narrative terms).[71] When we affirm the modality of "is," we are making a truth claim; when we affirm the modality of "ought" we are making a validity claim (just as when we go to an art gallery and affirm the beauty of a painting, we are making an aesthetic claim). When we affirm that something is "divine" (or, for that matter, "legal"), we are similarly attributing a linguistically constructed "modality" to it. We may therefore question whether the secular/religious distinction (or, for that matter, the "legal/moral" distinction) is ontological or itself a social construction of sense. But this is neither to deny nor to affirm the reality of either legal or religious experience. Greimasian semiotics is purely descriptive; its position on sense and reference (the latter being the concern of pragmatics rather than semantics) means that it cannot validate (or invalidate) truth claims within linguistic resources.

The Greimasian school looks for "basic structures of signification," and finds them in a "deep" level of sense construction based upon a particular model of narrative. The concept of narrative has become popular in the social sciences in recent years, albeit in the form of a range of different particular conceptions of what narrative is. In legal studies, too, narrative models of different kinds have been used for a number of different purposes. The semiotic approach of Greimas and his followers proceeds from first principles. It stresses the role of narrative in the deep structure of signification of *any* form of discourse. Thus, it is equally applicable to

plea: see text accompanying n.74 and n.100. See also n.93, on this issue in the context of the normative syllogism.

70 See further text accompanying n.146, below.

71 Cf. my "Mediation and Immediacy in the Jewish Legal Tradition" in a forthcoming conference volume (prepublication version available at www.academia.edu/s/171e34ccfc?source=link and http://ssrn.com/abstract=2800819).

both legal and religious discourses; it also provides a methodology for explaining how *we* make sense of particular discourses as "legal" or "religious."[72]

Greimas sought to extend the ideas of Saussure regarding the semantic structure of individual sentences by applying them also to "discourse." We have to make sense not merely of individual sentences, nor even of the relations of contiguous sentences, but also of texts as a whole. The folklorist Vladimir Propp had analyzed one hundred Russian folktales, and identified some thirty-one narrative themes in them, recurring in different forms. Through a reanalysis of this material, Greimas derived a much more abstract, general (and, as he claimed, universal) model in which his "basic structures of signification" ("*structures élémentaires de la signification*") consist of two axes:

(a) the syntagmatic axis of Saussure generated an "actantial" model, in which discourse makes sense in terms of underlying patterns of intelligible action. This is worth stressing: our sense-making capacities are primarily oriented towards making sense of human action, and in particular making sense of elements of human action which appear in a diachronic sequence.
(b) the associative (or "paradigmatic") axis generates choices (often structured as oppositions) of story elements which are used in the story-sequence (or "syntagm").

The combination of these two levels, Greimas claimed, represents the "deep level" of all discourse. We make such sense by understanding the data in terms of meaningful sequences of action. What is a "meaningful sequence of action" can be specified (the "syntagmatic axis,"). Thus the Greimasian theory claims to provide an account of the construction of the sense of behaviour (including speech behaviour), and not merely of the language we use to tell stories. In subsequent work, members of the Parisian school have applied the Greimasian scheme to many different forms of discourse and behaviour. And psychologists of perception endorse this approach, as when they note the phenomenon of "confabulation" – "fake perception" (my phrase) to make an otherwise non-meaningful sequence meaningful.[73]

The syntagmatic axis (the discursive version of the syntax of a sentence) is "semio-narrative": we can thus speak of a "narrative syntagm." Every human action, for

72 Cf. Ben-Menahem, *supra* n.57.

73 An example is given by A. Trankell, *The Reliability of Evidence: Methods for Analyzing and Assessing Witness Statements* (Stockholms: Beckmans, 1972), cited by S. Lloyd-Bostock, *Law in Practice* (British Psychological Society and Routledge Ltd., 1988), 6: A lawyer in a taxi saw the door of the car in front of him stop suddenly and one of the doors swing open. He also saw an old man lying in the road. He thought he had seen the old man fall out of the car or be pushed out. In fact the old man was a pedestrian who had previously been knocked down; he had never been in the car whose door had opened. Such confabulation can be explained in narrative terms: the lawyer here assumed that there was a link between things which he perceived in sequence. There is an operating assumption (in legal terms, a rebuttable presumption) that such sequences are meaningful, rather than being a mere series of unconnected events.

Greimas, begins with the establishment of a *goal*, which thereby institutes someone as the *subject* of that action, with the goal of *performing* it. In realizing the action, the subject will be helped or obstructed by other actions of other social actors. This help or obstruction will affect the "competence" of the subject to perform the action. The desired action itself will be achieved, or not achieved. But it is a characteristic of human action that the sequence does not finish there. Human beings reflect upon past actions. As a consequence, the syntagmatic axis of Greimas concludes with the concept of *recognition* (otherwise, "sanction"). Human action (whether real or fictional) thus appears meaningful in terms of a basic three-part "narrative" sequence, for which Greimasians have adopted the following technical vocabulary:

(1) "Contract": the institution of the subject through the establishment of goals and competences. The goals of action may be of any kind: they may include communicative goals.
(2) "Performance" (or nonperformance) of those goals.
(3) "Recognition" of that contract and performance (or nonperformance).

Any narrative involves a set of interactions, in the course of setting goals, performing them, and assisting or obstructing their accomplishment. At the "deep level," the theory sees these interactions as involving a set of abstract actors, termed *actants*, which appear in pairs: Sender-Receiver, Subject-Object, Helper-Opponent. A Sender invests a Receiver as Subject of the story, by communicating a goal to him/her (though the actual Sender and Receiver may be the same; in other words, the Subject may be self-motivated). In achieving this goal (normally involving action upon an "Object"), or performing this task, the subject may be assisted by a "helper," or obstructed by an "opponent." The figures of "helper" and "opponent" were derived from the plots of Propp's Russian folktales. Later, the "helper" and "opponent" disappeared from the model as independent *actants*, and were replaced by a more abstract notion of the presence or absence of the competences – the *savoir-faire* and *pouvoir-faire* – required to perform the action. In "recognition," too, a Sender sends a message to a Receiver, which produces the sense that the task is recognized as having been performed, not performed, well performed, badly performed, etc. The scheme may be represented diagrammatically as seen in Figure 5.1.

The paradigmatic axis is based on Saussurian and Lévi-Straussian foundations. At every point on the syntagmatic axis (as in the single sentence), there are choices to be made. But such choices are limited to things which may be substitutable, one for the other. At each point in the narrative syntagm, there exist conventionally defined semiotic constraints, as to what elements are substitutable for each other without altering the meaning of other elements in the syntagm. These constraints may reflect binary oppositions (analyzed in terms of the "semiotic square") or larger groups of substitutable elements, as in relations of "hyponymy." Discourse elements, just as individual words, have similar relations, and may similarly be substituted (or not substituted). Greimas, however, offers a more formal description of how this works.

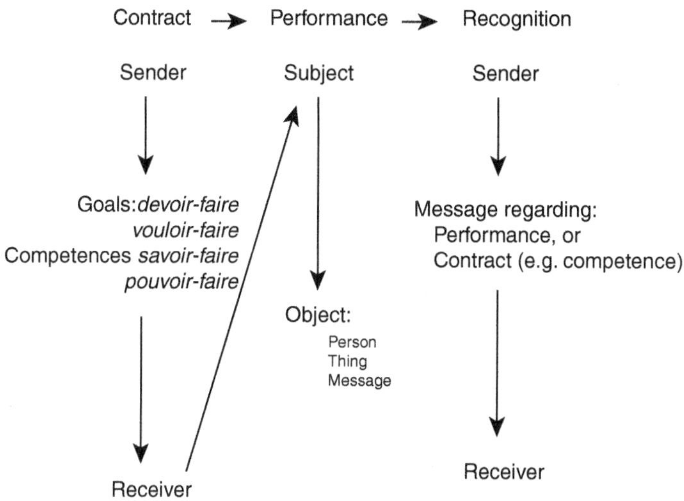

FIGURE 5.1 The Narrative Syntagm according to Greimasian Semiotics

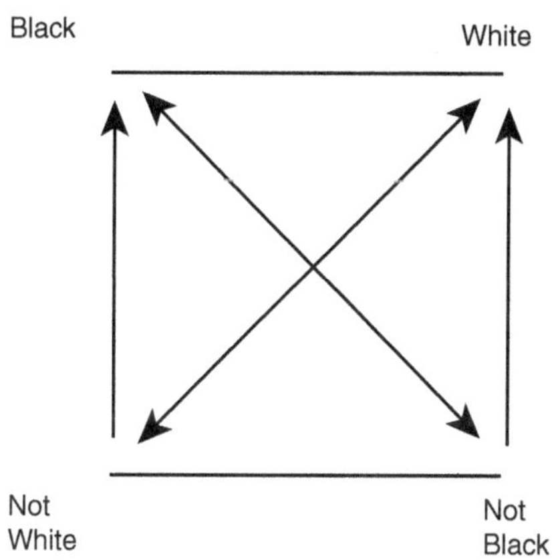

FIGURE 5.2 The Semiotic Square

Binary oppositional relationships, in particular, reflect a structure called the "semiotic square," in which "contradictories" and "contraries" are distinguished. Where two terms are contradictory, not only does the assertion of the one entail the negation of the other; the negation of the one entails the assertion of the other. In a conventional opposition (contrariety), on the other hand, the assertion of one term entails the negation of the other, but the negation of one term does not entail the assertion of the other. *Black* v. *White* is such a relationship: if something is black, it cannot be white, but if it is not black, it is not necessarily white, as seen in Figure 5.2.

"Opposites" like black and white, cat and dog, guilty and innocent may be analyzed in this way. Thus, in the conventional understanding of black and white as "opposites," we go up the sides of the square, in treating "white" as the privileged manifestation of "not black" (the contradictory of "black") and "black" as the privileged manifestation of "not white" (the contradictory of "white"). This may be illogical, but it aids considerably the construction of sense within social interaction (where we are not all logicians). It is this same process which prompts the lay assumption that a person found "not guilty" (the contradictory of guilty) is in fact "innocent," choosing to privilege that particular choice from amongst the possible senses of "not guilty." This also illustrates the proposition that the meanings of terms depends upon their internal sense relations rather than their referents in the outside world. "Not guilty" has different meanings in the English and Scottish legal systems, since the latter also provides the possibility of a "not proven" verdict.[74]

In the sending and receipt of messages regarding performance, which constitutes the "Recognition" part of the narrative syntagm, the evaluations thus communicated are often termed "modalities." They are not, however, confined to "evaluations" in the normal (judgmental) sense. They may include aesthetic and emotive evaluations. The behavior of a lawyer, for example, may be accompanied by such modalities as helpful, formalistic, polite, and efficient. Modalities may also be "deontic," expressive of different types of normativity: in Western legal systems, behavior may be permitted, required, or prohibited, while in Islamic jurisprudence it may also be recommended or disapproved.[75]

"Above" the "deep level," there is a level of construction of meaning contributing more directly to the meaning of the surface data (for Greimas, the "level of manifestation"), which may be termed "thematic."[76] Early in my career (and before my exposure to semiotics) I reviewed George Fletcher's *Rethinking Criminal Law*[77] and was particularly struck by his use of the notion of "collective images."[78] Fletcher argued that the technical intricacies of the common law of larceny, particularly in the seventeenth and eighteenth centuries, were best understood in terms of the relationship of different fact situations to the "collective image of acting like a thief." That collective image served as a kind of paradigm: if one asked people what their

74 See further Jackson, *Making Sense in Law*, *supra* n.1, 26–30; Bernard S. Jackson, "Truth or Proof?: The Criminal Verdict," *IJSL/RISJ* XI/33 (1998), 227–73.

75 Robert Brunschvig, "Logic and Law in Classical Islam," in *Logic in Classical Islamic Culture*, ed. G. E. von Grunebaum (Wiesbaden: Harrassowitz, 1970), 11; Robert Brunschvig, "Hermeneutique Normative dans le Judaïsme et dans l'Islam," *Accademia Nazionale dei Lincei, Rendiconti della Classe di Scienze morali, storiche e filologiche*, Ser. VIII vol. XXX, fasc. 5–6, pp. 1–20 (May–June 1975), at 5.

76 For the "thematic trajectory," see A. J. Greimas and J. Courtés, *Semiotics and Language. An Analytical Dictionary* (Bloomington: Indiana University Press, 1982), 344.

77 George Fletcher, *Rethinking Criminal Law* (Boston: Little, Brown and Coke, 1978).

78 B. S. Jackson, "Towards an Integrated Approach to Criminal Law: Fletcher's *Rethinking Criminal Law*," *The Criminal Law Review* (1979), 621–29. See further Jackson, *Law, Fact and Narrative Coherence*, *supra* n.1 100f., 108.

typical image of the activity of a thief was, the response was likely to be the nocturnal burglar. (Of course, collective images are temporally and culturally contingent.) From this it does not follow that the daytime pickpocket would not be regarded as within the collective image of acting like a thief (though it might generate its own independent collective image – thus burglar versus pickpocket). Clearly, there will be cases closer to or more distant from the paradigm: the daytime burglar, the nighttime thief who puts his hand in the window but not his body, etc. But the collective image was not merely a description of typical action; it also included a tacit social evaluation. *This* collective image of acting like a thief involved a particular frisson, a fear of the intruder, a horror of the crossing of territorial boundaries, with all the attendant danger which, socially, such boundary-crossing is thought to entail. We may translate such tacit social evaluations into our semiotic model, as the transfer of modalities: the activity of the thief is recognized as (though here, perhaps, not necessarily performed as) dangerous.

In my version of semiotic theory, I call such paradigms "narrative typifications of action."[79] From this example, three important elements of the notion of a "narrative typification" emerge. First, a narrative typification is not a definition in terms of necessary and sufficient conditions; as a model which informs our perception, it does not generate (as the positivist might wish) "demonstrable" judgments as to what is "within" or "outwith" the image. But it is capable of generating judgments of relative similarity. Second, such a typification is not a neutral description; it comes, always, laden with a form of evaluation (for even "indifference" is a form of evaluation). Third, some typifications belong to particular social and/or professional groups – "semiotic groups," distinguished one from another by the (often overlapping but still distinct) systems of signification operating within them.

However, there is no complete divide between semiotic groups, even those of the laity and professionals. Even though (institutional) Law and Religion are forms of secondary symbolization (using the primary, natural language in a particular, specialized way), they remain (being human constructs) parasitic upon social understandings, despite any ideological claims to autonomy, such as the notion of the "artificial reason of the law." It is a primary claim of the work I have done in legal semiotics that even lawyers cannot escape their own humanity and social settings. Underneath every legal formulation, the primary social understanding may be submerged, but not eliminated.

Greimasian semiotics stresses that both the narrative syntagm and narrative typifications of action are applicable not only to the content of a narrative

[79] See my "Thématisation et typifications narratives en droit," *Protée* 22/2 (1994), 57–68, in the special issue *Le lieu commun*, ed. E. Landowski and A. Semprini (Chicoutimi: Université du Québec, 1994); English version: "Thematisation and the Narrative Typifications of the Law," in *Law as Communication*, ed. D. Nelken (Andover: Dartmouth Publishing Co., 1996), 175–94, acknowledging also the work of W. L. Bennett and M. S. Feldman, *Reconstructing Reality in the Courtroom* (New Brunswick: Rutgers University Press, 1981).

(semantics), but also to the act of enunciation (or communication) of that narrative (pragmatics). Indeed, no complete understanding of the sense of the message itself is complete without making sense of the purpose of communicating it. I have called this the narrativization of pragmatics.[80] The enunciation of messages is as much an action as anything else which human beings do (as speech act theory has recognized). It is generally assumed to be meaningful action. We therefore have to ask whence derives its meaning. A Greimasian would claim that the very act of communication of a message is equally analyzable according to the model of the Greimasian and narrative syntax, and thus reflects (at the "deep level") the semio-narrative syntagm. But within any particular society or social group, what counts as a successful enunciation, and what type of enunciative meaning is attributed to it (assertion, threat, play, irony, etc.) are matters of internalized social knowledge (at the "thematic level"),[81] as indeed are the signs (at the "level of manifestation") of successful performance.

Application of the Greimasian model to issues of law and religion thus requires us to pose the following questions:

Who is the Subject of the act (whether linguistic or not) in question?

How is that Subject constructed, which entails:

(1) Who sends to (or invests with) the subject the appropriate modalities?
(2) What are the appropriate modalities in this particular case?

What is the act which the subject performs?

Who performs the recognition of that act?

How is that recognition constructed, which entails:

(1) Who sends to whom the appropriate modalities?
(2) Who receives them?
(3) What are the appropriate modalities in this particular case?

Crucial to the application of this model is the understanding of the existence of different semiotic groups, defined by their distinctive ways of constructing and communicating sense.[82] Thus, the same act may be understood (recognized) in quite different ways within different semiotic communities, not least because of their adoption of different semantic relations within the same natural language.

Space does not permit the giving here of a systematic account of the application of all aspects of the Greimasian model to "law," "religion," or "religious law." But it is not difficult to locate within the model the nature of the differences between secular law and religious law. Two issues may here be highlighted. First, the identity of the

80 For applications in the legal sphere, see text accompanying n.131.
81 See text accompanying n.131.
82 See further *Making Sense in Law, supra* n.1, 93–98.

sender who invests the subject with the desire/obligation/competence/authority to act. In secular legal theory this would normally be the state or constitution; generally, in religious law it would be God.[83] But our very use of the terminology of State, Constitution or God raises the very same (Saussurian) questions of sense and reference, to which there can be no objective answer within language.[84] A second issue is the forms of recognition which may be accorded, whether the act be one of a legal institution or a private individual. As noted above,[85] in western legal systems, behavior may be permitted, required, or prohibited, while in Islamic jurisprudence it may also be recommended or disapproved. The Halakhah does not have a formal typology of such modalities, but it is clear that there are forms of recognition which reflect the recommended[86] or disapproved, rather than the permitted, required, or prohibited.

VI GREIMASIAN SEMIOTICS APPLIED TO LAW (SECULAR AND RELIGIOUS)

In what follows, I attempt to summarize some of my earlier work on the application of semiotics to secular law and apply the same type of analysis to the *halakhah*, in order to clarify the areas of commonality, and those of difference.[87] It also provides an opportunity to show the interaction of various aspects of the semiotic model described in Section V, and even to add one or two refinements to it.

A *The Discursive Basis*

A fundamental starting point is the realization that "law," whether secular or religious, is in fact a collection of quite distinct discursive practices, linked by a set of inter-discursive claims. There is legislation, adjudication (which includes both decision-making and justification), and doctrine. Legislation puts forward rules applicable in general; adjudication seeks to resolve the disputes of individuals in

83 Assuming here that the subject of the legal performance is human; a different analysis may be required for the direct operation of divine law, without human involvement (on which, from a non-semiotic view, see §§1.1, 4.2–3 of my "Human Law and Divine Justice," *supra* n.40).

84 See text accompanying n.75.

85 *Ibid.*

86 E.g. *lifnim mishurat hadin*, "beyond (sometimes 'within') the line of the law." See Shmuel Shilo, "On One Aspect of Law and Morals in Jewish Law: *Lifnim Mishurat Hadin*," *Israel Law Review* 13 (1978), 359–90.

87 A major portion (pp. 21–35) of Jackson, *Journey*, *supra* n.1 addresses the question: "How different is religious law?" including sections on: Media and Mediation of Biblical law (23–26); The Language of "Biblical law" (26–27); Principles/Values of "Biblical law" (27–28);· Reiteration and (Forms of) Recognition in Biblical law (28); A unified system? Law and Narrative in the Bible (28–30); Legal concepts and institutions (30–32), observing, at 31: "The semiotician, rather, should ask (a) what are the narrative patterns of human behaviour reflected in such concepts?; and (b) by what process of recognition is the modality of 'legal' attributed to them?"?; Rabbinic Law: Rules, Truth or Trust (32–35).

the light of both legislation and whatever other sources of general rules are accepted by the particular system; doctrine encompasses both commentary on the reasons for particular areas of legislation and adjudication, and theorizing about the nature of the particular legal system or systems in general. When assessing the inter-discursive claims made in both adjudication and doctrine, we must start by examining how the "other" discourse is constructed in the discourse under consideration (typically, how the sense of a statute is constructed in the course of adjudication). And this involves not only an examination of the syntagmatic and paradigmatic structures of the "home" discourse, but also (so far as may be possible) its pragmatics: Who is communicating this message to whom, and for what purpose? Indeed, this emphasis on the individual discourse may be applied, reflexively, to the present exercise, and the particular senses of the "legal," "secular," and "religious" used in it, even if that discourse is thought to have incorporated a sense originating elsewhere (whether in literary or other sources).

There is no single, "natural," relationship between these different discursive practices. Different "legal systems" may construct them differently. For example, "doctrine" plays a far more important normative role in civil law systems than in the common law. For the *halakhah*, "doctrine" may take the form of *aggadah*, including, in biblical literature, narratives. Thus, for example, in studying the Book of Ruth, we must start by examining how the levirate and women's inheritance rights are understood in that narrative, before considering any possible relationship with the relevant pentateuchal laws.[88]

Of course, the Torah bears little resemblance to any modern legal document. The laws, even those found in the Pentateuch, are embedded in a wider narrative; they do not claim to be the enforceable law of a state, but are presented as divine revelations (or teachings)[89] of what such a law ought to be. They consist largely in concrete, individual rules rather than legal concepts and institutions. Biblical scholars have highlighted the "casuistic form" as typical of Biblical law. This form comprises two elements: a protasis (a conditional clause: "If . . . ") and an apodosis, stating the expected ("normative") consequences of such an action. The protasis contains the first two elements of the narrative syntagm: the "contract" (instituting the subject) and the "performance"; it does not indicate the third element (the "recognition") explicitly; instead, the apodosis provides a normative form of recognition. In the Jewish tradition, the latter may be either religious or sanctions of the type expected by nineteenth-century positivism (though in the religious tradition we cannot ignore the religious connotations of the death penalty). The religious forms

[88] See further B. S. Jackson, "Ruth, the Pentateuch and the Nature of Biblical Law: In Conversation with Jean Louis Ska," in *The Post-Priestly Pentateuch. New Perspectives on its Redactional Development and Theological Profiles*, eds. Konrad Schmid and Federico Giuntoli (Tübingen: Mohr Siebeck, 2015), 75–111.

[89] As is commonly recognized. the term *torah* means "instruction" rather than "law"; I have argued that there are strong affinities to the Biblical "wisdom" tradition: *Wisdom-Laws*, *supra* n.16, at 35–39.

of recognition are not confined to the ritual sphere, as may be seen from the responsum discussed below.[90]

There is a tendency among some commentators, both academic and rabbinic, to downplay the role of the biblical Torah text in their understanding of Jewish law: at most, the text of the Torah is to be understood through rabbinic eyes. But this in itself has major consequences. The Rabbis recognize the foundational character of the biblical text for the later tradition. In so doing, they have to grapple with the problems posed by the literary character of the biblical text (including its frequent linguistic ambiguity regarding modalities, particularly between permission and obligation). They construct the text as presumptively perfect in terms of human rationality, and thus adopt a hermeneutics which most commonly assumes comprehensiveness, consistency and lack of redundancy, reserving the residual safety net of superior divine cognition for difficulties which appear to defy human resolution.

The distinctiveness of the discourses of legislation, adjudication and doctrine has occasionally been recognized in both secular jurisprudence and the literature of the halakhah. For the former, we may cite in particular the work of Hans Kelsen. From the beginning, his basic conception of the norm had a distinctly semiotic tone: the norm, he argued, was to be understood as the meaning of an act of will.[91] It was thus a form of sense attributed to an act of human behaviour. In his later work, he stressed that the justification of the norm (even in terms of reference to other legal sources) was not part of the norm itself, and should not be treated as part of the science of jurisprudence.[92] He even abandoned the use of logical subsumption (of the particular case within a general norm) as a form of justification, on the grounds that both the general norm and the particular norm were the meanings of acts of human beings (legislators, judges) but there could be no logical connection between one such act of will and another. I have debated logical subsumption in linguistic terms with Neil MacCormick, stressing that the judge always has to make a decision as to the meaning of the general norm s/he is applying, even if that is endorsement of its conventional meaning.[93] On less philosophical grounds, both Scandinavian and

90 Text accompanying n.108.

91 Jackson, *Semiotics and Legal Theory*, *supra* n.1, 231–32; Jackson *Making Sense in Jurisprudence*, *supra* n.1, 100–02.

92 B. S. Jackson, "Kelsen between Formalism and Realism," *The Liverpool Law Review* VII/1 (1985), 79–93; Jackson, *Semiotics and Legal Theory*, *supra* n.1, 114–24; *Making Sense in Jurisprudence*, *supra* n.1, 243–57.

93 See N. MacCormick, *Legal Reasoning and Legal Theory* (Oxford: Clarendon Press, 1978), ch.2; Jackson, *Law, Fact and Narrative Coherence*, *supra* n.1, ch.2; N. MacCormick, "Notes on Narrativity and the Normative Syllogism," *IJSL/RISJ* IV/11 (1991), 163–74; B. S. Jackson, "Semiotic Scepticism: A Response to Neil MacCormick," *IJSL/RISJ* IV/11 (1991), 175–90; overall summary in Jackson, *Making Sense in Jurisprudence*, *supra* n.1, 245–55. MacCormick readily agreed that it is wrong to say that the major premise "refers" to the minor, in that reference (following Strawson) is a deictic activity which requires the presence of the minor premise at the time of the utterance of the major premise. (It thus belongs to pragmatics, what we do with a particular utterance, rather than its meaning.) MacCormick then sought to argue that it is correspondence of sense between the major

American legal realism are also skeptical about the relationship between legislation and adjudication.[94]

In the literature of the halakhah, Elon cites a story of regarding a *poseq* (R. Ḥayyim of Brisk) who wished not to hear the reasoning of a colleague charged with deciding a case (R. Isaac Elḥanan of Kovno), on the grounds that he respected the authority of the latter to make the decision, but did not wish to hear his reasoning, in case he disagreed with it.[95]

I have analyzed the Hart/Dworkin debate in terms of the discursive structures presupposed by each, using the semiotic square and Blanché's development of the square of logic into a hexagon[96] and concluded that the focus of Hart was on legislation (which could have gaps, reflecting Blanché's hexagon) while that of Dworkin was on adjudication (which could not have gaps, reflecting the semiotic square, with its conventional closure rule): for legislators, gaps could always be filled in the future; for judges, a decision had to be made in each particular case reflecting the best possible construction of the respective rights of the parties.[97] In the light of all this, I would argue that the conclusion of Ben-Menahem that "governance by judges rather than by rules is the primary feature of the talmudic legal system"[98] is no mere oddity of a particular religious system, but rather reflects the nature of the relationship between of decision-making and justification in general. I have argued, moreover, that decision-making is a private mental activity often involving subconscious invocation of particular forms of social knowledge,[99] while justification is a public communication to a particular audience, using the conventions and closure rules of that audience.[100]

and minor premises which admits of logical subsumption. But then, the legislator and the judge may attribute different senses to the words of the legislative norm. To this, MacCormick ultimately took the view that the relationship between the major and minor is one of denotation, understood as being that the minor premise must be within the range of *potential* reference of the major premise. But who, again, is to decide on such potential reference? It is hard to resist the critical conclusion that the use of logic in this area is a rhetorical device designed to create the illusion of objectivity. See also the subsequent debate in *IJSL/RISJ* XI (1998): Jori at 59–65; Jackson at 79–93; Touchie at 193–203; Jackson at 323–27.

94 *Making Sense in Jurisprudence*, *supra* n.1, chs. 5–6.

95 *Constructing*, *supra* n.1, at §3.3, from M. Elon, "More about Research into Jewish Law," in *Modern Research in Jewish Law*, ed. B. S. Jackson (Leiden: E.J. Brill, 1980), 66–111, at 89–90 n.52.

96 R. Blanché, *Les structures intellectuelles* (Paris: H. Vrin, 1966); for comparison of Greimas and Blanché, see *Semiotics and Legal Theory*, *supra* n.1, 86–99.

97 See further B. S. Jackson, "Hart and Dworkin on Discretion: Some Semiotic Perspectives," in *Semiotics, Law and Social Science*, ed. D. Carzo and B. S. Jackson (Reggio and Rome: Casa del libro editrice, 1985), 145–67; French version in *Archives de Philosophie du Droit* 34 (1989), 243–58; *Making Sense in Jurisprudence*, *supra* n.1, 200–05.

98 Text accompanying n.63, above, where, we may note, the "talmudic legal system" is implicitly equated with adjudication.

99 the "narrative typifications of action": see the text accompanying nn.79–80 above.

100 Jackson, "Internal and External Comparisons of Religious Law: Reflections from Jewish Law," *supra* n.23, at 182–83. However, the very use of terms such as "Jewish law" and "Islamic law," even of the notion of "religious systems of law," simply begs the vital questions. Judaism is a culture encompassing both a public sphere and a private sphere. Islam is the same. Judaism has the *halakhah*. Islam has

B *The Modalities of Recognition*

A full analysis of the "not guilty" verdict[101] indicates the following:

(1) People are not restricted to attributing a single modality to the action they are evaluating. "Guilty" and "not guilty" may be understood in terms of either "fact" or "proof" – or both: actually not guilty (= innocent) or not proved guilty (whether or not actually innocent).
(2) While the structure of particular modalities may be "binary," as in "Guilty" versus "Innocent," reflecting the most common form of sense, other, more sophisticated sense constructions are also possible, as in the Scottish triadic structure of verdicts, which is structured as a hyponomy.[102]
(3) Both the structure (binary or hyponomic) and the substance of modalities may vary between different semiotic groups (reflecting their particular discursive structures), this in itself reflecting the different narrative syntagms in which they are involved.[103] In general, binary structures are a feature of orally communicated "common sense" (the sense we share in common), while hyponomic are more characteristic of and derive from literacy-based discourse.[104] But even this, as other aspects of semantics, is subject to socio-environmental factors, as the great variety of words for "snow" in Eskimo languages shows.[105]
(4) In some cases even the semantic choices made at the paradigmatic level may themselves evoke narrative images.

I have stressed the link of narrative typifications of action (at the "thematic" level) with "tacit social evaluations."[106] The latter also function as manifestations of the "recognition" element of the narrative syntagm,[107] specifically by the sending of nonlegal modalities in relation to aspects of the "Contract" and/or "Performance."[108]

the *shari'a*. There is struggle within each of these cultures over the appropriation of the *halakhah/shari'a* to the spheres of the public or the private. Should they be viewed as law or as religion? Are these categories mutually exclusive? Clearly not. Are particular aspects of the *halakhah* and *shari'a* exclusively attributable to one or the other? Probably not. Are there tensions regarding the significance (public or private) to be attributed to particular rules within each tradition? Almost certainly, yes.

101 Text accompanying n.73.

102 *Semiotics and Legal Theory*, *supra* n.1, 35–41; *Making Sense in Law*, *supra* n.1, 24 and 148.

103 Cf. paragraph commencing before n.96.

104 On orality and literacy, see further text accompanying n.143.

105 David Robson, "Are There Really 50 Eskimo Words for Snow?" *New Scientist* (December 18, 2012), citing *SIKU: Knowing our Ice: Documenting Inuit Sea-Ice Knowledge and Use* (New York, NY: Springer, 2010), noting, inter alia, that the Inuit dialect spoken in Nunavik, Quebec, has at least fifty-three such terms.

106 Text accompanying n.77.

107 Text following n.73. This may also involve external actors, whose independent speech acts may also be understood in terms of the narrative syntagm.

108 As in the cases of the coin-tossing and apparently sleeping judges, in text accompanying n.135, below.

The nature and variety of institutional recognitions available within the halakhah, despite the absence of the typical sanctions available in a national legal system, is illustrated by a remarkable fifteenth-century responsum by R. Israel b. Ḥayyim of Brunn, which shows the weakness of the distinction between the legal and the religious in this context. A murder, of one Nissan, had occurred in the German town of Posen, committed by two people: "Simḥah" (in a state of drunkenness) and Naḥman (described by a witness as "ignorant and illiterate"). The latter had shown no remorse or penitence, and R. Israel indicates that there is nothing he can do about him. Nevertheless the responsum opens with a strong religious condemnation: "I name them both murderers, utterly guilty before the divine tribunal, but, (alas), beyond the jurisdiction of the human court!"[109] On the other hand, "Simḥah" was reported to have been "filled with remorse and seeks to repent." For him, R. Israel recommends as follows:

> He shall journey about as an exile for a full year. Every day he shall appear at a synagogue – or at least on every Monday and Thursday. He shall make for himself three iron bands, one to be worn on each of his two hands, which were the instruments of his transgressions, and one to be worn about his body. When he enters the synagogue, he shall put them on and pray with them on. In the evening he shall go barefoot to the synagogue. The *ḥazan* shall seat him (publicly) prior to the *Vehu Raḥum* prayer. He shall then receive a flogging and make the following declaration: "Know ye, my masters, that I am a murderer. I wantonly killed Nissan. This is my atonement. Pray for me." When he leaves the synagogue he is to prostrate himself across the doorsill; the worshipers are to step over him, not on him. Afterwards he is to remove the iron bands . . . After one year he shall continue his fasts on Mondays and Thursdays. He shall, for the rest of his days, carefully observe the anniversary month and the anniversary date of the killing. He shall fast at that time (the date) three consecutive days if he is healthy or only two days, the day of the wounding and the next day, the day of Nissan's death, if he is infirm. He shall, for the rest of his days, be active in all enterprises to free imprisoned Jews (i.e., hostages held by gentiles), charity, and the saving of lives. He shall work out an arrangement with his (Nissan's) heirs to support them properly. He shall ask their pardon and the widow's pardon. He shall return to God, and He shall have mercy on him.[110]

Here, it is the "sentencing" which constitutes the form of communal (or institutional) recognition which the respondent proposes. The regime includes a physical mirroring punishment, elements of public humiliation, and the public confession and acceptance of the punishment as an atonement. But that is not the only form of

[109] This is then explained, citing talmudic sources, in terms of the halakhic restriction of capital punishment to cases where there is only one assailant, thus avoiding problems of multiple causation.

[110] Translation by S. M. Passamaneck in *An Introduction to the History and Sources of Jewish Law*, *supra* n.18, at 346–50, reproduced, with permission, from J. Bazak and S. M. Passamaneck, *Jewish Law and Jewish Life* (New York: Union of American Hebrew Congregations, 1977), Book 7, 15–20. See further *Constructing*, *supra* n.1, §3.6.3, at 21–22; in more detail in Jackson, "The Practice of Justice in Jewish Law," *supra* n.32, at 41–45.

recognition provided within the responsum: The question and answer[111] both also use moral condemnation: both perpetrators are "wicked." This would be the primary form of recognition for the wider community: a social modality which evokes an image of a typical murder.[112] Indeed, R. Israel commences: "You have called Naḥman by his name Naḥman; you have called Simḥah a murderer. *I name them both murderers*."[113] Moreover, R. Israel concludes with reintegration within the community: "And since Simḥah has expressed remorse and seeks repentance and atonement, immediately upon his submission to the program of public degradations, he becomes our brother once again for every religious purpose."

Generally, we may think that the classification of the institutional sanctions, by the attribution of the modalities of the legal (in the secular sense) or the religious, represent a quite separate recognition process, of purely academic interest.[114] If so, this case provides an exception: the whole point of this regime, applied to Simḥah but not Naḥman, is that the offender must understand the religious significance of the regime, and indeed the community as a whole is being taught an important religious lesson in terms of how to treat offenders. Moreover, "legal" and "religious," as applied to the sanctions, are not here constructed in a relationship of "contrariety":[115] there are clear communal sanctions, partly of the physical nature, but they have a religious purpose, and depend upon the religious point of view of the recipient of those sanctions himself.

C Drafting, Decision-Making, and Narrative Typifications

The distinction between decision-making and justification is well illustrated in the legal context. Narrative structures underlie judicial decision-making, and frequently explain why a decision has been made in an area of legal difficulty and where the purely legal justification appears problematic, or eminently contestable. I have applied such an analysis, inter alia,[116] to *Riggs* v. *Palmer*,[117] the American case which

[111] Fully reproduced in Passamaneck's original, *supra* n.110.

[112] This will evoke both the biblical sources on murder, particularly the "*rotseax hu*" ("he is a murderer") in the cases described in Num. 35:16–18, which also specify the instrument used in the murder, and the social understanding of murder, with its modalities of cruelty, horror and loss.

[113] Emphasis in original. The form "*rotseaḥ-hu*" ("he is a murderer") is unusual in the Hebrew Bible, and was categorized by Daube as the "diagnosis form." See his discussion in "Some Forms of Old Testament Legislation," *Proceedings of the Oxford Society of Historical Theology* (1944), 36–46, at 39–42, and *Ancient Jewish Law. Three Inaugural Lectures* (Leiden: Brill, 1971), 100–06; further, Jackson, *Studies in the Semiotics of Biblical Law*, *supra* n.1, 49–51 (on the relationship of "naming" and "justification"), 95–96.

[114] Jackson, *Journey*, *supra* n.1, ss.5.1, 5.3; similarly, as regards "legal institutions," which function primarily as a convenient means of teaching and analyzing sets of interrelated rules. See further Jackson, "Introduction: Semiotics and Institutional Theory," *IJSL/RISJ* IV/12 (1991), 227–32.

[115] Text accompanying n.74.

[116] See also my analysis of a difficult line of English law cases of contracts induced by fraud as to identity of one of the parties: *Law, Fact and Narrative Coherence*, *supra* n.1, 101–06, and of the "Brother Daniel" case, discussed below (text commencing before n.122).

[117] 115 N.Y. 506, 22 N.E. 188 (1889); Jackson, *Making Sense in Jurisprudence*, *supra* n.1, 199–200, 208, 241–42; *Journey*, *supra* n.1, at 8–9.

Dworkin used in *Taking Rights Seriously* to demonstrate the need to use legal principles (and not merely legal rules) in deciding hard cases,[118] even though such principles might have to be inferred from the legal tradition, and would not pass Hart's "demonstrability" test.[119] Here, the courts agonized, in doctrinal terms, over whether a grandson who – knowing that he had been named his grandfather's heir in his will – had murdered him in order to secure and accelerate his inheritance, should be allowed to inherit, in the absence of any exclusion of such cases from the New York statute on wills. Ultimately, the New York Court of Appeals decided (by a majority of 2–1) that there was a principle of law, to be applied in this case, that "A person should not profit from his wrong." Dworkin rejected the view of Hart that the legal system consisted of rules only, so that if there was a gap in the law, it could only be filled by creation of a new rule by the exercise of judicial discretion. Against this, Dworkin argued that there was always a correct, or at least a best available, answer in the existing law, if the judges looked hard enough, even though only a "Hercules," a "lawyer of superhuman skill, learning, patience and acumen,"[120] might be able to persuade his colleagues of such. But once one looks at the facts in "common sense" social rather than purely legal doctrinal terms, one realizes that this narrative is so distant from the typical situation of testamentary succession, which presupposes peaceable if not loving (a "tacit social evaluation") family relationships, that it would "stink" (a nonlegal modality) to give the inheritance to the murderer. That means that we privilege the peaceable versus violent opposition in the narrative, and regard its deviation from the typical as sufficiently important to justify not applying the legal consequence normally associated with (peaceable) testamentary succession. In short, and despite the naive legal assumption that reasons stated by judges in their judgments represent fully and accurately the very bases of their decisions, we have to make a distinction between the private, mental processes of decision-making on the one hand, and the public, discursive processes of justification on the other. The "artificial reason of the law" may dominate in the latter, but the (no doubt culturally contingent) sense we have in common cannot be excluded at the psychological level.[121]

Both the syntagmatic axis and the paradigmatic (through narrative typifications) were prominent in the famous "Brother Daniel" case[122] decided under Israeli (not Jewish) law on who counted as a Jew for the purposes of Israel's Law of Return

[118] Dworkin, *Taking Rights Seriously*, *supra* n.10, at 23, 28–30.

[119] *Supra*, s. II, paragraph ending with n.6.

[120] Dworkin, *Taking Rights Seriously*, *supra* n.10, at 105.

[121] See my " Rationalité consciente et inconsciente dans la théorie du droit et la science juridique," *Revue interdisciplinaire des études juridiques* 19 (1987), 1–18; " Conscious and Unconscious Rationality in Law and Legal Theory," in *Reason in Law. Proceedings of the Conference Held in Bologna, 12–15 December 1984*, eds. Carla Faralli and Enrico Pattaro (Milan: Giuffrè, 1988), III.281–99.

[122] *Oswald Rufeisen* v. *Minister of the Interior*, H.C. 72/62 (Supreme Court of the State of Israel sitting as the High Court of Justice); a full English translation of the judgments is available in *Selected Judgments of the Supreme Court of Israel*, Special Volume, ed. A. F. Landau (Jerusalem: Ministry of Justice, 1971). For my analysis, see B. S. Jackson, "Brother Daniel: The Construction of Jewish

1950.[123] The petitioner, Oswald Rufeisen, was born in Poland of Jewish parents, reared as a Jew, and was active as a youth in a Zionist Youth movement. When the Germans occupied Poland he managed to infiltrate a German police station and was able to pass information to the local Jewish population, thus saving them from deportation (and worse). He then fled to the forest and joined a group of Russian partisans. There came a stage when he had to take refuge in a small Catholic nunnery. There, he converted to Catholicism, while still regarding himself as a Jew and adopting the name of "Brother Daniel." After the war he maintained his earlier commitment to emigrate to Israel and ultimately arrived there in 1958, claiming his right to Israeli citizenship as a Jew under the Law of Return. By a majority of 4–1, the Israel Supreme Court denied his petition, while allowing him to enter and ultimately obtain citizenship by naturalization. Rufeisin's story combines elements from different Jewish narrative stereotypes. We commence with an unremarkable narrative of a Jewish boy seeking to fulfil a Zionist ideal, proceed to the quite remarkable story of a war hero, and then to the story of a Jew who has converted (deserted) to Christianity. To make sense of all this, we need either to select and privilege some aspects of the story and suppress others, or to create a new synthesis and with it a new evaluation. We do not normally find the hero and the deserter united in a single person. Justice Silberg, for the majority, described his own "psychological difficulty" in the case and speaks in terms of conflicting evaluations: "But this sense of profound sympathy and obligation [to Rufeisen] must not be permitted to mislead us and to justify our profaning the concept of 'Jew' both in name and in meaning." The differences between the majority and minority on the court as to whether a Jew who had adopted Christianity could still be regarded as a Jew, I argued, depended on whether "Jew" and "Christian" were contraries within a semiotic square or whether they admitted of further possibilities (in accordance with the logic of Blanché). For the majority, they were contraries: a Jew could not be a Christian (and this, in the light of the malign history of Jewish-Christian relations, rather than on theological grounds).

But the differences between the majority and minority went beyond their conceptions of "a Jew" and extended to the Jewish nature of the State itself – whether it should be viewed simply as a continuation of the Diaspora experience (which maintained tradition in a defensive way) or as representing a rebirth, a fresh start. This latter issue, I suggested, reflects differences in constructing the relation between Past and Future, which could also be analyzed in terms either of the square or the hexagon. Justice Cohn, the one judge finding in favor of Rufeisen, contrasted the petitioner's openness on arrival at the Port of Haifa (observing: "Had he folded his gown, hidden his cross and concealed his creed, the gates would have been opened

Identity in the Israel Supreme Court," *IJSL/RISJ* VI/17 (1993), 115–46 (summarized in Jackson, *Journey*, *supra* n.1, s.3.4, at 16–19).

123 s.3[a]: "A Jew who has come to Israel and subsequent to his arrival has expressed his desire to settle in Israel may, while still in Israel, receive an *oleh*'s [immigrant's] certificate."

wide without protest") with the historic position of Diaspora Jews who, "loyal to their ancestral faith, donned the outward garb of the Christian religion so that they might continue to dwell in the lands beloved to them and harvest the fruit of their toils." Citing Isaiah xxvi, 2, "Open ye the gates that the righteous gentile which keepeth the truth may enter in," Justice Cohn argued that it was such openness which the State of Israel should now display, showing its own liberation from the constraints of the past.

There is much scope for examining the role of narrative typifications in both general norms and adjudication in Jewish law, but the issue presents itself differently according to the period, literature, and semiotic groups concerned. I confine myself here to the early period. In any legal system, the earlier we go back the more their general norms reflect ordinary speech rather than technical formulations. I have argued that many of the laws of the *mishpatim* of Exodus 21–22 reflect socially understood narrative typifications, even when those narratives are not fully stated. A simple but clear example is Exodus 22:2–3 (MT: 1–2),[124]

2 If a thief is found breaking in, and is struck so that he dies, there shall be no bloodguilt for him;
3 but if the sun has risen upon him, there shall be bloodguilt for him.

The biblical provision has appeared to many as badly drafted: the first verse, which allows self-help, makes *no* explicit mention of the time of the incident; the only explicit reference to the time occurs in the second verse, which denies the legitimacy of self-help during the day. It is in the light of that qualification, apparently, that the permission of self-help has to be restricted to the nocturnal incident. This would appear at first sight to be a very strange type of drafting. Apparently, the audience is first given the impression that self-help is *always* available, then this is qualified by denying its availability when the incident occurs during the day. Indeed, some scholars have wondered whether the second verse may be a later addition: originally the householder was entitled to kill the intruding thief at any time of day or night; later this form of self-help was restricted to the daytime intruder.[125] But if we pose the question of meaning of v.2 not in the (semantic) form of: "what situations do the words of this rule cover?" but rather in the (narrative) form of: "what typical situations do the words of this rule evoke?" then we are entitled to take into account the image of typical thieving presented in the book of Job:

***Job* 24:14, 16**
The murderer rises in the dark;
that he may kill the poor and needy

[124] Discussed in Jackson, *Studies in the Semiotics of Biblical Law*, *supra* n.1, at 75–77, under the heading "'Literal Meaning: Narrative versus Semantic Models'"; see also "Literal Meaning . . .., " *supra* n.6, at 438; *Wisdom-Laws*, *supra* n.16, at 26, 309–12 (and more generally at 23–39).

[125] Discussed and rejected in my *Theft in Early Jewish Law* (Oxford: The Clarendon Press, 1972), 204–06.

and in the night he is as a thief.
In the dark they dig through houses;
by day they shut themselves up;
they do not know the light.

This indicates that nocturnal activity was the primary image of acting like a thief. Exodus 22:2 did not have to make that explicit: it was part of the narrative image evoked by the words.

As regards decision-making, it may be tempting to suggest that many of the thirty talmudic instances of decision-making "not in accordance with the *Halakhah*" collected and analyzed by Ben-Menahem,[126] may repay analysis in this light. And indeed, some of them bear substantive comparison with *Riggs* v. *Palmer*, insofar as a party is penalized for immoral conduct which is technically legally valid.[127] More generally, it is not easy to elicit the social understandings underlying the talmudic sources. Later responsa appear to be a more fruitful ground, as in the murder case on which R. Israel b. Ḥayyim of Brunn was asked to advise,[128] and in which a host of socio-religious understandings are explicit. But here we are dealing with the equivalent of a modern "sentencing" decision, in which considerable discretion, within legal parameters, may be given to the judge. Jewish family law, however, continues to use narrative typifications of female behaviour, with social evaluations influencing legal outcomes: "it is better (for a woman) to dwell in grief than to dwell alone" (literally: in widowhood);[129] and the fear that a woman seeking divorce may in fact have "cast her eyes upon another man."[130]

D *The Narrativization of Pragmatics*

It is not only in the spheres of the content of adjudicatory decisions that the notion of narrative typifications comes into play. I have applied it to the secular trial process, distinguishing within it the "story in the trial" from the "story of the trial," the latter manifesting the narrativization of pragmatics.[131] We can ask about the Subject,

126 Ben-Menahem, *Judicial Deviation in Talmudic Law*, *supra* n.18.

127 E.g. "The Case of the Kidnapper" (Babylonian Talmud *Yevamot* 109b, commonly referred to as the Naresh case), discussed at Ben-Menahem, *Judicial Deviation in Talmudic Law*, *supra* n.18, at 41–50; "The Case of the Notorious Robber" (Babylonian Talmud *Baba Kamma* 96b). Ben-Menahem takes the view, however, that the talmudic approach reflected in these sources goes beyond the forms of judicial discretion which Dworkin appears to endorse: *ibid.*, at 155.

128 Text accompanying n.101.

129 *Tav lemeitav* ... first found in the Talmud (e.g. *Yevamot* 118b). On its history, see Shoshana Knol, *Agunah and Ideology* (Deborah Charles Publications for the Agunah Research Unit, University of Manchester, 2011) available at www.manchesterjewishstudies.org/publications/, esp. ch.2.

130 Already in Mishnah Nedarim 11:12. See Knol, *Agunah and Ideology*, *supra* n.129, esp. ch.3. Chapters 4–5 analyze the incidence of these two maxims in modern Israeli rabbinical court decisions (but including a section, at 137–44, on their combined use in six medieval and modern responsa); chapter 6 concludes the book by discussing the extent to which they influence the resolution of divorce cases.

131 Jackson, *Law, Fact and Narrative Coherence*, *supra* n.1, 112–29; Jackson, "Thematisation and the Narrative Typifications of the Law," *supra* n.79, at 187–92; Jackson, *Journey*, *supra* n.1, at 2, 7–8, 14, 19–21.

Performance, and Recognition of each of the plethora of different communicative acts within the trial process. In principle, the same model is applicable to religious institutions and discourse, and to the components of "religious law." Nor is recognition of the speech behavior of participants in any formal legal process restricted to legal modalities. In 1992, a case was reported of an American judge deciding to convict for speeding on the toss of a coin.[132] The case was not appealed, and so the conviction stood as legally valid. However, the judge was subsequently censured by the Judicial Conduct Commissioner of the State of Washington, on a complaint charging him with violating judicial canons governing the integrity of the court, the avoidance of impropriety and the impartial performance of duties.[133] Similarly, in an English case, *R.* v. *Langham and Langham*,[134] the defense appealed on the grounds that the judge "was, or appeared to be, asleep during part of the trial and thus justice was not seen to be done." The Court of Appeal refused the application for leave to appeal on the grounds of lack of evidence that the judge was actually asleep. Nevertheless it commented that if it was true that the judge *appeared* to be asleep, that "was a matter which the court would certainly deplore but was not a sufficient grounds for saying that justice was not seen to be done." Given the essentially private nature of proceedings of rabbinical law courts, official parallels to such adverse social recognitions are unlikely to be found. However, there is much in unofficial media sources deploring judicial behaviour in relation to women, particularly in divorce cases.

E *Authority, Truth, Trust, and Objectivity*

We may turn to semiotics for assistance also in understanding the notion of authority in the legal system. It is part of the competence – *pouvoir-faire* – with which the Subject (whether of the legislative or adjudicatory act) is invested. But what is the appropriate legal modality of recognition of that Subject's act? Normally, we would use the language of validity (the legal appropriation of true). But here as elsewhere, the argument advanced above about the relationship between truth and trust[135] becomes relevant, and is justified by the understanding that *semantics are necessarily mediated via pragmatics*. In short, the legal system cannot objectify itself so as to eliminate the dominance of persons over ideas. Of course, notions of political and legal authority are inculcated through education from an early age. But why do we trust in education? Because we trust our teachers, the delegates of our parents. Is the

132 Reported in the *Canadian Lawyer's Weekly*, April 1992, and discussed in Jackson, *Making Sense in Jurisprudence*, *supra* n.1, 119–21, as a test of an aspect of the legal theory of Kelsen.

133 Sources cited in Jackson, *ibid.*, at 120 n.44.

134 *Criminal Law Review* (1972) 457; discussed in Jackson, *ibid.*, at 119–20 n.43.

135 Text accompanying n.70, see further Jackson, "Trust in(g) Eric," in *As interações sensíveis: Ensaios de sociossemiótica a partir da obra de Eric Landowski*, ed. A. C. de Oliveira (São Paulo: Editions Estação das Letras e Cores e Editora CPS, 2013), 81–100; Jackson, "Philosophy of Law: Secular and Religious," *supra* n.43, at 52–55.

authority of the *gedolim*, regarded as the supreme halakhic scholars of the age, constructed through analysis of their works, or through trusting the judgements of others? Inevitably, for the most part it must be the latter, since intellectual access to such scholarship is restricted.

Modern secular law prides itself on its objectivity. The classic account of how this works is that of the legal philosopher H. L. A. Hart, for whom legal systems were characterized by the "union of primary and secondary rules." "Primary rules" were the rules of substantive law; "secondary rules" were the rules which determined how the legal system worked, and included in particular "rules of recognition" formulated so as to provide a "conclusive affirmative indication" as to whether a purported primary rule was (recognized as) valid or not. This model thus generated the "demonstrability thesis": with little exception, one could always know, objectively, what the law was.[136] One might, perhaps, expect a system of religious law to be even stronger ("more objective," if that were possible). But this turns out, in the case of Jewish law, not to be the case. The end result, in my view, is that the system depends on trust rather than truth, and what it "demonstrates" is the mediation of semantics via the narrativization of pragmatics.

In the course of a five-year research project which I directed at Manchester[137] on the vexed, practical problem of the "chained wife" (*agunah*) whose husband refuses to cooperate with the court in granting his wife a divorce (a *get*), thereby preventing her remarriage and rendering adulterous any subsequent relationship into which she may enter and the children thereof "illegitimate" (*mamzerim*), we discovered that what modern legal philosophers call the "rules of recognition" of the legal system remain, in Jewish law, subject to significant controversy. This, we found,[138] applied to (1) the rule of majority decision itself (often regarded as the most basic "secondary rule" of Jewish law); (2) the rule that, as amongst post-talmudic authorities, later opinions are followed in preference to earlier ones (*hilkheta kebatra'ei*), but leaving a *discretion* to the contemporary judge not to follow the later authority when that the latter's decision might have been different had he been aware of a (later discovered) earlier authority; (3) uncertainties also exist in such areas as the status of newly discovered MS sources; (4) the status and identification of the "leading authorities of the day" (*gedoley hador*).

Indeed, doubts as to what is authoritative in the system are so extensive that a (creative) doctrine of doubts has developed, granting *discretion* to be lenient in various types of case given the existence of different levels of doubt (*safeq*): a single doubt relating to an issue of rabbinic status is sufficient to justify exercising leniency;

136 On all this, see Jackson, *Making Sense in Jurisprudence*, *supra* n.1, at ch.7, including the extent to which Hart ultimately modified his view in the light of Dworkin's critique and his assertion that the legal system includes principles as well as rules.

137 See www.manchesterjewishstudies.org/agunah-research-unit/ with downloadable publications from its Publications page. See also Jackson, "Philosophy of Law: Secular and Religious," *supra* n.43, at 50–52.

138 For a summary, see Jackson, *Journey*, *supra* n.1, §IV.7. On point (i) see also text at n.42, *supra*.

a single doubt relating to an issue of biblical status is not sufficient to justify exercising leniency, but a double doubt is sufficient.[139] Yet reliance on these rules regarding doubt is discretionary. In the absence of any universally accepted central rabbinic authority, different rabbinic courts will exercise that discretion in different ways. Some may even deny that the discretion exists. Can there then be any objectively correct answer in such a situation? Despite the continuing endorsement by some influential rabbinic voices of a positivist-inspired objectivity, the better answer – and one, I would maintain, itself supported by Jewish tradition – is that the *halakhah* is based at least as much on the concept of trust[140] as on that of truth.[141]

We should not, moreover, assume a universal conception of "truth." The Rabbi, philosopher and theologian Steven Schwarzschild wrote: "In Judaism truth is primarily an ethical notion: it describes not what is but what ought to be,"[142] citing the association of truth with ethical notions in the Bible[143] and rabbinic literature.[144] Hermann Cohen designated the normative unity of cognition and ethics as "the fundamental law of truth."[145] And Martin Buber is said to have identified faith (*emunah*[146]) with truth, here conceived as interpersonal trust.[147] And such conceptions derive support from classical rabbinic sources, as is shown by the already cited[148] talmudic passage where a heavenly voice (*bat qol*) affirms apparently contradictory opinions of the rival rabbinic schools of Hillel and Shammai (*Erubin* 13b) in the words "these and these are the words of the living God," but concludes that in practice one should follow the views of the School of Hillel. The Talmud then asks: "what was it that entitled Beth Hillel to have the *halakhah* fixed in agreement with their rulings? – Because they were kindly and modest, they

139 See n.43, *supra*.

140 See the conclusion to Jackson, *Constructing*, *supra* n.1, at 24–25.

141 Whether the attribute of "truth" may be attached to legal propositions is discussed, in the secular context, by A. Pintore, *Il Diritto Senza Verità* (Torino: Giappichelli, 1996), translated as *Law without Truth* (Liverpool: Deborah Charles Publications, 2000).

142 S. Schwarzschild, "Truth," *Encyclopedia Judaica* (Jerusalem: Keter, 1973), XV.1414–15, at 1414. See further Jackson, "Some Preliminary Observations . . . ," *supra* n.49, at 201–02.

143 Peace (*Zechariah* 8:16), righteousness (*Malachi* 2:6ff.), grace (*Genesis* 24:27, 49), justice (*Zechariah* 7:9), and even salvation (*Psalms* 25:4ff.).

144 *Mishnah Avot* 1:18, "The world rests on three things – truth, justice, and peace."

145 H. Cohen, *Ethik des reinen Willens* (Berlin: B. Cassirer, 1904), ch.1.

146 *emunah* is frequently attributed to God in Jewish liturgy. In context, it clearly refers to human perception of God's trustworthiness, rather than to human adherence to any abstract truth-claim. Does this sell out any "hard" conception of truth? In the theological context, the believer may reasonably say: "My belief that X is true is based on my faith in the truthfulness / trustworthiness of my source of information (God), which is far more reliable than any attempt I might make at independent confirmation" (thus explicitly mediating semantics via a narrativized pragmatics). See further text accompanying n.161.

147 Schwarzschild, *supra* n.142, at 1415. See M. Buber, *Two Types of Faith* (London: Routledge & Paul, 1951), 7–12. On Buber's non-referential conception of truth, and its relation to the I-Thou relationship, see E. Levinas, "Martin Buber and the Theory of Knowledge," in *The Philosophy of Martin Buber*, ed. P. A. Schilpp (London: Cambridge University Press, 1967), 133–50, at 141–44.

148 See text accompanying n.49.

studied their own rulings and those of Beth Shammai, and were even so [humble] as to mention the action of Beth Shammai before theirs."

Though my conclusion regarding the relationship between truth or trust was arrived at largely through the above research project on contemporary Jewish divorce law, there is reason to suspect its pertinence also to secular law. Critical theorists have long maintained that the objectivity of the legal system is an ideological construction, designed to preserve while concealing the play of power, through invoking logic and in other ways.[149] Dworkin's invocation of Hercules as a "lawyer of superhuman skill, learning, patience and acumen"[150] may appear to be a giveaway, but even Hercules seeks to base trust in himself on rationality rather than intuition or other personal characteristics. But there are good semiotic reasons to prioritize trust: trust is an interpersonal relationship, thus integrally involved in pragmatics; truth (on the Saussurean approach to reference) is merely a claim, which must take account also of the narrativization of pragmatics.

F *The Medium: Orality and Literacy*

No semiotic account may properly ignore the media through which the message is communicated. Even where this is language, there remains an important distinction between orality and literacy. There are (associated) diachronic and cognitive aspects to the relationship, as seen in the important work of Walter Ong and Basil Bernstein.[151] We can trace the process by which oral norms of behaviour increasingly assume a literary form. In the Bible itself, Daube pointed to what is there an unusual feature of drafting. *Num.* 35:16–19 commences: "But if he struck him down with an instrument of iron, so that he died, he is a murderer; the murderer shall be put to death." As far as the (punitive) consequences ("recognition") of the act of striking are concerned, "he is a murderer" (*rotseax hu*) is logically redundant,[152] although verse 19 does add a further consequence of being "a murderer," allowing the avenger of blood to kill him when he meets him. So we have here a classification of the act, or more accurately the actor, to which a further normative consequence is attached. Daube called it the "diagnosis form," on the analogy of medicine.[153] Similarly, in

[149] Jackson, *Law, Fact and Narrative Coherence*, *supra* n.1, 180–90.

[150] Dworkin, *Taking Rights Seriously*, *supra* n.10, at 105.

[151] See in general Walter Ong, *Orality and Literacy* (London and New York: Methuen, 1982), and especially his concept of the "oral residue" in literacy; Basil Bernstein, *Class, Codes and Control* (London: Routledge and Kegan Paul, 1971), for his distinction between "restricted" and "elaborated" codes. See further Jackson, *Studies in the Semiotics of Biblical Law*, *supra* n.1, 71–75; *Making Sense in Law*, *supra* n.1, 77–88, 93–94.

[152] Cf. the famous argument of Alf Ross in his "realist" critique of legal concepts: "Tu-Tu," *Harvard Law Review* 70 (1957), 778–81; see further Jackson, *Making Sense in Jurisprudence*, *supra* n.1, 141–49.

[153] David Daube, "Some Forms of Old Testament Legislation," *Proceedings of the Oxford Society of Historical Theology* (1944), 39–43; David Daube, *Ancient Jewish Law* (Leiden: E.J. Brill, 1981), 100–06; Jackson, *Studies in the Semiotics of Biblical Law*, *supra* n.1, 49–51, 95–96.

commenting[154] on the development from the use of verbal forms ("if a man steals") to nominal forms, particularly the use of "action nouns,"[155] Daube, observed: "there has been some reflection on the activity in question, there is some trend towards instruction, systematisation, classification, perhaps, and the thing is becoming more of an institution" while stressing that such a development was by no means restricted to law but rather characterizes "much of the intellectual history of civilization."[156] But then, we must ask, *cui bono*? In whose discourse (in which "semiotic group") is such a development useful? We very quickly arrive at the (surely, obvious) conclusion that there is no single "legal" discourse: we need to distinguish between laity and professionals, and indeed subgroups within each.

One consequence of this is that there is no single, or privileged, form of "legal" interpretation. The closer a written text may be to its oral (social) origins, the more important the "oral residue" which remains submerged, in the form of "narrative typifications of action." It is not that the written form necessarily "defines" such typifications; rather, such typifications may be evoked by example.[157] This requires a different form of reading/understanding from that of modern law. In particular, there is no warranty whatsoever for applying the logic of "necessary and sufficient conditions" ("If" = "if and only if"). Rather, it becomes a matter of assessing the *relative similarity* of other cases to that offered in the text and to judge the utility of deciding similarly.[158] To take an example from my recent work on the Book of Ruth: the institution of levirate may be typified by Deuteronomy's "when brothers live together … " (Deut. 25:5) but should certainly not be restricted to that situation.

VII CONCLUSIONS[159]

In one important respect, our semiotic analysis makes a difference to the way in which we understand the relationship between law and religion, at least as regards religions which include a doctrine of revelation. The starting point of the narrative syntagm, the "Contract," involves the construction of a (human) subject, who in the legal context may be legislator or judge. In each case, it presupposes the transfer, through communicative means, of a "competence." For orthodox Judaism, the

154 David Daube, *Roman Law, Linguistic, Social and Philosophical Aspects* (Edinburgh: Edinburgh University Press, 1969), 11–63.

155 E.g. *gezel* for robbery; *genevah* and *gezelah* in the Bible referred to the property stolen or robbed. See further Jackson, *Studies in the Semiotics of Biblical Law*, *supra* n.1, ch.4, on the development of biblical legal drafting.

156 Daube, *Roman Law*, *supra* n.154, at 11–12.

157 Jackson, "Literal Meaning," *supra* n.6.

158 See further Jackson, *Journey*, *supra* n.1, s.4.2 and esp. nn.105–07; for comparison with Hart, see Jackson, "Trust in(g) Eric," *supra* n.135, at 84–85.

159 See also the methodological implications of this analysis in Jackson, *Journey*, *supra* n.1, §5.2 (at p. 37), first of which is the stress on the separate analysis of each individual discourse, as in the text accompanying n.88 above.

Sender of that competence is God. Revelation (in its various forms)[160] thus cannot be confined to theology;[161] it plays an integral part in the way we make sense of actual legal practices. Of course, human understanding of God as the source of revelation requires, from a semiotic point of view, the human attribution of particular modalities of competence and reliability to God, as Subject of the communicative act of revelation. "God" in human discourse is necessarily a human discursive construction, even though in so using it the claim is made that it refers to a real God. The existence of this God, not to mention its nature, is beyond human proof, notwithstanding the (largely anthropomorphic) heuristic devises which we use to get close to it. And essentially the same argument may be applied where "the Law" is personified as the Sender.

A sceptic may wish to go no further, and say that much of the "religious" discourse is an exercise in fictions. But even if we accept that human language cannot "refer" (in the strict sense) to matters which are not sensory and about which deictic (in the strict sense) statements cannot be made, this cannot prove the non-existence of such phenomena, any more than positive statements about them can prove their existence. On this argument, truth cannot be established by discursive means, even though the credibility or force of such statements can be explained in terms of interpersonal trust.

But there are issues where the tension is more acute. Take the example of a "cultural Jew," brought up in a household of moderate observance, who continues to observe some of the rituals, such as the Pesach seder, but without any sense of religious obligation. How do we characterize such a practice? Do we recognize it through the modality of "religious" or not? And can we make that judgment independent of the religious politics of any particular community (or semiotic group)? I am reminded, in this context, of the famous observation of Maimonides (in what appears to be its most authentic version) in relation to the eschatological fate of Noahides. They do merit the world to come, says Maimonides, but only if their observance of the Noahide commands is because they believe that they were given by God; otherwise, such Noahides (who observe those commands because of their rationality) may be regarded only as wise men.[162] All the more so, it may be argued, in relation to cultural Jews? But they too have an internal point of view, that of their own semiotic group, and if that group qualifies such behaviour as "Jewish," even if not as "religious," who are we to quarrel with the sense of Jewish identity

160 Not merely, for Judaism, the revelation of the Torah to Moses (including, for Orthodoxy, the Oral Torah), but also the charismatic inspiration attributed to the early judges (see 2 *Chronicles* 19:6, text at n.17, *supra*), which we may regard as a prototype of the original form of *semikhah*, together with prophecy, the "heavenly voice" (*bat kol*), and recourse to divination via the *urim* and *thumim*, or to the ordeal by bitter waters in Num. 5 (which the rabbis essentially abolished).

161 Contrast the view of Elon, as quoted in n.15, *supra*.

162 Laws of Kings 8:11. See Jacob Dienstag, "Natural Law in Maimonidean Thought and Scholarship (*On Mishneh Torah, Kings, VIII.11*)," *The Jewish Law Annual* VI (1987), 64–74, at 65f., on the textual issue.

which they construct? That, I may observe, was certainly the approach adopted by the late Justice Haim Cohn in the Shalit case and in his (wonderful) dissenting judgment in the case of Oswald Rufeisin ("Brother Daniel!").[163]

The overall effect of the argument of this paper may be a simple affirmation, at least in the following sense: the basics of sense construction, as understood by the Greimasian model, are the same for both law and religion. At the same time, the model allows for the identification of differences. But it also problematizes the value of the concepts themselves: who, we may ask, needs to talk about either "law" or "religion" as such? – a very different question from that of the characterization of particular acts or norms as "legal" or "religious." "Law As Religion: Religion As Law" is thus a secondary (or meta-) question addressing the relationship between institutional concepts rather than human behaviour in either its factual or normative dimensions. It may, however, figure large in the rhetoric of religious politics, whose full understanding requires us to narrativize the pragmatics (speech behaviour) of its participants.

[163] See text accompanying n.122.

6

Canonicity As a Defining Feature of Legal and Religious Discourse

A Programmatic Essay

Daniel Reifman

I INTRODUCTION

The theme of this volume – the affinity between law and religion – may be productively analyzed at a range of resolutions, from a microhistorical focus on specific religio-legal phenomena, to a broader perspective on how law and religion interact within particular societies or cultures, to an overarching comparison of law and religion as cultural discourses. However, the broader the scope of the analysis, the more pressing the issue of methodology becomes. Specific phenomena may be examined using any number of academic disciplines (history, sociology, cultural studies, gender or race studies, etc.), while a broader analysis demands a sure grasp of philosophy of religion, philosophy of law, or both. At its most all-encompassing, a study of the affinity between law and religion requires a methodology distinct from both philosophy of law and of religion which is able to analyze both fields using a single set of tools.

The field of semiotics is particularly well suited to this task, as it offers a technically precise definition of a discourse which can serve as a model for both religion and law. Following a brief survey of key concepts in semiotic theory, we will analyze some of the distinctive features of legal and religious discourse and then narrow our focus to an important feature that they share, namely their conservative character. Our goal is to develop a methodological framework for analyzing this common feature of law and religion. We will define conservativism in terms of the general properties of semiotic systems, and argue that this characteristic is an intrinsic feature of both religion and law, rather than a function of particular social or cultural circumstances.

II DEFINING DISCOURSES

The proper subject of semiotics is the sign – any discrete, repeatable representational form. A sign may be simple, which is to say irreducible – a phoneme, a letter, a physical movement; or it may be compound, which to say composed of smaller sign-units – a statement, a text, a ritual, a painting or photographic image. One of the key principles of semiotics is that meaning is not inherent in the form of the sign, but rather the product of relationships between signs. (Umberto Eco proffers that "properly speaking there are not signs, but only *sign-functions*."[1]) Hence an important aspect of semiotic analysis is the way that the meaning of any sign is determined by the *system* of signs within which it is situated. Language is one example of a semiotic system, but any system that conveys information through the medium of discrete, repeatable forms may be treated as the object of semiotic analysis. Semiotics is relevant to law not only because it is articulated using language, but more fundamentally because legal systems consist of a range of physical forms – terms, texts, images, practices, and procedures – which generate meaning and facilitate communication. The same is true of religion, science, the arts, or other material cultures – any of the systems of meaning that constitute human society.

An essential aspect of any sign system is the fact that its structure is that of a *network* rather than a hierarchy. Ferdinand de Saussure posits that sign systems generate meaning through patterns of difference between the component signs of the system, and it is only these patterns which divide the amorphous mass of semiotic space is into discrete units of signification. Thus, the most basic element of a sign's meaning is its *value* – its position within the semiotic network, as defined by the way its semantic range is demarcated from that of other signs in that network.[2] As Eco explains, semiotic values issue from within the system itself; "they are not defined in terms of their content . . . but in terms of the way in which they are opposed to other elements of the system and of the position which they occupy within it."[3]

While Saussure demonstrates the concept of value with regard to simple signs, such as phonemes and words, later semioticians such as A. J. Greimas, Julia Kristeva, and Michel Foucault explain that compound signs are also defined by their position within a network of similar signs. The difference between simple and compound signs is that a compound sign invariably has at least two layers of meaning, the first determined by the rules of a particular code regarding the combination of individual units, the second determined by the sign's position within the network of other compound signs within which it is situated. Foucault articulates the difference between these two layers in his distinction between a sentence and what he refers to as a "statement" (*énoncé*):

> [T]here is no statement in general, no free, neutral independent statement . . . : it is always part of a network of statements, in which it has a role, however minimal it may be, to play. Whereas grammatical construction needs only elements and rules in order to operate . . . the same cannot be said of the statement. There is no statement that does not presuppose others; there is no statement that is not surrounded by a field of coexistences, effects of series and succession, a distribution of

1 Umberto Eco, *A Theory of Semiotics* (Bloomington: Indiana University Press, 1976), 49 (emphasis in original).

2 *Course in General Linguistics*, eds. Charles Bally and Albert Sechehaye, trans. Roy Harris (Chicago: Open Court, 1983), 110–20.

3 Ibid., 73.

> functions and roles. If one can speak of a statement, it is because a sentence (a proposition) figures at a definite point, with a specific position, in an enunciative network that extends beyond it.[4]

Analyzed as a sentence, a series of words derives its meaning from the grammatical rules of a given language; analyzed as a statement, the same series of words derives its meaning from its position within a network of other statements – what Foucault refers to as an "enunciative field" or simply as a discourse.[5] Foucault's model thus explains how a given sentence may take on a range of meanings beyond its "literal" (i.e., grammar-determined) meaning depending on the discourse within which it is situated. At the risk of oversimplifying, we may say that semiotics as a field takes the set of tools designed to analyze language and uses them to analyze higher level discourses,[6] a discourse being nothing more than a structured network of compound signs. This is an important aspect of Kristeva's celebrated concept of intertextuality: the meaning of a literary text is determined not only by its internal structure but also by its relationship to other texts within a literary canon.[7]

Semiotics provides not only a technical definition of a discourse, but also an explanation of what it means for two discourses to be distinct from one another. Consider the relationship between law and morality, two discourses with a particularly complicated relationship. It is tempting to think of law and morality as part of an integrated normative system, in which moral precepts function as the overarching principles for legal adjudication – a position that has been articulated in various forms within modern legal theory.[8] Yet it is obvious

4 Michel Foucault, *The Archaeology of Knowledge*, trans. A. M. Sheridan Smith (New York: Pantheon, 1972), 99.

5 "[T]he term discourse can be defined as the group of statements that belong to a single system of formation; thus I shall be able to speak of clinical discourse, economic discourse, the discourse of natural history, psychiatric discourse;" ibid., 107–08.

6 This is not to imply that language is necessarily a paradigmatic semiotic system, only that it serves as a useful reference point due to its ubiquity. The question of whether language constitutes the primary semiotic system is in fact a topic of debate among semioticians. For opposing viewpoints, see Umberto Eco, "Peirce's Notion of Interpretant," *MLN* 91 (1976): 1457–72; and Émile Benveniste, "The Semiology of Language," in *Semiotics: An Introductory Anthology*, ed. Robert E. Innis (Bloomington: Indiana University Press, 1985), 226–46.

7 Julia Kristeva, "Word, Dialogue and Novel" in *Desire in Language: A Semiotic Approach to Literature and Art*, ed. Leon S. Roudiez, trans. Thomas Gora, Alice Jardine & Leon S. Roudiez (New York: Columbia University Press, 1980), 64–91.

8 The question whether one can define law as independent from morality was famously the subject of a debate between Lon Fuller and H. L. A. Hart. Fuller ("Reason and Fiat in Case Law," *Harvard Law Review* 59 [1946]: 376–95; "Positivism and Fidelity to Law: A Reply to Professor Hart," *Harvard Law Review* 71 [1958]: 630–72) argued that morality is necessary to provide content to the form of law, while Hart ("Positivism and the Separation of Law and Morals," *Harvard Law Review* 71 [1958]: 593–629; *The Concept of Law* [Oxford: Oxford University Press, 1961]) countered that law need not always correlate with morality. Ronald Dworkin followed Fuller's position on the necessary connection between law and morality, and incorporated this into a comprehensive theory of legal adjudication; " The Model of Rules," *University of Chicago Law Review* 35 (1967): 14–46; *Law's Empire* (Cambridge, MA: Harvard University Press, 1986).

that we frequently assign different moral and legal values to the same action: an act can be morally good but legally prohibited, or morally wrong but legally permissible. In contrast, an act cannot have two antithetical values within the same system: it cannot be simultaneously legal and illegal, or moral and immoral.[9] Hence to conflate law and morality with one another is to undermine a basic dimension of what it means for something to have legal or moral significance.

We can make the same point with regard to the relationship between religion and science. Peter Berger notes that if one defines religion (following Thomas Luckman) as reflecting the "human capacity for self-transcendence," one could conceive of modern science as a sort of religion.[10] Yet Berger rejects this as patently unhelpful, since "[i]f one does that, one is subsequently forced to define in what way modern science is *different* from what has been called religion by everyone else."[11] To wit, we instinctively categorize certain types of propositions about the world as scientific and others as religious. The discourses of religion and science constitute different sets of values (again in the semiotic sense of the term) that do not always correlate with one another.[12]

It is important to state that our concise definition of a discourse does not do justice to the vast internal complexity of each of the discourses we have mentioned. Any

9 This is not to say that there is never uncertainty or debate about what the legal or moral value of an action is, rather that states of uncertainty or debate are recognized as *failures* to assign value to that action. Below we will propose that moral discourse leaves much more room for such indecisiveness than does legal discourse.

10 The same could be said of many other definitions of religion, including the influential definition offered by Clifford Geertz that we will return to below.

11 Peter Berger, *The Sacred Canopy: Elements of a Sociological Theory of Religion* (Garden City, NY: Doubleday, 1969), 177.

12 We should acknowledge that the very notion of defining religion as a system of *meaning* has been challenged, notably by Talal Asad, who insists that "religion as practice, language, and sensibility set in social relationships rather than as systems of meaning": "Religious language – like all language – is interwoven with life itself. To define 'religion' is therefore in a sense to try and grasp an ungraspable totality. ...[D]efinitions of religion are embedded in dialogs, activities, relationships, and institutions ..." (Craig Martin, "*Genealogies of Religion*, Twenty Years On: An Interview with Talal Asad," *Bulletin for the Study of Religion* 43 [2014], 13–14).

See also Asad's oft-cited essay, " The Construction of Religion as an Anthropological Category," in *Genealogies of Religion: Discipline and Reasons of Power in Christianity and Islam* (Baltimore: Johns Hopkins University Press, 1993), 27–54.

I suggest that Asad's critique reflects an excessively narrow association of religious "meaning" with "belief." The model of semiotics we have proposed suggests a far broader conception of meaning, in which every form that facilitates cognition and communication may be analyzed as a sign. Hence all the various elements that Asad mentions – including those social practices and institutions necessary for the exercise of power (which Asad sees as integral to a proper understanding of religion) – derive their religious significance from their position within a complex network of signs. (Below we will propose that any semiotic network that we consider to be religious must *also* include certain propositions that we refer to as "beliefs.") Asad's description of religion as "an ungraspable totality" reflects the fact that religion – like all sign systems – is nothing more than the amalgam of many individual signs. Semiotics is precisely the study of how such amalgams function as coherent and discrete systems notwithstanding their fragmentary nature.

legal, religious, moral, or scientific system is made up of many different types of signs – not only spoken and written language, but also actions (practices, procedures, rituals, etc.) and two- or three-dimensional representational forms: art, architecture, food, clothing, etc. Even if we limit our definition of "discourse" specifically to linguistic elements, we are still faced with an enormous variety of terms, statements, texts, and formulae that are part of any cultural system. That is to say, closer analysis reveals each of these discourses to be further divided and subdivided into countless smaller networks of signs.[13] A fuller analysis of such internal divisions is beyond the scope of this study. However, below we will argue for the heuristic value of a simplified schematic of each of these discourses notwithstanding their internal complexity.

We should also note that value is only one element of a sign's meaning, reflecting the *oppositional* relationships between signs. Cultural scholars have often focused exclusively on the semiotic structures created by these oppositional relationships (hence the movement known as structuralism), thereby preventing a full appreciation of what semiotics has to offer to the study of human culture. After all, much of the semiotic functioning of cultural discourses – the way representational forms generate meaning and facilitate communication – comes from *positive* relationships between signs,[14] what Charles Sanders Peirce aptly describes as "the translation of a sign into another system of signs."[15] We will not address this dimension of semiotic theory, since this chapter is less concerned with the way individual discourses function as systems of meaning than with the differences between distinct discourses and their positions relative to one another within the broader array of contemporary society.

III THE SEMIOTIC CONCEPT OF CANONICITY

The notion that meaning is dependent on a network of individual signs affects how we analyze the *evolution* of languages and other discourses over time. One of Saussure's major contributions to linguistics was his insistence that language must be studied first and foremost synchronically as a network of mutually defining signs before it can be analyzed diachronically. This is not because languages are static (they are not), but rather because "language is a system of pure values, determined by nothing else apart from the temporary state of its constituent elements."[16] That is to say, from a semiotic perspective, any system of meaning is *all* structure; without

[13] See Yuri Lotman's discussion in *Universe of the Mind: A Semiotic Theory of Culture*, trans. Ann Shukman (London: I.B. Tauris, 2001), 138.

[14] On this point, see Robert A. Yelle's critique of earlier applications of semiotics to the study of religion; *Semiotics of Religion: Signs of the Sacred in History* (London: Continuum, 2012), 9–12, 24–26.

[15] *Collected Papers of Charles Sanders Peirce*, vol. 4, eds. C. Hartshorne and P. Weiss (Cambridge, MA: Harvard University Press, 1933), §127; quoted in Roman Jakobson, "A Few Remarks on Structuralism," *MLN* 91 (1976): 1537.

[16] Saussure, *Course in General Linguistics*, 80.

a clear picture of the patterns of difference among the components of the system at a given point in time, there is no "thing" to analyze. Thus the existence of any language or higher-level discourse necessarily depends on there being an accumulated body of signs to constitute it and to ensure its stability over time. For the same reason, Saussure insisted that linguistic evolution can be analyzed only in terms of changes to individual elements, not to the system as a whole: in order to for us to able to speak of change to the system, the structure that *is* the system cannot be destabilized.[17]

This property of semiotic systems – the fact that signs must inhere within the system in order for it to function – is an important aspect of what we refer to as *canonicity*. We often speak of a canon in terms of a set of *exemplary* units in a specific discourse: a body of outstanding works of literature or art, a collection of cases and statutes that are most often cited or studied in legal contexts,[18] a set of iconic experiments in scientific discourse.[19] In contrast, canonicity in the sense we are using it is a property of *all* units of a semiotic system: once a sign is accepted as an element of the system – a word is recognized as meaningful within a given language, a ruling is endorsed as legally authoritative, an experiment is recognized as scientifically significant – it becomes part of the internal structure of that system, and tends to inhere within it over time. Moshe Halbertal has referred to this as "formative canonicity," the way that terms and texts that have already been incorporated into a discourse continue to be "taught, read, transmitted, and interpreted" over time, effectively functioning as the "shared vocabulary" of a given society or profession.[20] In effect, the property of canonicity changes the shape of a semiotic system in relation to the axis of time: even when signs enter the system at different points in its history, their relationship to one another may be analyzed synchronically so long as they are in use at the same time. As Krsiteva explains regarding the significance of a literary canon, "Diachrony is transformed into synchrony, and in light of this transformation, linear history appears as abstraction."[21]

Our use of the term canonicity to refer to the way that semiotic systems retain their constituent elements over time is different than the way the term has been defined elsewhere in contemporary scholarship. For instance, Jonathan Z. Smith defines a religious canon as a structured catalog of religious objects or texts that has undergone "closure," which inevitably leads to its interpretation and application

17 Ibid., 79–98.

18 See Jack Balkin and Sanford Levinson, eds., *Legal Canons* (New York: NYU Press, 2000).

19 Thomas Kuhn explains that this is one sense in which we speak of "scientific paradigms": specific instances of particular scientific phenomena "which, employed as models or examples, can replace explicit rules as a basis for the solution of the remaining puzzles of normal science"; *The Structure of Scientific Revolutions*, 3rd ed. (Chicago: University of Chicago Press, 1996), 175.

20 Moshe Halbertal, *People of the Book: Canon, Meaning, and Authority* (Cambridge, MA: Harvard University Press, 1997), 3.

21 Kristeva, "Word," *supra* note 7, 65.

to a much broader range of phenomena.[22] Smith is certainly correct that the concept of canon is integral to the use of a set of signs as the basis for a far-reaching exegetical agenda. Yet his association of canonicity with closure is too simplistic: it is true that the initial process of canon-formation requires some sort of closure, roughly meaning a distinction between those forms that are "in" and those that are not, but there are many systems that we think of as canons that do not remain closed, and continue to accrue additional forms over time. For example, a canon of legal texts – those texts that are considered authoritative for legal practice and adjudication – may be expanded though various processes of recognition (executive or legislative actions, judicial rulings, etc.), some of which are invariably part of any legal system.[23] What distinguishes canons is not their closure to new elements, but rather their tendency to retain their constituent elements once they have been inducted.

While this tendency to retain sign elements is a defining characteristic of systems that we think of as paradigmatically canonical, the fact that any semiotic system depends on the existence of an accumulated body of signs indicates that *all* such systems must have this tendency to some extent; to wit, canonicity as we have defined it is a universal semiotic property, albeit a *variable* property. Strongly canonical discourses are *conservative* in the sense that existing elements to the system are preserved: they tend not to be displaced by new additions to the system nor do they become obsolete on their own. Weakly canonical discourses, on the other hand, may be characterized as *progressive*, in the sense that the component signs of those systems are frequently – and often actively – either displaced by new signs or simply discarded. However, even weakly canonical discourses are far more conservative than we normally assume them to be. To take the example that is the subject of Saussure's own work, language is not a system of meaning that we normally think of as canonical, and indeed it tends to be progressive in the way that it jettisons words and grammatical features over time: even texts from fifty years ago frequently strike us as dated. Yet the concept of formative canonicity accurately expresses the fact that the vast majority of any given language remains extremely stable over time, and *must* remain stable in order for the language to function. Saussure ascribes the inflexibility of language to a number of factors, among them the size and complexity of the networks of relationships between signs, as well as the large number of members of the linguistic community who use them. But regardless, he concludes that language's potential for change is appreciable only from a longitudinal perspective.[24]

Just as the essential property of canonicity is an inevitable corollary of the mechanisms by which semiotic systems operate, so, too, we may propose that the *degree* of canonicity of a given semiotic system is determined by its specific semiotic function, the particular type of meaning it generates. The central claim that we will

22 Jonathan Z. Smith, "Sacred Persistence: Toward a Redescription of Canon," in *Imagining Religion: From Babylon to Jonestown* (Chicago: University of Chicago Press, 1982), 44–52.

23 Hart, *The Concept of Law*, *supra* note 8, 97–120.

24 Saussure, *Course in General Linguistics*, 71–74.

make in this chapter is that legal and religious systems are strongly canonical relative to other human discourses (language, the arts, material culture, science, and morality), and that this aspect of law and religion stems from the essential character of these discourses rather than from contingent factors, such as the political functions that these systems often serve. Obviously we do not mean to say that political authority is irrelevant to the dynamics of religion or law; on the contrary, authoritative bodies are frequently decisive in the process by which religious or legal signs become formally recognized. However, we will propose that once a sign has been integrated into a legal, religious, or any other discourse, its longevity is largely independent of that authority, and dependent instead on the specific character of that discourse and its broader, apolitical function within human society.

In and of itself, the notion that law and religion are conservative discourses is admittedly rather intuitive. The innovative elements of our analysis are our definition of canonicity as a variable property of all sign systems, and the notion that the degree of canonicity of a given discourse is determined primarily by the kind of meaning it serves to convey rather than by contingent factors such as the presence or absence of institutional authority. Our assertion about the strongly canonical character of law and religion is obviously extremely broad, and probably impossible to defend solely through an accumulation of data. Hence instead of focusing on historical or contemporary examples of legal or religious conservativism, we will take the opposite approach: examining the essential elements of both legal and religious discourse to understand why we would *expect* each of them to retain its constituent elements over time. Our purpose in doing so is not to prove this thesis conclusively, but rather to develop an analytical framework to serve as the basis for future research.

IV A DIGRESSION: TWO METHODOLOGICAL OBJECTIONS

However, before we proceed, we need to address two methodological objections that our analysis may raise. First, is it really possible to generalize about so many different types of religions and legal systems? Surely any system's degree of canonicity is affected by the particular historical context in which it is situated and the specific nature of its component signs. Indeed, given our assumption that canonicity is a variable property of semiotic systems, it would seem reasonable to assume that just as different types of discourses may be strongly or weakly canonical, so, too, different discourses of the same type might not be canonical to the same degree. For example, there may be significant differences in the longevity of different modes of signs – performative (practices and rituals), material (art, architecture, food, clothing, etc.), or verbal signs (words and texts), as well as between oral and written verbal signs. Yet we will propose that these factors are secondary to the overall differences between law and religion on the one hand and other societal discourses on the other, such that religious and legal systems are conservative relative to other discourses within a particular society. If there is one set of contextual parameters that we must place on our analysis, it is that the concept of religion as we will analyze it is distinctive to the modern age, not because modern religion isn't contiguous with premodern systems of meaning, but because the relationship between religion and other societal discourses – or rather the extent to which religion and other discourses can be considered separate from one another – has changed so drastically in the modern era.

A second, more fundamental objection may be articulated as follows: It is a prevalent view in contemporary scholarship that discourses are not anchored in any sort of context-independent foundation, be it rational, epistemic, or metaphysical. From this methodological starting point, some scholars have asserted that in the absence of another basis for discursive meaning, it is only the dynamics of power that provides a given discourse with its substance or legitimacy. The notion that meaning is a function of power has been asserted in philosophy of religion by Talal Asad,[25] in philosophy of science by Paul Feyerabend,[26] and is a prominent strain of thought among critical legal theorists.[27] According to these scholars, it is not possible to describe a set of principles or characteristics that defines these discourses apart from the political structures that utilize them. The thesis we have formulated specifically downplays the significance of political authority in determining the character of these and other discourses, hence prompting the question: in the absence of reason, metaphysics, or even power as the basis for meaning, what factor allows each of these fields to function as a discrete, coherent discourse?

As we suggested above, the key to understanding the way discourses function is the concept of difference, which Saussure posits as the most basic element of meaning. Just as the meaning of individual signs is generated most fundamentally by patterns of difference within a structured network of signs, so, too, individual discourses acquire meaning through patterns of difference between distinct discourses within a broader cultural framework. Our analysis going forward will be devoted to identifying some of the key characteristics that distinguish between different discourses in contemporary society.

The notion that something as firm as meaning is ultimately rooted in something as amorphous as patterns of difference seems deeply counterintuitive. Depending on one's inclination, this makes it either a pivotal contribution of semiotics to critical analysis or a reason to be skeptical of semiotic theory. To readers who find themselves in the latter category, and who might still be inclined to view law, for example, simply as a veiled expression of power, we may note that more nuanced analyses of contemporary legal discourse have complicated the picture painted by critical legal scholars, showing how legal devices may also be used to challenge political authority and protect the disenfranchised.[28] This strongly suggests that the law has an

25 Asad, "Construction of Religion," *supra* note 12.

26 Paul Feyerabend, *Against Method*, 3rd ed. (London: Verso, 1993).

27 For example, see Joseph Singer, "The Player and the Cards," *Yale Law Journal* 94 (1984): 1–70.

28 For a summary of this scholarship, see Jack Balkin, "Critical Legal Theory Today," in *On Philosophy in American Law*, ed. Francis J. Mootz III (Cambridge: Cambridge University Press, 2009), 64–72.

independent dimension of meaning, which in turns allows it to be used for a variety of political ends.

V THE SEMIOTIC CHARACTER OF LEGAL AND RELIGIOUS DISCOURSE

Because semiotics analyzes any discourse as the amalgam of its constituent signs, understanding how discourses such as law or religion function differently from one another requires us to examine the kinds of individual statements and texts that we consider to be legal or religious in nature. Here we return to the problem of the internal complexity of each discourse: How can we characterize the system based on its constituent components if each discourse is comprised of so many different kinds of linguistic forms?

An instructive example for approaching this sort of problem is R. M. Hare's analysis of morality in his book, *The Language of Morals*.[29] Hare's approach is not explicitly semiotic, but he grapples with the same basic difficulty we have outlined here: how to articulate a unified definition of morality given the variety of statements within moral discourse. In the face of a pronounced bias among logicians toward indicative propositions (which can be measured against reality for their truth value), Hare argues that all moral judgments – even those formulated as indicative statements – necessarily entail prescriptive statements insofar as their purpose is to regulate behavior: "to guide choices or actions, a moral judgment must be such that if a person assents to it, he must assent to some imperative sentence derivable from it."[30] To wit, the function of moral discourse can be fulfilled only if ostensibly descriptive phrases are taken as implicitly prescriptive. In effect, Hare reduces the semiotic variety of moral discourse to a single type of form.

In the course of his analysis, Hare addresses two counterarguments for why indicative statements may independently be considered moral propositions. One counterargument is the concept of moral naturalism, broadly speaking the idea that moral values are a function of the natural world, or at least of human nature, such that morality may be reduced to a set of indicative statements about what is "good" or "right." Hare makes a compelling case that such statements are never merely descriptions of an ontological state, since the terms "good" and "right" necessarily reflect an evaluative dimension. Less convincing is Hare's analysis of a second type of indicative statement: moral assessments which allude – descriptively – to what others consider to be moral without the speaker herself offering any evaluative judgment. Hare refers to these as "inverted comma moral judgments," and rejects them as genuine value judgments.[31] Yet Hare's critics point out that his definition would exclude from moral discourse any statement by an amoralist, a moral

[29] R. M. Hare, *The Language of Morals* (Oxford: Oxford University Press, 1952).

[30] Ibid., 171.

[31] Ibid., 163–65.

hypocrite, or even a weak-willed individual regarding moral behavior, since none of these individuals are actually committing to the moral standards they describe; to exclude such a wide range of individuals as not true participants in moral discourse seems rather artificial. It is clear that the relationship between indicative and imperative statements within moral discourse is far more complex than Hare makes it out to be.

Nonetheless, Hare's assertion regarding the irreducibly prescriptive nature of morality is hard to dismiss entirely. Even if prescriptive statements cannot be implicated in the meaning of every individual moral proposition, we may conclude that they are essential to the semiotic constitution of moral discourse as a whole: the type of meaning we associate with any discourse called "morality" requires it to include a set of directly prescriptive statements, even as it may also include descriptive statements.[32] The relationship between these essential prescriptive statements and other, descriptive, statements is not one that can be reduced to logical deduction, or even one-to-one correspondence, but Hare is correct that a purely descriptive system cannot serve the basic function that morality does, namely to regulate human behavior. To wit, to claim that a certain statement has no prescriptive implications for anyone is to remove it from the realm of moral discourse. This formulation makes no claim about the source or basis for morality; it simply expresses how language we regard as moral operates as a system of meaning and communication.

This analysis provides a model for a simplified analysis of other types of discourses. For example, even though legal discourse, too, involves many different types of statements, we may say that law is irreducibly prescriptive in the sense that a set of directly prescriptive statements regulating human behavior – what H. L. A. Hart refers to as primary rules – is a necessary (though perhaps not sufficient) characteristic for a discourse to be called "law."[33] Alternately, if we follow Lon Fuller's thought experiment of an embryonic society developing social institutions *de novo* (he imagines a group of castaways afflicted by collective amnesia),[34] we might consider even a rudimentary regulatory system – consisting solely of directly prescriptive statements about the kind of behavior permitted, obligated, or prohibited in that society – to be identifiable as "law." Again, this analysis does not address the source or basis for the law, only the minimum necessary conditions for legal language to be meaningful: all legal statements that are not directly prescriptive are in some sense dependent for their meaning on directly prescriptive statements.

32 James Lenman articulates this point especially well: "The making of inverted commas moral judgements is clearly *parasitical* on the making of genuine moral judgements but not *vice versa* ... That is why we *cannot* imagine a world in which the only kind of moral judgements ever made are inverted commas moral judgments" (emphasis in original); " Moral Naturalism," *The Stanford Encyclopedia of Philosophy* (Spring 2014 Edition), ed. Edward N. Zalta, https://plato.stanford.edu/archives/spr2014/entries/naturalism-moral/.

33 Hart, *The Concept of Law*, *supra* note 8, 77–88.

34 Lon L. Fuller, "Reason and Fiat in Case Law," *Harvard Law Review* 59 (1946): 377.

Religion presents a more complex problem than law, given the range of systems that we might choose to include under that heading and the variety of modes of expression found within them: there is hardly an aspect of human culture that has not been touched in some way by religion. This complexity is reflected in the wide-ranging (and often amorphous) definitions that have been proposed by philosophers of religion. One may appreciate the sentiment that formulating a concise definition of religion – one that not only describes religion but also demarcates it from other related discourses – is a fool's errand.[35] Yet few would deny that a discourse would not be considered religious without some conception of reality and of humanity's place in it. This point is underscored by one of the most influential definitions of religion, that of Clifford Geertz: "[A] religion is (1) a system of symbols (2) which acts to establish powerful, pervasive and long-lasting moods and motivations in men (3) by *formulating conceptions of a general order of existence* and (4) clothing these conceptions with such an aura of factuality that (5) the moods and motivations seem uniquely realistic."[36] Or to return to our imagined embryonic society, we might consider a rudimentary system of prescriptive statements to be a legal system, but we would not consider it to be a religion unless it also contained a set of *descriptive* statements about our existence.[37] Hence we may define religion as irreducibly descriptive, at least relative to law.

VI CANONICITY IN RELIGION AND SCIENCE

The upshot of delineating religion in this way is that for all of the similarities between religion and law, there are essential aspects of religion that are best appreciated by contrasting it with another irreducibly descriptive discourse, namely science. Scientific discourse, too, consists of many different types of statements, yet it, too, must minimally consist of a set of descriptive statements about the natural world. If religion is strongly canonical in the sense that we defined it above, science constitutes a perfect foil of a descriptive discourse that is weakly canonical: it tends not only to change over time, but to change specifically by *discarding* of elements of the system. The most famous articulation of this idea is Thomas Kuhn's analysis of scientific revolutions as paradigm shifts – the rejection of one conceptual framework in favor of another. But Kuhn's idea merely reflects a broader trend within philosophy of science: since the middle of the last century, scholars have ceased advocating for a strictly cumulative model of scientific development. Rather, scientific progress invariably involves disposing of elements of the regnant paradigm – terms and

35 See William Arnal and Russell T. McCutcheon, *The Sacred Is the Profane: The Political Nature of Religion* (Oxford: Oxford University Press, 2013), 23–27.

36 Clifford Geertz, "Religion as a Cultural System," in *Anthropological Approaches to the Study of Religion*, ed. Michael Banton (London: Tavistock, 2004), 4; emphasis added.

37 This is not to say that beliefs necessarily occupy a privileged place within the structure of religious discourse (e.g., that other manifestations of religion should be seen as deriving from them). Rather, beliefs are especially significant insofar as they distinguish religion from other cultural discourses.

theories, models, experimental procedures, and even observations – that do not fit with new data collected and outstanding problems solved.[38]

The reason for this dynamic of scientific discourse may be attributed to one of the basic functions that science serves, to describe the workings of nature as accurately as possible; any element that does not fill this function is therefore abandoned. But regardless of the reason, the propensity of scientific discourse to discard elements of the system is reflected in the very different outcomes of scientific and religious upheaval. When fundamental elements of a given religion are called into question, it quite frequently results in the founding of a *new* religion, sect, or denomination alongside the old one. In contrast, while challenges to fundamental aspects of a given scientific paradigm invariably meet resistance, challenges which stand the test of time end up *transforming* the field rather than dividing it. Despite the many scientific debates and revolutions that have occurred over the past five hundred years, we still think of the scientific community as overwhelmingly unified (or rather, divided by field of interest rather than by ideology).

The notion that scientific progress is not strictly cumulative was articulated most forcefully by Karl Popper, who identified it as one of the defining elements of science. According to Popper, scientific inquiry is best characterized not by its use of inductive logic but rather by its use of *falsification* as a criterion for validity: "it must be possible for an empirical scientific system to be refuted by experience."[39] It is this element that makes scientific systems so prone to revision and upheaval: "What compels the theorist to search for a better theory ... is almost always the experimental falsification of a theory, so far accepted and corroborated."[40] Popper's proposal has been subject to extensive critique and refinement over the past half century. The most significant revision was offered by Imre Lakatos, who asserts that falsification results in the rejection of a theory only when a new, improved theory (one which "offers any novel, excess information compared with its predecessor")[41] is available to replace it. (He calls this "sophisticated falsificationism."[42]) Moreover, Lakatos maintains that falsifiability is meaningful only in the context of an overall

38 Kuhn's choice to focus specifically on instances of cataclysmic change – leading him to distinguish sharply between "normal" and "revolutionary" science – has been one of the most frequently challenged aspects of his work. Kuhn's critics charge that he underestimates the extent to which significant changes occur within the context of "normal" science – that is to say, without the drastic event of a paradigm shift. For an early articulation of this critique, see Stephen Toulmin, "Does the Distinction between Normal and Revolutionary Science Hold Water?" in *Criticism and the Growth of Knowledge*, eds. Imre Lakatos and Alan Musgrave (Cambridge: Cambridge University Press, 1970), 39–47. The point that we are making – that science is progressive or weakly canonical – does not take a stand on the debate between Kuhn and his critics as to whether scientific change is primarily incremental or abrupt.

39 Karl Popper, *The Logic of Scientific Discovery* (London: Routledge, 2002), 18.

40 Ibid., 90.

41 Imre Lakatos, "Falsification and the Methodology of Scientific Research Programmes," in *Criticism and the Growth of Knowledge: Proceedings of the International Colloquium in the Philosophy of Science*, eds. Imre Lakatos and Alan Musgrave (Cambridge: Cambridge University Press, 1970), 120.

42 Ibid., 116–22.

"research programme," consisting of a "hard core" of theory surrounded by auxiliary hypotheses; it is these auxiliary elements that are most subject to rejection due to falsification.[43] Yet regardless of the weaknesses in Popper's original thesis, it is difficult to deny that he has identified a critical aspect of scientific discourse. Whether we assess falsifiability on the level of an individual theory, a data set, or an integrated research program, a key element of what makes that unit of discourse *meaningful* in a scientific sense – what legitimates it as a point fit for discussion and debate within the scientific community – is the possibility that it will be rejected based on contradictory empirical evidence. Simply put, falsifiability is a property of the kind of meaning that we instinctively associate with modern science, and it is this element of science that makes it weakly canonical.

Popper proposed falsifiability not only as a positive description of scientific inquiry, but also as a criterion to demarcate science from pseudoscientific disciplines, such as Freudian psychoanalysis or Marxist historiography. In this regard, too, Popper's thesis has proven to be insufficient; philosophers of science now doubt that there is a single attribute that we can use to verify a given discipline as a science.[44] Yet again, Popper's thesis captures one important element of what distinguishes science from other disciplines, and particularly from modern religious discourse. A key attribute of many religious propositions – those statements we instinctively identify as religious in character – is that they are fundamentally *un*falsifiable. Although this point is rarely found in formal scholarly definitions of religion, it is famously the subject of Antony Flew's 1950 essay, "Theology and Falsification":

> Now it often seems to people who are not religious as if there was no conceivable event or series of events the occurrence of which would be admitted by sophisticated religious people to be a sufficient reason for conceding "There wasn't a God after all" or "God does not really love us then." Someone tells us that God loves us as a father loves his children. We are reassured. But then we see a child dying of inoperable cancer of the throat. His earthly father is driven frantic in his efforts to help, but his Heavenly Father reveals no obvious sign of concern. Some qualification is made God's love is "not a merely human love" or it is "an inscrutable love," perhaps – and we realize that such sufferings are quite compatible with the truth of the assertion that "God loves us as a father (but, of course . . .)." We are reassured again. But then perhaps we ask: what is this assurance of God's (appropriately qualified) love worth, what is this apparent guarantee really a guarantee against? Just what would have to happen not merely (morally and wrongly) to tempt but also (logically and rightly) to entitle us to say "God does not love us" or even "God does not exist"? I therefore put to the succeeding symposiasts the simple central

43 Ibid., 132–38.

44 For a balanced perspective on this point, see Martin Mahner, "Science and Pseudoscience: How to Demarcate After the (Alleged) Demise of the Demarcation Problem," in *Philosophy of Pseudoscience: Reconsidering the Demarcation Problem*, eds. Massimo Pigliucci and Maarten Boudry (Chicago: University of Chicago Press, 2013), 29–43.

questions, "What would have to occur or to have occurred to constitute for you a disproof of the love of, or of the existence of God?"[45]

Flew's analysis of religion is quite obviously meant to be critical, based on the assumption that falsification is a feature of all rational discourse: "Some theological utterances seem to, and are intended to, provide explanations or express assertions. Now an assertion, to be an assertion at all, must claim that things stand thus and thus; and not otherwise. Similarly an explanation, to be an explanation at all, must explain why this particular thing occurs; *and not something else*."[46]

That is to say, Flew considers an explanation to be substantive only if it can be tested against another possible explanation; he endorses falsificationism (as Lakatos defines it) as a standard for all meaning. Popper himself rejected this point in the same breath that he declared falsifiability central to scientific discourse: recognizing a particular statement as unfalsifiable does not render it meaningless, only meaningful in a different way.[47] The original respondents to Flew's essay, R. M. Hare and Basil Mitchell, demonstrate that human knowledge is comprised of an enormous variety of propositions, many of which, such as expressions regarding one's personal security (or insecurity) or faith in others (or lack thereof), are fundamentally not subject to empirical falsification.[48]

If we turn Flew's critique of religion on its head, we may offer a positive description of religions as systems designed to organize propositions that are not subject to empirical assessment.[49] And while they are hardly the only social systems to serve this function, they are among the most extensive and elaborate systems to do so. As Peter Berger observes, religion is more all-encompassing than other social nomoi in that it is nearly always cosmic in scope.[50] This is a critical point: as we mentioned above, Saussure posits that one of the factors which contributes to the invariability of a language over time – what we have called its canonicity – is the number of signs

45 Reprinted (with the original respondents and Flew's response) as " Theology and Falsification: A Symposium," in *The Philosophy of Religion*, ed. Basil Mitchell (Oxford: Oxford University Press, 1971), 13–22, at 15.

46 Ibid., 21 (emphasis original).

47 Popper, *Scientific Discovery*, *supra* note 39, 18n*3.

48 "Theology and Falsification," *supra* note 45, 15–20.

49 This distinction between falsifiable and unfalsifiable propositions does not lead to any particular approach to how religious signs should be understood. For example, a modern approach to reports of miracles might be to interpret them as psychological rather than epistemic (i.e., concerning knowledge of mind-independent phenomena), or even to view them as metaphors. Yet even those who assert that miracles are manifest in physical reality ascribe them to causes other than falsifiable, scientifically accepted principles.

An important consequence of the non-falsifiable nature of miracles is that the miraculous nature of an event can be established only negatively, by process of elimination. A good example of this is the Catholic Church's procedure of confirming miracles for sake of beatification, which is done by systematically ruling out scientific explanations of the event in question.

50 Berger, *Sacred Canopy*, *supra* note 11, 25–28. Hence insofar as religion is necessarily anthropocentric, it may be described as "the audacious attempt to conceive of the entire universe as being humanly significant" (28).

necessary to constitute the system, yielding a highly complex internal structure based on patterns of difference between the signs. Thus compared to other similar discourses (e.g., pseudosciences, superstitions), we would expect religions to be the least inclined to discard their constituent signs, since religious signs are more tightly enmeshed in the web of relationships that is a semiotic system.

As we indicated above, this division between science and religion is primarily a modern phenomenon. As our ability to make precise and uniform empirical observations has dramatically improved over the past half millennium, the distinction between falsifiable and unfalsifiable propositions has become increasingly relevant in the organization of human knowledge, and falsifiable propositions have coalesced into a distinct discourse with a different dimension of meaning.[51] Yet even if this distinction is contingent to our own historical period, it is critical to understanding the way that science and religion function in relation to one another within our time. The resistance of religion to change has become an increasingly pressing issue in the last generation with the rise of religious fundamentalism on the international stage. The perspective we have proposed explains why religion's resistance to change is inherent to religious discourse as it exists within modern society, rather than merely reflecting external (i.e., social, cultural, or political) forces.

VII CANONICITY IN LAW AND MORALITY

Following our proposal that legal systems be analyzed as irreducibly prescriptive, we may posit that the strong canonicity of law stems from the paramount importance of consistency in legal behavior and adjudication.[52] Consistency is an element of law that has not been well studied within philosophy of law, in part because it is so self-evident (what is a rule if not something applied consistently?), and in part because consistency in-and-of itself does not suffice to explain the many different purposes that law may have. Consistency may reflect the sociological need for order and stability, the religious value of consonance with the divine will or other cosmic forces, or moral concerns such as justice and fairness. But it is eminently clear that all systems that we refer to as "law" share this common feature.

One consequence of legal consistency is the predominance of rigid categories within legal discourse: cases deemed to be similar for purposes of legal behavior are

[51] This description follows Berger's definition of secularization as "the process by which sectors of society and culture are removed from the domination of religious institutions and symbols;" ibid., 107.

[52] One of the few scholars to explicitly discuss the importance of consistency to legal discourse is the German sociologist Niklas Luhmann, who identifies consistency in decision-making as the meaning of justice within modern legal systems; *Law as a Social System*, eds. Fatima Kastner, Richard Nobles, David Schiff and Rosamund Ziegert, trans. Klaus A. Ziegert (Oxford: Oxford University Press, 2004), 219. We are going further than Luhmann in proposing that this consistency is an operative principle of law in general, but a full exploration of Luhmann's distinction between premodern and modern law is beyond the scope of this chapter.

grouped together and assigned the same legal value (permissible/prohibited, obligatory/optional, liable/exempt, guilty/innocent, etc.). However, consistency demands not only that the legal system assign the same value to all similar cases at any one point in time, but also that any given case be treated the same as comparable cases that have been decided previously. This *diachronic* axis of consistency is reflected in the fact that, once established, legal rules are considered to remain in effect until formally amended or overturned (by what H. L. A. Hart refers to as the rules of change),[53] and behavior not governed by legal rules tends to remain ungoverned until formally addressed. Moreover, the way that those legal rules are applied is also expected to remain consistent over time: any legal subject may expect the outcome of her case to be the same as that of equivalent cases in the past. For the same reason, when existing laws are deemed *not* be relevant to the case at hand, law accords significance to an appeal to tradition, convention or the status quo: it is meaningful – though not always decisive – to claim before a legal authority, "But it has always been done this way." In sum, the paramount value of consistency determines that conservativism is hard-wired into the nature of legal discourse, rather than merely a product of the personal intransigence of judges or other legal authorities.

We may underscore this aspect of legal discourse by contrasting it with another irreducibly prescriptive discourse, namely morality. As with religion, the definition of morality is a highly contentious point, but the moral philosopher Bernard Gert convincingly posits that one of the key features of morality is that it is *informal*, meaning that it has "no authoritative judges and no decision procedure that provides unique answers to all moral questions."[54] In effect, Gert is observing that consistency in decision-making is *not* a central feature of moral discourse, since there is no context in which the moral values assigned to different cases need to be resolved with one another. This reflects a fundamental truth of moral reasoning: the moral value of a particular action is measured primarily by its accordance with broad moral principles and with its consequences for the well-being of those creatures that it impacts, and to a far lesser degree by its consistency within a category of comparable cases.

Gert's assertion has numerous implications for the nature of moral discourse. For our purposes, however, the key implication of Gert's thesis is the way that moral discourse relates to its own past. The relative unimportance of consistency within moral discourse means that, in contrast with law, arguments from tradition, convention or the status quo do not carry significant moral weight; in assessing the moral value of an action that will unambiguously benefit or harm another, coherence with past moral judgments tends not to be influential. This facet of moral discourse

[53] Hart (*The Concept of Law*, *supra* note 8, 60–64) considers the concept of legal continuity – that a law endures until such time as it is repealed – to be one of the key features that distinguish law from mere habit.

[54] Bernard Gert, *Morality: Its Nature and Justification*, revised ed. (Oxford: Oxford University Press, 2005), 11.

makes it far more responsive to shifting societal perspectives: without the need to cohere with past decisions, moral decisions can reflect what society presently considers to be right or good.

Analysis of the way that moral systems evolve over time is largely absent from major works in moral philosophy. When this aspect of morality is analyzed, it is almost always in reference to the idea of moral *progress*, the notion that humanity is advancing toward a more enlightened moral state. This idea is expressed in the abstract in Hegelian and Marxist historiography, and has been advocated in more concrete terms by Peter Singer.[55] Yet the notion that moral discourse is evolving in a positive direction remains highly controversial, caught up in disagreements as to whether there has been an improvement in overall human well-being,[56] as well as ideological debates over whether modern Western society's more permissive attitudes toward practices such as abortion or assisted suicide constitute progress or regress. The argument we are making avoids these controversies by putting forth a more modest position, namely that moral discourse is constitutionally prone to *evolution*, but not necessarily in a positive direction. Even if one rejects the idea of moral progress specifically, it is difficult to make sense of the ways that common morality has dramatically changed over the past several hundred years – on issues as varied as religious and racial diversity, slavery, gender roles, sexual mores (including but hardly limited to homosexuality), and treatment of animals – without acknowledging that the propensity for change is a central aspect of moral discourse.

More relevant to our thesis, this evidence for moral change underscores the relatively conservative nature of law. On nearly every one of these issues, changes to the law (e.g., banning slavery or discrimination) were most often responses to shifts in popular sentiment that had destroyed the moral consensus on that issue.[57] These are examples of law fulfilling one of its standard societal functions: to provide resolution on issues of irresolvable moral debate.[58] But the legal changes in these areas have frequently been preceded by the use of law to enforce the morally controversial status quo. To wit, not only does law change more slowly than morality, it also serves to *constrain* the implementation of moral change.

As with religious intransigence, legal intransigence is often attributed to extralegal – especially political – forces, but this assumes that law is merely a tool for the exercise of power, devoid of any independent dimension of meaning. Our analysis of legal

55 Peter Singer, *The Expanding Circle* (Princeton: Princeton University Press, 1981).

56 For a critical view on this point, see Theodor Adorno, *Minima Moralia: Reflections from Damaged Life*, trans. E. F. N. Jephcott (London: Verso, 2005), 53–56.

57 Religious diversity is a notable exception to this point, since laws establishing tolerance toward religious minorities in the modern period have often been motivated by political or economic considerations (as they have throughout history) rather than moral concerns, such that these legal changes sometimes precede corresponding shifts in moral sentiment.

58 As Gert explains, "[w]hen it is important that [moral] disagreements be settled, societies use political or legal systems to supplement morality. These systems do not provide a moral answer to the question; rather, the question, being regarded as unresolvable, is transferred to the political or legal system"; *Morality*, *supra* note 54, 11.

discourse offers a more nuanced explanation. Law is a discourse distinct from politics that is intrinsically predisposed to favor existing patterns of behavior and the attitudes and beliefs that attend them. This aspect of law makes it a useful tool for political authorities to maintain the status quo, but more generally makes it unsuited to serve as a vehicle for initiating social or cultural change.

VIII CONCLUSION

The semiotic property of canonicity refers to the extent to which systems of meaning such as languages and higher-level discourses retain their constituent elements over time. We have proposed that the discourses of religion and law have intrinsically strong degrees of canonicity, such that they function as predominant forms of "institutional memory" within human culture. While our analysis has mainly been a general, programmatic discussion, we have alluded to some of its specific implications, both for the internal dynamics of law and religion themselves, and for the frequent points of tension between law and religion and other cultural discourses. Although a fuller analysis is beyond the scope of this chapter, a further set of implications is the way that legal and religious terminology and concepts are frequently used within other discourses to express rigidity or durability, such as the way that sociologists analyze secular political commitments in modern society as "civil religion." It is our hope that the methodological framework that we have developed here will prove useful for discussing this phenomenon and conducting future research.

C

Legal-Theological Roots

7

Exceptional Grace

Religion As the Sovereign Suspension of Law[1]

Robert A. Yelle

I THE FIRST CUT: MAKING AND MAPPING DISTINCTIONS BETWEEN LAW AND RELIGION

What is law? What is religion? And what sort of relation is implied by their conjunction? Does the phrase "law and religion" describe a fusion, a dichotomy, or something else? Such questions might appear either too basic or unanswerable, depending on one's perspective. To complicate matters further, the directive posed to us by the editors of this volume is to look for areas of overlap – of congruence or even identity – between these two categories that are normally viewed as mutually exclusive. So, we must sketch a picture that recognizes identity-within-difference, or at least convergence-within-distinction, between law and religion.

In perusing the existing scholarly literature in the relevant disciplines, I find a basic lack of agreement, and thus of clarity, concerning what distinguishes and what unites "law and religion." For many lawyers who choose to operate strictly within the confines of doctrine, it is often taken for granted what both law and religion are. Law consists of the constitution, statutes, case law, and other authoritative norms that are the basis for deciding a case. Religion is a bit more problematic, but can be defined through the manner in which such legal sources have demarcated religion from nonreligion. The fact that "religion" (e.g. as "freedom of religion") appears in these sources of law is a clear indication that religion is something that is an object of law: a word, originally drawn from natural language, that must be given legal meaning and effect. Only recently have some dissenters begun to argue that the legal system constructs religion as an object, and thus brings it into being – or at least distorts and deforms it – in a manner that belies its independent existence.[2] When courts construe what legally protected "religion" is, they are, for all practical purposes, theologizing, and in this regard, filling the role formerly played by inquisitors when discriminating between

1 I would like to acknowledge the generous assistance of Bernard Jackson and Devin Singh, both of whom offered helpful suggestions for the revision of this paper.

2 Winnifred Fallers Sullivan, *The Impossibility of Religious Freedom* (Princeton: Princeton University Press, 2005; new ed. 2018) is the *locus classicus* for such arguments.

orthodoxy and heresy. Strictly speaking, the separation of law from religion that is supposedly the hallmark of legal secularism is impossible. This perspective obviously implies a form of mutual interdependence of law and religion, or at least a dependence of religion on law, but not, I think, of the sort intended by our editors.

What happens if we consider religion outside of the judicial process, and move beyond current legal doctrine to consider history and anthropology? Historians of religion, such as myself, are intimately familiar with the increasingly prevalent claim that "religion" is a second-order term that bears the imprint of modern, European (and thus post-Christian) culture and that, when used outside of this culture, must be applied with caution and, usually, an asterisk or scare quotes. There are also arguments that something like the idea of religion has been recognized and demarcated through concepts and special terms in premodern and non-Western cultures. (We shall see Ivan Strenski's version of this argument shortly.) This demarcation of "religion" is often against "politics," as in the medieval Catholic distinction between two spheres of authority: that possessed by the *sacerdotium*, or priestly power, and that of the *regnum*, or royal/imperial power. This distinction was arguably grounded in Holy Scripture, with Jesus's injunction to "Render therefore to Caesar"[3] and his disclaimer that "my kingship is not of this world,"[4] and was embodied in the legal institution of the Roman Catholic Church. So much of this background has rooted itself into our brains and languages that we (meaning English-readers) often assume the naturalness of the distinction between Church and State, here capitalized, as they often are, to signal their fictive personhood, or indeed metaphysical substantiality. Such a separation can hardly apply in the same way to cultures where this institutional division has not occurred.[5] Incidentally, this already highlights the erroneousness of the claim that the "separation of Church and State," without further qualification, is a distinctive feature of secular societies; the idea of such a separation grounded the Roman Catholic Church's claim to an independent authority.

What about the conjunction indicated by the term "religious law"? A few years ago I participated in a conference that posed the question whether religious law has a right to exist in modern, secular societies. The phrase "religious law" was understood by all, including myself, to describe the laws of particular religious communities: for example, Roman Catholic canon law, Jewish law, Islamic Shari'ah, etc. This makes sense under the current order, where an ostensibly secular and universal law confronts the normative traditions of communities that aim to practice a limited form of self-government and, perhaps, of legal pluralism. However, for more abstract and general scholarly purposes, this concept of "religious law" obviously depends on the prior definition of certain groups as "religious" and not merely as, for example,

3 Matthew 22, Mark 12, Romans 13. All biblical references are to the RSV unless otherwise specified.

4 John 18:36.

5 However, for an analysis of similar distinctions beyond European Christianity, see Rodney Needham, "Dual Sovereignty," in *Reconnaissances* (Toronto: University of Toronto Press, 1980), 63–105.

minority groups, diasporic cultures, or voluntary associations.[6] "Religious law" then means just the laws regulating such groups. This is clear enough, and may serve for some pragmatic purposes, but as it depends on circular reasoning, it lacks a theoretical foundation. The other meaning of "religious law" is laws pertaining to religious matters, and arguably runs into the same tautology or logical regress, unless we can identify what such matters are.

Historians used to debate whether law was originally religious or not, meaning whether in ancient times it would have made sense to speak of "law" and "religion" as separate domains. In the nineteenth century, Henry Maine argued that Hindu law, as represented by the *Laws of Manu*, was originally religious, as it more closely resembled Leviticus than the Roman Institutes. He extended this to all systems of law in their primitive stage of development: "For Manu, though it contains a good deal of law, is essentially a book of ritual, of priestly duty and religious observance; . . . There is no system of recorded law, literally from China to Peru, which, when it first emerges into notice, is not seen to be entangled with religious ritual and observance."[7] Maine's characterization of Hindu law followed earlier Christian parallels between Hindus and Jews, and reflected the idea that religious laws are not "proper" laws: not rational, modern, secular. This thinking was parochial: the Sanskrit term *dharma* (as in *Mānavadharmaśāstra*, one name for Manu's text) cannot be translated simply as either "law" or "religion"; it encompasses both of these concepts and extends also to ritual performances. The indigenous category describes a unified conception to which the composite term "religious law" may be applied only as an approximation, and an anachronistic one at that.

Arthur S. Diamond argued, conversely, that there was never a time when religion and law – meaning the norms that govern the mundane order – were not regarded as distinct.[8] David Daube took a moderate position on the question. Noting scholarly bias in favor of "the theory that in the early life of nations all precepts were religious precepts, the separation of law and religion being achieved at a more advanced stage of civilization," he declined to affirm or deny this theory, and argued that in any case it would not be appropriate to generalize from one culture, such as that of ancient Israel as reflected in the Hebrew Bible, to all cultures.[9] Moreover, Daube provided examples of the sacralization of law – "how legal ideas developed into religious ideas under the hands

6 See Naomi Goldenberg's argument that what we call "religions" are actually "vestigial states" and markers of ethnic nationhood. Naomi Goldenberg, "The Category of Religion in the Technology of Governance: An Argument for Understanding Religions as Vestigial States," in Trevor Stack, Naomi Goldenberg, and Timothy Fitzerald, eds., *Religion as a Category of Governance and Sovereignty* (Leiden: Brill, 2015), 280–92.

7 Henry Maine, "The Sacred Laws of the Hindus," in *Dissertations on Early Law and Custom* (London: John Murray, 1883), 1–25 at 5.

8 Arthur S. Diamond, *Primitive Law Past and Present* (London: Methuen, 1971), 47–49, 80, 89–91, 104, 109–13, 124–26.

9 David Daube, "Law in the Narratives," in *Studies in Biblical Law* (Cambridge: Cambridge University Press, 1947; reprint ed. Ktav Publishing, 1969), 1–73 at 1.

of priests and prophets"[10] – one of these being the borrowing of the idea of redemption from debt as a metaphor for salvation in Jewish and Christian traditions.[11] As this example is discussed in Section VI below, I leave it aside for now.

The question of whether law was "originally religious" is indeed quite difficult to answer, even if we focus only on the Hebrew Bible. On the one hand, as Maine already noted, we know that substantial parts of the Pentateuch concern "priestly duty and religious observance" or more bluntly "ritual." On the other hand, there is much of secular law there as well. In terms of historical development, it is noteworthy that the law codes of the Hebrew Bible appear much more "religious" in this sense than the older and related Code of Hammurabi. This is also true because the biblical laws, whether they have to do with ritual or secular matters (such as cases of assault or property damage), are presented as the product of divine revelation. Such observations imply a process of "sacralization" of law in the biblical milieu, along the lines of what Daube described. We know from other cultural contexts that "secular" and "religious" systems of rules can coexist: the *Arthaśāstra* or "Treatise on Politics" from ancient India is an example of the former, if there ever was one, and is of similar antiquity to the *Laws of Manu*: both are roughly two millennia old. Whereas *Manu* was written mainly by and for priests, there are examples of other, mainly later *dharmaśāstra* texts, such as the *Nāradasmṛti*, that are much more "secular," in the sense that they are more concerned with, for example, commerce, and with norms enforced by the court, and less with ritual matters and the afterlife.[12]

Much more is at stake here than ancient history. Secularization – meaning the separation of law from religion, and with this, the reciprocal independence of each from the other – is part of the autobiography of modernity. Paradoxically, the idea of secularism itself is not nonreligious, but indebted in complex ways to Christianity, as Ze'ev Falk noted:

> A few remarks must be made on the idea of the separation between law and religion. Separation, or rather secularization, may be defined as the emancipation of humanity from the religious dimension in general, and from clerical rule in particular. It must be understood that this has been a particular phenomenon in the history of Christianity, and must not necessarily play the same role in other religions, such as Judaism, Islam or mystical systems. Although many Christian churches resisted secularization, it is implied in the Christian dichotomy between *God* and *Caesar*, *Civitas Dei* and *Civitas Terrena*, as well as between *spirit* and *body*. Paul's spiritualization of biblical law, drawn to its logical conclusion, means irrelevance of law for salvation, which in turn calls for secularization of law.[13]

10 Ibid., 3.

11 Ibid., 39–62.

12 See discussion in Robert A. Yelle, *The Language of Disenchantment: Protestant Literalism and Colonial Discourse in British India* (New York: Oxford University Press, 2013), 146–47.

13 Ze'ev Falk, *Law and Religion: The Jewish Experience* (Jerusalem: Mesharim, 1981), 13.

Falk accordingly rejected Diamond's contention that law and religion were originally distinct in Judaism.[14] Falk's argument anticipated some more recent arguments, including my own, that secularization was originally a Christian idea that, already in Paul, was directed against Mosaic law. Paul's idea that the Gospel is a matter of grace (*charis*) rather than of law (*nomos*), or of the spirit rather than the letter of the law, sharpened a distinction between law and religion in a way that had profound consequences, not only for Christian-Jewish relations but also for the entire trajectory of European culture. I have traced how the traditional Christian division of the Mosaic law into three separate categories – natural or moral law, civil or judicial law, and ceremonial law – informed the separation of religion from both law and ritual, particularly during and after the Protestant Reformation.[15] The idea that the ceremonial law had been abrogated by the Gospel went back to Paul, but was deployed by Protestants against both Jews and Catholics in the process of redefining religion as a matter of belief or interior piety. These categories were not indigenous to Jewish tradition, although the latter did identify certain Mosaic ritual laws as *ḥukkim* or "statutes" and debated whether these were susceptible to rational explanation.[16] Evolutionary accounts of secularization echo older Christian supersessionist narratives according to which religion may have been originally "legalistic" and "political," but was freed from such mundane things by the Gospel. At the same time that religion became spiritual – a matter of grace – law and politics became nonreligious or secular. "Render therefore to Caesar," indeed. What was excluded (marginalized, disestablished) was largely ritual. This can be put tentatively into the form of an equation: (RELIGIOUS LAW) – (RITUAL) = (SECULAR LAW) + (SPIRITUAL RELIGION).

Comprehending the relationship between law and religion has been complicated dramatically by the legacy of Christian bias regarding the Mosaic law, Torah, or *halakhah*. Christian polemics against Judaism as legalistic and ritualistic accelerated during the Reformation, and influenced ostensibly scientific scholarship on the Hebrew Bible, such as Julius Wellhausen's reconstruction of the Pentateuch, which

14 Ibid., 17.

15 Robert A. Yelle, "Moses' Veil: Secularization as Christian Myth," in *After Secular Law*, ed. Winnifred Fallers Sullivan, Robert A. Yelle, and Mateo Taussig-Rubbo (Stanford: Stanford University Press, 2011), 23–42; "The Hindu Moses: Christian Polemics against Jewish Ritual and the Secularization of Hindu Law under Colonialism," *History of Religions* 49 (2009): 141–71, republished as ch. 5 of *The Language of Disenchantment*; "Imagining the Hebrew Republic: Christian Genealogies of Religious Freedom," in *Politics of Religious Freedom*, ed. Winnifred Fallers Sullivan, Elizabeth Shakman Hurd, Saba Mahmood, and Peter Danchin (Chicago: University of Chicago Press, 2015), 17–28; "'By Fire and Sword': Early English Depictions of Islam and Judaism as 'Impostures' or Political and 'Unfree' Religions," *Patterns of Prejudice* 53 (2020): 91–108.

16 "Dietary Laws," *Encyclopedia Judaica* (Jerusalem: Keter Publishing House, 1971), 26–45 at 42; see more generally Isaac Heinemann, *The Reasons for the Commandments in Jewish Thought, from the Bible to the Renaissance*, trans. Leonard Levin (Boston: Academic Studies Press, 2008). See also Diamond's claim (126) that in the Hebrew Bible *mishpatim* refers to legal as distinguished from religious and moral rules.

relegated many ritual laws, particularly those regarding sacrifice, to a later phase of priestly consolidation of the Torah in order to rob them of the prestige of origins.[17] For Wellhausen and many other Protestants, the contrast between "the law and the prophets" described a dichotomy between priestly law and true, inspired religion that aligned with the opposition between Judaism and (authentic) Christianity. In this way, the Gospel could be interpreted as a restoration of the original, prophetic impulse of ethical monotheism, against corruptions introduced by priests, first within Judaism and then within Roman Catholicism.

II THE SECOND CUT: *AUCTORITAS* VERSUS *POTESTAS*

The first attempt to make sense of "law and religion" has ended with an impasse. We have seen that in some cultures these are combined, while in others they are distinct; and that our propensity to regard them as describing two different domains of culture has been conditioned both by Christian theology and by secularism. In short, these are not natural and perennial categories, but cultural and, therefore, historically determined ones. We cannot, in fact, define what either "law" or "religion" in general is with cross-cultural, trans-temporal validity.

However, despite having contributed myself to the genealogical critique of the ostensibly secular opposition between law and religion, I do not think we need to abandon all hope of the possibility of finding something analogous to this distinction in many other societies. Such an analogy is necessarily structural, and systematic. It depends, not on any substantive definition of either law or religion, but rather on the recognition of the dynamic and fluid tension that characterizes the relationship between these two domains. This argument builds from the previously mentioned efforts to stabilize the category of religion as against that of politics. Ivan Strenski has argued that the opposition between religion and politics is better understood as that between *auctoritas* and *potestas*, or "authority" and "power."[18] These distinctions go back to republican Rome, where *auctoritas* originally referred to the ability of the Senate, inter alia, to authorize and thus legitimize an action that would be carried out by another who had *potestas*. In 494 CE, Pope Gelasius I sent a letter to Emperor Anastasius I Dicorus, in which he appropriated these terms to distinguish their respective spheres of authority:

> Two there are ... by which this world is chiefly ruled, namely, the sacred authority [*auctoritas sacrata*] of the priesthood and the royal power [*regalis potestas*]. Of these the responsibility of the priests is more weighty in so far as they will answer for the kings of men themselves at the [divine] judgment. Know ... that, although you [Emperor Anastasius] take precedence over all mankind in dignity, nevertheless you must piously bow the neck to those who have charge of divine affairs and seek from

[17] Robert A. Yelle, "From Sovereignty to Solidarity: Some Transformations in the Politics of Sacrifice from the Reformation to Robertson Smith," *History of Religions* 58, No. 3 (February 2019): 319-46.

[18] Ivan Strenski, *Why Politics Can't Be Freed from Religion* (Malden, MA: Wiley, 2010).

> them the means of your salvation. . . . For if the bishops . . . recognizing that the imperial office was conferred on you by divine disposition, obey your laws so far as the sphere of public order is concerned . . . With what zeal ought you to obey those who have been charged with the administration of the sacred mysteries?[19]

Gelasius' idea that the Pope's *auctoritas* and the Emperor's *potestas* governed different domains, but that the Pope ultimately, because of the greater importance of salvation, possessed the higher authority, came to be known as the doctrine of the Two Swords, and served as the basis for the Christian opposition between the spiritual and temporal powers, the ecclesiastical and civil laws, etc.[20]

Extending Gelasius's distinction beyond its original context of application, Strenski argues that religion is (mainly) a type of *auctoritas* that, for this reason, can never be finally and fully separated from politics, which is (mainly) a type of *potestas*. These two qualities exist in a dialectical relationship, in which religion is a second-order form of politics, as it were, that can lend meaning and legitimacy to the existing order, or conversely serve as a basis for contesting and even changing that order.

> While a given "religion" may display both *potestas* and *auctoritas*, no "religion" is conceivable without *auctoritas*. Yet, some religions are conceivable in the absence of *potestas*. But, on the other hand, while politics too reveals a mixture of both *potestas* and *auctoritas*, it is conceivable without *auctoritas*, but no political entity lacking *potestas* is conceivable. While elements of this definition are well rooted in everyday notions of religion, I think the definition takes us beyond mere recycling of everyday understandings of religion. It puts the notion of authority forward – ultimate, sacred, and transcendent authority, to be precise.[21]

Strenski thus describes a Venn diagram in which *auctoritas*/religion and *potestas*/politics overlap, but do not entirely converge. Indeed, he laments the loss of understanding of *auctoritas* as this has been collapsed into the mere exercise of worldly power or *potestas*, a collapse that he finds in, among others, Michel Foucault. Strenski attributes our inherited imbalance or rather conflation between these two qualities to the Pope's own power grab, his attempt to assert a plenary temporal *potestas* in addition to his spiritual *auctoritas*: "Both Church and emperor claimed to rule by virtue of their *potestas*. We thus think about power as a unified field rather than as an arena of complementary differences because the Church simply ceased representing the spiritual alone."[22] According to Strenski, the Roman Church was the first absolutist state, and the Pope the first absolute sovereign.[23] Strenski therefore appears to retell a version of the story of modernity as a decline – a fall from grace – that began either with the Investiture Controversy or a bit later, in the High Middle Ages.

19 Brian Tierney's translation, quoted in ibid., 75.
20 Ibid., 77 states that Gelasius' own formulation was effective for only two centuries.
21 Ibid., 52; see also 64, 91.
22 Ibid.; see also 80, 98, 116–18.
23 Ibid., 80–81.

Strenski generalizes the *auctoritas-potestas* distinction beyond its immediate historical context, applying it, for example, to the distinction between *Brahman* (priest) and *Kṣatriya* (ruler) and between *dharma* (justice) and *artha* (power) in ancient India.[24] Some would object to this generalization on the grounds that it makes a parochial, medieval Christian category appear universal. However, this objection is arguably itself too general, as any set of categories that might be deployed in cross-cultural comparison must originally be borrowed from some natural language and historical tradition. I am quite sympathetic to Strenski's effort to find a definition of religion in structural rather than essentialist terms. Having acknowledged that there is no *substantive* definition of religion that possesses any cross-cultural or trans-historical validity, we must pursue such structural or systems-theoretical redescriptions of religion, or abandon any engagement with the data.

Yet I think we can (and must) improve upon Strenski's effort. One route forward lies in mapping out more precisely what is meant by the distinction between *auctoritas* and *potestas*. As previously noted, this predates Gelasius, and actually goes back to pagan Rome, where the distinction was applied to describe two different types of political power.[25] The Senate had *auctoritas*, the power to authorize or legitimate an action, while the magistrate had *potestas*, the power to implement or carry out that action. Although the terms were not always used consistently through the centuries of the Republic and subsequent Empire, and *auctoritas* could be attributed to persons of esteem who lacked political office, a useful contemporary analogy would be to the distinction between legislative and executive power under the modern doctrine of separation of powers.

To understand this better, let's look at some of the later iterations of this distinction, as laid out in Table 7.1.

TABLE 7.1 Auctoritas *vs.* potestas *and related separation-of-power distinctions*

SOURCE	"RELIGION"	"LAW"
Ancient Rome	*Auctoritas*	*Potestas*
Two Swords in Medieval Christianity ca. 500–1500 CE	Ecclesiastical/ Spiritual Power (*Sacerdotium*)	Civil/ Temporal Power (*Regnum*)
Adolphe Thiers (19th c.)	"Ruling"	"Governing"
Emanuel Sieyès (late 18th c.)	Constituting Power	Constituted Power
Walter Bagehot (19th c.)	Dignified Power	Efficient Power
Modern parliamentary democracy	King/Queen (or President in some parliamentary systems)	Prime Minister

24 For a related discussion of this opposition in ancient India, see Robert A. Yelle, "Spiritual Economies beyond the Sacred/Secular Paradigm: Or, What Did Religious Freedom Mean in Ancient India?" in *Varieties of Religious Establishments*, ed. Lori Beaman and Winnifred Fallers Sullivan (Farnham, Surrey, UK: Ashgate, 2013), 15–32.

25 Strenski, *supra* note 18, 72–73, 93–94.

The distinction between *auctoritas* and *potestas* seems to have served as the basis for a number of later distinctions, each of which expressed the difference between a power that was exercised immediately and a power that was more remote from direct application and, perhaps by virtue of being above the fray, regarded as superior. Such appears to be the source of the distinction between "ruling" and "governing" expressed in Adolphe Thiers' famous line, "The king rules, but he does not govern" (*Le roi règne, mais il ne gouverne pas*);[26] as well as of Walter Bagehot's distinction between the "dignified" and the "efficient" parts of government in his work on *The English Constitution* (1867), where the "dignified" part refers to the mysteries of state embodied in the royal personage, which could be sullied by too close a contact with the messy affairs of the day-to-day business of government:

> No one can approach to an understanding of the English institutions, or of others which, being the growth of many centuries, exercise a wide sway over mixed populations, unless he divide them into two classes. In such constitutions there are two parts (not indeed separable with microscopic accuracy, for the genius of great affairs abhors nicety of division): first, those which excite and preserve the reverence of the population – the *dignified* parts, if I may so call them; and next, the *efficient* parts – those by which it, in fact, works and rules. There are two great objects which every constitution must attain to be successful, which every old and celebrated one must have wonderfully achieved: every constitution must first *gain* authority, and then *use* authority; it must first win the loyalty and confidence of mankind, and then employ that homage in the work of government. ... The Queen is only at the head of the dignified part of the constitution. The prime minister is at the head of the efficient part. The Crown is, according to the saying, the "fountain of honour;" but the Treasury is the spring of business.[27]

The nineteenth-century formulations of Thiers and Bagehot show a lingering reference to divine right, and also perhaps to the idea of the mystical body of the sovereign, as opposed to his (or her) natural body.[28] The separation of powers continues in the distinction between the Queen and Prime Minister in the United Kingdom and that between the President and Prime Minister in certain other parliamentary democracies. The United States, as is well known, vests executive power in a President who is no mere figurehead. However, none of these modern versions of the separation of powers is particularly theological. A version of the

26 *Le National* (January 20, 1830). The fuller version makes clear that this was an argument for limited monarchy: "Le Roi garde le trône, poste toujours menacé, pour qu'un ambitieux ne s'en empare pas. Le pays se gouverne sous ces yeux avec son assentiment et sa gloire, car on vient tous les ans le féliciter de la prospérité publique qu'il n'a pas faite mais qu'il a suffisamment faite s'il ne l'a pas empêchée. En un mot, il règne et le peuple se gouverne." Another version of this is "Le roi n'administre pas, ne gouverne pas, il règne." Thiers' famous statement was later to be quoted by Pierre-Joseph Proudhon, Max Weber, and Carl Schmitt, among others.

27 Walter Bagehot, *The English Constitution* (London: Chapman & Hall, 1867) (emphasis in original).

28 Ernst Kantorowicz, *The King's Two Bodies: A Study in Medieval Political Theology* (Princeton: Princeton University Press, 1957).

division of powers is also found in the distinction in business corporations between the Board of Directors and the Chief Executive Officer.

The distinction between *auctoritas* and *potestas* was – and perhaps still is – best understood as a distinction internal to politics. It was not originally a theological distinction at all, but rather became sacralized through its assimilation by Gelasius. Because, as indicated also by its contemporary versions, this distinction has to do with a separation of powers that can be of an entirely mundane, political or economic nature, it appears, at first glance, less than ideally suited for the work that Strenski assigns to it: namely, the expression of the distinction between religion and (worldly) politics.

III THE THIRD CUT: SOVEREIGNTY VERSUS LAW

Or perhaps it is just that we have not yet understood the full implications of the distinction between *auctoritas* and *potestas*. Here Giorgio Agamben can be helpful, although as a non-Latinist I cannot evaluate the accuracy of all of his contentions. Agamben includes an important discussion of the distinction in his work, *State of Exception*, which is itself part of the *Homo Sacer* series.[29] He assimilates *auctoritas* to the idea of a self-legitimating sovereignty that superintends and is capable of suspending the legal order, which is identified with *potestas*:

> Let us try to better define the nature of this "power that grants legitimacy" in its relation to the *potestas* of the magistrate and the people. ... Under extreme conditions ... *auctoritas* seems to act as *a force that suspends* potestas *where it took place and reactivates it where it was no longer in force*. It is a power that suspends or reactivates law, but is not formally in force as law. ... The juridical system of the West appears as a double structure, formed by two heterogeneous yet coordinated elements: one that is normative and juridical in the strict sense (which we can for convenience inscribe under the rubric *potestas*) and one that is anomic and metajuridical (which we can call by the name *auctoritas*). The normative element needs the anomic element in order to be applied, but, on the other hand, *auctoritas* can assert itself only in the validation or suspension of *potestas*. Because it results from the dialectic between these two somewhat antagonistic yet functionally connected elements, the ancient dwelling of law is fragile and, in straining to maintain its own order, is always already in the process of ruin and decay. The state of exception is the device that must ultimately articulate and hold together the two aspects of the juridico-political machine by instituting a threshold of undecidability between anomie and *nomos*, between life and law, between *auctoritas* and *potestas*. ... As long as the two elements remain correlated yet conceptually, temporally, and subjectively distinct (as in republican Rome's contrast between the Senate and the people, or in medieval Europe's contrast between spiritual and temporal powers) their dialectic – though founded on a fiction – can nevertheless

[29] Giorgio Agamben, *The Omnibus Homo Sacer* (Stanford: Stanford University Press, 2017), 230–42.

> function in some way. But when they tend to coincide in a single person, when the state of exception, in which they are bound and blurred together, becomes the rule, then the juridico-political system transforms itself into a killing machine.[30]

Explaining all of the nuances of this passage within the context of Agamben's larger project is impossible here. What is important is to recognize that he assimilates the distinction between *auctoritas* and *potestas* to that between sovereignty and law, in accordance with Carl Schmitt's understanding of sovereignty as the power to suspend the law or to declare a state of exception (i.e. a state of emergency). Rather than some weak, effete power of authorization, such as is still possessed by the English monarch, who technically speaking must assent to all laws approved by Parliament, and could in theory refuse to do so, the form of *auctoritas* described by Agamben is the fulsome power possessed by the sovereign prior to the taming of divine right during and after the seventeenth century. *Auctoritas* coincides with the power to intervene in a normative order by creating, suspending, or breaking (and potentially remaking) that order. A similar force was attributed by some Christian theologians in the High Middle Ages to God as an omnipotent sovereign, whose absolute power (*potentia dei absoluta*) was capable of disrupting or suspending the existing framework of laws (*potentia ordinata*) through miracles and divine commands.

Agamben further identifies *auctoritas* as a personal quality held by an *auctor*, such as a *pater*, *princeps*, or *dictator*.[31] He does not hesitate to identify this quality with Max Weber's notion of "charismatic authority": "'Charisma'–as its reference to Paul's *kharis* [grace] (which Weber knew perfectly well) could have suggested – coincides with the neutralization of law … ."[32] This reinforces the connection of *auctoritas* with sovereignty, understood as the power of ultimate decision held by one ruler (monarch) in his or her personal capacity. The danger according to Agamben is that, in modern times, *auctoritas* and *potestas* have collapsed together, so that there is no separation of powers, no relationship of checks and balances, but only totalitarian dictatorship. Table 7.2 (next page) may assist in appreciating these associations.

As I have demonstrated elsewhere, such theological ideas concerning absolute power shaped the background of the early-twentieth-century debate between Carl Schmitt and Max Weber.[33] Weber explicitly opposed charismatic authority to legal authority, and identified the former with the power to suspend the law: "genuine charismatic domination knows no abstract laws and regulations and no formal adjudication. … [I]in a revolutionary and sovereign manner, charismatic domination transforms all values and breaks all traditional and rational norms: 'It has been written … but *I* say unto

[30] Ibid., 234, 240 (the second passage is repeated at 1266; see also 1278–79) (emphasis in original).
[31] Ibid., 237–38.
[32] Ibid., 239.
[33] Robert A. Yelle, *Sovereignty and the Sacred: Secularism and the Political Economy of Religion* (Chicago: University of Chicago Press, 2019), ch. 2.

TABLE 7.2 *Sovereignty vs. law and related oppositions (after Agamben)*

SOURCE OF OPPOSITION	"SOVEREIGNTY"	"LEGALITY"
Ancient Rome	*Auctoritas*	*Potestas*
Christian scholastic idea of God's two powers	Absolute Power (*potentia/ potestas dei absoluta*)	Ordained Power (*potentia ordinata*)
Christianity (Paul, Romans)	Grace (*charis*)	Law (*nomos*)
Max Weber	Charismatic Authority	Legal/ Bureaucratic Authority

you . . . '"[34] (Weber quoted Jesus's statement from the Gospels twice as an illustration of charisma.) He argued further that charisma has declined in an increasingly bureaucratic modernity. Schmitt pointed out that such views echoed the radical Protestant attack on miracles, which coordinated with the prohibition of absolute sovereignty. Weber's account was not a neutral history, but a partisan "political theology."

There is, according to Weber and Schmitt, not only a structural opposition between sovereignty and law, but also an historical divide, according to which sovereignty has declined or been repressed in an increasingly rule-governed modernity. This historical process is what we call "secularization" or "disenchantment." Scrutinizing this process as it relates to law will help us further along the road to understanding the relationship between law and religion.

IV THE FOURTH CUT: THE DISENCHANTMENT OF LAW

In *Economy and Society*, Weber sketched a compelling account of the evolution of legal traditions away from the supposedly *ad hoc* justice imposed by dictators, khadis, prophets, and other charismatic figures. The early stage of society involved decision by fiat. The chieftain would pronounce a verdict without having to explain the reasons. This resembled very closely what we refer to in other contexts as divine command.[35] Oracles and ordeals were examples of the judicial processes appropriate to this stage. Weber explicitly invoked William Blackstone's eighteenth-century description of English common law judges as "oracles" to illustrate the traces of charisma in that legal tradition. Blackstone meant to laud their wisdom and discretion as interpreters or even deliverers of the inspired judgments of a divine justice. These verdicts were singular and independent; they were made on a case-by-case basis, through the judge's personal authority and not necessarily in strict reliance on prior judicial precedent. Such verdicts therefore appeared as a form of quasi-magic,

34 Max Weber, *Economy and Society*, ed. Guenther Roth and Claus Wittich (Berkeley: University of California Press, 1978), 1115; see also 243. See also Bernard Jackson, "The Prophet and the Law in Early Judaism and the New Testament," in *Essays on Halakhah in the New Testament* (Leiden: Brill, 2008), 13–31 at 21.

35 See discussion in Yelle, *Sovereignty and the Sacred*, *supra* note 33, ch. 2.

also as having pragmatic effect, much in the manner in which the ritual pronouncements of the Catholic Church worked *ex opere operato* to bring a new state into being. As we would now say, they were "speech acts."

The onward rationalization of the law involved shedding such vestiges of judicial charisma, although obliterating every trace of this was and remains impossible. This progressive disenchantment of the law formed the background of Schmitt's argument for bringing back an irruptive sovereignty. Schmitt's polemic depended on at least two arguments: first, that the disenchantment of sovereignty (charisma, miracle, divine command) was a choice or a dogmatic position taken by certain Protestant theologians, which could therefore be dismissed as a partisan "political theology"; and second, that sovereignty could not really be excluded in any case, as there would always be a need for an ultimate authority capable of making, suspending, or changing the law.[36]

Schmitt's opponents included the legal positivists, such as Hans Kelsen, who were the spiritual descendants of Jeremy Bentham. Bentham had already staked out a position, in its own way as extreme as Schmitt's, and at the opposite pole from his. Where Schmitt was all about the exception, Bentham did his best to exclude this, through the elaboration of a comprehensive, plain-language code (the "Pannomion") that would supposedly neither require nor allow any interpretation or discretion on the part of the individual judge.[37] Directly attacking Blackstone's idea that judges were "oracles," Bentham sought to remove the taint of arbitrary discretion from the common law by a thorough rationalization of its statutory basis. In this project he followed directly in the footsteps of certain Deists, such as Matthew Tindal, who had earlier attacked miracles, divine commands, and similar states of exception to natural law.

Both Bentham and Schmitt were extremists. Neither position was tenable. We still need both law and sovereignty. Yet the apparent fact that neither seemed quite willing to allow this suggests that modernity has reached a condition of polarization with respect to these two qualities. We have already seen echoes of this polarization or "breakdown" in both Strenski and Agamben, each of whom has diagnosed the collapse of the (formerly functioning) dynamic tension between *auctoritas* and *potestas*. The original lament of this sort arguably came from Weber, who described modernity not only as "disenchanted" and "rationalized," but also as an "iron cage" (*stahlhartes Gehäuse*).[38] Applied to law, this would represent the condition in which legal norms have lost all charismatic authority and, with this, their legitimacy and power to command obedience.

36 Carl Schmitt, *Political Theology: Four Chapters on the Concept of Sovereignty*, trans. George Schwab (Chicago: University of Chicago Press, 1985).

37 Robert A. Yelle, "Bentham's Fictions: Canon and Idolatry in the Genealogy of Law," *Yale Journal of Law & the Humanities* 17 (2005): 151–79.

38 Max Weber, *The Protestant Ethic and the Spirit of Capitalism*, trans. Talcott Parsons (New York: Charles Scribner's Sons, 1958), 181.

Whereas Weber's opposition between charisma and law now appears to capture rather precisely part of the modern condition, it is important to recognize and acknowledge what Schmitt already pointed out: namely, that the stark opposition between charisma and law itself represents a particular perspective that may with some justice be attributed to the Protestant exacerbation of the Pauline divide between *charis* and *nomos*.[39] As described in Section I of the present chapter, this is a dichotomy that appears indebted, on the one hand to Christian anti-Jewish polemics, on the other to Protestant anti-Catholic polemics. Both of these polemics insist that *charis* is not *nomos* – that grace has nothing to do with law. It is widely known that Weber's own framing of this dichotomy was influenced by Rudolph Sohm, the Protestant theologian who described the downfall in the early Christian community as having occurred when the original mode of charismatic leadership was replaced by a legally defined process of the election of bishops.[40] At that point, the Gospel was corrupted into the Roman Catholic Church. That Sohm's account was just a latter-day version of the Protestant trope that miracles ceased in the early church has been ignored by most scholars, certainly by those who still regard Weber's theory as scientific and "value neutral."

Is it really true that charisma is the antithesis of law? To begin to answer this question, I turn now to reflect upon the historical context out of which such categories emerged – namely, Hebrew biblical law – and specifically, to the question of what *charis* might have meant originally in the Gospels.

V THE FIFTH CUT: *CHARIS* VERSUS *NOMOS*, OR "JUSTICE AND RIGHTEOUSNESS"?

In a series of erudite and incisive essays, Bernard Jackson argues that law as depicted in the Hebrew Bible originally was not separate from charisma, but was dependent on the personal authority of the judge, who was regarded as the embodiment of justice.[41] The Pauline valorization of the "spirit" of the law over its "letter" still reflected a situation in which judgments were thought to be delivered through

39 Carl Schmitt, *Political Theology II: The Myth of the Closure of Any Political Theology*, trans. Michael Hoelzl and Graham Ward (Malden, MA: Polity Press, 2008), 66–67, 74.

40 See Robert A. Yelle, "'An Age of Miracles': Disenchantment as a Secularized Theological Narrative," in Robert A. Yelle and Lorenz Trein, eds., *Narratives of Disenchantment and Secularization: Critiquing Max Weber's Idea of Modernity* (London: Bloomsbury, 2021), 129-48 at 141–45.

41 I have drawn on very helpful comments from, as well as on the following essays by Bernard Jackson : "The Prophet and the Law," *supra* note 34; "Legalism and Spirituality: Historical, Philosophical and Semiotic Notes on Legislators, Adjudicators, and Subjects," in *Religion and Law, Biblical-Judaic and Islamic Perspectives*, ed. E. B. Firmage, B. G. Weiss and J. W. Welch (Winona Lake: Eisenbrauns, 1990), 243–61; "Constructing a Theory of Halakhah" (published in 2012 on http://jewishlawassociation.org/resources.htm); "Historical Observations on the Relationship between Letter and Spirit," typescript; *Wisdom-Laws: A Study of the Mishpatim of Exodus 21:1–22:16* (Oxford: Oxford University Press, 2006); "Justice and Righteousness in the Bible: Rule of Law or Royal Paternalism?" *Zeitschrift für Altorientalische und Biblische Rechtsgeschichte* IV (1998): 218–62.

divine inspiration. Originally, there was no contradiction between law and prophecy, such as was retrospectively (and anachronistically) projected onto the Hebrew Bible, especially by Christians. Prophets, like kings and other judges, were capable of delivering legal judgments, but also of suspending or changing the law. Law was seen as something more than a decision rule that was foreordained and meant to be applied strictly. Indeed, at first the law was not even written down; and even after it was committed to writing, such written rules were neither co-extensive with, nor exhaustive of, the whole of the law. Only gradually was the codified law applied more strictly and the prophetic dimension marginalized, as illustrated by the later Rabbinic story of Akhnai's oven, which expressed the exclusion of miraculous authority in favor of democratic decision by the rabbis. This development, as Jackson notes, appears to represent a defensive response to Jesus's prophetic message, which had placed charismatic authority in starker opposition to the law.[42] It was reinforced by the idea that prophecy had ceased, an idea that existed in Judaism before it was deployed by certain Church fathers against Christian heretics and, later, resuscitated by Protestants as a weapon against the Roman Catholic Church as well as enthusiasts within their own ranks.

Jackson invokes Weber's account of charisma and its institutionalization in the course of his account.[43] Both agree that charisma represents a sovereign power to suspend the legal norm in a particular instance, also by appeal to miracles and consultation with oracles.[44] Yet where Weber described a dichotomy between charismatic and legal authority, Jackson argues that the original form of authority in ancient Israel was "monistic," meaning that it combined charisma and law.[45] Only after prophetic charisma had been excluded as a source of justice, partly in response to the challenge posed by Christianity to the Law, did a "dualistic" system arise in Judaism, in which a written statute was interpreted by rabbis qualified through ordination (*semikhah*). Ordination itself had earlier been charismatic, but came to be conferred "as a result of qualification in the *yeshivah*."[46] This ancient history closely parallels Sohm's account of the institutionalization of authority in the early Christian community, which was adapted by Weber in framing the opposition between charismatic authority and legal/bureaucratic authority, or "office charisma" (*Amtscharisma*). Yet where Jackson describes this as a relatively late development that replaced an earlier "monistic" system, Weber (and, *a fortiori*, Sohm)

42 Jackson, "The Prophet and the Law," *supra* note 34, 29–30. Joseph Weiler explains Jesus's trial and condemnation as the Jewish community's response to his claim to suspend and rewrite the Law. The relevant biblical law according to Weiler is Deuteronomy 13:1–5. See Joseph H. H. Weiler, "The Trial of Jesus," *First Things* (June 2010), available at www.firstthings.com/article/2010/06/the-trial-of-jesus. Cf. Jackson, "The Prophet and the Law," 17.

43 Jackson, "Legalism and Spirituality," *supra* note 41, 253; "Constructing a Theory of Halakhah," *supra* note 39, 15.

44 Jackson, "Justice and Righteousness," *supra* note 41.

45 Jackson, "Constructing a Theory of Halakhah," *supra* note 41, 12.

46 Ibid. See also Jackson, "Historical Observations," *supra* note 41, 5–6.

described a permanent struggle between charisma and law that was illustrated already by the conflict between prophets and priests in the Hebrew Bible.[47]

The starkness of Weber's dichotomy reflects its theological origins. As Agamben (and Carl Schmitt and John Potts, among others) pointed out, the original, theological source for Weber's notion of charismatic authority was Paul's distinction between *charis* or grace and *nomos* or law, as employed in Romans, which paralleled some other Pauline oppositions, such as that between spirit and flesh, or spirit and letter.[48] This distinction has been fateful for the subsequent history of Christian-Jewish relations, as well as for the European Christian understanding of the relationship between law and religion as a disjunction and rigid dichotomy. But where does it come from?

Several points might lead us to expect that this opposition had an origin in law. One is Paul's claim to have been a student of Rabbi Gamaliel, an expert in Torah or law; another is the fact that Paul evidences a familiarity with legal concepts and forensic rhetoric; a third is that the term *nomos* had by this time become the standard word in Hellenistic Greek for "law"; a fourth is that, as used by Paul, *nomos* appears to be a designation for the Torah or the Mosaic law.[49] Weighing against this expectation is the traditional theological interpretation of *charis* as divine grace, which stands as a positive hindrance, if not an insurmountable obstacle. The theological perspective is that grace has literally nothing to do with law, that it comes out of the blue, *ex nihilo*, or as an uncaused cause. (This is, indeed, the source of the dichotomy.) We must attempt to get behind this perspective in order to appreciate what *charis* might have meant, precisely in relation to its original, Hebrew context.

A perusal of Strong's Concordance suggests that *charis* (grace, gift, credit, or thanks) was used by Paul in several instances specifically to denote the character or motivation of an action that exceeded what was required by the law.[50] For example, Romans 4:4 (NKJV) states: "Now to him who works the wages are not counted as grace [*charis*], but as debt." This usage parallels that in the Gospel of Luke.[51] At Luke 6:32–34 (NKJV), Jesus states:

> But if you love those who love you, what credit [*charis*] is that to you? For even sinners love those who love them. And if you do good to those who do good to you, what credit [*charis*] is that to you? For even sinners do the same. And if you lend to those from whom you hope to receive back, what credit [*charis*] is that to you? For even sinners lend to sinners, to receive as much back.

47 See Yelle, "'An Age of Miracles,'" *supra* note 40.

48 For discussion and references, see Yelle, *Sovereignty and the Sacred*, *supra* note 33, ch. 2.

49 Jackson, "Constructing a Theory of Halakhah," *supra* note 41, 17, points out that "law" is in fact not a good translation of Torah, which means something more like "instruction" and is broader than a collection of legal rules. Point taken, but in Paul's polemic it appears that the category of law is already undergoing a devaluation that is the topic of the present discussion.

50 Romans 4:4, 6:15, 11:6; Ephesians 2:8.

51 Luke 6:32–34, 17:9.

Charis here appears to refer to a principle of justice or mercy that suspends the strict application of a legal or commercial norm, such as that pertaining to the payment of wages or the repayment of debts. It has been suggested to me that *charis* here may be translating the Hebrew term *chesed*, which is usually rendered into English as "mercy."[52] This makes sense also in light of the understanding of Hebrew biblical law that Jackson has articulated, in which the application of law was not rigid but flexible, and was legitimated through the personal authority of the judge, who supposedly possessed divine inspiration. In such a system, precisely as Weber described, charismatic authority is capable of suspending otherwise valid legal norms. Jackson argues persuasively that such an expansive conception of justice was expressed by the common phrase *mishpat utsedakah*, or "justice and righteousness," discussed also by Moshe Weinfeld: "Weinfeld sees 'justice and righteousness' as particular responsibilities of the king, reflected in a number of institutions whereby he liberated his subjects from economic (and other forms of) oppression."[53] Such forms of liberation included the releases from servitude and debt that occurred in conjunction with the declarations of *deror* and *misharum*, which are described below. Jackson contends that in Weinfeld's account righteousness (*tsedakah*) "becomes a kind of equity, designed to temper the strictness of law, the latter being conceived (in modern terms) as the application of legal rules by judges who have no discretion to resolve disputes in any other way." Jackson's main disagreement with this interpretation is that it ignores the fact that judges also had the responsibility, discretion, and latitude to be "righteous" and, when necessary, to deviate from the strict letter of the law.

What is significant, in connection with our discussion of *charis* as a possible translation of *chesed*, is that this Hebrew term also appeared sometimes in such binomial formulas, as Weinfeld notes: "During the Second Temple period, the concept of 'justice and righteousness' developed and deepened. Instead of the pair of concepts, justice and righteousness . . ., we find righteousness and kindness (*tsedakah* and *chesed*), which acquired a broader meaning."[54] He glosses the latter term as follows: "*Chesed*, 'kindness,' is identical with goodness and mercy. It is not a characteristic that is congruous with strict justice, since if it were to be applied in court it would otherwise interfere with the execution of justice, which must be untempered by partiality."[55]

In other words, we have evidence of the prevalence of a concept of equity in the Second Temple period that appeared to function precisely as the notion of *charis* in the New Testament examples provided above. Whether or not *charis* was translating

52 This was suggested to me independently by both Bernard Jackson and Haim Shapira, personal communications.

53 Jackson, "Justice and Righteousness in the Bible," *supra* note 41. See also Moshe Weinfeld, *Social Justice in Ancient Israel and in the Ancient Near East* (Jerusalem: Magnes Press, 1995), 11ff., 17ff.; Jackson, "Constructing a Theory of Halakhah," *supra* note 41, 11.

54 Weinfeld, *Social Justice*, *supra* note 53, 19; see also 29.

55 Ibid., 36.

chesed, a version of this concept existed prior to the Gospel revelation, and was therefore not created out of nothing. This concept denoted, at its core, the power to suspend or deviate from a strict application of the law in the quest for a higher justice that was informed by mercy. As such, it referred to what we have been calling "sovereignty" as distinguished from "law." It would not be correct to regard *charis/chesed* as a nonlegal principle, any more than it would be correct to regard sovereignty as having nothing to do with law. I emphasize this point because many of us who come from a European, Christian background have been conditioned to regard grace as a nonlegal and specifically religious category. This understanding, I suggest, has been influenced by a particular reading of Paul, who indeed at times highlights the opposition between *charis* and *nomos* (or between the spirit and the letter of the law) to such an extent that these two principles no longer appear to belong together, as part of a comprehensive concept of justice. Paul's emphasis on the disjunctive rather than the conjunctive aspect of this binomial shaped the later idea of a separation between religion and law, as well as Weber's sharp bifurcation between charisma and legal authority.

VI THE SIXTH CUT: THE PARDON POWER AS ILLUSTRATION OF THE "RELIGIOUS" PRINCIPLE IN RELATION TO LAW

Let's take stock of where we are in the argument. The emerging picture suggests that our ordinary, common-sense understanding that law and religion are separate or even antithetical has been conditioned by secularism and, before this, by Christian theology, which (especially in its post-Reformation manifestations) has tended to identify religion as "wholly other," as transcendent of the mundane world. When religion comes into contact with law, it appears precisely as a zone of freedom, as a suspension of the law. Yet these very qualities are the same ones that identify what we call "religion" as a form of sovereignty, which is also characterized by the power to suspend the law, through the declaration of a state of exception.[56] If Christianity and secularism have introduced a "cut" between religion and law, as reflected in the dichotomy between *charis* and *nomos*, this cut performed an incision into the body of law itself, a body that was formerly unified in the person of the sovereign judge, who acted through divine inspiration. As Jackson put it, justice went from being "monistic" to "dualistic."

But is it really the case that religion may be nothing more than a particular expression of the power of the sovereign who suspends the law? Let us test this thesis again using the example of the pardon power. The pardon power provides an especially good case for a historical reconstruction because, among other things, we can trace it from our contemporary era all the way back to ancient Mesopotamia. As we have just seen, Weinfeld notes the debt releases called *andurarum* or

[56] This is the central argument of my book, *Sovereignty and the Sacred*, *supra* note 33.

misharum as examples of the sovereign's power to do equity.[57] Although the evidence is equivocal, in ancient Mesopotamia such debt releases appear to have coincided with several types of events: a threat to the polity resulting from foreign armies or a famine; the first full year of a king's reign; and the Akitu or New Year's festival.[58] These were sovereign acts that sometimes coincided with an actual state of emergency, in the event of which there were pragmatic reasons that counseled removing the burden of debt from citizens whose attentions should be focused fully on addressing the immediate threat.[59] When occurring at the beginning of the first full year of a king's reign, the debt release resembled a reset or "clean slate" that also served to create gratitude for the new ruler; in this respect it paralleled the acts of *largesse* that in later European contexts also coincided with the entry into sovereignty.[60] In the case that such a debt release synchronized with the New Year's festival, it had the additional connotation of a cosmic renewal in which the king, who according to some accounts underwent ritual humiliation, was subsequently victorious over the forces of evil. Agamben has seen in such festivals a "state of exception" that marks a moment in the life of sovereignty.[61]

In the Hebrew Bible, such suspensions of the law were called *deror* – liberation – and included release from debt (*shemitta*) as well as from slavery. During the Sabbatical, every seventh year, debts were canceled and slaves were freed. Every seventh Sabbatical, thus every forty-nine or fifty years, a Jubilee was declared, on which farmland was also returned to its original owners. Although there is some evidence that the Sabbatical was practiced, the Jubilee appears to have remained a piece of utopian social legislation. The main innovation in the Hebrew Bible as compared with the ancient Near Eastern precedent was to take this power out of the hands of the king and to place the cancellation of debts on a regular schedule. What was originally a sovereign act was converted into a legal institution.[62] However, kings or judges could still grant pardons in individual cases.

David Daube identified the incorporation of an originally legal idea of redemption into Jewish and Christian tradition as a central metaphor for salvation, a process

57 See also Jackson, "Legalism and Spirituality," *supra* note 41, 249.

58 My summary here relies on Michael Hudson and Marc Van de Mieroop, *Debt and Economic Renewal in the Ancient Near East* (Bethesda: CDL Press, 2002).

59 It should be noted that pardons frequently have been granted, not only following civil wars (in which case as applied to an entire class of persons they are more generally referred to as "amnesties"), but also in order to free individuals for conscription into the army in the case of a state of war. Examples may be found in more recent centuries, e.g. in the British Navy. See Willam Duker, "The President's Power to Pardon: A Constitutional History," *William and Mary Law Review* 18 (1977): 475–538 at 478.

60 Jean Starobinski, *Largesse*, trans. Jane Marie Todd (Chicago: University of Chicago Press, 1997).

61 Agamben, *The Omnibus Homo Sacer*, *supra* note 29, 222–29.

62 Jackson, "Justice and Righteousness," *supra* note 41, in accordance with his interpretation of biblical law as including the suspending power, suggests that the *deror* was a means to give effect to legal rights, rather than something regarded as separate from the law. This would certainly be true from the standpoint of a "monistic" conception of justice as he describes; however, it still seems to me that there is analytical value in distinguishing such sovereign acts from strictly legal ones, as we have seen in the course of our analysis.

that began already in the Hebrew Bible with the institutions of the Sabbatical and Jubilee years.[63] Gradually, the idea of a "redeemer" (*go'el*), one who buys something back from debt, and of a future redemption that involved a literal liberation from bondage, was extended to a more general idea of salvation:

> This idea [of redemption], of fundamental importance in the Old Testament and Talmud, in the gospels and all Christian doctrine, has its root in early law. It is one might justly say, an outstanding example of a legal notion being taken up and made into a religious notion by priests and prophets. ... In the end, the notion of redemption was even more spiritualized, and God thought of as redeeming His people not only from physical slavery but also from the fetters of sin and death.[64]

The importance to the identity of the Israelites of the deliverance from slavery in Egypt during the Exodus and the Conquest of Canaan served to reinforce this metaphor.[65] Daube focused on the root of the concept as "red-emption" or buying back,[66] although he noted that already in the case of most places in the Hebrew Bible where the notion of redemption appears, no actual payment is implied.[67] Still the concrete basis of this metaphor in a legal transaction shone through.[68] Daube contended that "that peculiar element from the socio-legal sphere, the idea of salvation by means of 'red-emption', ... occurs in no other system."[69]

In some cases, indeed, the use of the idea to denote the one who redeems the blood of the victim of a murder (*go'el ha-dam*), an archaic idea connected to the *lex talionis*, continued to inform the notion of a spiritual redeemer who removes the stain of sin and death.[70] Daube noted the application of this idea to Jesus in the Gospels, and added that "In the Middle Ages, the legal element in the idea of redemption by God ... At times perhaps ... was over-emphasized: salvation, with some theologians, became almost a business transaction."[71] Here he may have been referring to Anselm of Canterbury, whose explanation of the mechanism of salvation through Jesus' death on the cross in *Cur Deus Homo* has been interpreted by some critics as based on a crude materialism resting on feudal notions of justice and the institution of *Wergeld*, or payment as compensation for a homicide.

Redemption, as Daube understood it, is a legal concept that specifies the conditions under which a debt may be canceled or repurchased. It literally meant "buying back." The process that Daube described, namely the metaphorical extension into the religious domain of this originally legal or commercial idea, appears to represent

63 Daube, "Law in the Narratives," *supra* note 9, 39–62.
64 Ibid., 42.
65 Ibid., 52.
66 Ibid., 39.
67 Ibid., 41.
68 Ibid., 48.
69 Ibid., 60.
70 Ibid., 58–59.
71 Ibid., 61.

a key case of the sacralization of law. However, the situation is quite complex, and there are considerations that weigh against the conclusion that these ideas were ever purely legal, if by this is meant "nonreligious." To begin with, the notion of repurchasing something that has been devoted for sacrifice is a common one in the Hebrew Bible.[72] While this qualifies as an economic transaction, it also pertains to a key form of ritual praxis and, as such, can hardly be termed nonreligious. Significantly, in the uses of *charis* described in the preceding section, the idea of debt (or lending) appears, but there is no mention whatsoever of a legally defined repurchase. The notion of *charis* that appears in Paul and Luke coincides with that of the pardon in its original etymology as "*par don*," meaning by free gift rather than by obligation.

More importantly, in terms of the foregoing analysis, is that the liberation achieved by the *andurarum/deror*, like individual pardons, was a sovereign act, even when performed by a judge, rather than a legal act in the narrow sense. In the *deror* of the Hebrew Bible, this act has been legalized and routinized to some extent, although its close connections with sovereignty arguably persist.[73] This remained the case when subsequently, in Christian traditions, redemption was theologized as an act of divine grace, an act that was itself an expression of God's sovereignty and omnipotence. In 1300, long after the period Daube describes, the institution of the Jubilee was revived by the Popes as part of the economy of indulgences and penances that developed in the High Middle Ages. Starting from 1400, every twenty-five years (save in 1800, due to the Napoleonic wars) has witnessed a Jubilee in Rome that grants the compliant pilgrim a plenary indulgence from sin. This institution depends on the Pope's "power of the keys" or authority to bind and loosen the fetters of sin, and to open or close the doors of heaven. Such pardon powers are traditional attributes of sovereignty.

In recent centuries, this aspect of sovereignty is sometimes called the "dispensing power," meaning the sovereign's ability to dispense with or suspend a legal order. Because one of the main applications of this power consists of the granting of pardons, it has also been referred to as "the royal prerogative of mercy," which is one of the "absolute" as opposed to "ordinary prerogatives" of the king. It appears clear that this power was established through analogy to God's omnipotence. Kathleen Moore states: "Pardon has historically been understood as an act of grace, a gift freely given from a God-like monarch to a subject."[74] Daniel Franklin agrees: "Prerogative powers permitted the king to exceed the established laws of the state. This was considered permissible inasmuch as the king, as the embodiment of

72 See, e.g., Leviticus 27.

73 Yelle, *Sovereignty and the Sacred*, *supra* note 33, ch. 5.

74 Kathleen Moore, *Pardons: Justice, Mercy, and the Public Interest* (New York: Oxford University Press, 1989), 8–9. Moore appears to be closely paraphrasing Chief Justice John Marshall's statement in *United States* v. *Wilson* (1833) that "A pardon is an act of grace, ... which exempts the individual, on whom it is bestowed, from the punishment the law inflicts for a crime he has committed." 32 U.S. (7 Pet.) (1833) 150 at 159–60.

the state, was a representative of god on earth."[75] In his book on the development of habeas corpus, Paul Halliday traces this power to the same source, namely the divine right of kings:[76] "For that is what the royal power to create sanctuary or to grant pardon was: a miracle by which the normal rules of law, which might inflict the ultimate pains on the subject's body, were suspended."[77] As Halliday notes, habeas corpus, or the power to command that the king's subjects be brought before the Court of King's Bench for justice, often served as the preliminary to the granting of a pardon. The concept of "equity" advanced by the King's Bench, also in opposition to the "law" of the Court of Common Pleas, might be regarded as a lesser, related power.

Both Halliday and Franklin refer to the pardon as an example of the "absolute" as opposed to the "ordinary prerogative" of the king.[78] These were later names for what were called in the High Middle Ages the absolute and ordained powers, powers that were attributed originally to God and extended by analogy to human sovereigns, such as Popes and Emperors. (See Table 7.2.) Together with divine commands, the miracles in the Hebrew Bible were one of the chief sources of evidence for God's omnipotence.[79] It is this older idea of divine and royal sovereignty, founded on the miracle, that Schmitt contended had been excluded by the modern ascendancy of law. The pardon power is a residue of this absolute power.

The plenary extent of the pardon power is striking. A pardon was held by numerous authorities to remove the guilt as well as the punishment attaching to an offense. In the thirteenth century, Henry Bracton stated that the pardoned "is like a new born infant and a new man, as it were."[80] In the seventeenth century, Matthew Hale said that "Exemption from guilt and punishment comes properly enough under this title, *viz.* by pardon. . . . The king's pardon in such cases is so strong that it takes away the guilt *in foro humano* as well as the punishment."[81] In *Ex parte Garland* (1866), the US Supreme Court stated that a presidential pardon makes the pardoned "as innocent as if he had never committed the offense."[82] Both the idea of being born again, and that of granting dispensation from the guilt (or *culpa*) as well as the punishment (or *pœna*) attached to an offense, were originally theological ideas

75 Daniel P. Franklin, *Extraordinary Measures: The Exercise of Prerogative Powers in the United States* (Pittsburgh: University of Pittsburgh Press, 1991), 20.

76 Paul Halliday, *Habeas Corpus: From England to Empire* (Cambridge: Harvard University Press, 1989), 66–69.

77 Ibid., 72.

78 Ibid., 68, Franklin, *Extraordinary Measures*, *supra* note 75, 21–22.

79 For a general discussion, see Yelle, *Sovereignty and the Sacred*, *supra* note 33, ch. 2. For divine command in Judaism, see Jackson, "Constructing a Theory of Halakhah," *supra* note 41, 20–21.

80 Bracton, *De Legibus et Consuetudinebus Angliane* 3: 371, trans. S. Thorne (1879), quoted in Duker, "The President's Power," *supra* note 59, at534.

81 Matthew Hale, *The Prerogatives of the King*, ed. D. E. C. Yale (London: Selden Society, 1976), 260. See also Duker, "The President's Power," *supra* note 59, at 490, quoting Francis Winnington in a case involving Charles II's attempt to pardon before impeachment Thomas Osborne, the Earl of Danby.

82 71 U.S. 333 (1866) at 380.

applied in the case of penances and indulgences in the Roman Catholic Church. Although there are certain limits on the pardon power today, the roots of that power lie deep in the notion of absolute sovereignty formerly expressed by the divine right of kings.

Based upon the foregoing summary, we should have to conclude that the modern pardon power is not, as Daube thought, a "sacralized legal notion," but instead, as Schmitt put it, a "secularized theological notion." Aspects of the power arguably continue to betray its religious roots: for example, the fact that a discharge from all debts in bankruptcy occurs in the seventh year, like the Sabbatical year in the Hebrew Bible.[83]

VII CONCLUSION

However, the larger conclusion is that it in fact makes no sense to speak of "sacralization" or "secularization." These terms have significance only in the context of an understanding of what "religion" means. And the entire thrust of our analysis has been that religion (meaning "religion in general") does not exist as something separate from a total social order that is characterized by the dynamic interplay between law and sovereignty, defined as the authority to suspend the law. Where "religion" has emerged through the assertion of an independent sovereignty (as in the case of Gelasius, or already with Jesus), or in the form of a differentiated institution (such as the Roman Catholic Church), there is nothing, objectively speaking, that permits us to identify such a sovereign as "religious" except through its contrast with another mode of sovereignty that is defined, in opposition, as "secular." Even in this case, the doubleness (or duplicity?) of this opposition remains, since it continues to depend on the original interplay between sovereignty and legality (or *auctoritas* versus *potestas*), that is now itself reduplicated, through the Two Swords. Where Gelasius said, *Duo sunt*, Thomas Hobbes answered that the Church (*ekklesia*) was merely a political community like any other: "And therefore, a Church, such a one as is capable to command, to judge, absolve, condemn, or do any other act, is the same thing with a civil commonwealth ... Temporal and spiritual government are but two words brought into the world to make men see double and mistake their lawful sovereign."[84]

Hobbes's reduction of religion only aimed to prevent the multiplication and confusion of overlapping sovereignties. The recognition of religion as a form of politics does not remove the need for sovereignty itself, either as the power that

[83] I have been unable to trace the precise source of this provision, although the discharge itself appears to go back at least to the reforms passed under Queen Anne at the beginning of the eighteenth century in England.

[84] Thomas Hobbes, *Leviathan*, ed. Edwin Curley (Indianapolis: Hackett, 1994), chap. 39, sec. 5. See discussion in Robert A. Yelle, "Hobbes the Egyptian: The Return to Pharaoh, or the Ancient Roots of Secular Politics," in A. Azfar Moin and Alan Strathern, eds., *Sacred Kingship in World History: Between Immanence and Transcendence* (New York: Columbia University Press, in press).

superintends (and suspends) law, or as the hope for redemption, grace, or a higher form of justice. What we call "religion" has given voice to this hope, and often asserted a sovereign independence in its name.

I can no longer tell, at the end of this study, where law ends and religion begins. These two qualities appear to be intertwined, like Siamese twins or (as in the case of another metaphor deployed by Paul against the Law) Jacob and Esau, who struggled even in the womb for supremacy. Esau was entitled to rule by law, meaning the right of primogeniture. Yet he sold his birth right to Jacob, who also stole his brother's blessing which, although acquired through trickery, could not be recalled. The story of these twins suggests again that law is not enough, since its rigid forms can be broken or defeated. The question instead is, who shall be sovereign?

8

A Bad Man Theory of Religious Law (Numbers 15:30–31 and Its Afterlife)

David C. Flatto

I INTRODUCTION

In a recent survey of modern Jewish thought, Leora Batnitzky homes in on its central tension: Does Judaism – a tradition suffused with rules and rituals – constitute a religion?[1] If this term is understood to emphasize the centrality of faith and creed, it seems inapposite to the hyper-normativity of Judaism. But discarding this label would call Judaism's legitimacy into question, at least from the vantage point of many who contemplated this matter at the dawn of modernity. Much of the creativity in the conceptions of Judaism that were formulated by leading Jewish thinkers from the eighteenth century onward emanated from grappling with this seminal challenge.[2]

The origins of this tension are usually traced to the sweeping transformations introduced by Jewish emancipation, including the consequential encounters of Jewish thinkers with Christian (especially, Protestant) theology.[3] Prior to the eighteenth century, on the conventional account, Judaism was widely conceived of as a "religion of laws." But this characterization glosses over variations within a tradition that evolved over many centuries.[4] Thus, substantial scholarship has explored the critical dialectic between "law" and "spirituality" in medieval Jewish thought.[5] Even in classical writings, one can discern a subtle and suggestive discourse surrounding these themes.

[1] Leora Batnitzky, *How Judaism Became a Religion: An Introduction to Modern Jewish Thought* (Princeton, NJ: Princeton University Press, 2011).

[2] This is the primary thesis of Batnitzky. See also Abraham Melamed, *Dat: From Law to Religion, a History of a Formative Term* [Hebrew] (Bnai Brak: Hakibutz Hameuhad, 2014).

[3] Protestant theology posed various challenges to Judaism. One came from the Protestant emphasis on faith over works or law. Another came from its conception of religion as being less of a public affair, and more of an interior or private matter, which is beyond the coercion of others. More generally, Protestant thought identified religion as apolitical, and therefore separate from, and consistent with, the expanding nation-state. The analysis below mostly relates to the first of these themes (along with other extra-normative dimensions of religiosity relating to the spiritual attitude and character of a person). See note 7. Batnitzky, by contrast, is also focused on religion's political dimensions.

[4] Another limitation of the conventional account is that the nature of law within the Jewish tradition also evolved over the centuries (see, e.g., the brief analysis of Mendelssohn's ceremonial laws in the conclusion). This phenomenon deserves further exploration.

[5] See, e.g., Isadore Twersky, *Studies in Jewish Law and Philosophy* (New York: Ktav Pub. House, 1982).

The latter needs to be underscored in light of contrary claims currently being advanced in the field of religious studies. Decrying the anachronism of applying the concept of "religion" to premodern works, scholars have urged us to "imagine no religion" in conjuring up the world of antiquity and late antiquity. In this vein, a recently published book under this title argues that various terms that appear in classical writings are mistranslated as "religion" and "theology."[6] But the absence of analogous terminology in older works is hardly dispositive. While the mature constructs of modern theology may be only of late vintage, substantial "religious" impulses or emphases relating to beliefs,[7] attitudes, or values beyond the system of norms are arguably embedded in much historic material.[8] Only a careful excavation of early literature can reveal their imprints.

The chapter below turns back many centuries before the period covered by Batnitzky's survey in order to further interrogate various conceptions of "Judaism" that are reflected in formative writings from antiquity and late antiquity. It seeks to illuminate whether earlier iterations of "Judaism" were so fully aligned with law and praxis that they constituted the entirety of religious life and its ultimate achievement. Or, alternatively, whether one can already perceive in earlier traditional discourse an acknowledgment, or even an articulation, of a "religious" or "theological" nucleus apart from the normative order.[9]

Instead of an elusive attempt to reconstruct the core of "Judaism" (which has been ventured by others with debatable degrees of success),[10] one can gain precious insight about its essence by concentrating on its measure of sacrilege

6 See Carlin A. Barton and Daniel Boyarin, *Imagine No Religion: How Modern Abstractions Hide Ancient Realities* (New York: Fordham University Press, 2016). See also Brent Nongbri, *Before Religion: A History of a Modern Concept* (New Haven: Yale University Press, 2013).

7 In this chapter, when I speak of "law" I am referring to a system of norms, mostly comprised of discrete actions that are mandated or proscribed, based on prescripts in the Torah and related traditions. In general, the term "religion" is rather open ended, and can encompass different matters. See, e.g., Micah Gottlieb's review of Batnitzky, *How Judaism Became a Religion*, entitled, "Are We All Protestants Now?," *Jewish Review of Books*, Vol. 10 (Summer 2012). In this chapter, however, when I explore the contours of religion beyond the system of prescribed norms, I am referring to beliefs, attitudes, or commitments, or what may be conceived of as modes of relating faithfully to, or with, God. Beyond this, I am not suggesting particular, rigid definitions of "law" or "religion," and recognize the fluidity of these concepts over time, and in different contexts.

8 See Annette Y. Reed, "Partitioning 'Religion' and its Prehistories: Reflections on Categories, Narratives, and the Practice of Religious Studies," in *The Things We Study When We Study Religion*, ed. Leslie Dorrough Smith (Sheffield: Equinox, forthcoming).

Admittedly, there is a danger of universalizing phenomena that are more contextual or contingent, and in this respect the nomenclature can obfuscate as well as illuminate.

9 To be sure, much biblical, Second Temple and rabbinic literature focuses on matters that pertain to faith. Yet throughout this corpus (but see note 13), the core religious life is evidently structured around prescripts and commandments. See generally Menachem Kellner, *Must a Jew Believe Anything?* (London; Portland, OR: Littman Library of Jewish Civilization, 1999). The inquiry below interrogates whether this characterization is incomplete, and whether there is a significant sphere of religious life that exists apart from the normative field

10 See, e.g., George Foot Moore, *Judaism in the First Centuries of the Christian Era: The Age of Tannaim* 2nd ed. (Cambridge, MA: Harvard University Press, 1927); Solomon Schechter, *Some Aspects of*

or heresy.[11] What a tradition considers to be utterly contrary to its core reveals much about its foundations. This chapter therefore concentrates on conceptions of the "bad man" in early Jewish discourse to learn about where it draws its most fundamental lines.[12] In a concentrated form, this is vividly captured by the hermeneutic legacy of one seminal biblical passage.

A *A Biblical Source and Its Afterlife*

The conception of Judaism as a "religion of laws" derives in the first instance from the paramount role of norms in the Torah.[13] A plethora of commandments – including civil, criminal, cultic, and ritual prescripts – fill this corpus. Moreover, divine revelation at Sinai consists entirely of mandatory canons. In stipulating the observance of these laws, God enters into a binding covenant with Israel. By pledging its steadfast commitment to upholding these commandments, Israel in turn becomes a "priestly kingdom and holy nation" (Exodus 19:6). Legal obeisance is thus necessitated not for social or political reasons, but as a sacred imperative.[14] It is for this reason that when the term "Torah" is translated into Greek it is rendered as "*nomos*." The central theology of the Torah revolves around its laws.[15]

Rabbinic Theology (New York: Macmillan, 1910); and Ephraim E. Urbach, *The Sages, Their Concepts and Beliefs*, trans. Israel Abrahams (Cambridge, MA: Harvard University Press, 1987).

11 Any study of the "essence" of Judaism must contend with the elusiveness or nebulousness of this concept. This is further exacerbated by many renderings that have accumulated over the centuries (and is also muddied by loaded terms such as "religion" and "law," which are themselves open to variable definitions). Nevertheless, such an inquiry is too vital to strike down on peremptory grounds. Rather this seminal topic must be approached from multiple perspectives, which can contribute meaningfully to a broader account. This chapter aims to make a contribution in this vein by considering an aspect of this inquiry that has been largely overlooked.

12 The nomenclature of the "bad man" deliberately borrows from the famous American jurist Oliver Wendell Holmes, notwithstanding the very different connotation of this phrase in its original context. Writing in the "Path of the Law," a seminal late nineteenth century account of the nature of jurisprudence, Justice Holmes writes the following provocative words: "If you want to know the law and nothing else, you must look at it as a bad man, who cares only for the material consequences which such knowledge enables him to predict . . . " 10 *Harvard Law Review* 457, 459 (1897).

In this quintessential formulation of legal realism, Holmes stresses the significance of the real-world consequences of law for an offender. In this chapter, the subject matter and underlying argument is altogether different: If you want to know the degree to which a legalistic religion such as Judaism is exclusively defined by norms, you must (also) evaluate its conception of the ultimate sinner or transgressor.

13 In the rest of the Bible, the role of law is much less pronounced. See James L. Kugel, "Some Unanticipated Consequences of the Sinai Revelation: A Religion of Laws," in *The Significance of Sinai: Traditions About Sinai and Divine Revelation in Judaism and Christianity*, ed. George J. Brooke, Hindy Najman and Loren T. Stuckenbruck (Leiden; Boston: Brill, 2008), 1–4. In postbiblical literature, there are also less legalistic strands. See, e.g., John J. Collins, "How Distinctive was Enochic Judaism?" *Meghillot* 5–6 (2007): 1–18.

14 See James L. Kugel, *The Great Shift: Encountering God in Biblical Times* (Boston: Houghton Mifflin Harcourt Publishing Company, 2017) 177–86.

15 See Jon Levenson, *Sinai and Zion: An Entry into the Jewish Bible* (New Voices in Biblical Studies series; San Francisco: Harper & Row, 1985), 42–55; and James L. Kugel, *How to Read the Bible: A Guide to Scripture, Then and Now* (New York: Free Press, 2007), 260–79.

Numerous scholars have articulated this vital feature of the Torah, perhaps none more cogently than Moshe Greenberg.[16] Contrasting the nature of biblical law with earlier cuneiform codes of the Ancient Near East, Greenberg highlights the religious character of the former as its distinguishing essence. His description (which focuses particularly on biblical criminal law) culminates with the striking implications of this phenomenon:

> In the biblical theory the idea of the transcendence of the law receives a more thoroughgoing expression . . . .There is a distinctively religious tone here, fundamentally different in quality from the political benefits guaranteed in the cuneiform law collections. In the sphere of the criminal law, the effect of this divine authorship of all law is *to make crimes sins*, a violation of the will of God.[17]

Formulated more generally, according to the Torah, violating any law is tantamount to sinning against God.

Adducing support for this proposition, Greenberg singles out one Pentateuchal source, Numbers 15:30–31.[18] To appreciate how this source functions as a proof text requires further background. As will soon become evident, Greenberg, if anything, is understating the dramatic implications of these verses.

The middle section of Numbers 15 (verses 22–31) records a pericope (the "Numbers pericope") relating to different modes of violating an unspecified transgression, which is comprised of two parts. Part one (15:22–29) addresses the sacrificial atonement for an inadvertent transgression of a community or an individual,[19] while part two (15:30–31) describes the fatal punishment for an individual transgression that is committed "with a raised hand" (Hebrew "*beyad ramah*"). Due to the juxtaposition of the two parts, the latter phrase has been interpreted by most scholars, including Greenberg, to refer to a transgression that is committed intentionally[20]

16 Moshe Greenberg, "Some Postulates of Biblical Criminal Law," in *Studies in the Bible and Jewish Thought* 1st ed. (JPS Scholar of Distinction series; Philadelphia: Jewish Publication Society, 1995) 25–42.

17 Ibid., 28. Emphasis added.

18 Ibid., 29.

19 Numbers 15 refers to an inadvertent transgression of the community (15:24–26) and an individual (15:27–29). The topic of atonement for an inadvertent transgression is also addressed in Leviticus 4, which refers to these same two bodies, as well as two other figures (an anointed priest and a leader), and contains somewhat different regulations. The relationship of Number 15 to Leviticus 4 is much debated by commentators and scholars. See the references cited in the next two notes.

20 See Rashi on Numbers 15:30, who defines "*beyad ramah*" as "*be-mezid*." Among modern scholars, see Baruch A. Levine, *Numbers 1–20: A New Translation with Introduction and Commentary* 1st ed. (Anchor Bible series; New York: Doubleday, 1993) 396; Aryeh Toeg, "A Halakhic Midrash in Numbers 15.22–31," [Hebrew] *Tarbiz* 43 (1973–74): 1; Jacob Licht, A *Commentary on Numbers* [Hebrew] (Jerusalem: Magnes Press, 1985–91), 92; Aharon Shemesh, *Punishments and Sins: From Scripture to the Rabbis* [Hebrew] (Jerusalem: Magnes Press, 2003), 58; and Bennie H. Reynolds, "The Expression *Beyad Ramah* in the Hebrew Bible and the Dead Sea Scrolls and the Legacy of the Holiness School in Essene Legal Texts," *JBL* 132.3 (2013): 589, 604. See also Jacob Milgrom, *Numbers* (New York: JPS, 1990), 96, 122 and Appendix 35.

In general, Shemesh's analysis of the Numbers pericope, as well as its subsequent exegesis in Qumran and rabbinic literature, is highly illuminating.

(a dissenting viewpoint interprets it as a publicly defiant act, which seems to be the meaning of "*beyad ramah*" elsewhere in the Bible).[21] The contrast between the two parts of the pericope on this (majority) reading is plain. Whereas an inadvertent transgression can be atoned for by (a specific regimen of) sacrifices, an intentional transgression cannot, and is instead punished harshly.

What is the nature of the transgression discussed in this pericope (in either part)? The verses invoke the generic formulation of the transgression of the "commandments."[22] This implies that the second part of the pericope refers to an intentional violation of *any* prohibition.[23]

In light of this, the second part's description of the gravity of a single violation and its ensuing punishment is startling (far exceeding Greenberg's measured formulation that a violation constitutes a sin). Here are the verses in full:

> [30]But whoever acts intentionally (*beyad ramah*), whether a native or an alien, blasphemes (*megadef*) the Lord, and shall be cut off (*venikhrata*) from among the people. [31]Because of having despised the word of the Lord (*devar Hashem bazah*) and breached his commandment (*mitsvato hefer*), such a person shall be utterly cut off (*hikaret tikaret*) and bear the guilt (*avonah bah*).

A person who intentionally violates the law – any law – blasphemes God, the ultimate form (or act) of sacrilege. By transgressing God's word, he or she despises it; and by failing to uphold a commandment, he or she annuls it. An act of such gravity saddles its perpetrator with guilt. Echoing an ominous refrain, Scripture declares a ruthless punishment of excision for the transgressor (variants of the term *karet* appear three times in these verses).[24] More than a sin (Greenberg's characterization), a violation of

Note that this chapter mostly focuses on "*beyad ramah*" as a key phrase. In addition, the interpretations of other – arguably interrelated – terms, phrases, and clauses in these verses are also significant. See notes 54 and 77.

21 See Targum Onqelos on Numbers 15:30, who defines "*beyad ramah*" as "*be-resh gali*," bare-headed (i.e., an idiom for a brazen posture). Certain modern scholars likewise posit a "gap theory" in construing this pericope: While 15:22–29 refers to an inadvertent transgression, 15:30–31 glosses over an intentional violation and instead addresses the impact and punishment of a brazen transgression. See Roy Gane, *Cult and Character: Purification Offerings, Day of Atonement, and Theodicy* (Winona Lake, IN: Eisenbrauns, 2005), 204–13; Joel S. Baden, "The Structure and Substance of Numbers 15," *Vetus Testamentum* 63 (2013): 359; Timothy R. Ashley, *The Book of Numbers* (Grand Rapids: Wm. B. Eerdmans Publishing Co., 1993), 288; Host Seebass, *Numeri* (Neukirchen-Vluyn: Neukirchener, 1995), 146–47; and Aryeh Amihay, *Theory and Practice in Essene Law* (New York: Oxford University Press, 2017), 94. The dissenting viewpoint is informed in part by the semantic of the term "*beyad ramah*" elsewhere in Scripture. See note 32.

22 The opening verse of the pericope, Numbers 15:22, refers to "all of the commandments," which presumably means a single violation of any of them. When the passage shifts to the transgression of an individual (whether inadvertent or "*beyad ramah*"), it clearly relates to a single violation, as reflected in the formulations of 15:27, 31.

23 In theory, this can refer to violating any negative commandment or abrogating any positive commandment, but it is plausible to limit it to the former category. See Toeg, "A Halakhic Midrash in Numbers 15.22–31," 3–4.

24 *Karet* is usually understood as a divine punishment, but there is a dissenting viewpoint in modern scholarship. See Shemesh, *Punishments and Sins*, 59.

a norm according to these verses constitutes a shattering transgression which evokes a devastating response. The pericope emphatically projects legal obeisance as the measure of religious devotion.[25]

In an important analysis of this pericope, Aryeh Toeg likewise draws attention to the extraordinary rhetoric it employs when describing the consequences of a single transgression (i.e., blaspheming God, etc.). In order to account for this charged language, Toeg posits that these verses are formulated with a "prophetic vocabulary" that conveys the experiential dimension – rather than the normative implications – of sin.[26] By appealing to an alternate genre to explain these verses, Toeg rightly magnifies their religious intensity. But their semantic cannot be stripped of its normative content which is integral to their meaning.[27] Rather, the brunt of these verses emanates from the way they yoke religion and theology to legal obeisance. Only by conceiving of religion as primarily filtered through law, can such radical verses about the consequences of a transgression be comprehended.[28]

Given the potency of these verses, the question of their legacy becomes critical. These verses confront all subsequent readers and interpreters, who must determine whether they can assimilate, or abide by, their plain, and radical, implications about the theological weight of law. Alternatively, if they reinterpret these verses (by rendering "*beyad ramah*" and its other loaded phrases in a different manner) to refer to something other than an intentional violation of law as the root of religious blasphemy this will inevitably lead to a revised construction of the theological

25 Presumably, the pericope operates within a covenantal framework which adds to the gravity of each legal violation. See, e.g., Gane, *Cult and Character*, 212. This is certainly how these verses are understood in Qumran literature. But see the references to an alien (*ger*) in Numbers 15:26, 29, 30, which may complicate matters. See Christiana van Houten, *The Alien in Israelite Law* (Sheffield: JSOT Press, 1991), 149–51.

26 See Toeg, "A Halakhic Midrash in Numbers 15.22–31," 1–20 (the extraordinary rhetoric is highlighted ibid., 2). See also Michael Fishbane, *Biblical Interpretation in Ancient Israel* (Oxford: Oxford University Press, 1985), 189–94, 223–24.

27 In any event, it is apparent from the analysis below that certain early biblical interpreters understood the verses in this pericope to have normative significance.

28 Even then, certain scholars feel the need to further contextualize the underlying ideology of the Numbers pericope. For example, Toeg associates it with Leviticus 19's particular conception of commandments as an inexorable expression of the divine will (which is captured in the refrain "I am God" that is reiterated throughout the litany of commandments recorded in Leviticus 19). In such a scheme, breaching any commandment constitutes a clear affront to God. See "A Halakhic Midrash in Numbers 15.22–31," 17–19. Israel Knohl, in turn, links it to the interpersonal relationship between man and God that is intrinsic to "Holiness" theology. See "The Sin Offering Law in the 'Holiness School' (Numbers 14.22–31)," in *Priesthood and Cult in Ancient Israel*, ed. Gary A. Anderson and Saul M. Olyan (JSOTSup 125; Sheffield: JSOT Press, 1991), 192–203.

While these scholarly theories have a certain appeal, they may situate the Numbers pericope in too narrow a frame. As Greenberg intimates (but understates), this pericope's ideology is in consonance with the legalism of Sinai and much of the Pentateuch, even if its implications are striking. In any event, such theories are not relevant for the postbiblical (i.e., Second Temple and rabbinic) legacy of the Number's pericope. But see Reynolds, "The Expression *Beyad Ramah*," 591, 04–605, about the nexus between Holiness theology and the Qumran scrolls.

sphere. The exegesis of these verses thus serves as a prism for subsequent interpreters to negotiate the foundational relationship between religion and law.

Notwithstanding the singular tone and content of the Numbers pericope, it takes on much significance in early postbiblical exegesis.[29] Below I will examine two sets of exegetical traditions which (for the most part) advance profoundly different approaches toward these consequential verses. A dominant trope in Qumran literature, where these verses have a surprisingly pervasive afterlife, builds upon their plain sense in constructing a religious world view structured around the normative order. In contrast, rabbinic literature largely pivots in another direction, articulating novel forms of religious heresy that are increasingly differentiated from the sphere of law. While both traditions contain counter voices and overlap to a certain extent, their overall divergent emphases are unmistakable. These diverse traditions advance alternate paradigms of law and religion.

II QUMRAN LITERATURE

The distinct formulations and verses of Numbers 15:30–31 figure prominently in the Qumran corpus, especially in a couple of passages I will analyze below. In fact, Elisha Qimron notes that the Scrolls routinely employ the Scriptural term "*beyad ramah*" as a standard label for an intentional transgression (alongside other terms for an inadvertent one, such as "*shogeg*"), instead of the common biblical and rabbinic term, "*mezid*."[30] This usage reflects that the Numbers pericope is often understood at face value in this corpus (i.e., following the majority reading).

If the term "*beyad ramah*" signifies an intentional violation, however, it should not be construed merely as a technical term. As Aryeh Amihay has argued, this phrase evidently retains a loaded biblical resonance in Qumran.[31] While Amihay bases this term's fuller semantic upon several biblical passages (such as Exodus 14:8, Numbers 33:3, etc.), most of the Qumran references that invoke this term appeal specifically to Numbers 15:30 (as recently stressed by B. Reynolds).[32] As noted, in the Numbers pericope the term means any intentional transgression; and violating any such

29 The Numbers pericope also has an important afterlife in early Christian literature, with an emphasis on the sin of blasphemy. See, e.g., Mark 3:28–29; Matthew 12:32; Luke 12:10. Highlighting this particular sin may reflect a somewhat distinct interpretive tradition of the Numbers pericope. See note 70. See also David Flusser, "Some of the Precepts of the Torah from Qumran (4QMMT) and the Benediction Against the Heretics," [Hebrew] *Tarbiz* 61 (1992): 336–38; and Yair Furstenburg, *Purity and Community in Antiquity* [Hebrew] (Jerusalem: Magnes Press, 2016), 61.

30 Qimron further argues that the term "*zadon*" of Deuteronomy 17:12 is deliberately transformed to "*beyad ramah*" in 4Q159. In 4Q171 both terms are used. See Elisha Qimron, "On Unintentional and Intentional Sins in the Dead Sea Scrolls: A Study in the Terms Used for Their Designation," [Hebrew] *WCJS* 10a (1990) 103–10.

31 See Amihay, *Theory and Practice in Essene Law*, 93–99.

32 See Reynolds, "The Expression *Beyad Ramah*," 589. There are certain historic and exegetical passages in Qumran that seem to appeal to other scriptural references of the term "*beyad ramah*" where the semantic is a brazen, public, defiant or haughty act. See ibid., 600–04.

transgression, according to the pericope, constitutes a blasphemy against God. By repeatedly citing this term, then, Qumran authors are presumably evoking this meaning, and making its strong nexus between law and religion a centerpiece of their ideology (a secondary set of Qumran texts discussed below function differently).[33] In certain Qumran texts this ideology is in fact especially pronounced. Building upon the Numbers pericope, they project normative perfection as essential to the religious identity of the sect, and therefore consider transgressions to be particularly damaging to the religious fabric of the community.[34]

A vivid instance of the latter is found in the opening passage of the foundational rules of the Community (the "rules of volunteering") in 1QS 5.[35] Explicitly invoking the term "*beyad ramah*" toward the end, the passage throughout expands on its themes. After delineating the formative covenant of the sectarian community, which revolves around punctilious observance of the laws of Moses as explicated by the priestly sons of Zadok, the passage draws a stark contrast between its members and the wicked sinners. A new initiate to the community must openly pledge his allegiance:

> He should swear by the covenant to be segregated from all the men of injustice who walk along the path of wickedness. (1QS 5:10–11)

The Scroll's account of the latter is particularly significant:

> For they are not included in his covenant since they have neither sought nor examined His decrees in order to know the hidden matters (*nistarot*) in which they err by their own fault and because they intentionally violated (*beyad ramah*) revealed matters (*niglot*). (1QS 5:11–12)

Invoking the terminology of the Numbers pericope, the passage extends its scope to encompass a collective rather than an individual, and to repeat violations rather than a single transgression. Further, it conflates the two parts of the pericope in characterizing the "men of injustice." Negligently violating hidden, that is, unrevealed, prohibitions (corresponding to the inadvertent transgression of Numbers 15:22–29)[36]

33 Qimron describes the Qumran corpus as less developed in its vocabulary for intentionality than rabbinic literature, which uses the terminology of "*mezid*." However, the deployment of "*beyad ramah*" seems deliberate and purposeful in this oeuvre, as intentional violations are tantamount to a grave sin in Qumran theology.

34 See also Gary A. Anderson, "The Interpretation of the Purification Offering (*Hatat*) in the *Temple Scroll* (11QTemple) and Rabbinic Literature," *JBL* 111 (1992): 17–35, who argues that according to Qumran exegesis Numbers 15 is the primary source for inadvertent transgressions. It records the general rule, while Leviticus 4 addresses the special sacrificial rites for the consecration of the Tabernacle (in contrast, rabbinic exegesis identifies Leviticus 4 as the primary source that records the general rule, while Numbers 15 addresses the case of idolatry, at least according to a well-known rabbinic tradition discussed below).

35 For further analysis, see Aharon Shemesh and Cana Werman, *Revealing the Hidden: Exegesis and Halakhah in the Qumran Scrolls* [Hebrew] (Jerusalem:Mosad Bialik, 2011),246–54.

36 On the relationship between the concealed or unrevealed teachings of the sect, and inadvertent transgressions, see Aharon Shemesh and Cana Werman, "Hidden Things and their Revelation," [Hebrew] *Tarbiz* 66 (1997): 471–82; Shemesh and Werman, *Revealing the Hidden*, 81–83;

as well as intentionally violating revealed ones (corresponding to the intentional transgression of 15:30–31), the ignoble sinners are those who continually transgress the law. They are fated to a ravaging punishment, an intensification of the damning fate of Numbers 15:

> this is why wrath will rise up for judgment in order to effect revenge by the curses of the covenant, in order to administer fierce punishments for everlasting annihilation (*kalah*) without there being any remnant. *Blank* (1QS 5:12–13).[37]

Expanding upon the Numbers pericope in these various ways, the passage magnifies the stakes of legal obeisance.

Another remarkable passage with a similar ideological thrust appears later in (certain recensions of) 1QS. Establishing a penal scheme for a sectarian member who violates a single transgression, it relies explicitly on the Numbers pericope. In its bold implementation of the biblical template, it likewise revises certain of its salient features.

The passage opens by underscoring the meticulous normative standards demanded from members of the sect (referred to here as the "council of holiness"):[38]

> *Blank* These are the regulations by which the men of perfect holiness shall conduct themselves, one with another. All who enter the council of holiness of those walking in perfect behavior as he commanded. (1QS 8:20–21)

What happens when a member violates these binding rules depends on the mode of the offense. Initially, the passage relates to an intentional violation ("*beyad ramah*"), based on Numbers 15:30–31:

> anyone of them who breaks a word of the law of Moses intentionally (*beyad ramah*) or fraudulently (*remiyah*) will be banished from the Community council and shall not return again . . . . (1QS 8:21–23).

Next, the passage relates to an inadvertent transgression based on the earlier verses of the Numbers pericope (Numbers 15:22–29):

> However if he acted inadvertently (*bi-shegaga*) he should be excluded from pure food and from the council and they shall apply the (following) regulation to him: ≪He may not judge anyone and [he may] not [be a]sked any advice for two whole years≫ ... if he has not sinned again through oversight until two full years have passed. *Blank*. (1QS 8:24–27)

Shani Tzoref, "The 'Hidden' and the 'Revealed': Progressive Revelation of Law and Esoterica," [Hebrew] *Meghillot* 7 (2009): 157–90; and Gary A. Anderson, "Intentional and Unintentional Sin in the Dead Sea Scrolls," in *Pomegranates and Golden Bells* (Winona Lake, IN: Eisenbrauns, 1995), 54–57.

37 See Jacob Licht, *Rule Scroll: A Scroll from the Wilderness of Judea: 1QS, 1QSa, 1QSb* (Jerusalem: Mosad Bialik, 1965), 132 (who compares this passage to 1QS 2:15 and 4:13); and note the allusions to Deuteronomy 29:19; Ezekiel 24:8; and Proverbs 15:1.

38 Scholars debate whether the council is equivalent to the community or not. See Shemesh, *Punishments and Sins*, 80–82.

This passage shares the orientation of the 1QS 5 passage, but each is more exacting in certain respects. Both underscore that transgressions violate the core religious identity of the sectarian community. The 1QS 8:20–27 passage further states that a single intentional violation leads to banishment from the Sectarian community.[39] In other words, it affirms the plain sense of Numbers 15:30–31 in all its severity.[40] The passage diverges (at least in focus), however, from the 1QS 5 excerpt in terms of who responds to the intentional transgressor. Whereas 1QS 5 describes the intensified punishment of divine annihilation (*kalah*)[41] for transgressors, according to 1QS 8 the penal agent is the communal council who administers a punishment of expulsion. Indeed, in this sense 1QS 8 departs from the Numbers pericope, as well. According to the Numbers pericope, an intentional transgressor who sins against God receives a heavenly punishment of excision (repeated threefold in the verses), and an inadvertent one atones by bringing a sin offering. In 1QS 8 these are translated into communal punishments to be meted out by the council, the former by expulsion and the latter by way of a temporary ban.[42]

In order to illuminate the crux of 1QS 8, Aharon Shemesh attempts to reconstruct its theological underpinnings by linking it to other sections of the Rule of the Community and the Damascus Covenant.[43] For instance, he argues that an intentional transgressor is expelled by the council because his actions expose him as a "son of darkness," as described in 1QS 3 (or, perhaps more explicitly as a "wicked person," as described in 1QS 5). This also implies that following his ejection by the council, the transgressor will be vanquished by God.[44] Similarly, Shemesh explains the temporary expulsion of an inadvertent transgressor as based upon a larger theology of exile in the Scrolls.[45] As intriguing as these cross references are, they gloss over the locus of this passage, which is brought into sharper relief by its juxtaposition with 1QS 5. Instead of a heavenly damning of sinners, here the

39 This exacting standard may be an outgrowth of the intensified covenantal commitment among the members of the sectarian community. Dedicating to embodying a religious ethos of legal perfection, the community purges deviants as a way of maintaining this commitment. Note also that the scriptural references in 1QS 8 omit mention of the *ger* (alien) that appears in Numbers 15. See note 25. See generally Bilha Nitzan, "The Concept of the Covenant in Qumran Literature," in *Historical Perspectives: From the Hasmoneans to Bar Kohba in Light of the Dead Sea Scrolls*, eds. David Goodblatt et al. (Leiden: Brill, 2001), 85–104. See also Menahem Kister, "Marginalia Qumranica," [Hebrew] *Tarbiz* 57 (1988): 315–25.

40 There are various other related passages in Qumran literature. See Anderson, "Intentional and Unintentional Sin in the Dead Sea Scrolls," 51–52; and Shemesh, *Punishments and Sins*, 65–67, 72–80.

41 See also 1QS 4:14.

42 See also Simeon Chavel, "Numbers 15.32–36 – A Microcosm of the Living Priesthood and Its Literary Production," in *The Strata of the Priestly Writings: Contemporary Debate and Future Directions* (Zurich: AThANT 95, 2009), 45–56.

43 See Shemesh, *Punishments and Sins*, 60–82.

44 Shemesh, *Punishments and Sins*, 62 links this to a doubling of *karet* in Num 15:31, but it is more likely that it is based on an exegesis that construes "*karet*" as "*kalah*." In any event, according to Shemesh, the sectarian actors are abetting the divine punishment.

45 See Shemesh, *Punishments and Sins*, 67–72.

theological drama all plays out within the normative structure of the community. The religious constitution of the community is preserved by normative perfection; the spiritual state of an individual member turns on his legal obeisance; and his theological destiny is determined by the council's penal pronouncement. Religion is filtered through law, and law alone.

Several passages in the Qumran corpus offer variants of this paradigm.[46] In the proximate 1QS 8:15–17 passage, for instance, an intentional transgressor ("*beyad ramah*") is punished with (temporary) exile (not a permanent expulsion). According to CD 10:3, such a figure is only disqualified from delivering testimony. In other words, he remains nominally within the sectarian community, but is pushed to its margins in terms of his legal and social status.[47] Both of these sources likewise operate within a religious worldview that is highly legalistic (i.e., where an intentional transgression elicits a legal response, and the boundaries of the religious community are maintained by legal sanction), but calibrate the penal and social consequences in a different, and more lenient, manner. All three texts (CD 10, 1QS 8:15–17 and 20–27) echo the Numbers pericope in treating an intentional transgression as a decisive breach of the community's religious ethos of legal perfection.

Certain scholars attribute the severe Qumran punishment of an intentional transgressor recorded in 1QS 8:20–27 to the reality of sectarian life where maintaining social conformity was feasible.[48] While this context may make such an arrangement attractive or at least possible, it is hardly inevitable. When considered alongside the various passages surveyed above, 1QS 8 emerges as one response among several alternatives.[49]

Other Qumran writings (such as 1QS 6–7, 4Q266, frag. II, 4Q270, frag. 7i, 15–19), in fact, diverge from this paradigm and do not define the religious fabric of the sectarian community in normative terms. Operating with a dual construct similar to 1QS 8:20–27 (and arguably based upon its Scriptural foundation, the Numbers pericope), these texts crucially differ in terms of what triggers a harsher response. Instead of invoking the phrase "*beyad ramah*," they introduce terms like "*moes*," to despise, or "*libgod*," to rebel, to characterize the underlying wrong.[50] In other words, the grounds for expulsion from the community is a brazen rejection of God and the

46 Shemesh and Anderson downplay the significance of, or gloss over, these variants, but this is not convincing. See Shemesh, *Punishments and Sins*, 80–82; and Anderson, "Intentional and Unintentional Sin in the Dead Sea Scrolls," 57, n. 20.

47 The underpinnings of this legal-sociological construct, and its analog in the later rabbinic category of a *rasha*, require separate treatment. I explored aspects of this topic in a lecture entitled, "Who is Wicked? Adapting Witness Qualification Standards in Rabbinic Law" (Columbia University Conference in Honor of David Weiss Halivni, New York, NY, May 2005).

48 See Anderson, "Intentional and Unintentional Sin in the Dead Sea Scrolls," 53. Even if the sectarian milieu enabled such a scheme, it is still worth reflecting upon the religious axioms of such a system, which is my aim above.

49 See also 4Q159 which may even refer to a death penalty for a violation committed "*beyad ramah*," although this is far from certain. See Reynolds, "The Expression *Beyad Ramah*," 598.

50 These terms may be interpretations of the Scriptural terms "*beyad ramah*" and/or "*megadef*."

religious values of the community.[51] The foundational sin is thus not committing a legal violation, but repudiating the community's principal commitments. Prefiguring certain aspects of rabbinic literature, this strand reflects a secondary voice in the Qumran corpus.[52]

The dominant strand in Qumran writings, however, advances a religious order bounded within a normative frame. Here, the Numbers pericope openly serves as a foundational text, and "*beyad ramah*" (in its plain sense) functions as a pivotal term.[53] Further, a couple of passages expand upon this legalistic foundation in ways that exceed Scripture. 1QS 5 envisions a bloc of transgressors, a foil to the community, who will suffer divine castigation; and 1QS 8 circumscribes a covenantal community whose religious ethos is defined by law, and whose boundaries are controlled by law. By accentuating, augmenting, and implementing the striking paradigm of the Numbers pericope, this strand epitomizes a conception of Judaism as a religion of laws.

III RABBINIC LITERATURE

The primary rabbinic source that elaborates on the Numbers pericope – a range of homilies in the Sifre spread over two sections (111–12) – contains certain traces of the legalistic sectarian position.[54] In its opening paragraph (111), the Sifre records the well-known view of the rabbis which interprets the Numbers pericope as referring specifically to the transgression of idolatry (more on this shortly),[55] but first the

51 See the sources and analysis in Shemesh and Werman, *Revealing the Hidden*, 254–73.
Also, CD 3:9–19 sounds like the contrast to the inadvertent sinners who are the forerunners of the sect are the sinning Israelites who completely reject and abandon the covenant (i.e., they are more than intentional sinners), pace Shemesh and Werman, *Revealing the Hidden*, 257–58.

52 This secondary Qumran tradition arguably follows the minority reading of the Numbers pericope. See note 21.

53 See Anderson, "The Interpretation of the Purification Offering," 33.

54 The analysis below will trace legalistic and extra-legalistic strands in the early rabbinic exegesis of the Numbers pericope. These correlate to a certain extent with whether the phrase "*beyad ramah*" from the latter part of the pericope is rendered as an intentional or brazen act. In addition, there are other variables in the rabbinic understanding of this part that are consequential, including whether its subject matter is any (and all) prohibition(s), idolatry, or some other form of "heresy" (which perhaps does not depend on a discrete act); whether other Scriptural terms, such as "*megadef*," "*devar Hashem bazah*," "*mitsvato hefer*," etc., are treated as independent or integrated phrases, and how they are interpreted; and the nature of the *karet* punishment recorded in this part. I will relate to several of these variables below. All references to the Sifre below are to the edition of Menahem Y. Kahana, *Sifre on Numbers: An Annotated Edition* [Hebrew] (5 vols.; Jerusalem: Magnes Press, 2011–15).

55 This rabbinic interpretation of Numbers 15 is informed to some extent by the rabbinic interpretation of Leviticus 4. According to rabbinic exegesis, Leviticus 4 discusses the general rule of sin offerings for inadvertent transgressions (*korban hatat*), which applies to all inadvertent transgressions of *karet* prohibitions (but see Louis Finkelstein, *Sifra on Leviticus*, Vol. 1 (New York: Jewish Theological Seminary Press, 1990), 199; and Noam Zohar, *The Sin Offering in Tannaitic Literature* (MA dissertation, Hebrew University, 1988), 128–31; and see also the broad definition of *karet* advanced by Shemesh alluded to in note 61, which needs to be balanced with Shemesh's remarks referenced in note 74). On this understanding, neither biblical source applies to lesser (i.e., non-*karet*) prohibitions

midrash considers (and subsequently rejects) another option (Sifre 111, ed. Kahana, lines 1–5):

> "But if you unintentionally fail to observe all these commandments (Numbers 15:22)"[56]: ... Scripture here speaks of idolatry. You say idolatry, *but perhaps (it speaks of his transgressing) all of the commandments of the Torah* ... (emphasis mine).[57]

And similarly in the continuation of the midrash (ibid., lines 5–7):

> "And it shall be, if by the eyes of the congregation it were done in error (Numbers 15:24)" – Scripture hereby singles out one mitzvah. And which is that? (the injunction against) idolatry. You say it is idolatry, *but perhaps it is (any) one of all the mitzvoth stated in the Torah* .... (emphasis mine)

In other words, the midrash registers the plain sense of Scripture (presumably following the majority reading).[58] In fact, certain rabbinic traditions arguably

(which generally are punishable with lashes when violated intentionally, and have no sacrificial requirement when violated inadvertently). See also Anderson, "The Interpretation of the Purification Offering," for further discussion.

A comprehensive evaluation of the rabbinic interpretation of Numbers 15 must thus be evaluated alongside the rabbinic understanding of Leviticus 4 and other scriptural passages relating to the *karet* punishment; as well as the general penology and sacrificial system according to the rabbis. This chapter's scope, however, is more narrow in focus. The rabbinic interpretations of Numbers 15 necessarily advance certain theological perspectives, and evaluating their underpinnings is its primary concern.

56 This Sifre passage addresses the first part of the Numbers pericope, but this hermeneutic likely informs how the rabbis read the latter part as well. In the continuation of the Sifre, there are alternate renderings of the latter part, but they probably do not reflect upon how the rabbis read the first part of the pericope (since requiring a sacrifice on such alternate grounds is difficult to fathom). But see Nahmanides on Numbers 15:22, who presents an alternate plain sense reading of the first part of the pericope.

57 The literal verse refers to all the commandments; the continuation of the pericope refers to a single commandment. See note 22.

58 Arguably, this Sifre tradition is aware of the sectarian position recorded in Qumran literature. This conjecture may also be reflected in the reference to the covenant in the continuation of the midrash ("Just as one who transgresses all of the commandments ... breaks the covenant ... ") which is not mentioned in the verses, but may be implicit in certain Qumran elaborations on these verses. See note 39.

A further clarification is in order: The majority and minority readings turn on whether to construe the term "*beyad ramah*" in the latter part of the pericope as an intentional or brazen act, but both readings generally assume that this section involves any prohibition. Rabbinic discourse, by contrast, suggests that it may refer to any prohibition, idolatry, or another form of "heresy." So when the paragraph above states that the midrash registers the plain sense of the pericope this means, minimally, that the rabbis are aware that the Numbers pericope can be referring to any or all commandments (rather than idolatry), but does not necessarily mean that sinning "*beyad ramah*" is to be construed as acting in an intentional manner. Nevertheless, this construction seems likely. To wit, this clearly seems to be the understanding of "*beyad ramah*" according to the rabbinic tradition that the pericope addresses the sin of idolatry (i.e., verses 30–31 are referring to an *intentional* violation of idolatry; see Rashi on Numbers 15:30). The continuation of the paragraph above lists other rabbinic traditions that may likewise follow the majority reading of the pericope. Later on, the chapter will evaluate rabbinic traditions in the Sifre and elsewhere that follow the minority reading.

interpret (the latter part of) the Numbers pericope in this manner. Thus, Sifre 112 (ed. Kahana, line 50) records an exegetical gloss attributed to R. Akiva on Numbers 15:31,[59] "a soul—who sins intentionally (*mezidah*)."[60] Likewise, the teaching of R. Hanania b. Gamliel in tractate Makkot (3:15) that "one could lose their life for committing just one sin" may echo this position.[61]

Most rabbinic constructions of the Numbers pericope, however, eschew the literal interpretation for a variety of reasons, and do not identify a single violation of any prohibition as the root of the religious rupture which is depicted in its verses. A central question raised by these alternative hermeneutics is whether they signal a different conception of religion. On the literal understanding of the Numbers pericope (i.e., the majority approach), the essence of religion is comprised of legal obeisance; and therefore violating the law severs one's relationship with God and the religious community. Do these other rabbinic readings operate with a similar template, or present a different kind of religious order that is not solely structured around norms?

The most familiar rabbinic interpretation of the Numbers pericope – advanced in lieu of the plain meaning in the paragraph above – limits its subject matter to the prohibition of idolatry.[62] The following paragraph addresses the opening part of the pericope:

> "But if you unintentionally fail to observe all these commandments (mitzvoth) (Numbers 15:22)": ... Scripture here speaks of idolatry. ... (Sifre 111, ed. Kahana, lines 1–5)

59 This teaching of R. Akiva (if it originated in this context, see the parallel reference in the next note) may be in tension with his teaching about the doubling of *karet*, analyzed below.

60 See Sifre 70 (ed. Kahana, lines 6–8). See also the successive teachings in Sifre 112 about the cascading effects of a sin (ed. Kahana, lines 41–45); and Sifre Zuta on Numbers 15:22, 30.

61 This is how Shemesh interprets this teaching (which also assumes that the punishment of *karet* can be supplanted with lashes, at least when the latter are a suitable alternative punishment). See *Punishments and Sins*, 95.

Note that Shemesh even argues that the well-known position of the Sifre described in the next note accords with the plain sense of the pericope (and the narrow focus on the sin of idolatry refers to other parts of the pericope), a claim which is more questionable. See *Punishments and Sins*, 82ff.

62 The well-known rabbinic tradition that limits the Numbers pericope to the sin of idolatry (or other prohibitions of a similar scale) has certain halakhic implications. First, according to this tradition, the Numbers verses establish that idolatry is punishable by (the standard) *karet* (punishment). See *m. Ker.* 1:1. Moreover, the verses inform the general scope of sin offerings for inadvertent transgressions (*korban hatat*): atonement is only required for inadvertent transgressions of *karet* prohibitions. See Sifre Numbers 112 (cited in note 64), and Sifra *Hova* 1:7 (note the continuation of the Sifra considers, but rejects, alternate classifications of severe prohibitions that may be considered to be on a similar scale to idolatry).

Yet, this rabbinic tradition also raises questions (beyond the glaring issue that there is scant textual evidence to link the Numbers pericope to idolatry). Why would Scripture dedicate a discrete (part of a) pericope to the intentional sin of idolatry, as opposed to all other *karet* prohibitions? Further, why do the pericope's verses employ extraordinary rhetoric? At first blush, there is nothing halakhically distinct about an intentional violation of idolatry that differentiates it from other *karet* prohibitions (in contrast with the inadvertent case, where the sacrificial requirements for atoning for the sin of idolatry are anomalous). See Nahmanides on Numbers 15:22, whose comments may help address this issue by linking this rabbinic tradition with his understanding of the pericope's plain sense. This will not, however, explain the rabbinic tradition on its own terms. But see *b. Hull.* 5a.

Similarly, a subsequent paragraph (Sifre 112, ed. Kahana, lines 59–61) interprets the latter part as involving an intentional violation of idolatry.[63]

At first blush, narrowing the Numbers pericope in this manner still assumes a religious order that is defined by norms, but only deems an intentional violation of a severe prohibition to have the dire consequences described in the pericope's latter part. This is the implication of a related Sifre teaching that groups idolatry with other legal prohibitions of a similar scale (i.e., prohibitions which are punishable by *karet*).[64] It is also possible that idolatry is singled out as a cardinal prohibition which is in a category of its own, or emblematic of all the commandments.[65] The first paragraph concludes in this vein (Sifre 111, ed. Kahana, lines 5–10):

> It is, therefore, written "And if you err and do not do all of these commandments (Numbers 15:22)": This comes to define the one commandment. Just as one who transgresses all of the commandments divests himself of the yoke (*poreq ol*), and breaks the covenant (*mefer berit*), and reveals the Torah (*megaleh panim ba-Torah*), so, he who transgresses one commandment (idolatry) does the same, as it is written, "to destroy His covenant (turning to the worship of other gods . . .) (Deuteronomy 17:2–3)." And the covenant is nothing other than Torah, as it is written, "These are the words of the covenant, etc. (Deuteronomy 28:69)."

But this justification raises another possible explanation for why the Sifre distinguishes this particular sin. Idolatry is not just a cardinal prohibition, but a flagrant betrayal of God. Arguably, this is the underlying thrust of the above passage (committing idolatry divests oneself of the yoke, etc.).[66] The fundamental theological affront of idolatry is likewise underscored in a neighboring passage in the Sifre that employs a somewhat cryptic metaphor to capture its audacity.[67]

63 This interpretation is also presumed in *m. Hor.* 2:6 and throughout tractate Horayot (Mishnah and Tosefta); as well as in Sifra *Hova* 1:7, Sifre Zuta on Numbers 15, and various *baraitot*. See also Shemesh, *Punishments and Sins*, 91–93; and Anderson, "The Interpretation of the Purification Offering," 19–20.

Of course, a collateral effect of narrowing the pericope to the sin of idolatry, or the alternate renderings explored below, is to reduce the stakes of violating a generic prohibition. This may be part of the rabbinic design. I thank Professor Benny Porat for emphasizing this point.

64 "'An individual who sins unintentionally (Numbers 15:29)'– R. Yehudah b. Betheira says: . . . Just as serving idolatry is distinct in that it is an act in which deliberate transgression is punishable by *karet* (excision), and unwitting transgression by a sin-offering, so all who act unwittingly must be an act where deliberate transgression is punishable by *karet* (excision) and unwitting transgression by a sin-offering" (Sifre 112, ed. Kahana, lines 34–36).

65 In theory, one could imagine grouping idolatry with a smaller set of severe prohibitions, such as murder and adultery. See, e.g., *y. Peah* 1:1 (which also adds the prohibition of *lashon hara*). But this possibility is not hinted at in this context.

66 An alternate formulation is that idolatry constitutes a profound rejection of the foundations of Judaism, including the yoke, the covenant, etc. In either case, the brunt of the transgression is less about a prohibited normative action than about what it signifies religiously.

67 "'[he] blasphemes the Lord (Num 15:30)' – R. Eliezer b. Azariah says, As a man would say to his neighbor: 'You have scraped out the dish (of food) and diminished it.' Issi b. Akavya says, As one would say to his neighbor: 'You have scraped out the entire dish and left nothing in it' (Sifre 112, ed. Kahana,

These alternate explanations reflect two different ways of conceptualizing the prohibition of idolatry:[68] a normative perspective, where idolatry is classified as a "first-degree" offense; and a theological perspective, where idolatry epitomizes the ultimate religious betrayal.[69] Notably the other two specific prohibitions that surface in rabbinic constructions of the Numbers pericope – committing blasphemy against God[70] and rejecting the rite of circumcision[71] – share a similar duality. These are cardinal commandments, where the violation and heresy are interwoven.

A A *Novel Series of Rabbinic Interpretations of the Numbers Pericope*

The rabbinic interpretations of the Numbers pericope examined so far are thus arguably grounded in a traditional normative discourse.[72] In other passages, however, the Sifre betrays a decidedly different tone.[73] When unmoored by the midrash

lines 46–48)." See also Sifre Zuta on Numbers 15:24. There are other traditions in the Sifre that compare idolatry to a rejection of the Decalogue, but their meaning is more equivocal.

68 Idolatry is a prohibited act which signifies a theological stance. Still, a given discourse may place greater emphasis on one of these dimensions.

69 See Sifre Deuteronomy 221 and *m. Sanh.* 6:4, which refer to idolatry and blasphemy as unique sins that undermine a foundational principle (*pashat yado ba-ikar*). According to the rabbis, both of these cardinal prohibitions may be alluded to in Numbers 15:30–31. See the next note. See also David Henshke, "For a Hung Body Is an Affront to God: On the Difference in Exposition between the Sages and the Sectarians and the Mishnah and the Tosefta," [Hebrew] *Tarbiz* 69:4 (2000): 510–14.

70 The term *megadef* (in Numbers 15:30) is interpreted by *Hazal* as a (second) reference to idolatry or a discrete sin of blasphemy (see *b.Ker.* 7a-b; a sugya which also cites Sifre 112). See Henshke, "For a Hung Body is an Affront to God," 513. According to the former tradition, the term focuses on a blasphemous act of idolatry or its blasphemous consequences (which may be indicative of a theological discourse).

The latter tradition interprets this term to refer to a discrete sin of blasphemy. Accordingly, the verse refers both to the prohibition of idolatry (either "*beyad ramah*" or "*devar Hashem bazah*") and blasphemy ("*megadef*"). See also *m. Ker.* 1:1 which lists idolatry alongside blasphemy as prohibitions punishable by *karet*, presumably based on this verse; and *m. Sanh.* 7:4 which also lists them sequentially.

There also may be a distinct exegetical tradition which interprets the verse as solely focused on the sin of blasphemy. See note 29.

71 See Sifre 112 (ed. Kahana, lines 53–56) and *m. Avot* 3:11 cited below.

72 Even if idolatry has a certain duality, as described above, it remains an established norm. Still, the idolatry hermeneutic of this pericope may enable a pivot to a different kind of theological discourse, especially since approaching it solely on normative grounds arguably does not account for the pericope's content and extraordinary rhetoric. See note 62.

73 For further analysis of various sections of the Sifre and other parallels in rabbinic literature, see Kahana, *Sifre on Numbers* on Sifre 111–12; Shemesh, *Punishments and Sins*, 88–95; Chaim J. Milikowsky, "*Gehenna* and 'Sinners of Israel' in the Light of *Seder Olam*," [Hebrew] *Tarbiz* 55 (1986): 311–43; and Chaim J. Milikowsky, *Seder Olam: Critical Edition, Commentary and Introduction* [Hebrew] (Jerusalem: Yad Ben Zvi, 2013) on S. Olam 3. See also Toeg, "A Halakhic Midrash in Numbers 15.22–31," 2–3, 19–20; Flusser, "Some of the Precepts of the Torah from Qumran (4QMMT)," 333–74; Adiel Schremer, *Brothers Estranged: Heresy, Christianity and Jewish Identity in Late Antiquity* (Oxford; New York: Oxford University Press, 2010), 33, 79–81; Jenny R. Labendz, "Know What to Answer the Epicurean: A Diachronic Study of the 'Apiqoros in Rabbinic Literature," *Hebrew Union College Annual* Vol. 74 (2003): 175–214; Jonathan Klawans, *Heresy, Forgery, Novelty: Condemning, Denying, and Asserting Innovation in Ancient Judaism*

from its plain sense, the pericope is open hermeneutically, with each verse, and even each clause, potentially pregnant with distinct meanings.[74] A string of rabbinic traditions fill this interpretive void in striking ways.[75]

Beyond their notable number and range, these traditions diverge– to varying degrees– from the interpretation of "*beyad ramah*" as an intentional transgression.[76] Rather than limiting the pericope to a particular prohibition, and assimilating it into a familiar halakhic discourse where religiosity is measured by legal obeisance, they posit novel dimensions or forms of irreligiosity.[77] Ultimately, the Sifre here transitions into an altogether different discourse of sin and punishment.[78] Wittingly or not, the rabbis here

(New York: Oxford University Press, 2019), 67–72; David Michael Grossberg, *The Meaning and End of Heresy in Rabbinic Literature* (PhD diss. Princeton University, 2014), 192–211; and David Michael Grossberg, *Heresy and the Formation of the Rabbinic Community* (Tubingen, Germany: Mohr Siebeck, 2017), 55, 76–77, 152.

74 Toeg argues that these Sifre interpretations, which revolve around non-idolatrous sins, are homiletic and ideological in nature; they serve as a secondary layer within the Sifre that complements its halakhic core, which maintains that the subject of the pericope is idolatry. See Toeg, "A Halakhic Midrash in Numbers 15.22–31," 19–20. See also Ishay Rosen Zvi and Adiel Schremer, "Hagadot al Dofi," [Hebrew] *Teudah* 31 (2021) 381; and, in a different vein, Shemesh, *Punishments and Sins*, 93, n. 103. But most of these Sifre interpretations seem to be discrete traditions that stand on their own (as opposed to passages such as Sifre 112, ed. Kahana, lines 57–59, or the Talmudic materials cited by Toeg, which clearly seem to be supplementary traditions that are homiletic in nature). In any event, this argument misses a crucial point. Fundamentally, the idolatrous and non-idolatrous interpretations recorded in the Sifre are elaborating on two alternate constructions of "*beyad ramah*." The former renders this phrase as an intentional act (i.e., the majority reading), and the latter renders it (and other terms in these verses) as referring to various modes of sac-religiosity (i.e., the minority reading, largely following the Targum's tradition of "*be-resh gali*"). See note 77. This basic difference, in turn, has profound theological stakes for the legacy of the Sifre pericope that have gone unnoticed: Whether religiosity is normatively bounded, or has other extra-normative, and arguably more essential, dimensions.

75 Note that I am not denying that there might have been sociological or polemical factors (e.g., anti-sectarian or anti-Christian, etc.) that influenced rabbinic discourse in these paragraphs and similar texts, as emphasized by other scholars. My argument is that scholarship has largely overlooked the significance of the Numbers pericope in prompting or enabling the rabbis to fill an interpretive void. Moreover, wittingly or not, through their hermeneutics the rabbis developed new religious terminology and concepts, and more generally, constructed elements of a distinct theological sphere. At the same time, I agree that the impetus for rabbis to engage in this discourse and the specific content with which they filled this void was likely informed by the socio-religious context in which they lived.

76 In a related vein, they also disagree about whether to interpret "*beyad ramah*" as involving a transgression that is violated by a discrete act (with different degrees of intentionality), or not.

77 These novel forms should be seen as articulations that align with the minority reading of the Numbers pericope, following the Targum's interpretation (see note 21). Once "*beyad ramah*" is not rendered as an intentional transgression, but as some mode of sac-religiosity (with or without an underlying act), other phrases from the latter part of the pericope may be understood to signify additional modes. Accordingly, this section of the Sifre also construes such other phrases. In contrast, the previously analyzed Sifre traditions that follow the majority reading presumably interpret these verses in a more integrated manner that focuses on a transgression and its consequences (but see note 70). The different Sifre traditions also seemingly diverge on how to interpret the pericope's punishment of *karet*. See the last paragraph of Section III below.

78 For more general accounts of sin in rabbinic literature, see, e.g., Adolf Büchler, *Studies in Sin and Atonement in the Rabbinic Literature of the First Century* (London: Oxford University Press, 1928);

articulate elements of a religious worldview that is not bound within the normative order.

Here are the relevant excerpts from the Sifre on Numbers 15:30–1 (Sifre 112, ed. Kahana, lines 37–57):[79]

(1) "But whoever acts intentionally (*beyad ramah*) (Numbers 15:30)" – This is one who reveals the Torah (*megaleh panim ba-Torah*), like Menasheh ben Hezkiah.

(2) "[he] blasphemes the Lord (Numbers 15:30)" – This is one who sits and renders a ridiculous homily in front (alt. to the face) of the Lord (*Ha-Maqom*), saying (for example): "He should not have written in the Torah 'And Reuven went [in the days of the wheat harvest ...] (Genesis 30:14)'" ....[80]

(3) "Because of having despised the word of the Lord (Numbers 15:31)" – This is a Sadducee. "and breached his commandment (Numbers 15:31)" – This is a heretic (*apiqoros*).

(4) Another interpretation: "Because of having despised the word of the Lord (Numbers 15:31)" – This is one who reveals the Torah (*megaleh panim ba-Torah*). "and breached his commandment (Numbers 15:31)" – This is one who breaks the covenant (*mefer berit*) of the flesh (circumcision). From here R. Elazar Hamodai said: One who desecrates the offerings, cheapens the festivals, breaks the covenant (*mefer berit*) (of circumcision) of our father Abraham or reveals the Torah (*megaleh panim ba-Torah*) – even if he has performed many commandments, it were best to thrust him from the world.

(5) If he says: "The entire Torah I accept, except for this one matter" – [This is] "Because of having despised the word of the Lord (Numbers 15:31)." "The entire Torah he (Moses) said from the mouth of the Holy One but this thing he said on his own" – [This is] "Because of having despised the word of the Lord (Numbers 15:31)". ...[81]

The Sifre's range of interpretations covers uncharted terrain that lies beyond the familiar normative landscape. According to many scholars, Paragraph (1) refers to the violation of a prohibition in a brazen or defiant manner,[82] which arguably

Solomon Schechter, *Some Aspects of Rabbinic Theology* (New York: Macmillan, 1910), ch. 14; Stanley Wagner, "Religious Non-Conformity in Ancient Jewish Life" (DHL dissertation, Yeshiva University, 1964); Urbach, *The Sages, Their Concepts and Beliefs*, 420–523; George Foot Moore, *Judaism in the First Centuries*, Vol. I, 460–96; Milikowsky, "*Gehenna* and 'Sinners of Israel' in the Light of *Seder Olam*"; Labendz, "Know What to Answer the Epicurean"; and Gary A. Anderson, *Sin: A History* (New Haven, CT: Yale University Press, 2009), 95–110.

79 I have translated these excerpts based on the Kahana edition, and added an enumeration. See his notes for manuscript variants, which have little influence on my broader argument.

80 See the references in note 87.

81 See the parallel traditions cited in Kahana, *Sifre on Numbers*, 805–06.

82 This depends on the meaning of the phrase "*megaleh panim ba-Torah*." The interpretation herein follows Kahana and Naeh, who interpret this as an open or public, i.e., brazen, transgressive act. This

expresses, if you will, a mens rea of heresy or insurrection;[83] Paragraph (2) and certain parts of Paragraph (4) involve various disdainful attitudes; Paragraph (3) refers to a heretical or sinful persona, rather than a prohibited act or mode of conduct;[84] and other parts of Paragraph (4) and Paragraph (5) describe a rejection of the covenant, Scripture or law. In sum, the sins depicted in these sections of the Sifre are attitudinal, ideational, or theological.

One can sort this catalog of sins (alongside others referenced in proximate passages in the Sifre) across a spectrum that ranges from standard norms to increasingly novel ones, with a waning link to formal praxis.[85] Beginning with an intentional violation of a single or all commandment(s) (which the Sifre at least registers), the Sifre refers to: a violation of an arch commandment; (arguably) a violation of an arch commandment that is expressive of a rejection of a core theological principle (God's supremacy or the covenant); a violation of a single commandment in a defiant manner (arguably expressing a mens rea of heresy or insurrection); a rejection of the (normative) authority of Scripture or the law; a disdainful attitude toward religious institutions (such as holidays or sacred objects); a rejection of a core theological principle (e.g., resurrection); a heretical or sinful persona (that transcends any particular transgression, attitude, or idea);[86] and (arguably) a betrayal or

interpretation can be traced back to the Targum's translation of "*be-resh gali*" (see note 21), as "*megaleh panim*" may well be an extension of that phrase. See, e.g., *b. Eruv.* 69a. There are also alternative interpretations of "*megaleh panim ba-Torah*" that associate it with a brazen rejection, or exegesis, of the Torah. See the discussions in Kahana, *Sifre on Numbers*, 797; Grossberg, *The Meaning and End of Heresy*, 186–211; Menahem Kister, "Studies in 4QMiqsat Maase Ha-Torah and Related Texts: Law, Theology, Language and Calendar," [Hebrew] *Tarbiz* 68 (1999): 327, n. 42; Shimon Sharvit, "Hermeneutic Traditions and their link to Scribal Traditions of the Mishnah," in *Studies in Rabbinic and Biblical Literature and in the History of Israel: In Memory of Professor Ezra Z. Melamed* [Hebrew] (Ramat Gan: Bar-Ilan Press, 1982), 120–21; and Moti Arad, *Sabbath Desecrator with Parresia: A Talmudic Legal Term and its Context* [Hebrew] (New York: Jewish Theological Seminary, 2009), 213–27.

83 Such a brazen act can be conceived of as a more flagrant form of violating a norm; a violation with a deleterious social impact; or, as stated in the paragraph above, an act of insurrection or a mode of expressing heresy.

Interestingly, the Sifre never refers in this context to a repeat offender, like a *meshumad*, or a *mumar lehachis*. Other rabbinic sources do. See, e.g., *t. Sanh.* 13:5; and Sifra *Nedava* 2:3. There are also other rabbinic sources that may relate to a mens rea of heresy or insurrection. See, e.g., the suggestive formulation in Sifra *Behuqotai* 2:2.

84 An evaluation of this irreligious persona depends on whether a Sadducee and/or an *apiqoros* is classified based on his or her: anti-halakhic praxis; belonging to a distinct social group; or espousing a problematic theology. See the references in note 86.

85 The precise (conceptual) ordering is debatable; the above represents one plausible way to sort these sins in such an array.

I tend to read the Sifre here as being inchoate, as the discourse explores the boundaries of religious sins. The novel renderings of the Sifre may or may not be mutually exclusive.

86 The nature of the "heresy" is presumably not rooted in any one specific transgression, but a broader heretical orientation. The midrash's subject has shifted from a violation, to a sin, to a sinner.

On the definition and status of the heretic, see Milikowsky, "*Gehenna* and 'Sinners of Israel' in the Light of *Seder Olam*," 329–37; Labendz, "Know What to Answer the Epicurean," 177–89; Grossberg, *Heresy and the Formation of the Rabbinic Community*, ch. 5; and Christine Hayes, "Legal Realism

blasphemy of God. A conventional normative framework is expanded to encompass increasingly original sins of a theological nature.

At times, the shift in discourse evident in the Sifre is more subtle, but also revealing. Consider in this vein a notable difference in emphasis among a couple of the paragraphs cited above. Paragraph (5) describes a challenge to the authority of the Torah and its precepts – either by rejecting the Torah's integrity or by limiting the scope of its divine origins. The sacrilege is not measured by a violation of law per se, as much as by undermining the stature of the Torah or the legal traditions. Still, the heresy in question implicates the supreme standing of biblical law.

A seemingly related interpretation (2), however, discards these normative trappings. Here the rabbis likewise describe an impugning of Scripture, but the critique is expressed as scornful mockery.[87] Moreover, this interpretation – which construes the Scriptural words, "[he] blasphemes the Lord (Numbers 15:30)" – depicts the jeering homilist confronting Scripture's Author, "sit[ting] and render[ing] a ridiculous homily in front (alt. to the face) of the Lord .... " Moving beyond the status of Scripture and the law, the heretical challenge targets God, as it were. Note that on its terms, the homilist-blasphemer is not denying the divinity of the Torah, but challenging God's immaculate wisdom that is manifest in it. The crux of the verbal assault is personal.

B *The Triad As Reflecting a Shift in Rabbinic Discourse*

A more dramatic shift in the rabbinic discourse surrounding the Numbers pericope can be discerned when one focuses on the literary record of three phrases that appear in the Sifre and elsewhere in rabbinic literature: "*megaleh panim ba-Torah*," "*mefer berit*," and "*poreq ol*."[88] In Paragraph (1), the Sifre invokes the phrase "*megaleh panim ba-Torah*;" and in the opening part of Paragraph (4), the commentary on one lemma refers to it as well, while the commentary on the next lemma refers to "*mefer berit*." As discrete phrases, they presumably designate distinct prohibitions.[89]

and the Fashioning of Sectarians in Jewish Antiquity," in *Sects and Sectarianism in Jewish History*, ed. Sacha Stern ; IJS Studies in Judaica series (Leiden; Boston: Brill, 2011), 133–44. For a helpful overview of the scholarly debate about heresy, see Michal Bar-Asher Siegal, *Jewish-Christian Dialogues on Scripture in Late Antiquity* (New York: Cambridge University Press, 2019), 7–17.

87 See Kahana, *Sifre on Numbers*, 797–99; Aharon Shemesh, "Traces of Sectarian Halakha in Tannaitic Literature" [Hebrew] *Meghillot* 2 (2004): 91–101; Hananel Mack, "What Else Did King Manasseh of Judea Discover in the Torah," [Hebrew] *Meghillot* 2 (2004): 105-11; and Rosen Zvi and Schremer, "Hagadot al Dofi."

88 For a list of references, see Kahana, *Sifre on Numbers*, 805 n. 105. For an extended analysis, see Grossberg, *The Meaning and End of Heresy*, 183–211.

89 For example, "*mefer berit*" on its own presumably means not being circumcised (still, it may express – or may over time signify – something more); "*mefer berit*," as an element within the triad (and perhaps in certain other sources), may refer to the heresy or insurrection involved in not being circumcised, or a rejection of the covenant (perhaps even the Sinai covenant). The latter can have theological and/or social implications. A full analysis is beyond the scope of this chapter.

However, in an earlier passage in Sifre 111 (cited below), these two phrases, preceded by "*poreq ol*," form a litany of three offenses. This same triad is recorded in several places in rabbinic literature. Beyond individuated offenses, they seem to comprise a single category (either they share a common denominator, or are conflated into a single wrong).[90] The very formulation of a triad may reflect a revised conceptualization of grave sin.

What is the nature of this triad, and how is it (or are they) violated? A partial response can be gleaned from the hermeneutic elaboration recorded in Sifre 111 (ed. Kahana, line 8):

> ... one *who transgresses all of the mitzvoth* divests oneself of the yoke (*poreq ol*), and breaks the covenant (*mefer berit*), and reveals the Torah (*megaleh panim ba-Torah*) ... (emphasis mine).

As represented in this passage, the triad is not a label for a sin(s), but the derivative consequence(s) of a cumulative transgression. One who violates all the commandments[91] causes the drastic fallout that is captured by this threefold formulation. The triad is thus associated with established norms.[92]

What is fascinating is that elsewhere (in tannaitic literature) the nature of the triad (or a couple of its elements) differs. In three tannaitic sources – Mishnah Avot, Baraita Shavuot, and Tosefta Sanhedrin – the triad is projected as a stand-alone sin (or sins), which is unrelated to other violations. Moreover, each of these tannaitic sources accents different characteristics of the triad that diverge from conventional norms.

Thus, the Mishnah in Avot (as it is paraphrased in the latter part of Paragraph (4) of the Sifre) includes two of the triad's elements on a list of egregious modes of conduct or postures that can hardly be designated as standard violations. This is further implied by the conclusion which states (in the Sifre's rendition) that if any item on the list was infringed, "even if he has performed many commandments, he deserves to be thrust from the world."[93] The enumerated items differ from conventional prohibitions, and their gravity exceeds the ordinary normative metric.[94]

90 The latter suggestion is the thesis of Grossberg, *The Meaning and End of Heresy*, 183–211.

91 The continuation of the passage refers to the transgression of idolatry: "so, he who transgresses one mitzvah (idolatry) does the same, as it is written, 'to destroy His covenant (turning to the worship of other gods ...) (Deuteronomy 17:2–3).' And the covenant is nothing other than Torah, as it is written, 'These are the words of the covenant, etc. (Deuteronomy 28:69)'."

92 It is difficult to place this source and the ones cited below in chronological order. As a result, it is difficult to know whether the triad formulation emerged within a normative context, or was transplanted from a non-normative context.

93 The Mishnah's rendition is, "even if he has accomplished good deeds (commandments), he has no share in the world to come." See Kahana, *Sifre on Numbers*, 804–05 (who also lists other significant variants). The Mishnah (and perhaps the Sifre's rendition of the Mishnah as well) should thus be added to the notable references to the world to come evaluated below, and offers further evidence of a penological shift that is manifest in the rabbinic discourse regarding these novel forms of sin.

94 On this reading, the Mishnah is stating that regardless of one's normative record, he or she should be cast out on account of these enumerated sins.

A *baraita* recorded in the Talmud underscores another essential characteristic of the sui generis triad:[95]

> Rabbi Judah the Prince says: For all transgressions that are stated in the Torah, whether one repented, or whether one did not repent, Yom Kippur atones, except for one who divests oneself of the yoke (*poreq ol*), and reveals the Torah (*megaleh panim ba-Torah*), and breaks the covenant (*mefer berit*). For these, if one repented, Yom Kippur atones, and if not, Yom Kippur does not atone.

Unique among all sins in terms of atonement,[96] the triad is openly contrasted with standard halakhic violations. Only the triad demands a more intensive atonement procedure in which repentance is indispensable (a requirement which arguably derives from the rabbinic interpretation of the final clause of Numbers 15:31, "and bear the guilt (*avona bah*)").[97] In other words, the *baraita* classifies the triad as a more weighty category of sin(s).[98] To the extent that the triad consists of foundational, theological sins or heresies that are based on the sinner's interior attitude or state, the necessity of repentance seems particularly apt.[99]

95 See *y. Sheb* 1:6, *y. Yom* 8:6, *b. Sheb* 13a, *b. Yom* 85b.

96 There are different ways to evaluate the core of a religion, even within a so-called "bad man" approach. This chapter focuses on the exegesis of a foundational text about a cardinal sin and its grave consequences. Another way is to consider which sins mandate the most demanding forms of penitence or atonement. A third path is to evaluate which kinds of sinners forfeit their share in the world to come. As is evident from this chapter, there may be a degree of overlap among these indicia. Other methods can also be explored, including: Who is branded as a *rasha, min, meshumad, apiqoros*, etc.? Which sins receive the harshest punishments? Which sins are inviolable even under great duress? Which sins are singled out as especially severe in halakhic or aggadic discourse? Etc.

97 See Sifre 112, ed. Kahana, lines 66–67.

98 The hierarchy of sins in terms of atonement and repentance requires discrete analysis. See, e.g., *m. Yom.* 8:8, *t. Yom.* 4:5–9, and Mekh. R. Ishmael, *Bahodesh Parsha* 7 (ed. Horowitz, 227–29).

99 Strikingly, The Talmud (e.g., *b. Shev* 13a) links this heightened demand of repentance to the double formulation of *karet* in Numbers 15:31, capturing the centrality of the Numbers pericope for the adumbration of rabbinic theology. This specific prooftext is also the source for a punishment in the world to come according to R. Akiva, as explained in the next paragraphs. While the Talmud contrasts these two exegetical renderings of the double formulation, they seem to cohere conceptually: The triad warrants a distinctive, spiritual punishment and demands a distinctive, spiritual process of repentance. In other words, repentance may be especially apt for a religious, extra-legalistic, sin, and such a sin when unrepented may warrant a punishment in the world to come. Indeed, in the Sifre 112 (ed. Kahana, lines 62–67), they seem to operate in tandem. See also Shemesh, *Punishments and Sins*, 87–90, who notes that the potential for repentance is not stated in the verses and is an innovation of R. Akiva (which may differ from R. Yishmael in *t. Yom.* 4:6–8). But note that this "innovation" is a lessening of an extraordinary punishment of forfeiture of the world to come, a crucial point that is glossed over in his analysis. See note 113. So there is an internal consistency to R. Akiva's approach to this pericope: A theological sin necessitates a spiritual punishment, but can also be redressed through repentance. See also Saul Lieberman, *Tosefta Ki-Feshuta*, Vol. 4 (New York: Jewish Theological Seminary of America, 1992), 826.

Parenthetically, it is interesting to note the rhetoric of the Talmudic sugya (*b. Shev.* 12b–13a) in its characterization of other sins (aside from the triad). The Talmud refers to an intentional violation of a prohibition as an insurrection (*mered*), and to one who refrains from repenting for a violation as one who sustains his or her insurrection (*omed bemirdo*). Thus, even violating a standard prohibition constitutes an insurrection for the Talmud (and evidently an even more acute religious rupture is caused by the sin of the triad).

Finally, a third tannaitic source, a Tosefta Sanhedrin passage linked to *m. Sanh.* 10:1 (knows as the opening Mishnah of *Pereq Heleq*), betrays other essential characteristics of the triad.[100] The Mishnah records a list of beliefs that preclude a person from a share in the "world to come (*olam haba*),"[101] including a person who denies resurrection (from the Torah),[102] rejects the notion of "Torah from Heaven," and an *apiqoros*.[103] *T. Sanh.* 12:9 adds the triad (as well as one who pronounces the divine name)[104] to this list.

The placement of the triad alongside these other wrongs implies that they all share a similar quality. All are arguably theological or creedal sins.[105] What elsewhere is conceived of as a triad involving normative violations is now associated with heresies.

A crucial signal of the theological nature of the Tosefta's discourse here is the striking punishment it declares for breaching the triad – a forfeiture of a share in the world to come. Notice how this diverges from the standard penology of rabbinic literature. Ranging from lashes to capital punishment (and encompassing *karet* and *mitah beyedei shamayim*),[106] the standard penology is imminent and corporeal. In contrast, the forfeiture described in the Tosefta is deferred and (perhaps also) noncorporeal.[107] Or to formulate it differently, it is a heavenly punishment that fits a theological sin.[108]

100 For more on Mishnah and Tosefta *Heleq* (and the parallel passage in *Seder Olam*), see the references cited in notes 73 and 86; and the discussion and references in David M. Grossberg, *Heresy and the Formation of the Rabbinic Community* (Heidelberg: Mohr Siebeck, 2017), 110–15.

101 The first line in the printed editions is a later addition, and the original core of the Mishnah is composed of only these three items. See Israel Jacob Yuval, "All Israel Have a Portion in the World to Come," in *Redefining First-Century Jewish and Christian Identities: Essays in Honor of Ed Parish Sanders*, ed. Fabian E. Udoh (Notre Dame, IN: University of Notre Dame Press, 2008), 114–38 (who also evaluates the Jewish-Christian polemical dimensions of this Mishnah and other related sources).

102 There are different recensions of this line. See Adiel Schremer, "Negotiating Heresy: Belief and Identity in Early Rabbinic Literature," in *Canonization and Alterity: Heresy in Jewish History, Thought, and Literature*, eds. Gilad Sharvit and Will Goetsche (Berlin: de Gruyter, 2020), 43, n. 40.

103 Strikingly, each of these three types of sinners are alluded to in Sifre Numbers 111–112, ed. Kahana: line 52 (*apiqoros*), line 57 (related to Torah from heaven), and line 74 (related to resurrection). See also Kahana, *Sifre on Numbers*, 812.

104 This latter item, too, is based on Numbers 15:30. See Shemesh, *Punishments and Sins*, 75.

105 See Milikowsky, "*Gehenna* and 'Sinners of Israel' in the Light of *Seder Olam*," 329–37.

106 These divine punishments are also part of the ordinary penological scheme. See also Aharon Shemesh, *The Punishment of Flagellation in Tannaitic Sources* [Hebrew] (PhD dissertation, Bar-Ilan University, 1994), ch. 7; and Shoval Shafat, *The Interface of Divine and Human Punishment in Rabbinic Thought* [Hebrew] (PhD dissertation, Ben-Gurion University, 2011), 25–30.

107 The nature of the world to come is debated in scholarship. See Milikowsky, "*Gehenna* and 'Sinners of Israel' in the Light of *Seder Olam*," 320–21. A punishment involving the world to come may target the sinner's body and soul (see *t. Sanh.* 13:2–5); or is one of privation, at least as represented in the Mishnah. Other sinners listed in the Tosefta (*t. Sanh.* 13:4) and Seder Olam (the latter part of ch. 3) commit carnal sins – i.e., "*begufan*" – and their posthumous punishment is of a different nature. See ibid., 336.

108 See also *y. Pe'ah* 1:1.

The roots of this transfiguration can be traced back to a different passage in the Sifre. Recall how the Numbers pericope records variants of the term *karet* three times in delineating the punishment for sinning "*beyad ramah*." Certain rabbinic hermeneutics interpret these verses to be referring to a standard form of *karet*. For instance, the rabbinic tradition that identifies the pericope's transgression as idolatry must understand the verses in this manner (since *karet* is clearly specified as the punishment for idolatry alongside numerous other prohibitions enumerated on a seemingly exhaustive rabbinic list).[109] But other traditions in the Sifre examined above that construe the pericope as referring to novel forms of sinning cannot brook this interpretation[110] (since these sins are not included on this rabbinic list).[111] Moreover, these are not the kinds of sins that warrant standard punishments, which are only meted out for prohibited actions. As the conception of the pericope's underlying sin evolves in the Sifre, the punishment must as well. This seems to be the implication of R. Akiva's teaching in Sifre 112 (ed. Kahana, lines 62):

> "shall be utterly cut off (*hikaret tikaret*) (Numbers 15:31)": "cut off (*hikaret*)" – in this world; "utterly cut off (*tikaret*)" – in the world to come (*olam haba*). These are the words of R. Akiva . . .[112]

Upon introducing the world to come, the rabbinic discourse surrounding the Numbers pericope withdraws from the standard penology of the halakhah and enters into a new realm.[113] What justifies this shift is in part the extraordinary rhetoric of the verses, including its ringing (and anomalous) repetitions of *karet*. An intensification

[109] See *m. Ker.* 1:1. By identifying idolatry as the subject matter of the Numbers pericope, this rabbinic tradition distinguishes the unique sacrifices delineated in the pericope from the standard *hatat* regulations delineated in Leviticus 4 (which according to the rabbis are required for inadvertent transgressions of other *karet* prohibitions). At the same time, this rabbinic tradition streamlines the punishment for an intentional violation specified in the latter part of the pericope with the generic category of *karet*.

[110] Note, however, that even the novel interpretations of Numbers 15:30–31 probably interpret the first part of the pericope as referring to idolatry. See note 56.

[111] See *m. Ker.* 1:1; nor are they referred to as punishable by *karet* elsewhere in the Bible or rabbinic literature (see Shemesh, *Punishments and Sins*, 59).

[112] The (slightly emended) source continues (lines 62–64): "R. Yishmael says: But since it says, 'blasphemes the Lord, and shall be cut off (Num 15:30),' are there then three excisions in three worlds? Rather, what is meant by 'shall be utterly cut off (Num 15:31)' – the Torah speaks in the language of man."

Whether R. Ishmael disagrees with R. Akiva is less certain. The Talmud (*b. Sanh.* 64b and 90b) states that he agrees with R Akiva. But see Kahana, *Sifre on Numbers*, 808–09, who argues that, according to the Sifre, R. Yishmael may demur. The latter seems likely. According to R. Yishmael, the sin of the Numbers pericope is idolatry (see *Sifre* 112, ed. Kahana, lines 59–61), which is punishable by standard *karet* (see *m. Ker.* 1:1).

[113] My analysis above, which contends that rabbinic penal discourse here enters into a new penal realm, parts ways with Aharon Shemesh, *Punishments and Sins*, 75, 87–90, 93–95. In the medieval commentators, there is a similar debate about whether the *karet* in these verses, and in the teaching of R. Akiva, is sui generis or belongs to the generic category of *karet*. Contrast the position of Maimonides, Hilkhot Teshuvah 8:2, with Nahmanides on Leviticus 18:29. See also the important summary of the Abarbenel on Numbers 15:30. But even Maimonides' position is more complex. See Hilkhot Teshuvah 3:6–14; and Guide for the Perplexed 3:41.

of *karet*, according to this homily, signals a qualitative transformation. At another level, the shift is a function of nascent definitions of "*beyad ramah*" and the other key terms of the pericope in the Sifre.[114] As the religious rupture of the Numbers pericope defies a formal-normative discourse (which is also reflected in the revised conception of the triad that is recorded in the three tannaitic sources), a corresponding theological punishment must be formulated (or appealed to) by the Rabbis.[115] While the former discourse dominates rabbinic literature,[116] the latter – which is reserved for the most solemn religious sins or sinners – emerges in the rabbinic unpacking of this pericope.[117] These discursive traditions of the Sifre contribute to the formation of rabbinic theology, including its doctrines of penitence and the world to come.[118]

IV CONCLUSION

The Numbers Pericope encapsulates in a few verses a seminal dimension of biblical religion. Employing exceptional rhetoric, Scripture describes a sinner's frontal assault on the divine realm which leads to a catastrophic fallout. What precisely is the sin? The plain sense of Scripture according to most commentators is that

I offered initial reflections on these themes in a lecture entitled, "The Hermeneutics of Heresy," at the British Association for Jewish Studies Conference in Oxford, England, July 2019.

114 Toeg is right to emphasize the pericope's extraordinary rhetoric describing the underlying sin, impact and punishment. See "A Halakhic Midrash in Numbers 15.22–31," 2; and the discussion near note 26 above. But labeling this terminology as a prophetic account of a legal transgression (i.e., as offering a different perspective on the impact of violating a normative prohibition; see "A Halakhic Midrash in Numbers 15.22–31," 18–19) is misleading according to the rabbis' novel discourse which responds to the charged language of this pericope. For the rabbis, the pericope is religious and theological in tone and substance. In this spirit, the rabbis further articulate its extra-normative dimensions, ranging from the original sins they enumerate, to a heightened requirement of repentance for such sins, to an alternate penology relating to the world to come.

115 The Tosefta and Seder Olam also refer to more conventional sinners who receive a different posthumous punishment. See note 107.

116 Rabbinic Judaism is hyper-legalistic in its focus. See, e.g., Moshe Halbertal, "The History of Halakhah and the Emergence of Halakhah," *Dine Israel* 29 (2013): 1–23. One telling indication of this is the manner in which theological commitments in the Bible, such as the call to love and fear God, are translated by the rabbis into concrete halakhic norms. Yet, the rabbis also developed theological ideas and doctrines (including outside the realm of aggada), notwithstanding the generalization of various scholars to the contrary. See also Milikowsky, "*Gehenna* and 'Sinners of Israel' in the Light of *Seder Olam*," 337; as well as the alternate perspective of Grossberg, *Heresy and the Formation of the Rabbinic Community*.

117 The layout of tractate Sanhedrin seems to transition between these two discourses. Most of the tractate is devoted to standard halakhah and penology; but *Pereq Heleq* addresses a different – and arguably more severe – kind of sin (i.e., a theological rejection or betrayal) and punishment (i.e., a divine, eternal, and perhaps also noncorporeal one).

118 There may of course be additional factors shaping rabbinic discourse in these spheres relating to sociological or polemical concerns (see note 75) or theological challenges involving questions of theodicy.

a person intentionally violated any biblical prohibition. A breach of norms amounts to divine blasphemy.

When one examines the early reception history of this pericope in Qumran literature these themes are mostly intensified, even as a secondary voice is also registered. The Scrolls regularly invoke the terminology of the pericope to refer to any intentional violation, and central passages in the Rule of the Community use it as a template for delimiting the normative boundaries of the sectarian community. In one passage, the apparatus of law is further deployed to ensure legal obeisance, which is vital for the community's socio-religious integrity. Law structures the community's core religious identity.

Yet in a later exegetical phase recorded in rabbinic literature a marked metamorphosis transpires.[119] Despite certain traces of the plain sense of the Numbers pericope, rabbinic hermeneutics largely reject the notion that its subject matter is a standard prohibition. The striking rhetoric of the pericope is instead reinterpreted by the rabbis through a series of transformative teachings. Despite the dominance of halakhah in the spiritual worldview of the rabbis, these homilies expose an essential religiosity that eclipses the universe of norms. Likewise, notwithstanding the usual focus of the rabbis on concrete actions with this-worldly consequences, here the rabbis explore a spiritual sphere and anticipate the world to come.[120] New theological frontiers, hinted at in the verses, receive preliminary formulations in the suggestive exegesis of the rabbis.

What began as a paradigm of religion structured through law in the Bible, and served as a foundational text in the Qumran corpus for the sectarian legal-religious imaginary, becomes a platform for the rabbis to adumbrate a theological world beyond the strict contours of law. In subsequent chapters, this novel hermeneutic becomes the basis for crucial expansions. Thus, the theological tropes that rabbinic traditions identified within the Numbers pericope and began to unpack, have a rich and varied afterlife in the Medieval period.[121] By the early modern period referred to at the outset, Judaism receives robust articulations as a religion that move well beyond the pericope.

Nevertheless, a striking echo of the pericope's motifs can be discerned in an important passage written by Moses Mendelssohn, the figure who, according to Batnitzky, "invented" the (early modern) idea of Jewish religion.[122] Expounding on the interplay between law and religion in the Bible in his landmark work *Jerusalem*, Mendelssohn offers a characterization that recalls (or, more precisely anticipates)

119 Another significant difference between Qumran and rabbinic writings in this context is that the former place much emphasis on the social-communal consequences of sinning, which is less apparent in the latter. Still, the rabbis are also sensitive to its social dimensions, albeit in more subtle ways that are reflected in their classifications and rhetoric.

120 In contrast, Qumran literature, which contains an extensive theology and eschatology, focuses on the normative dimensions of this pericope, and its immediate social consequences. Still, the gap between the present and the eschaton in the sectarian mindset may not be so vast, at least in certain respects.

121 See note 113.

122 Batnitzky, *How Judaism Became a Religion*, 4. I thank Professors Sharon Flatto and Edward Breuer for their guidance with this material.

the synopsis of Moshe Greenberg (who adduces the pericope as "Exhibit A") cited above:[123]

> ... in this nation, civil matters acquired a sacred and religious aspect, and every civil service was at the same time a true service of God ... the public taxes were an offering to God; and everything down to the least police measure was part of the divine service.[124]

A proximate passage notably formulates the converse dynamic as well:

> ... Every sacrilege against the authority of God, as the lawgiver of the nation, was a crime against the Majesty, and therefore a crime of state. Whoever blasphemed God committed lese majesty ...[125]

In other words, law and religion are deeply intertwined in the Bible.

More significant than the overlapping characterization of Greenberg and Mendelssohn, however, is its contrasting implications for each thinker. Greenberg's account, as elaborated upon above, suggests a convergence between these realms, as religion operates within a normative framework. But Mendelssohn marshals it to advance a more capacious conception of the religion of Judaism. By the early modern period the religious orientation is evidently too pervasive to be otherwise confined. On the contrary, the ceremonial laws, for Mendelssohn, are consonant with, and also constitutive of, religion writ large (as the term would be understood by his Protestant interlocutors).[126]

Supplementing a universal category of rational faith, Judaism contains historical truths and ceremonial rules. These latter precepts,[127] which must be embraced

123 The political dimensions of his characterization are crucial for Mendelssohn and for appreciating the larger claims at stake in his argument, but are less germane to the religious dimensions explored in this chapter.

For more on the political dimensions, see Edward Breuer, "Mendelssohn's Jewish Political Philosophy," in *Moses Mendelssohn: Enlightenment, Religion, Politics, Nationalism*, eds. Michah Gottlieb and Charles H. Manekin (Baltimore, MD: University of Maryland Press, 2015), 1–48; and Eric Nelson, "From Selden to Mendelssohn: Hebraism and Religious Freedom," in *Freedom and the Construction of Europe: New Perspectives on Philosophical, Religious, and Political Controversies*, ed. Martin Van Gelderen and Quentin Skinner (Cambridge, MA: Harvard University Press, 2013), 105–14.

124 Moses Mendelssohn, *Jerusalem, or, On Religious Power and Judaism* (trans. Allan Arkush; Hanover, MA: Brandeis University Press, 1983), 128.

125 Ibid., 129.

Interestingly, Mendelssohn's other discussions of blasphemy and sacrilegious behavior may share certain similarities with the minority reading of the Numbers pericope. See ibid., 36, 129–30.

126 See also Batntizky, *How Judaism Became a Religion*, 27–28, who especially emphasizes the apolitical and nonrational aspects of the ceremonial laws.

127 Scholars have attempted to tease out some of the subtler implications of Mendelssohn's notion of ceremonial laws. See, e.g., Michah Gottlieb, *Faith and Freedom: Moses Mendelssohn's Theological-Political Thought* (New York: Oxford University Press, 2011), ch. 2; Gideon Freudenthal, *No Religion Without Idolatry: Mendelssohn's Jewish Enlightenment* (Notre Dame, IN: University of Notre Dame Press, 2012), ch. 6; and Elias Sacks, *Moses Mendelssohn's Living Script: Philosophy, Practice, History, Judaism* (Bloomington, IN: Indiana University Press, 2017), ch. 2.

voluntarily, are fulfilled with one's body, as well as one's heart, mind, and soul. They serve as a living script, rousing a practitioner, and inspiring his or her contemplation of metaphysical and moral ideals. Transitory in nature, these ceremonial laws foster an authentic religious experience, and evade the fetishism of idolatry. Alongside their praxis, their subjective and communal meaning is continually interpreted and revised. A more elastic form of law thus affords a more expansive religiosity.

For some other early modern thinkers following in Mendelssohn's wake (e.g., Abraham Geiger and Hermann Cohen), the ceremonial norms are mostly relinquished, and faith, reason, and ethics flourish in their place.[128] Whether through a framework of norms, or without one, conceptions of Judaism as a religion have continued to evolve ever since. From a tradition dominated by laws in much of its formative strata, "Judaism" has thus gradually developed rich discourses of theology, which are grafted onto, situated alongside, or advanced in lieu of the normative order. Indeed, in certain modern iterations, Judaism does not just make room for theology, but is even stunningly recast as the quintessential religion.

[128] See Batntizky, *How Judaism Became a Religion*, 36–40, 52–59.

9

Soviet Law and Political Religion

Dmytro Vovk

I INTRODUCTION

At the beginning of the 1950s my PhD supervisor was a doctoral candidate at the Kharkov Law Institute, where he was preparing to defend his doctoral dissertation on Soviet law. His work "Soviet legislation" addressed purely legal issues like the nature of Soviet laws, the interlinks between law and legislation, and the hierarchy of legal acts in the Soviet Union. Just as his department recommended that his dissertation be defended before a special council responsible for conferring his degree, Joseph Stalin issued an article, "Marxism and the Problems of Linguistics." Even though Stalin's article had little to do with my supervisor's dissertation, his department immediately ceased preparing for his defense and returned his dissertation so that he could consider the conclusions of Stalin's opus. Their reactions were not reflections on the quality of his dissertation, or even the doubtless, outstanding scientific significance of Stalin's works (even if he did write them himself). Rather, they believed no research could justifiably be complete without quotes from the Soviet chief's most recent works, or from Marx, Engels, and Lenin for that matter – all of which were used in debates as final arguments, the truth that needed no elaboration or defense, in the same way that medieval theologians used to cite the Bible, Church Fathers, or Aristotle.

Around the same time, my supervisor's own supervisor and the head of his department had a habit of restricting his lectures to only enrolled students. If he spotted an unfamiliar person, he would leave the classroom out of a reasonable fear of being misunderstood. In Soviet times he did not write a word, but his academic views lived on in the memories and academic works of his students. It was precisely the terror felt by those living under totalitarianism: fear that discussing or lecturing on certain topics, such as the Law of the Twelve Tables or types of legal rules, might put the speaker under suspicion of contradicting Marx or Lenin, even though these men never wrote on the same issues. This understanding reminds me of an older fear of crossing a thin and twisted line that separates theology from heresy.

One can easily detect religious language in Soviet legal texts, namely, in constitutional acts. The USSR's Constitution of 1924 opens with Apocalyptic imagery: the world has been broken into two camps – a socialist kingdom of good where peace, freedom, and equality reign supreme, and a capitalist hell where inequality, slavery, pogroms, and chauvinism rule. Religious rhetoric runs through other Soviet constitutional texts, as well. In the 1919 Constitution of the Ukrainian Socialistic Soviet Republic, an individual's duty to work is supported with an almost direct quote from St. Paul: "He who does not work, neither shall he eat."

Soviet philosophy of law was grounded on Lenin's interpretations of Marxism, ideas that had an almost sacramental character through the assumed infallibility of their authors whose correctness was predetermined in the absence of scientific or any other kind of criticism. Several key conceptions (for example, the messianic role of the state and politicization of law) were implied from Lenin's version of Marxism and influenced Soviet law on both philosophical and practical levels, including the Soviet understanding of legality and human rights.

This chapter explores religious features of Soviet law and argues that the source of this religiosity was not internally legal, but was political and implied from Soviet totalitarianism,[1] which can be described as a form of political religion. This conception suggests that totalitarian regimes (re)produce a religious means of grounding and implementing their own power over society. Moreover, at the core of totalitarian political power, there always lies an overarching goal, in pursuit of which the state frees itself from any legal restrictions. Thus, the conception of political religion is a suitable intellectual tool for studying certain aspects of Soviet law because it unpacks the concepts and principles of Soviet Law more fully than traditional analytical approaches.

This does not mean that Soviet law or totalitarian law in general cannot be considered according to the usual dichotomy, "law – arbitrariness," as was

[1] I do not explore here whether democratic legal systems have similar religious features. My intuition is that they do. Robin West writes about the faith that Americans have in their Constitution (Robin West, R. (2016). "Law's Emotions." *Rich. J. L. & Pub. Int.* 19, 344–45). Otfried Höffe suggests that human rights – the key element of liberal political and legal systems – constitute a modern civil religion: (S. Gosepath and G. Lohman (eds.) (2008). *Filosophiya prav liudyny* [Philosophy of Human Rights] (pp. 32). Kyiv: Nika-Centre Publishing House). They play the same role that the Christian claim regarding man being made in the image of God once did. Human beings differ from all other beings because they have rights. The contemporary mainstream Western discourse of human rights is a discourse of the moral grounds of rights, their scope, their balance with other values, and the limits of government interference, but it is not a discourse about whether they exist. To frame the question in that way would be absurd. Individual rights are taken as a given, as almost an object of confidence. The same confidence is palpable in the American Declaration of Independence, when it refers to the "self-evident" truth of "inalienable Rights," or the Treaty on European Union that was "inspired" by the universal value of "the inviolable and inalienable rights of the human person." And the same is true for the solemn language of democratic constitutions and inaugural oaths of democratically elected presidents (the Bible can sometimes be found nearby), in the almost eschatological narrative of the history of human rights (from the darkness of rightlessness to the light of equal rights for all), in the cultish character of those who fought for human rights (Martin Luther King, Nelson Mandela), and in the victims of glaring violations of rights (Emmet Till).

done by Gustav Radbruch,[2] H. L. A. Hart,[3] Harold Berman,[4] or Dennis Lloyd (with different conclusions).[5] But traditional approaches do not adequately illuminate the nature of Soviet law. G. W. Paton wrote that Soviet law was "a sword for the executive and not a shield for the private citizen,"[6] that is to say, that Soviet law was the arbitrariness of the state. Soviet law, however, could be a shield, at least for politically loyal individuals in civil, family, and labor relationships or even in some relations with public power, and could be a sword in any legal situations against political dissidents, persons, or social group suspected of disloyalty. A political-religion perspective helps to demonstrate and explore this ambiguity.

Finally, two reservations should be made with respect to the scope and focus of my research. First, applying the political-religion conception presupposes a broad meaning of religion, which cannot be reduced to historical religions and faith traditions. When I argue that some features or elements of the Soviet legal system were religious by their nature or some doctrines and ideas beyond Soviet law were religiously justified, I do not try to argue that religions as social institutions in any way presuppose or support totalitarian political systems per se. I only mean that totalitarian political regimes are inclined to sacralize their power and employ religious tools in order to sustain themselves. This usually has some influence on the legal systems of totalitarian countries. This chapter should not be considered as a Voltaire-like critique of religion.

Second, in this chapter I explore only state-made law and pay almost no attention to informal regulation that may sometimes, especially in private-law issues, replace formal legal rules.[7] While law is not limited to state-made law, I limit my commentary because political religion influenced mostly the Soviet formal legal system, including legislation, court practices and legal doctrines developed by legal scholars and taught in law schools. At the same time, comparative research of formal and informal normative regulation in the Soviet Union,[8] can add a lot to our understanding of how legal and public-power institutions function in totalitarian political regimes.

[2] Radbruch, G. (2006). "Statutory Lawlessness and Supra-statutory Law." *Oxford Journal of Legal Studies* 26(1), 1–11.

[3] Hart, H. L. A. (2012). *Concept of Law* (3rd ed., pp. 210–12). Oxford: Oxford University Press; Hart, H. L. A. (1957). "Separation of Law and Morals." *Har. L. Rev.* 71, 616–18.

[4] Berman, H. J. (1958). "Soviet Law and Government." *Mod. L. Rev.* 21(19), 22; Berman, H. J. (1955). "Soviet Justice and Soviet Tyranny." *Colum. L. Rev.* 55, 805–06.

[5] Lloyd D. (1976). *The Idea of Law* (pp. 204). London: Penguin Books.

[6] Paton, G. W. (1946–47). "Soviet Legal Theory." *Res Judicatae* 3, 62.

[7] See, e.g., Ellickson, R. (1991). *Law without Order: How Neighbors Settle Disputes*. Cambridge, MA: Harvard University Press.

[8] See, e.g., Leacock, E. B. (1972) "Introduction and Notes." In F. Engels *The Origin of the Family, Private Property, and the State: in the Light of the Researches of Lewis H. Morgan*. New York, NY: International Publishers.

II THE SOVIET POLITICAL REGIME AS POLITICAL RELIGION

The history of politics can easily be written as the history of politics and religion. Many perennial political questions have been answered religiously. For example, questions including whether the state or kingdom differs from a band of robbers (even if the only actual difference has always been whether the robbers were roving or stationary), why the state must be obeyed, and why it has the right to use force, have found answers in the divine status of ancient monarchs, St. Paul's pronouncements about all authorities being established by God,[9] the status of the monarch as head of the Church, the medieval doctrine of the divine right of the king and corresponding myths, symbols, and rituals, and so on. Religion includes political power in a metapolitical context of what Leo Strauss once called "imaginary perfection,"[10] and ties it to the transcendent forces and otherworldly aims animating human life, that is, the City of God, salvation, or heaven.

Religion and religiously sanctioned law thereby normativizes relations between man and the political order. If the monarch is one of the gods or the son of god or Heaven, or the government is of God, then the power of the government appears to be a part of the eternal divine order and should itself observe God's commands rather than acting arbitrarily. The fear and powerlessness which man felt towards the sovereign reflect the sovereign's corresponding fear and powerlessness towards the might of gods and the duty to rule according to divine prescriptions, where the ruler and ruled share a perspective of responsibility before God. Things on the ground, of course, were more complicated, appealing to sources of political legitimacy as well as to a monarch's own perception of his divinely determined power – regarding the former, a certain political form would imply divinely legitimated rule, where the religious legitimation of government power became intertwined with elements of political representation (for example, Roman Republic), and regarding the latter, we would do well to consider the numerous denunciations of Old Testament prophets against unjust monarchs or corrupt judges.

The secularization of politics and law changes this pattern. Secularization significantly reduced religious dimension of the political discourse. Politics becomes exclusively or mostly an inner-worldly matter. Recalling a historical study by Christopher Hill, Jeffrey Stout points out that already in the middle of the seventeenth century, citations to scripture in the English Parliament provoked laughter, reflecting the decline of the Bible's public discursive authority.[11] Likewise, the divine right of kings did not prevent the High Court of Justice established by Parliament from sending Charles I to the gallows.

9 Rom. 13:1

10 Strauss, L. (1989). "Three Waves of Modernity." In *Introduction to Political Philosophy* (pp. 86). Detroit, MI: Wayne State University Press.

11 Stout, J. (2004). *Democracy and Tradition* (pp. 94–95). Princeton, NJ: Princeton University Press.

Despite increasing secularization, faith and a religious way of arguing for power, symbolism, and rituals did not completely disappear from politics. Emilio Gentile writes that in the modern period there occurs a transition from the sacralization of political power to the sacralization of the political system.[12] In other words, politics itself acquires the rhetoric of religion, distinct only in that the content, according to Eric Voegelin's categories, no longer transcends the world but becomes immanent to it.[13] Belief, commitment, and practice shifted direction to the things of this world – homeland, humanity, class, race, and the relation between ruler and ruled, who are either charmed (Georg Simmel) or frightened (Eric Fromm) by the ruler. Gentile talks about two forms of this secular religion: civil religion and political religion. He writes:

> Civil religion is the conceptual category that contains the forms of sacralization of a political system that guarantee a plurality of ideas, free competition in the exercise of power, and the ability of the governed to dismiss their governments through peaceful and constitutional methods. ... Political religion is the sacralization of a political system founded on an unchallengeable monopoly of power, ideological monism, and the obligatory and unconditional subordination of the individual and the collectivity to its code of commandments.[14]

The totalitarian state pretends to be more than a form of government – it sees itself as the ruler of history, the creator of a new society or socioeconomic formation, the source of world revolution, the protector of race or nation, the keeper of an identity that is under threat. This sacred mission justifies the government's monopoly on political and economic power, its total control over society, and any arbitrariness because, as totalitarians often claim, these bring about the stated ultimate end. In this sense, any real totalitarian state is a mix of fear and prospective happiness, or "paradise on this side of the grave,"[15] where fear of an omnipotent and omniscient machine of unbounded power is compensated for by an officially sanctioned expectation for future happiness: communist class-less society or the Thousand Year Reich.

Here I do not separately discuss the question of whether political religions appear to copy or make a travesty of traditional religion.[16] It seems to me that the aims of totalitarianism, such as totalitarian monopolization of power and control over society and individuals, their behavior, and consciousness, pushes this political system toward a wide (and perhaps twisted) employment and reproduction of secularized religious patterns and concepts. For totalitarian regimes, religion

[12] Gentile, .E. (2006). *Politics as Religion*. (G. Staunton Trans., pp. XIV). Princeton, NJ: Princeton University Press.

[13] Voegelin, E. (1986). *Political Religions* (DiNapoli & Easterly Trans., pp. 14). Lewiston, NYE. Mellen Press.

[14] Gentile, *Politics as Religion*, *supra* note 12, p. XV.

[15] Schumpeter, J. A. (2006). *Capitalism, Socialism and Democracy* (pp. 6). Oxford: Routledge.

[16] Baehr, P. (2010). *Hannah Arendt, Totalitarianism and the Social Sciences*. Stanford, CA: Stanford University Press; Gregor, A. J. (2012). *Totalitarianism and Political Religion: An Intellectual History*. Stanford, CA: Stanford University Press; J. Augustejn, P. Dassen and M. Janse (eds.). (2013). *Political Religion beyond Totalitarianism*. New York: Palgrave-Macmillan.

appears to be a suitable method for achieving these aims[17]. Even still, certain islets of ideology-free political and legal institutions, like contracts in civil law, appear to be an exception. We can examine the Soviet political regime as a form of political religion, including its official communist ideology and supported cults, myths, symbols, practices, and public institutions, on which Lenin and his party of Bolsheviks monopolized and sustained their power.

The Leninist and Stalinist interpretation of Marxism constituted the basis of Soviet communism. Marx's teaching about the inevitable proletariat revolution and the construction of a communist class-less and government-less society is a combination of a scientific knowledge and a prophecy of the last who shall become the first, of the City of God on Earth. This is worth dwelling on because such an interpretation of class struggle takes matters beyond the limits of politics and economics. The liberation of the proletariat along with the whole of humanity becomes a question of the battle of good and evil, of ridding injustice from this world,[18] and not simply a response to political obstructions and an unjust distribution of economic resources. Therefore, it should come as no surprise that Marxism, as Bjarne Melkevik writes,[19] quickly became the object of a cultish and almost religious devotion of those who, believing in the Communist Manifesto, waited and, by their actions, catalyzed the creation of a communist "association in which the free development of each is the condition of the free development of all."[20]

Lenin's interpretation of Marxism intensified this religious component in three key ways by appropriating Marx's teachings to his own political goals. First, Lenin rejected any interpretation of Marxism that offered to minimize class struggle and make use of the evolutionary path without revolution.

Second, citing Marx and Engels, Lenin established that the transition from capitalist society into communism requires one additional step. Revolution does not do away with government but instead replaces bourgeois government with a transitional, proletariat government, which will begin to dissolve or to "wither away" with the disappearance of class contradictions.[21] The dictatorship of the proletariat (specifically, Lenin and his party's dictatorship)[22] is therefore the only

17 In "Terrorism and Communism" Leon Trotsky wondered how to make the bourgeoisie obey if the proletariat state had no "future [transcendent] penalties" and "priests' hell" (Trotsky, L. (1961). *Terrorism and Communism. A Reply to Karl Kautsky* (M. Shachtman Trans., pp. 22). Ann Arbor, MI: The University of Michigan Press). For him the answer was terror. However, terror would not be effective and a political order would not be stable without ideology that engaged most of the population.

18 Baehr, *Hannah Arendt, supra* note 16, p. 93.

19 Melkevik, B. (2010), *Marxisme et Philosophie de Droit : le Cas Pasukanis* (pp. 7). Paris: Buenos Books International.

20 K. Marx and F. Engels (1985). *The Communist Manifesto* (pp. 105). London: Penguin Books.

21 Lenin, V. (1932). *State and Revolution* (pp. 15–16). New York: International Publishers.

22 Lenin exclaimed in a letter to the People's Commissar for Justice, Dmitry Kursky: "The State is us, us, deliberate workers, us, communists." Lenin, V. (1970). *Polnoe sobranie sochineniy* [Complete works] (5th ed., Vol. 44. pp. 397). Moscow: Izdatel'stvo politicheskoy literatury.

path to building communism. Lenin underlined that the exploiters can be defeated in one stroke but cannot be destroyed in one stroke,[23] because after the revolution the proletariat dictatorship should preserve itself and be strong enough for battle with the bourgeoisie and its sympathizers. Stalin added concerns about growing class struggle during the transition to communism and the impossibility of dissolving the state while being surrounded by capitalist countries; these concerns demanded an even more powerful state that would be prepared for battle against enemies from within and from without.[24] As a result, even the officially sanctioned death of the state became a question of the distant future. After breaking through resistance from the class of exploiters, the USSR was proclaimed to be for all people and appeared as the necessary facilitator of society, even all of humanity in a new class-less world, where according to Lenin, each could "receive from society, without any control over the labor of the individual citizen, any quantity of truffles, automobiles, pianos, etc."[25] This messianic role allowed the state to justify any actions in relation to the society and to each individual.

Third, like many religions have throughout their history,[26] Lenin's version of Marxism refused to entertain any criticism. The texts of Marx, Engels, Lenin, and Stalin (during his rule) became official dogma, whereas all other versions of Marxism were declared to be perversions or slander. Lenin began a tradition of interpretation according to which verifying Marx and Engels's conclusions appeared an absurd task. The trouble was that there were internal contradictions in Marx's works, as is almost unavoidable whenever all of a thinker's works, including even his or her letters, are accepted as a single whole.

Soviet ideologists overcame internal contradictions in Marxism-Leninism like the internal contradictions in the Bible. Like medieval scholastics, Lenin and his followers juggled quotations in order to resolve conflicts of interpretation and showed that the problem was not with the contradictions but with misunderstanding "correct" revolutionary Marxism – correctly understanding was a symbol of faith open only to Bolsheviks and no one else.[27] Lenin devoted his main theoretical work,

[23] Lenin, V. (1952). *The Proletarian Revolution and the Renegade Kautsky* (pp. 48). Moscow: Foreign Languages Publishing House.

[24] Stalin, J. (1942). *Leninism: Selected Writings* (pp. 98). New York: International Publishers. Accordingly, Andrey Vyshinsky argued that the State could only dissolve when all countries became socialist (Vyshinsky, A. (1948). *Issues of Theory of State and Law* (pp. 227). Moscow: State Publishing of Law Literature; Vyshinsky, A. (1948). *The Teachings of Lenin and Stalin on Proletarian Revolution and the State* (A. Rothstein. trans., pp.116–17). London: Soviet News. The irony was that when Engels wrote about strengthening public power during the growth of class contradictions within the state, he meant the bourgeois state, not the state where the proletariat revolution succeeded (Leacock, Introduction, *supra* note 8, p. 230).

[25] Marx and Engels, *The Communist Manifesto*, supra note 20, p. 80.

[26] Cf. Saint Paul's phrase "for there must be also heresies among you" (1 Cor. 11:19) with Medieval practices of persecution of heretics.

[27] For example, Lenin wrote that when Marx had spoken about the "future statehood of communist society," he did not contradict the basic view of communism as a stateless society (Lenin, *State and Revolution*, *supra* note 21, p. 84).

"State and Revolution," to "resuscitate the real teaching of Marx on the state" and rid it of "opportunistic distortion."[28] The word "distortion" is revealing. This is the rhetoric of battling heresy, not of "scientific" discussion. As Joseph Schumpeter wrote about Marxism generally, for an orthodox Marxist, as for any orthodox believer, an opponent is not merely in error but in sin.[29]

In this sense, the absence of any political rights in the Soviet system is completely logical. In liberal political systems the critics of the state occupy the same moral position as supporters of the state. But if politics becomes religion, then political rights (the freedom of association for critics of the state, a multi-party system, etc.) encroach on an exclusively true political order, just as religious liberty encroaches on the exclusive truth of a state religion. Critics of the state are then seen as guilty of the same sin as heretics or atheists. Carl Schmitt was completely frank in one of his works of the Nazi period: "Now [after the coming to power of the Nazis] there is no equality but rather an absence of discrimination between the enemy of the state and its friend, between a comrade of the people and a stranger."[30]

Contradictions between official ideology and reality were overcome by way of what Hannah Arendt called the totalitarian "contempt for factuality."[31] All actions of the regime that contradicted its own ideology or officially stated aims were considered unreal, nonexistent. In this way, there were no workers obligated to labor in slavery-like conditions in Soviet plants and factories because Lenin's workers were the "vanguard" of working people and masters of the universe,[32] who "will scarcely allow anyone to trifle them."[33] Thus, there was no actual Supreme Council of the USSR – a caricature of Parliament without any actual influence, where deputies were always voting for drafts worked out by the bureaucracy beforehand – because Marx criticized bourgeois democracy for the arbitrariness of its executive power and the lack of parliamentary control over it,[34] and because Marx called the parliamentary regime the regime of unrest that lived by discussion and thrived in conflict.[35]

28 *Id.*, p. 6–7.
29 Berlin, I. (1957). "The Silence in Russian Culture." *Foreign Affairs* 36(1), 5.
30 Schmitt, C. (2001). *State, Movement, People: the Triadic Structure of the Political Unity. The Question of Legality*. (S. Draghic ed. and trans., pp. 4). Corvalis, OR: Plutarch Press. This observation is worth considering insofar as it shows a rhetorical similarity between criticism of political sin (being an enemy of the state) and religious criticism of individual rights, for which many religions use the objection of "difference" to arguments about equality and discrimination. The exclusion of women from certain kinds of professions or activities does not appear to be discriminatory because men and women are legally equal, but different and have different social roles.
31 Power, S. (2004). "Introduction." In H. Arendt, *Origins of Totalitarianism* (pp. 590). New York: Schocken Books.
32 Lenin, *The Proletarian Revolution*, *supra* note 23, p. 39.
33 Lenin, *State and Revolution*, *supra* note 21, p. 85.
34 Fine, B. (2002). *Democracy and the Rule of Law: Marx's Critique of the Legal Form* (pp. 112). Caldwell, NJ: Blackburn Press.
35 Marx K. (1996). "The Eighteenth Brumaire of Louis Bonaparte" (pp. 71). In T. Carver (ed. And trans.) *Marx: Later Political Writings*. Cambridge: Cambridge University Press.

The messianic role of the state in forming a new society of Soviet people and in moving toward communism was supplemented by the teaching that developed Marxism-Leninism in all spheres of social life, even the most unexpected. The religious nature of Soviet communism presumed and demanded a capacity to create a complete picture of the world in which all the primary questions of human life would find answers. "Marxism will be able to do everything," assures a character in Andrei Platonov's dystopian novel *The Foundation Pit*. This teaching could be applied everywhere from science to sex: Marxism-Leninism could go so far as to teach how, in fact, genetic mutation happens or that one could only enter into sexual relations with partners of the same social class.

The institutional dimension of Soviet political religion comprised not only the state but also the Party and mass state-funded associations of young people, artists, writers, and so on. Membership in these movements, just like belonging to a state religion in many nonsecular states, was not just a way of immersing the population in official ideology from the moment one first stepped foot outside the family into kindergarten or primary school; it was also a way of determining privileges or, what was more common, it was a condition of nondiscrimination.

As with traditional religions, Soviet political religion had its own mythology, its own cults and anti-cults, rituals, and "holy" places. These applications legitimized the political regime and intensified the population's loyalty and controllability. Further, the mythology amplified the supposedly scientific foundation of the Soviet system and reinforced the emotional scaffolding required to support official activities; but above all, it instilled in people's minds that picture of the world which was most useful for a totalitarian regime. All the while communism battled traditional religion, which it perceived as an ideological and political contestant for authority and power. We can deduce that traditional religion presented such a threat from Marx's emotional determination of religion as "the opium of the people"[36] and the "mystification" from which one's conscience needs to be freed,[37] or from Lenin's comparison of believing in God to a necrophilia.[38]

On an ideological level, as David Walsh writes, "the presence of a divine Creator jeopardized the whole project of human self-salvation through revolutionary action,"[39] while on a political level, churches and religious communities presented, as Hannah Arendt said, the natural "objective enemy"[40] meaning part of the class of

36 Marx, K. (1970). *Critique of Hegel's 'Philosophy of Right'*. (Jolin & O'Malley Trans., J. O'malley ed., pp. 131) Cambridge: Cambridge University Press.

37 Marx, K. (1996). "Critique of the Gotha Programme" (pp. 225). In T. Carver (ed. and trans.) *Marx: Later Political Writings*. Cambridge: Cambridge University Press.

38 Lenin, V. (1969). *On Religion* (pp. 39). Moscow: Progress Publishers.

39 Walsh, D. (1995). *After Ideology: Recovering the Spiritual Foundations of Freedom* (2nd ed., pp. 122). Washington, DC: Catholic University of America Press. Walsh provides evidence from Marx demonstrating that Marx viewed religion as an ideological opponent or competitor rather than an element alien to his worldview.

40 Power, Introduction, *supra* note 31, p. 11.

exploiters or an element of the government machine. Soviet official atheism solves both of these problems. It allows the government, as Walter Lippmann put it, to appropriate for itself the functions and prerogatives of God.[41] Besides that, communist atheism serves to justify the act of rejecting one's freedom of conscience in the interest of the Communist Party's (or really, the state's) war against religion, interpreted as a war for freeing believers from "incorrect" convictions that, as one Soviet scholar argued, stand in the way of their happiness.[42]

The dogmas, teachings, and practices of the Soviet political regime impacted the normative systems of Soviet society. There never were a set of morals that expressed purely class struggle. Communist morality in the USSR was more accurately a mix of commitment to communist ends, patriotism, universally shared human values, and the rules of cohabitation. The same can be said of Soviet law. Although it was of course impacted by the teachings of Marxism-Leninism and bolstered by the nature of the Soviet state, Soviet law was not completely severed from its past and even shared a number of traits with Western law. In this sense, the USSR legal system was reminiscent of the legal system of a nonsecular country, where religious law could compete with local customs or secular laws and could even dominate over them without being able to completely supersede them.

III THE SYMBOL OF FAITH IN SOVIET LAW[43]

The symbol of faith in Soviet law is a set of ideas or dogmas that exhibit the influence of Soviet political religion on Soviet law. These ideas concern the nature of Soviet law, its role in society and in the movement toward communism, how law interacts with politics and the State, and its relationship with bourgeois law.

Marxism-Leninism considers law to be a part of the superstructure above the economic base, that is, above the relationship of production and exchange. The first section of the Communist Manifesto begins with the claim that the history of all hitherto existing societies has been the history of class struggle.[44] Where the means of production generate a surplus for exchange, there exist classes and class struggle. The economically dominant class, which owns the means of production and appropriates the surpluses, strengthens its dominance over other classes by way of political and legal institutions. Law, therefore, entrenches formal inequality among people of different classes. In this sense, the bourgeois state and its law institutionalize the dominance of the bourgeoisie as the ruling class over the proletariat and similarly oppressed social groups.[45]

41 Lippmann, W. (1989). *Public Philosophy* (pp. 83). New Jersey: Transaction Publishers

42 Mchedlov, M. (1982). *Religiya i sovremennost'* [Religion and the Present] (pp. 243). Moscow: Gospolitizdat.

43 Karl Marx used the similar term "articles of faith" as a set of political ideas that are above criticism in his Letter to W. Bracke (Available at: www.marxists.org/archive/marx/works/1875/letters/75_05_05.htm).

44 Marx and Engels, *The Communist Manifesto, supra* note 20, p. 79.

45 *Id.*, pp. 92–93.

The socialist revolution consists in the formerly oppressed proletariat, along with their collaborators, forcefully taking power into their own hands and installing a dictatorship of the proletariat that governs in the interests of working-class people. After crushing the resistance from the class of exploiters, particularly after establishing public ownership of the means of production, the state becomes an all-people's government. Law in this state likewise appears to be for all people, meaning that it serves the interests of all people rather than of specific classes. This, as Lenin once said, is "bourgeois law without the bourgeoisie" or, in other words, law that strengthens formal equality, but does not entrench class oppression. Lenin wrote that as the first step of communism, the socialist state maintains formal equality in the distribution of products of consumption insofar as equal amounts of labor ensure equal wages (the principle "from each according to his ability to each according to his work"). Therefore, the bourgeois legal principle of formal equality is used as a means of destroying classes, and the socialist state's legal system became "bourgeois law without [the class dominance of] the bourgeoisie."[46] The contents of the law as well as politics, religion, or art are determined by the nature of economic relations and class struggle in a particular historical period. Rembrandt's paintings or Dickens's novels, medieval *droit coutimier* and the formal equality of bourgeois law, elections and human rights, God and marriage, all express the economic conditions of life in a given society and its class contradictions. When economic order changes, so too does the ideological form of that society's understanding and expression.

What does this mean for law?

First, law is a victim of history. From this perspective, when we reach the communist end of history, law as an instrument of coercion will wither away. It follows that the destiny and fate of Soviet lawyers was to witness the withering of that to which they had dedicated their professional lives, and by their actions to draw nearer the death of law.

Second, if law is determined by economics, its independent influence on social development is very limited. The legal form is necessary for substantiating the new economic order. It serves as a tool for nationalizing the property of capitalists, for the pursuit of class enemies, and for strengthening the position of the Communist Party. Nevertheless, law on its own cannot change the existing economic order, changes in the economic structure of society must precede changes in legal structure.

Moreover, if the most important existential question concerns changing the economic order, then for the sake of building a society without class contradictions, the state can use any element of the superstructure as an ideological weapon in the struggle of good (the socialist state on its way to communism) versus evil (the capitalist system). This struggle does not determine the content of any law, administrative act, judicial decision, or lecture at any law school, not to mention books or films, but it does mean that there was always the possibility their content could be so

[46] Lenin, *State and Revolution*, *supra* note 21, p. 82.

determined. If the state needed it, then law and the courts (as well as textbooks of Roman law, children's cartoons, or even Shakespeare's plays) could be mobilized in defense of the political system. Paul Ricoeur writes:

> Once it is assumed that these [juridical, political, religious, and cultural] spheres have no autonomy, then the Stalinist state is possible. The argument is that since the economic basis is sound and since all the other spheres are merely reflexes, shadows, or echoes, then we are allowed to manipulate the latter spheres in order to improve the economic basis.[47]

At least as applied to law, this state is as Stalinist as it is Leninist. Lenin proclaimed that the interests of the revolution are higher than the formal rights of a democratically elected, representative body.[48] In other words, if the revolution demands it, or, if Lenin believes that the revolution demands it, then legal procedures can be neglected. In his letter to Dmitry Kursky, Lenin directly insisted on fast, expedient, revolution-based show trials against political enemies of the Soviet government. He emphasized the role of Party influence on judges and members of the revolutionary tribunal for the achievement of this end.[49] In this demand for political violence against enemies, sanctified by court decisions, it is easy to see Stalin's upcoming show trials against enemies of the people as the new role of legal form in installing a socialist world. From the perspective of political religion, the legal form is valuable insofar as it lines up with the avowed or actual goals of the Soviet political regime, above all ensuring loyalty to the government and its politics. For that reason, several times in his letter Lenin emphasized the role of his party in "improving" the work of judges and officials.[50] He meant that law should be primarily influenced by state aims, that legal principles such as the presumption of innocence or due process are less significant than political expediency. The aims and needs of political religion are higher than legal principles, and when it is expedient to do so, law serves as one of the methods of achieving a political goal.

Third, as part of the preliminary stage preceding the onset of communism, the epoch of socialism is characterized by its own socialist law, which is radically different from bourgeois law. Even dressed in clothes of human rights or democracy, bourgeois law always exhibits class coercion and inequality, while socialist law always exhibits exactly the opposite. Lenin wrote: "Take the fundamental laws of modern states, take their administration, take the right of assembly, freedom of the press, or 'equality of all citizens before the law,' and you will see at every step evidence of the hypocrisy of bourgeois democracy."[51]

47 Ricoeur, P. (1986). *Lectures on Ideology and Utopia* (G. H. Taylor ed., pp. 155). New York: Columbia University Press.

48 Lenin, *The Proletarian Revolution*, *supra* note 23, p. 75.

49 Lenin, *Polnoe sobranie*, *supra* note 22, p. 396–97.

50 *Id.*, p. 397.

51 Lenin, *The Proletarian Revolution*, *supra* note 23, p. 34.

This framing allows Soviet legal science to look at bourgeois law in the same way that Vladimir Mayakovsky looked at the New York bourgeoisie in the poem "Broadway":

> I am in ecstasy from the city of New York.
> But I will not take the cap from my head.
> The Soviets have their own pride:
> on the bourgeoisie we look from above.[52]

From this perspective, in bourgeois law there is not, nor could there be, guarantees of "real" human rights or "real" justice; instead there are only legal norms, procedures, and institutions, through which capitalists ensure their political dominance and the bondage of exploited classes.

Support for this assertion of Soviet legal scholars was found in Arendt's "contempt for factuality," an alternative world of past, present, and future law, often quite distant from how things actually were. In 1938, when Stalin's terror reached their peak, a famous Soviet scholar of criminal procedure still portrayed the Soviet judiciary as independent and obedient only to the law.[53] In the same year, Andrey Vyshinsky explained the need to establish individual fault in every concrete crime despite being aware of the practice of punishing family members of enemies of the people.[54] In a different work, Vyshinsky concluded that the principle distinction of Soviet constitutionalism is the actuality of constitutional rights and the actual ability to use them; in contrast he said that bourgeois constitutional law is an artful perversion of reality, proclaiming rights that cannot be realized.[55] In reality, as a rule, everything was exactly the opposite – Soviet constitutions declared the right of members of the Soviet federation to secession, but in fact, the legal mechanism of secession was never established.

IV THEOLOGY OF SOVIET LAW

Here I explore how the theology of Soviet law developed its symbol of faith by way of four interrelated doctrinal problems: (1) the "death" of law; (2) the correlation of socialist and bourgeois law; (3) the links between law and politics; and (4) the economic nature of law (the base–superstructure problem). The term "theology" is, of course, relative. I use it to show that in the studies of Soviet lawyers there was no clear-cut distinction between philosophy of law and religious interpretations of Marxism-Leninism. Samuel I. Shuman compared Soviet philosophy with

52 Translated by Carlotta Chenoweth.

53 Strogovich, M. (1939). *Priroda Sovetskogo ugolovnogo processa I printsip sostyazatelnosti* [Nature of Soviet Criminal Procedure and Principle of Adversary] (pp. 39). Moscow: Law Press of People's Commissariat of Justice of the USSR.

54 Vyshinsky, A. (1938). *Sudebnie rechi* [Trial speeches] (pp. 109). Moscow: Uridischeskoye izdatel'stvo NKJu SSSR.

55 Vyshinsky, *Issues of Theory of State and Law*, *supra* note 24, p. 133.

a "theological exegesis rather than anything likely to be identified as the professional product of people like Plato, Kant or Hume."[56] The theology of Soviet law nevertheless also pursued quite practical aims of the totalitarian political regime: the centralization of power, maximum interference with all aspects of social life, control over society, and the loyalty of the population and its obedience.

The "death" of law is, perhaps, the simplest point in the symbol of faith. According to Marxism-Leninism, as law does not exist without the coercive power of the state, both must wither away together after the high phase of communism has come. But class struggle demands more state power to defend the achievements of the Russian Revolution rather than less power through withering away. Because "withering away" means gradual weakening of law rather than immediate disappearance, Soviet jurisprudence turned suddenly from expecting withering away as an actual future development of law to withering away as a process just beyond the horizon of events.

Prominent Soviet legal scholar, Evgeny Pashukanis suggested that law would pass away after private property was liquidated and a planned economy was established. As Bjarne Melkevik pointed out, for Pashukanis, the withering away of law must follow the withering of market society, but not due to a voluntary political decision or any ideological discourse.[57] However, in later works, Pashukanis provided an important qualification. If he first spoke about the withering away and gradual dissolution of law during the transition to communism, then later, leaning on Marx's and Lenin's conception of bourgeois law without the bourgeoisie, Pashukanis wrote about Soviet law as "the legacy of a bourgeois epoch that was to outlive the bourgeoisie": law would exist while there was a relation of equivalency between labor and wage,[58] and, as a consequence, material inequality of individuals. Similar thought that law would wither away only after full material equality within society was reached was articulated by Pyotr Stuchka[59] and Mikhail Reysner. The latter noted that a "formula that provides unequal treatment of unequal people will kill law."[60] The discussion was summarized by Andrey Vyshinsky in a very illustrative way:

> Law will wither away only when people will have gotten so accustomed to following the main rules of community life that they will follow them without any coercive force. Before that, however, total control, strong labor and community discipline, and total subordination of the whole work of the new society to a really democratic state is still needed.[61]

56 Shuman, S. I. (1959). "Soviet Legality as Revealed by Soviet Jurisprudence." *Wayne L. Rev.* 5, 213.

57 Melkevik, *Marxisme et Philosophie de Droit*, *supra* note 19, p. 48.

58 Pashukanis, E. (1980). *Izbrannie proizvedeniya po obschey teorii prava I gosudarstva* [Collected Works on General Theory of Law and State] (pp. 50, 55). Moscow: Nauka Press.

59 Stuchka, P. (1932). *Revolutsionnaya Rol Prava i Gosudarstva* [Revolutionary Role of Law and State] (pp. 102). Moscow: Soviet Legislation Press.

60 Reysner, M. (1925). *Pravo, Nashe Pravo, Chuzhoe Pravo, Obschee Pravo* [Law, Our Law, Foreign Law, Common Law] (pp. 259). Leningrad; Moscow: Gosudarstvennoye izdatel'stvo.

61 Vyshinsky, *Issues of Theory of State and Law*, *supra* note 24, p. 44.

That was the end of the discussion. After Vyshinsky, the withering away of law was never discussed seriously in Soviet legal jurisprudence. Predictably, the utopia in which absolutely everyone follows absolutely all of society's rules, in which all are ready to work to the extreme in order to receive an equal number of Lenin's "truffles, cars, and pianos," failed to materialize, unlike the second part of Vyshinsky's observation regarding total control and subordination.

The idea of "bourgeois law without the bourgeoisie" was also employed to compare socialist and bourgeois law. Any law expresses the will of the ruling class and is to be supported coercively by the state. Stuchka wrote that socialist law was transitional; it accompanied the transition from capitalism to communism.[62] It was the law of a class and it was coercive, but it was law of a special kind. Socialist law does not serve as a means by which the minority oppresses the majority. Rather, socialist law embodies the unified will of the proletariat and serves the interests of all working people. Though it was still the law of formal equality and material inequality, Vyshinsky argued that Soviet law did include some elements of material equality: the social ownership of the means of production, an equally available social right to education, healthcare, pensions, social support for large families, etc.[63] Vyshinsky emphasized that all these benefits were granted by "the Soviet power" and "the Soviet state."[64] Hence, the state acted as manager and de facto owner of public wealth and distributor of social goods, which only strengthened the paternalistic relationship with society so favorable for a totalitarian regime.

Relations between law and politics, the third point under discussion, were an intrinsic part of Soviet discourse on the nature of law and its validity. During the 1920s and early 1930s, there were competing versions of the Marxist approach to law in Soviet jurisprudence, including Pashukanis's "the commodity exchange theory of law," where primary elements of law are legal relations of commodity exchange between autonomous and formally equal subjects;[65] Stuchka's law as a system of social relations that expresses the will of the ruling class and are enforced by its organized power (that is, usually by the state);[66] Yakov Magaziner's law as a system of obligatory rules that are established and protected by the state but created by society itself and shaped in concrete administrative or judicial decisions;[67] and Mikhail Reisner's theory of class intuitive law, a combination of the class approach and Leon Petrażycki's psychological theory.[68]

62 Stuchka, P. (1964). *Izbrannie proizvedeniia po marksistsko-leninskoy teorii prava* [Selected Works on Marxism-Leninism Theory of Law] (pp. 102). Riga: Latvian State Press.

63 Vyshinsky, *Issues of Theory of State and Law*, *supra* note 24, p. 43.

64 *Id.*

65 Pashukanis, *Izbrannie proizvedeniya po obschey teorii prava I gosudarstva*, *supra* note 58, p. 78, 113.

66 Stuchka, *Revolutsionnaya Rol Prava i Gosudarstva*, *supra* note 59. p. 9.

67 Magaziner, Y. (2006). *Izbrannie raboty po obschey teorii prava* [Selected Works on General Theory of Law] (pp. 68–70). Saint Peterburg: Yuridichesky Center Press.

68 Reysner, *Pravo, Nashe Pravo, Chuzhoe Pravo, Obschee Pravo*, *supra* note 60, p. 117, 130.

These theories seem to be more sociological (or some combination of sociological approaches and legal positivism). The validity of law is connected not only with the establishment of laws by a certain legal authority, but also with its real action within society. Sociological theories of law conflict with the logic of a totalitarian system that is not ready to recognize and accept any permanent restrictions on its lawmaking power or right to influence and change society using legal means. The prospect of finding law in real administrative and court practices, but not in legislative acts, seems tempting, of course; public officials and judges could thereby manipulate laws for the will of the state or the party. But in giving too much discrete power to small cogs in the machine, it contradicts the totalitarian aim of concentrating and centralizing power. Instead of following the will of the highest authority, these channels would create their own legal regulation and rely on their legal conscience rather than on the laws they professionally apply.

Moreover, pluralistic debate about the nature of law was hardly compatible with the totalitarian system. Disagreement and confrontation of ideas were discouraged; differences of opinion, philosophical schools, factions, or parties would be harmful for social cohesion and loyalty to the state. Isaiah Berlin argued that this was why after Stalin gathered strength, he stopped all ideological debates and announced the victory of this or that (randomly chosen) school.[69] Andrey Vyshinsky unified the variety of approaches to law in the late 1930s.[70] He defined law as follows:

> Law is a system of rules of behavior expressing the will of the ruling class and it is established by the legislator, as well as by the customs and rules of community life sanctioned by the state, the application of which is guaranteed by the state coercively in order to protect, to strengthen, and to develop social relations and orders that are beneficial and favorable for the ruling class.[71]

For Vyshinsky, legal rules always express the will of the ruling class and are always established or sanctioned by the state. Thus, the will of the ruling class cannot be articulated against the Soviet state – the first state in the world where the proletariat revolution has won and social justice has been done. Moreover, due to its messianic mission, the state understands this will better than the ruling class itself. For that reason the state is authorized to establish not only rules that express the actual will of the ruling class, but also anything that will be favorable for the proletariat and all working people in the future ("in order … to develop social relations"). Thus,

69 Berlin, "The Silence in Russian Culture," *supra* note 29, p. 13.

70 These debates literally ended: Stuchka and Reisner died. As to Reisner, whose daughter was close to Leon Trotsky, there is little doubt about his fate if he would have lived to see the Great Terror. Pashukanis and some of his followers were shot as "enemies of people." What is remarkable here is that the tragic end of Pashukanis' life was not mentioned in the volume of his works published in the USSR in the 1980s, although it was an open secret, even abroad. Lon L. Fuller mentioned this fact in a paper from 1948 (Fuller, L. L. (1949). "Pashukanis and Vyshinsky: A Study in Development of Marxian Legal Theory." *Mich. L. Rev.* 47, 1159).

71 Vyshinsky, *Issues of Theory of State and Law*, *supra* note 24, p. 83.

Vyshinsky's theory presupposes no institutions or procedures capable of, to borrow Radbruch's terminology, "supra-statutory law" against "statutory lawlessness." Some Soviet lawyers argued that because there was no antagonism between the state and individuals in Soviet society, there were also no disputes between the state and private persons and, consequently, that there was no need for judicial review of administrative acts (individual acts are meant here, but judicial review of normative acts seems to be even more absurd in this regard).[72]

Such a combination of the legislative will of the state and the will of the ruling class that is exclusively expressed by the state, is the way to argue the core principle of the Soviet law: the so-called "socialist legality" that is strict observance of legal rules (norms of the law) by all persons and entities except the state itself, which, due to its political aims and with reference to the will of people and the benefits for the ruling class, is able to deviate from these rules, ignoring or arbitrarily changing them. The state acts here as an oracle of class will and the exclusive lawmaker – an almighty "legal God." This God makes his "covenant"[73] with the chosen Soviet people, the only people that has jumped to a new socialist grade of social development. This God requires obedience to "commandments" in order to reach perfection or transition to communism. It is the communist aim, rather than any legal construction, that commands the mutual loyalty of the State and the people.[74] The state punishes those who deviate from commandments, both to those who violate legal rules and those who express political disloyalty.[75] In the covenant, the state itself is not limited by rules or principles, for it is guided by its messianic aim.

This does not mean that the state always exercised its power arbitrarily and the application of legal rules is always uncertain. Soviet law could protect individuals against the state when the state allowed it. For example, an employee dismissed unfairly could be reinstated after filing a lawsuit or making a claim to a competent state body or even appealing to the local chapter of the Communist Party. Yet an employee fired for a political joke or a student dismissed from university for involvement with the dissident movement had no chance of an effective remedy regardless of the formal reason for dismissal. At any moment the state could ignore any legal procedure, rule, or principle when it came to individuals or social or ethnic groups that qualified as "traitors," "enemies of the people," or "dissidents" because

72 Abramov, S. N. (1947). "V sovetskom prave ne mozhet byt administrativnogo iska." [There Cannot Be Administrative Lawsuits in Soviet Law] *Socialist Legality* 3, 48; Studenikina, M. S. (1974). *Gosudarstvenniy Kontrol v Sphere Upravleniya* [State Control in the Sphere of Governance]. Moscow: Uridicheskaya literatura.

73 cf. Gen. 17:2.

74 Just as mutual loyalty of the Nazi state and people is founded on ethnic identity, as indicated by Carl Schmitt (Schmitt, *State, Movement, People*, *supra* note 30, p. 48).

75 Throughout Soviet history, expression of political disloyalty, such as anti-Soviet propaganda and intentionally false statements about the Soviet state, remained a formal crime according to Soviet criminal law.

political aims weighed more heavily than any rules or principles. This is precisely when law becomes terror.

Vyshinsky's approach prevailed until Stalin's death and was later condemned and partly rejected by post-Stalin Soviet legal science. Subsequently, some Soviet philosophers and legal theorists continued their commitment to the base–superstructure dichotomy, to class theory, coerciveness, and normativity as core features of law, but they also tried to work out less statist conceptions of law, including a focus on judicial process. For example, they sought strict and unconditional observance of legal procedures by state bodies and public servants, and to their definitions of law they added legal relations, legal conscience, and subjective rights and responsibilities, along with legal rules.

In the late 1970s, the most prestigious Soviet law journal, "Soviet State and Law," organized a series of debates on how law was to be understood. All scholars participating in the event cited Marx, Engels, Lenin, Leonid Brezhnev, and decrees of the latest Congress of the Communist Party. None were prevented from defending rather different concepts and characteristics of law: law as legislation, law as state will, law as something broader than positive law, distinctions between societal law and official law, etc. Although these debates were presented as returning to or revisiting a "correct" Marxism, it is hard to imagine that the participants were converted Marxists. Like the Bible in the English Parliament of the seventeenth century, in the late USSR legal ruminations on the withering away of law could only provoke a smile. Scholars instead sought out a compromise between their views on law and the symbol of faith in Soviet law that they could not ignore. For instance, Leningrad University's Lev Yavich wrote that law not only subordinated individuals to the means of production but also was a way of enabling their creativity.[76] For Yavich, law was most certainly determined by society's economic system and class relations, but it also guaranteed a certain amount of individual freedom, even in terms of feudal or bourgeois law. This methodological trick, as well as the relevant increase of the importance of law and legal regulation within the Soviet state, demonstrated the gradual ideological weakening of soviet political religion in the legal arena.

Olympiad Ioffe, one of the participants in the "Soviet State and Law" debates and a brilliant Soviet specialist in civil law and Roman law, was deprived of his professorship in the early 1980s for permitting his daughter to immigrate to Israel. After that Ioffe was compelled to immigrate to the United States where he found work at several American universities. His works from this time demonstrate an adequate assessment of Soviet jurisprudence that is free from repetition of Marxist-Leninist dogmas,[77] including those he relied upon in the debates. The same seems to be true for most of the other participants in that discussion. After the dissolution of the

[76] Yavich, L. (1985). *Suschnost Prava* [The Essence of Law] (pp. 10). Leningrad: Leningrad University Press.

[77] Ioffe, O. (1985). *Soviet Law and Soviet Reality*. Dordrecht; Boston: Kluwer Academic Publishers.

USSR in 1991, some of them became natural-law philosophers, others legal positivists and legal sociologists. Most ideas of Soviet law (withering away of law, class approach, "base–superstructure") never again played an important role in their research.

V INFLUENCE WITHIN THE LEGAL SYSTEM

Now I show how the ideas that derived from Soviet law's symbol of faith worked in practice. This is not easy to do within the parameters of a single section in this chapter. Nevertheless, to that end I will look at four phenomena in Soviet law – uniqueness, publicness, politicization, and socialist legality – to clarify how and to what extent each of these phenomena influenced the legal system of the Soviet Union.

Uniqueness. Soviet law was considered radically different from the law of bourgeois (capitalist) states. Historically, Soviet law differed from Russian Imperial Law, and Soviet Law was geographically removed from Western law. Western comparativists employed the term "socialist legal family"[78] to distinguish Soviet law and the legal systems of other socialist countries that emerged after World War II from civil law and common law.

Political uniqueness was necessary for criticizing Western law and legal values. *Rechtsstaat* was called "a mirage that came to replace religious ideology."[79] The rule of law was stigmatized as a cult,[80] and human rights were considered to be rights for the rich. Meanwhile, Soviet legal science offered the doctrine of a "truly" lawful state, for in the Soviet conception of socialist democracy, even a peasant from a remote village could be elected to the highest legislative body and could formally work as a deputy, all judges were elected by representative bodies (formally elected as well), and human rights derived from the "social nature" of human beings,[81] that is, from their affiliation with and loyalty to a socialist political and economic order.

Yet the uniqueness of Soviet law, both in its historical and geographical dimensions, was relative. Although for Lenin everyone could be a judge,[82] the Soviet government promptly turned toward written, codified law created by professionals for application by professional servants and lawyers. In this sense, Soviet law had features similar to both the law of the late Russian Empire[83] and the law of Continental European states. Private law contained many legal institutions

78 K. Zweigert and H. Kőtz (1987). *Introduction to Comparative Law* (2nd ed., Vol. 2, T. Weir trans.). Oxford: Clarendon.

79 Pashukanis, *Izbrannie proizvedeniya po obschey teorii prava I gosudarstva, supra* note 58, p. 131.

80 Tumanov, V. (1971). *Burzhuaznaya pravovaya ideologiya. K kritike ucheniy o prave* [Bourgeois Legal Ideology. Critique of Theories of Law] (pp. 68). Moscow: Nauka.

81 *Id.*, p. 346.

82 P. Beirne & A. Hunt (1990). "Law and the Constitution of Soviet Society: The Case of Comrade Lenin" (pp. 74). In P. Beirne (e.) *Revolution in Law: Contribution to the Development of Soviet Legal Theory (1917–1938)*. Armonk, NY: M. E. Sharpe, INC.

83 Nikolay Timasheff wrote: "It is more than Soviet law; it is Russian law, grounded in Russian history" (Timasheff, N. (1950). "Is Soviet Law a Challenge to American Law?" *Fordham L. Rev.* 19, 182).

resembling those found in capitalist legal systems (e.g., contract of sale, which, Stuchka argued, would never be socialist; damages; the mutual rights and responsibilities of spouses; etc.). Ioffe provided a number of examples of Roman law's influence on Soviet law,[84] thereby establishing even more links between the socialist and civil-law families.

Some rules, procedures, and doctrines of Soviet law were unique due to the features of Soviet political religion. I explore some of them in the context of publicness and the politicization of Soviet law and socialist legality.

The *publicness* of Soviet law means extreme expansion of public-law regulation in the Soviet legal system, as well as in every totalitarian system. Totalitarian regimes tend to centralize power and to interfere greatly in the private space; limiting civil society and family life enables the regime to centralize and exert its power over society. Lenin wrote, "We recognize nothing private; for us everything in the economic field is public law."[85] Soviet lawyers therefore dismissed the civil-law distinction between public and private law.

In constitutional and administrative law, publicness determines the characteristics of centralization, which in the Soviet case meant three things: the strict subordination of lower state and Communist Party bodies to higher ones; the fakeness of Soviet federalism; and the denial of any separation of powers; disproportionate state interference with family, labor, and civil-law relations. For example, all economic relations with the state involved related to administrative, but not civil, law. It is worth contrasting the concept of "personal" property, as applied to the means of consumption, with the almost completely banned "private" property as applied to the means of production – under this construction one could buy a car for his or her personal, noncommercial needs but could not buy a harvester to harvest crop for selling. In labor law, the state ultimately limited the terms of labor contracts that employers and employees were free to negotiate, including remuneration, schedule, specific requirements, and incentives, etc., because work itself was a duty, not an individual right. Those who were able to work but did not might be prosecuted. Publicness of law also meant that state interests took priority over private interests. Thus, for example, the theft of state property was punished more severely than the theft of private property.

Politicization, that is, the dominance of politics, over law, had a variety of expressions. First, both the law and the state officially defended communist ideology. Article 6 of the Soviet Constitution of 1977 described the teachings of Marxism-Leninism as the basis for social development and characterized the Communist Party as the "ruling and directing force of Soviet society." One is tempted to think of the Party as a Marxist "church." But rather than a separate institution, the Party was part of an enormous state machine, especially after Stalin's "cleansing." It had no

[84] Ioffe, O. (1982). Soviet Law and Roman Law, *B.U. L. Rev.* 62, 701.

[85] Lenin, *Polnoe sobranie*, *supra* note 22, p. 396.

interests of its own separate from those of the state. Article 6 is dedicated, then, not to the Party's role as a political institution, but to the defense of Soviet communism by public power and legislation and to compelling popular loyalty to this ideology and its institutional embodiment, the Soviet state.

Second, politics and state interests may be excluded from ordinary legal regulation. Under Stalin, legislative provisions and legal procedures sanctified terror against political opponents, certain social and ethnic groups, and the whole of society. For this purpose, criminal codes and special decrees established an extremely wide and uncertain corpus delicti of political crimes, such as participation in anti-Soviet organizations. For this purpose, criminal codes and special decrees established an extremely wide and vague *corpus delicti* of political crimes, such as participation in anti-Soviet organizations, though none of that was enough, and some of Stalin's potential or real opponents and "objective enemies" were simply murdered. After Stalin's death, the state continued to persecute dissidents. Trials against politically disloyal persons were a light version of Stalin's show trials. Still, though they did not presuppose the accused's active self-incrimination, the judge, prosecutor, advocate, and accused all knew the outcome ahead of time even in these post-Stalin trials. Beyond politically motivated imprisonment, other legal tools of oppressing dissidents were exercised, including dismissal, internal and external exile, revocation of citizenship, and forced treatment in psychiatric medical institutions for nonexistent illnesses. The state selected punishments based on political reasons rather than legal provisions.

Politics was significant not only when dealing with political opponents of the state; politics could also be a reason for violating *res judicata* or giving ex post facto effect to criminal law in nonpolitical cases. In the early 1960s, a highly publicized trial began in Moscow against people accused of illegal commercial activity and trading currency (the infamous Rokotov-Faibishenko case). The convicted offenders were sentenced to the maximum imprisonment of eight years, but under pressure from the Soviet chief, Nikita Khrushchev, the Presidium of the USSR Supreme Council enacted two decrees that increased the maximum sentence to fifteen years and, later, to the death penalty. Afterwards, the court reviewed the case, applied new decrees ex post facto, and sentenced the defendants to death.

Socialist legality. Strictly speaking, Soviet law did not begin with the idea of obedience to state-made laws, but rather with a revolutionary legal conscience of state officials and lawyers. After the immediate cancellation of all legal acts of the Russian Empire, Pyotr Stuchka, who was a legal theorist, a People's Commissar for Justice, and head of the Supreme Court of the USSR, advised judges to be guided by their class consciousness when hearing cases.[86] Following Stuchka's advice, judges and officials should resolve individual cases according to the Party's consideration of

[86] Stuchka, P. (1924). *Klassovoe Gosudarstvo i Grazhdanskoe Pravo* [Class State and Civil Law] (pp. 10). Moscow: Krasny Pechatnik.

what is good or bad for the proletariat revolution and for Soviet power. In a more purified form, this would be Orwell's world of total legal uncertainty, a world without any strict or predictable procedures or terms, as well as without any written laws.

As I wrote above, legal regulation based on class consciousness would appear to be attractive and convenient for a totalitarian system. A legal system of this kind, however, disseminates power among a great number of officials and judges who make law every day. (And these are different "laws," so to speak, because the lawmakers' legal consciousness could not be identical, therefore giving rise to what Herbert Hart called the "plurality of [legal] systems".[87]) Officials and judges all become authoritative lawmakers, which contradicts the totalitarian centralization of power. In response, the Soviet government issued a huge number of decrees, instructions, and orders strictly limiting the arbitrary power of its officials and bodies in order to regulate state actors but leave space for situations when the state may be interested in maintaining legal uncertainty. The regime's aim was not to give officials unlimited discretion, but to allow them to ignore legal rules while prosecuting political opponents or using the forced labor of imprisoned persons so that, if or when it was needed, the state could punish those officials for arbitrariness.

The main difference between socialist legality and legality as an element of the Western rule of law doctrine is that, in the latter case, legality should be interpreted in the light of other principles (human rights, legal certainty, due process etc.) that ensure the quality of laws, secure their appropriate application, and subordinate the state to law. Socialist legality subordinates the individual to state laws and decrees, leaving the state itself to follow legal provisions at its discretion, according to whether or not the interests of the ruling class or the whole Soviet people, that is, the interests of the state, demand that it deviate from these provisions. Following laws became its own objective without any justification by stronger principles (human rights, for example). Under this guiding principle, it only makes sense that the USSR considered all legal acts performed during the Nazi occupation of its territory as void, even though it would have been more reasonable not to nullify all marriages or real estate contracts but to consider every case separately.

Socialist legality ultimately limits the number of cases where individuals are permitted to lawfully deviate from legal rules. In particular, Soviet criminal law prohibited self-defense if there was a chance of running away or calling the police for help. This might mean that if you were attacked by someone in a dark alley, you could not defend yourself if you were a professional runner or if there was a chance that a police officer was around the corner. In civil law, legislation always prevailed over contracts. Thus, socialist legality served as a tool of state control over both society and individuals and established total dependence on the state even in the private space.

87 Hart, *Concept of Law*, *supra* note 3, p. 25.

VI CONCLUSION

Vyshinsky and I happened to be separated by one generation of jurists; we were only a handshake apart. I began this chapter with a story about my PhD supervisor, who as a graduate student participated in a conference where Vyshinsky was a keynote speaker and who wrote his dissertation at a time when Vyshinsky's legal thought was settled dogma.

Today, the constitutions of all the Post-Soviet states are filled to the brim with provisions regarding the rule of law and the government's accountability to individuals. In each of these constitutions we can find a solid catalogue of human rights and all of the usual principles that usually accompany a stable democracy – separation of powers, constitutional and judicial review, due process, and so on. Yet a number of very different political regimes operate on the basis of these (rhetorically similar) constitutions, ranging from the severe autocracies in Central Asia to the Baltic democracies in the European Union.

To be sure, this state of affairs arises from various economic, political, and social causes. What interests me is the levity with which post-Soviet societies approach their constitutions, treating their own, relatively recent, founding political and legal documents as if they were mere declarations or as if they were mandatory, though not especially practical, attributes of all independent states.

Precisely this attitude indicates that the primary element of the Soviet legal tradition was the politicization of law; law's subordination to politics survives in Post-Soviet societies. If, after the collapse of the USSR, all viable political goals as well as support from Western countries called for the adoption of liberal constitutions, then why not do so? But if a liberal attitude with regard to morality, or the fundamental, or due process, does not answer our social needs or to our societal aims or traditions, then why not ignore them?

A proper farewell to Soviet law tradition will only come about when law acquires a value independent of politics, that is, when law is no longer subordinated to politics. This can be conceived as a movement away from a theology to a philosophy of law. I am not calling for a "legal enlightenment," that is, the liberation of a legal system from irrational grounds. Like all values, legal values, especially human rights, always carry an emotional commitment. In contrast, law must no longer be regarded as just a means of carrying out political decisions and as the subject of political manipulation.

Only then can we expect a break with Soviet political religion, which allowed for the certain exercise of legal rules only to the extent that the state found them useful in carrying out its designated function of moving society ever closer to a brave new world.

10

International Law as Evangelism

Kevin Crow

I INTRODUCTION: "A BARGAIN ABOUT GOD AND NATURE"

This chapter suggests that the rise of the UN's development and human rights regimes share many parallels with the development of American Christianity, especially after the Evangelical pivot away from the Social Gospel after World War II. In exploring the many intersections of post–World War II internationalism and Evangelicalism, it suggests that the rise of certain UN values should be considered at least partly an expression of law as religion. That is, some international law is sanctified as universal truth, or presented as a "savior," while some political speeches can be considered secularized versions of the American Evangelical take on Jesus's call to "go and make disciples of all nations."

In broad strokes, the chapter explores the influence of a distinct form of American Evangelicalism, which took form during the century before the adoption of the Universal Declaration of Human Rights (UDHR) in 1948 but which overtook Mainline Protestantism in America as the dominant "political theology" after World War II.[1] At the same time as the UN human rights mission floundered during the Cold War,[2] Evangelicalism became a dominant force first in the ideological outlook of many Americans and then in the American political sphere.[3] The UN turned its focus to Bretton Woods progeny, adopting and promoting a new

[1] Accounts of this are provided in various forms by, inter alia, MATTHEW AVERY SUTTON, AMERICAN APOCALYPSE: A HISTORY OF MODERN EVANGELICALISM (2014); ERNEST R. SANDEEN, THE ROOTS OF FUNDAMENTALISM: BRITISH AND AMERICAN MILLENARIANISM, 1800–1930 (1970); GEORGE M. MARSDEN, FUNDAMENTALISM AND AMERICAN CULTURE (2006); ADAM LAATS, FUNDAMENTALISM AND EDUCATION IN THE SCOPES ERA: GOD, DARWIN, AND THE ROOTS OF AMERICA'S CULTURE WARS (2010); STEPHEN SPECTOR, EVANGELICALS AND ISRAEL: THE STORY OF AMERICAN CHRISTIAN ZIONISM (2008); MARK HUTCHINSON & JOHN WOLFFE, A SHORT HISTORY OF GLOBAL EVANGELICALISM (2012); RANDALL BALMER & LAUREN F. WINNER, PROTESTANTISM IN AMERICA (2002); RUSSELL SANDBERG, LAW AND RELIGION (2012); RELIGIOUS RULES, STATE LAW, AND NORMATIVE PLURALISM: A COMPARATIVE OVERVIEW (Rosetta Bottoni, Renaldo Cristofori, and Silvio Ferrari eds., 2016).

[2] See MICHAEL IGNATIEFF, AMERICAN EXCEPTIONALISM AND HUMAN RIGHTS (2005); see also JOHANNESS MORSINK, THE UNIVERSAL DECLARATION OF HUMAN RIGHTS: ORIGINS, DRAFTING, AND INTENT (1999).

[3] See SUTTON, *supra* note 1.

universalist mission: "development." While this mission began as an inwardly focused European project, it grew, especially during the years following the Cold War, into an outwardly focused extra-Western mission with goals now described as "inextricably linked" to those of human rights.[4] In parallel, and especially after the Cold War, Evangelicals embraced a new globalism that saw greater engagement with international development as a means to maximize individual impact, both for the evangelizer and for the evangelized.[5]

While "development" in law describes an economic process that is dependent upon the external condition of capitalism,[6] "development" as a concept has long been associated with "natural" processes, as inevitable as the passage of time.[7] While philosophers David Hume and Adam Ferguson contested the idea that "development" could ever be understood as "continuous growth" – they were both writing in some form on the inevitable decline of nations[8] – it was their contemporary Adam Smith who carried the day. Smith's descriptions of capital economics are well known: an inevitable force, an "invisible hand" guiding the "progress of opulence," the "necessity" of which is imposed by the "natural . . . order of things."[9] Indeed, the voices comprising the dominant philosophy of the West, and the founding texts of economics as a discipline, presented "development" not as a *choice* but as a *necessity*.[10] American Evangelicals have a similar understanding of the progression of history.[11]

Like "development," the Universal Declaration is infused with beliefs that human rights are "natural," necessary, and just. Specifically, that document articulates rights as if their validity for anyone depends upon their validity for everyone. Many of these rights are presented as innate; all are presented as universal. Perhaps because of this, even some prominent lawyers assume the ratification of the UDHR had some form of universal consent at its genesis.[12] But this has never been the case. The UDHR very much reflects American, Christian, and Evangelical values. At the very least, it presupposes a natural law formulation that sanctifies the

4 European Commission on Democracy and Human Rights, EIDHR, Mission Statement, www.eidhr.eu/democracy-human-rights-development (last accessed April 24, 2017).

5 Melani McAlister, The Kingdom of God Has No Borders: A Global History of American Evangelicals (2018).

6 The economic concept of "development" is one that strives toward "convergence" regarding several criteria, including education, per capita spending power, GDP, etc. The project of "convergence" assumes a capitalist market economy.

7 See *e.g.* Charles Darwin, On the Origin of Species (1859).

8 Gilbert Rist, The History of Development (1997).

9 See Adam Smith, The Wealth of Nations (1776).

10 See *e.g. id.*

11 To dispensational protestants, history progresses in a series of predetermined stages, as revealed by *Revelation* 20 and 21, and other biblical passages.

12 Comment based on a public speech delivered by Supreme Court of Canada Judge Rosalie Abella at the Conference on Constitutional Adjudication: Between "Pluralism" and "Unity," Luiss University, Rome (May 6, 2017). Abella made reference to the universal consensus that "we" had regarding human rights in the decades following World War II.

mere status of "humanity."[13] Adjectives such as "inherent," "inalienable," and verbs such as "born" are used throughout the Declaration in alluding to the source of the rights it enshrines.[14] The UDHR also speaks of "the fundamental attributes of the individual" and the "essential rights of man," and while the lawyers who crafted the final draft went to great lengths to avoid references to "God" as "Nature" in the text, there was one exception in the Preamble's assertion that people are "by nature endowed with reason and conscience."[15] The essential idea is that rights are derived from the virtue of being human, to be recognized rather than created by humans and human institutions. On this view, sovereignty is likewise rooted in the individual rather than the group.

But these conceptions of human rights are far from necessary. This was obvious at the outset in many ways. For example, not a single Communist nation voted to approve the language in the finalized draft, primarily based on objections that the draft improperly conceptualized the relationship of the individual to the State.[16] The draft assumed in many instances that individual rights were more important than group rights.[17] Had the six Marxist states entered a "no" vote, the draft would not have become enshrined as the document we read today,[18] but these states, along with South Africa (abstaining due to continued apartheid) and Saudi Arabia (abstaining due to objections about family rights) – took the abstention role as an act of diplomacy; one that would allow the draft to move forward without indicating the complicity of abstaining states.[19] This symbolically if not procedurally undermined the UDHR's universalist claims at its very genesis: it suggested that the document was ideologically unsound or immature.[20]

While some might dismiss the idea that Christianity infused the UDHR by pointing to the diversity of its drafters,[21] that dismissal would ignore the fact that all three ideological authors – including the predominant two[22] – spent their entire

13 Michael Ignatiff describes this process in his Tanner Lectures delivered at Human Rights as Politics, Human Rights as Idolatry, Princeton University Center for Human Values (April 4–7, 2000).

14 Art. 1–8, Universal Declaration of Human Rights (December 10, 1948); see also MORSINK, *supra* note 2, ch. 8.

15 UDHR, Preamble.

16 The lack of "true" universality regarding competing views of the appropriate conceptualization of group versus individual rights was also evident in contemporary human rights related debates regarding how to frame the crimes charged at Nuremburg, for example, in Lauterpacht's emphasis on protecting the individual through the crime against humanity of "mass murder" versus Lemkin's emphasis on creating the elevated crime of genocide to encapsulate the moral weight of targeting a "group" as more severe than merely targeting a large number of individuals.

17 MORSINK, *supra* note 2.

18 Unanimous ratification was a precondition to the legitimacy of its "universal" claim, so by abstaining rather than dissenting, the abstaining parties allowed the voting parties to proceed with a claim of unanimity. See *id.*

19 See *id.*

20 IGNATIEFF, *supra* note 2.

21 See *e.g.* MARY ANN GLENDON, THE FORUM AND THE TOWER: HOW SCHOLARS AND POLITICIANS HAVE IMAGINED THE WORLD FROM PLATO TO ELEANOR ROOSEVELT (2011).

22 Although Eleanor Roosevelt was present for the discussions, by her own journal accounts and counter to popular American myth, she did not participate as the discussion of the "two learned gentlemen"

adult lives seeped in American Christian ideology. One was an American Christian, one passionately embraced Evangelicalism, and the two non-Americans had spent most of their adult lives in the USA and had received their prolonged higher educations from American universities.[23] While Peng Chun Chang spent the vast majority of his formative years and adult life in the USA eventually receiving a PhD from Columbia, Charles Malik since boyhood attended evangelical schools founded by US missionaries in Lebanon, eventually attending the American University in Cairo and earning a PhD from Harvard. If Malik had his way, the UDHR would make direct reference to "God," but he settled for an expression of the "God"-assumption in the idea of "inherent" rights – a hard-fought concession according to the record.[24] Later in life, in an essay honoring then-famous tele-evangelist Billy Graham published in the *Journal of the Evangelical Theological Society*, Malik declared that "the Bible is the source of every good thought and impulse I have," and expressed an apocalyptic longing for Jesus to "return and judge the living and the dead."[25] Back in 1948, Chang was able to curtail Malik's fervor with quotes from Confucius as the two pinpointed "universal" truths for the UDHR.[26]

In the place of "God and Nature," the UDHR enshrines beliefs about the individual that carry elements of both "God and Nature." The human is "God"-like because human rights elevate humanity above all else; the planet and all other species are functional instruments over which the human has domain. The human is also "Nature" because the UDHR's rights come not from creation or cognition but from mere existence. The element of "nature" is especially important to the present role of the UN's development mission because, as already noted, the concept of development itself is often assumed to be a necessary, inevitable occurrence.[27]

The year following the adoption of the UDHR saw President Truman's now infamous Point Four 1949 Inaugural Speech,[28] which encouraged a new globalist

quickly went over her head. See *id.* The drafting committee, distilled from eighteen discussants, consisted of Eleanor Roosevelt, Peng Chun Chang, and Charles Malik. The actual drafting was largely the handiwork of Canadian lawyer John Humphrey, with a few slight revisions from French lawyer René Cassin. See IGNATIEFF, *supra* note 2.

23 This was true of both Peng Chun Chang and Charles Malik. While Chang was a committed Humanist, Malik published an account of his evangelical beliefs regarding God's call to Americans: Charles H. Malik, *The Two Tasks*, 23 J. EVANG. THEOL. SOC. 289 (1980).

24 MORSINK, *supra* note 2, at 284.

25 Malik, *supra* note 23, at 290.

26 See ELEANOR ROOSEVELT, ON MY OWN 77 (1958).

27 See Kevin Crow, *The Concept of "Development" in International Economic Law: Three Definitions and an Inquiry into Origin*, 14 MANCHESTER J. INT'L ECON. L. 148 (2017).

28 The full text of Truman's Point Four is as follows: "[W]e must embark on a bold new program for making the benefits of our scientific advances and industrial progress available for the improvement and growth of underdeveloped areas. More than half the people of the world are living in conditions approaching misery. Their food is inadequate. They are victims of disease. Their economic life is primitive and stagnant. Their poverty is a handicap and a threat both to them and to more prosperous areas. For the first time in history, humanity possesses the knowledge and skill to relieve suffering of these people. The United States is pre-eminent among nations in the development of industrial and

development mission. His speech came at the same time as Cold War tensions or ideological prematurity froze out human rights – the UN's original *raison d'être*.[29] Point Four's mission is exemplary of American Exceptionalism. Here, I suggest that it parallels Evangelicalism in ways that are immediately striking. First, it recalls the desperate straits – the horror of hunger and want – in which more than half the world's population live (the "unsaved" other). Second, it presents the good news (gospel) that, "for the first time in history," (a singularity, a Messianic notion) an answer is at hand that will bring happiness and make it possible for lives to be transformed. Third, this will not come to pass without agency: energies must be mobilized to produce more, to invest, to work, to expand trade. Finally, in the end, if the chance is seized and people agree to the efforts required, an era of happiness, peace, and prosperity will dawn from which everyone stands to benefit. This cluster of ideas can also be viewed as an expression of quasi-religious faith in American approaches to social and economic governance –as a call for *International Law as Evangelism*.[30]

The speech can be more critically viewed as replacing the English colonial language of the "white man's burden" to "civilize the savages" with a triumphalist "responsibility" to bring "democracy" and "rule of law" to "underdeveloped nations."[31] At the same time as the UN's primary mission morphed from human rights to development, the organization turned increasingly to NGOs that were already engaged in the international proliferation of projects like education, poverty-reduction, and what would today be known as "capacity building."[32] Initially, the biggest of these were missionary organizations, responding to Jesus's command – "go and make disciples of all nations" – long before the UN was hatched, and boasting global networks that the UN hoped to mobilize.[33] While many of the largest of this first wave had Catholic and Protestant roots, by the time the "third wave" of Christianity began to emerge in "developing" nations in the 1980s,[34] most of these

scientific techniques. The material resources which we can afford to use for assistance of other peoples are limited. But our imponderable resources in technical knowledge are constantly growing and are inexhaustible." President Harry S. Truman's Inaugural Address of January 20, 1949, in Department of State Bulletin, January 30, 1949, p. 123.

29 See UN Charter, Preamble.

30 I use the term "evangelism" rather than "evangelicalism" for the title of this chapter because "evangelism" more directly describes a behavior or way of thinking about law that is facilitated by the UDHR and the BWIs, whereas Evangelicalism refers to a more specific ideology.

31 For a general overview of criticisms in this vein, see Martti Koskenniemi, The Gentle Civilizer of Nations: The Rise and Fall of International Law: 1870–1960 (2004); also compare Ignatieff, *supra* note 2, with Samuel Moyn, The Last Utopia: Human Rights In History (2010); see also Samuel Moyn, Christian Human Rights (2015).

32 For a recent, controversial, and likely now defunct articulation of the American concept of "capacity building," see the Trans-Pacific Partnership's Chapter of the same name. Before its demise on the first day of Donald Trump's Presidency in 2017, the TPP was the largest proposed free trade agreement ever to include both "developed" and "developing" countries.

33 *E.g.*, Catholic NGOs such as the Salvation Army and the International Committee of the Red Cross. There were also evangelical networks such as the Young Men's Christian Association (YMCA) and others.

34 Katharina Hofer, *The Role of Evangelical NGOs in International Development: A Comparative Case Study of Kenya and Uganda*, 38, 3 African Spectrum 375 (2003).

organizations had largely secularized their international activities, sometimes as a precondition for UN funding.[35] However, in executing UN development initiatives – a task that has fallen exponentially to NGOs since the conclusion of the Cold War[36] – these NGOs gained increasing ability to set preconditions for international assistance both through global prominence and through "consultant" status.[37]

In painting a picture of international human rights and development law as Evangelism, this Chapter proceeds in broad strokes. This is somewhat of a necessity for the chapter's aim; volumes would be needed to explore each of the movements it references in full. The chapter also makes no claims about the specific mindsets of individuals working within the organizations or agencies mentioned; it is rather analyzing the social movements that produced and reshaped human rights and development during the immediate post–World War II moment to the present day. Thus, in broad strokes, the following sections will map the departure of dominant Christian ideology from mainline "Social Gospel" Protestantism to an increasingly political form of Evangelicalism after World War II (Section II); the Evangelical globalism that emerged from Jesus's call to "make disciples of all nations" and its parallels in the Bretton Woods and outgrowths of Truman's Point Four vision of "development" (Section III); interactions between Evangelical organizations and parallels to Evangelical thought as the UN shifted its focus from human rights to development (Section IV); and some concluding remarks on how international lawyers might – given the existence of a good dose of Abrahamic (if not Christian) ideological infusion in UN institutions – (re)imagine how international law might respect multiple ideologies at the same time (Section V).

II FROM "SOCIAL GOSPEL" TO EVANGELICALISM

Postmillennialism and Premillennialism describe differing doctrinal beliefs regarding the present stage of human history as it relates to the apocalyptic prophecies of the Book of Revelation in the Protestant Bible. Postmillennialists interpret Revelation Chapter 20 as a promise that Jesus Christ's "second coming" will occur *after* a period of 1,000 years during which Christian ethics will globally thrive.[38] Postmillennialists hold that, prior to this Christian Millennium, the church is equipped with the teachings and gospel of Jesus and charged with a Great Commission to "go and make disciples of all nations … teaching them to obey everything I have commanded you."[39] Once the Church has executed this work, the doctrine holds, the Christian Millennium will commence, and only after the

35 See *id.*; see also KAMARI MAXINE CLARKE, FICTIONS OF JUSTICE: THE INTERNATIONAL CRIMINAL COURT AND THE CHALLENGE OF LEGAL PLURALISM IN SUB-SAHARAN AFRICA (2009).

36 *Id.*

37 See *id.*; see also IGNATIEFF, *supra* note 2.

38 See *e.g.* SUTTON and other sources cited *supra* note 1.

39 *Matthew* 28:19 (New International Version).

conclusion of that Millennium will Jesus's physical return to Earth occur.[40] Between the American Revolution and the American Civil War (1776–1861), Postmillennialism was by far the prevalent doctrine amongst American Protestants. In the decades following the Civil War, Postmillennialists began to take less seriously the supernatural elements of their religious belief. Influential theologians, such as William Newton Clarke, found that the Bible was not "infallible and supernatural" but rather a "natural and normal" ethical guide to inform our behavior here on earth.[41] The Kingdom of Heaven was not otherworldly, but a description of ideals for this world; it was not external but internal.[42] On this view, Christians had a duty to ensure that social and economic systems responded to the call in Jesus's Matthew 6:10 prayer: "Thy Kingdom come. Thy will be done, on earth as it is in heaven."[43] This was the Social Gospel: a belief that humans had a duty to create heaven-like conditions on earth coupled with a belief that the end of the world was nowhere in sight. Thinking along these lines dominated "mainline" Protestantism in America from roughly the 1880s until the 1930s.

By contrast, Premillennialists believe that the physical coming of Jesus will occur *prior* to the 1000-year Christian Millennium, and that followers of Jesus will ascend into heaven at that time by means of Rapture.[44] The dominant American Pre-Millennialist school is known as "Dispensationalism." Dispensationalists hold that, after the Rapture, there is a seven-year period of "tribulation" after which Jesus will return again with his saints (this is based on an equation derived from Revelation 20 and 21). After this return, the Christian Millennium will begin.[45] The distinctive feature in the theology of Dispensationalism is the belief that history is divided into several sections, each exhibiting the same characteristics: God reveals himself to humanity, humanity is asked to obey, humanity fails to obey, God judges humanity and introduces a new period of probation. (Adam's fall, Noah's Ark, Abraham's calling, Moses's exodus, Christ's birth, the current age of the church.[46]) Dispensationalists believe the earth is currently nearing the end of the 1000-year Rapture-inducing period of sin. Scholars in many fields have offered accounts of how this mindset affects the individual's relationship to the earth, the individual's relationship to society, and the individual's relationship to other

[40] See *e.g.* SUTTON and other sources cited *supra* note 1.
[41] *E.g. id.*
[42] *E.g.* BALMER & WINNER, *supra* note 1.
[43] *Matthew* 6:10 (King James).
[44] *Id.*
[45] *Id.*
[46] "And I saw thrones, and they sat upon them, and judgment was given unto them: and I saw the souls of them that were beheaded for the witness of Jesus, and for the word of God, and which had not worshipped the beast, neither his image, neither had received his mark upon their foreheads, or in their hands; and they lived and reigned with Christ a thousand years. But the rest of the dead lived not again until the thousand years were finished. This is the first resurrection. Blessed and holy is he that hath part in the first resurrection: on such the second death hath no power, but they shall be priests of God and of Christ, and shall reign with him a thousand years." *Revelation* 20:4–6 (King James).

individuals.[47] Some have noted that Premillennialism absolves its adherents of a strong sense of responsibility for social amelioration. Others have noted that, if the earth is "fallen" and social evils are the result of the devil's influence, rather than focus on bringing about social conditions that allow individuals to realize God's kingdom on earth, the more essential project is to prepare oneself and others for heaven. This is where Evangelicalism finds its primary orientation.[48]

The causes of Evangelicalism's rise to prominence since World War II are obviously manifold; too vast to explore in great detail here. But some economic perspectives, particularly from Barro and McCleary,[49] note that it is not the particular sect or interpretation that boosts social appeal so much as the *sincerity* of belief in faith and religion. The economist's view suggests that greater diversity in the supply of religions combined with religion's exposure to America's "sink or swim" capital markets led to a Christianity of increased "quality" to seize market share (if quality is measured through a religion's ability to secure capital from its followers).[50] Where quality is determined by devotion, although it is difficult to accurately measure "sincerity," American Evangelicals appear unique in the *type* of religious sincerity they hold as compared to other predominantly Protestant cultures.[51] In other fields, some suggest that, as the First World War claimed millions of lives from 1914–19 and as the Great Depression set in after 1929, the Premillennial message of impending doom became more palatable to a population living on the fringes of death and economic ruin.[52] Still others suggest that a sincere belief in the merits of the Free Market rendered Premillennial theology's "fallen world" doctrines a plausible explanation for the failures of *laissez faire* Capitalism.[53] At least one common thread that runs throughout the explanations for Evangelicalism's rise is the observation that a cultural majority in America sought some form of "light in the darkness": an interpretation of scripture that could not only inspire sincerity on a personal level, but also explain the inconsistency of war and economic depression with the belief that Godliness and Capitalism brought peace and prosperity.[54]

Whatever spurred its rise, this "light in the darkness" ideal kept Evangelicals largely apolitical until after World War II. For the first half of the 1900s, Evangelicals rejected the political process as a component of "modernity," bent on reinterpreting God's word to cater to the lax moral standards of a corrupted society.[55] One influential scholar describes early Evangelicals as a "loose, diverse, and changing federation of

47 See *supra* note 1.

48 See Sutton, Marsden, Sandeen, Balmer & Winner, all *supra* note 1.

49 Robert Barro & Rachel McCleary, *Religion and Economic Growth* (Nat'l Bureau of Econ. Rsch., Working Paper No. 9682, 2003), https://scholar.harvard.edu/files/barro/files/religion_and_economic_growth_2003.pdf (accessed May 12, 2017).

50 *Id.*

51 See especially Sandeen, Marsden, and Sutton, *supra* note 1.

52 See Balmer & Winner, *supra* note 1.

53 See Marsden, *supra* note 1.

54 Sutton emphasizes this narrative.

55 See Marsden, *supra* note 1.

cobelligerents united by their fierce opposition to modernist attempts to bring Christianity into line with modern thought."[56] Evangelicalism certainly had intellectual foundations, but it was also reactionary, suspicious of institutions as corruptors of the faith.[57] In the mid-1920s until the 1950s, the drive to keep Christianity "pure" created a situation in which Evangelicals were "determinedly sectarian and isolated from the American cultural mainstream."[58] The exclusion from politics was a voluntary, even doctrinal, component of the belief.

In many ways, Harold Ockenga led the charge of Evangelicalism's new political engagement. Long before Richard Nixon spoke of the "silent majority" in the early 1970s, Harold Ockenga spoke of the "unvoiced multitudes."[59] He viewed FDR's inaction on sexual licentiousness and Eleanor's support of interracial marriage as a sign that it was time to "clean house at Washington" (a slogan not unlike Trump's "drain the swamp").[60] This thread was picked up by Jerry Falwell, Billy Graham, and eventually Ronald Reagan, all three of whom spoke of the "moral majority."[61] Falwell and Graham both eventually held official positions as "spiritual advisors" to presidents – Graham was advisor to Nixon, Bush, Reagan, and Clinton. Ockenga, Falwell, Graham, and Fuller formed the National Association of Evangelicals (NAE) in 1942, and over the next fifteen years, this organization crafted "a culturally savvy, professional Evangelical engagement with public life that helped Americans make sense of the post-War apocalyptic reminders of imminent violence, horrific persecution, inhumanity, and destruction."[62] According to the NAE, the "American Century" had arrived, and it was the "wholehearted" responsibility of America as the "most powerful nation in the world" to "exert upon the world the full impact of our influence."[63] The NAE held influence over Evangelical doctrine that is difficult to overstate, and it unrelentingly linked country with faith. The NAE's "American Century" paralleled the rise of modern Evangelicalism as a political force.

III "MAKE DISCIPLES OF ALL NATIONS"

When the UDHR was drafted, the Social Gospel still held dominant sway on American culture, especially amongst the intellectual elite who participated in its creation.[64] But in

56 *Id.*

57 Billy Graham's son, Franklin Graham, founder of a major international "development" provider, has come under fire for comments indicating as much.

58 JOEL A. CARPENTER, REVIVE US AGAIN: THE REAWAKENING OF AMERICAN FUNDAMENTALISM (1997).

59 See Harold Ockenga, "Unvoiced Multitudes" in *Evangelical Action! A Report of the Organization of the National Association of Evangelicals for United Action* (1942).

60 SUTTON, *supra* note 1.

61 Jerry Falwell formed an organization under this name in 1979.

62 See SUTTON, *supra* note 1.

63 Henry Luce, *The American Century*, LIFE, February 17, 1941. This article predated the NAE, but Luce spoke on behalf of many of its founders.

64 Esteemed international lawyers such as Humphreys and Cassin, and colleagues such as Eleanor Roosevelt and Malik.

the decades following the UDHR's ratification, Evangelicalism rose to the fore both ideologically and politically. The rise of Evangelicalism, along with its Dispensationalist understanding of history as progressing in distinct phases toward a definite end, correlated with a shift in the UN's focus from an organization predominantly engaged in the propagation of rights to an organization predominantly engaged in various forms of "development": educational, democratic, and of course, economic.[65] This is not to say that Evangelicals caused this shift. But even while Evangelicalism cannot be said to have directly created it, from the perspective of powerful Evangelicals such as World Vision's Robert Peirce and Frank Phillips, the rise of the global development project a gave secular form of financial backing to Jesus's call to Evangelical missionaries in Matthew 28:19–20: "Therefore go and make disciples of all nations, baptizing them … and teaching them to obey everything I have commanded you."

There are many parallels to note between Evangelical globalism – the specific belief that one has a "responsibility" to bring one's way of life to those that are living in other ways – and the UN's human rights and development missions. Evangelicalism's characterizations of "unreached people groups" are often those development institutions characterize as "least developed." And like the Social Gospel, human rights as an ideal spread not because it overtly serves the interests of a few powerful states but primarily because it presents itself as advancing the interests of the powerless. Just as missionaries have done since the days of Jesus, human rights imbedded itself into the soil of cultures and worldviews independent of the West, promising that it could sustain ordinary peoples' struggles against unjust States and oppressive social practices – that anyone could be "saved."[66] Perhaps the UDHR was appealing in these contexts not as a representation of universal norms, not as an expression of some intrinsic good of humanity, but as "salvation." The salvationist promise was deliverance from humanity's potential for depravity.

This is not to say that the UDHR was drafted in an Evangelical or even Abrahamic vacuum. Many delegates participated on its committee. But after initial debates, only three delegates actually participated in the crafting of the UDHR's initial provisions: Roosevelt, Malik, and Chang. Although some place Roosevelt at the helm due to her position as Chair, both Roosevelt's and Malik's diaries and letters, along with the resulting draft of the UDHR and other official records, indicate that Malik, a fervent Evangelical, dominated the discussion. The discussion itself took place within a broader emerging framework. While the UDHR has become important to our present, it was born amongst a crowd of appeals to international juridical means to prevent the repetition of wartime atrocities, including the UN Charter of 1945;[67] the

65 See ECOSOC and UNDP mission statements. See also "development" initiatives from US Dep't of State.

66 See SUTTON, *supra* note 1.

67 Outlawing aggressive war between states.

Genocide Convention of 1948;[68] the revision of the Geneva Conventions of 1949;[69] and finally the International Convention on Asylum of 1951.[70] Nevertheless, the Abrahamic influence on the precise shape of these international mechanisms is well documented and virtually undeniable.[71]

In this light, an Evangelical layperson would likely understand the UDHR's text or the Point Four speech not with reference to international relations, law, or global economics, but with reference to concepts familiar in daily religious life. Point Four mirrors the call of the Gospel: America must "go" and "mak[e] the benefits of our scientific advances available" for all "underdeveloped areas" teaching the "inadequate[ly]" nourished "victims of disease" with "primitive and stagnant" economies how to "relieve the suffering" through America's Messianic "knowledge and skill."[72] And in order to ensure that disciples are made "of all nations," ratifying international human rights covenants has become a condition of entry for new states joining the UN.

IV FROM HUMAN RIGHTS TO "DEVELOPMENT"

The worldwide spread of human rights norms is sometimes seen as a moral consequence of economic globalization.[73] The US State Department's annual report for 1999 on human rights practice around the world describes human rights and democracy – along with "money and the Internet" – as one of the three universal languages of globalization.[74] While this may too easily imply that human rights are a style of moral individualism that have elective affinity with the economic individualism of the global market,[75] it can certainly be said that the narratives advanced by the US State Department view human rights and development as advancing hand in hand.

This was not always so. Although there was certainly enthusiasm amongst newly decolonialized States for especially the "self-determination" provisions in the UDHR at its outset, and although some of those States sought to mobilize the

68 Protecting religious, racial, and ethnic groups against extermination.
69 Strengthening noncombatant immunity.
70 Protecting the rights of refugees.
71 See *e.g.* Oona Hathaway & Scott J. Shapiro, The Internationalists: How a Radical Plan to Outlaw War Remade the World (2017).
72 Direct quotes from Point Four, full text cited in footnotes to Section I above.
73 *Id.*
74 U.S. Dep't of State, Annual Report on Global Human Rights Practice (1999).
75 Such an explanation fails to recognize the antagonistic dimensions of the relation between human rights and money, between moral and economic globalization. Antagonism can be seen, for example, in the campaigns by human rights activists against the labor and environmental practices of the large global corporations. T. F. Homer-Dixon, Environment, Scarcity and Violence (1999); O. Mehmet, E. Mendes, & R. Sinding, Towards a Fair Global Labour Market: Avoiding a New Slave Trade (1999); see also Amnesty Int'l, *Human Rights: Is It Any of Your Business?* (2000); Carnegie Council on Ethics and International Affairs, *Who Can Protect Workers' Rights? The Workplace Codes of Conduct Debate*, 2 Human Rights Dialogue (2000).

UDHR in international relations, more critical voices have convincingly shown that the UDHR lacked a shared "universalist" understanding to begin with,[76] and therefore lay largely dormant until it was revitalized as part of a broader economic agenda,[77] or a mobilizing utopic vision, at the end of the Cold War.[78] The United Nations and the Bretton Woods Institutions were hatched after roughly a decade in which the New Deal and the "Social Gospel" saturated religious and political life in the United States.[79] The work of UK economist John Maynard Keynes, whose most famous book advocated for central spending in excess of tax revenue during times of economic stagnation,[80] was also influential in shaping how the IMF and World Bank conceptualized the central goal of Bretton Woods – international economic cooperation.[81] All of these ideas (New Deal, Social Gospel, Keynesianism) elevated a community rather than individualized approach to economic policy, which is a far cry from the individual primacy attributed to the UDHR today. Thus, in the original split of development and human rights, one might conceptualize the Bretton Woods institutions as expressing the Social Gospel's communalism and human rights as expressing its emphasis on the intrinsic worth of individual human beings.

As already noted, the "development" institutions were initially "inwardly" focused toward the States that created them. Once the institutions were established, and once Europe was rebuilt and increasingly interdependent, the development mission turned "outward" toward Africa, Asia, and South America, beginning in the mid-1970s under Nixon and accelerating ever since. The UN Charter demanded that its values be accorded to all nations "without distinction" without much consideration paid to the idea that distinction might at times be a good thing.[82] Thus (again in very broad strokes), as a large influx of new states (former colonies) opted into GATT 1948 and other trade agreements in the late 1950s and 1960s,[83] and as increased production capacities and urbanization in "developed states" coincided with an increase in global demand for commodities, the (in)ability of former colonies to produce those primary goods ushered in the Kennedy Round in 1963.[84] It was the Kennedy Round

76 Samuel Moyn, The Last Utopia: Human Rights in History (2010); see also Samuel Moyn, Christian Human Rights (2015).

77 Jessica Whyte, The Morals of the Market: Human Rights and the Rise of Neoliberalism (2019).

78 See Moyn, The Last Utopia, *supra* note 76.

79 For an enriching discussion on the social ideologies underlying the New Deal, see Heinz Elau, *Neither Ideology nor Utopia: The New Deal in Retrospect*, 19 Antioch Rev. 523–37 (1959).

80 See John Maynard Keynes, The General Theory of Employment, Interest, and Money (1936).

81 See United Nations Monetary and Financial Conference, *Final Act and Related Documents, Bretton Woods, New Hampshire*, July 1 to July 22, 1944, https://fraser.stlouisfed.org/files/docs/historical/eccles/036_17_0004.pdf.

82 See UN Charter Preamble.

83 This was largely the result of a wave of new post-Colonial states in Africa and Southeast Asia, and a corresponding rise in global demand for commodities.

84 The Kennedy Round was the sixth session of GATT negotiations, held in Geneva between 1964 and 1967. It was spurred by the US Trade Expansion Act in 1962, which authorized then-President Kennedy to conduct mutual tariff negotiations with other states. The negotiations were planned in 1963, but unfortunately, Kennedy was assassinated before they took place in 1964.

that legally incorporated for the first time Truman's "development" as a goal of the emerging international economic legal order, and it later migrated back to primary UN organs through the ECOSOC and the UNDP.[85]

While US resistance to outcome-driven human rights tribunals was present from the start,[86] it conversely embraced "security and predictability"-driven international economic tribunals. Economic tribunals – ICSID arbitration and the WTO's DSU – rose along with the shift in development's luminary away from Keynesian influence. The reasons for the massive overhauls that broke through in the 1980s are manifold, but the tides seem to have turned partially as a result of the Oil Shock of 1973[87] – itself fueled by Richard Nixon's departure from the "gold standard" guaranteed at Bretton Woods – and partially as a result of neoliberal economic policies in the 1980s that took the place of Keynes, bolstered by the Evangelical resistance to all things Communist during the same period.[88] Indeed, the Reagan and Thatcher administrations in the 1980s advocated outright anti-Keynesian approaches to economics in a "conscious effort" to reposition and recalibrate "ideas and expectations about the appropriate role of government, the importance of private enterprise, and the virtues of markets."[89] Those administrations successfully mobilized anti-communist fervor against the idea of government economic planning in general.

In the decades prior to Reagan, at least two pivotal factors drove the UN to entrench "development" in international law. First, the Cold War constituted the "Third World" as an ideological battleground of the major powers,[90] so that new States or national liberation movements were able to benefit from the support of influential protectors (sometimes switching from one to another).[91] Second,

85 Economic and Social Council, established in 1945; UN Development Programme, established in 1965 as an organ of the ECOSOC.

86 See Morsink, *supra* note 1.

87 The oil crisis itself is part of the Bretton Woods legacy. When President Nixon decided to take the US dollar off the gold standard in 1971, it meant that foreign states, including OPEC states, could not redeem their US foreign exchange reserves for gold, as established by the Bretton Woods Agreement of 1944. This collapse of the dollar's value and booming cost of gold hurt many OPEC countries, and when Nixon took the additional step of requesting $2.2 billion in military aid to Israel to fight Egypt in 1973, OPEC reacted by placing an embargo on oil exports to the United States, sending the country into a recession. See *e.g.* Kimberly Amadeo, *OPEC Oil Embargo: Causes and Effects of the Crisis*, The Balance, 21 January 2017.

88 Keynesian policies came to an end in 1971, when Nixon put a stop to the fixed exchange rate of the US dollar. Floating exchange rates are now the norm amongst major world economies. See *The Bretton Woods Conference, 1944*, U.S. Dep't of State, https://2001-2009.state.gov/r/pa/ho/time/wwii/98681.htm.

89 Stephen Gill & David Law, The Global Political Economy: Perspectives, Problems and Policies (1998).

90 The term "Third World" was first used by Alfred Sauvy in an article entitled *Tiers Monde, une planète* (L'Observateur, August 1952), which compared the colonial or ex-colonial countries to the Third Estate of the *Ancien Régime* in France. He referred to a short 1789 book by Abbé Sieyès which posed the famous formula: "What is the Third Estate? Everything. What has it been so far within the political order? Nothing. What does it ask? To be something."

91 See Ignatieff, *supra* note 2.

Communist-Capitalist antagonism blocked the UN decision-making system, because the effective veto of the permanent members of the Security Council could be used to prevent any action under Chapter VII of the Charter "with respect to threats to the peace, breaches of the peace, and acts of aggression."[92] The organization was thus forced to recalibrate its mission to areas of greater international consensus, which included a (then vague) promise of "development."[93] By the time Ronald Reagan stood at the Brandenburg Gate in West Berlin and famously demanded that "Mr. Gorbachev tear down [the Berlin] wall!,"[94] "development" – through the UN and the international legal instruments that took cues from its institutions – was fully incorporated as a legal instrument in the emerging field of international economic law.[95] But while "development" became entrenched in international law during the fiercest decades of the Cold War,[96] it was not until after the collapse of the Berlin Wall that the neoliberal philosophy emerged as the global preference for ordering both the domestic and the international economy.[97] Neoliberalism's proponents believed in the market above all to determine an efficient allocation of resources;[98] foundational neoliberal assumptions like those in Ricardian "comparative advantage" became the assumed logic guiding new approaches to international trade and investment law in the 1990s.[99] Neoliberalism stressed privatization of public enterprises,[100] liberalization of flows of investment,[101] and global governance of trade and investment.[102] Obviously, these were not new ideas that suddenly emerged after 1989, but they did become

92 The UN intervention in Korea had been formally "recommended" on June 27, 1950 by the Security Council (in the absence of the Soviet representative), but the conduct of operations drew its authority from the General Assembly, which, in Resolution 355/V of 3 November 1950 – the so-called Uniting for Peace or Acheson Resolution – substituted itself for a Security Council again paralyzed by the return of the Soviet delegate. This episode, legally murky as it was, demonstrated the UN's incapacity to act in accordance with the provisions of the Charter.

93 See generally *id.*; see also Arturo Escobar, Encountering Development: The Making and Unmaking of the Third World (1995).

94 Ronald Reagan's speech at the Brandenburg Gate came during the closing years of the Cold War, on June 17, 1987, in response to Soviet leader Mikhail Gorbachev's consistent signaling to Western powers that he was open to economic restructuring and to working toward the resolution of long-standing tensions with the United States. However, Gorbachev met resistance from his own regime and from East German leader, Erich Honecker. The Berlin Wall was built in August 1961 to prevent East Germans from fleeing communist rule and escaping to West Germany. Its sudden destruction in November 1989 symbolized the fall of communism worldwide.

95 See *e.g.* generally Jean Rey, Report on the Kennedy Round, June 1967.

96 1950s McCarthyism, 1960s Cuban Missile Crisis, 1970s Vietnam War.

97 Neoliberalism reached the peak of its influence in the 1990s, although it emerged as a philosophy and garnered varying degrees of influence during several earlier periods. See Jamie Peck, Constructions of Neoliberal Reason (2010).

98 See generally Chicago School economists in the vein of Milton Freidman, Capitalism and Freedom (1962).

99 See *e.g.* M. Sornarajah, Resistance and Change in the International Law on Foreign Investment (2015).

100 *Id.*

101 *Id.*

102 *Id.*

bound together as a sort of "package deal" in what John Williamson famously coined the "Washington Consensus" – ideas as old as "motherhood and apple pie," but tied together and remarketed as a surefire toolkit for "economic development."[103] This set of policies was embraced by the Washington-based international economic institutions: the World Bank, the International Monetary Fund, and the (now Geneva-based) World Trade Organization.[104] Today it represents a convergence of ideas, debatably synonymous with George Soros's concept of "market fundamentalism"[105] that emanates not only from Washington, but from the entire developed world.

By the 1990s the Washington Consensus was considered widely as the basis of US economic success. The national interest required government agencies to take such a stance: The USA's economy prospered as a result of multinational corporations being able to produce and market goods abroad while sourcing raw materials from abroad for use at home.[106] Predictably, other States that benefitted, that is, the most economically powerful States, rallied around the neoliberal globalist approach. Thus, the economic provisions that began at the Kennedy Round in 1963 and traveled through the UNCTAD in 1964,[107] the UNDP in 1965,[108] the UNSC's so-called Second Development Decade Resolution in 1970,[109] before becoming hierarchized in the Enabling Clause of 1979,[110] became entrenched through the Marrakesh Agreement and the establishment of the WTO in 1995.[111] Alongside these developments, "New International Economic Order" (NIEO) efforts that began at the Asia-Africa Conference in 1955 and served the "Third World" through

103 John Williamson, *A Short History of the Washington Consensus*, first published in 1998, Williamson's essay was republished in Narciss Serra and Joseph Stiglitz (eds.), THE WASHINGTON CONSENSUS RECONSIDERED: TOWARDS A NEW GLOBAL GOVERNANCE (2008), p. 14; DAVID HARVEY, A SHORT HISTORY OF NEOLIBERALISM (2005); STEPHAN GILL, POWER AND RESISTANCE IN THE WORLD ORDER (2008) (arguing that global governance on the basis of market dominance was locked in by rules). See also Alvaro Santos, *The World Bank's Uses of the "Rule of Law" Promise in Economic Development*, in THE NEW LAW AND ECONOMIC DEVELOPMENT (David Trubek and Alvaro Santos eds., 2006).

104 Of course, the term "Washington Consensus" is not entirely accurate, as noted by Joseph Stiglitz and others. Firstly, it is not a "consensus" in the strict sense, but rather, a convergence of ideas. And secondly, it is not exclusive to Washington, but rather a concept emerging from the entire developed world. See *id.*

105 Market fundamentalism, according to Soros, is the idea that markets are "value free," a function of pure mechanical or mathematical truths, unattached to ethics or morals. See *e.g.* George Soros, *Capitalism versus Open Society*, FINANCIAL TIMES, October 30, 2009.

106 As one indicator, between 1990 and 2000, the US GDP nearly doubled, from 5.5 to 9.8 trillion dollars. See *US Business Cycle Expansions and Contractions*, NATIONAL BUREAU OF ECONOMIC RESEARCH, www.nber.org/cycles/cyclesmain.pdf.

107 UN Conference on Trade and Development, http://unctad.org/en/Pages/Home.aspx.

108 UN Development Programme, www.undp.org.

109 S. C. Res. 2626/XXV, (October 24, 1970).

110 GATT, *Differential and More Favourable Treatment Reciprocity and Fuller Participation of Development Countries*, L/4903 (November 28, 1979) www.wto.org/english/docs_e/legal_e/enabling1979_e.htm.

111 Marrakesh Agreement Establishing the World Trade Organization, April 15, 1994, 1867 U.N.T.S. 154.

a series of UN Resolutions mostly in the 1970s found themselves dead in the water when economically developed States failed to get on board with an alternate convergence of ideas – what one might call the "Bandung Consensus" – that is, economic sovereignty, corporate regulation under international law, and permanent sovereignty over natural resources, amongst other proposals. In sum, in the 1990s, it became settled that international economic law's job was to increase the size of the pie, not to redistribute it.

Increasing the size of the pie, however, meant more international resources should be spent on infrastructural, educational, and institutional development in developing States. While trade and investment legal regimes ensure that private interests are protected against States and that States are protected against discriminatory trade practices amongst themselves, the UN and Bretton Woods Institutions could not leave development entirely to the private sector. In formal development initiatives, the role of NGOs has expanded significantly since the United Nations Development Programme (UNDP) was established in 1965, and almost exponentially since the conclusion of the Cold War. Scholars writing on UN Initiates in the Global South in 2004 had already noted that the "UN's Economic and Social Council [ECOSOC] now grants consultative status on its work to 2,234 NGOs from around the world."[112] Citing a 1999 paper on the "Politics of Development" and an ECOSOC report from 2003,[113] one scholar compares this number to the mere forty-one NGOs that were similarly involved in the 1940s:

> Even the World Bank, often primarily focused on large-scale development and infrastructure projects, recognizes NGOs as vital to its work. In 1998, 50 percent of the projects it approved incorporated NGO participation, a marked increase from 1973, when only 6 percent of Bank projects involved NGOs. The growth in number, scope and profile of African NGOs over the last thirty years mirrors these general trends among Southern NGOs.[114]

In part because of the purported "weakness" of postcolonial governments, powerful human rights and rule of law NGOs have become recognized and institutionalized as part of the UN's post–World War II development mission. Their members tend to speak from a place of authority on issues that affect indigent communities, and some have been able to influence national and international spheres of public policy by expanding into new geographic sites and engaging in unprecedented partnerships.[115] In tandem, during the immediate post–Cold War period between 1991 and 2001, the government-sponsored development assistance flowing from individual Western

[112] Sarah Michaels, Undermining Development: The Absence of Power among Local NGOs in Africa (2004).

[113] Michael Chege, *Politics of Development: Institutions and Governance*. This was a background paper prepared for the World Bank's "Africa in the 21st Century" project (Global Coalition for Africa, 1999).

[114] Michaels, *supra* note 112.

[115] *Id.*

states fell by an estimated 25 percent,[116] which further increased global demand for UN-funded NGO assistance.

The most prominent non-faith-based NGOs in today's transnational landscape – such as Amnesty International and Human Rights Watch – fight for human rights as an ideological contest for the establishment of what James Ferguson has argued grants membership and access to "Western" institutional power: the power of information, the power of capital, the power of mobility.[117] Increased acquisition of such powers depends on the acceptance of certain development and human rights agendas. While AI and HRW do not receive state funding to do so, they are largely operated by individuals who held human rights-related positions in US Government or in UN Agencies; the boards of directors of both organizations are populated overwhelmingly from US and European firms and philanthropic organizations. Religious NGOs, by contrast, increasingly receive direct funding from the USA.[118]

Where does Evangelicalism fit into this picture? We have seen that the UDHR and development missions carry ideological parallels with the development of American Evangelical thought. We have also noted that Evangelicalism has played an ever-increasing role in American politics since World War II. Here, I want to suggest that an intertwining of these parallel ideologies emerged with the UN's increasing reliance on NGOs at the turn of the twenty-first century. The United States placed increasing pressure on the UN to adopt Evangelical-supported policies predominantly associated with reproductive health. In 2001, George W. Bush spearheaded domestic legislation aimed at increasing Evangelical involvement in global development projects,[119] and in 2002, the Bush administration withheld hundreds of millions of dollars in funding from the UN Fund for Population Activities, the WHO, and NGOs with reproductive programs in developing countries.[120] The Trump administration did the same thing in 2017 and 2019.[121] Meanwhile, conservative evangelical NGOs boosted their presence at UN policy forums. As Jennifer Butler observed in 2000, only the most conservative Christian groups are represented at the UN,[122] sometimes joining forces with Islamic conservatives and politically conservative think tanks such as the Heritage Foundation on areas of common interest such as "halt[ing] the expansion of sexual and political rights for gays,

[116] Clarke, *supra* note 35 citing Vangelis Vitalis, *Official Development Assistance and Foreign Direct Investment: Improving the Synergies*, presented at Organization for Economic Co-operation and Development's Global Forum on International Investment: Attracting Foreign Direct Investment for Development, Shanghai, December 5–6, 2002 (p. 3), online at www.oecd.org/dataoecd/54/61/2764550.pdf (accessed May 14, 2017).

[117] James Ferguson, Global Shadows: Africa in the Neoliberal World Order (2006).

[118] See Clarke, *supra* note 35; see also Hofer, *supra* note 34.

[119] See the Bush Administration's so-called Faith-Based and Community Initiatives (2002).

[120] Hofer, *supra* note 34.

[121] Edward Wong, *Trump Administration Expands Anti-Abortion Policies with New Overseas Funding Rules*, N.Y. Times, March 26, 2019.

[122] Jennifer Butler, *The Religious Right at the Beijing +5 PrepCom*, 15 Glob. Pol'y F. (2000).

women, and children."[123] Since the late 1990s, international conservative organizations have increasingly mobilized in support of "pro-family" or "anti-LGBT" values across faith lines.[124] While many of these organizations emerged from Western Catholic and Protestant states, the reactionary approach of Evangelicalism has found allies in many non-Christian states. One fascinating outcome of this phenomenon is the ability of the Evangelical movement to claim universality when it comes to the principle of a right but particularity when it comes to the definition. Specifically, where the UDHR declares a universal right to marriage in Article 16, Evangelicals insist that the "men and women" to whom this right belongs be defined as heterosexual units, not as individual men and women with the freedom to marry other individuals, whether men or women. The ability of conservative Evangelicals to exercise this type of political influence through domestic and international institutions has inspired conservative groups from other denominations to lobby the UN as well.[125]

The backdrop for the influence of American Evangelical organizations through UN institutions had been set long before the turn of the twenty-first century. In the immediate post–World War II era, international Evangelical NGOs were the organizations best equipped to internationalize the shifting mission of the UN – they had the skills and the infrastructure to mobilize Western resources to achieve social goals abroad.[126] This is because Christian missionaries "did development first" along its non-investment-based dimensions such as education, medical aid, and technology transfer. By the time Truman produced his secularized call to spread American values to all nations in his Point Four speech, evangelical organizations like The Salvation Army and The American Red Cross had already existed for the better part of a century, and already boasted an impressive global spread.[127] As the Social Gospel that nourished those organizations gave way to Evangelicalism during the Cold War years, new global organizations like YWAM, Bethany, World Vision, and Samaritan's Purse also rose to prominence.[128] This new guard of global missionary organizations differed from their Social Gospel ancestors in that they placed individual experience at the fore: not only a conversionary agenda with respect to the evangelized but also a transformative experience with respect to the evangelizer.[129] Many of these organizations took advantage of Reagan, Clinton, and Bush-era incentives to increase government involvement with Evangelical organizations abroad.[130]

123 Colum Lynch, *Islamic Bloc, Christian Right to Team Up to Lobby U.N.*, Wash. Post, June 17, 2002.

124 Barro & McCleary, *supra* note 49.

125 Hofer, *supra* note 34.

126 Carpenter, *supra* note 58.

127 The Salvation Army and the Red Cross (including the American Red Cross) both had extensive global networks by the late 1800s. Multiple sources confirm this, but see *e.g.* Edward H. McKinley, Marching to Glory: The History of the Salvation Army in the United States, 1880–1992 (1995).

128 Hofer, *supra* note 34.

129 McAlister, *supra* note 5.

130 *Id.*

World Vision and Samaritan's Purse in particular took advantage of government "development" funding to advance global initiatives through longstanding state cooperation when other Evangelical NGOs were wary of government funding as a potential infringement on religious autonomy. Both organizations – World Vision and Samaritan's Purse – were founded by Evangelical minister Bob Pierce (who believed Christianity was the cure for Communism),[131] both focus on "international development," and both receive substantial "development" and "humanitarian aid" contracts from the USAID and from the UN.[132] Along with a growing number of Evangelical groups, World Vision has consultative status with UNESCO and partnerships with UNICEF, UNHCR, ILO, WHO, and other Evangelical groups around the world. With a stronger missionary focus, Samaritan's Purse specializes in emergency relief and infrastructural projects related to water, sanitation, nutrition, medical care, and public health.[133] It receives USAID funding and works closely with UN development initiatives around the globe.[134] It has come under fire for intermingling US government initiatives with religion, most publicly for requiring USAID recipients to sit through prayer meetings prior to receiving aid,[135] and its President Franklin Graham (cofounder and son of famed Evangelist Billy Graham) has openly described non-Evangelical religions as inherently "evil."[136]

These are two examples of many. But a systematic analysis of every Evangelical organization engaged in the UN's development project is beyond the scope of this Chapter, and not necessary to demonstrate the central point: the concept of "development" in international law reflects Evangelical ideology, and the latter has sought to shape the former's contours as it migrated from the UDHR to ECOSOC, the UNDP, the World Bank, and the multitude of NGOs now engaged in the project of international development. I do not present this as "good" or "bad." Indeed, in many ways it is unsurprising that international human rights and development efforts turned to Evangelical organizations in expanding development projects during and after the Cold War. As political scientist Robert Woodberry has expertly shown, "conversionary protestants" were responsible for creating many of the social preconditions that led to the world's most successful democracies (high literacy rates, mass education, voluntary organizations, and newspapers).[137] Perhaps it is precisely because these preconditions facilitated democracy that they became

[131] Information derived from the websites of these organizations, available at www.samaritanspurse.org, and at www.wvi.org, respectively (last accessed May 15, 2017).

[132] *Id.* See also Hofer, *supra* note 34; Clarke, *supra* note 35.

[133] Information on the organization available at www.samaritanspurse.org (last accessed May 15, 2017).

[134] Hofer, *supra* note 34; Clarke, *supra* note 35.

[135] See *e.g.* David Gonzalez, *U.S. Aids Conversion-Minded Quake Relief in El Salvador*, N.Y. Times, March 5, 2001, www.nytimes.com/2001/03/05/world/us-aids-conversion-minded-quake-relief-in-el-salvador.html (last accessed May 15, 2017).

[136] See *e.g.* Laurie Goldstein, *Top Evangelicals Critical of Colleagues Over Islam*, N.Y. Times, May 8, 2003, www.nytimes.com/2003/05/08/us/top-evangelicals-critical-of-colleagues-over-islam.html (last accessed 15 May 2017).

[137] Robert Woodberry, *The Missionary Roots of Liberal Democracy*, 106 Am. Polit. Sci. Rev. 244 (2012).

cherished cultural goals in the American psyche, and while a multitude of complexity has gone into the shaping of the present international legal status quo, one can rationally speculate that, in part, the UN secularized these cherished Western cultural goals at its founding and in many subsequent instruments, retrospectively rationalizing them through the language of modernity, and then began to institutionalize them in part through "development."

But while it took the better part of two decades to mobilize the international resources and institutions that would – in this comparison – "minister" to the "underdeveloped," the structure of Point Four parallels Evangelicalism in ways that are immediately striking. First, it recalls the desperate straits – the horror of hunger and want – in which more than half the world's population live (the "unsaved" other). Second, it presents the good news (gospel) that, "for the first time in history" (a Messianic notion), an answer is at hand that will bring happiness and make it possible for lives to be transformed. Third, this will not come to pass without agency: energies must be mobilized to produce more, to invest, to work, to expand trade. Finally, in the end, if the chance is seized and people agree to the efforts required, an era of happiness, peace, and prosperity will dawn from which everyone stands to benefit.

The fact that Truman's speech parallels a secularized version of the "truth" as proclaimed by Evangelicalism may have contributed to American "faith" in Truman's "development." But the underlying belief fueling this "faith" was shared not only by the Christian world but, insofar as a Messianic message is conjured, by everyone who belonged to a salvationist religion.[138] In the years since 1949, rhetorical techniques have been used again and again in declarations affirming the necessity of "development" as the only solution to the problems of humanity.[139] And in much the same way questioning religious belief was frowned upon within the Church, questioning "development" as such is frowned upon by international lawyers, economists, and human rights activists alike.[140] "Unsaved" people groups as characterized by Evangelical missionaries parallel the "underdeveloped" nations as categorized by the UN. The World Bank's largest concentration of development projects exist in areas that correlate with Luis Bush's 10/40 window – an often used Evangelical visual tool to point to the area of the earth most in need of "saving."[141] This aligns to the ideological legacy of the UDHR in ways too close to seem entirely coincidental. As Charles Malik – one of the two ideological fathers of the UDHR – wrote in a 1980 contribution to the Journal of the Evangelical Theological Society:

> Jesus Christ is my Lord and God and Savior and Song day and night. I can live without food, without drink, without sleep, without air – but I cannot live without

[138] See Marie-Dominique Perrot, Gilbert Rist & Fabrizio Sabelli, La Mythologie programmée: L'économie des croyances dans la société moderne (1992).

[139] *Id.*, at 196–97.

[140] This statement is based on the observations of Gilbert Rist (1997).

[141] See Luis Bush & Beverly Pegues, Move of the Holy Spirit in the 10/40 Window (1999).

> Jesus. Without him I would have perished long ago. I live in and on the Bible for long hours every day. The Bible is the source of every good thought and impulse I have. In the Bible God himself, the Creator of everything from nothing, speaks to me and to the world directly – about himself, about ourselves and about his will for the course of events and for consummation of history. And believe me: Not a day passes without my crying from the bottom of my heart, "Come, Lord Jesus!" I know he is coming with glory to judge the living and the dead, but in my impatience I sometimes cannot wait and I find myself in my infirmity crying with David, "How long, Lord?" And I know his kingdom shall have no end.[142]

Many of the tenets of Malik's Evangelicalism – from the individualistic focus, to the emotional witness, to the apocalyptic yearning – are also identifiable in the UDHR. Through the extension granted by Point Four and existing international religious networks, the UN's development project echoes Evangelicalism's call to spread the neoliberal gospel to all nations. In other words, it can be considered a form of evangelism.[143]

V CONCLUSION

The UN human rights institutions and the Bretton Woods institutions mirror to some degree religious beliefs that are deeply seeded in the Evangelical ethos. This is *International Law as Evangelism*. Today, UN and USAID development funding, empowered by Christianity-infused human rights texts, enable Evangelical missionary organizations to transcend state and international government in the spread of conservative goals: the World Congress of Families, which promotes anti-LGBT laws internationally on the basis of UDHR Article 16;[144] the Alliance Defending Freedom, which draws its funding from American corporations such as the former Blackwater Security Group and represents Christian clients in international courts;[145] World Vision, which receives USAID funding and regularly bids on UN development contracts, but has the authority to impose conditions on communities that receive benefits of those contracts;[146] and many others. Obviously, USAID and the UN support a great many organizations and projects whose goals are not aligned with Evangelicals, but it does not fund organizations from other religious sects under the umbrella of "development." Thus, in addition to providing a social context

142 Malik, *supra* note 23.

143 See note 30.

144 UDHR Article 16 describes the right to marry and form a family. The language of the article specifically refers to "men and women" in defining the right, but the Article does not restrict the right only opposite sex couples.

145 See *e.g.* Dimitrova v. Bulgaria, App. No. 39084/10, Eur. Ct. H.R. (2015), finding violations of freedom of thought and religion. For information on the organization's funding, see www.adflegal.org/issues/international. Blackwater changed its name to Academi after a long series of controversies related to the execution of its US government contracts in Iraq tainted its name.

146 Clarke, *supra* note 35; see also Ignatieff, *supra* note 2.

characterized by a universalizing impulse, Evangelical organizations have also been strikingly active in reshaping UN and US development spending and decision-making.

While religious influence on domestic legal systems is well-documented and relatively uncontroversial in many instances, the dominant influence of any ideology infusing the construction and interpretation of international law should be resisted. This is not to say that ideology is not continuously and inevitably present in how we understand what is "good" or even "right" – of course it is. But perhaps if international lawyers start with a recognition that international law is infused with ideology, we can move beyond claims that present any particularized expression of the "good" or "right" as universal. From there, perhaps we can imagine how international law might express and respect multiple ideologies at the same time.

D

Religious Conceptions of Law

11

"Enjoin Them upon Your Children to Keep" (Deuteronomy 32:46)

Law as Commandment and Legacy, or, Robert Cover Meets Midrash

Steven D. Fraade[*]

I INTRODUCTION

On April 26, 2004 I attended a one-day conference at the Yale Law School on "Rethinking 'Nomos and Narrative': Marking Twenty Years Since Robert Cover's Essay." My modest contribution to that occasion was subsequently published as "Nomos and Narrative Before *Nomos and Narrative*," in the *Yale Journal of Law and the Humanities*, in which I explored some of the history of the dynamic intersection of "nomos and narrative" in Judaism from antiquity to modern times, mainly through an assembly of rabbinic texts.[1] Here I wish, once again, to pay tribute to Robert Cover by critically engaging another of his essays, "Obligation: A Jewish Jurisprudence of the Social Order" (first published in 1987 in the *Journal of Law and Religion*).[2] I shall do so by bringing for our close reading pleasure an early rabbinic

* This chapter was first presented at a conference on "Jewish Law and the Modern State," Yale University Law School, New Haven, CT, March 5, 2017. Thanks to Alan Appelbaum, Michal Bar-Asher Siegal, Joseph David, David Flatto, Zeev Harvey, Marc Herman, Hannan Hever, Berachyahu Lifshitz, Maren Niehoff, Ishay Rosen-Zv, Yonatan Sagiv, and Eliyahu Stern for having read or heard and astutely commented upon earlier versions of this paper, to Anthony Kronman for critical insights in response to the original oral delivery, and to Benjamin Porat for help in defining the subject. Finally, I wish to thank the two anonymous reviewers for their penetrating insights.

1 Steven D. Fraade, "Nomos and Narrative Before Nomos and Narrative," *Yale Journal of Law and the Humanities* 17 (2005): 81–96; republished in Steven D. Fraade, *Legal Fictions: Studies of Law and Narrative in the Discursive Worlds of Ancient Jewish Sectarians and Sages*, Supplements to the Journal for the Study of Judaism 147 (Leiden: Brill, 2011), 17–34.

Cover's essay first appeared as, "The Supreme Court, 1982 Term – Forward: Nomos and Narrative," *Harvard Law Review* 97 (1983), 4–68; reprinted as "Nomos and Narrative," in *Narrative, Violence, and the Law: The Essays of Robert Cover*, ed. Martha Minow, Michael Ryan, and Austin Sarat (Ann Arbor: The University of Michigan Press, 1992), 95–172. On *nomos* (law) being the Greek word consistently employed by the third-century Jewish Greek translators of the Pentateuch for the scriptural Hebrew word *torah* (teaching), the consequences of which have been enormous, see Fraade, "Nomos and Narrative," *supra* n. 1, 83–85 (as well as *Legal Fictions*, *supra* n. 1, 20–21).

2 Robert Cover, "Obligation: A Jewish Jurisprudence of the Social Order," *Journal of Law and Religion* 5, no. 1 (1987): 65–73. It was reprinted in *Narrative, Violence, and the Law*, *supra* n. 2, 239–48. My page citations will be to the reprint. The essay was first given orally at the Columbus School of Law, Catholic University

text of midrash (scriptural commentary) that is highly relevant to Cover's theme and remarkable for its honesty and prescience, qualities shared with Cover. For the Rabbis, and the Hebrew Bible before them, there can be no law without religion or religion without law, however we might define those slippery terms.

II ROBERT COVER ON JEWISH LAW AS COMMANDMENT OR OBLIGATION

In his aforementioned essay on "Obligation" (Hebrew: *mitzvah*, but more broadly understood by Cover as "incumbent obligation" [239]), Cover draws a sharp contrast (but with caveats) between western secular jurisprudence, which is based on individual *rights*, and Jewish religious jurisprudence, which is based on collective (but also individual) *obligations*. Thus, for example, in the former, justice is served by fulfilling the *rights of individuals* to, say, receive affordable medical care, whereas in the latter, it is the *obligation of the collective* to provide it.

Cover argues that each such system of law (or legal discourse) is founded and sustained by a distinctive narrative or "myth." Thus, modern individual "rights" are rooted in the *secular* mythos of a social contract, whereas Jewish "commandments" are rooted in the *religious* mythos of an all-encompassing divine (or Mosaic) revelation that enjoins those commandments upon *all* of Israel, including future generations, standing at Mt. Sinai.[3] Here is Cover in his own words:[4]

> The basic word of Judaism is obligation or mitzvah. It, too, is intrinsically bound up in a myth – the myth of Sinai. Just as the myth of social contract is essentially a myth of *autonomy*, so the myth of Sinai is essentially a myth of *heteronomy*. Sinai is a collective – indeed, a *corporate* – experience. The experience at Sinai is not chosen. The event gives forth the words which are commandments. . . . All law was given at Sinai and therefore all law is related back to the ultimate heteronomous event in which *we were chosen – passive voice*. (emphases added)

of America, as Cover's contribution to the Symposium "The Religious Foundations of Civil Rights Law," sponsored by the Interdisciplinary Program in Law and Religion, on April 19, 1986.

3 See Deut. 29:13–14: וְלֹא אִתְּכֶם לְבַדְּכֶם אָנֹכִי כֹּרֵת אֶת־הַבְּרִית הַזֹּאת וְאֶת־הָאָלָה הַזֹּאת: כִּי אֶת־אֲשֶׁר יֶשְׁנוֹ פֹּה עִמָּנוּ עֹמֵד הַיּוֹם לִפְנֵי יְהוָה אֱלֹהֵינוּ וְאֵת אֲשֶׁר אֵינֶנּוּ פֹּה עִמָּנוּ הַיּוֹם ("I make this covenant, with its sanctions, not with you alone, but both with those who are standing here with us this day before the Lord our God and with those who are not with us here this day" [NJPS]), taken by some commentators (e.g., the Palestinian targumim) to refer to (and obligate) all future generations. Thus the "myth of Sinai" is not just that the Torah was divinely commanded to Israel there and then, but that all subsequent generations are equally bound by virtue of their have been proleptically included. The universal legal question of whether a constitution can obligate successive generations to fulfill the commitments undertaken by its predecessors is famously discussed in Thomas Jefferson's letter of September 6, 1789 to James Madison in the *Papers of Thomas Jefferson*, most recently accessed at https://jeffersonpapers.princeton.edu/selected-documents/thomas-jefferson-james-madison. See also below, n. 54.

4 Cover," Obligation," *supra* n. 2, 240.

Cover acknowledges that for most of Jewish history, Jews have not exercised the coercive, sovereign authority necessary to enforce most of the commandments, understood as having been initially commanded by God through Moses, his prophetic agent. Again, citing Cover:[5]

> The Jewish legal system has evolved for the past 1900 years without a state and largely without much in the way of coercive powers to be exercised upon the adherents of the faith. … The Jewish legal apparatus had not had the autonomous use of violence at its disposal for two millennia which are, indeed, for all practical purposes the period in which Jewish Law as we know it came to be. In a situation in which there is no centralized power and little in the way of coercive violence, it is critical that the *mythic center of the Law reinforce the bonds of solidarity*. Common, *mutual reciprocal obligation* is necessary. The myth of divine commandment creates that web. (emphases added)

According to Cover,[6] even when Jewish law created plenty of space for divergent legal interpretations and rulings, it predicated that polysemy or legal pluralism not on individualism, per se, but on the myth of a single, divine, originary, commanding voice.[7] This renders the system of commandments qua commandments (and not simply as "good deeds") all the more remarkable for its persistence and relative continuity over thousands of years in the absence of a centralized, politically (as distinct from socially) coercive enforcement of judicial sovereignty. Even so, Cover argues, the system is predicated on its subjects' understanding their obligations as stemming from the collective self-understanding of, passively speaking, "being commanded."[8]

Cover acknowledges that rights-discourse and duties-discourse are not impervious to one another, often producing hybrids that belie the secular (rights) versus religious (commandments) dichotomy. Thus, one can just as easily identify secular systems based on duties-discourse (e.g., communism, fascism), as one can justify systems based on rights-discourse that are founded on religious principles or myths (e.g., the US

5 Ibid., 242–43.

6 Ibid., 243.

7 On interpretive polysemy and legal pluralism in classical rabbinic sources, see the following: Steven D. Fraade, "Rabbinic Polysemy and Pluralism Revisited: Between Praxis and Thematization," *AJS Review* 31 (2007): 1–40 (as well as *Legal Fictions*, *supra* n. 1, 427–75); Steven D. Fraade, "Response to Azzan Yadin-Israel on Rabbinic Polysemy: Do They 'Preach' What They Practice?" *AJS Review* 38 (2014): 339–61; Steven D. Fraade, "'A Heart of Many Chambers': The Theological Hermeneutics of Legal Multivocality," *Harvard Theological Review* 108 (2015): 113–28.

8 For a thorough treatment of the problematic reception of commandments in post-enlightenment, secularized Jewish societies, see Arnold Eisen, *Rethinking Modern Judaism: Ritual, Commandment, Community* (Chicago: University of Chicago Press, 1998). For theological reflections on Jewish law as commandment, see Benjamin D. Sommer, *Revelation and Authority: Sinai in Jewish Scripture and Tradition*, Anchor Yale Bible Reference Library (New Haven: Yale University Press, 2015), esp. 99–146.

Declaration of Independence). As Cover indicates, this is not simply a function of modernity:[9]

> Now, just as the social contract theories generated Hobbes and others who bore a monstrous and powerful collective engine from the myth of individualism, so the Sinaitic myth has given rise to *counter myths* and accounts which stress human *autonomy*. The rabbinic accounts of law-making autonomy are very powerful indeed, though they all conclude by suggesting that everything. … everything was given at Sinai. And, of course, therefore, all is, was, and has been commanded – and we are obligated to this command. (emphases added)

In the end, "Sinai and social contract both have their place" as dynamically intersecting mythoi of jurisprudence.[10]

The midrashic text that we will shortly examine asks, how can the commandments (and the Sinai/Moses myth[11] upon which they rest) be obligatory for all time, that is, be upheld and transmitted across the generations, especially in the absence of political and judicial sovereignty and in the reality and cacophony of human autonomy? As we shall see, the midrash is a beautiful example of an ancient rabbinic text that reads a "counter myth" of *legal autonomy* into the heteronomy of Scripture.

III THE HEBREW NOUN *MITZVAH* AND VERB *TZIVAH*

Before doing so, however, a few words are required regarding the meaning of the noun *mitzvah* (commandment or obligation) and the verb from which it derives, *tzivah*, (to command or enjoin). As Cover indicates, this is the core word for biblical/ Jewish law as being divinely commanded and obligatory (alongside many other words for law).[12] But this verb, *tzivah*, has another, less widely attested and acknowledged meaning, or shade of meaning, that being to will possessions or instructions to one's heirs in anticipation of one's death, as in an "ethical will."[13] But the two

9 Cover, "Obligation," *supra* n. 2, 241.

10 Ibid., 248.

11 Since the book of Deuteronomy is narratively framed as Moses's teachings (see Deut., 1:5) forty years after the revelation at Sinai, Moses here can be thought of as a forty-year extension of Sinai, in terms of Cover's "myth of Sinai."

12 For some random examples of the noun and verb used biblically with respect to divinely or Mosaically commanded laws, see Exod. 19:7; 25:22; 34:34; 35:1; Lev. 6:3; 27:34; Num. 30:1; 36:13; Deut. 1:3; 4:2, 5; 5:15, 28; 6:1–2, 6, 25; 11:13; 15:15; 24:18, 22; 30:8; 31:10; 34:9; Mal. 3:22. I calculate the frequency of occurrence of such words among the books of the Pentateuch as follows, indicating rounded frequency per 1,000 words: Genesis 1.3, Exodus 3.2, Leviticus 2.9, Numbers 2.8, Deuteronomy 6.2. Note the significantly higher frequency of occurrence in the book of Deuteronomy. For a broader linguistic treatment of *mitzvah* in tannaitic rabbinic corpora, see Tzvi Novick, *What Is Good, and What God Demands: Normative Structures in Tannaitic Literature*, Supplements to the Journal for the Study of Judaism 144 (Leiden: Brill, 2010).

13 See Frances Brown, S. R. Driver, and C. A. Briggs, *A Hebrew and English Lexicon of the Old Testament* (Oxford: Clarendon, 1907), 845b; Gen. 18:19; 49:29, 33; 50:16; 2 Sam. 17:23; 1 Kgs. 2:1; 2

meanings are close to and sometimes bleed into one another (both being forms of instruction), as in the following biblical verse, Deuteronomy 33:4, referring to Moses at the very end of his life and career, introducing what might be termed Moses's ethical will, or "blessing," (Deuteronomy 33) to the tribes: "Moses charged us with (the) Teaching (Torah), as the heritage of the congregation of Jacob" (New Jewish Publication Society (NJPS) adapted).[14] The poetic parallelism of this verse would suggest an alignment between the verb to charge (*tzivah*) and the noun for heritage (*morashah*). By this understanding, Moses, at the very end of his life and leadership, is more likely to have enjoined the people to embrace what is now their heritage than to have commanded them collectively to obey its laws. We are here, after all, in the midst of a rhetorical discourse of admonition rather than that of law as commandment, even though the difference is a subtle and unstable one. Alternatively, the parallelism might suggest what began as Moses's command soon became the heritage of the successive generations of Israelites. This meaningful ambiguity (commandment/legacy) both foreshadows and enables the radical midrashic reading of Deuteronomy 32:46 that we are almost ready to engage.

IV THE BIBLICAL CONTEXT: MOSES'S SWAN SONG

Deuteronomy 32, the scriptural lection *Ha'azinu* ("give ear"), is Moses's swan song, just prior to his death at the ripe old age of 120, after 40 years of unsought leadership of the Israelites in their epic journey from Egypt to the edge of the Promised Land. In Cover's mythic-narrative sense, Moses's oration is Sinai's

Kgs. 20:1; Isa. 38:1. It is not until rabbinic literature that the nominal form *tzava'ah*, for a will or testament, is evidenced in b. Bava Batra 147a. See Avraham Even-Shoshan, *Hammillon Heḥadash* (Jerusalem: Kiryath Sepher, 1979), vol. 5, 2207b. For Hebrew ethical wills across history, see Israel Abrahams, ed., *Hebrew Ethical Wills* (Philadelphia: Jewish Publication Society of America, 1926; repr. 1976). For ancient exempla, attributed to biblical patriarchs, see James H. Charlesworth, ed., *Old Testament Pseudepigrapha*, vol.1 (Garden City, NY: Doubleday, 1983), 773–995.

14 There is no definite article in the Hebrew for "(the) Teaching (Torah)." The word *torah* (teaching, instruction) in the book of Deuteronomy can refer to Deuteronomy as a whole (or to some parts thereof), as in Deut. 1:5; 17:18, 19; 31:11, 12. For Deuteronomy's expanded understanding of *torah*, see, most recently, John J. Collins, *The Invention of Judaism: Torah and Jewish Identity from Deuteronomy to Paul* (Oakland, CA: University of California Press, 2017), 21–43 ("Deuteronomy and the Invention of the Torah"). However, here it can refer just to the present section (Deut. 33) or to divine/Mosaic teaching more abstractly. In later times the word would denote the Pentateuch as a whole, and in still later times, as we shall see, to the totality of Torah teaching, both scriptural ("written") and rabbinic ("oral"). See below, nn. 20–22. Sir. 24:23 (LXX) equates the Torah of our verse with the "book of the covenant" (cf. Exod. 24:7; 2 Kgs. 23:2). For a variety of midrashic understandings of "heritage" in this verse, see Sifre Deut §345 (ed. Finkelstein, 402), on which see Steven D. Fraade, *From Tradition to Commentary: Torah and Its Interpretation in the Midrash Sifre to Deuteronomy* (Albany: State University of New York Press, 1991), 56–60. For the continuing importance of this verse in Jewish religious culture and education, see Jeffrey H. Tigay, *The JPS Torah Commentary: Deuteronomy* (Philadelphia: Jewish Publication Society, 1996), 321–22; 407 n. 40. For this verse standing for the Torah as a whole, see b. Sukka 42a; b. Bava Batra 14a.

forty-year extension. The book of Deuteronomy is Moses's paraphrastic reprise of the laws and narratives of the past forty years. It is full of pathos regarding Moses's repeatedly denied petitions to God to be able to see his epic mission to its completion across the Jordan River.[15] Throughout Deuteronomy, Moses worries and warns the people that without his charismatic prophetic leadership, upon settling in the Land and enjoying its bounty (and mixing with its non-Israelite inhabitants), they will grow complacent, forgetting their history and abandoning the commands to their great covenantal peril. Deuteronomy is Moses's last chance to inoculate them, rhetorically speaking, against this feared or anticipated outcome.

V THE MIDRASHIC COMMENTARY (SIFRE TO DEUTERONOMY §335)

The scriptural lemma (Deuteronomy 32:46) is part of the conclusion to Moses's *Ha'azinu* song. Its midrashic commentary divides the verse into two halves, so that each half receives its own discrete interpretation. We shall later return to the question of whether the two exegetical units form a larger whole, or just two distinct units that are editorially placed in sequence according to the order of the scriptural verse.[16] Here's the verse (32:46a–b in bold), together with its surrounding verses, to give a sense of its scriptural context:[17]

[מה] וַיְכַל מֹשֶׁה לְדַבֵּר אֶת־כָּל־הַדְּבָרִים הָאֵלֶּה אֶל־כָּל־יִשְׂרָאֵל׃
[מו-א] וַיֹּאמֶר אֲלֵהֶם שִׂימוּ לְבַבְכֶם לְכָל־הַדְּבָרִים אֲשֶׁר אָנֹכִי מֵעִיד בָּכֶם הַיּוֹם
[מו-ב] אֲשֶׁר תְּצַוֻּם אֶת־בְּנֵיכֶם לִשְׁמֹר לַעֲשׂוֹת אֶת־כָּל־דִּבְרֵי הַתּוֹרָה הַזֹּאת׃
[מז] כִּי לֹא־דָבָר רֵק הוּא מִכֶּם כִּי־הוּא חַיֵּיכֶם וּבַדָּבָר הַזֶּה תַּאֲרִיכוּ יָמִים עַל־הָאֲדָמָה אֲשֶׁר אַתֶּם עֹבְרִים אֶת־הַיַּרְדֵּן
שָׁמָּה לְרִשְׁתָּהּ׃

15 For a detailed analysis of the of Moses's failed petition in Sifre Deuteronomy, see Steven D. Fraade, "Sifre Deuteronomy 26 (ad Deut. 3:23): How Conscious the Composition?" *Hebrew Union College Annual* 54 (1983): 245–301.

16 This is a common question in interpreting midrashic commentary as a redacted collection of discrete exegetical comments. For consideration of this question, pursued with respect to another section of the Sifre Deuteronomy commentary, see Fraade, "Sifre Deuteronomy," *supra* n. 15, 245–301.

17 Unless otherwise indicated, I transcribe the text according to MS London 341, with slight adjustments. I was able to access it from microfilm. This manuscript is adopted by the data base of the Academy of the Hebrew Language (*Ma'agarim*), since MS Vatican 32, which is generally preferred, is not extant here. Louis Finkelstein's standard edition (384–85) significantly departs from this and related manuscripts in the last lines of this section of the midrash, which I shall discuss in due course. I only indicate variants to this manuscript when they affect the meaning significantly enough as to have a bearing on my argument. I have treated this passage previously, although in different detail and for different purpose, in *From Tradition to Commentary*, *supra* n. 14, 119–20, with notes. The Sifre to Deuteronomy is an anthology of tannaitic (70–220 CE Palestine) exegetical traditions, redacted in the mid- to late third century CE. For a brief critical introduction, see Menahem Kahana, "Sifrei," in Encyclopaedia Judaica, ed. Michael Berenbaum and Fred Skolnik, 2nd ed., vol. 18. (Detroit: Macmillan Reference USA, 2007), 562–64.

[45] And when Moses finished reciting *all* these words to *all* Israel,
[46a] he said to them: Take to heart [lit.: set your heart toward] all the words with which I have warned you this day.
[46b] Enjoin them upon your children, that they may observe faithfully all the words of this Teaching (Torah).
[47] For this is not a trifling thing for you: it is your life; through it you shall long endure on the land that you are to possess upon crossing the Jordan. (NJPS)

V PART 1

Here is the midrash's commentary to the first half of verse 46, following MS London:

"ויאמר אליהם שימו לבבכם לכל הדברים [אשר אנכי מעיד בכם היום]" (דברים ל"ב:מ"ו): צריך אדם שיהו עיניו ולבו ואוזניו מכוונין לדברי תורה. וכן הוא אומר,"בן־אדם [שים לבך ו]ראה בעיניך ובאזניך שמע (ושים לבך) את כל אשר אני (דבר אליך) [מדבר אתך] [לכל־חקות בית־ה' ולכל־תורתיו] ושמת לבך למבוא הבית (ל)[ב]כל מוצאי המקדש" (יחזקאל מ"ד:ה). והרי דברים קל וחומר, ומה בית המקדש שנראה בעיני(ה)ם ונמדד ביד צריך אדם שיהו עיניו ולבו ואוזניו מכוונין, דברי תורה שהן כהררין התלויין בסערה על אחת כמה וכמה.

"He said to them: Take to heart [lit.: set your heart toward] all the words [with which I have warned you this day]" (Deuteronomy 32:46a): A person needs to direct his eyes and his heart and his ears toward words of Torah. And so it says, "O mortal, [mark well] [lit.: set your heart], look with your eyes and listen with your ears to all that I tell you [regarding all the laws of the Temple of the Lord and all the instructions concerning it.] Note well [lit.: set your heart toward] the entering into the Temple and all who must be excluded from the Sanctuary" (Ezekiel 44:5). We may argue *a fortiori ad minore* (*qal vaḥomer*; from light to heavy or the reverse): If in the case of the Temple, which could be seen with the eyes and measured with the hand,[18] a person needed to direct his eyes and his heart and his ears (toward it), then how much more should this be with words of Torah, which are like mountains suspended by a hair.

While the idiom "to set one's heart (=mind) toward" would seem to denote mental engagement with or concentration on divine or Mosaic instruction, the midrash, based on the parallel use of the same idiom in Ezekiel 44:5, but there combined with the senses of seeing and listening, concludes that in Deuteronomy 32:46a too, Moses is exhorting the people to actively and intensely engage "words of Torah," not just mentally, but visually and aurally as well, in effect, with the totality of one's sensing self.[19]

18 For measuring the heavenly Temple, see Ezek. 40:3–42:20; Zech. 2:1–5; Rev. 11:1–2.

19 For the triad of heart (=mind), eyes, and ears, see Deut. 29:3; Isa. 6:10; 32:3–4a; Jer. 5:21. For the combination of seeing and hearing of revelation, see Exod. 20:15 (18), as rabbinically (and Philonically) interpreted, as discussed in my article, "Hearing and Seeing at Sinai: Interpretive Trajectories," in *The Significance of Sinai: Traditions about Sinai and Divine Revelation in Judaism and Christianity*, ed. George J. Brooke, Hindy Najman, and Loren T. Stuckenbruck, Themes in Biblical Narrative 12 (Leiden: Brill, 2008), 247–68 (as well as *Legal Fictions*, *supra* n. 1, 501–22). For the

Before proceeding, however, we should note that the expression "words of Torah," construed here broadly as including both scriptural and non-scriptural (oral) rabbinic teaching,[20] is without direct scriptural antecedent. In the present context, the phrase "words of Torah" does not appear in the first half of the verse (46a), but is the result of a midrashic importing of it from the second half of the verse (46b: "all the words of this Torah") to the first (46a: "all the words"). The expression "the words of Torah" within the Pentateuch only appears in the book of Deuteronomy, where it occurs nine times, but always modified by the demonstrative pronoun "this" (as in verse 46b), referring to some form of the book of Deuteronomy or a part thereof,[21] as in Deuteronomy 1:5, where "this Torah" introduces the book of Deuteronomy, or the bulk thereof, that follows. The expression "the words of Torah" appears only five more times in the rest of the Hebrew Bible, but always with the definite article "the."[22] The more inclusive (rabbinic) expression "words of Torah" (without the definite article or demonstrative pronoun) *never* appears scripturally or, for that matter, in any pre-rabbinic Jewish text (e.g., the Dead Sea Scrolls). By contrast, the expression appears 13 times in the Mishnah, 15 in the Tosefta, and 190 times in the tannaitic midrashim, in the latter predominantly (145/190) in commenting on the book of Deuteronomy.

Returning to our midrash, the parallel expressions of Moses's call to the people to pay close mental and multi-sense attention to his "words of Torah" and God's call to Ezekiel to pay close attention to the envisioned heavenly Temple do not constitute an analogy between equals. Rather, by an argument of *qal vaḥomer* the midrash says that if such multi-sense engagement is divinely demanded with respect to the seemingly solid, stable, and tangible Temple, *how much more* should it be required of the precariously fragile, unstable, and intangible "words of Torah."

The metaphor of "mountains suspended by a hair" demands a brief detour. The phrase appears in only one other tannaitic textual context, that being m. Ḥagigah 1:8 and its related t. Ḥagigah 1:9 and t. ʿErubin 8:23. There it metaphorically denotes a class of laws (e.g., Sabbath laws) with "little Scripture and many laws," meaning that this class of laws has little in Scripture upon which to "lean" (according to the Tosefta). The Sifre Deuteronomy commentary is unique in its

visual aspects of rabbinic textuality, see Rachel Neis, *The Sense of Sight in Rabbinic Culture: Jewish Ways of Seeing in Late Antiquity* (Cambridge: Cambridge University Press, 2013).

20 On the rabbinic phrase "words of Torah" denoting both biblical and rabbinic oral Torah, see Fraade, *From Tradition to Commentary*, *supra* n. 14, 258 n. 219. See especially Sifre Deut. 306 (ed. Finkelstein, 339): "So too words of Torah are all one, but they comprise *miqrāʾ* (Scripture) and *mišnâ* (oral teaching): *midrāš* (exegesis), *hălākôt* (laws), and *haggādôt* (narratives)." For treatment, see Fraade, *From Tradition to Commentary*, *supra* n. 14, 97.

21 Deut. 17:19; 27:3; 27:8, 26; 28:58; 29:28; 31:12, 24; 32:46. For the later expression "the Torah," see Neh. 8:18; 2 Chr. 34:14.

22 Josh. 8:34; 2 Kgs. 23:24; Neh. 8:9, 13; 2 Chr. 34:19.

use of this metaphor to characterize "words of Torah" in their entirety. Should we read the Sifre in light of the Mishnah and Tosefta, as saying that all "words of Torah," that is, all of rabbinic law, are fragile by reason of having "little Scripture and many laws," that is, few scriptural hooks upon which to hang or from which to derive its laws? I would prefer not to do so, but to read the expression in Sifre Deuteronomy in its own right, thereby preserving the radical ambiguity of its reason for characterizing rabbinic "words of Torah" in their entirety as being "like mountains suspended by a hair." One could imagine other reasons for this fragility besides the abundance of rabbinic laws with respect to their meager scriptural bases, for example, the difficulty of committing such a large corpus of laws and cacophonous legal debate to memory and oral recitation, and hence the danger of their being lost.[23] This would link, as we shall see, the two parts of the midrash to one another. In any case, the *qal vaḥomer* argument is ironic, since at the time the midrash was composed, the physical Temple (but not its heavenly prototype) had long been destroyed, while the unstable "words of Torah" had survived, perhaps thanks to the multi-sense attention lavished upon them by their midrashic tradents over the generations.

V PART 2

As radical as is this self-admission of comprehensive rabbinic legal fragility, the midrash's comment to the second half of the biblical verse is even more radically honest, and potentially subversive. The end of the passage, as we shall see, is

[23] This is a fear frequently expressed in tannaitic texts, including in Sifre Deut. See Shlomo Naeh, "ʾOmanut ha-zikkaron: mivnim shel zikkaron ve-tavniyot shel tekst be-sifrut ḥazal," in *Meḥqerei Talmud III: Talmudic Studies Dedicated to the Memory of Professor Ephraim E. Urbach*, eds. Yaakov Sussmann and David Rosenthal (Jerusalem: Magnes, 2005), 543–89; Fraade, *From Tradition to Commentary*, *supra* n. 14, 105–19 (on Sifre Deut. §48); Marc Hirshman, *The Stabilization of Rabbinic Culture* 100 C.E.–350 C.E.: *Texts on Education and Their Late Antique Context* (Oxford: Oxford University Press, 2009), 31–48 ("Sifre Deuteronomy: The Precariousness of Oral Torah"). For the view that the fear here is one of loss of memory, especially of the Oral Torah, see the commentary to the Sifre by David Pardo (1719–92). On the textual reading, "like mountains suspended by a hair," see the excellent discussion by Michal Bar-Asher Siegal, "Mountains Hanging by a Strand? Re-Reading Mishnah Ḥagigah 1:8," *Journal of Ancient Judaism* 4 (2013): 235–56; מיכל בר-אשר סיגל, "לפשר הביטוי 'כהררים התלויים בשערה' (משנה, חגיגה א, ח)", *Leshonenu* 76.1-2 (5774/2004): 137–48, whose argument for replacing the word "mountains" (*hararim*) with one that denotes "dry desert bushes" (*ḥararim*) is more relevant to the Mishnah and Tosefta than to the Sifre (where there are no manuscript variants to *hararim*), and in any case would not change the meaning of the passage for my present argument. The Hebrew word used here for the plural "mountains" (*hararim*; construct form, *harerei*) is found both in Scripture (twelve times) and in tannaitic texts (sixteen times). For the former, see Num. 23:7; Deut. 8:9; 33:15; Jer. 17:3; Hab. 3:6; Ps 30:8; 36:7; 50:10; 76:5; 87:1; 133:3; Song. 4:8. For the latter (in addition to Sifre Deut. §335; m. Ḥag.. 1:8; t. Ḥag. 1:9; and t. Erub. 8:23), see Sifre Deut. §353 (ed. Finkelstein, 414.1–2; five times); Midrash Tanaʾim Deut. 33:15 (ed. Hoffman, 217; three times); Mek. R. Ishmael Amalek 1 (ed. Horovitz-Rabin, 177.1); Mek. R. Shimʿon bar Yoḥai Exod. 17:8 (ed. Epstein-Melamed, 119.22); Sifra Mek. Demiluʾim 37 (ed. Weiss, 46a.3); Sifre Num. §161 (ed. Horovitz, 223.7). The frightening image of a mountain (Sinai) cut off and suspended in the air, can be found in the Mekhilta of R. Ishmael Baḥodesh 3 (ed. Horovitz-Rabin, 214.17, with note).

particularly difficult, and likely corrupt, in the opinion of several commentators, here following MS London:[24]

"אשר תצום [את בניכם לשמר]": אמר להם, "צריך אני להחזיק טובה שתקיימו את התורה אחרי. אף אתם צריכין (אתם) להחזיק טובה לבניכם שיקיימו את התורה אחריכם." מעשה שבא רבינו מלדקיא ונכנס רבי יוסי ברבי יהודה ורבי אלעזר בן יהודה וישבו לפניו. אמר להן, "קרבו לכ[א]ן וקרבו לכ[א]ן. צריך אני להחזיק לכם טובה שתקיימו את התורה אחרי. אף אתם צריכין להחזיק טובה לבניכם ש(ת)[י]קיימו את התורה אחריכם." אילו אין משה גדול הוא ואילו אחר וקיבלנו תורתו לא הייתה תורתו שוה [כלום] על אחת כמה (שהָיו רצים)[25] וכמה. לכך נאמר, "אשר תצום [את בניכם לשמר]."

"Enjoin them upon your children to keep" (Deuteronomy 32:46b): He (Moses) said to them: "I should be grateful[26] if you would maintain the Torah after me (=my death). Similarly, you should be grateful to your children if they would maintain the Torah after you." It once happened that when our Rabbi [Judah the Patriarch] came from Laodicea (in Asia Minor), Rabbi Jose the son of Rabbi Judah [bar Ilai] and Rabbi Eleazar the son of Judah[27] entered and sat before him. He said to them: "Come close! Come close! I should be grateful to you if you would maintain the Torah after me. Similarly, you should be grateful to your children if they would maintain the Torah after you."[28] Had Moses not been great, or had he been

[24] MS London 341, with minor adjustments. See above, n. 17. This manuscript is, by and large, consistent with MS Berlin 151, *Yalquṭ Shim'oni*, the First Printing (Venice, 1546), *Liqutei Aggadot Sifre* (MS Oxford 937, photocopies of which were provided to me by Yonatan Sagiv), being French-Ashkenazi-Italian in provenance. For those noting that the text at the end of the passage, in all its attestations, is corrupt, see the commentaries ad loc. of Eliezer Naḥum (ca. 1660–1746) (מגומגם ["confused"]), David Pardo (מגומגם מאד ["very confused"]), and Louis Finkelstein (1895–1991) (המעתיקים שבשו את כל המאמר ["the copyists ruined the whole passage"]).

[25] The words within parentheses are a scribal error, and are marked as such by the scribe. This is presumably an error of *homoioteleuton*, since the words שהיו רצים appear in the Sifre's next comment (§336, ed. Finkelstein, 386 line 4), also in conjunction with the expression, על אחת כמה וכמה. My thanks to Yonatan Sagiv for pointing this out.

[26] Literally, "I need to give you credit." Compare m. 'Abot 2:8; 6:6. For "be grateful," see Marcus Jastrow, *A Dictionary of the Targumin, the Talmud Bavli and Jerushalmi, and the Midrashic Literature* (New York: Choreb, 1926), 444b; Eliezer ben Yehuda, *A Complete Dictionay of Ancient and Modern Hebrew*, vol. 3 (Jerusalem: Makor, 1980), 1491b (Hebrew), citing our Sifre passage. See also Rashi to Num. 25:12, cited by *Aruch Hashalem*, ed. Alexander Kahut, vol. 3, 361–62, under the entry "חזק"and the sub-entry :"החזיק טוב" "'את בריתי שלום'. שתהא לו לברית שלום. כאדם המחזיק טובה וחנות למי שעושה עמו טובה אף כאן פירש לו הקב"ה שלומותיו." ("'My covenant of peace': It should be for him a covenant of peace. Just as a person is grateful and gracious to one who does him a favor, so here the Holy One, Blesed Be He, assured him of his peace"). Finally, see Z. Ben-Ḥayyim, תיבת מרקה *[Tibåt Mårqe]: A Collection of Samaritan Midrashim* (Jerusalem: The Israel Academy of Sciences and Humanities, 1988), 58 (n. 2 to n. 15), for החזיק טובה as the equivalent of Aramaic אחסן טבו. My thanks to Berachyahu Lifshitz for having brought the last to my attention.

[27] These are not otherwise known to have been students of Rabbi Judah the Patriarch. See Ofra Meir, *Rabbi Judah the Patriarch: Palestinian and Babylonian Portrait of a Leader* (Tel-Aviv: Hakibbutz Hameuchad, 1999), 137–38 (Hebrew). For variant names, see Finkelstein's critical apparatus ad loc.

[28] I take what follows not to be the "words" of Rabbi Judah the Patriarch, but of the anonymous midrashist or redactor.

someone else,[29] and had we received his Torah,[30] would it not have been worth [a thing]?[31] How much more so![32] Therefore it says, "Enjoin them [upon your children to keep]."[33]

Before further unpacking this midrash, it should be noted that a different, shorter, more easily rendered strand of this midrashic tradition, especially the lines beginning with "Had Moses not been great," appears to have been preserved in a Byzantine-Yemenite tradition, as evidenced in *Midrash Ha-Gadol* and *Midrash Leqaḥ Ṭov*, here citing from the former:[34]

או אינו אלא משה רבן שלנביאים שאלולי אחרים ש(ת)קיימו את תורתו מה היתה תורתו שווה.

Were it not for Moses, the greatest of the prophets,[35] and had not others maintained his Torah, what would his Torah have been worth?

[29] The text's syntax here (ואילו אחר) is difficult and its meaning unclear. I will return to the word אחר below. I take it to mean that had Moses not been such a great prophet, or had the Torah-giver been someone else (inferior) altogether. But see below, n. 36.

[30] Note the switch here from second-person singular to first-person plural ("we") here. I understand "his Torah" to refer to the Torah of "someone else." and "we" to be the perpetual we of the text's readers/auditors. See below at n. 52.

[31] Compare the expression אינו שוה כלום ("it is not worth a thing"), appearing three times in the Sifra, four times in the Babylonian Talmud, and eleven times in the aggadic midrashim. I take this sentence to be rhetorical, and in disbelief: would not the Torah have had value regardless of its "author"? Note that in the commentary to the Sifre attributed to RaBad ("Pseudo-RaBaD") (ed. Basser, 315), the commentator comments with a single word, בתמיה ("in disbelief").

[32] I understand this enigmatic statement to mean, "How much more so is it to be valued since it was given by none other than the great Moses and maintained, generation to generation, ever since!" My explanatory insertion is necessary to make sense of the text, especially the awkward, "How much more so." For similar understandings, see the eighteenth-century commentary to the Sifre, *Zera' 'avraham* by R. Abraham Yequti'el Zalman Lichtstein, as well as that of R. Moses David Abraham Treves Ashkenazy (1780–1856) in his commentary to the Sifre, *Toledot 'adam*. For additional readings and suggested meanings, see Herbert W. Basser, *Midrashic Interpretations of the Song of Moses* (New York, Frankfort on the Main, Berne: Peter Lang, 1984), 263–65; Herbert W. Basser, *In the Margins of Midrash: Sifre Ha'azinu Texts, Commentaries, and Reflections* (Atlanta: Scholars Press, 1990), 157, 181. Ishay Rosen-Zvi has suggested to me that a rhetorical understanding of "how much more so" to mean that the value of the Torah is in itself and in subsequent generations having received and maintained it, and not in its having originated with Moses. Its value is all the greater ("how much more so") for having been passed down from generation to generation regardless of its originator. Stated differently, "Who wrote the Bible?" is irrelevant to its value as having been continually transmitted and received.

[33] I understand this to mean, "*You* (in each generation) are to enjoin (command) them upon your children," even if they had been originally commanded by someone else, but all the more so since they were commanded by the great Moses.

[34] *Midrash Ha-Gadol* Deut. 32:46 (ed. Fisch, 737); also included in *Midrash Tanna'im* ad loc. (ed. Hoffmann, 205) with minor variants; *Midrash Leqaḥ Ṭov* ad loc. (ed. Buber, 120). The unique relationship between *Midrash Ha-Gadol* and *Midrash Leqaḥ Ṭov* is evidenced by the fact that they alone have the following sentence in the above story of Rabbi Judah the Patriarch: לא זז מקרבן עד שקרבן לפני רגליו ("He [Rabbi] did not cease urging them to come closer until they were as close as his feet"). For a stematic chart showing this textual branch, see Menahem Kahana, "Prolegomena to a New Edition of the Sifre on Numbers" (PhD dissertation, Hebrew University, 1982), 276 (Hebrew).

[35] *Midrash Leqaḥ Ṭov* has גדול העולם ("the greatest in the world").

Note that instead of the word אחר ("other"), as in MS London and its family of witnesses, which I argued was awkward, we have אחרים ("others"), which could have been abbreviated as אחר' and subsequently miscopied as אחר, which makes less sense here than אחרים. Thus, hypothetically, a prior un- or less-corrupted text behind both versions could have been, … אילו אין משה גדול הוא ואילו[לא] אחר[ים] קיבלו תורתו ("Had Moses not been so great, and/or had others not received his Torah … "). Interestingly, no witness to this part of the midrash includes both אחר and אחרים, suggesting that this is a differentiating marker between the two main recensions of the text: MS London and company (with אחר, referring to a law-giving leader other than Moses) and *Midrash HaGadol – Midrash Leqaḥ Ṭov* (with אחרים, referring to the successive generations of recipients after Moses).[36] Note also that the *Midrash HaGadol – Midrash Leqaḥ Ṭov* recension lacks the concluding (and awkward in MS London and its allied witnesses) expression על אחת כמה וכמה ("how much more so"), as well as the concluding citation of the lemma, לכך נאמר ("as it is said … "). It is possible that these are editorial accretions added for purposes of stylistic consistency. Although as collections, these midrashic anthologies are considerably later than the Sifre, they may at times preserve texts and traditions that are earlier than the manuscript evidence for the Sifre itself.[37]

Two modern rabbinic scholars have significantly emended the text of the Sifre here, using the printed edition (virtually identical to MS London), but pulling it into accord with the *Midrash Ha-Gadol – Midrash Leqaḥ Ṭov* tradition. Thus, the Gaon R. Elija of Vilna (the GRA) (1720–97), in "his emendations," renders our difficult concluding lines as follows:

משה גדול הוא ואלו לא באו אחרים לא היתה תורתו שוה אנו על אחת כמה וכמה כול.

> Moses was great, but if others had not come (to receive it), his Torah would not have been worth (a thing). How much more is this the case for us!

Similarly (but without acknowledged awareness of the GRA's emendation), Louis Finkelstein renders the end of our midrash as follows:

אילו אין משה גדול ואילולא אחרים קבלו תורה על ידו לא היתה שוה. [אנו] על אחת כמה וכמה. לכך נאמר,"אשר תצום את בניכם".

[36] It has been suggested to me that the word אחר in MS London and its related witnesses be taken in the temporal sense of "after" (as previously in אחרי ["after me"] and אחריכם ["after you"]). This too, however would require emendation: אילו אין משה גדול הוא ואילו אחר (ו)קיבלנו תורתו לא הייתה תורתו שוה [כלום ("If Moses had not been great, and if after [him] (and) we had received his Torah, would his Torah have not been worth [a thing]?"). Consider as well Deut. Rab. 8:6, commenting on Deut. 30:11–12: "'It is not in the heavens': Moses said to them: So that you should not say another (אחר) Moses will arise and bring us a different (אחרת) Torah from the heavens." My thanks to Berachyahu Lifshitz for bringing this text to me attention.

[37] For this possibility, see Kahana, "Prolegomena," *supra* n. 34, 265 (Hebrew). Note that two of the modern commentators to the Sifre who consider its text to be corrupt (see above, n. 24), David Pardo and Eliezer Naḥum (ed. Kahana, 432), appear to favor the *Midrash Ha-Gadol – Midrash Leqaḥ Ṭov* recension, and paraphrase the Sifre's text accordingly.

> With all of Moses's greatness, had no one received his Torah, it would not have been worth [a thing]. How much more is this the case [for us]![38] Therefore it says, "Enjoin them upon your children [to keep]."

Notwithstanding these text-critical challenges at the end of the midrashic passage, and my preference for the *Midrash Ha-Gadol – Midrash Leqaḥ Ṭov* recension, the various versions share some important exegetical features. In order to understand and appreciate them, it is first necessary to recognize an aspect of the biblical verse that might at first have gone unnoticed by the non-midrashist. We might have expected Moses to enjoin his immediate audience to observe the commandments once they had crossed over the Jordan River and entered the land, but without any longer the advantage of his charismatic, prophetic teaching and leadership. However, the biblical verse has Moses enjoin, rather, his audience to command *their children* to observe[39] all of the Torah's commandments, presumably in perpetuity (as would seem to be the implied meaning of verse 47).[40] Thus, in Moses's final days, his public role as commander and teacher in chief is not transmitted so much to future national leaders (e.g., Joshua according to Numbers 27:12–23; Deuteronomy 31:2–8; and 34:8–9; or Ezra according to Nehemiah 8:1–8) as to the succession of parents and future parents in the private setting of the family or home.[41]

Turning to the midrashic comment to the second half of the verse (32:46b), it paraphrases Moses's speech to the people in a strikingly altered form and emotional

38 The word אנו ("for us") is provided by Finkelstein to make sense of the sentence, but is, as he admits, missing in all manuscripts. As we have seen, the GRA makes the same insertion into the Sifre's text ("How much more is this the case *for us*!"). This expression (including "for us") appears thirty-four times in classical rabbinic literature, twenty-seven of which are in the aggadic midrashim, but this is its only occurrence in the tannaitic corpora. It will be discussed below. Note that in a printed edition of *Yalquṭ Shim'oni* (Jerusalem, 1960), 678, the word עכשיו ("now") is inserted within square brackets where Finkelstein and the GRA insert אנו ("for us"), in either case bringing the midrashic lesson to the present readers of the text.

39 The Hebrew verb employed here, *lishmor*, is commonly used biblically for keeping commandments or fulfilling obligations. See, for example, Exod. 12:17; 23:15; Deut. 5:1, 12; 29:8. In rabbinic Hebrew, it gains as well the sense of preserving (*leqayyem*) teachings in one's memory. See Fraade, *From Tradition to Commentary*, *supra* n. 14, 258 n. 222.

40 Note the emphasis on transmission to both one's children and children's children (grandchildren). For a similar emphasis, see Deut. 4:9; 31:13; Exod. 10:2. Since Deut. 34:9 states that the present generation of Israelites "heeded him [Moses], doing as the Lord had commanded Moses," it might be assumed that Moses's was more worried about the next generation, not yet part of his audience, than the present generation. Compare Mek. R. Ishmael Beshallaḥ 1 (ed. Horovitz-Rabin, 80.6–10), commenting on Exod. 13:19: "He [Joseph] made the children of Israel surely swear" that they would carry his bones with them when they left Egypt. The doubling (infinitive absolute) of the verb "swear" in the biblical Hebrew is midrashically interpreted to mean that the Israelites, and Joseph's brothers in particular, not only swore themselves, but legally obligated their children as well under the oath.

41 For the intellectual/pedagogical preoccupation of Deuteronomy see Tigay, *The JPS Torah Commentary*, *supra* n. 14, xvii–xviii. For other examples, see Deut. 1:5; 4:1, 5, 9; 5:1; 6:7, 20–25; 11:19; 17:18-19; 31:11–13.

tone. No longer is Moses the authority figure who commands absolute obedience to "all the words of this Teaching (Torah)," but a suppliant who implores the people not only to maintain themselves the "words of Torah" after his impending death, but to beseech their children to do the same. Subtle as the change is, the verb *lishmor* (observe) in the biblical text is replaced by *leqayyem* (to maintain, which rabbinically denotes as well study and memorization) in the midrash.[42] Impotent, as it were, any longer to command, Moses must employ moral persuasion in the hope that the people will both maintain the words of Torah and, perhaps even more importantly, transmit them to the next generation, and for it, implicitly at least, to do the same in turn in perpetuity.

As if to signal, from the advantage of hindsight, that Moses and the successive generations of Israelites succeeded in so fulfilling and transmitting the Torah laws, we are suddenly transported forward in time approximately fourteen hundred years to the study, as it were, of R. Judah the Patriarch, who as purported editor of the Mishnah, the earliest and most consequential digest of rabbinic Torah law, might be (and is) thought of as a latter-day Moses. R. Judah the Patriarch, we may infer, is either toward the end of his life or anticipating it ("after me"). He, we are told, has just returned from a mission of some sort to Laodicea (probably the one on the Lycus), a heavily hellenized Roman provincial city in Asia Minor (modern-day Turkey), with a substantial Jewish (and Christian) population. From the story, we do not know what R. Judah the Patriarch experienced there, but it would seem to have caused him to worry about the present and/or future state of Judaism in a highly hellenized environment. Inviting two students to come close (doubly expressed in some witnesses such as MS London), thereby indicating perhaps intimacy, but also urgency, he says to them, in the words of the midrash, *exactly* what Moses said to the people at the end of his life, some fourteen hundred years earlier. In this context, "children" could mean biological offspring or "students," intellectual offspring, or both.[43] The pathos here is similar to that of Moses in his waning days. With all the learning and authority that R. Judah the Patriarch commands, he cannot successfully command or coerce his students, but can only implore them to fulfill and transmit what he has imparted to them to their children/students, and so on. R. Judah the Patriarch is clearly portrayed here as a latter-day Moses, perhaps also implying a parallel in status between their respective Torahs (Written and Oral), and the fragile nature of both.[44]

The absolute identity of the midrashic words of Moses to those of Rabbi Judah the Patriarch, and the similarity and shared pathos of their situations, might lead us to

42 See above, n. 39.

43 See Sifre Deut. §34 (ed. Finkelstein, 61) to Deut. 6:7: "'Impress them upon your children' (וְשִׁנַּנְתָּם לְבָנֶיךָ): These are your students. Similarly, you find that in every place students are called children."

44 For the dialectical tension between the two, see Yair Furstenberg, "The *Agon* with Moses and Homer: Rabbinic Midrash and the Second Sophistic," in *Homer and the Bible in the Eyes of Ancient Interpreters*, ed. Maren R. Niehoff, Jerusalem Studies in Religion and Culture 16 (Leiden: Brill, 2012), 299–328.

overlook some fundamental differences between them. Moses is *publicly* addressing the whole Israelite people, while Rabbi Judah the Patriarch is *privately* (and intimately) addressing two of his students (their being two allows Rabbi Judah the Patriarch to employ the same second-person plural forms of address as does Moses). There is a shift from a great leader *publicly* enjoining the "corporate" Israel, to a later great teacher who does so *privately* to two individuals (and their children/students). Thus, Moses's message and role, as midrashically construed, has become more individualized (and intimatized) with time, as, presumably, it has become for the "we" of the midrash's presumed audience,[45] who as *autonomous individuals*, may be moved (or not) to compliance by the rhetoric of *mitzvah* as legacy. Both Moses (as midrashically reinvented) and Rabbi Judah the Patriarch seek not just immediate observance of the commandments, but long-term maintenance of "words of Torah," now entrusted to internalizing textual study among small groups of masters and disciples, rather than to mass acceptance of the laws by the people as a whole.[46] Survival of Torah depends as much on its private as public transmission through performance.[47]

Note as well the subtle role reversal of master and students (or "patron" and "clients"). While they come, presumably, with the intent of paying their respects to Rabbi Judah the Patriarch (note the hierarchical language of "they entered and sat before him"), it is he who is now revealed to be dependent on their "favor." The honor that they expect to bestow upon him is now reversed, being no longer an expression of his superior status but of his total dependence upon them to carry forward his teaching.[48]

45 This occurs in both strands of the tradition. See above, n. 30 for the MS London tradition, and above, n. 38 and below at n. 52, for the *Midrash Ha-Gadol – Midrash Leqaḥ Ṭov* tradition as incorporated by the GRA and Finkelstein in their emendations.

46 Free choice, but with sharp covenantal consequences either way, is a central theme running through the book of Deuteronomy, but see, in particular, Deut. 11:26–28; 30:15–30. The shift to the more local, intimate, and individualized didactic relation of Judah the Patriarch to his students, might reflect the social reality of the rabbinic "movement" of the time of the Sifre's composition and redaction (second-third century CE), comprised as it was of small master-disciple study circles. See, for example, Shaye J. D. Cohen, "The Rabbi in Second-Century Jewish Society," in *The Cambridge History of Judaism, vol. 3, The Early Roman Period*, eds. W. Horbury, W. D. Davies, and J. Sturdy (Cambridge and New York: Cambridge University Press, 1999), 922–90.

47 For more on this tension, see Natalie B. Dohrmann, "Can 'Law' Be Private? The Mixed Message of Rabbinic Oral Law," in *Public and Private in Ancient Mediterranean Law and Religion*, ed. Clifford Ando and Jörg Rüpke, Religionsgeschichtliche Versuche und Vorarbeiten 65 (Berlin: De Gruyter, 2015), 187–216.

48 I am indebted to Ishay Rosen-Zvi for these suggestions. For Rabbi Judah the Patriarch (and his successors) receiving the salutation (*salutatio*) due to a patron, see Aharon Oppenheimer, *Rabbi Judah ha-Nasi* (Jerusalem: The Zalman Shazar Center, 2007), 52–53 (Hebrew). For patronage salutations and gifts in early rabbinic literature, see Mekhilta of R. Shimʿon bar Yoḥai to Exod. 22:24 (ed. Epstein-Melamed, 212). For the "gift economy" and patronage more broadly in the ancient world, see Phebe Lowell Bowditch, *Horace and the Gift Economy of Patronage*, Classics and Contemporary Thought 8 (Berkeley: University of California Press, 2001), esp. 31–63 ("The Gift Economy of Patronage"). For patronage in ancient Jewish societies more broadly, see Seth Schwartz,

The full pathos of Moses's words (and by extension, those of R. Judah the Patriarch) is indicated in the concluding sentence of the midrashic commentary, regardless of which textual strand one prefers to follow. In either case, the critical role of transmission across the generations (whether by children or by students) is emphasized, while the commanding role of Moses (and of R. Judah the Patriarch) is sidelined. Moses's prophetic greatness does not ensure the "maintenance" of Torah teaching, but rather is contingent upon it, that is, upon the reception, fulfillment, and transmission of his words (understood to encompass the totality of rabbinic "words of Torah")[49] by successive generations, not of prophetic leaders (as in the "chain of transmission: in the opening lines of Pirqe ʾAvot), but of teachers and parents able to impress the laws and teachings of his Torah upon their students and children to both observe and transmit. Otherwise, we are told, it is as if Moses's Torah (and, we might infer, Moses himself, and, by extension, R. Judah the Patriarch) would not have been of any worth or consequence.[50]

The midrash, at least as explicitly emended by the GRA and by Finkelstein, and as less boldly asserted by MS London's introduction of "we,"[51] makes one final, gigantic, temporal leap, as it were, this time to the present of the text's auditors, with another argument of *qal vaḥomer* (although not fully tagged as such and absent in the *Midrash Ha-Gadol – Midrash Leqaḥ Ṭov* recension): Just as Moses's (that is, his Torah's) worth, with all of his greatness, was entirely contingent on his ability to impress the responsibility of transmission on the minds and hearts of his successors, how much more is that the case "for us"(*ʾanu*), who, shrink before the greatness of Moses (and by association, before that of R. Judah the Patriarch). Or, as MS London expresses it, the maintenance and transmission of the Torah is contingent on "us" rather than on Moses's prophetic greatness and revelatory authorship. Even had he not been so great, or not been the Torah's commander to begin with, "we" would still have been expected to receive, maintain, and transmit it in perpetuity. How much more so with Moses and his greatness! Nevertheless, the Torah could have been maintained (or not) by "us" without him. Ironically, "we," in effect, are now the equals (at least) of Moses and R. Judah the Patriarch in bearing the weight of the continuity of the chain of transmission. They are as dependent on "us" to maintain their "words of Torah" as "we" are dependent on them for the "words of Torah"'s prophetic and canonical authority. Although not explicitly stated here by the Sifre, "our" inclusion as the latest link in this chain is midrashically effected by the biblical verse's prescient reference in 46a to "this day," as if signaling the longue durée of the perpetual present, in which every successive day is signified by "this day."[52]

Were the Jews a Mediterranean Society? Reciprocity and Solidarity in Ancient Judaism (Princeton: Princeton University Press, 2009).

49 See above, n. 20.

50 See above, n. 31.

51 See above, n. 30.

52 For this exegesis in Sifre Deut, see §33 (ed. Finkelstein, 59), to Deut. 6:6; §41 (ed. Finkelstein, 86), to Deut. 11:13; §58 (ed. Finkelstein, 124), to Deut. 11:32; §153 (ed. Finkelstein, 206-207), to Deut. 17:9 and

VI CONCLUSIONS

In conclusion, let me first address the question of whether the two halves of our midrash constitute a whole, greater than the sum of its parts, even as each can stand perfectly well on its own. Both halves are honest yet radical in emphasizing the precariously fragile, unstable nature of "words of (rabbinic/oral) Torah," especially as transmitted orally through study and memorization. The first does so by comparing "words of Torah" to "mountains suspended by a hair," referring either to their tenuous scriptural warrants (as in the parallel in m. Ḥagigah 1:8), or to the tenuous task of their retention and transmission through memorization, at any moment liable to being severed from their roots by the cutting of their hairline suspensions.[53] The second does so by emphasizing the inter-generational human challenge to observing and transmitting "words of Torah" from teacher to student and parent to child, *without* the ability (already with Moses) of being able to command absolute fidelity.

Not only do the two halves of the midrash share with each other the rhetorical argument of *qal vaḥomer* (but not as explicitly in the second half), but they both do so with irony, reversing the seemingly obvious designation of "heavy" and "light": the Temple is no more sturdy than the fragile "words of Torah," and Moses (and R. Judah the Patriarch by association) is no greater than his successors when it comes to obligating the next generation to observe the commandments. "Our" "words of Torah" are as fragile as were theirs, and "we" are as impotent as were they to command obedience from our children and/or students. In the end, all "we" can do is *implore* them (as were "we") to carry forward the charge, based on a rhetoric, no longer of Sinai-based commandment, but of cross-generational fidelity to legacy.

Thus, in addition to (or between) Cover's rhetorical, mythic vectors of law as social contract (rights) and law as Sinaitic revelation (commandments), we might interpose that of law as legacy, which draws upon and nourishes both, without necessarily negating or superseding either: upon the myth of Sinai for its diachronic, inter-generational transmission of commandments (even without an immediate Commander-in-Chief or Lieutenant Commander), while upon the myth of social contract for its synchronic creation of sympathetic communities. Both can instill and inspire "bonds of solidarity," as Cover terms them, whether vertically or horizontally. But so too can law as historically transcendent legacy, extending both back to Sinai in shared memory and forward through the present of shared community to the next generation (at least) in unassured anticipation and aspiration. Stated differently, Moses retains (at least for now) his greatness, but it remains precariously dependent upon "our" bonds of both collective and individual solidarity with both one another and with his legacy. In that regard, we might compare Edmund Burke's

§345 (ed. Finkelstein, 402), citing Deut. 29:9. See Fraade, *From Tradition to Commentary*, *supra* n. 14, 256 n. 196. By my count, "this day" appears forty-two times in the Book of Deuteronomy. For all of Israel, throughout the generations, having been included in the revelation and obligation at Sinai "this day," see above, n. 3.

53 See above, n. 23.

understanding of the inter-generational grounding of law in society. For example, "[The state] becomes a partnership not only between those who are living, but between those who are living, those who are dead, and those who are to be born."[54]

Circling back to Cover, we can say that a central mythic component of the Jewish legal legacy is the self-understanding of "being commanded." Even the anarchist in Cover would recognize law as commandment and law as legacy (like nomos and narrative) as two dialectical sides of the same coin, both being expressed by the same Hebrew verbal root, *tzivah*. Similarly, we might say (if we had a three-sided coin), that Cover's two foundational myths of law as contract (rights) and law as revelation (commandments) can only be deepened by their integration with law as legacy, which incorporates both rights and obligation.

54 See Edmund Burke, *Reflections on the Revolution in France* (1890), ed. Frank M. Turner (Rethinking the Western Tradition, New Haven: Yale University Press, 2003), 81–83 (here 82). Burke continues: "But one of the first and most leading principles on which the commonwealth and the laws are consecrated, is lest the temporary possessors and life-renters in it, unmindful of what they have received from their ancestors, or of what is due to their posterity, should act as if they were the entire masters; that they should not think it among their rights to cut off the entail, or commit waste on the inheritance, by destroying at their pleasure the whole original fabric of their society; hazarding to leave to those who come after them a ruin instead of an habitation – and teaching these successors as little to respect their contrivances, as they had themselves respected the institutions of their forefathers. By this unprincipled facility of changing the state as often, and as much, and in as many ways, as there are floating fancies and fashions, the whole chain and continuity of the commonwealth would be broken. No one generation could link with the other. Men would become little better than flies of a summer" (81), or "like mountains suspended by a hair." For a philosophical meditation on the necessary confidence in a "collective afterlife" (and the potential consequences of its termination) for human projects including law, see Samuel Scheffler, *Death and the Afterlife*, with commentaries by Susan Wolf, Harry G Frankfurt, Seana Valentine Shiffrin, and Niko Kolodny, ed. and intro. Niko Kolodny (Oxford: Oxford University Press, 2013), relating to Moses on p. 35. See also above, n. 3.

12

"Between Man and God" and "Between Man and His Fellow"

Categories in Polemical Context

Itzhak Brand

I INTRODUCTION

The distinction between precepts that are "between Man and God" (*bein adam la-maqom*) and those that are "between Man and his fellow" (*bein adam le-ḥavero*) is generally taken to be a general consensus view, going back to its first appearances in the talmudic corpus. Due to the distinction's simplicity, few have dealt with it, including its historical context. But an examination of the tannaitic literature, where the two categories were documented, reveals that there was disagreement about the distinction between them.

This chapter will present the disagreement in its historical context, proposing that it should be viewed in light of a latent dispute pitting the talmudic sages, especially those of the second and third generations at Yavneh, against the early Christian literature that was contemporary with them, and perhaps also the Roman law of that period. The chapter will also address the related issue of the arrangement of the Ten Commandments on the two Tablets of the Law. Early Christianity mostly saw the separation between two units of the Ten Commandments as a clear expression of the distinction between the two types of precepts, but a widespread sages approach rejected such a categorical distinction and thus also the division of the Ten Commandments onto two tablets.

II BELLORIA THE CONVERT'S QUESTION

The distinction between the two categories of precepts, "between Man and God" and "between Man and his fellow,"[1] appears to have been first documented in the academy at Yavneh in the second and third generations of the tanna'im, in the reply

[1] This applies to these categories literally. The idea of a distinction between types of norms, religious and social, is very old and can be found already in Philo, in Roman law, and in early Christianity. See below, Section V.B (Philo); Appendix A (Roman law); Section V.C (early Christianity).

by Rabbi Jose the Priest, one of Rabban Johanan ben Zakkai's disciples,[2] to a question posed to Rabban Gamaliel of Yavneh. Belloria, a Roman matron who had converted to Judaism, asked Rabban Gamaliel as follows: Belloria the convert once asked Rabban Gamaliel: It is written in your Torah: "The great, mighty, and awesome God who favors no one [and will not take bribes]" (Deuteronomy 10:17), and elsewhere it is written: "The Lord shall show favor to you and give you peace" (Numbers 6:26). In short: Does the Lord pardon sinners or does he reject their appeals for forgiveness? When Rabban Gamaliel, for whatever reason, did not respond, Rabbi Jose the Priest spoke up:

> I will tell you a parable. To what is this matter comparable? To a person who lent his friend one hundred dinars and fixed a time for repayment of the loan before the king, and the borrower took an oath by the life of the king that he would repay the money. The time arrived, and he did not repay the loan. The delinquent borrower came to appease the king for not fulfilling the oath that he had sworn by the life of the king, and the king said to him: For my insult I forgive you, but you must still go and appease your friend. Here also the same is true: Here, the verse that states: "The Lord shall show favor to you," is referring to sins committed between man and God, which God will forgive; there, the verse that states: "God favors no one," is referring to sins committed between a person and another, which God will not forgive until the offender appeases the one he hurt.

This is how the contradiction was resolved, until Rabbi Akiva came with a different explanation:

> Here the verse is referring to the time before one's sentence is issued, when God shows favor and forgives; and there the verse is referring to the time after the sentence has been issued, when He no longer forgives.[3]

Rabbi Jose the Priest holds that divine justice must be unbiased – "who favors no one and will not take bribes"; this applies to transgressions between Man and his fellow.[4] However, God does grant absolution for transgressions between man and God,[5]

2 Zechariah Frankel, *Darkei hamishnah* (Tel Aviv, 1958/9), 94 n. 3; Gedalia Alon, *The Jews in Their Land in the Talmudic Age*, 70–640 C.E., Vol. 1 (Jerusalem, 1980), 104.

3 B *Rosh Hashanah* 17b–18a Hebrew according to JTS MS 218 (270 EMC); translation from the William Davidson Talmud (at www.sefaria.org.il/Rosh_Hashanah.18a.1?lang=he&with=all&lang2=he, accessed March 8, 2017).
Var. lect. : בלודיא | Most MSS: בלוריא; Munich 140: ברוריא.
בתורתכם | Haim Z. Dimitrovsky, *Śeride Bavli* II.1 (New York: Jewish Theological Seminary, 1979), 233: בתורה.
כאן בעברות שבין אדם לחברו כן בעברות שבין אדם למקום | Munich 95 (and Ed. Venice and Dimitrovsky): כאן בעבירות שבין אדם למקום כאן בעבירות שבין אדם לחבירו | London, BL, Harl. 5508 (400): כאן בעבירות שבין אדם לשמים (בסיפא):

4 The problem of God's favoritism appears in several locations in talmudic literature and is resolved in various ways. See Menahem Kahane, *Sifre Bamidbar, Annotated Edition, Part II* (Jerusalem, 2011), 324.

5 It is possible that Rabbi Jose the Priest's distinction is based on the context of the two verses cited. The verse that follows "who will not show favor or take bribes" (Deut. 10:17) concerns interpersonal

because they affect only Him, and a king can pardon offenses of *lèse majesté*.[6] The text and style of the baraita suggest that Rabbi Jose's statement was made in a polemical context, and especially because he is responding to the query of a convert who was formerly a Roman matron.[7] Her question is belligerent and polemical, beginning "it is written in *your* Torah."[8] The term used to describe

matters: "Who executes justice for the orphan the widow, and loves the stranger, giving him food and clothing" (v. 18). On the other hand, "the Lord will show you favor" is part of the priestly blessing (Num. 6:22–27), as part of a string of the Lord's favor bestowed on the Israelites through the use of the divine name – clearly in the domain of human-divine relations.

6 The parable of the king and the creditor is based on a well-known practice in the Greco-Roman world, where oaths invoking the ruler's life were common. See Saul Lieberman, *Greek in Jewish Palestine: Hellenism in Jewish Palestine* (New York, 1994), 192–93; Samuel Krauss, *Paras ṿe-Romi ba-Talmud u-va-midrashim* [Persia and Rome in the Talmud and Midrash] (Jerusalem, 1947), 65–68. The distinction between the king's law and heavenly law in relation to false oaths ("for my insult I forgive you, but you must still go and appease your friend.") represents a well-known and mirror-image situation in Roman law. See the Code of Justinian 82.11.1: "The punishment for perjury oath will be imposed on them by God. ... We do not expect that the punishment for perjury will be imposed on them by a human"; ibid., 6.3.21 (Ulpian): If a person took an oath and subsequently died, and is found to have perjured himself, according to Marcellus, "the religious aspect of the oath shall be taken into account." See also Krauss, *Paras ve-Romi*, 68: "Among the Romans, an earthly court did not punish perjury, because judgment is [left for] God."

Scholars of Roman law have different views about how the courts' recusal from cases of perjury should be understood. Some have seen it as a result of the fundamental separation that Roman law maintained between religious law and secular law. See Fritz Schulz, *Classical Roman Law* (Oxford, 1951), 370: an injury to the gods is a matter for the gods ("Deorum iniuria diis curae"). Another opinion is that the prosecution of perjury is reserved to the gods because of procedural considerations: the legal system's limited ability to take effective action against perjurers. In general, the law resorts to religious tools only as a last resort, when other legal instruments cannot be used. This is the case for curses and oaths, where the difficulty of enforcement leads to a dependence on religious "tools." See Alan Watson, *The State, Law, and Religion: Pagan Rome* (Athens, GA: 1992), 49–50. For a broader discussion of the distinction between religious law (*ius divinum*) and human/secular law (*ius humanum*) in Roman law, see Appendix A.

7 Shmuel Klein, "Shalosh matanot tovot" [Three good presents], *Zion* 1 (1926), 12; Adolf Büchler, *The Economic Conditions of Judæa after the Destruction of the Second Temple* (London: Jews' College, 1912), 66–67; Moshe David Herr, "The Historical Significance of the Dialogues between Sages and Roman Leaders" [Hebrew], *Proceedings of the Fifth World Congress of Jewish Studies*, Division IV (1969): 282–83; Gedalia Alon, *The Jews in Their Land in the Talmudic Age*, 70–640 C.E., Vol. 2 (Jerusalem, 1984), 561 (Belloria is Valeria); Tal Ilan, *Lexicon of Jewish Names in Late Antiquity*, vol. 1 (Tubingen, 2002), 50, and 344.

8 "It is written in your Torah" declares the questioner's attitude towards the Torah – *your* Torah, not *ours*. However, Ezra Zion Melamed, *Midreshei halakhah shel ha-tana'im ba-talmud ha-bavli* (Jerusalem, 1988), 347, n. 4, had difficulty with this formulation and proposed deleting "your Torah": Belloria is a convert, not a non-Jew. So too Dimitrovsky, *Śeride Bavli*. However, in all manuscripts the text is "it is written in your Torah." The tenor of this phrasing is usually critical and belligerent. See, for example: M *Avodah Zarah* 3:4 (the query addressed by Proclos son of Philosophos to Rabban Gamaliel) and Abraham Wasserstein, "Rabban Gamaliel and Proclus of Naucratus", *Zion* 45 (1980): 257–67; *Mekhilta de-Rabbi Ishmael, Ba-ḥodesh* 6, Horowitz & Rabin ed., 226 (a philosopher and Rabban Gamaliel); B *Berakhot* 32b (a *hegmon* and a pious man); B *Avodah Zarah* 17a (Jacob of Kefar Saknia, "one of the disciples of Jesus the Nazarene," asked Rabbi Eliezer), and the parallel in *Ecclesiastes Rabbah* 1:3. See also David Rokeaḥ, "Ben Sitra is Ben Pantera – Clarification of a Philological-Historical Problem", *Tarbiẓ* 39 (1969): 9–12. In one case, a Jewish sage uses this formulation in a polemic against the Kuthites (Samaritans). See J *Sotah* 7:5 [21c], eds.

R. Jose's intervention, *nitpal lah* – "he dealt with her"[9] – is also typical of polemic encounters.[10]

Rabbi Jose's words, possibly uttered in the heat of debate, remained unchallenged until Rabbi Akiva offered an alternative reply. The locution "until Rabbi Akiva came and taught" appears several times in talmudic literature, where it signals a homiletic or ideological revolution and significant innovation by Rabbi Akiva, generally in the field of halakhah.[11] The use of this locution, then, indicates that Rabbi Akiva's proposal is not meant only as an additional reply to Belloria's question and is not simply a homiletic exegesis. Rather, it is an innovation on a matter of principle, stating that divine judgment is not contingent on the type of positive actions or transgressions attributed to a person, but on the stage of divine judgment: after the sentence has been rendered, the divine judgment is final and cannot be undone. But until then, God can forgive all transgressions, including those between two individuals. Thus, Rabbi Akiva denies the distinction between types of transgressions and holds that divine justice deals in the same fashion with all transgressions, whether they offend God or other human beings.

Later we will try to understand Rabbi Akiva's position on this matter of principle in light of the polemic. First, though, we will examine another tannaitic exegesis, in which Rabbi Akiva again opposes the distinction between transgressions towards God and transgressions towards human beings.[12]

Academy of the Hebrew Language, 934: "Rabbi Eleazar son of Rabbi Simeon said: I told the Kuthite scribes: You have forged your Torah and have not done yourselves any good, because you wrote into your Torah near Elonei Moreh Shekhem. . ." See also: *Midrash Tanna'im* Deut. 15, 10, Hoffman ed., 84 (a philosopher and Rabban Gamaliel).

9 *Niṭpal le* [he responded to] implies a quarrelsome and sometimes even belittling reply to an antagonistic questioner. See, for example, B *Eruvin* 64b (Rabbi Ila'i to a non-Jew); B *Bava Batra* 115b and B *Menaḥot* 65a (R. Johanan ben Zakkai to Sadducees); *Megillat Ta'anit*, ed. Vered Noam (Jerusalem, 2004), 61 (R. Johanan ben Zakkai to a Boethusian). See also Ben Yehuda Dictionary, s.v. טפל, 1910 ("began to speak and argue with"); Krauss, *Paras ṿe-Romi*, 66.

10 Parables ("I shall use a parable to explain what this matter is like") are used in many non-polemical contexts as well, but are especially common in polemical contexts. See: David Stern, "Tafkido shel hamashal be-sifrut Hazal" [The function of the parable in rabbinic literature], *Jerusalem Studies in Hebrew Literature* (1985): 92 n. 5. For additional sources see: *Avot de-Rabbi Nathan*, Recension B, ch. 8, ed. Schechter, 24; *Mekhilta de-Rabbi Ishmael*, *Ba-ḥodesh* VI, 226; B *Shabbat* 108a; B *Bava Batra* 10a; B *Sanhedrin* 91a; B *Avodah Zarah* 54b–55a.

11 In most cases, this term describes the halakhic revolution that Rabbi Akiva introduced by determining that the halakhah is according to the rulings of the School of Hillel, and not the School of Shammai's rulings, which had previously been the norm. See: J. N. Epstein, "Le-mishnat Rabbi Yehuda (le-ḥeqer meqorot ha-mishnah)," *Tarbiẓ* 15 (1943): 5 ("R. Akiva ruled in support of the House of Hillel"); Avraham Goldberg, "Tannaim in the generation of R. Judah the Prince," *Proceedings of the World Congress of Jewish Studies* 6 (1973): 92–94; Shmuel Safrai, "The Decision in Favor of the School of Hillel in Yavneh," *Proceedings of the World Congress of Jewish Studies* 7 (1977): 40–41. See also: M *Ma'aser sheni* 5:8; M *Nedarim* 9:6 (and parallel, T *Nedarim* 5:1, ed. Lieberman, 114); T *Pesaḥim* 1:7, ed. Lieberman, 142; T *Mo'ed qatan* 2:10, ed. Lieberman, 371; ibid. 2:14, 372; *Sifra*, *Metzora*, *Zavim*, vol. 3, 79c (and parallel, B *Shabbat* 64b); B *Qiddushin* 57a (and parallel, B *Bekhorot* 6b); B *Bava Metzia* 62a.

12 Rabbi Jacob Ettlinger noted the link between Rabbi Akiva's two homilies in *Arukh la-ner*, *Niddah* 70b: "And regarding the fact that Rabbi Akiva was uncomfortable with Rabbi Jose the Priest's resolution, we can say *that he is consistent with his own position:* . . . that if one does not repent sins against his fellow,

III RABBI ELEAZAR BEN AZARIAH'S HOMILY

The distinction between transgressions against God and those against other human beings returned to the academy (*beit midrash*) at Yavneh in the following generation, raised by Rabbi Eleazar ben Azariah:

> "For on this day He shall atone for you [to purify you from all of your sins; before the Lord you shall be purified]" (Leviticus 16:30) . . .
>
> For transgressions between man and God, Yom Kippur atones; for transgressions between Man and his fellow, Yom Kippur does not atone, until he conciliates his fellow.
>
> R. Eleazar b. Azariah expounded this as follows: "Of all of your sins before the Lord you shall be purified": For matters between yourself and God, you are pardoned; for matters between yourself and your fellow, you are not pardoned until you conciliate your fellow.[13]

As pertains to Yom Kippur, the distinction between the categories (precepts that apply between Man and God and those that apply between Man and his fellow) is anchored in the biblical text. In his homily, Rabbi Eleazar ben Azariah repunctuates the verse in a way that implicitly creates a category of "transgressions between Man and God": "From all of your sins before the Lord – you shall be purified" (Leviticus 16:30). That is, there is a category of "transgressions before the Lord," for which alone there is atonement and purification. Yom Kippur itself atones only for sins "before the Lord," but not for "matters between yourself and your fellow."

Here too Rabbi Akiva seems not to accept the distinction between two categories, or the homily through which they are derived. The last mishnah in tractate *Yoma* presents a homily by Rabbi Akiva that parallels that of R. Eleazar ben Azariah:

> R. Akiva says, Happy are you, Israel! Before whom are you purified, and who purifies you [of your transgressions]? Your Father Who is in heaven. For it is said, "Then will I sprinkle pure water upon you, and ye shall be pure"; and it is also said, "The ritual bath [*lit.* Hope] of Israel is the Lord"; even as a ritual bath purifies the impure, so does the Holy One, Blessed be He, purify Israel.[14]

Rabbi Akiva is responding to Rabbi Eleazar ben Azariah's homily. According to his reading, the Israelites are purified before God. Rather than reading "from all your sins *before the Lord* – you shall ye be purified," he reads "From *all* your sins – before the Lord you shall be purified."[15] That is, "before the Lord" does not apply to the

then what sinned against God is not forgiven either. Thus partial repentance will be of no benefit, since 'from *all* your sins before God shall you be purified.' So Rabbi Akiva, consistent with his position and not holding such an opinion, is uncomfortable with this answer, and [instead] reconciles the texts: here, before the final judgment, and there after the final judgment." See also below, nn. 17 and 48.

13 *Sifra, Aḥarei mot* 5:8, acc. to MS Vatican 66.

14 M *Yoma* 8:8–10, MS Kaufman.

15 Regarding the argument about how the two homilies punctuate the verse, see: Mordechai Breuer, *Ṭaʿamei ha-miqra be-21 sefarim u-ve-sifre emet* [The cantillation marks in the 21 books and Job-Proverbs -Psalms] (Jerusalem Mikhlalah, 1982), 375; Simcha Kogut, *Ha-Miqra, ben ṭeʿamim le-farshanut*

sins, limiting them to those between human beings and God, but to the quality of purification: the Israelites are purified before God, who purifies them himself;[16] the atonement worked by Yom Kippur and the purification by God apply both to transgressions against God and those against one's fellow human beings.[17]

In this homily, too, Rabbi Akiva seems to take issue with the distinction that Rabbi Eleazar ben Azariah makes between types of transgressions. We may conclude that this distinction is a matter of disagreement among the tanna'im. Rabbi Akiva does not accept it because he believes that transgressions against one's fellow are also transgressions against God.[18] What is the import of his position?

IV A DISAGREEMENT WITH A POLEMICAL BACKGROUND

In this section, we will examine Rabbi Akiva's position in the context of a debate that raged, mainly below the surface, between his notion and various positions taken by early Christian thinkers. Above, with reference to Belloria the convert, we noted the polemical elements in the background of this first appearance of the distinction between the two categories of "Man and God" and "Man and his fellows." In that

[Correlations between biblical accentuation and traditional Jewish exegesis] (Jerusalem, 1996), 64, 125–26. Rabbi Akiva's reading is consistent with the placement of the cantillation marks in the MT. Rabbi Eleazar's reading is according to the Temple tradition. See Maimonides, *Mishneh Torah*, Laws of the Yom Kippur Service, 2:7: "During each of the three confessions, he [the high priest] would intend to complete the Tetragrammaton with those blessing [reciting *barukh shem kevodo le'olam va'ed* – Blessed be His glorious name forever and ever], and he would [then] say to them 'you shall be purified' [completing the verse]." In other words, there was a pause in the reading of the verse by the high priest between "The Lord" and "you shall be purified." The source of this tradition seems to be Jose ben Jose's liturgical poem *Atta konanta*, which the Geonim knew. See: Aaron Mirsky, *Piyyuṭei Yose ben Yose* [Jose ben Jose's liturgical poems] (Jerusalem, 1977), 13–14, 162, 164, 169; *Teshuvot ha-ge'onim ha-ḥadashot* [The new responsa of the Geonim], ed. Simcha Emanuel, § 115, 23. On the other hand, see: Zvi Malachi, *Ha-avodah le-yom ha-kippurim—ofyah, toldoteha, ve-hitpatḥutah ba-shirah ha-ivrit* [The Yom Kippur service: character, history, and development in Hebrew poetry] (Jerusalem, 1974), 19–20.

In addition to the disagreement about the punctuation of the verse, there is also an hermeneutical disagreement about the word "before." According to R. Eleazar ben Azariah, it means "in the eyes of" ("designating the one who calculates or evaluates"), meaning: "your sins before God" are the sins in God's eyes – "between you and Him." According to Rabbi Akiva, however, "before" "designates the object of the activity" or the "direction," and "before God shall you be purified" means that the purification is directed towards God. See: Eliezer Rubinstein, "Lifnei ṣ. sh. [Before ṣ. sh.] *Leshonenu* 40 (1975): 58–64. See also *BDB*, s.v. פנה (Oxford, 1957), 816–17; *KBL*, s.v. פנה (Leiden, 1996), 942; Menachem Zvi Kaddari, *Dictionary of biblical Hebrew*, s.v. פנים (Ramat-Gan, 2006), 865.

16 See Kogut, *Ha-miqra*, 64; Ettlinger, *Arukh la-ner*.

17 Rabbi Akiva's homily deduces general purification from all transgression from two verses: First: "And I shall throw upon you pure water and you shall be purified; I shall purify you *from all your impurities and from all your fetishes*" (Ezek. 36:25). The second: "Hope of Israel! O Lord! All who forsake You shall be put to shame" (Jer. 17:13), which refers to the sins referenced in the preceding verses, including those against God (17:1–3) and those against human beings (v. 11).

18 Other sources preserve a different tradition about Rabbi Akiva's position. See Numbers Rabbah, 11:7, MS Munich 97. Cf.: Midrash Hagadol, Numbers 6:26, ed. Z. M. Rabinowitz (Jerusalem, 1997), 95.

story, we identified linguistic and literary features relevant to a polemic, but the matter at dispute is not obvious.

Belloria's question seems to be testing the limits of divine forgiveness, and, thus, of divine justice. Rabbi Jose the Priest's answer may be taken as tactical and superficial: transgressions between a man and his fellow do not fall under the purview of divine justice and fall into the exclusive jurisdiction of human instances. As in the parable, a debt to one's fellow does not concern the king.[19] Rabbi Jose the Priest's proposal evidently satisfied the second generation at Yavneh. Later, however, Rabbi Akiva rejected it by asserting that divine judgment applies also to transgressions between Man and his fellow, which, like those between man and God, can be pardoned only until the final verdict has been rendered.

The tannaitic discussion centers on the legal and religious status of the norms of personal conduct. A similar question seems to have been at the center of a polemic between Rabbi Akiva and early Christianity.

In Jerusalem, Jesus responds to a question posed by one of the Pharisee "experts in the law": "Which is the great commandment in the law [Torah]?"[20] He replies:

> And he said to him, "You shall love the Lord your God with all your heart, and with all your soul, and with all your mind. This is the great and first commandment. And a second is like it, You shall love your neighbor as yourself. On these two commandments depend all the law and the prophets" (Matthew 22:34–40).[21]

A few decades later, Rabbi Akiva replied to the same question in a completely different way (*Sifra, Qedoshim* II 4:12):

> "'And you shall love your fellow as yourself" (Leviticus 19:18)—Rabbi Akiva says: This is a great rule in the Torah." Ben Azzai says: "This is the book of the genealogy of Man [, on the day God created Man, He made him in the divine image]" (Genesis 5:1) is an even greater rule than that.[22]

19 Compare with n. 6 above.

20 Jesus's words were originally a "great rule in the Torah," mistranslated into Greek as "a great commandment." See David Flusser, "The Ten Commandments and the New Testament," in *'Aśeret ha-dibberot bi-re'i ha-dorot* [The Ten Commandments through the generations], ed. B. Z. Segal (Jerusalem, 1986), 180; Serge Ruzer, "Ṣemed ha-ṣivvuyim 've-ahavta' bi-vrit ha-ḥadashah u-ve-sereh ha-yaḥad" [The double love precept in the New Testament and in the Rule of the Congregation], *Tarbiẓ* 71 (2002): 354, n. 5.

21 Similarly in Mark 12:28–31 and Luke 10:25–28. See Victor Paul Furnish, *The Love Command in the New Testament* (London, 1972), 33–34; Victor Paul Furnish, "Love of Neighbor in the New Testament," *Journal of Religious Ethics* 10 (1982): 327–34. See also: Ruzer, ibid.

22 *Sifra, Qedoshim* 2:4.12, MS Vatican 31. It is uncertain whether the core of the debate between Ben Azzai and Rabbi Akiva is exegetical or theological. If the latter, Ben Azzai sees loving one's fellow as a social and moral obligation ("the genealogy of Man"), whereas Rabbi Akiva sees it as also a religious obligation (see immediately below). If the former, Ben Azzai too holds that loving one's fellow is a religious obligation and is building mainly on the end of the verse: "This is the book of the genealogy of Man … *in God's image made He him*" (Gen. 5:1). See Rabbi Joseph Saul Nathansohn, *Ziyyon vi-yrushalayim*, on *J Nedarim* 9:4 (Vilna: 1925/6), 30b.

Rabbi Akiva, unlike Jesus,[23] focuses on a single golden rule – love your fellow.[24] Of course, we should not conclude from this that Rabbi Akiva discarded the precept to love God; he also ruled, based on the verse, "And you shall love the Lord your God with all your might" (Deuteronomy 6:5), that this applies "even if He takes your life."[25] It appears, rather, that Rabbi Akiva believed that the obligations to love one's fellow and love God are interlinked, just as the verse itself links the two domains of relationships: "And you shall love your fellow as yourself, *I am the Lord*" (Leviticus 19:18).[26] In other words, the declaration "I am the Lord" follows the commandment to love one's fellow in order to teach that loving one's fellow is not only a human and social matter but in fact derived from the obligation to honor God, because God made humans in the divine image.[27]

23 Jesus's view about the two rules was accepted in the Jewish world of the late Second Temple period, earlier echoes of it can be found at least since *Jubilees*. See George Foot Moore, *Judaism in the First Centuries of the Christian Era*, II (Cambridge, MA, 1955), 86; below, n. 50; David Flusser, *'Aśeret ha-dibberot*, 168–69, 172–74 at nn. 21–27, and 177 at nn. 35–36 (David Flusser, *Yahadut bayit sheni, ḥakhameha ve-sifrutah* [Second Temple Judaism, its sages and literature] (Jerusalem, 2002), 164–65, 168–69, 173; Ruzer, "Ve-ahavta," 362–65. Flusser holds that some talmudic sages supported the demand for double love (of God and of fellow). See David Flusser, "A New Sensitivity in Judaism and the Christian Message," *Harvard Theological Review* 61 (1968): 112–13. However, Flusser, *'Aśeret ha-dibberot*, at n. 28, holds that there is no explicit expression of this position in talmudic literature, in deference to Rabbi Akiva's authority.

For another discussion about similar polemic between R. Akiva and early Christianity, see Appendix B.

24 M. Weinfeld, "Julius Wellhausen's Understanding of the Law of Ancient Israel and Its Fallacies," *Shnaton: An Annual for Biblical and Ancient Near Eastern Studies* 4 (1980): 69: "The two elements – the love of God and the love of his fellow, were merged by R. Akiva, the most prominent representative of the Pharisees" (as opposed to the Christian separation between the two). It appears that Rabbi Akiva's position is based on Hillel's statement in B *Shabbat* 31a (MS Oxford 366): "On condition that you teach me the entire Torah. . . . He said to him: that which is hateful to you, do not do to your fellow." See Theodor's note in *Genesis Rabbah with Minhat Yehudah*, J. Theodor and Hanoch Albeck, eds. (Jerusalem, 1965), 237; Israel Abrahams, *Studies in Pharisaism and the Gospels* (New York, 1967), 21–24.

25 J *Berakhot* 9:5 [14b], ed. Academy of the Hebrew Language, 75, and B *Berakhot* 61b (the words of Rabbi Akiva himself); *Sifre*, Deuteronomy 32, ed. Finkelstein, 55 (the words of Rabbi Eliezer, his teacher). See also: Abrahams, *Pharisaism*, 19.

26 Baruch J. Schwartz, *T°rat ha-qedushah: iyyunim ba-ḥuqqah ha-k°hanit she-ba-T°rah* [The holiness legislation: studies in the Priestly Code] (Jerusalem, 1999), 323: "The repetition of the formula 'I am the Lord' . . . indicates . . . that [the author] does not see the precepts between Man and his fellow as an independent category but rather as precepts between Man and God"; Martin Buber, *Darko shel Mikra: 'iyunim bi-defuse-signon ba-Tanakh* [The way of Scripture: studies in the Hebrew Bible's stylistic patterns] (Jerusalem, 1978), 104: "What we have here is not a moral command but a faith-related command. . . . Inasmuch as human beings are Mine, I command you in this matter." For an opposite formulation, see Flusser, *'Aśeret ha-dibberot*, 178: "We may assume that according to this anthropocentric approach . . . the first rule, which is love of God, is seen as included in the overall rule of love for one's fellow." Such a reading is common in Kabbalah and Hasidism. See, e.g., Haim Vital, *Liqquṭei Torah nevi'im u-ketuvim, Qedoshim* (Tel Aviv, 1972/3), 190 (in the name of R. Isaac Luria); *Toledot Ya'akov Yosef*, Qedoshim (Medzhybozh, 1816/7, 73a); *Qedushat Levi ha-shalem*, II (Jerusalem, 1957/8), 414; *Sefat Emet*, Korach, 5656.

27 So too the early-fourth century church father Lactantius: "The very same thing you granted to Man is granted to God, because Man is God's image." See: Lactantius, "Divine Institutes" 6.10, in *The Divine*

V THE TWO TABLETS

The polemic between some of the tanna'im and early Christianity about the relationship between one's duties to God and those to other people can be examined from an additional perspective: the arrangement of the Ten Commandments on the two Tablets of the Law.

A *The Division*

The notion that the Ten Commandments were divided between the two Tablets of the Law appears frequently in medieval Jewish philosophy and biblical commentaries.[28] The idea is that the Ten Commandments were divided equally: the first five, commandments "between Man and God," were written on one tablet, and the second five, commandments "between Man and his fellow," were written on the second tablet. Various considerations seem to lie behind this separation, both practical and textual.

Let us begin with the practical considerations. In the ancient Near East, most texts were written on a single tablet. Hence breaking up a rather short text onto two tablets may well indicate some internal distinction between the two parts, and the division of the commandments between the tablets might be the result of this distinction.[29] Moreover, the Decalogue is a fundamental and important text, one that should be committed to memory. The division into two sets of five is convenient for this purpose, because it is common to use the fingers to tally memorized items, and two sets of five corresponds to the fingers on each hand.[30]

Institutes: Books I–VII, Trans., Mary Francis McDonald (Washington, DC, 1964), 417. See also Abrahams, *Pharisaism*, 18, 20.

It is possible that this is how Rabbi Tanhuma interpreted Rabbi Akiva's words. See *Genesis Rabbah* 24:5, ed. Theodor and Albeck, 237: "Rabbi Akiva said: 'Love your neighbor as yourself' is the greater rule; lest you say 'since I have been debased, let my fellow be debased.' Rabbi Tanhum said: If you have done so, know whom you are debasing: 'In God's image made He him.'" It is unclear whether this is an interpretation of or addition to Rabbi Akiva's statement. It could even be a contrary position, similarly to the disagreement between Rabbi Akiva and Ben Azzai (above, n. 22): Rabbi Akiva stresses the human and social aspect, "like you": because I have been debased, may my fellow also be debased; whereas Rabbi Tanhuma stresses the religious aspect: it is God who is debased.

28 See, e.g., Ibn Ezra, Nahmanides, and Abravanel (below, nn. 32, 34); David Kimhi on Isa. 5:12; Joseph Albo, *Sefer ha-Iqqarim*, 3:26.

29 James L. Kugel, *The Bible as It Was* (Cambridge, MA, 1997), 381.

30 See Eduard Nielsen, *The Ten Commandments in New Perspective: A Traditio-Historical Approach*, trans. David J. Bourke (Naperville, IL, 1968), 34. This idea was first proposed by Rabbi Joseph ben David of Saragossa, a student of Rabbi Nissim of Gerona, in his commentary on the Torah, ed. Feldman (Jerusalem, 1973, 171); and, after him, Moshe ben Simeon of Frankfurt (eighteenth century) in his commentary on the *Mekhilta* (below, n. 49), *Zeh yenaḥamenu* (Amsterdam, 1712, 48b), and nineteenth–century commentators on the midrash – R. Joseph Zundel and Rabbi Zev Wolf Einhorn, on *Song Rabbah* 5:12. See also: Edward L. Greenstein, "The Rhetoric of the Ten Commandments," in *The Decalogue in Jewish and Christian Tradition*, Henning Graf Reventlow and Yair Hoffman, eds., (New York, 2011), 6, n. 22. A hint to this effect is found in the *Mekhilta* (below, n. 46), which

There are also textual considerations. Several literary and philological elements distinguish the first five commandments from the second five. Commandments six through ten (as found in Deuteronomy 5:17–18) are linked by the conjunctive *vav*, whereas the first five commandments are separate statements.[31] In addition to this syntactic difference, there are a number of literary differences as well. God's name appears (either as *Elohim* or as the Tetragrammaton) in each of the first five commandments, but never in the second five.[32] All those in the first group are lengthy and include their rationales and in some cases the reward or sanction for their observance or violation; whereas the second five are short and laconic,[33] absolute prohibitions with no explanation or stated reward.[34]

B *Philo: The Roots of the Idea*

Given these reasons – both the practical and the textual – the bipartite division of the commandments and the corollary distribution between the two tablets appear quite logical. However, the first explicit mention of this division seems to be by Philo of Alexandria, in his treatise on the Ten Commandments:[35]

> He divided the ten into two sets of five which He engraved on two Tables. … The superior set of five. … Thus one set of enactments begins with God the Father and

compares the Tablets of the Law to hands, based on the verse "His hands are rods of gold, studded with beryl" (Song of Songs 5:14). See also: *Numbers Rabbah* 13:15; *Song Rabbah* 5:14; *Tanḥuma, Eqev*, 9.

31 Moshe Weinfeld, *'Aśeret ha-dibberot u-qeri'at shema': gilguleihen shel haṣharot emunah* (Tel Aviv, 2001), 39.

32 *Pesiqta rabbati* 21, MS Parma 3122, ed. Ish Shalom, 99: "Adrianus (may his bones be ground) asked Rabbi Joshua ben Hananiah. He said to him: … The first ten [*sic*!] precepts that the Holy [One blessed be He] gave, His name is found in them. … But the latter five precepts … His name is not found in them"; Abraham Ibn Ezra, short commentary on Exodus 20:1: "Therefore, the [divine] name is mentioned in these five precepts (whereas there is no [divine] name in the other five), because these five are between Man and the Creator"; Abravanel on Exodus 20 (eighth question) and Deut. 5:6; Weinfeld, *'Aśeret ha-dibberot*, 86.

33 The second tablet contains precepts that are obligations of natural morality and based on the principle of reciprocity, so they require no rationale. By contrast, the precepts on the first tablet are religious and spiritual obligations, and therefore require explanation and persuasion. See Moshe Weinfeld, *The Anchor Bible, Deuteronomy 1–11* (New York, 1991), 245; Greenstein, "The Rhetoric of the Ten Commandments," 7.

34 Nahmanides on Ex. 20:13: "And here, [He] has mentioned the reward for some of the commandments, and not for others, such as in the second commandment 'a zealous God,' in the third 'for [the Lord] will not clear,' in the fifth 'so that [your days] last long'; whereas in the others He did not mention a punishment or reward. And this is because the last five commandments are for the benefit of Man, and their reward accompanies them."

35 Philo seems to have been influenced by the common distinction between "divine law" and "human law" that emerged from classical Greek philosophy and literature, going back to the pre-Socratics, and later in the Stoa. See: Christine Elizabeth Hayes, *What's Divine about Divine Law? Early Perspectives* (Princeton, 2015), 55–56 (See also her reference to Martens, inn. 3); E. E. Halevi, *'Erkhei ha-aggadah ṿeha-halakhah le-or meqorot yevaniyim ṿe-laṭiniyim* [The principles of aggadah and halakhah in light of Greek and Latin sources], I (Tel Aviv, 1979), 210–11 and n. 2. A similar distinction exists in Roman law. See above, n. 6.

> Maker of all, and ends with parents who copy His nature by begetting particular persons.[36]
>
> . . . the fifth commandment on the honour due to parents . . . He placed on the border-line between the two sets of five; it is the last of the first set in which the most sacred injunctions are given and it adjoins the second set which contains the duties of man to man.[37]

Philo's division of the commandments between the two tablets derived from his fundamental view of both the tablets and the Torah precepts in general. He believed that the tablets, and the Ten Commandments written on them, included all the precepts,[38] which were divided into two main branches or main headings:

> But among the vast number of particular truths and principles there studied, there stand out practically high above the others two main heads: one of duty to God as shewn by piety and holiness, one of duty to men as shewn by humanity and justice . . .[39]

Thus the bipartite division of the commandments, which, for Philo, include all the precepts, reflects the two categories of precepts: the first tablet deals with "duty to God," and the second with "duty to men."

C *The Christian World*

Philo's thesis has echoes in the Christian world. The idea of the distinction between the two tablets can be found as early as Paul's Epistle to the Romans, at least partially and indirectly.[40]

> Owe no one anything, except to love one another; for he who loves his neighbor has fulfilled the law. The commandments, "You shall not commit adultery, You shall not kill, You shall not steal, You shall not covet," and any other commandment, are summed up in this sentence, "You shall love your neighbor as yourself." Love does no wrong to a neighbor; therefore love is the fulfilling of the law.[41]

36 Philo, "De Decalogo" #50, in *Philo VII*, trans. F. H. Colson (LCL, 1984), 31.

37 Ibid., #106, 61. See: Yehoshua Amir, "Aśeret ha-dibberot al-pi Filon me-aleksandria," in Segal, *'Aśeret ha-dibberot*, 122; Flusser, "Aseret ha-dibberot," 180; Moshe Greenberg, "The Decalogue Tradition Critically Examined," in *Studies in the Bible and Jewish Thought* (Philadelphia, 1995), 300.

38 Philo, *De Decalogo*, #154; ibid., #19. See also: Suzanne Daniel-Nataf, introduction to *De Decalogo*, in Philo, *Ketavim* [Writings] II (Jerusalem, 1991), 185–86 [Hebrew]; Harry Austryn Wolfson, *Philo; Foundations of Religious Philosophy in Judaism, Christianity, and Islam* II (Cambridge, MA, 1968 [1947], 181–82, 201–02; See also: ibid., I, 128; II, 304–05. Regarding the talmudic sages' position on this matter, see Efraim Elimelech Urbach, *The Sages, their Concepts and Beliefs*, trans. Israel Abrahams (Jerusalem, 1975), 844–47.

39 Philo, *De Specialibus Legibus II*, #63. See also Wolfson, *Philo*, II: 395.

40 For a discussion of Philo's possible influence on Paul's attitude towards the Ten Commandments, see: Gottfried Nebe, "The Decalogue in Paul, Especially in His Letter to the Romans," in *The Decalogue in Jewish and Christian Tradition*, 58–60. For other parallels between Philo's and Paul's interpretations of the Ten Commandments, see ibid., 64–65.

41 Romans 13:8–10. See, similarly, Mark 10:19; Matthew 5: 21, 27, 43. The idea of emphasizing the precepts between man and his fellow (the second tablet) as the main part of the Torah comes from

Paul writes that the second five commandments are summed up by the core rule of loving one's neighbor as one's self. While he does not explicitly mention Jesus's "double core rule" of loving God and loving one's fellow, it is possible that he hints at it when he mentions "any other commandment" and "the law." If so, the first five commandments are summed up by the other commandment to love – "You shall love the Lord your God."[42]

D *The Talmudic Literature*

We have seen that the idea of a distinction between the first five and the second five commandments, and their separate inscription on the two Tablets of the Law, originated with Philo and was taken over by early Christianity and the Church Fathers. The idea was also common in the rabbinic scholarship of the Middle Ages. Now we must ask how the talmudic sages viewed this idea.

There does not seem to have been a consensus among them on this matter. The majority position opposed the idea of the distinction, holding that all ten commandments were written on each of the two tablets, possibly on both sides. The division into five on each tablet was a minority opinion:

> How were the tablets written?
>
> Rabbi Ḥananiah ben Gamaliel says: "Five on one tablet and five on the other tablet." This is as is written: "And he wrote them on two stone tablets" (Deut. 4:13): five on one tablet and five on the other tablet.
>
> And our rabbis say: "Ten on one tablet and ten on the other tablet." This is as is written (Deut. 4:13): "He declared to you the covenant that He commanded you to observe, the Ten Commandments . . . ": ten on one tablet, and ten on the other tablet.
>
> Rabbi Shimon ben Yohai said: twenty on one tablet and twenty on the other tablet. As is written: "And he wrote them on two stone tablets" (Deut. 4:13): twenty on one tablet and twenty on the other tablet.
>
> Rabbi Simai says: forty on one tablet, and forty on the other tablet. "From this side and from that side they were written" (Ex. 32:15): a tetragon (solid with four written faces).[43]

Jesus, and he repeats it in various contexts. See: Robert M. Grant, "The Decalogue in Early Christianity," *The Harvard Theological Review* 40 (1947), 2–4, 6; below, note 50 (*Didache*).

42 Flusser, "Aseret ha-dibberot," 169–70; Nebe, "The Decalogue in Paul," 58, 80–83. According to Nebe, ibid., 81, it is possible that "all other precepts" refers to the first tablet, and "therefore love is the fulfillment of the entire Torah."

If the idea of the division of the commandments between the two tablets is not stated outright in Romans, though it could be inferred from the text, it does appear, explicitly and systematically, in Augustine. See Appendix C.

43 J *Sheqalim* 6:2 [49d] (ed. Academy of the Hebrew Language), 625; J *Sotah* 8:1 [22d], 940. See also *Exodus Rabbah* 47:6 (according to Jerusalem, NLI, MS ~24 5997): "[This] teaches that the first and latter [commandments] were [different] <the same>. How were the Ten Commandments arranged? Five on one tablet and five on [the other] tablet, according to Rabbi Judah. Rabbi Nehemiah says: Ten on one tablet and ten on [the other] tablet, as is stated 'And when Moses descended from the

For most of the tanna'im, the Ten Commandments constitute a single indivisible unit. Because the Ten Commandments are described as written on two tablets and on both of their sides, they must have been written twice on each tablet, for a total of four times, and possibly even on all four sides of each tablet, for a total of eight times. The minority opinion[44] is not comfortable with the notion of such repetition and consequently divides them between the two tablets, five on each.[45]

We might propose that the disagreement here is relevant to the distinction between the types of precepts – those "between Man and God" and "between a man and his fellow." That is, perhaps the minority opinion divides the commandments into five on each tablet because it supports this distinction. However, examination of Rabbi Hananiah ben Gamaliel's homily in the *Mekhilta* reveals that this is not the case:

> How were the Ten Commandments arranged? Five on the one tablet and five on the other.
>
> On the one tablet was written: "I am the Lord thy God." And opposite it on the other tablet was written: "Thou shalt not murder." This tells that if one sheds blood is accounted to him as though he diminished the divine image. . . .
>
> On the one tablet was written: "Thou shalt have no other god." And opposite it on the other tablet was written: "Thou shalt not commit adultery." This tells that if one worships idols it is accounted to him as though he committed adultery, breaking his covenant with God. . . .
>
> On the one tablet was written: "Thou shalt not take [the Lord your God's name in vain]." And opposite it on the other tablet was written: "Thou shalt not steal." This tells that he who steals will in the end also swear falsely. . . .
>
> On the one tablet was written: "Remember the Sabbath day," and opposite it on the other tablet was written: "Thou shalt not bear [false witness against your fellow]." This tells that one who violates the Sabbath as it were bears witness before He who spoke and the world came into being that He created his world in six days and did not rest on the seventh, and one who keeps the Sabbath bears witness before He who spoke and the world came into being that He created his world in six days and rested on the seventh . . .
>
> On the one tablet was written: "Honor your father [and your mother," and opposite on the other tablet was written: "Thou shalt not covet." This tells that one who covets will end up bearing a son who curses his father and honors those who are not his father.
>
> It was for this that the Ten Commandments were arranged five on one tablet and five on the other.—These are the words of Rabbi Ḥananiah, the son of Gamaliel.

mountain' this were written" (this is mistaken citation, and it *probably should be*: "And Moses [turned and] descended from the mountain, . . . on this side and on that side they were written" [Ex. 32:15]).

44 In addition to Rabbi Hananiah ben Gamaliel, Rabbi Judah also holds this position. See *Exodus Rabbah* 47:6 (previous note).

45 The minority view appears as the consensus position in *Mekhilta de-Rabbi Yishmael* (next note). This was also Philo's position (above, n. 36): "He divided the ten into two sets of five each which He engraved on two tables." See also Josephus, *Antiquities*, III 6.8 (§138): "Within this ark he deposited the two tables, whereon had been recorded the ten commandments, five on each of them, and two and a half on either face" (trans. Thackeray, LCL, vol. 4).

> And the sages say: ten on one tablet, and ten on the other tablet, as it is written: "And these words spoke the Lord to all your congregations … " and "Your two breasts are like two fawns … " (Song of Songs 4:5) and "His hands are rods of gold … " (ibid. 5:14).[46]

For Rabbi Hananiah ben Gamaliel, the division of the commandments between the tablets is actually meant to negate the distinction into two categories; their parallel inscriptions ("On the one tablet was written … and opposite on the other tablet was written … ") emphasized their integration and complementary nature.[47] The complementarity goes both ways. On the one hand, precepts "between a man and his fellow" are also "between Man and God." Murder is not only a transgression between human beings but also between humans and God, inasmuch as one who spills blood has also assaulted God's image;[48] similarly, theft may lead to false oaths. On the other hand, precepts "between Man and God" are linked to those "between a man and his fellow": an idolater is like an adulterer, and one who observes or violates Shabbat is like a witness standing before the judges.[49]

46 *Mekhilta de-Rabbi Yishmael, ba-Ḥodesh* 8, trans. Lauterbach, 731.

47 It is possible that Rabbi Hananiah's homily is in agreement with Sages' idea that the two tablets were identical ("twins of a gazelle," Song 4:5). See Tamar Kadari, "'Tokho raṣuf ahavah': al ha-Torah ke-ra'ayah bi-derashot tanna'im le-shir ha-shirim" ["'Within It Was Decked With Love': The Torah as the Bride in Tannaitic Exegesis on Song of Songs], *Tarbiẓ* 71(3/4) (2002): 401. The word כנגד, *keneged*" [which Lauterbach translated as "opposite it"] can be applied physically to the writing on the tablets, meaning the sixth commandment was written on the same line as and opposite the first commandment, the seventh opposite the second, and so on. But it can also be interpreted symbolically as referring to the content of the commandments, meaning that they correspond, matching and complementing each other. This is the interpretation of the *Mekhilta, Pesiqta Rabbati* 21 (Shklov 1806), 34c: "The five first Commandments opposite (*keneged*) the last [five]." Later it states that the Ten Commandments were corresponding to (*keneged*) the ten utterances with which the world was created, or corresponding to (*keneged*) the Ten Plagues. For the two senses of *keneged*, see: Shlomo Naeh, "'Ezer ke-negdo,' 'keneged ha-mashḥitim'" [Forgotten Meanings and a Lost Proverb], *Leshonenu* 59(2) (1996): 108–11 (which shows how *keneged* can be both a positional and a comparative preposition).

48 Yair Lorberbaum, "'Al reṣaḥ, 'onesh mavet, ve-ha-adam be-ṣelem Elohim be-sifrut Ḥazal" [On murder, capital punishment, and man's creation in the divine image in talmudic literature], *Pelilim* 7 (1998), 239–42, 253–56. Lorberbaum (241) proposes that the *Mekhilta*'s homily is based on Rabbi Akiva's midrash (*Genesis Rabbah* 34:9, ed. Theodor-Albeck, 326): "Anyone who spills blood is considered to have reduced the [divine] image. Why? Because 'He who spills the blood of man, etc. [by man shall his blood be spilled, because in His image did God make man]' (Gen. 9:6)." The identification of human blood and the divine image "blurs the semantic barrier between God and Man, thus blurring the distinction between precepts between Man and God and precepts between Man and his fellow." See also: Yair Lorberbaum, *Ṣelem Elohim: halakhah ve-aggadah* [The divine image: halakhah and aggadah] (Jerusalem and Tel Aviv, 2004), 301–02, 354–58. Rabbi Akiva's and the *Mekhilta*'s homilies are compatible with Rabbi Akiva's rejection of any distinction between types of precepts. See above, at nn. 12 and 17.

49 Moshe Greenberg, "Mesoret 'aśeret ha-dibberot bi-re'i ha-biqqoret" [The Ten Commandments tradition in light of criticism], in: *'Aśeret* ha-dibberot *bi-re'i ha-dorot*, 90: "The homily … hints at the reciprocal relationship between the precepts between Man and God and those between Man and his fellow. And the switch of the starting point of each statement from one set of five to the other one, emphasizes the equal value of the two sets"; *Zeh yenaḥamenu* (above, n. 30): "That these were opposite those, so one who violates [a precept] on this side is deemed to have violated [a precept] n the other side."

We conclude that the tanna'im rejected the notion that the Decalogue has two subsets – commandments "between Man and God" and those "between Man and his fellow." First, the idea of such a division has no explicit source in talmudic literature.[50] Second, in the sources that do discuss the arrangement of the Ten Commandments on the two tablets, the majority opinion rejects the idea and holds that all ten were written as a single unit. Third, the minority opinion, which posits a physical division of the Ten Commandments onto two separate tablets, believes that this division was meant to lead to an integrated reading. This does not accord with the idea that the Decalogue falls into two subsets and instead supports a harmonization of the different categories of commandments.[51]

50 Urbach notes an early midrashic source that includes the "double love" homily, followed by a detailed list of the second five commandments with regard to the obligation to love one's fellow. This would seem to support the idea of separation. See: *Sefer Pitron Torah* [The book of the solution of the Torah], ed. Efraim Elimelech Urbach (Jerusalem, 1978), 79–80 (*Sefer Pitron Torah*, ed. Malachi Beit-Arié, facsimile of MS Heb. 40 5767, 63–64): "As the sages said: *all the precepts in the Torah* depend on two verses: the first, '*And you shall love the Lord your God*' (Deut. 6:5); the second, '*And you shall love your fellow as yourself*' (Lev. 19:18); that two hundred forty-eight positive precepts all depend on 'and you shall love the Lord your God, etc.'. . .. and the negative precepts depend on 'And you shall love your fellow as yourself.'. . .'*And you shall love your fellow as yourself*' is the epitome of all the negative precepts stated in regards to a human being. . . . *Thou shalt not take the Lord's name in vain* and *thou shalt not murder* and *thou shalt not commit adultery*, and *thou shalt not steal* and *thou shalt not bear* [false witness] and *thou shalt not covet*." Urbach (*Pitron Torah*, ibid) conjectures that "the statement comes from an early source." But it does not appear to come from the talmudic sages, as Urbach himself says elsewhere. See Efraim Elimelech Urbach, "Ma'amadam shel 'aśeret ha-dibberot ba-'avodah u-va-tefillah" [The status of the Ten Commandments in the Temple service and in prayer], in *'Aśeret ha-dibberot bi-re'i ha-dorot*, 136 ("a parallel midrash, though from a later source"). See also above, n. 23.

The source may be the *Didache*, a Jewish-Christian text. See Flusser, *Yahadut u-meqorot ha-naṣrut* [Judaism and the sources of Christianity] (Tel Aviv, 1969), 235–36, 244–47. The regnant position dates the text to the second half of the first century CE. See Huub van de Sandt and David Flusser, *The Didache: Its Jewish Sources and its Place in Early Judaism and Christianity* (Minneapolis: Fortress Press, 2002), 48–49. Indeed, in the *Didache* there is a parallel to the homily in *Pitron Torah*: "There are two ways, one of life and one of death… The way of life, then, is this: First, you shall love God who made you; second, your neighbour as yourself; and all things whatsoever you would should not occur to you, do not also do to another." See *The Didache*, 1:1–2, ed. Kurt Niederwimmer (Minneapolis, 1988), 59–77. Subsequent to the "double love" homily, a detailed list of the commandments on the second tablet appears later in the *Didache* (2:2–7). See Sandt and Flusser, *The Didache*, 56; and, in greater detail, Huub van de Sandt, "Essentials of Ethics in Matthew and the Didache: A Comparison at a Conceptual and Practical Level," in *Early Christian Ethics in Interaction with Jewish and Greco-Roman Contexts*, eds. Jan Willem van Henten and Joseph Verheyden (Leiden, 2013), 245–51. However, as we saw above (around n. 41), such a model existed in early Christianity. Hence it stands to reason that the passage in question is Christian and not by the talmudic sages. See Philip S. Alexander, "Jesus and the Golden Rule," in *Hillel and Jesus: Comparisons of Two Major Religious Leaders*, eds. James H. Charlesworth and Loren L. Johns (Minneapolis: Fortress Press, 1997), 162–64. Some hold that the passage is a synthesis of Jewish and Christian sources. See Grant, "The Decalogue in Early Christianity," 9. This seems likely, because the text was influenced by various sources – Jewish, sectarian, and Christian (see Sandt and Flusser, *The Didache*, 56–57, 59, and 70–80).

51 The harmonization is also expressed in the parallel that the talmudic sages drew between the first two sections of the *Shema* and the Ten Commandments. See J *Berakhot* 1:4 [3c] (p. 9). This parallel

It appears, then, that a widespread position of the talmudic sages rejects the idea of a division of the precepts into those "between Man and his God" and those "between Man and his fellow." All the tanna'im oppose the early Christianity approach that maintained this division. This may support the possibility that the issue was an item of dispute between Jews and Christians.

VI FINAL THOUGHTS

Above we discussed the relationship between the two "wings" of halakhah – the "religious" and the "sociolegal" – in the rabbinic literature, and against the background of the parallel Jewish-Christian debate. We chose to focus on those aspects that we see as primary, from a philological-historical approach to the rabbinic literature. However, there are clearly other aspects that may affect the question of the relationship between the two wings. Here, briefly, are three of them:

A. Legal theory aspect: One of the basic tools used to organize a scientific system is taxonomy.[52] Legal taxonomy sorts and organizes the law, dividing it into families, branches, groups, etc. Three types of legal taxonomy can be differentiated:[53]
   (1) Formal taxonomy classifies and explains law from a theoretical perspective, and has no normative or practical ambitions.[54]
   (2) Functional taxonomy defines the framework of the dispute between litigants and helps resolve them. This mode of organization may have a normative influence, although it is indirect and focused on the particular case and its outcome.
   (3) Rational taxonomy is the most activist of the three. It offers a normative explanation and meaning, and thus influences decision-makers in both the legislature and the judiciary.

   The distinction between the types of precepts might be made in any of these taxonomies. In the tannaitic literature it appears in the attempt to

effectively paces all the precepts under the joint title of the two sections: the precept to love God. See: Abrahams, *Pharisaism*, 28; Aharon Oppenheimer, "Removing the Decalogue from the *Shema* and Phylacteries: the Historical Implications," in *The Decalogue in Jewish and Christian Tradition*, 99–100. See also Urbach, "'Áśeret ha-dibberot," 133. He asserts that the Jewish-Christian debate about the recitation of the Ten Commandments during prayer stemmed from the early Christian emphasis on the interpersonal precepts. See above, at nn. 41 and 42. This is why, the talmudic sages dropped the recitation of the Ten Commandments from the liturgy and included them under the rubric of the precept to love God, including those that clearly apply among human beings.

52 On taxonomy as a phenomenon from a philosophical perspective, see M. Härlin and P. Sundberg, "Taxonomy and Philosophy of Names," *Biology and Philosophy* 13 (1998): 233–35.

53 Emily Sherwin, "Legal Taxonomy," *Legal Theory* 15 (2009): 25–54.

54 Formal taxonomy has another goal: mapping law in order to transfer information from one legal system to another. Such a method is especially common in comparative law. See Ugo Mattei, "Three Patterns of Law: Taxonomy and Change in the World's Legal Systems," *The American Journal of Comparative Law* 45 (1997): 6.

resolve a theological and exegetical problem, evidently in the context of the Jewish-Christian polemic. This distinction might therefore be formal, and perhaps even functional. However, it is doubtful whether it also claims to define a general theological and legal position.

B. The epistemological aspect: The human mind may relate to different and contradictory factors within a single system in two polar ways. One of them is dichotomous and dualistic.[55] Here reality is seen as separate entities: the metaphysical is distinct from the physical, and the divine from the natural. Therefore, according to this method, in a normative system there will be a separation between the legal wing and the religious wing.

Another method proposes a harmonious and complementary approach.[56] It sees disparate and even contradictory phenomena as different and complementary facets of a single harmonious entity.[57] Torah law completes what is missing in natural morality and human law, and views civil law as simultaneously religious law. In this way, the precepts "between man and his fellow" may also be an aspect of "between man and God."[58]

C. The religious aspect: Ernst Akiva Simon distinguished two paradigms of religion: "Catholic" and "Protestant." The Catholic pattern is total: religion is involved in every aspect of life; and just as God is present everywhere and everything is subject to His authority, so too all normative systems are subordinate to religion. The Protestant paradigm is "softer." Here religion is flexible

55 Dualism has many types and applies to many domains. On theistic dualism (the Creator's relationship with Creation), see Leroy Rouner, "Dualism," *The Westminster Dictionary of Christian Theology* (London, 2002), 166. On dualism in the context of the psychophysical problem (the relationship between mind and body), see Howard Robinson, "Dualism," *The Stanford Encyclopedia of Philosophy*, ed. Edward N. Zalta, available at: https://plato.stanford.edu/entries/dualism/; W. D. Hart, "Dualism," in *A Companion to the Philosophy of Mind*, ed. Samuel Guttenplan (Oxford, 1996), 265–68.

56 The complementary approach describes, in very domains of knowledge, complementary relations between causes that are different or opposing in quantum physics, in the wake of Niels Bohr, see: Simon Saunders, "Complementarity and Scientific Rationality," *Foundations of Physics* 35 (2005): 417–47; Niels Bohr, "Causality and Complementarity: Supplementary Papers," in *Philosophical Writings of Niels Bohr*, eds. Jan Faye and Henry J. Folse, vol. IV (Woodbridge, 1998), 164–69. In the social sciences (complementarianism: men and women as complementary sexes), see, e.g., Prudence Allen, "Man-Woman Complementarity: the Catholic Inspiration," *Logos* 9 (2006): 87–105 (the Catholic stance); online at www.laity.va/content/dam/laici/documenti/donna/filosofia/english/man-woman-complementary-the-catholic-inspiration.pdf. In tort law, see Izhak Englard, "The Idea of Complementarity as a Philosophical Basis for Pluralism in Tort Law," in *Philosophical Foundations of Tort Law*, ed. David G. Owen (Oxford, 1995), 183–95.

57 In the talmudic corpus, the dominant position about the mind-body problem is monistic and harmonizing. See Julius Guttmann, *The Philosophy of Judaism: The History of Jewish Philosophy from Biblical Times to Franz Rosenzweig*, trans. David W. Silverman (Northvale, NJ, 1988), 51–52; Urbach, *The Sages* [Heb.], 190–98. See also Nissan Rubin, *Qeṣ ha-ḥayyim: ṭiqsei qevurah bimqorot ḥazal* (Tel Aviv, 1997), 54–64; Lorberbaum, *Ṣelem Elohim*, 192–93, n. 81.

58 On the connection between the normative separation and the overall confrontation between dualism and harmonism, see my "Commandments between Man and God and between Man and His Fellow – Between Separation and Completion: A Medieval Debate" (unpublished).

and liberal regarding aspects of life that are not clearly religious and grants them autonomy.[59]

The "Catholic" paradigm will not acknowledge a distinction between precepts that are between man and God and precepts that are between man and his fellow. The "Protestant" paradigm can do so. About a century ago there was a sharp debate between representatives of the two modes, with regard to the application of halakhah as a legal system in a modern Jewish state.[60] The secular wing affiliated with the Hebrew Law Society called for a separation between "religious law" and "civil law." The religious Zionist wing opposed this vehemently:

> If for other peoples, religion and state are two domains, ... for the Jewish people both of them, religion and state, are bound together and connected, and anyone who would separate them is cursing the people's soul. Our Torah contains not only precepts between man and God, but also precepts between man and his fellow and between man and his country ...[61]

The ideas presented in this chapter may support the latter position. The controversy hovers above the question of the separation that took place in its infancy during the second and third generations in Yavne. A reexamination of the statements by the tanna'im, against the background of the Jewish-Christian debate of those years, may lead to the conclusion that the rabbinic literature tends to reject the distinction and to combine the precepts between man and his fellow with those between man and God.

APPENDIX A (NOTE 6): BETWEEN *IUS DIVINUM* AND *IUS HUMANUM* IN ROMAN LAW

Roman law distinguishes religious law from secular law. It recognizes both *fas* (divine law or sacred law) and *ius* (human law). According to the definition by Servius Sulpicius Rufus, "*fas* relates to religion, and *iura* to humans" ("Ad religionem fas, ad homines iura pertinent").[62]

59 Akibah Ernst Simon, *Ha'im od yehudim anaḥnu?* (Jerusalem, 1982). For a recent discussion of Simon's stance, see Avi Sagi, "Ha'im od yehudim anaḥnu," in *Hamishim le-arba'im ushemoneh*, ed. Adi Ophir (Jerusalem; Tel Aviv, 1999), 79–87.

60 For an extensive discussion, see Amihai Radzyner, "Hamishpaṭ ha'ivri bein 'le'umi' le-'dati': ha-dilema shel ha-tenu'ah ha-datit-le'umit," *Meḥqerei Mishpat* 26 (2010): 110–18.

61 Yehuda Leib Hakohen Fishman, "Ha-ṣiyonut ha-datit ṿe-hitpatḥutah," *Ezkerah* 5 (1936): 121. For a critique of the "catholic" stance of religious Zionism, see Sagi, "Ha'im od yehudim anaḥnu." See also Avi Sagi, "*Ṣiyonut datit: bein segirut liftiḥut*," in *Yahadut pnim va-ḥuṣ: di'alog bein olamot*, eds. A. Sagi, D. Schwartz and Y. Stern (Jerusalem, 2000), 124.

62 See Servius, *In Vergili Georgica*, 1.269. For different senses of this distinction, see: Leon ter Beek, Divine Law and the Penalty of *Sacer Esto* in Early Rome," in *Law and Religion in the Roman Republic*, ed. Olga Tellegen-Couperus (Leiden, 2012), 11–12; Watson, *The State, Law, and Religion* (see above n. 6), 94, n. 1. See also Watson, ibid., 86.

For a parallel distinction between the objects of religious law (*ius divinum*) and human/secular law (*ius humanum*), see Gaius, *Institutiones* 2.2–2.8. And at length, James Rives, "Control of the Sacred in

The roots of this distinction is in the Twelve Tablets. There, in the first foundations of Roman law, we encounter a paradox: law is strictly secular in nature, even though intended for an especially religious society.[63] The background here is sociopolitical: in the early fifth century BCE, in the wake of a severe socioeconomic crisis, tension emerged between the ruling elite (the Patricians) and the masses (the Plebeians). The Plebeians organized themselves in various political groups and demanded a written code to regulate the relations between the citizen and the state.[64] The written law – the Twelve Tablets – was enacted for the Plebeians; but religious laws were removed from it, because that applied to the Patrician religious establishment.[65] Thus the sociopolitical tensions created a paradox of legal theory and a normative tension between the "religious" and the "legal."[66]

The gulf in Roman law between "divine" law and the "law" deepens in the wake of the Christian influence on Roman law.[67] This influence is already discussed in the second half of the fourth century, in the *Liber quaestionum* attributed to Ambrosiaster.[68] In various passages the author describes Paul's separation of human law from divine law and the adoption of this Pauline idea by Roman law.[69]

APPENDIX B (NOTE 23): RABBI AKIVA AND EARLY CHRISTIANITY – ANOTHER POLEMIC

It is possible that Rabbi Akiva's integration of love for one's fellow and love for God is at the heart of another polemic between him and early Christianity:

> Love all these (disciples and *am ha'-ares*) and hate the sectarians, apostates and the informers . . .

Roman Law," in *Law and Religion in the Roman Republic*, ed. O. E. Tellegen-Couperus (Leiden and Boston: Brill, 2012), 166–68; Watson, *The State, Law, and Religion*, 55–57.

63 Watson, *The State, Law, and Religion*, 73. See also ibid., 1. On the secular character, see further Clifford Ando, "Religion and *ius publicum*," in *Religion and Law in Classical and Christian Rome*, eds. Clifford Ando and Jorg Rupke (Stuttgart, 2006), 129, 132–40. Even though law has a secular character, it bears the clear indirect imprint of religious social practices. For example, the source of the civil contract *(stipulatio)* is religious *(votum)*. See Watson, *The State, Law, and Religion*, 39–43. Similarly, the religious oath also is employed in the private and civil realm (ibid., 44–45 and 78–79).

64 See T. J. Cornell, *The Beginnings of Rome* (London and New York, 1995), 242–71.

65 Thus (according to Ulpian, *Digestia* 1.1.1.2), religious matters are part of public law, whereas civil law is part of private law. See Elizabeth DePalma Digeser, "Religion, Law and the Roman Polity: The Era of the Great Persecution," in *Religion and Law in Classical and Christian Rome*, eds. Clifford Ando and Jorg Rupke (Stuttgart, 2006), 70.

66 Watson, *The State, Law, and Religion*, 78.

67 Sophie Lunn-Rockliffe, *Ambrosiaster's Political Theology* (Oxford, 2007), 54–56.

68 On the author's identity and the historical and theological background of the work, see: ibid., 12–17, 33–50; Alexander Souter, *The Earliest Latin Commentaries on the Epistles of St. Paul: A Study* (Oxford, 1927), 39–48.

69 Andrew S. Jacobs, "Papinian Commands One Thing, Our Paul Another": Roman Christians and Jewish Law in the *Collatio Legum Mosaicarum et Romanarum*," in *Religion and Law in Classical and Christian Rome*, eds. Clifford Ando and Jorg Rupke (Stuttgart, 2006), 95–97.

[Rabbi Akiva says: "Yet it says,] 'But thou shalt love thy neighbour as thyself: I am the Lord. And why is that? Because I [the Lord] have created him. Indeed! If he acts as thy people do, thou shalt love him; but if not, thou shalt not love him."

Rabbi Simeon ben Eleazar says: "This matter was stated with a great oath: 'And you shall love your fellow as yourself [because] I am the Lord,' who faithfully pays rewards and extracts punishment."[70]

Both the text and meaning of Rabbi Akiva's homily are doubtful. According to our version (in footnote 71), the homily seems to be based on the declaration "I am the Lord" that is attached to the injunction to love one's fellow.[71] This declaration bases

[70] *Avot de-Rabbi Natan* [The Fathers According to Rabbi Nathan], Recension A, chapter 16 (MS New York, JTS 25); trans. Judah Goldin (London, 1956), 86. For textual variants, see, at length: Louis Finkelstein, *Mavo le-masekhtot Avot ve-Avot de-Rabi Natan* [Introduction to Tractates Avot and Avot de-Rabbi Nathan] (New York, 1950), 47–51; Menahem Kister *Iyyunim be-Avot de-R. Natan: nusaḥ, arikhah u-farshanut* [Studies in Avot de-Rabbi Nathan: text, redaction, and interpretation] (Jerusalem, 1998), 69–70; H. G. Becker, *Avot de-Rabbi Natan: Synoptische Edition beider Versionen* (Tübingen, 2006), 170–71. The statement is attributed to Rabbi Akiva in all textual witnesses except the first printed edition (Venice, 1550). Finkelstein (*Mavo*, 49–50), holds that the first clause ("Yet it says . . . [created him]") is Rabbi Akiva's, but the end ("those who act/do not act like one of your people") is not. According to the first clause, the fact that human beings are created in the divine image requires that we love everyone, including evildoers. But the second clause limits the love for one's fellow to those who "act like one of Your people." Given this contradiction, Finkelstein proposes that this is a hybrid text: Rabbi Akiva's authentic homily in the first clause is followed by another, even though it "is not by Rabbi Akiva at all and is only an interpretation and addition to the main point of the *baraita* and the words of the first authority" (and see, phrased differently, ibid. 49, n. 88). It is possible that ideology (tolerance and universalism) is lurking in the background of Finkelstein's proposal. See Jonathan Howard , "Ela ehov et kullam" [Rather, love everyone], *Ma'agalim* 8 (2013): 106–10. Kister (*Iyyunim*, 168), adopts Finkelstein's hypothesis of a hybrid text: "These are two completely different things, and their linkage creates a meaningless statement." However, his solution is just the opposite: the second clause is based on a common tannaitic homily (167), implying that it is Rabbi Akiva's original homily; but the first clause is rare and likely a later and inauthentic supplement (ibid., 70 and n. 160; idem, "Bein ma'amarei yeshu la-midrash" [Jesus's statements and the Midrash], *Meḥqerei yerushalayim be-maḥshevet Yisrael* II, (1981/2), 14, n. 27). Either way, the hybrid text thesis requires further study, based on Rabbi Simeon ben Eleazar's dictum in *Avot de-Rabbi Nathan*, Recension A, chapter 16, and the parallel statement by Rabbi Hananiah the Temple prefect (*Avot de-Rabbi Nathan*, Recension B, ch. 26, MS Parma 2785 [MS Schechter, 53]: "That on which the entire world depends on, a tradition (oath) was said about it from Mount Sinai: If [you] hate your fellow *whose deeds are as bad as your deeds – I am the Lord*, a judge who will punish that person; and if you love your fellow *whose deeds are proper, like your deeds – I am the Lord*, merciful and who has mercy upon you." For this parallel, see: Flusser, "Judaism and the Christian Message," 114–15; Kister, *Iyyunim*, 167–168. In this homily, Rabbi Hananiah combines "I am the Lord" (as an oath) with the limitation of the precept to love to those who behave appropriately. However, "I am the Lord" in this version does not refer to the Creator of all humanity, but to the God who commands and judges. In any event, here the combination seems to be original. Kister goes on to reject this consideration (ibid., 168 and 70 n. 159), but without presenting a decisive argument.

[71] It is possible that the formulation of the limitation – "if he acts *as thy people do*" – hints that the homily draws on the parallel between the command to love one's fellow and the adjacent precepts in the Torah: "You shall not hate your *brother* in your heart; you shall surely reprove *your fellow* and bear no sin for him. You shall not avenge nor bear a grudge against *the members of your people*. . ." (Lev. 19:16–17). See Kister, "Ma'amarei yeshu," 41, n. 27; Kister, *Iyyunim*, 167. These precepts do not protect everyone, but only members of one's close circle. See *Sifra*, *Qedoshim* 2:4, ed. Weiss, 89b: "You may

the obligation to love one's fellow on the fact that all human beings were created in the divine image: "And you shall love your neighbor as yourself [I the Lord have created him]."[72] A person who shirks his connection to God and does not act "like one of your people" is not worthy of his fellow's love.[73]

Jesus opposed this. In the Sermon on the Mount he prescribes love for all:

> You have heard that it was said, 'You shall love your neighbor and hate your enemy.' But I say to you, Love your enemies and pray for those who persecute you, so that you may be sons of your Father who is in heaven; for he makes his sun rise on the evil and on the good, and sends rain on the just and on the unjust. ... You, therefore, must be perfect, as your heavenly Father is perfect.[74]

Jesus is familiar with the traditional homily ("you have heard") that limits the love of one's fellow by excluding the wicked,[75] but turns it on its head: Yes, love for one's fellow derives from "I am the Lord." But precisely for this reason one must love also

take revenge and hold a grudge against others" (meaning non-Jews; see David Henshke, "Ḥametz shel aḥerim" [The leaven of others], *Te'udah* 16–17 (2001): 164–66); Aaron Shemesh, "Ha-mavdil bein bnei 'or livnei ḥoshekh bein yisra'el la-'amim" [Who distinguishes between the sons of light and the sons of darkness, between Israel and the nations], in *Atarah le-ḥayyim*, eds. D. Boyarin et. al. (Jerusalem, 2000), 211 and nn. 8, 9; Ruzer, "Ve-ahavta," 365–67. For other and even contradictory readings of the set of social precepts, see Schwartz, Torat ha-qedushah, 317–23. Another approach sees the homily as based on an alternative vocalization of the verse: *ra'akha* "your evil person" instead of *re'akha*, "your fellow." In other words, it is obligatory to love not only one's partners in right religious and social conduct, but also those who behave badly. See: Herbert Basser, "Hed le-midrash qadum bi-vrit ha-ḥadashah" [An Echo of Early Midrash in the New Testament],*Proceedings of the World Congress of Jewish Studies* 11 (div. C vol. I) (1993): 124–26. This is implausible: First, because it is passed on a faulty reading of the text in a way not employed in the tannaitic literature; see Shlomo Naeh, "Ein em la-masoret o: ha'im darshu ha-tanna'im et ketiv hatorah shelo ki-qri'ato hamequbbelet?" [Did the Tannaim Interpret the Script of the Torah Differently from the Authorized Reading?" *Tarbiẓ* 61(3/4) (1992): 407–10. Second, if the homily was based on an alternative reading of the verse, the homilist should have made that plain. The explanation proposed here is based on interpreting the words *re'akha kamokha* [your fellow like you] – a person who is like you; or on "I the Lord – made him."

72 Compare Rabbi Akiva's statement in M *Avot* 3:14: "*Beloved* is man, because he is *created in the image* [of God]. ... Beloved are Israel, because they are called *children of God*" with Jesus's homily (Matt. 5:45): "And you shall love your fellow as yourself...so that you shall be children to your father in heaven."

73 With regard to the homily in the first clause, see *Avot de-Rabbi Nathan*, cited above at n. 70: "*And hate (the sectarians)!* ... And so too David used to say 'O Lord, I hate those who hate You'" (Ps. 139:21; parallels: T *Shabbat* 13:5, ed. Lieberman, 58–59: "*Sectarian* books ... they and references to them should be blotted out; and it is in reference to them that the verse said: 'O Lord, I hate *those who hate You*'"). Similarly, *Avot de-Rabbi Nathan*, Recension A, ch. 9, MS New York: "Lest a person keep company with a *bad person* or an *evil person*... [as is written 'Should you help the wicked and love those who hate the Lord?'" (2 Chron. 19:2). The same follows from the Gaon of Vilna's emendation of the homily: "Yet He says 'And you shall love your fellow as yourself I am the Lord.' Why? '*Because I created him*,' and if he performs acts of justice and righteousness you shall love him, *and if not, you shall not love him*."

74 Matt. 5:43–48.

75 Ruzer, "Ve-ahavta," 355, n. 13. Flusser believes that this is a Sadducean homily: "it is extremely difficult to assume" that it is Pharisaic. See David Flusser, *Yahadut u-meqorot ha-naṣrut* (ibid. n. 50), 227–28.

one's enemies and the wicked, because they too are the children of their Father in Heaven, who is perfect, and who does not distinguish in his mercies, whose sun shines and rains fall on righteous and wicked alike.[76]

The two homilies – Rabbi Akiva's and Jesus's in the Sermon on the Mount – share an assumption: that "And you shall love your fellow as yourself" and "I am the Lord" are linked. Both assume a connection between the obligation to love one's fellow and *imitatio Dei*, but apply the latter in different ways: Rabbi Akiva infers that only fellow-men who follow in the path of the Lord are worthy of love, whereas Jesus preaches that it is God's love of all His creatures and benevolence towards them – including our enemies and the wicked – that is to be emulated.

It is possible that underlying this unspoken debate between Rabbi Akiva and early Christianity is the relationship between obligations towards God and obligations towards other human beings. Rabbi Akiva integrates the two categories and makes one depend on the other: those who breach their obligations to God do not merit the fundamental right at the basis of societal norms.[77] Early Christians rejected this link and viewed the two types of duties as parallel, separate, and independent. Love for one's fellow is mandatory, even if it indirectly detracts from God's honor.

APPENDIX C (NOTE 42): THE DIVISION OF THE TEN COMMANDMENTS IN AUGUSTINE

The idea of the division of the commandments between the two tablets appears, explicitly and systematically, in Augustine.[78] He presented the "golden rule" as the basis for the Ten Commandments and proceeded to explain their division between the two tablets accordingly:

> So that one commandment [the commandment to love] contains two [the commandment to love God and the commandment to love one's fellow], those two contain ten, those ten contain them all.[79]

76 Kister, "Ma'amarei yeshu," 13–14. The Christian position also adopts an attitude of distancing oneself from and hatred of sinners. The integration of hatred and love creates a complex paradox. See: Liu Qingping, "On a Paradox of Christian Love," *Journal of Religious Ethics* 35 (2007): 681–94.

77 The categorical distinction between the two contradicts Rabbi Akiva's position and fits in with a widespread attitude in the Second Temple period and in later of early Christianity. See above, n. 23. See also Flusser, "'Aśeret ha-dibberot," near n. 28.

78 Many date Paul's Epistle to the Romans to 55–58 CE (although a minority opinion, held by Gerd Lüdemann, holds for 51 CE). See F. F. Bruce, *The Epistle of Paul to the Romans: An Introduction and Commentary* (Leicester, 1983), 12; James D. G. Dunn, *Romans 9–16* (Dallas, 1988), XLIII–XLIV. Augustine's homily is about 350 years later, and was apparently written after 412. See *Augustine through the Ages: An Encyclopedia*, ed. Allan D. Fitzgerald et al. (Grand Rapids, 1999), 633–40, 774–89.

79 John E. Rotelle, ed., *Sermons on the Old Testament* (1–19), *The Works of Saint Augustine*, Vol. III/1, *Sermon* 9.16 (Brooklyn, 1990), 273. For a discussion of the idea of the division of the Ten Commandments between the two tablets in Augustine's thought, see also Wilhelm Geerlings, "The Decalogue in Augustine's Theology," in *The Decalogue in Jewish and Christian Tradition*, above n. 30, 112.

According to Augustine, the allocation of the Ten Commandments among the tablets is not five and five. Rather, there are three commandments that refer to love of God (the first, which is belief "I am the Lord" and "You Shall have no other gods"; the second (in the Christian enumeration), the prohibition against vain oaths – "Thou shalt not take the Lord's name in vain"; and the third (still in the Christian enumeration, remembering and observing the Sabbath), and seven commandments that refer to love for one's fellows (including the precept of honor one's parents).[80] Thus Augustine finalizes the division into two categories; henceforth the precepts that apply between Man and God are distinct from those that apply between Man and his fellow.[81]

80 John E. Rotelle, ed., *Sermons on the Saints (273–305A), Vol. III/8, The Works of Saint Augustine, Sermon 278.6.* (New York, 1994), 53; Geerlings, "The Decalogue," 117; G. B. Sarfatti, "Luḥot ha-berit ke-semel ha-yahadut" [The Tables of the Covenant as a Symbol of Judaism], *Tarbiẓ* 29 (1960): 388–89. Several other explanations for this division have been proposed. Some have suggested that there must be precisely three commandments referring to God, to match the Holy Trinity. See: *Corpus Christianorum: Series Latina*, ed. K. D. Daur (Turnhout, 1953), vol. 33, 103; R. H. Charles, *The Decalogue: Being the Warburton Lectures* (Edinburgh, 1923), 17, n. 1. According to Greenstein ("The Rhetoric of the Ten Commandments"), the division into three and seven commandments allows for a quantitative balance between the tablets, given that the first five commandments are significantly longer than the second five.

81 Luther followed Augustine in dividing the Ten Commandments into three and seven. See Henning Graf Reventlow, "The Ten Commandments in Luther's Catechisms," in *The Decalogue in Jewish and Christian Tradition*, above n. 30, 139–40. See also Laurence Vaux, *A Catechisme Christian Doctrine* (Manchester, 1583), 48 (at www.aloha.net/~mikesch/vaux.htm#48). For a discussion of other ways of dividing the Ten Commandments in the Christian world, see: Jonathan Hall, "St. Augustine and the Decalogue," 5–6, 9, at: http://decalogue.atwebpages.com/AugustineDec.pdf ; Charles, *The Decalogue*, ibid.; Sarfatti, "Luḥot ha-berit," 389, n. 123.

13

Christian Feasts and Administration of Roman Justice in Late Antiquity

Silvia Schiavo

I INTRODUCTION

Law as religion and religion as law: these expressions evoke the intertwining of two experiences, the legal one and the religious one, which characterizes every society, ancient and modern.

In pagan Rome the interconnection between *fas* and *ius* led to noteworthy consequences. Think, for example, about the role of the *pontifices*, not only in the religious dimension, but also in the interpretation and creation of law or, further, the close connection, in various legal and government contexts, between the magistracies and the sacerdotal colleges.[1]

In this work, however, our attention is drawn towards late antiquity and the relationship between the Christian religion and imperial legislation on administration of justice.

We will look at the problem of the articulation of the "times" of trials which, from a certain moment onwards, took on the Christian dimension of time as a new point of reference, examining how Christianity managed to influence the rhythms of the judicial administration.

Since the second century, the central Christian feasts were Sunday and Easter, both referred to the resurrection of Christ. As time has gone on, particularly at a local level, also commemoration of great martyrs took on importance. Unlike the pagan and Judaic feasts, Christian holidays were not connoted by a specific quality, there being no distinction between a "sacred" day and a "profane" day, since every day is a day of the Lord. As Jerome explains, the resurrection of Christ is celebrated every day, but some days are established for meetings between Christians, so as not to let people's faith diminish and so that there is more joy in the mutual meeting.[2]

[1] General outline in A. Watson, *The State, Law and Religion: Pagan Rome*, Athens – London, 1992. For various perspectives on the relationship between law and religion in Rome, see the essays in C. Ando , J. Rüpke (eds.), *Religion and Law in Classical and Christian Rome*, Stuttgart, 2006. A view of the Roman Republic is provided by the works collected in the recent volume: O. Tellegen-Couperus (ed.), *Law and Religion in the Roman Republic*, Leiden-Boston, 2012.

[2] Hier. *Ep. ad Galatas*, 2,4, PL 24, c. 596. On these aspects, see A. Di Berardino, *Cristianizzazione del tempo civico nel IV secolo*, in B. Luiselli (ed.), *Saggi di storia della cristianizzazione antica*

However, a considerable change took place over the fourth century. In fact, the old pagan Roman calendar was based on a different conception, according to which sacred time took on a different meaning compared to profane time: think of the distinction between *dies fasti,* devoted to commercial activities and trials and *dies nefasti,* during which significant jurisdictional and political activities were not permitted.[3]

Based on these principles, legislation began to move in a similar direction and the Christian articulation of time very slowly became intertwined with the civil calendar, influencing it profoundly. The emperors used "religious time" to articulate "legal time."

This happened, for example, through the establishment of some of Christian feasts as *feriae publicae,* thanks to the recognition of some days or periods of the year for the accomplishment or suspension of certain acts; in parallel with the abolition of pagan public sacrifices and *feriae* connected with pagan feasts, which became ordinary working days.[4] Another important instrument used by the emperors was the prohibition of spectacles on Christian feasts:[5] games and theatrical performances distracted believers from Christian services and this is confirmed by many invectives in the works of the Fathers of the Church.[6]

e altomedievale, Rome, 2006, p. 186 ss., to which we refer for some observations contained in this first paragraph.

3 See, among many others, K. L. NOETHLICHS, *Revolution from the top? Orthodoxy and the persecution of heretics in imperial legislation from Constantine to Justinian,* in C. ANDO, J. RÜPKE (eds.), *Religion and Law in Classical and Christian Rome,* Stuttgart, 2006, p. 118; J. RÜPKE, *Religion in Republican Rome. Rationalization and Ritual Change,* Philadelphia, 2012, p. 94 ss.; *Id., Rationalizing Religious Practices: the Pontifical Calendar and the Law,* in O. TELLEGEN-COUPERUS (ed.), *Law and Religion,* cit., p. 85 ss.; G. FORSYTHE , *Time in Roman Religion. One Thousand Years of Religious History,* New York-London, 2012, p. 21 ss.; U. AGNATI, *Costantino e la scansione cristiana del tempo (Cod. Iust. III 12,2 e Cod. Th. II 8,1),* in *L'indagine e la rima. Scritti per Lorenzo Braccesi,* I, Roma, 2013, p. 23 ss.; *Id., Constantine's Statutes on Sunday Rest. Social and Juridical Remarks,* in *Calumet-Intercultural Law and Humanities Review,* II, 2015, p. 1 ss., with notes 1 and 2.

4 On the above, see in particular M. BIANCHINI, *Cadenze liturgiche e calendario civile fra IV e V secolo. Alcune considerazioni,* in *Atti dell'Accademia Romanistica Costantiniana. Atti del VI Convegno internazionale,* Perugia, 1986, now in M. BIANCHINI, *Temi e tecniche della legislazione tardoimperiale,* Torino, 2008, p. 234, with an indication of other literature; D. BAUDY, *Prohibitions of Religion in Antiquity: Setting the Course of Europe's Religious History,* in C. ANDO, J. RÜPKE (eds.), *Religion and Law,* cit., p. 110 s.; M. R. SALZMAN, *On Roman Time. The Codex-Calendar of 354 and the Rythms of Urban Life in Late Antiquity,* Berkeley, Los Angeles, Oxford, 1990, p. 235 ss. who stresses that, while in the mid-fourth century "Pagan cult reigned virtually unchallenged," in the second half of the century Christian emperors attempted "to disassociated paganism from the culture and civic life of the empire."

5 For this profile, we refer particularly to E. Franciosi, *Dies festos nullis volumus voluptatibus occupari. Spettacoli e feste cristiane nella legislazione postclassica e giustinianea,* in F. BOTTA (ed.), *Atti del Convegno "Il diritto giustinianeo fra tradizione classica e innovazione",* Torino, 2003, p. 53 ss., and more recently A. DI BERARDINO, *Cristianizzazione del tempo civico,* cit., p. 187 s. which equally refers to the legislation abolishing spectacles during Christian feasts.

6 For example, John Chrysostom complained that, in Constantinople, churches were empty during spectacles while the people crowded into the circus: *De Anna, sermo* IV I, PG LIV, c. 660. Observations on the meaning of the prohibition of *spectacula* during Christian feasts in N. SPINETO,

Through the filter of the imperial constitutions, Christian feasts (such as Sunday, Easter, Pentecost, Christmas, Epiphany)[7] gradually came to be placed alongside civil feasts such as *dies Natalis* and the emperor's assumption of the throne[8] and became a powerful instrument for spreading the Christian message. All of this particularly follows the Edict of Thessalonica issued in 380, after which the most significant testimonies, which will be analyzed herein, are placed.[9]

It was not a complete replacing of the Roman calendar, because the "Christian time" started working alongside the "Pagan time." The attempts of Christian emperors to make pagan festivals and holidays illegal were only partially successful: they were celebrated also in the fifth and sixth centuries. They progressively lost their original religious meaning, rather becoming a matter of popular custom and culture.[10]

Nevertheless, the new way of organizing social time brought with it a set of symbols, rites, ceremonies, and values,[11] eventually conditioning people's daily lives.

Our attention will focus on texts that cover the *dies dominicus* and the Easter cycle. Hence, some constitutions will be examined through which Sunday and the days of the Easter cycle are used to influence and govern the times of trial, in particular (but not only) through the establishment of the obligation to suspend certain activities.

The statutes we will examine, chronologically to be placed after the 380, come mostly from the Theodosian Code. Later, some of them have been incorporated into the Justinian one. With reference to the two codifications, consequently, a complete, definitive picture emerges, showing that the Christian festivals have profoundly impacted the civil calendar.

It must however be pointed out that the various laws, at the time of their promulgation, were destined to different geographical areas, and were therefore measures in response to specific local needs, or that reacted to particular problems.

De spectaculis: aspetto della polemica antipagana, in A. Saggioro (ed.), *Diritto romano e identità cristiana. Definizioni storico-religiose e confronti interdisciplinari*, Rome, 2005, p. 220 ss. On the problem of contested Roman festivals in the fourth century, see F. Graf, *Roman Festivals in the Greek East. From the Early Empire to the Middle Byzantine Era*, Cambridge, 2015, p. 128 ss.

7 In general, on Christian feasts, see A. Di Berardino, *Tempo sociale pagano e cristiano nel IV secolo*, in A. Saggioro (ed.), *Diritto romano e identità cristiana*, cit., p. 104 ss. The list of Christian feasts is provided in CTh. 15,5,5, the constitution of Theodosius II issued in 425 through which Epiphany and Christmas became known as *feriae publicae*. The constitution, along with the passages of CTh. 2,8,18 and CTh. 2,8,19, is also included in C.3,12,6 (see A. Scarcella, *La legislazione di Leone I*, Milan, 1997, p. 329, note 29).

8 For a general outline, see M. Bianchini, *Cadenze liturgiche e calendario civile*, cit., p. 248 s.

9 *Id.*, p. 235.

10 Important evidence is given by the Calendar of *Polemius Silvius* (448–49 AD), from Gaul, in which many pagan festivals and *ludi* are reported, probably the ones the author considered still useful and necessary and that at the time were commemorated together with the Christian holidays. See M. R. Salzman, *On Roman Time*, cit., p. 239 ss. For a different stance, see A. Di Berardino, *Christian Liturgical Time and Torture (Cod. Theod.* 9,35,4 *and* 5), in *Augustinianum*, 51,1, 2011, p. 192, who talks about a gradual substitution of the pagan time by the Christian one.

11 In this regard, A. Di Berardino, *Tempo sociale pagano e cristiano nel IV secolo*, cit., p. 98.

Where possible, we will try to highlight these aspects, emphasizing the occasion in which the various constitutions were issued.

II CONSTANTINE AND THE "*DIES SOLIS*"

However, before examining the legislation on *dies dominicus* and the Easter festivity, it is first necessary to look at some measures of the Constantinian era, very well-known and debated among scholars, that is, two constitutions through which contractual activities and trials were suspended on the *dies Solis*.

They were C. 3,12,2(3), from C. 3,12 *De feriis* and CTh. 2,8,1, from CTh. 2,8 *De feriis* : formally two distinct measures, both addressed to Elpidius *vicarius urbis Romae*, the former issued on March 3, 321 and the latter on July 3 of the same year, but which some scholars consider to be two fragments of a single law.[12] Anyway, the constitutions were initially applied only in the West, and after the victory over Licinius they were extended also to the Eastern provinces.[13]

> C. 3,12,2(3). Imp. Constantinus A. Helpidio. Omnes iudices urbanaeque plebes et artium officia cunctarum venerabili die solis quiescant. ruri tamen positi agrorum culturae libere licenterque inserviant, quoniam frequenter evenit, ut non alio aptius die frumenta sulcis aut vineae scrobibus commendentur, ne occasione momenti pereat commoditas caelesti provisione concessa. PP. V. non. Mart. Crispo II et Constantino II conss. (a 321).[14]
>
> CTh. 2,8,1. Imp. Constantinus A. Helpidio. Sicut indignissimum videbatur, diem solis, venerationis sui celebrem, altercantibus iurgiis et noxiis partium contentionibus occupari, ita gratum ac iocundum est, eo die, quae sunt maxime votiva, compleri. Atque ideo emancipandi et manumittendi die festo cuncti licentiam habeant, et super his rebus actus non prohibeantur. PP. V. non. Iul. Caralis, Crispo ii. et Constantino ii. Caess. Conss. (a 321).[15]

12 See O. Seeck. *Regesten der Kaiser und Päpste für die Jahre 311 bis 476 n. Chr.*, Stuttgart, 1919, p. 62, according to which both laws refer to March 321; M. Bianchini, *Cadenze liturgiche e calendario civile*, cit., p. 235; S. Corcoran, *The Empire of the Tetrarchs. Imperial Pronouncements and Government. A. D. 284–324*, Oxford, 1996, p. 164, note 188; p. 312. J. Gothofredus, *Codex Theodosianus cum perpetuis commentariis*, Lipsiae, 1736, p. 137 which seems to exclude the two laws being a single measure, stating that they are two distinct constitutions addressed at different times to *vicarius urbis Helpidius*.

13 Soz. *Hist. Eccl.* 1,8. On this problem: A. Di Berardino, *Christian Liturgical Time*, cit., p. 195.

14 "Emperor Constantine Augustus to Helpidius. All judges and the people in the city should rest, and the work in all crafts should cease, on holy Sunday. But the people in the country may freely and lawfully apply themselves to cultivating their fields, so that the benefit conferred by the providence of God may not perish in an instant, since it often happens that grain can be sown in the furrows and vines planted in the trenches on no better day. Posted March 3, in the consulship of Crispus, for the second time, and Constantine, for the second time." (English Translation in B. W. Frier *et al.* (eds.), *The Codex of Justinian. A New Annotated Translation with Parallel Latin and Greek Text Based on a Translation by Justice Fred H. Blume*, I, Cambridge, 2016, p. 346.

15 "Emperor Constantine Augustus to Helpidius. Just as it appears to Us most unseemly that the Day of the Sun (Sunday), which is celebrated on account of its own veneration, should be occupied with legal altercations and with noxious controversies of the litigation of contending parties, so it is pleasant

Constantine intervened with C. 3,12,2 establishing that on the *dies Solis* the activities of all judges and inhabitants of the cities must have rest and that only inhabitants of the countryside could work in the fields. With CTh. 2,8,1 the emperor underlined that litigation must stop, in place of which suitable space should be left for the activities he referred to as *votiva compleri*. The only acts that could be accomplished were emancipations and manumissions, due to their non contentious nature.[16]

In relation to the time relationship between the two texts, the opinion of Gothofredus appears worthy of consideration, according to which CTh. 2,8,1, where the emperor talks about the past (*sicut indignissimum videbatur*), follows C. 3,12,2 from a chronological viewpoint: hence Constantine first established the prohibition of all judicial activities and, for the inhabitants of the cities, the suspension of all activities. The rule was different for the inhabitants of the countryside, who could continue their agricultural work.[17] At a later date, through the measure referred to in CTh. 2,8,1, the emperor is considered to have extended the range of permitted exceptions, stating that emancipations and manumissions could also be performed on Sundays.[18]

The texts mentioned, as has been seen, contain a reference to the *dies Solis*, an expression connoted by a certain amount of ambiguity, since it can be attributed both to the pagan solar cult and to Christian thought, which indicates Sunday as the day of the Lord.[19]

and fitting that those acts which are especially desired shall be accomplished on that day. 1. Therefore all men shall have the right to emancipate and to manumit on this festive day, and the legal formalities thereof are not forbidden. Posted on the fifth day before the nones of July at Cagliari in the year of the second consulship of Crispus and Constantine Caesars." (English translation in C. Pharr, *The Theodosian Code and Novels and the Sirmondian Constitutions. A Translation with Commentary, Glossary and Bibliography*, Princeton, 1952, p. 44.)

16 See J. Gothofredus, *Codex Theodosianus*, I, cit., p. 137, which summarizes the contents of CTh. 2,8,1 stating: "discrimen igitur facit Constantinus inter actus contentiosae et voluntariae Iurisdictionis." Gothofredus notes that in the Visigothic *Interpretatio* there is a mistake. In fact, it mentions the possibility of *gesta conficere* when the emperor Constantine refers to the fulfillment of the acts of emancipation and manumission and not to the drafting of the related *gesta* certifying the successful emancipation.

17 On the possible meaning of this exception, see *infra*, in this paragraph.

18 See J. Gothofredus, *Codex Theodosianus*, I, cit., p. 137, according to which CTh. 2,8,1 was not the first of Constantine's measures to ratify the prohibition to perform activities on Sundays – the previous one was therefore C. 3,12,2. An interesting perspective is that of K. M. Girardet, *L'invention du dimanche: du jour du soleil au dimanche. Le dies Solis dans la législation et la politique de Constantin le Grand*, in J. N. Guinot, F. Richard (eds.), *Empire chrétien et Église aux IVe et Ve siècles. Integration ou "concordat"? Le témoignage du Code Théodosien*, Paris, 2008, p. 346, according to which CTh. 2,8,1 is part of a rescript urged by Elpidius himself in order to obtain clarifications on C. 3,12,2, regarding the disparity of treatment between pagans and Christians. In fact, Christians were already authorized to proceed with *manumissio in ecclesia*. A different approach is presented in E. Moreno Resano, *El dies Solis en la legislación constantiniana*, in *Antiquité Tardive*, 17, 2009, p. 292, according to which these are fragments of the same imperial constitution.

19 On the use of the expression *dies solis* also among Christians and Christian emperors to indicate the day of the Lord see U. Agnati, *Constantine's Statutes on Sunday Rest*, cit., p. 10.

As we know, scholars have always been divided on the question and diverging interpretations of these texts have also been provided in recent times.

To briefly summarize the discussion, it is first necessary to remember that some of the words used by Constantine, that is, *venerabilis dies Solis* and *dies Solis veneratione sui celeber*, and the absence of motivations that openly refer to Christian thought, point towards the preeminent will of the emperor to reconnect with the cult of the sun, to which Constantine and the members of his family were dedicated prior to the conversion to Christianity.[20] Therefore, Constantine's choice of terminology would make it possible to relink his provisions to the cult of the sun[21] while not being able to fully deny the fact that this choice would give life to a sort of compromise between the Christian and the pagan worlds, thus allowing a not too clear position to be taken, during years which were undoubtedly still a time of transition. Hence, Christians benefited, although indirectly, from Constantine's provisions.[22]

On the other hand, for an opposite interpretation (already identifiable for example in the comment that J. Gothofredus dedicates to CTh. 2,8,1)[23] Constantine intended to impose respect for the Christian feast of Sunday, *dies dominicus*, by still calling it *dies Solis*.[24] According to this different stance, the

20 See L. De Giovanni, *Costantino e il mondo pagano*, Naples, 1977, p. 108, who, regarding CTh. 2,8,1, underlines how sun worship certainly influenced the emperor in some way and that the subject of assimilation to the sun recurs until the complete decline of Licinius (even after the disappearance of the pictures of the sun from coins, around the year 320). See also M. Bianchini, *Cadenze liturgiche e calendario civile*, cit., p. 235. On the importance of the cult of the sun for the Constantine dynasty, see the recent P.O. Cuneo, *Anonymi Graeci oratio funebris in Constantinum II*, Milan, 2012, p. 95 ss.

21 Among others, A. H. M. Jones, *The Decline of the Ancient World*, London, 1966, p. 41 s.; P. R. Coleman-Norton, *Roman State and Christian Church*, I, London, 1966, p. 83 s.; W. Rodorf, *Sunday. The History of the Day of Rest and Worship in the Earliest Centuries of the Christian Church*, London, 1968, p. 163 s.; A.S. Scarcella, *La legislazione di Leone I*, cit., p. 331, note 35, M. Wallraff, *Constantine's Devotion to the Sun after 324*, in *Studia Patristica*, 34, 2001, p. 256 ss.; E. Moreno Resano, *El dies Solis en la legislación constantiniana*, cit., p. 289 ss.; *Id.*, *La ley constantiniana del dies solis en su context politico y legislativo*, in *Studia Historica*, 27, 2009, p. 187 ss.; G. Forsythe, *Time in Roman Religion*, cit., p. 153. General outline in U. Agnati, *Constantine's Statutes on Sunday* Rest, cit., p. 10 ss.

22 See, among others, E. Moreno Resano, *El dies Solis en la legislación constantiniana*, cit., p. 303. On the ambiguity of the law see M. R. Salzman, *On Roman Time*, cit., p. 236.

23 See J. Gothofredus, *Codex Theodosianus*, I, cit., p. 137, who starts his comment by stating: "Dies solis, seu Dominico, est haec Constantini M. constitutio: cuius de eodem altera, verum prior tempore ad eundem Helpidium hoc ipso anno extat *Cod. Iustinianeo lex* 3. *Hoc. Tit.*"

24 Also with reference to this different interpretation, the literature is very vast. We will limit ourselves to remembering B. Biondi, *Il diritto romano cristiano*, I, Milan, 1962, p. 162 ss.; P. Bonetti, *Dies Solis e dies dominicus nella legislazione imperiale romano-cristiana*, *"Boll. Scuola di perfezionamento e di specializzazione in dir. del lavoro e della sicurezza sociale Univ. Trieste"*, 9.25–27, 1963, p. 13 ss.; A. Di Berardino, *La cristianizzazione del tempo nei secoli IV-V: la domenica*, in *Augustinianum*, 47, 2002, p. 97 ss.; *Id.*, *Tempo sociale pagano e cristiano nel IV secolo*, cit., p. 95 ss.; *Id.*, *Cristianizzazione del tempo civico nel IV secolo*, cit., p. 179 ss.; K. M. Girardet, *L'invention du dimanche: du jour du soleil au dimanche*, cit., p. 341 ss.; P. Siniscalco, *Il cammino di Cristo nell'Impero romano*, Bari, 2009, p. 170; U. Agnati, *Constantine's Statutes on Sunday Rest*, cit., p. 4 ss.; G. Anello, *The Rest and the West. The Legacy of Constantine's Rules Concerning the Dies Dominica: Anthropological Notes*, in *Calumet-*

constitutions with which we are dealing are connected with the Christian cult[25] on the basis of different signs.

In particular, it should be considered that in the legislation of the Christian emperors of the fourth century who, through different measures, attempted to overcome the paganism that still covered civil society (we will look at some examples below), the expression *dies Solis* is used to indicate Sunday without any pagan connotation. This implies that it may also be used in this sense in Constantine's texts,[26] and not in relation to the cult of the sun. Again, it should not be forgotten that in the Christian conception Christ had been considered the *Sol Iustitiae* for some time, and that the cult of the sun had certainly had a strong influence on the Christian worship.[27]

To this it must be added that Constantine pursued policies that clearly distinguished Christian feasts from Jewish ones. Think about the Council of Nicaea, during which the independence of the Christian Easter with respect to Passover was established with the identification of a common date for all the Christian communities.[28] Since the emperor most probably issued a measure (which we do

Intercultural Law and Humanities Review,1, 2015, p. 1 ss.; P. F. BRADSHAW , M.E. JOHNSON, *The Origins of Feasts, Fasts and Seasons in Early Christianity*, London, 2011, p. 25 ss. J. RÜPKE, *The Roman Calendar from Numa to Constantine. Time, History and the Fasti*, Chichester-Malden, 2011, p. 165: "Although the ruling is delivered in a religiously neutral form, there can be no doubt that its motivation is Christian. In the law's wording, *venerabilis* refers to a cult practice that must comprehend more than an astrologically favourable disposition on the 'day of sun'."

25 This is the position expressed recently by U. AGNATI, *Constantine's Statutes on Sunday Rest*, cit., 4 ss.

26 See particularly U. AGNATI, *Constantine's Statutes on Sunday Rest*, cit., p. 10 ss. The scholar also reminds us that in the writing of Christian authors, Sunday is often talked about using the expression *die Solis*: for example in Justin Martyr (1 *Apol.* LXVII 3); in Gregory of Tours (*Hist. franc.* III 15), while Tertullian uses *dies dominicus* when addressing Christians (*De idol.* XIV 7), and *dies Solis* when addressing pagans (*Apol.* XVI, 1). A collection of constitutions of Christian emperors in which the expression *dies Solis* is used in relation to the Christian Sunday can be found in A. DI BERARDINO, *La cristianizzazione del tempo nei secoli IV-V: la domenica*, cit., p. 101.

27 See U. AGNATI, *Constantine's Statutes on Sunday Rest*, cit., p. 13 ss., with a collection of sources. On these aspects see also M. BIANCHINI, *Cadenze liturgiche e calendario civile*, cit., p. 236, which highlights the fact that the name *Sol Iustitiae* in relation to Christ dates back a long way (as far as Justin Martyr); and G. FORSYTHE, *Time in Roman Religion*, cit., p. 133 ss.

28 As testified by Eusebius, *Vita Constantini* III, XVI–XX: according to the writer, the most important result of the council was not the solution to the Arian question, rather the identification of the date for Easter. On these aspects see A. M. RABELLO, *L'observance de fêtes juives dans l'Empire romain*, in H. TEMPORINI , W. HAASE (eds.), *Aufstieg und Niedergang der Römischen Welt: Geschichte und Kultur Roms im Spiegel der Neuren Forschung*, II, 21.2, Berlin-New York, 1984; A. M. RABELLO, *The Jews in the Roman Empire: Legal Problems, from Herod to Justinian*, Aldershot, Burlington Usa, Singapore, Sydney, 2000, p. 1309 ss.; A. DI BERARDINO, *L'imperatore Costantino e la celebrazione della Pasqua*, in G. BONAMENTE , F. FUSCO (eds.), *Costantino il Grande*, I, Macerata, 1992, p. 363 ss.; M. DELCOGLIANO, *The Promotion of the Constantinian Agenda in Eusebius of Caesarea's on the Feast of Pascha*, in S. INOWLOCKI , C. ZAMAGNI, *Reconsidering Eusebius. Collected Papers on Literary, Historical and Theological Issues*, Leiden, 2011, p. 39 ss.; U. AGNATI, *Constantine's Statutes on Sunday Rest*, cit., p. 20 ss. It should also be observed that until the second half of the fourth century, i.e. until the Council of Laodicea, from a liturgical point of view Sunday had still not taken on a precise physiognomy; some oriental communities continued, for example, to observe Saturday. The fact that Christians united on Sundays to pray and celebrate the Eucharist was more a custom than an

not know) on respecting Saturday for Jews,[29] it is very likely that with the constitutions of C. 3,12,2 and CTh. 2,8,1, Constantine also intended to promote the Christian cult, connoting the day of *dies Solis* as a holiday to be considered the day of the Lord, and not as being connected with the cult of the sun.

Therefore, the two constitutions allegedly aimed to favor Christians who, free from any civil and trial-related commitments, could dedicate Sunday to rest for praying,[30] without the risk of any negative consequences. Through Constantine's decrees, Sunday was therefore taken away from judicial and commercial activities, which by their very nature were forebears of hostility, exchange of money, and the risk of fraud.[31] In fact, as pointed out, in CTh. 2,8,1 acts such as emancipations and manumissions remain outside the emperor's provisions.

It is difficult to know which position to take within this debate and to opt for one interpretation over another.

However, an aspect that appears to be significant is that of the sure "appropriation" by Christians of Constantine's constitutions. We refer to the operation led by some writers who see the aforementioned measures as indisputably connected with Sunday as the day of the Lord.

First of all, Eusebius of Caesarea.[32] In the *Vita Constantini*,[33] the writer mentions various times Constantine's legislation on the *dies Solis*, highlighting its connection with the Christian cult.[34]

According to Eusebius, Constantine established that the most important day of the week, the one that "really comes first" be dedicated to prayer and belong to the

obligation. On these aspects see M. Bianchini, *Cadenze liturgiche e calendario civile*, cit., p. 236 ss., with further bibliographical indications. For a collection of texts from which it emerges how important it was to the ecclesiastical hierarchies that the believers attended the Sunday service, see U. Agnati, *Constantine's Statutes on Sunday Rest*, cit., p. 24 ss.

29 Eusebius, *Vita Constantini* IV,18,2. See U. Agnati, *Constantine's Statutes on Sunday Rest*, cit., p. 19.

30 According to U. Agnati, *Constantine's Statutes on Sunday Rest*, cit., p. 22, it is not a question of protecting rest in itself, rather for the purpose of the Christian cult and prayer. Different stance in J. Rüpke, *The Roman Calendar from Numa to Constantine*, cit., p. 166.

31 See again U. Agnati, *Constantine's Statutes on Sunday Rest*, cit., p. 23.

32 This is highlighted by J. Gothofredus, *Codex Theodosianus*, I, cit., p. 137.

33 On the work, and on the reliability of Eusebius, see in particular A. Cameron , S. Hall, *Eusebius. Life of Constantine, Introduction, Translation and Commentary*, Oxford, 1999, p. 6 ss., with a discussion of the problem of the citation of Constantine's imperial legislation within the work.

34 It is not possible to establish whether the writer is referring here precisely to CTh. 2,8,1 and C. 3,12,2 or to other measures with similar content of which we are not aware. The testimony of Eusebius of Caesarea on this point is considered by many, including A. Di Berardino, *La cristianizzazione del tempo nei secoli IV–V: la domenica*, cit., p. 110 ss.; J. Rüpke, *The Roman Calendar*, cit., p. 165; U. Agnati, *Constantine's Statutes on Sunday Rest*, cit., p. 8. See also the observations of K. M. Girardet, *L'invention du dimanche: du jour du soleil au dimanche*, cit., p. 349 ss., according to which the words of Eusebius (with general indications without stopping to look at any concrete circumstances or exceptions) confirm the existence of a general rule of rest on the *dies solis* (to be interpreted in the Christian sense) prior to 321, presumably straight after the conversion of Constantine. CTh. 2,18,2 and C. 3,12,2 according to the scholar are some exceptions to a previously established rule. In the same regard see R. Soraci, *Dies solis e dies Domini. Dai riti mistagogici al culto cristiano*, in V. Aiello , L. Di Salvo (ed.), *Salvatore Calderone (1915–2000). La personalità scientifica*, Messina, 2010, p. 242 s.

Lord.[35] Again, the author reminds us that the emperor ordered all citizens of the empire to rest on the days of the Savior, and people were also required to respect Saturdays. The writer specifies that this probably happened to remember the actions which according to tradition were performed by the Savior.[36] Finally, he stated that the provincial governors were obliged to observe the day of the Lord; the emperor also required them to honor the festivities of the martyrs and to celebrate the feasts of the Church: all this according to Constantine's wishes.[37]

The words of the bishop of Caesarea describe Constantine's interventions as being undoubtedly connected to the Christian cult, focused on respecting Sunday as the day devoted to prayer.[38] In the perspective adopted by Eusebius the strong link between Constantine and Christianity emerges, without any doubt; it is also significant that in Eusebius, *Vita Constantini*, IV,XVIII,2 a "parallel" intervention is remembered in relation to respecting Saturday, most likely addressed to Jews.[39]

Scholars who sustain the connection of C. 3,12,2 and CTh. 2,8,1 with the cult of the sun do not consider the words of Eusebius to be reliable, believing that he must have been motivated by apologetic reasons.[40]

Eusebius of Caesarea was not alone in underlining the connection between Constantinian legislation and the Christian cult. The testimony of Sozomen of Gaza also suggests the same, stating that Constantine established the obligation to observe the day of the Lord.[41] He underlines that the function of Constantinian legislation[42] is to respect Sunday as a day devoted to the Lord, through the prohibition to perform judicial and contractual acts: Sunday must instead be used for prayer, therefore believers are exonerated from any activities that could hinder the spirituality of the day in any way.

35 Eusebius, *Vita Constantini*, IV, XVIII, 1.

36 *Id.*, 2.

37 *Id.* On this see K. L. Noethlichs, *Revolution from the Top?*, cit., p. 117.

38 A. Di Berardino, *La cristianizzazione del tempo nei secoli IV–V: la domenica*, cit., p. 111, notes also that in Eusebius, *Vita Constantini* IV, XVIII–XIX the writer also talks about the need to celebrate the *dies solis* by the army. See also Eusebius, *Laudes Constantini* IX,10, where the writer reminds us again that Constantine established that a day must be devoted to prayer: again here it talks about the first day of the week, the day of the Lord and the Savior.

39 It is very likely that the measures relating to Saturday issued by Constantine, and interpreted by Eusebius in the Christian sense, allowed Jews to abstain from work on Saturdays. On these aspects see S. G. Hall, *Some Constantinian Documents in the Vita Constantini*, in S. N. C. Lieu , D. Monserrat (eds.), *Constantine*, London, 1998, p. 101 ss. On the problem, see also U. Agnati, *Constantine's Statutes on Sunday Rest*, cit., p. 18 ss. The point made by Eusebius is also confirmed by CTh. 16,8,20, Honorius's and Theodosius's constitution issued in 412 in which the emperors, within the context of a series of provisions in favor of Jews, confirm respect for Saturdays referring to various previous imperial constitutions which, unfortunately, have not been kept.

40 A critical stance on the interpretation of the bishop of Caesarea is shown, for example, by M. Wallraff, *Constantine' s Devotion to the Sun after 324*, cit., p. 260, who considers the testimony to be unreliable and reproposes the idea that Constantine's constitutions referred to the cult of the sun. See also E. Moreno Resano, *El dies Solis en la legislación constantiniana*, cit., p. 304.

41 Soz. *Hist. Eccl.* I,8, II.

42 J. Gothofredus, *Codex Thedosianus*, I, cit., p. 137, relates Sozomen's passage with CTh. 2,8,1.

Sozomen also offered an opening on the reason why Constantine dictated such rules, suggesting that Sunday was the day on which Christ rose again, hence beating death.[43] It was therefore a "Paschal" day of the week and, as such, was to be celebrated.[44]

In short, these testimonies show that beyond what should have been the original meaning of Constantine's measures, C. 3,12,3 and CTh. 2,8,1 (or similar measures) were immediately linked to Christianity and therefore perceived as a way of enhancing Christian worship.[45]

Returning now to the contents of the two Constantinian laws, they establish abstention from all judicial and contractual activities, with the exception of emancipations and manumissions. Again, as has been seen in C. 3,12,2 the emperor asked for the work of the inhabitants of the cities to stop, while those living in the countryside could continue their activities if necessary.[46]

There has been some discussion as to the meaning of this exception. According to scholars who consider the law to be connected to the Christian cult, it was a prudent stance by the emperor, who did not want to impose a law inspired by Christianity on the inhabitants of the countryside who were connected to paganism.[47]

As for judicial activities, specifically of interest to us, the words of the emperor point towards the suspension on Sundays of all proceedings. This is the starting point to be considered for looking now, in greater depth, at the problem connected with the relationship between Christian feasts and administration of justice.

III CHRISTIAN SUNDAY FROM VALENTINIAN II TO LEO

The suspension of judicial and contractual activities on Sunday is found in 386, in a western constitution by Valentinian II. For those who already see a link to Christianity in the Constantinian constitutions, this text surpasses all related ambiguities, presenting a definitively Christian connotation of the *dies Solis* and

43 There are mentions of Sozomen's testimony in A. Di Berardino, *La cristianizzazione del tempo nei secoli IV e V: la domenica*, cit., p. 111; *Id.*, *Tempo sociale e pagano*, cit., p. 103.

44 See also John 20,19 and Justin Martyr in the *Prima Apologia* (LXVII, 8).

45 See E. Moreno Resano, *El dies Solis en la legislación constantiniana*, cit., p. 304. It is to be remembered that from the point of view of the councils, it was necessary to wait for the Council of Laodicea (the date of which is uncertain, but presumably in the second half of the fourth century) which establishes that believers were to honour Sundays by abstaining from work. On this point see M. Bianchini, *Cadenze liturgiche e calendario civile*, cit., p. 237, with note 8.

46 As for the problem of contractual activities which should have been banned, E. Moreno Resano, *El dies solis en la legislación constantiniana*, cit., p. 296, considers that all commercial activities in urban centers were prohibited, whereas it was still possible to perform small activities in rural centers, also in light of CIL. III, 4121, an inscription that commemorates the institution, by the emperor Constantine, of a market (*nundinae*) to be held on the *dies Solis* at the bath complex of *Aquae Iasae*. According to scholars, the inscription dated back to shortly before the legislation passed in 321.

47 On this issue, see the thoughts put forward by U. Agnati, *Costantino e la scansione cristiana del tempo*, cit., p. 27 s., who goes over the ancient debate testified by Serv. *Dan. ad Verg. Georg.* I, 268. A different approach can be find in J. Rüpke, *The Roman Calendar from Numa to Constantine*, cit., p. 166.

contributing to the idea that Sunday is the day of the Lord.[48] On the other hand, according to those who believe Constantine was still connected to the cult of the sun, it is the first intervention envisaging the suspension of judicial and contractual activities on the Christian Sunday.[49]

The constitution was issued in Aquileia by Valentinian II, probably under the deep influence of his mother, Justina.[50]

It is CTh. 2,8,18, from the title *De feriis*, also reported by the compilers of the *Codex Theodosianus* in CTh. 8,8,3 and CTh. 11,7,13:[51]

> CTh. 2,8,18. Imppp. Gratianus, Valentinianus et Theodosius AAA. ad Principium Praefectum praetorio. Solis die, quem dominicum rite dixere maiores, omnium omnino litium, negotiorum, conventionum quiescat intentio; debitum publicum privatumque nullus efflagitet; nec apud ipsos quidem arbitros vel iudiciis flagitatos vel sponte delectos ulla sit agnitio iurgiorum. et non modo notabilis, verum etiam sacrilegus iudicetur, qui a sanctae religionis instinctu rituve deflexerit. Proposita III non nov. Aquileiae, accepta viii k. dec. Romae Honorio n.p. et Evodio conss. (a. 386).[52]

If we accept the theory according to which Constantine had already imposed respect for the Christian Sunday, the text is undoubtedly placed in a continuous line with those provisions, more clearly defining the connection with Christian thought and outlining the conception of the feast in the Christian sense. Significantly, the expression *dies Solis* is specified here through the words … *quem dominicum rite dixere maiores* … .[53]

48 As mentioned in the preamble, a further series of constitutions contains the provision of prohibiting the organization of all kinds of spectacles, which could interfere with the meaning of the religious feast. See, for example, CTh. 2,8,20 and CTh. 15,5,2. On these aspects of late imperial legislation, see abundantly E. Franciosi, *Dies festos nullis volumus voluptatibus occupari*, cit., p. 56 ss.; M. R. Salzman, *On Roman Time*, cit., p. 239 stresses that pagan festivals and holidays nevertheless continued to be celebrated.

49 For the different positions, see, among many, M. Bianchini, *Cadenze liturgiche e calendario civile*, cit., p. 248 and note 38; A. S. Scarcella, *La legislazione di Leone I*, cit., p. 331, note 35; E. Franciosi, *Dies festos nullis volumus voluptatibus occupari*, cit., p. 56 ss.

50 J. Gothofredus, *Codex Theodosianus cum perpetuis commentariis*, II, Lipsiae, 1737, p. 618.

51 Some extracts of this constitution can also be found in the title *De feriis* of the *Codex Iustinianus*, in C. 3,12,6, together with passages from another text, CTh. 2,8,19.

52 "CTh. 2,8,18. Emperors Gratian, Valentinian, and Theodosius Augustuses to Principius, Praetorian Praefect. On the Day of the Sun, which our ancestors rightly called the Lord's Day, the prosecution of all litigation, court business, and suits, shall be entirely suspended. No person shall demand the payment of a public or a private debt, nor shall there be any cognizance of controversies before arbitrators, whether they have been requested in court or chosen voluntarily. 1. That person shall be adjudged not only infamous but also sacrilegious who turns aside from the inspiration and ritual of holy religion. Posted on the third day before the nones of November at Aquileia: November 3. Received on the eighth day before the kalends of December at Rome in the year of the consulship of Emperor Designate Honorius and of Evodius-November 24, 386." (English translation in C. Pharr, *The Theodosian Code*, cit., p. 44).

53 A. Di Berardino, *Tempo sociale pagano e cristiano*, cit., p. 103 underlines that the expression *dies solis* is maintained here, specified through the words *quem dominicum rite dixere maiores*, hence understandable both for pagans and Christians.

Again, another common thread connects CTh. 2,8,18 with a previous law of Valentinian I, which established that on the *dies Solis* Christians could not be subjected to tax collection,[54] whereas in a later one, CTh. 2,8,19 issued in 389, Sunday, still known by the expression *dies Solis*, was listed among the feast days.[55] Here Theodosius states that "all days shall be court days" enumerating exceptions, among which *dies solis* and holy Paschal days, with the seven preceding and following days.[56]

Coming to an in-depth analysis of the contents of the constitution, Valentinian II requires that on the *dies Solis/dominicus* all proceedings and contractual activities be suspended, including acts before arbitrators.

All this is confirmed further in the *Interpretatio* that accompanies the text (CTh. 8,8,3) in the *Breviarium Alaricianum*:

> Int. ad CTh. 8,8,3. Die Solis, qui Dominicus merito dicitur, omnium hominum actio conquiescat, ut nec publicum nec privatum debitum requiratur, nulla iudicia neque publica neque privata fiant. Quod qui non observaverit, reus sacrilegii teneatur.[57]

The interpreter grasps the extent of the prohibition ratified by the emperor, which covers all *iudicia*, *privata* or *publica*.

As underlined in the commentary of J. Gothofredus (on CTh. 8,8,3), the measure therefore has a very extensive scope of application.

Ratione causarum, since according to the constitution, all types of proceedings must be suspended. *Ratione personarum*, because no-one, on the day of the Lord, can be involved in judicial proceedings: the provision also relates to non-Christians. *Ratione iudicum*, given that proceedings in front of judges are stopped but also those run by arbitrators, whether such arbitrators are called upon by judges or magistrates, or spontaneously chosen by the parties.[58]

54 CTh. 8,8,1. Regarding this constitution, following the comment of Gothofredus (J. Gothofredus, *Codex Theodosianus*, II, cit., p. 615 s.), a "sectorial" provision is to be highlighted, in the sense that the constitution only regards tax collection. An extremely significant aspect lies in the fact that here the emperor is still talking about the *dies Solis* defining it as *qui dudum faustus habetur*, hence showing the awareness of a previous discipline governing the theme of Sunday. Gothofredus also notes that the constitution only related to Christians.

55 On these texts see A. Di Berardino, *Tempo sociale pagano e cristiano*, cit., p.104 and recently F. Graf, *Roman Festivals in the Greek East*, cit., p. 105 ss. Some parts of CTh. 2,18,8, of CTh. 2,8,19 and of CTh. 15,5,5 converge in C. 3,12,6.

56 On CTh. 2,8,19 see M. R. Salzman, *On Roman Time*, cit., p. 236; F. Graf, *Roman Festivals in the Greek East*, cit., especially p. 114 ss.

57 Interpretation: "On the Day of the Sun (Sunday), which is deservedly called the Lord's Day, lawsuits of all men shall cease, so that non-payment of either a private or public debt shall be exacted. There shall be no trials, either public or private. If any person should not observe this regulation, he shall be held guilty of sacrilege" (English translation in C. Pharr, *The Theodosian Code*, cit., p. 209).

58 J. Gothofredus, *Codex Theodosianus*, II, cit., p. 617.

On this aspect, the connection has been noted with what was already provided for in the late classic period in a passage by the jurist Ulpian, who talked about the inefficacy of the *sententia arbitris* issued on feast days.[59]

Again, it is to be pointed out that in 469 the emperors Leo and Anthemius, with a constitution that we know through the *Codex Iustinianus*, C. 3,12,9 (11), and about which we will talk shortly,[60] underlining the prohibition of judicial activities on Sundays, allowed litigants to conclude agreements and transactions which, again according to J. Gothofredus, could be favored by recourse to arbitrators.[61]

An aspect that appears particularly significant to us comes from the grave consequences envisaged in the event of violating the rules dictated in the constitution. Anyone who did not respect these rules, infringing the Sunday rest (*qui a sanctae religionis instinctu rituve deflexerit*) was to be considered not only infamous (*notabilis*) but also sacrilegious (*sacrilegus*).

Hence, in the case in question, *crimen sacrilegii* is applicable, as on the other hand also clarified by the *Interpretatio*:[62] this is an important reinforcement of the discipline.[63] The emperors used Sunday as a day for suspending judicial proceedings and contractual activities for a decisive thrust towards the spread of the Christian religion and to do so the instrument of criminal sanctions was also necessary.

As mentioned above, there is another important text, by the emperors Leo and Anthemius, C. 3,12,9(11), focusing on respect for Sundays, as well as other Christian feasts, which returns, among other issues, to the suspension of judicial activities.[64]

59 D. 4,8,36 (Ulp. libr. 77 ad ed.). See K. H. ZIEGLER, *Das private Schiedsgericht im antiken römische Recht*, Munich, 1971, p. 187.

60 See *infra*, in this paragraph.

61 J. GOTHOFREDUS, *Codex Theodosianus*, II, cit., p. 617.

62 The stance of A. S. SCARCELLA, *La legislazione di Leone I*, cit., p. 329 does not appear to be convincing, according to which in the constitution in question, only moral reprobation was to be expressed against anyone violating the provisions relating to Sundays. Observations on the term *sacrilegus* in the constitution can be found in R. BRATOŽ, *Aquileia tra Teodosio e i Longobardi*, in G. CUSCITO (ed.), *Aquileia dalle origini alla costituzione del ducato longobardo*, Trieste, 2003, p. 483. On *crimen sacrilegii* in late antiquity, see in general O. ROBINSON, *Blasphemy and Sacrilege in Roman Law*, in *The Irish Jurist*, 8, 1973, especially p. 364 ss.; *Id.*, *The Criminal Law of Ancient Rome*, London, 1995, p. 84; B. SANTALUCIA, *Diritto e processo penale nell'antica Roma*, Milan, 1998, p. 290: in late antiquity it was conceived as a crime against Christian religion. Again, offenses against priests and places of worship are also included in this area, as is failure to comply with the legislative and administrative provisions of the emperor. In CTh. 16,2,25 and CTh. 16,5,8 the *sacrilegium* is referred to with reference to heretics: see C. HUMFRESS, *Orthodoxy and the Courts in Late Antiquity*, Oxford, 2007, p. 236.

63 In CTh. 8,8,2 in relation to the prohibition to collect taxes from Christians, a sanction is envisaged. In fact, general reference is made to *periculum*.

64 It is also necessary to remember that in C. 3,12 *De feriis* there is a text, C. 3,12,6(7) which merges passages of CTh. 15,5,5 (constitution of Theodosius II dated 425) with CTh. 2,8,18 and CTh. 2,8,19; there is also a reference here to the need to observe Sundays, indicated by the expression *dies Solis*: C. 3,12,6(7), 4–5.

The constitution, which dates back to 469, was placed by Justinian's compilers in C. 3,12 *De feriis,* a title which shows the by then established link between the Christian festivities and the civil calendar:[65]

> C. 3,12,9(11). Impp. Leo et Anthemius AA. Armasio pp. Dies festos, dies maiestati altissimae dedicatos nullis volumus voluptatibus occupari nec ullis exactionum vexationibus profanari. 1. Dominicum itaque diem semper honorabilem ita decernimus venerandum, ut a cunctis exsecutionibus excusetur, nulla quemquam urgueat admonitio, nulla fideiussionis flagitetur exactio, taceat apparitio, advocatio delitescat, sit idem dies a cognitionibus alienus, praeconis horrida vox silescat, respirent a controversiis litigantes, habeant foederis intervallum, ad se veniant adversarii non timentes, subeat animos vicaria paenitudo, pacta conferant, transactiones loquantur. 2. Nec tamen haec religiosi diei otia relaxantes obscaenis quemquam patimur voluptatibus detineri. nihil eodem die sibi vindicet scaena theatralis aut circense certamen aut ferarum lacrimosa spectacula: etiam si in nostrum ortum aut natalem celebranda sollemnitas inciderit, differatur. 3. Amissionem militiae, proscriptionem patrimonii sustinebit, si quis umquam hoc die festo spectaculis interesse vel cuiuscumque iudicis apparitor praetextu negotii publici seu privati haec quae hac lege statuta sunt crediderit temeranda. D. v id. Dec. Constantinopoli Zenone et Marciano conss. (a. 469).[66]

With the constitution in question, provision is therefore made for all the Christian feasts. It is very significant that the names of each feast are not listed: reference is hence only made to "festal days, the days dedicated to the Highest Majesty." This is probably a sign of the then established awareness of the people of the meaning of Christian feasts and the religious duties resulting therefrom.[67]

Respect for such feasts implies abstention from civil activities and from amusements, *voluptates.* With particular regard to the *dies dominicus*, Leo and Anthemius provide for it being dedicated to rest and prayer, therefore a series of activities,

65 In that regard, E. Franciosi, *Dies festos nullis volumus voluptatibus occupari*, cit., p. 63 s.

66 "C. 3,12,9(11). Emperors Leo et Anthemius to Armasius, Praetorian Prefect. We do not want the festal days, the days dedicated to the Highest Majesty, to be taken up with pleasures or profaned by vexatious demands. 1. We decree therefore that the Holy Lord's Day shall always be honored and venerated and excused from all executions of judgments. No summons shall disturb anyone; no exaction for providing surety shall be made; the clerks of the court shall be silent; let advocates retire from court; trials shall not be held on that day; the harsh voice of the auctioneer shall not be heard; litigants shall relax from controversies and have respite from their contracts; let adversaries come together without fear, let reciprocal penitence enter their minds; let pacts be made and settlements speak loudly. 2. But despite allowing this leisureliness on a day dedicated to God, We permit no one to give himself over to unseemly pleasures. The day shall not be open for the theater, the competition of the circus, or the tearful spectacle of wild beasts. If Our birthday or the day when We came to the throne should fall on Sunday, its celebration shall be deferred. 3. If anyone ever attends spectacles on that festal day, or if any clerk of a judge should believe that he can rashly violate the provisions of this law under the pretext of public or private business, he shall suffer the loss of his office and confiscation of his property. Given December 9, at Constantinople, in the consulship of Zeno and Marcianus (469)." (English translation in B. W. Frier *et al.* (eds.), *The Codex of Justinian*, I, cit., p. 645 s.).

67 The consideration is, again, by E. Franciosi, *Dies festos nullis volumus voluptatibus occupari*, cit., p. 66.

meticulously listed in the constitution, were to be suspended: exactions, *admonitio*, which was an introductory act of trials, *advocatio*, that is, the activities of lawyers; and all trials (*cognitiones*) were suspended[68].

With reference to vivid images that communicate the harshness of the procedural activities, the emperor provided for the *horrida vox* of the town crier (*praeco*) to be quiet and for litigants to take a break from the disputes in which they were involved (*respirent a controversiis litigantes*), so that a truce could be created between them.

The only activity still possible was that leading to the conclusion of agreements and transactions, clearly perceived as being compatible with the festivity considering their nature as instruments for pacification.

It was mentioned above that in CTh. 2,8,18 the prohibition of judicial activities on the *dies Solis* also related to arbitrators, both appointed by a judge and by the litigants themselves and that passage of the constitution is also referred to in the Justinian code, in C. 3,12,6.

J. Gothofredus noted a different stance in CTh. 2,8,18 with respect to Leo's subsequent law.[69] Can a contrast between the two provisions be effectively recognized? We do not think so: while the constitution of 386 intended to stop the judicial activities of arbitrators, Leo and Anthemius probably referred to out-of-court activities for concluding agreements and transactions.

Alongside these prescriptions, it was also prohibited to hold spectacles. Within the context of a path already marked out previously, the emperors provided that on religious days, to be dedicated to prayer and contemplation, no theatrical performances or circus events or spectacles involving beasts could be held, not even to celebrate the birthday or accession to the throne of the emperor.

The spectacles are here specified with the word *voluptates*, amusements, as in previous laws collected in the Theodosian Code. Describing *ludi* as *voluptates*, the Christian emperors tried to disassociate the spectacles themselves from the pagan holidays to which they were originally connected, indicating them as cultural events, without a religious meaning.[70]

In the final part of the constitution, some sanctions were provided for against anyone violating the various prohibitions. *Amissio militiae* and *proscriptio patrimonii* are mentioned, that is, loss of public office and confiscation of assets, to be applied both to anyone taking part in spectacles on days dedicated to festivities, and to the

68 For the analysis of Leo's text see A. S. Scarcella, *La legislazione di Leone I*, cit., 328 ss.

69 J. Gothofredus, *Codex Theodosianus*, II, cit., p. 617.

70 Pagans continued to appreciate their religious meaning, while Christians had a different approach; starting from 392 the emperors legislated against these spectacles on Sundays and then on other Christian holidays (see CTh. 2,8,20; 2,8,21; 2,8,23; 2,8,24). On the problem M. R. Salzman, *On Roman Time*, cit., p. 237 ss. For the reconstruction of the imperial legislation, starting from 392 AD., which prohibits the performance of spectacles on Christian feasts, see also E. Franciosi, *Dies festos nullis volumus voluptatibus occupari*, cit., p. 56 ss. It can perhaps be sustained that the prohibition of the celebration of *spectacula* was complementary to the suspension of judicial activities, and was used by the emperors, although in a gradual way, as a means of spreading Christianity within the context of a society that was still profoundly pagan.

clerk of any judge marring them with the excuse of public or private proceedings. With reference to the suspension of civil activities and proceedings, we have seen that negative consequences had already been envisaged, as the application of *crimen sacrilegii*.[71]

This constitution from certain viewpoints seems to conclude the *iter* undertaken by other emperors, perhaps by Constantine himself, an *iter* that aimed to push people to respect Christian feasts and, in particular, Sundays. It has been said that the emperor showed his desire to give a moral and religious imprint to judicial activities, not only by considering the *dies dominicus* as a solemn feast day, but also as a day of conciliation and penance. Hence there is undoubtedly an idea of the establishment of justice being profoundly influenced by what was by then the State religion.[72]

It should be pointed out, again, that the reiterated need for emperors to intervene to promote respect for Sundays probably indicates the great difficulty in ensuring compliance with such provisions.

IV SUNDAY, PRECAUTIONARY CUSTODY AND BISHOPS IN A CONSTITUTION BY HONORIUS

Sunday as a feast day is also taken into consideration in an important imperial constitution by Honorius, issued in Ravenna (409 AD). The text comes from the Theodosian title *De custodia reorum*, dedicated to precautionary custody in prison, applied both in civil and criminal suits.[73] Again here, the Christian feast is used by the emperor, in some way, as an instrument for controlling and managing some stages of the procedure, and as a mechanism for spreading Christian thought. The text is:

> CTh. 9,3,7. Impp. Honorius et Theodosius AA. Caeciliano praefecto praetorio. Post alia: iudices omnibus dominicis diebus productos reos e custodia carcerali videant et interrogent, ne his humanitas clausis per corruptos carcerum custodes negetur. Victualem substantiam non habentibus faciant ministrari, libellis duobus aut tribus diurnis vel quot existimaverint, commentarienses decretis, quorum sumptibus proficiant alimoniae pauperum. Quos ad lavacrum sub fida custodia duci oportet,

[71] In CTh. 2,8,18 but that clearly did not apply according to Leo and Anthemius, and, then, from Justinian's perspective.

[72] On these aspects of the text, see the considerations of A. S. Scarcella, *La legislazione di Leone I*, cit., p. 332. Of certain interest there is also a canon of *Concilium Tarraconense* dated 516 (can. IV, Mansi, col. 541 s.), prohibiting the clergy from passing judgment on Sundays, which was actually allowed on other days, with the exclusion of criminal proceedings. It is striking that conciliar sources actually include provisions of this kind following compliance with imperial legislation. This canon is mentioned in C. Ventrella Mancini, *Tempo divino e identità religiosa. Culto rappresentanza simboli dalle origini all'VIII secolo*, Turin, 2012, p. 188, note 63.

[73] The law is also reported in *Codex Iustinianus* (C. 1,4,9), in the title *De episcopali audientia*. On precautionary imprisonment, see, among others, M. Bianchini, *Cadenze liturgiche e calendario civile*, cit., p. 250; A. Lovato, *Il carcere nel diritto penale romano dai Severi a Giustiniano*, Bari, 1994.

multa iudicibus viginti librarum auri et officiis eorum eiusdem ponderis constituta, ordinibus quoque trium librarum auri multa proposita, si saluberrime statuta contempserint. Nec deerit antistitum christianae religionis cura laudabilis, quae ad observationem constituti iudicis hanc ingerat monitionem. Dat. VIII. kal. febr. Ravennae, Honorio VIII. et Theodosius III. aa. conss. (a. 409).[74]

With this constitution, Honorius imposes some positive changes to the conditions of prisoners through the application of the observance of the *dies dominicus*.

In fact, the emperor orders that on Sundays judges must investigate the condition of prisoners, by meeting them and obtaining information from them. In particular, they were to check that the detainees were not subject to any treatments against *humanitas* and ensure that the *commentarienses*, appointed to manage the prisons and the custody of the detainees,[75] saw to providing sustenance for them and that the prisoners were taken to the baths under *custodia*.

If the judges or their *officia* did not enforce these provisions, they would be fined twenty pounds of gold (while the high-ranking members of the office staff three pounds of gold). Again, the emperor established that the bishops were to be involved, guaranteeing assistance and religious comfort for the detainees, also dealing with controlling the officials.[76]

The constitution marks an important step forwards in the discipline relating to precautionary imprisonment, a sector already affected by different imperial interventions (particularly, by constitutions that aimed to make the situation of the detainees less harsh, or to accelerate proceedings to make imprisonment as short as possible).[77]

74 "CTh. 9,3,7. Emperors Honorius and Theodosius Augustuses to Caecilianus, Praetorian Prefect. (After other matters) On every Lord's Day, judges shall inspect and question the accused persons who have been led forth from the confinement of a prison, lest human needs be denied these prisoners by corrupt prison guards. They shall cause food to be supplied to those prisoners who do not have it, since two or three libellae a day, or whatever the prison registrars estimate, are decreed, by the expenditure of which they shall provide sustenance for the poor. Prisoners must be conducted to the bath under trustworthy guard. Fines have been established, fixed at twenty pounds of gold for the judges and the same weight of gold for their office staffs, and for the high ranking members of the office staffs fines of three pounds of gold have been set, if they should scorn these very salutary statutes. For there shall not be lacking the laudable care of the bishops of the Christian religion which shall suggest this admonition for observance by the judge. Given on the eighth day before the kalends of February at Ravenna in the year of the eight consulship of Honorius Augustus and the third consulship of Theodosius Augustus – January 25, 409." (English translation in C. Pharr, *The Theodosian Code*, cit., p. 229).

75 On the *commmentarienses*, recently, see L. Minieri, *I commentarienses e la gestione del carcere in età tardoantica*, in *Teoria e storia del diritto privato*, IV, 2011, p. 1 ss.

76 On the contents of the constitution, see in particular M. Bianchini, *Cadenze liturgiche e calendario civile*, cit., p. 251; A. Di Berardino, *La cristianizzazione del tempo nei secoli IV-V: la domenica*, cit., p. 105; A. Lovato, *Il carcere nel diritto penale romano*, cit., p. 209 ss.; C. Corbo, *Paupertas. La legislazione tardoantica*, Napoli, 2007, p. 173 s.; L. Minieri, *I commentarienses*, cit., p. 32.

77 See, for example, CTh. 9,3,1 = C. 9,4,1, of Constantine and CTh. 9,3,6 of Theodosius I. On the constitutions referred to herein, see M. Bianchini, *Cadenze liturgiche e calendario civile*, cit., p. 250 as well as the observations of A. Lovato, *Il carcere nel diritto penale romano*, cit., p. 197 ss.

The interesting aspect here for us lies in the close connection between the innovations introduced by Honorius and the festivity of Sunday. According to some scholars, the *dies dominicus* is used by the emperor for spreading the Christian message further, a message which must find practical application in an environment of pain and suffering as prison is, even though it has also been highlighted that Honorius had an "affected" attitude, which was not actually guided by a profound sense of justice.[78]

The final part of CTh. 9,3,7 is also significant, which provides for the involvement of bishops in the assistance to prisoners,[79] an involvement which on one hand can be seen as a sign of Christian charity and on the other could be interpreted as the necessary integration of a state organization that was inefficient in itself.[80]

From this point of view, it has to be stressed that Honorius himself issued other constitutions involving bishops in various frameworks of civil life; this could be seen as a sign of the decadence of the public system of the Western empire at that time.[81]

From this point of view, it may be interesting to remember that in the sixth century, within the *Concilium Aurelianense* V dated 549, rules are established that are very similar to those that can be read in Honorius' constitution. In fact, *intuitu miserationis*, it is provided that anyone in prison must be visited by the archdeacon or by the manager of the church; in compliance with the divine precepts, with mercy, they should be assisted in their needs. Again, the bishop was to appoint a diligent and faithful person, who saw to finding the essential items for prisoners; the bishop himself was responsible for providing the necessary supplies, to be taken from the episcopal residence.[82] It seems worthy of attention that in conciliar sources, rules of this type are testified for the sixth century. From this point of view, on the other hand, the emperors appear in the front line, anticipating models that were to be imposed subsequently in the conciliar canons[83].

78 Some evaluations on this can be found in M. Bianchini, *Cadenze liturgiche e calendario civile*, cit., p. 251 s.

79 See also *Sirm.* 13, the further constitution of Honorius dated 419, through which the emperor agreed that bishops could enter the prisons.

80 See also M. Bianchini, *Cadenze liturgiche e calendario civile*, cit., p. 254, which reminds us that the *lex* shows the gradual growth of the power of bishops in the cities and states that the requirement of the presence of bishops here cannot easily be related to Justinian's provisions of 529 contained in C. 9,4,6, where the presence of bishops in prisons is separated from the *dies dominicus*.

81 For a list of the imperial provisions that led to the progressive involvement of bishops in civil issues see J. Gothofredus, *Codex Theodosianus cum perpetuis commentariis*, III, Lipsiae, 1738, p. 45; Gothofredus describes Honorius' laws as interventions against the cruelty of the times. On these problems, see M. Bianchini, *Cadenze liturgiche e calendario civile*, cit., p. 252 ss.

82 *Concilium Aurelianense* V, a. 549, can. XX, in Mansi, IX, col. 134.

83 The affinity between can. XX of the *Concilium Aurelianense* and CTh. 9,3,7 is underlined by J. Gothofredus, *Codex Theodosianus*, III, cit., p. 46. On the relationship between the constitution of Honorius and the canon, see also C. Ventrella Mancini, *Tempo divino e identità religiosa*, cit., p. 188.

V PASCHAL PERIOD AND CRIMINAL TRIALS: TWO CONSTITUTIONS BY THEODOSIUS I

Among the imperial interventions relating to Christian feasts subsequent to the Edict of Thessalonica significant for judicial activities in general, various constitutions placed between 380 and 408 are reported. With these measures, through similar mechanisms to that seen in relation to the Sunday feast, the emperors govern the Paschal period in a "special" way.

On this point it is useful to remember, as already mentioned in the second paragraph, that the Christian Easter was originally celebrated in relation to the Jewish one, and that Constantine was the first emperor to treat this festivity *ex professo*. During the Council of Nicaea in 325 a single date was determined for all the Christian communities, to be celebrated on a Sunday.[84]

Over the course of the fourth century, the Christian Easter and the pre-Paschal period developed greatly from a liturgical and organizational point of view, also thanks to the legislative interventions of the Christian emperors.[85] Think, just by way of example, about the important laws on Paschal *indulgentia*, obviously inspired by the dimension of forgiveness which cannot be dealt with here.[86]

We will approach these constitutions in chronological order, examining interventions relating to torture and criminal proceedings.[87]

[84] On these aspects, as well as the authors referred to in Section II, see also A. Di Berardino, *Christian Liturgical Time and Torture*, cit., p. 191 ss., with literature cited in note 26. The testimony of Athan. *Ep. ad Afros episcopos* 2, PG 26, c. 1032 is significant. See C. Ventrella Mancini, *Costantino e il dissenso: i concili e la sua visione sociale*, in *Rivista di Diritto romano*, XIII, 2013, p. 7.

For an overview of the history of Easter, Lent and the Holy week, see P. F. Bradshaw, M. E. Johnson, *The Origins of Feasts, Fasts and Seasons in Early Christianity*, cit., p. 39 ss.

[85] See the observations of A. Di Berardino, *Christian Liturgical Time and Torture*, cit., p. 195 ss. The scholar remembers the recognition of a period of preparation for Easter that was progressively longer and a subsequent period. On Lent see also M. Bianchini, *Cadenze liturgiche e calendario civile*, cit., p. 239, note 18.

[86] See M. Bianchini, *Cadenze liturgiche e calendario civile*, cit., p. 240, note 19, according to which granting amnesty for Easter could not be placed on the same plane as the constitutions that provided for the adaptation of the time scales of the judicial administration to Christian feasts. In fact, similar measures had already been issued to mark certain events or occasions. On the theme of Paschal amnesty, for example, G. Bassanelli Sommariva, *Il giudicato penale e la sua esecuzione*, in *Atti dell'Accademia Romanistica Costantiniana. XI Convegno internazionale*, Naples, 1996, p. 57; A. Di Berardino, *Cristianizzazione del tempo civico*, cit., p. 191 ss.

[87] The Easter period, defined by the words *diebus quindecim paschalibus* (for which see C. 3,12,6(7)) is also taken into consideration in CTh. 2,8,21 of Theodosius, dated 392. These days were also used by the emperor to affect judicial and contractual activities, which seem to undergo a complete suspension: CTh. 2,8,21. Imppp. Valentinianus Theodosius et Arcadius Tatiano PP. *Actus omnes seu publici seu privati diebus quindecim paschalibus sequestrentur.* Dat. VI. K. iun. Constantinopoli Arcadio A. ii et Rufino conss. (a. 392). The version of the constitution accepted in *Codex Iustinianus*, C. 3,12,7(8) is also interesting: C. 3,12,7 (8). Imppp. Valentinianus Theodosius et Arcadius AAA. Tatiano pp. *Actus omnes seu publici seu privati diebus quindecim paschalibus conquiescant. in his tamen emancipandi et manumittendi cuncti licentiam habeant, et super his acta non prohibeantur.* Dat. VI. K. iun. Constantinopoli Arcadio A. ii et Rufino conss. (a. 392).

The first constitution, CTh. 9,35,4, was issued by Theodosius just a month after the Edict of 380, when the emperor was still in Thessalonica, and it was accepted in CTh. 9,35 *De quaestionibus*. It was also included in *Codex Iustinianus*, under the title C. 3,12 *De feriis* (C. 3,12,5):

> CTh. 9,35,4. Imppp. Gratianus Valentinianus et Theodosius AAA. Albuciano vicario Macedoniae. Quadraginta diebus, qui auspicio cerimoniarum paschale tempus anticipant, omnis cognitio inhibeatur criminalium quaestionum. Dat. VI. Kal. April. Thessalonicae, Gratiano A. V. et Theodosio A. I conss. (a. 380).[88]

The constitution establishes the important and noteworthy rule according to which all criminal proceedings were suspended during Lent.[89]

The text is not clear as the expression *cognitio criminalium quaestionum* is used here. The word *quaestio*, as we know, usually refers to torture, to the application of *tormenta*, which in the Roman criminal trial was used both in relation to defendants and to witnesses. In fact, the title 9,35 of *Codex Theodosianus*, *De quaestionibus* contains constitutions dedicated to various profiles connected with the discipline of such inquiry measure.[90] However, in Theodosius's provision, it appears to be used with a more general meaning, that is, related to all criminal proceedings.[91] For confirmation of this see, for example, *Interpretatio* of the constitution within the *Breviarium Alaricianum*:

> Int. ad CTh. 9,35,4. Diebus quadrigesimae, pro reverentia religionis, omnis criminaliter actio conquiescat.[92]

As can be noted, the correspondence with the text from the *Codex Theodosianus* is not perfect: Justinian's version of the constitution also reproduces part of the Constantinian CTh. 2,8,1 dedicated to the *dies Solis* (which, as we remember, was not referred to by the Justinian compilers). In particular, there is a point in which Constantine allowed emancipations and manumissions to be performed, actions that were considered compatible with the Christian feast. Hence, this derogation was used, within the Code of Justinian, with reference to the fifteen Paschal days, through combining two constitutions that originally referred to different feasts.

88 "CTh. 9,35,4. Emperors Gratian, Valentinian, and Theodosius Augustuses to Albucianus, Vicar of Macedonia. During the forty days which anticipate the Paschal season by the auspicious beginning of cerimonies, all investigation of criminal cases through torture shall be prohibited. Given on the sixth day before the kalends of April at Thessalonica in the year of the fifth consulship of Gratian Augustus and the first consulship of Theodosius Augustus – March 27, 380." (English translation in C. PHARR, *The Theodosian Code*, cit., p. 251).

89 On calculation of the forty days of Lent, see P. F. BRADSHAW, M. E. JOHNSON, *The Origins of Feasts, Fasts and Seasons in Early Christianity*, cit., p. 109 ss.

90 For a general analysis of the contents of CTh. 9,35, see M. BIANCHINI, *Cadenze liturgiche e calendario civile*, cit., p. 238 ss.

91 See J. GOTHOFREDUS, *Codex Theodosianus*, III, cit., p. 278 who underlines that the inclusion of the title *De quaestionibus* of the *Codex Theodosianius* in the constitution is the result of a misinterpretation by the compilers. Its placement in Justinian's code is more correct, in C. 3,12 *De feriis*. *Contra*, C. PHARR, *The Theodosian Code*, cit., p. 251: the author translates *omnis cognitio criminalium quaestionum* as "all investigation of criminal cases through torture" (see note 88).

92 Interpretation: "During the days of Quadragesima, in reverence for religion, all criminal actions shall be in abeyance." (English translation in C. PHARR, *The Theodosian Code*, cit., p. 251).

The interpretation clarifies the idea that the constitution is directed towards the general suspension of criminal proceedings (it says *omnis criminaliter actio conquiescat*). Further, with respect to Theodosius's text, the *ratio* of the imperial intervention is also explained: *pro reverentia religionis*, in reverence for religion.

Therefore, the constitution aims to introduce a cause for the suspension of all activities relating to criminal proceedings, including the application of torture, during the period of Lent before Easter. Clearly, all this is related to the idea of forgiveness and rebirth connoting the Paschal period, which Theodosius decides to use as a way of governing and influencing the time scales of the criminal trial, providing for the suspension thereof.

As has been highlighted, the suspension of the criminal proceedings and torture during the period of Lent is established *intuitu temporis*, that is, considering the peculiarities and sacredness of the moment in time. Up to now, exemptions from the application of *tormenta* were envisaged, for example, *intuitu personae*, with regard to the *status* taken on by the party who was to be subjected to torture, and never in relation to the time in which the use of this measure of inquiry was used.[93]

The expression of "forty days" reflects the duration of Lent in the Illyricum and in Greece: it was a law issued concerning the Macedonian provinces.[94] By scholars who believe that through CTh. 2,8,1 and C. 3,12,2 Constantine continued to move in a pagan context, the innovative importance of Theodosius's constitution is underlined. It appears to be the first measure by a Christian emperor to envisage the interference between the liturgical festivities and the civil (judicial) calendar. It also appears to be the first testimony of the adaptation of the time scales of the judicial administration to the reality of Christianity.[95]

Some years later, the emperor Theodosius returned to the subject through a new constitution, in 389. The constitution is addressed to the praetorian prefect of the East,[96] while the previous one was applied in the Illyricum.[97] Therefore, we read CTh. 9,35,5:

> CTh. 9,35,5. Imppp. Valentinianus Theodosius et Arcadius AAA. Tatiano P.P. Sacratis quadragesimae diebus nulla supplicia sint corporis, quibus absolutio expectatur animarum. Dat. VIII. Id. Septemb. Foro Flaminii, Timasio et Promoto conss. (a. 389).[98]

93 See M. Bianchini, *Cadenze liturgiche e calendario civile*, cit., p. 240. In relation to the prohibition of torture for certain parties (e.g. the *honestiores*), see, among others, P. Garnsey, *Social Status and Legal Privilege in the Roman Empire*, Oxford, 1970, p. 213 ss.

94 A. Di Berardino, *Christian Liturgical Time and Torture*, cit., p. 202, stresses that it is not possible to know if it was applied also in the other provinces; for the year 380 probably it had not concrete application elsewhere.

95 In that regard, see the reflections of M. Bianchini, *Cadenze liturgiche e calendario civile*, cit., p. 290.

96 It was issued at the *Forum Flaminii*, a Roman municipality, after Theodosius' first visit to Rome. See A. Di Berardino, *Christian Liturgical Time and Torture*, cit., p. 215.

97 On these issues see in particular J. Gothofredus, *Codex Theodosianus*, III, cit., p. 277, as well as the observations of M. Bianchini, *Cadenze liturgiche e calendario civile*, cit., p. 291.

98 "CTh. 9,35,5. Emperors Valentinian, Theodosius, and Arcadius Augustuses to Tatianus, Praetorian Prefect. On the consecrated days of the Quadragesima, during which time the absolution of souls is awaited, there shall be no corporal punishment. Given on the eighth day before the ides of September

A very similar precept is established here to the one found in the previous measure, although more restricted; whereas CTh 9,35,4 provided for the suspension of all criminal proceedings, here the emperor's attention concentrates only on the *supplicia corporis*, hence exclusively on the application of torture, which is suspended during Lent. It therefore follows that on the basis of this law, in the East, there was no limitation of the criminal trial as a whole, rather only in relation to the use of *tormenta* against *rei* and witnesses.

From the comment dedicated by Gothofredus to the constitution clues also emerge that allow some hypotheses to be put forward on the events that led to its promulgation, although only in brief. In fact, Gothofredus also points out that in literary sources, particularly in the work of John Chrysostom,[99] a revolt is remembered that took place in Antiochia, in relation to which the criminal trial was held during Lent that year. The revolt, caused by the imposition of new taxes, led to the destruction of some statues of the emperor.

It appears that during the trial the judges made use of torture against witnesses in such a cruel way as to push the bishop Flavianus to appeal to the emperor to ask for his intervention, which would actually have led to the issue of the law of CTh. 9,35,5.[100]

The law, which refers in part to the contents of the previous one[101], prohibits the use of *supplicia* during Lent with a very clear reason: it is a time reserved for *absolutio animarum*. During this period, bodies had to be left in peace: "Non sunt seculari iudicio corpora supplicio afficienda, quando a caelesti iudicio absolutio animarum expetitur."[102]

Lent is thus dedicated to penitence, reconciliation, conversion and admission of guilt: the constitution therefore reflects the evolution which over the course of the fourth century the conception of the Paschal period underwent.

The reciprocal forgiveness has become a fundamental aspect of this moment, and the Lenten preaching insisted a lot on the idea of Christian mercy. The idea under the law by Theodosius was probably the same inspiring legislation on amnesty: the celebration of Easter leads to the necessity of pardon for persons tormented by judicial investigation under torture and the fear of punishment.[103]

at Forum Flaminii in the year of the consulship of Timasius and Promotus – September 6, 389." (English translation in C. PHARR, *The Theodosian Code*, cit., p. 251).

99 99 *De statuis*, 13,137.

100 In that regard, see J. GOTHOFREDUS, *Codex Theodosianus*, III, cit., p. 278. It is to be noted that according to M. BIANCHINI, *Cadenze liturgiche e calendario civile*, cit., p. 241, note 21, this hypothesis is not very likely. Since an insurrection of Antiochia was testified in 387 and the law of Theodosius being dated to two years later, it would mean that some defendants, two years after the events, were still in prison and on trial. All of this cannot be excluded considering the fact that precise time limits for precautionary custody had not been established, as far as we are aware, until Justinian's era. A different stance can be found in A. BERARDINO, *Christian Liturgical Time and Torture*, cit., p. 202 s.

101 That, according to A. BERARDINO, *Christian Liturgical Time and Torture*, cit., p. 203, seemed not to be known by Libanius or Chrysostom writing on the facts of Antiochia.

102 That is, when absolution of souls is required, there shall be no corporal punishments. See J. GOTHOFREDUS, *Codex Theodosianus*, III, cit., p. 278.

103 See CTh. 9,38,4; observations in A. DI BERARDINO, *Christian Liturgical Time and Torture*, cit., p. 198.

Moreover, it cannot be excluded that through this constitution Theodosius intended to involve in some way the work of the priests in the penitential ministry, ensuring that confessions were obtained without the judges having to resort to the application of *tormenta*.[104] From this point of view, it is interesting to note that, according to John Chrysostom, during the trial after the insurrection in Antiochia, the judges themselves suffered for the torture, because they were forced to be instruments of an awful tragedy:[105] application of torture seems to be, first of all, a problem for the torturers.

The constitutions seen now, as mentioned, originally regarded the Illyricum and the Eastern prefecture.

However, it is quite possible that even in the Western part of the Empire there was legislation that aimed to prevent the application of torture during the Paschal period or connected with certain Christian feasts.

In *De obitu Valentiniani consolatio*[106] Ambrosius reconstructs the reaction of the emperor Valentinian in relation to a query from the praetorian prefect regarding a criminal trial: the response points towards excluding all types of cruelty during the days defined as *sancti*:[107] *respondit ut nihil cruentum sanctis praesertim diebus statueretur.*[108] It is not unlikely that the reference is to a prohibition to apply the inquiry measure of torture.

VI THE CASE OF *LATRONES ISAURI*

It has therefore been seen that with reference to Lent, criminal proceedings and torture undergo an important suspension *intuitu temporis*, hence connected with the particular nature of the reference time. However, this does not prevent the emperors from intervening, also providing for important derogations, dictated by contingent reasons.

Still on the subject of the relationship between the Paschal period and criminal procedure, and in particular suspension of torture, there is in fact a constitution of Theodosius II that we must remember, since it introduces a significant exception to the prohibition expressed in the previous constitution. This is the text, dated 408:

> CTh. 9,35,7. Impp. Honorius et Theodosius AA. ad Anthemium pp. Provinciarum iudices moneantur, ut in Isaurorum latronum quaestionibus nullum quadragesimae nec venerabilem pascharum diem existiment excipiendum, ne differatur sceleratorum proditio consiliorum, quae per latronum tormenta quaerenda est,

104 On all this, see M. Bianchini, *Cadenze liturgiche e calendario civile*, cit., p. 242 s. The author actually excludes the constitution being only inspired by Christian mercy.

105 *De statuis*, 13,137. A. Di Berardino, *Christian Liturgical Time and Torture*, cit., p. 198.

106 On this work by Ambrosius, see in particular E. Peretto, *Testo biblico e la sua applicazione nel De obitu Valentiniani di Ambrogio*, in *Vichiana. Rassegna di studi filologici e storici*, 18, 1989, p. 99 ss.

107 See J. Gothofredus, *Codex Theodosianus*, III, cit., p. 278. A. Di Berardino, *Christian Liturgical Time and Torture*, cit., p. 216, points out that, to refer to the period of Lent, John Chrysostom uses the expression *sancta quadragesima* while Agostino talks about *sancti dies*.

108 *De obitu Valentiniani consolatio*, 18.

cum facillime in hoc summi numinis speretur venia, per quod multorum salus et incolumitas procuratur. Dat. V kal. Mai. Constantinopoli Basso et Philippo conss. (408).[109]

The emperor admonishes the judges of the provinces who were not to suspend the application of torture against *latrones Isauri* during Lent and on Easter day. As we know, the Isaurians can be attributed with numerous raids and, in particular, they can be blamed for the depredation, between 404 and 408, of South and East Asia Minor, of the Diocese of the East and the island of Cyprus.[110]

It is therefore a constitution that contains emergency rules, clearly dictated to reinforce the instruments available to the *iudices* when it was time for them to try those responsible for such actions.

The explanation that the emperor provides on the need for such exceptional treatment is very significant: ... *cum facillime in hoc summi numinis speretur venia, per quod multorum salus et incolumitas procuratur.* Theodosius II states that the application of torture on *latrones Isauri* is justified for reaching safety and welfare of many: and in view of this divine forgiveness can be easily obtained.

The words of the emperor combine requirements for justice and religious aspects perhaps even more clearly than what happens in the other constitutions examined up to now: the application of Christian time, previously also used for governing civil and legal activities (criminal trial, application of torture, etc.) finds a limit here depending on contingent requirements.

It is perhaps possible to make out a connection with what was established by Constantine in C.3,12,2: as will be remembered, by ratifying abstention from work on the *dies Solis*, Constantine had however allowed work in the fields, clearly for reasons of "public utility";[111] Theodosius II, again to satisfy practical needs (in the case in question security and safety), established the possibility for the judges to resort to torture also on days considered as feasts.[112]

109 "CTh. 9,35,7. Emperors Honorius and Theodosius Augustuses to Anthemius, Praetorian Prefect. The judges of the provinces shall be admonished that in the examination under torture of the Isaurian brigands, the betrayal of the wicked plans of the brigands shall not be deferred, although such betrayal must be sought through the torture of the brigands. They shall not suppose that any day of the Quadragesima or the holy day of Easter shall be excepted, since pardon of the Highest Divinity is very easily hoped for in regard to such action, by which the safety and welfare of many are obtained. Given on the fifth day before the kalends of May at Constantinople in the year of the consulship of Bassus and Philippus – April 27 (February 26), 408." (English translation in C. Pharr, *The Theodosian Code*, cit., p. 251).

110 On all of this see essentially E. Stein, *Histoire du bas-empire. 1.1. De l'etat romain a l'etat byzantine, Texte*, Bruges, 1959, p. 238. There is reference to the various episodes that featured the Isaurians as protagonists in the thread of testimonies of Ammianus Marcellinus and Zosimus, in J. Gothofredus, *Codex Theodosianus*, III, cit., p. 280.

111 On this problem in C. 3,12,2 see J. Rüpke, *The Roman Calendar from Numa to Constantine*, cit., p. 166 ss.

112 See J. Gothofredus, *Codex Theodosianus cum perpetuis commentariis*, III, cit., p. 280.

Within the context of the *Codex Iustinianus* derogation to the right of torture appears to be wider. In fact, by including the constitution in C. 3,12 *De feriis*, the compilers made a significant change to the text:

> C. 3,12,8(10). Impp. Honorius et Theodosius AA. Anthemio pp. Provinciarum iudices moneantur, ut in quaestionibus latronum et maxime Isaurorum, nullum quadragesimae nec venerabilem pascharum diem existiment excipiendum, ne differatur sceleratorum proditio consiliorum, quae per latronum tormenta quaerenda est, cum facillime in hoc summi numinis speretur venia, per quod multorum salus et incolumitas procuratur. D. v. k. Mai. Constantinopoli Basso et Philippo conss. (a. 408).[113]

Justinian's version of the constitution says *in quaestionibus latronum et maxime Isaurorum*: this means that the judges were free to apply torture during Lent and on Easter day against all *latrones*, and not only against Isaurians.[114]

VII CONCLUSION

The collection of constitutions examined herein has enabled us to reconstruct, although briefly, how the Christian emperors used some of the Christian feasts to influence the civil calendar, with special regard to the administration of justice.

It is an operation pursued particularly following the Edict of Thessalonica of 380 but that could possibly have its roots further back in time if we accept the idea that Constantine's constitutions on the *dies Solis* already had a Christian connotation, as many scholars believe.

These statutes are originally intended for different regions, issued to respond to particular, local needs. Think, for example, at CTh. 9,3,7 by Honorius. Involving the bishops on Sunday for the benefit of those in pre-trial detention in prison, the emperor dictated a measure justified by practical, contingent needs of integration of an inadequate public apparatus. Or to CTh. 9.35.5, of Theodosius I, who suspended torture during Lent probably following what happened after the revolt of Antiochia, when even the judges were horrified by the harshness of torture. Again for local needs, the same emperor re-enacts the torture during Lent, when the Isaurian thieves came into consideration.

In spite of the different motivations behind the various constitutions, it is possible to glimpse a common line gradually brought forward by the emperors: the occasion of the

113 "Emperors Honorius and Theodosius Augusti to Anthemius, Praetorian Praefect. Let the judges of the provinces be warned not to think that they should omit any of the forty days of Easter or even the holy day of Easter itself in examining bandits (under torture) and especially the Isaurians, so that the disclosure of criminal conspiracies, which is to be sought through the torture of bandits, may not be deferred, since for this purpose, through which the safety and peace of many is secured, pardon from the Almighty is unquestionably hoped for. Given April 27, in the consulship of Bassus and Philippus at Constantinople (408)." (English translation in B. W. Frier *et al.* (eds.), *The Codex of Justinian*, I, cit., p. 645 s.).

114 On this aspect of the Justinian version of the constitution, see R. Bonini, *Ricerche di diritto giustinianeo*, Milan, 1990, p. 120 and note 85.

Christian feasts is taken for the introduction of measures soothing brutal aspects of trials and administration of justice; also the pagans could benefit from these measures.[115]

Through imperial legislation, what we can define as "Christian time" became, at least with reference to certain sectors, the "time of law."

The Roman emperors began articulating time based on the liturgical days, and the most important Christian feasts became reference points for handling judicial activities[116] and, more generally, for a new social organization.

Reference was made in the first paragraph to the fact that the emperors apply, in their constitutions on the times of the trial, a pattern that comes from the pagan world, where there was a distinction (unknown to Christianity) between *dies fasti* and *dies nefasti*. We remembered Jerome in the first paragraph, for whom every day, without distinction, is a feast, because the resurrection is celebrated every day.

From this point of view it is possible to state that the pagan culture, through law, had an important impact on Christianity. These imperial constitutions led to a significant outcome: exactly as happened in the Roman pagan world, the days of Christian feasts took on a particular connotation which made them different from the others. Sacred time therefore obtained a special connotation, a *qualitas* that it did not have before.

A quick examination of the language used by the emperors in the different measures clarifies this point. Think, for example, about one of the constitutions dedicated to Sunday (CTh. 2,8, 18) where the emperor states that who does not respect the Sunday is a *sacrilegus*, because he turns aside from the inspiration and ritual of holy religion. Again, in Leo's constitution, Christian feast days are defined as *dies festi* and are connoted as special, since they are days dedicated to the Highest Majesty. In the measures on the suspension of torture during Lent, Theodosius I states that this period has a singular quality, being reserved for absolution of souls.

At the same time, the opposite assumption is also true: through imperial legislation, Christianity, with its liturgical feasts, has a strong impact on the Roman world.[117] Contractual and legal activity, precautionary imprisonment, the criminal trial, and torture are governed also considering the liturgical requirements of Christians.

This means that the importance of the feasts leaves the "private circle" of Christian communities and meets with the "public circle," contributing to regulating times and social organization, with deep consequences (in a much wider perspective) on the Western world.[118]

A significant example of "law as religion" and "religion as law."

115 See A. Di Berardino, *Christian Liturgical Time and Torture*, cit., p. 220.

116 M. Bianchini, *Cadenze liturgiche e calendario civile*, cit., p. 255 ss. Note how what is described appears to be a specular mechanism with respect to the one used by the Church which, starting from Constantine's era, started to take on similar administrative structures to the imperial ones.

117 In that regard, still in relation to CTh. 2,18,1 and C. 3,12,2, G. Anello, *The Rest and the West*, cit., p. 4.

118 See *id.*, p. 4, with reference to Constantine's legislation on the *dies Solis*.

E

Law in Formation: Religious Perspectives

14

Law as a Problematic Aspect of Religion

Paul's Skepticism in a Broader Jewish Context

Serge Ruzer

I INTRODUCTION

In his pioneering studies, E. P. Sanders described late Second Temple Judaism as "covenantal *nomism*" in the sense that while the demands of the law as derived from the Torah constitute a core element of the covenantal relationship between God and Israel, the covenant is not exhausted by its law-centered aspect. It includes additional foundational components like election, God's faithfulness, his mercy, and mechanisms of atonement and reconciliation. As the title of his book where the term was first introduced indicates,[1] it is in conversation with views found in the epistles of Paul, penned mostly during the 50s of the first century CE, that the scholar was able to portray this more nuanced picture of the contemporaneous Judaism. No wonder – Paul, a member of the nascent Jesus movement, a messianic offshoot of broader Judaism, provides many examples of coping with the law-centered tenets of religion juxtaposed to those of God's mercy revealed in messianic redemption. This chapter attempts to further clarify certain aspects of Sanders' important intuition.

Paul uses extensively the term *nomos* (law) with a variety of meanings: sometimes this may refer to a universal law, archetypal law of the cosmos, which, as already the Hellenistic Jewish second-century BCE *Letter of Aristeas* argued, essentially overlaps with the law revealed in the Torah.[2] I, however, focus here on the cases where the particular Jewish meaning of *nomos* as related to Torah is clearly indicated by the context. This focus will allow to revisit the issue of Paul's grasp of the interactions between various parts of the Torah-centered law and their standing vis-à-vis other aspects of the covenant. Contextualizing Paul's strategies against the backdrop of the

[1] Ed P. Sanders, *Paul and Palestinian Judaism: A Comparison of Patterns of Religion* (Philadelphia: Fortress Press, 1977). See also Ed P. Sanders, "'A Covenant to the People, a Light to the Nations': Universalism, Exceptionalism, and the Problem of Chosenness in Jewish Thought," *Jewish Studies Quarterly* 16.1 (2009): 23–55.

[2] The equation that would be later propagated by Philo, see discussion in Christine Hayes, *What Is Divine about Divine Law?* (Princeton and Oxford: Princeton University Press, 2015), 122–24. That the outlines of universal law were available to the Gentiles without the Torah and thus they are responsible for fulfilling it, seems to be indicated in Rom 2:12: "All those who sinned without the law/Torah will also perish without the law/Torah."

variety of early Jewish thought patterns, I would argue that while propagating a singular, Jesus-centered, message – in many cases explicitly directed at Gentile fellow-travelers – Paul also addresses concerns of his implicit Jewish audience. His arguments thus echo and bear witness to a broader intra-Jewish awareness of the problematic aspect of the notion of religion as first and foremost law.

II TORAH AND THE WORKS OF THE TORAH

Scholars have long recognized nascent Christianity's multifaceted nature reflected in various, sometimes contradictory, emphases found within the Jesus movement during the first decades of its history. Attitudes to the demands of Jewish religious law, as expressed, on the one hand, in the Book of Acts, and, on the other hand, in Paul's authentic letters provide a telling example of such unresolved tension. According to Acts, in the times of messianic redemption those Gentiles who become part of the Jesus movement are exempt from embracing some ritual markers of belonging to Judaism. However, the continuing faithfulness of Jewish believers in Jesus to these precepts is never questioned, but rather presented as harmonious with their adherence to Jesus the Messiah (Acts 15:1–29; 21:18–25).[3] As a matter of fact, it seems that even Gentiles willing to embrace some positive Mosaic ritual prescriptions, preached in the Diaspora synagogues, are welcome to do so or, at least, not reprimanded for this inclination.[4]

Paul's writings, however, are distinguished by a different and clearly polemical emphasis, unequivocally denying the capacity of Judaism's ritual prescriptions to contribute to the cleansing of the hearts. These prescriptions might have had such

[3] Thus the author characteristically insists – in a balancing act compensating for the tragic Stephen episode in Acts 7 – that not only the first Jerusalem-based apostles but also Paul, returning to the city in the wake of his praiseworthy missionary successes among the non-Jews in the Diaspora, remained faithful to the Temple, undoubtedly the core element of Jewish ritual observance of the day (Acts 2:46; 21:26). See Hans Conzelmann, *Acts of the Apostles: A Commentary on the Acts of the Apostles* (Hermeneia; Philadelphia: Fortress, 1987), 24. For discussion of the narrative strategies throughout Acts, see, for example, Steven G. Wilson, *The Gentiles and the Gentile Mission in Luke-Acts* (Cambridge: Cambridge University Press, 1973); Robert L. Brawley, *Luke-Acts and the Jews: Conflict, Apology, and Conciliation* (Atlanta, GA: Scholars Press, 1987); Serge Ruzer, "Crucifixion: The Search for a Meaning vis-à-vis Biblical Prophecy. From Luke to Acts," in *Mapping the New Testament: Early Christian Writings as a Witness for Jewish Biblical Exegesis* (Leiden: Brill, 2007), 187–99. See also Justin Taylor, "Paul and the Jewish Leaders at Rome: Acts 28:17–31," in *Paul's Jewish Matrix*, eds. Thomas G. Casey and Justin Taylor (Rome: Gregorian and Biblical Press, 2011), 311–26. But cf. Martin Hengel, "The Beginnings of Christianity as a Jewish-Messianic and Universalistic Movement," in *The Beginnings of Christianity: A Collection of Articles*, eds. J. Pastor and M. Mor (Jerusalem: Yad Ben-Zvi, 2005, 85–100; Martin Hengel, *The Atonement: The Origins of the Doctrine in the New Testament* (Philadelphia: Fortress Press, 1981). In Hengel's view, the insight that the fulfillment of Torah ritual demands in general (and, more specifically, those connected to Temple worship) has lost its ability to effect forgiveness of sins and a place in the world-to-come, constituted a salient marker of the early Jesus movement as a whole almost from its inception, and thus distinguished it from broader Judaism.

[4] See Acts 15:21.

a capacity in the past; but in the messianic era, it is exclusively identification with and "sharing" in the Messiah's expiating death, and belief in his resurrection, that constitute the path leading to salvation – by grace and not by acquired merit. It is in this either-or context characterizing the Epistle to the Galatians that Paul comes to view those "external" precepts as harmful, as blocking the way to individual justification in the eyes of God through grace (Gal. 2:21, cf. Rom. 3:20): "I do not nullify the grace of God; for if justification were through the law (*nomos*, Torah?), then Christ died to no purpose." Moreover, those who still put their hope in the "works of the law (Torah)" are bringing upon themselves "law's/Torah's curse" (Gal 3:10–11, 6:15). The argument in chapter 2 of the epistle, where the phrase the "works of the *nomos*," obviously central for Paul's thinking there, is used repeatedly and emphatically, strengthens the understanding that *nomos* here means specifically the Torah of Israel (Gal. 2:15-16):[5]

> We ourselves, who are Jews by birth and not Gentile sinners, yet who know that a man is not justified by works of the law (ἐξ ἔργων νόμου), but through faith in Jesus Christ/the Messiah, even we have believed in Christ/the Messiah Jesus, in order to be justified by faith in Christ, and not by works of the law (οὐκ ἐξ ἔργων νόμου), because by works of the law (ἐξ ἔργων νόμου) shall no one be justified.

The Epistle to the Galatians is explicitly addressed to Gentile followers of Jesus in Galatia, who are under pressure from some representatives of the Jewish section of the movement to embrace Judaism's ritual practices, first of all circumcision so that the Jews and the Gentiles of the messianic group can become one community, for example, eat together (Gal. 2:11–14).[6] One then is justified in viewing the "works of the Torah" language as belonging to the discussion of that core issue – in other words, the phrase seems to designate the ritual markers of Jewish tradition. Therefore, the "works of the law, ἔργα νόμου," that Paul expresses doubts with regard to their effectiveness (Gal. 2:15–21) should be understood in this context in a limited sense – namely, as designating those practices prescribed by the Torah that serve as "identity badges" separating Jews from their Gentile neighbors. They are thus distinguished from the "core commandments" defining God's covenant with Israel or the Torah (νόμος) proper, such as the Decalogue and Leviticus 19:18 – passages that indisputably retain their centrality in the apostle's interpretation of the messianic salvation in Jesus, as forcefully expressed, e.g., in Gal 5:14.[7] Such an understanding of the "works of the law" finds corroboration in the מעשי התורה (*ma'asei ha-torah*, the works of the Torah) usage attested in 4QMMT from

5 The English quotations from the Old and New Testaments throughout this chapter are from the RSV.

6 For discussion of the nature of the "Galatian crisis," see, for example, Francis Watson, *Paul, Judaism, and the Gentiles: Beyond the New Perspective* (Grand Rapids, MI; Eerdmans, 2007), 100–08.

7 See James D. G. Dunn, "Works of the Law and the Curse of the Law (Galatians 3:10–4)," *NTS* 31.4 (1985): 523–42. For a criticism of Dunn's thesis, see Charles E. B. Cranfield, "The Works of the Law in the Epistle to the Romans," *JSNT* 43 (1991): 89–101; Dunn's response is found in his "Yet Once More 'The Works of the Law': A Response," *JSNT* 46 (1992): 99–117.

Qumran, where the phrase denotes ritual precepts, marking the proper observance of the Temple cult, corrupted according to the composers of the document by the current priestly leadership.[8] This ritual understanding is further confirmed when Paul reiterates the core opposition mentioned above (Gal. 5:2): "Now, I, Paul, say to you that if you receive circumcision, Messiah/Christ will be of no advantage to you."

Such a reading, highlighting the Gentiles within the Jesus movement as Paul's intended audience, supports the interpretation suggested by a number of influential scholars subscribing to what is now customarily called the New Perspective on Paul. Among them Krister Stendahl, John Gager, and Paula Fredriksen, who emphasized the specific context in which Paul's harsh statements concerning the (works of the) Torah were meant to resonate – namely, the non-Jewish addressees of the apostle's writings.[9] It was argued, moreover, that Paul's claim that pious Gentiles do not have to observe the positive ritual precepts of the Torah, for example, perform circumcision (whereas the prohibition of participating in idol worship was emphatically upheld by Paul with regard to the Gentile fellow travelers too),[10] in fact followed an accepted, particularly in the Hellenistic Diaspora, Jewish perception. Namely, even in the last days, the Gentiles will join the redemption in accordance with the pattern found in the biblical prophecy, that is, as Gentiles, without blurring the borderline between Israel and the nations. Following Isaiah's prophecy, the nations will come to the mountain of the Lord to serve him together with the Jews and become privy to the core messages of God's Torah, while remaining ethnically and culturally distinct from the people of Israel.[11] According to this influential approach,

8 4Q398 (4QMMT e), Frags. 14–17, 2:2–8; 4Q399 (4QMMT f), 1:11. See Dunn, "Works of the Law"; Joseph A. Fitzmyer, "Paul's Jewish Background and the Deeds of the Law," in *According to Paul: Studies in the Theology of the Apostle* (Mahwah, NJ: Paulist Press, 1993), 8–35, esp. 21–23. For a variety of appraisals – mostly differing from Dunn's – of the link observed here between Paul and 4QMMT, see Martin G. Abegg, Jr., "Paul, 'Works of the Law' and MMT," *BAR* 20:6 (1994): 52–61, 82; idem, "4QMMT, Paul, and 'Works of the Law'," in *The Bible at Qumran: Text, Shape, and Interpretation*, ed. Peter W. Flint (Studies in the Dead Sea Scrolls and Related Literature; Grand Rapids, MI: Eerdmans, 2001), 203–16, esp. 205–06; Tom N. Wright, "Paul and Qumran," *BR* 14.5 (1998): 18–54, esp. 54; Jacqueline C. R. de Roo, "The Concept of 'Works of the Law' in Jewish and Christian Literature," in *Christian-Jewish Relationships through the Centuries*, eds. Stanley E. Porter and Brook W. R. Pearson (Sheffield: Sheffield Academic Press, 2000), 116–47. It deserves notice that it is in this context that Paul moves to talk about Abraham, for whom his faith "was reckoned as righteousness" (Gen. 15:6) long before he was circumcised (Gal. 3:6–9).

9 See, for example, Krister Stendahl, *Final Account: Paul's Letter to the Romans* (Minneapolis, MN: Augsburg Fortress, 1995); John Gager, *Reinventing Paul* (Oxford: Oxford University Press, 2000), 43–75; Paula Fredriksen, "Judaism, the Circumcision of Gentiles, and Apocalyptic Hope: Another Look at Galatians 1 and 2," *JTS* 42 (1991): 532–64.

10 As, for example, in 1 Cor. 10:14–22.

11 See Isa. 2:1–4; Paula Fredriksen, "Judaism, the Circumcision of Gentiles." Correspondingly those are, in fact, Paul's opponents within the Jesus movement, insisting on "Judaizing" Gentiles who have embraced Jesus as the Messiah of Israel, who act as innovators here. Their stance may be seen as a reaction to the perceived delay in the arrival of the end and the corresponding changes in the projected redemption scenario – a longer historical perspective or, alternatively, the upcoming catastrophic phase of wars and disasters – with both perspectives engendering a need for socially consolidating the Jesus movement (ibid., pp. 558–61).

the demands to Gentiles wishing to become part of Israel's vocation are basically two: abandoning idol worship for the sake of worshipping the one God and adopting a truly moral behavior derived from the allegiance to the Creator.[12] Paul therefore followed here a beaten track, and since he addressed Gentiles only, he obviously did not intend to introduce any drastic reevaluation of the Torah vis-à-vis Jews.[13]

This new view of Paul clearly has its merits. However, as I argued elsewhere, the context of Galatians indicates that besides the Gentile fellow-travelers Paul must have had an additional, hidden, audience in mind – namely, those Jewish propagandists from within the movement, whose pressure on the Gentile members of the community prompted the apostle's response.[14] In fact, the opening line of the passage under discussion too points to a supposed intra-Jewish logic of the argument (Gal. 2:15–16): "We ourselves, who are Jews by birth and not Gentile sinners . . . know that a man is not justified by the works of the Torah . . ." One is therefore prompted to ask if the apostle's collation of a hierarchical distinction between the hard-core commandments of the Torah and the peripheral "ritual markers" of Judaism with the claim that those ritual "works of the Torah" do not actually contribute to achieving the righteousness epitomized in the Torah's foundational precepts, could resonate within the Jewish milieu too.

As noted above, this kind of outlook was somehow reflected in the general Hellenistic Jewish attitude toward Gentile sympathizers. The awareness of the hierarchical relationships between ritual markers of Judaism and its moral precepts is expressed in the second century BCE *Letter of Aristeas*. The Jewish sages there, also addressing Gentile audience, both emphasize the shared ethical values of the Torah and general Hellenistic outlook and try to argue for the usefulness – though they are not obligatory for the Gentiles – of Jewish ritual prescriptions as "helping devices" in educating our souls in their path to moral perfection.[15] It seems, however, that the hierarchical division – based on a variety of principles and with a different outcome – was applied to intra-Jewish religious discourse too, as aptly expressed in a well-known passage from the famous first century CE Jewish Hellenistic author, Philo of Alexandria:

> *There are some who, taking the laws in their literal sense as symbols of intelligible realities, are over-precise in their investigation of the symbol, while frivolously*

[12] This is, apropos, the approach reflected in Romans 1.

[13] According to this new approach, the age-long erroneous perception of Paul as a rebel against the Torah is a result of an anachronistic reading of his epistles in light of a later Christian outlook that emerged in different socio-historical circumstances of a clear-cut division and border marking. For example, Fredriksen has highlighted that some later notions emerging in the wake of and as a reaction to the destruction of the Temple, with Jewish followers of Jesus being gradually marginalized, were completely foreign to Paul's thinking. See Paula Fredriksen, "Paul, Purity, and the 'Ekklesia' of the Gentiles," in *The Beginnings of Christianity*, eds. J. Pastor and M. Mor (Jerusalem: Yad Ben-Zvi Press, 2005) 205–17, esp. 215–16.

[14] See Serge Ruzer, "Paul's Stance on the Torah Revisited: Gentile Addressees and the Jewish Setting," in *Paul's Jewish Matrix*, eds. Thomas G. Casey and Justin Taylor (Rome: Gregorian & Biblical Press, 2011), 75–97.

[15] See R. H. Charles (ed.), *Letter of Aristeas* (Oxford: The Clarendon Press, 1913), 139–68.

> *neglecting the letter. Such people I, for my part, should blame for their cool indifference, for they ought to have cultivated both a more precise investigation of things invisible and an unexceptionable stewardship of things visible.* As it is, as if living alone by themselves in a wilderness, or as if they had become discarnate souls, knowing neither city nor village nor household nor any company of humans at all, transcending what is approved by the crowd, they track the absolute truth in its naked self. These men are taught by Sacred Scripture to be concerned with public opinion, and to abolish no part of the customs ordained by inspired men, greater than those of our own day.
>
> For all that the Seventh Day teaches us the power of the un-originate and the non-action of created beings, let us by no means annul the laws laid down for its observance, kindling fire, tilling the earth, carrying burdens, instituting changes, sitting in judgment, demanding the return of deposits, recovering loans, or doing all else that is permitted in non-festal seasons. And though it is true that the Feast is a symbol of spiritual joy and of thankfulness to God, let us not bid adieu to the annual seasonal gatherings. And though it is true that circumcision indicates the excision of pleasure and all passions and the removal of the godless conceit under which the mind supposed itself capable of engendering through its own powers, let us not abrogate the law laid down for circumcising. For we shall be neglecting the Temple service and a thousand other things if we are to pay sole regard to that which is revealed by the inner meaning. We ought rather to look on the outward observances as resembling the body, and their inner meaning as resembling the soul. Just as we then provide for the body, inasmuch as it is the abode of the soul, so we must attend to the letter of the laws. *If we keep these, we shall obtain an understanding of those things of which they are symbols*, and in addition, we shall escape the censure and accusations of the multitude.[16]

Philo tellingly attests to a variety of Jewish attitudes toward the "external" precepts of the Torah – from neglecting to upholding them – all of which acknowledge the above division and share the conviction that the true meaning of the commandments is the "internal" one. Philo himself clearly ascribes to this consensual appraisal and confirms the priority of the inner meaning of the Torah precepts. Unlike some of his Jewish contemporaries, however, whom he criticizes for their readiness to drop ritual observance altogether and deal directly with the mending of their "inner man,"[17] Philo – a responsible member of the community who recognizes the constraints of our physical and social existence – upholds the validity of the ritual side of Jewish tradition as befitting external means for "gradually educating one's soul." Nevertheless, the problematic tension between the two divisions (or interpretations) of the law lingers: As aptly observed by Christine Hayes, while Philo's move aspired to strengthen the ritual aspect of the Mosaic Law, it could inadvertently "*enable* precisely that which Philo here protests."[18]

[16] Philo, *Migration of Abraham* 89–93 (emphasis added).
[17] Ibid., 89–93.
[18] Hayes, *What is Divine about Divine Law?*, 124 (emphasis in original).

Such dichotomist perceptions seem to have not been limited to the Greco-Roman Diaspora only. Though evidence concerning the early proto-rabbinic tradition is scarce and relatively late, it may indicate that the idea of a twofold partition of the bulk of religious precepts was known and duly discussed in the Land of Israel too. Suffice it to quote a tradition ascribed to none other than the second-century codifier of the Mishnaic law himself (*m.* ʾ*Abot* 2.1):[19]

> R. Judah the Prince said: Which is the proper course that a man should choose for himself? That which is an honor to him and elicits honor from his fellow men. Be as scrupulous about a light precept (מצוה קלה) as of a weighty one (כחמורה), for you do not know the reward allotted for each precept. Balance the loss incurred by the fulfillment of a precept against the gain and the accruing from a transgression against the loss it involves. Reflect on three things and you will never come to sin: Know what is above you – a seeing eye, a hearing ear, and all your deeds recorded in a book.[20]

One notes a partial overlap of terminology between our early third-century Mishnah and Matthew 5:19 (τῶν ἐντολῶν τούτων τῶν ἐλαχίστων, "the least of these/ the light commandments") – an overlap that points to the terminology's early provenance. Moreover, not unlike Philo (and Jesus in Matthew 5:19!),[21] the Mishnah votes for the importance of the efforts to fulfill precepts ostensibly not belonging to the core of the Torah. Though the reasons may be different, the "peripheral" commandments are seen here too as being in the final account expedient for a person's "balance of merits." And again, like Philo, the Mishnah mirrors an alternative approach, which it polemically rejects. Finally, while the dichotomy itself emerges as a shared feature of a whole spectrum of traditions, its character – namely, what commandments are seen as belonging to either category – may vary considerably. Thus, as distinct from Philo with his dichotomy between internal/spiritual and external meaning of the commandment, the Mishnah – similarly, for example, to Jesus' stance in Matthew 23:23 – seems to understand both categories as pertaining to the realm of deeds.[22]

19 Cf. Matt. 23:23 "Woe to you, scribes and Pharisees, hypocrites! For you tithe mint and dill and cummin, and have neglected the weightier matters of the law, justice and mercy and faith; these you ought to have done, without neglecting the others."

20 The English translation of Mishnaic material in this paper follows Herbert Danby, *The Mishnah* (Oxford: Oxford University Press, 1950).

21 "Whoever then relaxes one of the least of these commandments and teaches men so, shall be called least in the kingdom of heaven; but he who does them and teaches them shall be called great in the kingdom of heaven."

22 Matt. 23:23: "Woe to you, scribes and Pharisees, hypocrites! For you tithe mint and dill and cummin, and have neglected the weightier matters of the law, justice and mercy and faith; these you ought to have done, without neglecting the others." Cf. ʾ*Abot* 1.1, 3.13 ("the fence around the Torah"). The nature of the dichotomy – or hierarchy – indicated in Matthew 5 warrants further discussion. See Serge Ruzer, "Antitheses in Matthew 5: Midrashic Aspects of Exegetical Techniques," in Serge Ruzer, *Mapping the New Testament: Early Christian Writings as a Witness for Jewish Biblical Exegesis* (Leiden: Brill, 2007), 11–34.

If in the tractate ʾAbot the "light" commandments are presented as *potentially* expedient for God's approval, another telling Mishnaic tradition speaks of the fateful eschatological transformation of the individual – that is, the gift of the holy Spirit and the resurrection – as *conditioned* by the sequence of efforts at fulfilling, inter alia, ritual (external, secondary) observances (*m. Sotah* 9.15):

> R. Pinhas son of Yair says: "Expediency brings to cleanness, cleanness brings to purity, purity brings to chastity, chastity brings to holiness, holiness brings to meekness, meekness brings to the fear of sin, fear of sin brings to righteousness, righteousness brings to the spirit of holiness (holy spirit), and the holy spirit brings to the resurrection of the dead, and the resurrection of the dead comes through Elijah of blessed memory. Amen."

The historical context here is that of the destruction of the Temple and anticipation of redemption. Yet it stands to reason that the singling out of certain ritual observances as crucial for obtaining righteousness and eventually redemption is linked and point to an older topic – as does the previously discussed mishnaic passage.

To sum up, all the reviewed sources express awareness of one or another kind of distinction between primary and secondary (meaning of) Torah precepts, thus allowing to contextualize Paul's arguments within broader Jewish trends. While in the final account these sources uphold the validity of the secondary, for example, ritual, commandments, they indirectly attest to the possibility of an alternative tendency to dismiss those commandments as not crucial – an attitude they polemicize against.[23] Paul in Galatians therefore may be viewed as reflecting that alternative tendency; and his daring move could have been helped by the fact that he first came to discuss the issue while addressing a non-Jewish audience, which as noted, was perceived from the beginning as not obliged to the ritual identity markers of Judaism.

III THE CORE DEMANDS OF THE TORAH LAW

Having rejected the auxiliary value of the ritual precepts, Paul states explicitly what constitutes the true core of the Torah law, unswervingly obliging in the Messianic era – namely, Leviticus 19:18 precept "love your neighbor as yourself" (Gal. 5:14–15): "For the whole law (ὁ γὰρ πᾶς νόμος) is fulfilled in one saying (ἐν ἑνὶ λόγῳ), 'You shall love your neighbor as yourself'. But if you bite and devour one another take heed that you are not consumed by one another." Further on, in Galatians 5:22–23, the apostle clarifies the expectations from interpersonal relations, derived from the Leviticus 19:18 directive: "love, joy, peace, patience, kindness, goodness, faithfulness, gentleness, self-control; with regard to such there is no measure (limitations)."[24]

23 At least in the case of Philo, it is clear that we are not dealing with a polemical response to Paul, but in my opinion the same goes, e.g., for the ruling from *m. ʾAvot* 2.1.

24 Supposedly, an early reflection of the Rabbinic terminology of אין שיעור (no measure/limitations) – e.g., in *y. Yoma* 5.4.

It turns out, however, that Paul is not only pessimistic with regard to the ritual exercises' capacity to help one achieve the perfection of the great love command, but in fact denies the ability to fulfill it through any efforts of our own. According to the apostle, the very nature of the foundational demands of the religious law is such that we are unable to satisfy them however hard we try – it is only through the intervention of the divine agency of the Spirit that the mission can be accomplished. In other words, our only hope to achieve the true righteousness propagated by law, namely, to fulfil the above lofty aspects of the Lev 19:18 precept – is to be endowed with the Spirit (Gal. 5:5–16, 22, 24–25):

> *For through the Spirit, by faith, we wait for the hope of righteousness. . . . But I say, walk by the Spirit, and do not gratify the desires of the flesh. . . . . But the fruit of the Spirit is love, joy, peace, patience, kindness, goodness, faithfulness, gentleness, self-control* . . . And those who belong to the Messiah Jesus have crucified the flesh with its passions and desires. If we live by the Spirit, let us also walk by the Spirit. [emphasis added]

Thus, whereas the validity (usefulness) of the "secondary" law precepts is questioned, with regard to the indisputable core elements of the Torah-related righteousness it is our ability to fulfill them that is negated. We will return below to the motif of the Spirit as the great enabler, as well as to that of Jesus's atoning death, but for now suffice it to note that such an appraisal appears to undermine the whole function of the Torah as covenantal law.

It is possible to try interpreting this deeply seated skepticism in Galatians too as directed specifically at the Gentiles – in accordance with a broader Jewish perspective on Gentiles as "sinful by nature," reflected, as we have seen, in Galatians 2:15 ("We ourselves, who are Jews by birth and not Gentile sinners"). According to this interpretation, therefore, it is only through the intervention of the Spirit that the "Gentile nature" could be reformed and the Gentiles become capable of fulfilling the Torah's great commandment. However, as already the beginning of the slightly later Epistle to the Romans testifies, ostensibly addressing concerns of both Gentile and Jewish segments of the community in Rome,[25] that basic inability to cope with the Torah as law was viewed by the apostle as characteristic of Jews as well.[26]

In Romans, that "final account" of Paul's writing,[27] characteristically, the issue of ritual markers so central to Galatians takes a back seat,[28] with the epistle focusing

25 See, for example, John Murray, *The Epistle to the Romans*, vol. 1 (Grand Rapids, MI: Eerdmans, 1959), xviii–xxii; Norman Perring and Dennis C. Duling, *The New Testament: An Introduction* (San Diego et al.: Harcourt Brace Jovanovich, 1982), 187; Joseph A. Fitzmyer, *Romans: A New Translation with Introduction and Commentary* (London: Chapman, 1992), 31–34; cf. Gager, *Reinventing Paul*, 101, who while believing – in accordance with the New Approach tendency – that Romans likewise targets exclusively the Gentile audience, concedes that this epistle does speak "about Jews" too.

26 See Romans 2.

27 See Krister Stendahl, *Final Account: Paul's Letter to the Romans* (Minneapolis: Fortress Press, 1995).

28 See, for example, Rom. 3:20.

instead on the basic incapacity of both Gentiles and Jews to properly respond to the core demands of God's law.[29] The Gentiles' failure is explained already in Romans 1 as resulting – in accordance with broader patterns of Jewish propaganda – from betrayal of the belief in one Creator. As for the Jewish failure, highlighted in Romans 2 in respect to one Decalogue precept, it receives its comprehensive explanation later on, in Romans 7.[30] Finding unconvincing the attempts to interpret the reasoning in Romans 7 as targeting exclusively the "Gentile predicament,"[31] I therefore side with those who discern here Paul's grim diagnosis of the human condition, *Jews included*.[32] In the final account, what is central to my argument is that whoever are the explicit intended addressees of the reasoning in Romans 7, we should take into account – the move already probed above with regard to Galatians – the implicit Jewish audience too. The apostle's pessimistic appraisal is characteristically complemented with the quantum leap, leading from the earlier impotence vis-à-vis the demands of the law imposed from outside to the new mode of existence (Romans 7:4–6):

> Likewise, my brethren, you have died to the Torah/law through the body of Christ/the Messiah, so that you may belong to another, to him who has been raised from the dead in order that we may bear fruit for God. [5] While we were living in the flesh, our sinful passions, aroused by the law, were at work in our members to bear fruit for death. [6] But now we are discharged from the law, dead to that which held us captive, so that we serve not under the old written code but in the new life of the Spirit.

The appearance of the favorite Pauline expression "bear fruit" collated with the centrality of the Spirit, duly noted in the earlier discussion of Galatians 5, indicates that the "freedom from the law" here does not at all mean lawless frivolity. It rather designates a new stance "in the Spirit," finally enabling one to fulfill the core Torah commandments, which was impossible when one's relation to the law was

[29] Romans thus presents itself as a continuation of the discussion in Galatians, with Paul striving to clarify his position and "to ward off potential and actual misreadings of his (earlier) arguments" (Gager, *Reinventing Paul*, 103).

[30] Rom. 7:1 ("Do you know, brethren – for I am speaking to those who know the law/Torah . . . ") is one more indication of the epistle's engagement with the concerns of the Jewish component of the community in Rome; see note 26 above.

[31] As, for instance, in the Stowers' claim that "the persona of Romans 7," for whose sake Paul performs here the speech-in-character act, "can only be a gentile" (Stanley K. Stowers, *A Rereading of Romans: Justice, Jews & Gentiles* (New Haven & London: Yale University Press, 1994), 277). Stowers bases his assessment, inter alia, on his observation that the "sin as power" pattern of thought, is "not typical of the Hebrew Bible/Old Testament . . . but rather . . . of Homer and Greek poets" (ibid., p. 272), ignoring later, and more relevant, Jewish evidence. See also note 34 below and discussion there. Stowers views Romans as a whole in terms of exclusively Gentile intended audience (ibid., pp. 32–33, *pace*, e.g., Wernerm G. Kümmel, *Introduction to the New Testament*, 17th rev. ed. (Nashville: Abingdon Press, 1975), 307–10).

[32] Cf. Fitzmyer, *Romans*, pp. 473–77, where Romans 7 is understood as presenting the case of the human Ego.

that of vis-à-vis externally ordered obligation. In fact, Paul himself continues to clarify the matter (Romans 7:7-12):

> What then shall we say? That the law is sin? By no means! *Yet, if it had not been for the law, I should not have known sin.* I should not have known what it is to covet if the law had not said, "You shall not covet." [8] But *sin, finding opportunity in the commandment, wrought in me all kinds of covetousness.* Apart from the law sin lies dead . . . [10] the very commandment which promised life proved to be death to me. [11] *For sin, finding opportunity in the commandment, deceived me and by it killed me.* [12] *So the law is holy, and the commandment is holy and just and good.* Did that which is good, then, bring death to me? By no means! *It was sin, working death in me through what is good* . . . [emphasis added]

So, the law "is good" and it opens one's eyes, teaching what sin is, but, unfortunately the law does not provide one with the capability to resist sin (cf. Romans 3:20). Moreover, in our encounter with the just demands of God's law, sin manages to exploit our pervert nature (evil inclination?),[33] turning the commandment into temptation to disobey it. The problematic side of the "written code" is idiosyncratically emphasized here, though Paul takes care to piously ascribe the blame not to the Torah itself, which is holy, but to the defective human condition – and Jews are clearly not exempted.

In the following programmatic passage, Paul further elaborates on the issue, this time pointing to our "being flesh" as the real culprit (Romans 7:14–25):[34]

> We know that **the Torah/law is spiritual**; but I am carnal, sold under sin. [15] I do not understand my own actions. For I do not do what I want, but I do the very thing I hate. [16] Now if I do what I do not want, I agree that the law is good. [17] So then it is no longer I that do it, but sin which dwells within me. [18] *For I know that nothing good dwells within me, that is, in my flesh. I can will what is right, but I cannot do it.* [19] For I do not do the good I want, but the evil I do not want is what I do. [20] Now if I do what I do not want, it is no longer I that do it, but sin which dwells within me. [21] So I find it to be *a law* that when I want to do right, evil lies close at hand. [22] For *I delight in the law of God, in my inmost self,* [23] but *I see in my members another law* at war with *the law of my mind* and making me captive to the *law of sin which dwells in my members.* [24] Wretched man that I am! Who will deliver me from this body of death? [25] Thanks be to God through Jesus Christ our Lord! So then, I of myself serve *the law of God* with my mind, but with my flesh I serve the *law of sin.*[35]

[33] See discussion in Serge Ruzer, "The Seat of Sin in Early Jewish and Christian Sources," in *Transformations of Inner Self in Ancient Religions*, eds. Jan Assmann and Guy G. Stroumsa (Leiden: Brill, 1999), 151–65.

[34] See Ephraim E. Urbach, *The Sages: Their Concepts and Beliefs* (Jerusalem: Magnes Press, 1987), 472, who argues that such a localization of the sinful inclination in the body – in other words, the dualism of body and soul – while current "in the Hellenistic world, and also in Jewish Hellenism," was not characteristic of the rabbinic Sages.

[35] Whether the "I" of the passage provides a glimpse of Paul's own autobiographical exposure or represents the "speech in character" rhetorical device only, is an intriguing and much debated question. It is, however, irrelevant for the present discussion (emphasis added).

Telling is the variety of meanings in which the word "law" ($\nu\acute{o}\mu o\varsigma$) is used. First, the law is God's Torah addressed to our inner man, to our mind (*nous*) – thus it is "spiritual" (cf. Philo's position discussed above). However, when devoid of the Spirit, our response to God's law is "carnal," which means transgressing the commandment we are supposed to fulfill, thus succumbing to the "law of our bodily members," a sinful negative of God's holy Torah.[36]

According to Paul, this pitiful stance vis-à-vis God's law will continue until the body, which, as it were, pulls us down, is metaphorically "put to death" overwhelmed by the Spirit. The belief in Jesus' atoning death, combined with the notion of our bodies' metaphorical "death to sin," seems to reflect – and drastically modify – here a broader idea that until the very moment of physical death we all, even the righteous ones, are destined to incessantly struggle with sin. This is, for example, how this idea is expressed in the rabbinical midrash *Genesis Rabbah* (9.5):[37]

> "And lo, very good" (Genesis 1:31). [What is very good?] It is death. Why was the death ordained [even] for pious ones? [Because] all the time when they are [still] alive they spend fighting their evil impulse. [Only] when they die, they [may at last] rest.

This death-centered perception of final transformation is characteristically collated in Paul with the belief in the liberating function of the Spirit (Romans 7:24–8:4):

> Wretched man that I am! Who will deliver me from this body of death? [25] Thanks be to God through Jesus Christ/the Messiah our Lord! So then, I of myself serve the law of God with my mind, but with my flesh I serve the law of sin. 8:1 There is therefore now no condemnation for those who are in Chris/the Messiaht Jesus. [2] For the law of the Spirit of life in Christ/the Messiah Jesus has set me free from the law of sin and death. [3] *For God has done what the law, weakened by the flesh, could not do*: sending his own Son in the likeness of sinful flesh and for sin, he condemned sin in the flesh, [4] *in order that the just requirement of the law might be fulfilled in us*, who walk not according to the flesh but according to the Spirit. [emphasis added]

One notes that the crux of Paul's reasoning is the aspiration to finally be able to fulfill "the just requirements of the Torah."[38] The Torah is helpless: even if it still has a very

36 As I suggested in an earlier study, Paul may be here a witness to a pristine phase in a trajectory leading in later rabbinic sources to the idea that each bodily member is tasked with fulfilling the specific commandment assigned to it by the Torah. See Serge Ruzer, "The Seat of Sin."

37 The English quotation is from the *Midrash Rabbah*, ed. and tr. by H. Freedman (London: Soncino Press, 1939). See discussion in Serge Ruzer, "The Death Motif in Late Antique Jewish *Teshuva* Narrative Patterns and in Paul's Thought," in *Transformations of Inner Self*, eds. Assmann and Stroumsa (Leiden: Brill, 199), 151–65, esp. 158–62.

38 In contradistinction to what was until only a few decades ago the traditional view of Paul, which ascribed to the apostle the conviction that the dawn of the messianic era in its very essence heralded a divorce from the Jewish religious outlook centered on the Torah and its commandments. Statements on the Torah's (partial) validity and absolute holiness were correspondingly explained away as secondary and/or dictated by the needs of the mission. This appraisal had a long history in theological thought – both among Christians, who embraced this position as their own and among

important function to accomplish – namely, to highlight and strengthen the awareness of one's sins (Romans 3:20) – it also exposes one to the cunning of the evil impulse and, most important, does not provide the means to overcome humanity's built-in sinful inclinations and follow God's commandments (Romans 9:31).

At the end of the chapter, I will return to the characteristic collation of Jesus' atoning death and the gift of the Spirit as two complementing "enablers." Right now, however, I am going to ask to what extent this pessimistic appraisal of our inherent ability to cope with God's Torah as law was Paul's idiosyncratic contribution to the religious discourse or, alternatively, a reflection of an intuition of a much broader currency in the Jewish world.

It goes without saying that the call for the earnest effort to try to fulfill Torah commandments as the sure path to righteousness was characteristic of Jewish covenantal outlook as a whole, to which there are multiple attestations. The telling passage from Mishnah *Abot* 2.1, addressed above, is a fine example of such an outlook. An influential trend in rabbinic tradition also viewed the Torah as antidote to the evil impulse, even if its effectiveness is not always thorough.[39] However, by the time Paul was addressing the topic, a substantially different intuition, derived from an essentially pessimistic appraisal of a person's ability to gradually build the edifice of righteousness by his/her own efforts, had also been voiced in Jewish tradition. It was even enticingly suggested that this pessimistic appraisal was intrinsic to the Pharisaic religious outlook, which propagated the expansion of the scope of the commandments by means of reinterpretation (Oral Torah) to the realm of intentions ("the inner man") – a demand that further aggravated the impossibility of the task.[40] Later rabbinic sources also bear witness to such a tendency, with the sometimes inevitable conclusion, mentioned above, that nothing short of death can cure one's sinful inclination. I have dealt at length elsewhere with rabbinic responses to this conundrum;[41] it will suffice to say here that in such a context a variety of remedies were suggested, such as: trust in last-minute repentance, trust in God's merciful benevolence, and belief in the expiating function of one's death.

In eschatological thinking, however, this basically pessimistic assessment engendered aspirations for the last-days transformation of the nature of man's stance vis-à-vis God's law. This tendency, in fact, goes back to classical biblical

Jews (those who paid attention), who disapproved of it, including Judeo-Christians of the early centuries. Its various modifications have also been adopted, *mutatis mutandis*, by many influential scholars. For a review, see Gager, *Reinventing Paul*, 3–42. Characteristically, even Alan F. Segal ("Torah and *Nomos* in Recent Scholarly Discussion," *SR* 13:1 (1984): pp. 9–27) subscribed to this view at an earlier stage, claiming that "Paul deliberately revalued Torah" following "his radical conversion experience" (ibid., 27). The scholar seems to have later modified this assessment; see Alan F. Segal, *Paul the Convert: The Apostolate and Apostasy of Saul the Pharisee* (New Haven, CT: Yale University Press, 1990).

39 See Urbach, *The Sages*, pp. 472–73, 483–85.

40 Ellis Rivkin, "Pharisaic Revolution," inEllis Rivkin *The Shaping of Jewish History: A Radical New Interpretation* (New York: Scribner, 1971).

41 Ruzer, "The Death Motif"; "The Seat of Sin," in *Transformations of Inner Self*, 151–65, 367–91.

prophecy, with a famous example provided by Jeremiah, who speaks of a "change of heart" imposed by God "from outside" – and not the steadfast efforts invested in pious ritual actions, temple sacrifices included – as the only way to righteousness, remission of sins and redemption (Jeremiah 31:31–34):

> 31 "Behold, the days are coming," says the LORD, "when I will make a new covenant with the house of Israel and the house of Judah, 32 not like the covenant which I made with their fathers when I took them by the hand to bring them out of the land of Egypt, my covenant which they broke, though I was their husband, says the LORD. 33 But this is the covenant which I will make with the house of Israel after those days," says the LORD: "I will put my Torah/law within them, and I will write it upon their hearts; and I will be their God, and they shall be my people. 34 And no longer shall each man teach his neighbor and each his brother, saying, – 'Know the LORD,' for they shall all know me, from the least of them to the greatest, says the LORD; for I will forgive their iniquity, and I will remember their sin no more."

It is only this inner transformation enforced by God that makes the observance of the core stipulations of God's covenant possible.[42] Characteristically, in another famous oracle, that of Ezekiel, this eschatological transformation is further described in terms of receiving the gift of Spirit (Ezekiel 36: 24–29):

> 24 For I will take you from the nations, and gather you from all the countries, and bring you into your own land. 25 I will sprinkle clean water upon you, and you shall be clean from all your uncleannesses, and from all your idols I will cleanse you. 26 A new heart I will give you, and a new spirit I will put within you; and I will take out of your flesh the heart of stone and give you a heart of flesh. 27 *And I will put my spirit within you, and cause you to walk in my statutes and be careful to observe my ordinances.* 28 You shall dwell in the land which I gave to your fathers; and you shall be my people, and I will be your God. 29 And I will deliver you from all your uncleannesses; and I will summon the grain and make it abundant and lay no famine upon you. [emphasis added]

Compared to *m. Sotah* 9.15 quoted above, the passage from Ezekiel outlines an inverted sequence – instead of the righteousness, forgiveness of sins, gift of the Spirit and redemption as the crowning outcomes of earnest efforts to fulfill God's precepts, including the ritual ones focused on the cleanness-uncleanness dichotomy, the very ability to act righteously is presented here as conditioned by the prior intervention by God that changes one essentially with the "stroke of the spirit." This perception

42 It has been suggested that, in fact, Jeremiah already did not view certain elements of the ritual – namely, those pertaining to Temple sacrifices – as part of the obligatory core stipulations. See Moshe Weinfeld, "Jeremiah and the Spiritual Metamorphosis of Israel," ZAW 80 (1976): 17–56, esp. p. 32, who proposes that the prophet might have perceived the new covenant as associated not with formal statutes but exclusively with the "circumcision of the heart." Jeremiah might have also expressed a broader prophetic tendency to harbor reservations toward the priestly aspect of the Jewish religion.

would be later picked up in the *Rule of the Community*, drastically modified in accordance with the Qumranic double predestination belief. A powerful expression of that pattern of religious thinking is found in the closing section of the *Rule* (1QS 11.7–17):[43]

> *To those whom God has selected he has given them as everlasting possession; until they inherit them in the lot of the holy ones.* 8 He unites their assembly to the sons of the heavens ... to be an everlasting plantation throughout all future ages. 9 However, *I belong to evil humankind to the assembly of wicked flesh; ... the assembly of worms ... of those who walk in darkness ...* 10 For to man (does not belong) his path, nor to a human being the steadying of his step; since judgment belongs to God, 11 and from his hand is the perfection of the path. By his knowledge everything shall come into being, and all that does exist he establishes with his calculations and nothing is done outside of him. ... 13 he will free my soul from the pit and make my steps steady on the path; 14
>
> ... in his justice he will cleanse me from the uncleanness of the human being and from the sin of the sons of man, ... so that I can extol God for his justice ... Blessed be you, my God, who opens the heart of your servant to knowledge! 16 Establish all his deeds in justice, ... to be everlastingly in your presence, as you have cared for the selected ones of humankind. 17 *For beyond you there is no perfect path and without your will, nothing comes to be.* [emphasis added]

According to the *Rule*, the God-imposed transformation is (a) the only possible avenue to achieving the righteousness and (b) conditioned on the predestined election. The flesh-spirit dualism characteristic of the Dead Sea Scrolls, as well as of Paul in Romans 7,[44] is only hinted at here (the "flesh" being incapable of following God's will, line 9, cf. Matthew 26:41); the Spirit, however, is clearly perceived elsewhere in the same scroll as both cleansing the person's "inner man" when the last days come, and revealing God's ultimate mysteries (1QS 4.20–23):

> Meanwhile, God will refine, with his truth, all man's deeds, and will purify for himself the configuration of man, ripping out all spirit of deceit from the innermost part 21 of his flesh, and *cleansing him with the spirit of holiness from every irreverent deed.* He will sprinkle over him the spirit of truth like lustral water (in order to cleanse him) from all the abhorrences of deceit and from the defilement 22 of the unclean spirit. *In this way the upright will understand knowledge of the Most High, and the wisdom of the sons of heaven will teach those of perfect behavior.* For these are those selected by God for an everlasting covenant 23 and to them shall belong all the glory of Adam. [emphasis added]

The heavenly mysteries revealed to those "refined by God" are identified as a new interpretation of the Torah precepts, pertaining to the pre-eschatological "age of

43 The English translation of Qumranic material in this chapter follows Wilfred G. E. Watson *in The Dead Sea Scrolls Translated*, ed. F. García Martíne (Leiden: Brill, 1994) (electronic version).

44 See discussion in David Flusser, "The Dead Sea Sect and Pre-Pauline Christianity," in David Flusser, *Judaism and the Origins of Christianity* (Jerusalem: Magness, 1988), 23–74.

wickedness" in the *Damascus Document* 6, whereas both the necessity of the initially enforced action of the holy Spirit for obtaining righteousness and its cardinal effect as preventing one from sinning against God in the future are again highlighted in the Qumranic *Thanksgiving Hymns* (1QH 4.17–26):

> *[I give you thanks, Lord,] for the spirits you have placed in me . . . .to confess my former sins, to bow low and beg favour* [19] *for [. . .] of my deeds and the depravity of my heart. Because I wallowed in impurity, [I separated myself] from the foundation [of truth] and I was not allied with* [. . .] [20] To you does justice belong, blessing belongs to your Name for ever! [Act according to] your justice, [21] free [the soul of your servant,] the wicked should die! However, *I have understood that [you establish] the path of the one whom you choose* [22] *and in the insight [of your wisdom] you prevent him from sinning against you,* you restore his humility through your punishments, and by your ord[eals streng]then his heart. [23]
>
> [You, Lord, prevent] your servant from sinning against you . . . . [25] [. . .] *for your servant is a spirit of flesh. Blank* [26] [I give you thanks, Lord, because] *you have spread your holy spirit upon your servant* [. . .] his heart . . . [emphasis added]

The emphasis on election/gift of the Spirit as the precondition for fulfilling the Torah precepts is expressed with particular force and clarity in Qumranic texts – not least, thanks to its being linked there to the double predestination concept.[45] However, it stands to reason that outside of this idiosyncratic linkage, the late Second Temple revival of the intuition found already in Ezekiel 36 was not restricted to their sectarian eschatologically oriented milieu.[46] Paul then may be viewed as an important witness to this tendency.

IV CONCLUSION

My reading suggests that in both Galatians and Romans, Paul repeatedly addresses the challenge of the νόμος (law) component of Jewish religion. The apostle's rhetorically amplified statements there attest to a variety of nonharmonized

45 Moreover, the gift of the Spirit features in some Qumranic texts as a self-definition of the covenanters. Thus, for example, in fragments of the *Damascus Document* found at Qumran, "the anointed/messiahs by his/the holy Spirit" or "the messiahs of (his) holy Spirit" (משיחי רוח הקודש/משיחי רוח קודשו) serve as the community's collective self-definition (See 4Q266 ii, 2:12 (= CD-A 6) and 4Q 270 ii, 2:14). In other passages, a shorter title, "the anointed of the holiness" (משיחי הקודש), denotes the whole community of the covenanters – as distinguished from the Qumranic priestly elite, those belonging to the "Aaronic anointing see, e.g., 4Q266 iii, 2:9; 4Q267 2, 6; 4Q269 iv, 1:2; see Serge Ruzer, "The New Covenant, the Reinterpretation of Scripture and Collective Messiahship," in idem, *Mapping the New Testament*, 215–39.

46 The following passage by Philo seems to indicate that a similar emphasis, albeit without a characteristic link to the Spirit, was probed also in a non-eschatological Hellenistic Jewish context: "God has . . . promoted goodly natures apart from any manifest reason, pronouncing no action of theirs acceptable before bestowing his praises upon them. . . . the prophet says that Noah found grace in the sight of the Lord God (Gen 6:8) when as yet he had . . . done no fair deed, etc." (Philo, *Leg.* 3.77–79).

appraisals – from the Torah precepts being "good and holy" to constituting an obstacle on the way to true righteousness. In accordance with the latter emphasis, the centuries-long Christian tradition ascribed to Paul the conviction that in the messianic era, following Jesus's salvific death, the Jewish religious outlook centered on the Torah and its commandments becomes obsolete. Trying to cope with the apostle's statements on the Torah's (partial) validity and absolute holiness this tradition explained them away as, for example, dictated by the tactical constraints of the mission. Various modifications of this appraisal have also been adopted, *mutatis mutandis*, by some influential modern scholars.[47]

There have been also a number of inroads in recent research, alleviating this picture of Paul's substantial reversal of the attitude to the Torah law, including the law's ritual aspects. Most prominently, the scholars propagating the so-called New View of Paul forcefully argued for a context-related interpretation of Paul's criticism of Torah ritual precepts as directed exclusively toward Gentiles. If so, there is no reason at all to view it as radical – and no reason to think that he called for annulling the Torah obligations of the Jews. The issue of Torah observance or deeds-grace controversy can moreover be viewed as not part of the initial core of the apostle's teaching of messianic salvation, but rather one of the secondary themes evoked in response to varying circumstances – most notably, the appeal to non-Jewish addressees. This study approached the issue from a different angle. Not denying Paul's very particular circumstances, it aimed at discerning in the apostle's reasoning a reflection of broader Jewish awareness – within the covenantal nomism outlook – of the problematic side of the law as religion's foundational aspect.

I started with a discussion of Paul's "works of the Torah/law" usage featuring prominently in Galatians, which gives support to the suggestion that this phrase should be understood, similarly to its Hebrew parallel in the Dead Sea Scrolls, in a limiting sense of ritual markers. The context of the epistle indicates that those are the distinguishing positive ritual markers of Judaism, circumcision et al. that Paul tries to discourage his Gentile addressees within the Jesus movement from adopting. The apostle's argument is that the ritual elements of the law are, in fact, not helpful in our attempts to achieve true righteousness. The position, that those are only the core demands of the Torah – embracement of monotheistic faith and worship and of proper morals – and not the details of ritual law that are expected from Gentile God-fearers, was, in fact, current among Hellenistic Jews. Paul therefore may be viewed as riding upon an existing tendency. Though the apostles' polemical stress on the dilemma of either Jewish ritual or Jesus' atoning death, is definitely his singular trademark.

I suggested, however, that Paul's insistence that "secondary" ritual observances do not contribute to achieving true righteousness epitomized in the Torah's foundational demands, "Love your neighbor as yourself" (Leviticus 19:18), was also aimed at

47 See note 38 above.

his "hidden audience" – those Jewish members of the movement, whose influence on the Gentile fellow-travelers he is trying to repel. To clarify that intra-Jewish logic of the argument, I reviewed a number of early Jewish sources attesting to the variegated divisions of the Torah law into "primary" and "secondary" sections. Though in the final account, all these sources uphold the "righteousness value" of the "secondary" (external, ritual) observances – for example, as assisting in fulfillment of the foundational moral demands – they clearly betray the backdrop disagreements and polemic. This strengthens the probability that Paul's negation of the ritual's auxiliary value, first triggered by the concrete polemical situation vis-à-vis his Gentile addressees, was in the final account meant to have a broader appeal. Since in the intra-Jewish discourse it was likewise a matter of contention, Paul might have consciously related to some aspects of this contention.

However, it turns out that Paul's doubts with regard to the usefulness of the ritual precepts for our aspiration to achieve righteousness are part of his more substantial skepticism. The apostle in fact argues that one is incapable of fulfilling the Torah's foundational moral demands, those "just requirement of the law," through one's own efforts at all. In the Epistle to the Romans, he further elaborates on that, blaming our "being in flesh" for the basic impotence in coping with God's law. The chapter shows that side by side with more optimistic appraisals of the man-versus-Torah-as-law conundrum, this pessimistic one was not unknown in broader Jewish tradition, representing, moreover, a long-standing tendency within it.

Having briefly related to rabbinic responses to this pessimistic appraisal of human nature that focused on mechanisms of repentance and God's forgiveness, I noted that traditions of eschatological flavor alternatively attest to the aspiration for the last-days transformation. They are often expressed in terms of receiving the Spirit, which would finally make feasible the fulfillment of God's commandments. According to my reading, Paul inherited from broader patterns of Jewish thought not only the pessimistic diagnosis of human condition vis-à-vis God's demands in the "externally imposed" law, but also the eschatological solution of the problem through the gift of the Spirit. One of the characteristic features of Paul's argument is the coupling of this inherited motif of broader circulation with the "sectarian" argument, ascribing the same enabling function to Jesus's salvific death.

In the final account, my investigation brings me to the conclusion that the crux of the apostle's reasoning was not the annulment of the Jewish religious outlook centered on the Torah and its commandments. It was rather the perception of the deeply problematic nature of the human predicament in face of God's will as epitomized in the code of law. This seasoned pessimism was coupled with the eschatological hope for the inner transformation induced by the Spirit that would finally enable us to live up to the just demands of God's Torah. With regard to both these motifs, as well as to the perception of the hierarchical division between peripheral and core precepts, Paul's writings may be viewed as an illuminating witness to broader intuitions of Jewish tradition. The apostle, however, retains his idiosyncratic singularity thanks to the addition of the atoning death of the Messiah as a complementing enabler of that eschatological metamorphose, and, of course, to the conviction that this metamorphose is already somehow present among his addressees.

15

When Law Meets Theology

Legality and Revelation in the Jewish, Islamic, and Zoroastrian Traditions in the Abbasid Period

Yishai Kiel

I INTRODUCTION

Recent decades have seen growing interest in the interplay of law and religion, moving beyond the constitutional context (freedom of religion) and other practical legal concerns, to explore the broader dynamics of law and religion as "sciences" and classification systems.[1] The underlying assumption of research in the field has typically been that "law and religion are distinct spheres and sciences of human life, but they exist in dialectical interaction, constantly crossing-over and cross-fertilizing each other."[2] This working assumption, however, rests, to a large extent, on the uncritical acceptance of certain binary distinctions entrenched in Western legal culture and the history of Christianity,[3] compartmentalizing the notions of *logos* and *nomos*, law and faith, letter and spirit, and church and state. These distinctions can be traced back to the Greco-Roman dichotomy between divine (or natural) and positive law,[4] on the one hand, and antinomian tendencies pervading ancient Christianity, especially Paul's writings,[5] that reject the very idea that *nomos*, in the sense of positive law, can be a medium of revelation and manifestation of God's word and wisdom. The absence, moreover, of a distinctive category for

[1] The literature is vast. See, e.g., HAROLD BERMAN, THE INTERACTION OF LAW AND RELIGION (1974); HAROLD BERMAN, FAITH AND ORDER: THE RECONCILIATION OF LAW AND RELIGION (1993); LAW AND RELIGION (Gad Barzilai ed., 2007); Perry Dane, *Constitutional Law and Religion*, in A COMPANION TO PHILOSOPHY OF LAW AND LEGAL THEORY 119, 119–22 (2nd ed. Dennis Patterson ed., 2010).

[2] JOHN WITTE, JR . & FRANK S. ALEXANDER , CHRISTIANITY AND LAW: AN INTRODUCTION 1 (2008). For one recent example of this discourse, see Rafael Domingo, *Theology and Jurisprudence: A Good Partnership?* 32(1) J.L & RELIG. 79 (2017) (arguing for the restoration of a "dialogue" between theology and jurisprudence, since "interactions, synergies, and communication between sciences play an important role in the development of a scientist's knowledge").

[3] See JOSEPH DAVID, JURISPRUDENCE AND THEOLOGY IN LATE ANCIENT AND MEDIEVAL JEWISH THOUGHT (2014).

[4] CHRISTINE HAYES, WHAT'S DIVINE ABOUT DIVINE LAW? EARLY PERSPECTIVES 54–89 (2015).

[5] This is hardly the only possible reading of Paul. Indeed, Paul's view of the law is complex, "at times, his attitude toward the law is mildly positive, at times neutral, and at times harshly critical and condemnatory." (*id.*, at 141). For the inconsistency in Paul's treatment of the law see HAYES, DIVINE LAW, *id.*, at 140–64 and the vast literature cited.

religion and the religious sphere in premodern contexts,[6] even within the confines of the Western tradition, further obscures the discursive categorization of law and religion as distinct, yet interacting, orders of classification.

When we cast our gaze beyond the Western and Christian traditions, however, we encounter a range of alternative possibilities that blur the Western bifurcation and defy the compartmentalization of law and religion.[7] According to David Novak, commenting on law and religion in the Jewish tradition, "while today many regard law and religion as separate spheres and sciences of life, Judaism has long regarded these phenomena as overlapping, if not virtually identical."[8] Similar observations can constructively be made for other non-Western legal and religious traditions, such as Islam, Zoroastrianism, and Brahmanic Hinduism, to name just a few. In such contexts, it would perhaps be more productive to replace the discourse of law *and* religion, tendentiously assuming the existence of distinct spheres and orders of classification interacting with each other, with one of law *as* religion and religion *as* law, as framed by the present volume, reflecting the essential "fuzziness" of these categories, which can represent two sides of the same coin.

One need not envision a dichotomy between "Western" and "non-Western" approaches to law and religion. It is simply that we can gain a more nuanced and variegated appreciation of these intersecting and overlapping spheres, by a conscious attempt to evade bifurcated modes of analysis entrenched in Christianity and Western legal culture, in search of alternative models beyond the confines of the Occident. The present article, centered on Jewish, Islamic, and Zoroastrian perceptions of revelation and legality in the Abbasid period – offers yet another example of the problematization and unsettling of the "law and religion" paradigm by non-Western and non-Christian discourses.

The first centuries of the Abbasid period[9] – between the mid-eighth and early-eleventh centuries – roughly corresponding to the late Geonic era in rabbinic periodization, can arguably be seen as a landmark in the development of Jewish, Islamic, and Zoroastrian jurisprudence. This is not to say of course that the beginnings of Jewish, Islamic, and Zoroastrian law – in the sense of comprehensive systems of positive law – should be traced to this juncture. Indeed, the Jewish and Zoroastrian legal traditions are firmly rooted in late antiquity,[10] as reflected in the

6 See Brent Nongbri, Before Religion: A History of a Modern Concept (2013); Carlin Barton & Daniel Boyarin, Imagine No Religion: How Modern Abstractions Hide Ancient Realities (2016).

7 The literature is vast. See, e.g., Religion, Law and Tradition: Comparative Studies in Religious Law (Andrew Huxley ed., 2002).

8 David Novak, *Law and Religion in Judaism*, in Christianity and Law, *supra* note 2, at 33; The Cambridge Companion to Judaism and Law 2–3 (Christine Hayes ed., 2017).

9 For historical overviews of the period, see Michael G. Morony, Iraq after the Muslim Conquest (1984); Muhammad Q. Zaman, Religion and Politics under the Early Abbāsids: The Emergence of the Proto-Sunnī Elite (1997); Amira K. Bennison, The Great Caliphs: The Golden Age of the 'Abbasid Empire (2009).

10 The chronological limits of late antiquity are rather elusive. Certain scholars still do not include the rise of Islam within the confines of late antiquity, see, e.g., The Formation of the Islamic World,

detailed legal systems contained in the classical talmudic corpus,[11] on the one hand, and the Zoroastrian Zand (the Pahlavi translation and commentary on the Avesta)[12] and collection of Sasanian case law,[13] on the other hand. Islamic law is likewise rooted in late antiquity, as much of early Islamic law is indebted to pre-Islamic traditions and customs (including Roman, Sasanian, Jewish, and local Arabian law and custom).[14]

Notwithstanding the late-ancient origins of these legal traditions, the distinctive Islamicate[15] legal culture that emerged in Iraq and its surroundings under the early

Sixth to Eleventh Centuries, The new Cambridge History of Islam, Vol. I (Chase F. Robinson ed., 2011). To date, most scholars, however, do include the inception of Islam within late antiquity, see, e.g., Thomas Sizgorich, *Narrative and Community in Islamic Late Antiquity*, 185(1) Past & Present 9 (2004); Thomas Sizgorich, Violence and Belief in Late Antiquity: Militant Devotion in Christianity and Islam (2008); Robert G. Hoyland, *Early Islam as a Late Antique Religion*, in The Oxford Handbook of Late Antiquity 1053 (Scott Fitzgerald Johnson ed., 2012). Recently, Lena Salaymeh has suggested extending late antiquity to ca. 800 (while altogether discarding the conceptions of the "formative" and "classical" periods in Islamic legal history). See Lena Salaymeh, The Beginnings of Islamic Law: Late Antique Islamicate Legal Traditions 7–8 (2016). In the present context, I use the term "late antiquity" somewhat more conservatively, extending it only to the rise of Islam in the seventh century.

11 That talmudic law amounts to a cohesive legal system, see Hanina Ben-Menahem, *Talmudic Law: A Jurisprudential Perspective*, in The Cambridge History of Judaism, vol. 4: The Late Roman–Rabbinic Period 877 (Steven T. Katz ed., 2006).

12 For the pre-Islamic date of the Zand and its jurists see, e.g., Alberto Cantera, Studien zur Pahlavi-Übersetzung des Avesta 164–239 (2004); Shai Secunda, *On the Age of the Zoroastrian Sages of the Zand*, 47 Iranica Antiqua 317 (2012). The eighth book of the *Dēnkard* summarizes the contents of the (mostly lost) twenty-one *nasks* ("books") of the Avesta and Zand. But cf. Michael Stausberg, *The Invention of a Canon: The Case of Zoroastrianism, in* Canonization and Decanonization: Papers Presented to the International Conference of the Leiden Institute for the Study of Religions (LISOR) 257, 264–66 (9–10 Jan. 1997, Leiden; Arie van der Kooij & Karel van der Toorn eds., 1998) ("the twenty-one *nasks* of the *dēn* catalogued in *Dēnkard* book 8 are an attempt at classifying the entire religious tradition and not specifically the Avestan corpus as has been commonly assumed by the previous generation of scholars").

13 The *Mādayān ī Hazār Dādestān* ("Book of a Thousand Judgements"), a collection of real and hypothetical case law, was compiled in the first-half of the seventh century prior to the Islamic conquest of Iran. See Maria Macuch, Rechtskasuistik und Gerichtspraxis zu Beginn des siebenten Jahrhunderts in Iran: Die Rechtssammlung des Farrohmard i Wahrāmān 9–10 (1993); Maria Macuch, *Mādayān ī hazār dādestān*, in Encyclopædia Iranica (online edition; available at www.iranicaonline.org/articles/madayan-i-hazar-dadestan).

14 See, e.g., Wael Hallaq, A History of Islamic Legal Theories: An Introduction to Sunnī uṣūl al-fiqh 7–15 (1997); Wael Hallaq, The Origins and Evolution of Islamic Law 24–25 (2005). Some jurists, such as the eighth-century Ḥanafī legal scholar Abū Yūsuf (d. 798), went as far as consciously granting binding legal status to ancient pre-Islamic customs that are neither confirmed nor abolished or altered by Islamic law.

15 Marshall Hodgson was the first to coin the term "Islamicate" as referring "not directly to the religion, Islam, itself, but to the social and cultural complex historically associated with Islam and the Muslims, both among Muslims themselves and even when found among non-Muslims." See Marshall G. S. Hodgson , The Venture of Islam: Conscience and History in a World Civilization, Vol. 1, 59 (1974); See also Salaymeh, *supra* note 10, 9 ("The category of Islamicate is a heuristic tool that enriches our understanding of Islamic legal history by recognizing that Islamic law, from its beginning, structured relationships between and among Muslims and non-Muslims. The result was Islamicate legal syncretism").

Abbasid Caliphate was marked by an unprecedented level of reflexivity, systematization, professionalization, and theorization of the law. This is manifest in the gradual shift from oral to written culture; the transformation from anonymous and collective authorship to specialized legal works attributed to named jurists; the institutionalization of academies and cross-regional legal "schools"; the professionalization of judges and jurisconsults; the coming of age of legal hermeneutics; and the emergence of legal theory and reflexive engagement with the nature of the law.[16] In this context, Jewish, Islamic and Zoroastrian authors endeavored to provide a clearer definition of the law's "roots" (*uṣūl al-fiqh* to use the prevalent vernacular), and articulate its basic "rule of recognition," identifying the authoritative legal sources and setting criteria for legal validity.

In this context, several Jewish, Islamic, and Zoroastrian authors, who seem to have shared a postclassical consciousness vis-à-vis earlier generations, sought to confine their legal systems' jurisprudential sources (and, implicitly, the legal sources available to judges and jurisconsults) to the canonical textual manifestation of God's revelation. The assertion that the system's legal sources are confined to the textual articulation of God's revelation was connected, not only with the gradual shift from oral to written culture, but also with an ongoing process of normative and theological canonization,[17] in which compilations of earlier legal traditions came to be regarded as binding legal "sources" in a jurisprudential sense and theological manifestations of the divine will. In this context, a similar voice was echoed in Jewish, Islamic, and Zoroastrian circles in the Abbasid period insisting on the textual confinement of God's law to closed textual corpora – the Torah and Mishnah-cum-Talmud, the Quran and Hadith, and the Avesta and Zand – and facilitating a process by which these corpora came to be regarded as binding legal "codes" and the exclusive, complete, and authoritative articulation of God's revelation.[18]

From a legal theoretical perspective, the idea that the law is exhausted by its textual-statutory articulation (rather than being custom-based or judge-made) is consistent with legal formalism, an important dimension of which is the reductive confinement of the law to an exhaustive and self-contained body of norms, often manifest in the form of a comprehensive statutory code.[19] The textual-statutory

[16] The literature exploring these processes is exceedingly vast. For a summary, see the description and references listed in Yishai Kiel, A Jurisprudential Reading of Rav Sherira's Epistle and Legal Responsa in the Light of Rabbinic, Islamic and Zoroastrian Legal Culture 16–22 (PhD dissertation; The Hebrew University of Jerusalem, 2020).

[17] For the relationship between normative and theological canonization, on the one hand, and textual canonization (the establishment of a textually crystallized and thematically fixed version of a sacred work), see Ahmed El-Shamsy, The Canonization of Islamic Law: A Social and Intellectual History 3–4 (2013).

[18] The connection between canonization, limitation, confinement and closure will be discussed below. See generally Jonathan Z. Smith, *Sacred Persistence: Towards a Redescription of Canon*, in Imagining Religion: From Babylon to Jonestown 48 (1982).

[19] On legal formalism, see, in general, Judith N. Shklar, Legalism: Law, Morals, and Political Trials (1964); Duncan Kennedy, *Legal Formality*, 2 J. Leg. Stud. 351 (1973); Fredrick Schauer, *Formalism*,

demarcation of the law is also consistent with a formal interpretation of the notion of "legality" and the "rule of law,"[20] entailing the law's generality, accessibility, prospectiveness, coherence, clarity, stability, and predictability.[21] From a theological perspective, the textual-statutory confinement of God's law reflects the perception of God as legislator and "author" of the law, at the expense of human participation in the revelatory and legislative processes.

The idea that God is the legislator and author of a textually confined body of law, containing stable and predictable laws, to which all (including the sovereign) are subject, is not a trivial one and, in fact, has a history that requires unpacking. In the context of the ancient Near East, something approximating a theological version of the "rule of law" can be found, as early as the first half of the first millennium BCE, in the Bible[22] and, to some extent, in the young Avesta and Old Persian inscriptions.[23] The idea that God is the author of

97 YALE L.J. 509 (1988); Ernest J. Weinrib, *Legal Formalism: On the Immanent Rationality of Law*, 97 YALE L.J. 949–1016 (1988); D. Lyons, *Legal Formalism and Instrumentalism – A Pathological Study*, 66 CORNELL L. REV. 949 (1988); Brian Leiter, *Positivism, Formalism, Realism* 99 COLUM. L. REV. 1138 (1999); Larry Alexander, *"With Me, It's All or Nothing": Formalism in Law and Morality*, 66 U. CHI. L. REV. 530 (1999); Martin Stone, *Formalism*, in THE OXFORD HANDBOOK OF JURISPRUDENCE AND PHILOSOPHY OF LAW 166–205 (Jules L. Coleman, Kenneth Einar Himma & Scott J. Shapiro eds., 2002); Ernest J. Weinrib, *Legal Formalism*, in A COMPANION TO PHILOSOPHY OF LAW AND LEGAL THEORY 327–38 (Dennis M. Patterson ed., 2008).

20 See LON FULLER, THE MORALITY OF LAW 46–90 (1964 [rep. 1969]). For more recent discussions, see, e.g., Andrei Marmor, *The Rule of Law and Its Limits*, in LAW IN THE AGE OF PLURALISM 3 (2007); Andrei Marmor, *The Ideal of the Rule of Law*, in A COMPANION TO PHILOSOPHY OF LAW AND LEGAL THEORY 666 (2nd edition; Dennis Patterson ed., 2010); Jeremy Waldron, *The Rule of Law*, in THE STANFORD ENCYCLOPEDIA OF PHILOSOPHY (2016) (available online at https://plato.stanford.edu/archives/fall2016/entries/rule-of-law/); Jeremy Waldron, *The Concept and the Rule of Law*, 43 GEORGIA L. REV. 1 (2008); SCOTT SHAPIRO, LEGALITY 388–400 (2011). For the debate over the moral vs. formal nature of the "rule of law" and principles of "legality," see, e.g., FULLER, *id.*, at 200–23; H.L.A Hart, *Book Review: Lon Fuller. The Morality of Law*, 78 HARV. L. REV. 1281 (1965); Ronald Dworkin, *Elusive Morality of Law*, 10 VILLANOVA L. REV. (1965); MATTHEW KRAMER, IN DEFENSE OF LEGAL POSITIVISM: LAW WITHOUT TRIMMINGS (2003); NIGEL SIMMONDS, LAW AS A MORAL IDEA (2007); JOSEPH RAZ, THE AUTHORITY OF LAW: ESSAYS ON LAW AND MORALITY 210–31 (2009).

21 For a useful summary of Fuller's principles of "legality," see Colleen Murphy, *Lon Fuller and the Moral Value of the Rule of Law*, 24 LAW & PHIL. 239, 240–42 (2005).

22 See, e.g., Bernard M. Levinson, *The First Constitution: Rethinking the Origins of Rule of Law and Separation of Powers in Light of Deuteronomy*, 27(4) CARDOZO LAW REVIEW 1853 (2006) (demonstrating Deuteronomy's division of political power into separate spheres of authority and the subordination of each branch to the authority of the law).

23 I refer specifically to Xerxes' reference to "the law set down by Ahura Mazda," as distinct from the law of the king, and the Avestan underpinnings of this stance. See Yishai Kiel, *Reinventing Mosaic Torah in Ezra-Nehemiah in the Light of the Law (dāta) of Ahura Mazda and Zarathustra*, 136(2) JOURNAL OF BIBLICAL LITERATURE 325 (2017). See also Yaakov Elman, *Contrasting Intellectual Trajectories: Iran and Israel in Mesopotamia*, in ENCOUNTERS BY THE RIVERS OF BABYLON: SCHOLARLY CONVERSATIONS BETWEEN JEWS, IRANIANS, AND BABYLONIANS IN ANTIQUITY 7, 13–14 (Shai Secunda & Uri Gabbay eds., 2014) ("in vital respects Israelite religion and Zoroastrianism stood apart from Sumero-Akkadian religion even in Achaemenid times. Both had become, or were in the process of becoming, scriptural religions, that is, religions whose central doctrines were embodied in a revelation vouchsafed to a prophet in the form of a long compilation, though it would be more than a millennium before

a prescriptive legal "code," which developed in ancient Israel and Iran, stands in contrast to the prevailing paradigm in the ancient Near East, according to which the gods were perceived as guardians of justice who authorize the laws of the kings by establishing them and conferring upon them the principles of justice and the wisdom essential to fulfill their role. In this context, the laws were generally produced and authored by the kings, not the gods, and known by their names.[24]

Later expressions of the compatibility of the idea of God as legislator and author of the law and the formal principles of the "rule of law" can be gleaned, for example, from Josephus's interpretation of theocracy[25] or the Quranic emphasis on the subjection of prophets and sovereigns to God's law.[26] In the present context, I seek to highlight the significance of a particular juncture in the convoluted history of the interplay of legality and revelation, as manifest in Jewish, Islamic, and Zoroastrian thought in the Abbasid Near East.

Zoroastrianism's 'scripture' would be written down"). For the history of "divine law" in ancient Israel see, e.g., MICHAEL LEFEBVRE, COLLECTIONS, CODES AND TORAH: THE RE-CHARACTERIZATION OF ISRAEL'S WRITTEN LAW (2006); HAYES, DIVINE LAW, *supra* note 4; JOHN COLLINS, THE INVENTION OF JUDAISM: TORAH AND JEWISH IDENTITY FROM DEUTERONOMY TO PAUL (2017).

24 HAYES, *id.*, at 31–36. See also BERNARD LEVINSON , LEGAL REVISION AND RELIGIOUS RENEWAL IN ANCIENT ISRAEL 27 (2008) ("Israelite scribes introduced into the ancient world a new idea: the divine revelation of law. Accordingly, it was not the legal collection as a literary genre but the voicing of publicly revealed law as the personal will of God that was unique to ancient Israel"). Cf. LEFEBVRE, *supra* note 23, at 1–30 (arguing for the nonlegislative and nonprescriptive nature of ancient Near Eastern law in general and the essential conformity of biblical law to this model) and Raymond Westbrook, *What Is the Covenant Code?* in THEORY AND METHOD IN BIBLICAL AND CUNEIFORM LAW: REVISION, INTERPOLATION AND DEVELOPMENT 15–36 (Bernard M. Levinson ed., 2006). Also compare the Akkadian examples discussed in Peter Machinist & Hayim Tadmor, *Heavenly Wisdom*, in THE TABLET AND THE SCROLL: NEAR EASTERN STUDIES IN HONOR OF WILLIAM W. HALLO 146, 146–47 (1993); KAREL VAN DER TOORN, SCRIBAL CULTURE AND THE MAKING OF THE HEBREW BIBLE 207–11 (2007); Uri Gabbay, *Akkadian Commentaries from Ancient Mesopotamia and Their Relation to Early Hebrew Exegesis*, 19 DSD 267 (2012).

25 David Flatto, *Theocracy and the Rule of Law: A Novel Josephan Doctrine and Its Modern Misconceptions*, 28 DINE ISRAEL 5–30 (2011) (rejecting the popular and scholarly perception of theocracy, which is often used to designate fundamentalist religious leadership that undermines the "rule of law" and constitutional values, suggesting instead an opposite notion of theocracy, developed by Josephus, that is grounded in the "rule of law" and constitutional values). See also RE´MI BRAGUE, THE LAW OF GOD: THE PHILOSOPHICAL HISTORY OF AN IDEA (2007); RAN HIRSCHL, CONSTITUTIONAL THEOCRACY (2010).

26 WAEL HALLAQ, THE IMPOSSIBLE STATE: ISLAM, POLITICS, AND MODERNITY'S MORAL PREDICAMENT 48–73 (2013) (arguing for a robust constitutional paradigm in Islam as early as the Quran itself and rejecting Western scholarship's assumption of the impossibility of such a constitutional organization in Islamic governance); Wael Hallaq, *Quranic Magna Carta: on the Origins of the Rule of Law in Islam*, in MAGNA CARTA, RELIGION AND THE RULE OF LAW 157–76 (Robin Griffith-Jones & Mark Hill QC, 2015). (providing a "constitutional" reading of Q. 3:79: "It is not for a human [prophet] that Allah should give him the Scripture and authority and prophethood and then he would say to the people, 'Be servants to me rather than Allah,' but [instead, he would say], 'Be pious scholars of the Lord because of what you have taught of the Scripture and because of what you have studied'," which asserts the separation of powers and the supremacy of God's law over the sovereign).

The Jewish, Islamic, and Zoroastrian legal traditions generally hold that, alongside the authoritative revelation vouchsafed in the Torah, Quran, and Avesta, respectively, God imparted additional normative directives connected with the rabbinic idea of *torah she-be-ʿal pe* (Oral Torah) revealed at Sinai alongside the Written Torah,[27] the Islamic concept of *sunna* (the traditions, practices, and sayings associated with the Prophet Muhammad) complementing the Quran,[28] and the Zoroastrian notion of the *dēn*, expressing the totality of the Zoroastrian Tradition.[29] While Hebrew *torah she-be-ʿal peh*, Arabic *sunna*, and Pahlavi *dēn* ultimately came to be associated with textually demarcated legal corpora, they initially seem to have denoted an amorphous body of oral tradition.[30] In the early Abbasid period, several jurists argued for the authority of a textually-demarcated version of this "body of oral tradition" and the statutory and "codificatory" confinement of God's law to the corpora of the Mishnah-cum-Talmud, Hadith, and Zand (in addition to the Torah,

27 For the development and meaning of the rabbinic notion of *torah she-be-ʿal peh* see, e.g., Gerald Blidstein A *Note on the term 'Torah she-be-ʿal peh,* 42(3–4) TARBIZ 496 (1973); MARTIN S. JAFFEE, TORAH IN THE MOUTH: WRITING AND ORAL TRADITION IN PALESTINIAN JUDAISM, 200 BCE–400 CE (2001); Yaʿaqov Sussman, *'Torah she-be-ʿal peh' – peshuṭa ke-mashmaʿa: koḥo shel qotzo shel yod*, in MEḤQERE TALMUD 3:289 (3 vols.; Yaʿaqov Sussman & David Rosenthal eds., 2005); David Weiss Halivni, *The Breaking of the Tablets and the Begetting of the Oral Law: A History of 'Torah Sheb'al Peh'*, in JERUSALEM STUDIES IN JEWISH THOUGHT: IN MEMORIAM OF GERSHOM SCHOLEM (1897–1982) Vol. 2, 137–63 (Joseph Dan ed., 2007); Israel Y. Yuval, *The Orality of Jewish Oral Law: from Pedagogy to Ideology*, in JUDAISM, CHRISTIANITY, AND ISLAM IN THE COURSE OF HISTORY; EXCHANGE AND CONFLICTS 237–90 (Lothar Gall & Dietmar Willoweit eds., 2011); Natalie B. Dohrmann, *Can "Law" Be Private? The Mixed Message of Rabbinic Oral Law,* in PUBLIC AND PRIVATE IN ANCIENT MEDITERRANEAN LAW AND RELIGION 187–216 (Clifford Ando & Jörg Rüpke eds., 2015).

28 For the concept of *sunna* in early Islam see PATRICIA CRONE AND MARTIN HINDS, GOD'S CALIPH: RELIGIOUS AUTHORITY IN THE FIRST CENTURIES OF ISLAM 58–80 (1986); G.H.A Juynboll, *Some New Ideas on the Development of Sunna as a Technical Term in Early Islam*, 10 JERUSALEM STUDIES IN ARABIC AND ISLAM 97 (1987); JOSEPH LOWRY, EARLY ISLAMIC LEGAL THEORY: THE RISĀLA OF MUḤAMMAD IBN IDRĪS AL-SHĀFIʿĪ 165–205 (2007); See also the recent collection in THE SUNNA AND ITS STATUS IN ISLAMIC LAW: THE SEARCH FOR A SOUND HADITH (Adis Duderija ed., 2015).

29 For the concept of *dēn* in Zoroastrianism, see Prods Oktor Skjærvø, *The Zoroastrian Oral Tradition as Reflected in the Texts, in* THE TRANSMISSION OF THE AVESTA 3, 20–25 (Alberto Cantera ed., 2012); Yuhan Vevaina, *Enumerating the Dēn: Textual Taxonomies, Cosmological Deixis, and Numerological Speculations in Zoroastrianism*, 50 HISTORY OF RELIGIONS 111 (2010). For other meanings associated with Pahlavi *dēn* (in relation to Av. *daēnā* and New Persian and Arabic *dīn*), see Mansour Shaki, *Dēn*, in ENCYCLOPÆDIA IRANICA 7: 279–81 (available online at www.iranicaonline.org/articles/den). It would seem that much of the semantic range of Pahlavi *dēn* is already present in the Young Avestan *daēnā*. The latter term, which in the Old Avesta seems to refer primarily to a mental faculty that "sees" in the other world and guides the sacrifices, assumes in the Young Avestan texts several additional meanings, one of which is the totality of Ahura Mazdā's teachings and traditions (but not his "religion" as often translated). See Kiel, *Reinventing Mosaic Torah, supra* note 23, at 343–44.

30 For the initially amorphous nature of *sunna* see, for example, LOWRY, EARLY ISLAMIC LEGAL THEORY, *supra* note 28, at 168 ("Most often, however, the term *sunna* appears in the general sense of "tradition," "precedent," or "time-honored way of doing things"); for *dēn*, see, e.g., Stausberg, *The Invention of a Canon, supra* note 12, at 266 ("It shows the tendency to identify the Avesta with the religious tradition. This tendency is the result of an unconscious application of a Jewish, Christian, or Muslim concept of 'canonical scripture' to Zoroastrian material"). For *torah she-be-ʿal peh*, see, e.g., Halivni, *The Breaking of the Tablets, supra* note 27.

Quran, and Avesta), which were rhetorically presented as the exclusive manifestation of God's law and the complete embodiment of his revelation.

The emerging theoretical assertion of the textual-statutory confinement of God's law and revelation – connected with a strong emphasis on God's "authorship" of the law, on the one hand, and the principles of "legality," on the other hand – is consistent with a shift in the conceptualization of legal authority, in which context communal authority underwritten by a personal and mimetic relationship between master and student was gradually replaced by impersonal, textual, and hermeneutic authority,[31] while a deontic perception of legal authority was replaced by an epistemic one centered on the jurists' knowledge of posited textual sources.[32]

The legal theoretical shift was, at times, more declaratory and rhetorical perhaps than reflective of the actual legal mode of operation. This can be gleaned from the varying levels of willingness of jurists to incorporate other legal "sources" competing for prominence, such as "extra-canonical" textual traditions, "post-canonical" enactments, customary law, precedent, consensus, and independent reasoning not based on the canonical textual sources. In a similar manner, it has been correctly observed that the mere claim of a legal system to be of divine origin does not suffice, in itself, to indicate that it is actually "religious" in any practical sense.[33] But even insofar as rhetoric is concerned, one must pay close attention to the subtleties of the claim to divine origin, by interrogating the notions of "legal revelation" and "divine law" and delving into the meaning of the linkage posited between the legal and the divine. The various law codes of the ancient Near East, the laws of the Pentateuch, Greco-Roman discourses of natural law, and Manu's laws all claim to be "divine" in one sense or another, but the meaning and significance of this assertion differ considerably from one cultural context to another.

In the course of the present discussion, I will employ a distinction between personal-authorial and impersonal-formal claims concerning the law's "divine" nature;[34] between "participatory" and "stenographic" theories of revelation reflective

31 For personal and impersonal constructions of legal authority, see Martin S. Jaffee, *A Rabbinic Ontology of the Written and Spoken Word: On Discipleship, Transformative Knowledge, and the Living Texts of Oral Torah*, 65(3) JOURNAL OF THE AMERICAN ACADEMY OF RELIGION 525–49 (1997); Hanina Ben-Menahem, *Two Talmudic Understandings of the Dictum 'Appoint for Yourself a Teacher'*, in THINKING IMPOSSIBILITIES: THE INTELLECTUAL LEGACY OF AMOS FUNKENSTEIN 288 (Robert S. Westman & David Biale eds., 2008); Yishai Kiel, *Filial Piety and Educational Commitments: A Talmudic Conflict in Its Cultural Context*, 21 JEWISH STUDIES QUARTERLY 297 (2014).

32 For "epistemic" and "deontic" authority, see RICHARD T. DE GEORGE, THE NATURE AND LIMITS OF AUTHORITY (1985). Cf. Max Weber's classification of authority into charismatic, traditional, and legal-rational: Max Weber, *The Three Types of Legitimate Rule, in* 4(1) BERKELEY PUBLICATIONS IN SOCIETY AND INSTITUTIONS 1 (1958). For the shift in the conceptualization of legal authority from late antiquity to the early medieval period in Jewish, Islamic, and Zoroastrian law, see the preliminary remarks in Yishai Kiel, *The Authority of the Sages in the Babylonian Talmud: A Zoroastrian Perspective*, 27 SHENATON HA-MISHPAT HA-IVRI 131 (2012–13).

33 Hanina Ben-Menahem, *Is Talmudic Law a Religious Legal System? A Provisional Analysis*, 24 J.L. & RELIG. 379, 383 (2008–09).

34 See, e.g., HAYES, DIVINE LAW, *supra* note 4, at 1–4 (juxtaposing the personal biblical conception of divine law with the formal and impersonal sense of Greco-Roman discourses of divine law, according

of the relative role of humans vis-à-vis the divine in shaping the revelatory content;[35] and between "retrieval" versus "constitutive" paradigms of transmission in legal systems that look back to a defining moment of revelation.[36] We will see that, in the Abbasid period, the Jewish, Islamic and Zoroastrian legal traditions reflect an increasingly stronger "authorial" and "stenographic" rhetoric of God's law (undermining the role of human agency in the legal process), on the one hand, and an emphasis on the textual confinement of the law, consistent with the formal principles of "legality," on the other hand. Paradoxically, then, it is precisely when the law is said to be thoroughly theologized (rather than secularized) that it acquires its clearest legalistic facets, reflecting the law's generality, accessibility, prospectiveness, coherence, clarity, stability, and predictability. Indeed, the "religious" and the "legal" are mutually enforcing.

The textual demarcation of the law and its theologization are generally characteristic of Jewish, Islamic, and Zoroastrian thought in the Abbasid period. In this article, I will center on three exemplary authors in particular, Rav Sherira Gaon (906–1006), head of the Rabbinic academy at Pumbeditha; Muhammad b. Idrīs al-Shāfiʿī (767–820), the so-called "architect" of Islamic jurisprudence; and Mānuščihr, a ninth-century Zoroastrian jurist and high priest. These authors were chosen for two main reasons. First, these authors do not only rhetorically declare the canonical status of the Mishnah-cum-Talmud, Hadith, and Zand (alongside the Torah, Quran, and Avesta), but practically seek to subordinate or otherwise subject extratextual legal sources and methodologies – such as consensus (*ijmāʿ*, *ham-dādestānīh*, *haskamah*); reason and discretion (*ra'y*, *istiḥsān*, *istiṣlāḥ*, *meh-dādestānīh*, *sevara*, *shiqul ha-da'at*) and custom/practice (*'amal*, *'urf*, *'āda*, *kardag*, *minhag*, *ma'ase*) – to the canonical textual sources against the backdrop of competing tendencies prevalent among their contemporaries and predecessors.[37] Second, these authors address the canonical status of the textual-statutory sources systematically in the form of epistolary essays intended, among other reasons, to establish and

to which the law is divine by virtue of certain qualities inherent in it, i.e., rationality, truth, universality, and unchangeability).

35 See, e.g., Benjamin D. Sommer, Revelation and Authority: Sinai in Jewish Scripture and Tradition 2 (2015). ("Participatory" theories of revelation typically hold that the law constitutes a mixture of revelation and human responses to the divine will, while the law is created through a constant dialogue and the joint efforts of God and humans. "Stenographic" theories of revelation, on the other hand, typically hold that the law in its entirety was "handed down" and articulated by God).

36 See, e.g., Moshe Halbertal, People of the Book, Canon, Meaning and Authority 54–81 (1997) (the "retrieval" model grounds the authority of the law in a complete and perfect moment of revelation, while eliminating human agency and creativity. The jurists and exegetes merely reconstruct, unearth, and retrieve the content related at the initial moment of revelation. The "constitutive" model, on the other hand, holds that the jurists and exegetes possess the authority to constitute the law itself).

37 For a detailed discussion of these issues and the various approaches among Jewish, Islamic, and Zoroastrian jurists to "noncanonical" legal sources (e.g., "extra-canonical" textual traditions, "post-canonical" enactments, customary law, precedent, consensus, and independent reason not based on the canonical textual sources), see Kiel, Jurisprudential Reading, *supra* note 16.

ground the idea of the demarcation of God's law in a specific textual corpus. Thus, they played a particularly crucial role in articulating the stakes of the normative and theological canonization of their respective religious traditions during the Abbasid period, arguing for the textual confinement of revelation in designated corpora.[38]

In terms of social history, the Jewish, Islamic, and Zoroastrian jurists in the Abbasid period can be seen as members of dynamic normative communities engaged in a continuous effort to create legal meaning, while negotiating their particular legal identities within the broader framework of Islamicate legal culture. As such, these jurists were not "influenced by" or "resistant to" the surrounding legal culture, so much as they were an integral part of it, while having at the same time to balance their particular legal heritage with broader cultural identities. This is no less true for culturally "conservative" jurists, such as Sherira, Shāfiʿī, and Mānuščihr, who were, at one and the same time, members of a particular religious and normative tradition and the broader Islamicate legal culture.

Revisiting the theory of communal autonomy of religious minorities under Islam, Uriel Simonsohn[39] has argued that the consolidation of legal autonomy was an ideal fostered by religious and legal elites on both sides of the border, whose authority depended on the construction of such boundaries.[40] The practice "on the ground," however, transgressed these confessional aspirations, as evident from the fact that Jews and Christians regularly availed themselves of Muslim courts,[41] a practice which extended to other Islamicate minorities such as Zoroastrians.[42] It seems, however, that the "murky" boundaries between the various normative communities inhabiting Iraq and its surroundings in the Abbasid period were not simply the outcome of "popular" defiance of elite aspirations, as the Jewish, Islamic, and Zoroastrian authorities themselves shared deep structures of meaning (whether or not they cared to acknowledge it) and a postclassical consciousness connected with the idea of the textual-statutory demarcation of God's law.

38 For the connection between canonization, limitation, and textual closure see the "classical" treatment by Smith, *Sacred Persistence*, *supra* note 18.

39 Uriel Simonsohn, A Common Justice: The Legal Allegiances of Christians and Jews under Early Islam 6–10 (2011).

40 Compare Daniel Boyarin, Border Lines: The Partition of Judaeo-Christianity 1–33 (2004) (arguing that despite the attempts of the inspection-officers/heresiologists on both sides of the Jewish-Christian border to protect and maintain the borders, people were smuggling ideas and practices the whole time.)

41 Simonsohn, Common Justice, *supra* note 39, at 6–10. For a similar juxtaposition of elite aspirations vs. a murky situation on the ground (although not in the context of Iraqi legal culture), see recently Eve Krakowsky, Coming of Age in Medieval Egypt: Female Adolescence, Jewish Law, and Ordinary Culture (2017).

42 See the curious account of Zoroastrians under Islam in Sherman Jackson, *Islam and the American Common Good*, 1(1) The Journal of Islamic Faith and Practice 27, 35 (2018). I would like to thank Ahmed El-Shamsy for this reference.

II CANONIZING GOD'S LAW IN SHERIRA'S EPISTLE

This section will center on Sherira's account of the transmission history of the Oral Torah initially revealed at Sinai (alongside the Written Torah) and particularly the "constitutional" moment of the Oral Torah's textual crystallization in the Mishnah and, ultimately, in the Talmud. In this context, Sherira makes unprecedented claims about the legal and theological status of these works, claims which can be illuminated by contemporaneous reconstructions of the legal and theological status of the Quran and Hadith in the Islamic tradition and that of the Avesta and Zand in the Zoroastrian tradition.

Sherira opens his famous epistle[43] with the following statement concerning the canonical status of the Mishnah:

> Thus, we have witnessed that the six orders (of the Mishnah) were all arranged by our holy Rabbi (Rabbi Yehudah the Patriarch), so that we can recite them (systematically) one halakhah after another; one may not add (to the Mishnah) nor subtract from it.[44]

The idea that one may not add to the Mishnah nor subtract from its content and words seems to paraphrase Deuteronomy 4:2 ("You must neither add anything to what I command you nor take away anything from it"), thus aligning the unchangeable, static, and canonical status of the Pentateuch with that of the Mishnah as textual embodiments of the Written and Oral Torah, respectively. By pointing out the unchangeable nature of the Mishnah at the outset of the epistle, Sherira seems to set the stage for the ensuing discussion, in which he will make the case for the unique jurisprudential and theological status of the Mishnah, as the ultimate source of Jewish law and the complete and authoritative textual articulation of God's revelation.

43 On Sherira's epistle see, in general, Gerald Blidstein, *Ra'ayon torah she-be-'al peh ve-toldotav be-iggeret rav sherira gaon*, 4 DAAT 5 (1980); reprinted as *Oral Torah: Ideology and History in the Epistle of Sherira Gaon*, in RELIGIOUS KNOWLEDGE, AUTHORITY, AND CHARISMA: ISLAMIC AND JEWISH PERSPECTIVES 73 (Daphna Ephrat & Meir Hatina eds., 2014) (further references will be to the English version); ROBERT BRODY, THE GEONIM OF BABYLONIA AND THE SHAPING OF MEDIEVAL JEWISH CULTURE 20–25 (1998); Robert Brody, *On the Sources for the Chronology of the Talmudic Period*, 70 TARBIZ 75 (2000); Robert Brody, *Epistle of Sherira Gaon*, in RABBINIC TEXTS AND THE HISTORY OF LATE ROMAN PALESTINE 253 (Martin Goodman & Philip Alexander eds., 2010); Isaiah Gafni, *On the Talmudic Chronology in Iggeret Rav Sherira Gaon*, 52 ZION 1 (1987); Isaiah Gafni, *On Talmudic Historiography in the Epistle of Sherira Gaon*, 73 ZION 271 (2009). See also ADAM BECKER, FEAR OF GOD AND THE BEGINNING OF WISDOM 107–10 (2006); Adam Becker, *The Comparative Study of 'Scholasticism' in Late Antique Mesopotamia: Rabbis and East Syrians*, 34 AJS REVIEW 91 (2010); GERSON COHEN, SEFER HA-KABBALAH 50–56 (1967); Joseph David, *As Explained in the Book of Adam: The History of Halakha and the Mythical Perception of History in the Late Geonic Period*, 74(4) TARBIZ 577, 594–95 (2005); Simcha Gross, *When the Jews Greeted Ali: Sherira Gaon's Epistle in Light of Arabic and Syriac Historiography*, 24(2) JEWISH STUDIES QUARTERLY 122 (2017); KIEL, JURISPRUDENTIAL READING, *supra* note 16. For the only critical edition of the epistle see IGGERET RAV SHERIRA GAON (Hebrew, B. M. Lewin ed., 1921).

44 IGGERET, *id.*, at 7 (French recension).

Sherira's claims on behalf of the Mishnah, to be sure, are hardly trivial. Whatever its authors intended for it, the Mishnah, prior to the late Geonic period, was not perceived as the exclusive and complete articulation of the Oral Torah,[45] and certainly not as a binding legal "code."[46] While the amoraim and redactors of both Talmuds situated the Mishnah (or parts thereof) at the center of their interpretive endeavor (thus reflecting some degree of "canonicity"), they consciously and regularly deviated from the Mishnah's rulings[47] on the basis of both textual and nontextual legal traditions.[48] Sherira's assertion, by contrast, according to which "one may not add (to the Mishnah) nor subtract from it," seems to suggest the equivalence of the Pentateuch and Mishnah as exclusive, binding, and complete textual articulations of God's Written and Oral Torah.

Assuming the Mishnah's antiquity, the questioner – Jacob b. Nissim Ibn Shahin in the name of the Rabbanite community of Qayrawan – suggests that the Mishnah was composed in piecemeal fashion, a process stretching back to the early Second Temple period (notwithstanding the Sinaitic origin of the Oral Torah).[49] In his response, Sherira draws a distinction between the content of the Oral Torah, which

45 See, e.g., David W. Halivni, *The Reception Accorded to R. Judah's Mishnah*, in JEWISH AND CHRISTIAN SELF-DEFINITION, Vol. 2, 204 (E. P. Sanders ed., 1981); Mayer I. Gruber, *The Mishnah as Oral Torah: A Reconsideration*, 15 JOURNAL FOR THE STUDY OF JUDAISM IN THE PERSIAN, HELLENISTIC AND ROMAN PERIOD 112 (1984). In fact, the few talmudic references to a theory of an Oral Torah suggest a much more amorphous and dynamic body of tradition. See especially Halivni, *The Breaking of the Tablets*, *supra* note 27 (arguing that only in the post-talmudic period does the doctrine of the Oral Torah reach its "mature" form, according to which Moses received at Sinai every last detail of rabbinic tradition that will unfold throughout history. At this point, the Oral Torah becomes as static and unchangeable as the Written Torah). Cf. Samuel Safrai, *Oral Torah*, in THE LITERATURE OF THE SAGES, VOL. 1: ORAL TORA, HALAKHA, MISHNA, TOSEFTA, TALMUD, EXTERNAL TRACTATES 35–119 (Samuel Safrai ed., 1987).

46 See, e.g., Yaakov Elman, *Order, Sequence and Selection: The Mishnah's Anthological Choices*, in THE ANTHOLOGY IN JEWISH LITERATURE 53, 54–55 (David Stern ed., 2004) (pointing out the Mishnah's lack of cohesiveness, internal contradictions, unresolved disputes, duplications, lack of comprehensiveness in terms of the topics covered, and lack of organization in terms of the noncontextual arrangement of the material). See also Avraham Goldberg, *The Mishna: A Study Book of Halakha*, in THE LITERATURE OF THE SAGES, VOL. 1: ORAL TORA, HALAKHA, MISHNA, TOSEFTA, TALMUD, EXTERNAL TRACTATES 211–62 (Samuel Safrai ed., 1987); Ishay Rosen-Zvi, *Introduction to the Mishnah, in* THE CLASSIC RABBINIC LITERATURE OF ERETZ ISRAEL: INTRODUCTIONS AND STUDIES, VOL. 1, 47–48 (2 vols., 2018).

47 See, e.g., Halivni, *The Reception Accorded to R. Judah's Mishnah*, *supra* note 45, 204–12. By contrast, Geonic deviation from the Mishnah (and its authoritative interpretation in the Babylonian Talmud) is marginal. See UZIEL FUCHS, THE GEONIC TALMUD: THE ATTITUDE OF BABYLONIAN GEONIM TO THE TEXT OF THE BABYLONIAN TALMUD 171 (2017) ("It is true that the later Geonim decided, here and there, not in accordance with the Talmud and, sometimes, interpreted the Mishnah against the grain of its talmudic interpretation .... But, those were all *rare exceptions*" [my translation and emphasis]).

48 Cf. Rosen-Zvi, *Introduction to the Mishnah*, *supra* note 46, at 2 (arguing that the Mishnah in the early amoraic period was regarded as "a complete and binding corpus").

49 IGGERET, *supra* note 43, at 5 (French recension): "And as for your inquiry concerning how the Mishnah was written, and whether the members of the great assembly started writing it, and the sages of every generation wrote parts of it, until Rabbi came and sealed it." (ודשאלתון כיצד נכתבה המשנה אם אנשי כנסת הגדולה התחילו לכתוב וכתבו חכמי כל דור ודור מקצתה עד שבא רבי וחתמה). The question seems to allude to the position of Rav Sa'adya as recorded in *Sefer Ha-Galui*. See HANOCH ALBECK, INTRODUCTION TO THE MISHNAH 65–66 (1959); Rosen-Zvi, *Introduction to the Mishnah*, *supra* note 46, at 12n. 51. For *Sefer Ha-Galui* see most recently RAV SAADYA GAON, in THE FOCUS OF

can be traced back to Sinaitic revelation, and which was well-known to the early sages, and its textualization-crystallization in the Mishnah[50] (albeit in oral form).[51] As explained by Robert Brody,

> there was no need in Second Temple times for a specific formulation of the tradition, which was universally agreed upon and understood; each master was free to transmit the material to his students in any style he chose. It was only with the crisis surrounding the destruction of the Temple that misunderstandings and doubts proliferated and the need for an established text was perceived, and only in the days of R. Judah the Prince was the time ripe for the production of such a text, which was immediately recognized as the canonical Mishnah.[52]

The Oral Torah's textualization-crystallization realized in Rabbi's codificatory project is described in the epistle in the following manner:

> And authority was bestowed upon Rabbi (from Heaven) together with his Torah, for his entire generation was subservient to him all of his days. As we have learned (*b. Git.* 59a): Rava the son of R. Abba said, and some say (it was) R. Hillel the son of Rabbi: from the days of Moses until Rabbi, we have not found Torah and authority combined in one person (lit. "in one place") . . . In his days, the rabbis were spared all persecution due to the love (Emperor) Antoninus had for him. He (=Rabbi) then decided to arrange/systematize the law, so that the rabbis would recite it uniformly rather than each his own version. Since, those early rabbis before the destruction of the Temple did not require this (=a crystallized version of the Oral Torah) since it is an oral Torah and they did not receive the rationales of known matters in the form of the Written Torah. Rather, the rationales were preserved in their hearts, and each of them taught his students just as a person conveys a matter to his friend in whatever manner of speech he fancies. And as they convened in the Temple and the academies, the legal matters arranged in their hand, with authority and without fear and anxiety, they were aided from Heaven insofar as the underlying rationales of the Torah were as clear to them as the law given to Moses at Sinai . . . And in the days of Rabbi, their matters were aided, so that the words of the Mishnah were just as they were pronounced by the Almighty and they were like a sign and a wonder. But Rabbi did not compose (these matters) on his own accord (lit. "out of his own heart"). Rather, (they were) the words recited by some of those early rabbis.[53]

The Mishnah's status as the complete and ultimate textual embodiment of God's Oral Torah is reflected in the assertion that "the words of the Mishnah were just as they were pronounced by the Almighty." While Sherira acknowledges and discusses

Controversies in Baghdad: Saadya's Sefer ha-Galuy and Mevasser's Two Books of Critique of Him 80–167 (Joshua Blau & Joseph Yahalom eds., 2019).

50 See Blidstein, *Oral Torah*, *supra* note 43.

51 At least according to the French recension (MS Aleppo) of Rav Sherira's Epistle, which is generally regarded as more reliable than the Spanish one, the author was acutely aware of the oral nature of the Mishnah's compilation. See Brody, Geonim, *supra* note 43, at 21–22.

52 *Id.*, at 278–79.

53 Iggeret, *supra* note 43, at 21–23 (French recension).

the specific historical circumstances that led to the compilation of the Mishnah by Rabbi many years after the moment of the Sinaitic revelation, he insists on the fact that the final product of the Mishnah reflects the exact words pronounced by God to Moses.

Elsewhere in the epistle, Sherira alludes to social convention and the consensus of the sages and nation at large as constitutive of the Mishnah's jurisprudential status as the ultimate source of rabbinic law.[54] In this passage, however, he seems to ground the Mishnah's unique status in divine providence and inspiration.[55] Talya Fishman[56] notes in this regard that Sherira makes unprecedented claims, not only about the legal status of the Mishnah, but also about its theological status, portraying Rabbi as an agent in a divinely guided project aimed at a comprehensive textual articulation of the Oral Torah. It is God who revealed the Oral Torah to Moses at Sinai and it is he who, after many generations, guided the compilation of the Mishnah, so as to systematically articulate its accurate words. The divine characteristics of the Mishnah are manifest, accordingly, in the providential support that accompanied its production, which is reflected in the fact that Rabbi encountered no objection or difficulty, from within or from without the rabbinic community, to hinder his ambitious compilation project. The Mishnah's "divine" status is further reflected in its textual, stylistic, and organizational "perfection."[57] "And when everyone saw the beauty of the Mishnah's arrangement and the truth of its reasoning and the precision of (its) words, they all abandoned those (other) tannaitic teachings they had been reciting."[58]

Fishman further notes in this context that Sherira's allusions to divine guidance and the stylistic and linguistic "perfection" of the Mishnah are reminiscent of contemporaneous Islamic rhetoric concerning the Quran's inimitability (*i'jāz al-Qur'ān*).[59] Like the Quran's inimitable and miraculous nature, which is believed to be manifest in its perfect style, the uniqueness of its language, and its concise nature,[60] Sherira emphasizes the Mishnah's textual, stylistic, and organizational "perfection" in rather similar

54 Yishai Kiel, *Reinventing Yavneh in Sherira's Epistle: From Pluralism to Monism in the Light of Islamicate Legal Culture*, in STRENGTH TO STRENGTH: ESSAYS IN HONOR OF SHAYE J. D. COHEN 515 (Brown Judaic Studies ed., 2018).

55 This duality in the epistle was briefly noted in Blidstein, *Oral Torah*, *supra* note 43, at 83.

56 Talya Fishman, *Claims about the Mishnah in the Epistle of Sherira Gaon: Islamic Theology and Jewish History*, in BEYOND RELIGIOUS BORDERS: INTERRELIGIOUS INTERACTION AND INTELLECTUAL EXCHANGE IN THE MEDIEVAL ISLAMIC WORLD 65, 67 (David Freidenreich & Miriam Goldstein eds., 2012).

57 See TALYA FISHMAN, BECOMING THE PEOPLE OF THE TALMUD: ORAL TORAH AS WRITTEN TRADITION IN MEDIEVAL JEWISH CULTURES 41 (2011).

58 IGGERET, *supra* note 43, at 30 (French recension).

59 Fishman, *Claims about the Mishnah*, *supra* note 56, at 67; FISHMAN, PEOPLE OF THE TALMUD, *supra* note 57, at 41–42, 249n. 131. For the doctrine of *i'jāz al-qur'ān*, see Richard C. Martin, *Inimitability* in ENCYCLOPÆDIA OF THE QURAN 2:526 (available at https://referenceworks.brillonline.com/entries/encyclopaedia-of-the-quran/inimitability-EQCOM_00093).

60 These facets, I might add, are emphatically stressed throughout Shāfi'ī's epistle on legal theory. See, e.g., SHĀFIʿĪ, RISĀLA, 53–71 [THE EPISTLE ON LEGAL THEORY: A TRANSLATION OF SHĀFIʿĪ'S RISĀLA 22–28 (Joseph Lowry trans., 2015)].

terms. While Jewish authors more commonly participated in this type of discourse by arguing for the perfection and conciseness of scripture (often in response to Islamic claims of *taḥrīf* ["distortion, falsification"]), Sherira seems to extend the contours of this discourse by making similar claims about the Mishnah.

Sherira further grounds the authority of the Mishnah in a myth, according to which the closure and canonicity associated with Rabbi's codificatory project were predestined and prophesied in the "Book of Adam:"[61] "As explained in the Book of Adam: Rabbi and R. Nathan are the end of Mishnah."[62]

The narrative and mythical framework in which Sherira couches his jurisprudence lends itself to a "Coverian" analysis focused on the interplay of nomos and narrative[63] and the grounding of legal cultures in constitutional "myths."[64] In line with Robert Cover's view of the normative sphere as one defined not only by statutes and legal institutions but also by narratives and myths providing meaning to the law, I read the providential support guiding Rabbi's codificatory project, the miraculous alignment of the Mishnah's wording with the Sinaitic articulation of the Oral Torah, and the predestination of Rabbi's endeavors prophesied in the "Book of Adam," as the narrative context for Rav Sherira's jurisprudence. In this framework, the textual-statutory confinement of the Oral Torah and the view of the Mishnah as "authored" and articulated by God are confirmed and validated through the narrative and mythical framework.[65]

Rav Sherira's jurisprudential claims on behalf of the Mishnah, however, are not simply upheld by the mythical and narrative framework. While the miraculous and divine characteristics of the Mishnah indeed support its unique status, it is not entirely clear how the myths surrounding the Mishnah square with its jurisprudential construction as the ultimate source of Jewish law. Does the Mishnah's exclusive jurisprudential status rest on its divine and miraculous qualities or on the positivist notion of social convention reflected in the consensus of the sages and nation at large. As in Cover's model, the sphere of narrative and myth does not simply and

61 For Sherira's employment of the "Book of Adam" see David, *As Explained in the Book of Adam*, *supra* note 43.

62 IGGERET, *supra* note 43, at 59 (French recension), based on *b. B. Metz.* 85b–86a. Sherira further argues based on the talmudic tradition that, "in this manner, (rabbinic) instruction accumulated generation after generation until Ravina at whose time it ceased. As Samuel, the astronomer, had seen written in the Book of Adam: Ashi and Ravina are the conclusion of instruction" (IGGERET, *id.*, at 69). See also IGGERET, *id.*, at 28: "And our rabbis have taught that even Adam took joy in R. Akiva's Torah, when the Holy One, blessed be he, showed him every generation and its sages."

63 See Robert Cover, *The Supreme Court, 1982 Term – Forward: Nomos and Narrative*, 97(4) HARV. L. REV. 4 (1983).

64 See Robert Cover, *Obligation: A Jewish Jurisprudence of the Social Order*, 5(1) JOURNAL OF LAW AND RELIGION 65, 66 (1987) (juxtaposing the foundational myths of Sinai and the Social Contract, which underly the Jewish and Western legal cultures).

65 For another example of Sherira's use of jurisprudential myths see Kiel, *Yavneh*, *supra* note 54 (regarding the founding rabbinic "council" at Yavneh)

uncomplicatedly uphold the nomos, but rather often problematizes its very assumptions.

Sherira's declaratory statements concerning the divine nature, not only of the Oral Torah per se, but also of its textual articulation in the Mishnah, reflect a "stenographic" model of revelation and a rhetoric of divine "authorship" of the law, as opposed to weaker interpretations of the law's divine origins underlying the "participatory" model of revelation. This seems to accord with the rhetoric of other late Geonic authorities, most notably Saʿadya, whose claims on behalf of God's "authorship" of the Oral Torah were often described as rhetorical overstatements/exaggerations, likely motivated by the Karaite challenge to rabbinic authority.[66] The revelatory model upheld by Saʿadya reflects the comprehensiveness and singularity of the Sinaitic revelation, the content of which might be "retrieved" by jurists, but is not "constituted" by them, and the rejection of "participatory" interventions in the content revealed.[67] Sherira's assertions to that effect might similarly be construed as ideologically motivated rhetoric countering Karaite claims.[68]

66 For Saʿadya's 'overstatements' in this regard and his anti-Karaite agenda, see, e.g., Brody, Geonim of Babylonia, *supra* note 43, at 96–99, 244–48; Marina Rustow, Heresy and the Politics of Community: The Jews of the Fatimid Caliphate 25–26 (2008); Jay Harris, How Do We Know This? Midrash and the Fragmentation of Modern Judaism 79 (1995); Eliezer Schlossberg, *Ha-pulmus be-yeṣirato shel rav saʿadya gaon* 126–27 Sinai 305 (2000–01); Marc Herman, Systematizing God's Law: Rabbanite Jurisprudence in the Islamic World from the Tenth to the Thirteenth Centuries 39–42 (PhD dissertation; University of Pennsylvania 2016); Marc Herman, *Prophetic Authority in the Legal Thought of Saadia Gaon*, 108(3) Jewish Quarterly Review 271, 278–81 (2018).

67 According to this approach, rabbinic midrash (ostensibly deriving the law by means of scriptural exegesis) should be regarded as an attempt to scripturally ground preexisting laws already known to the exegetes through tradition, rather than "real" law-generating activity. This paradigm associates midrash with "retrieval" rather than "constitution." The "retrieval" model is related theologically to the "authorial" and "stenographic" paradigms of revelation, both upholding the completeness and singularity of the Sinaitic revelation, while downplaying human involvement in the revelatory process. In addition to the studies by Halbertal (*supra* note 36) and Sommer (*supra* note 35) mentioned above see also Harris, How Do We Know This, *supra* note 66, at 73–102; Yohanan Silman, Qol gadol ve-lo yasaf: torat israel ben shelemut le-hishtalmut 39–69 (1999).

68 His hyperbolic rhetoric notwithstanding, Sherira advocates a somewhat more moderate version of the Oral Torah's revelatory status in comparison with Saʿadya. Robert Brody observes in this regard that, "In addition to literary crystallization … Sherira is willing to allow for a substantial degree of historical evolution in the specific contents of the Oral Torah, while at the same time maintaining the extreme antiquity of the tradition as a whole. Aside from doubts and controversies concerning the details of earlier traditions, new problems arose from time to time, which had to be resolved by analogy with established tradition. The essence of his position appears to be that all the later ramifications were contained *in potentia* in the earliest tradition and would have been clear to the earliest authorities had they considered these questions" (Brody, Geonim of Babylonia, *supra* note 43, at 279). Indeed, it would seem that Sherira's "formalistic" and "legalistic" rhetoric is complicated by the role (however limited) he assigns to human agency in the legal process. Compare with Maimonides' "cumulative" paradigm outlined in Halbertal, People of the Book, *supra* note 36, at 59–63. For the differences between Saʿadya and Sherira in this regard see Harry Fox, *Neusner's The Bavli and Its Sources, A Review Essay*, 80(3–4) Jewish Quarterly Review 353–54 (1990); Herman, Systematizing God's Law, *supra* note 66, at 63–64.

It must be stressed that the assertion of the textual-statutory demarcation of the Oral Torah (however rhetorical and hyperbolic) represents an unprecedented claim in rabbinic thought. The (few) talmudic sources that clearly subscribe to a theory of a dual Torah given at Sinai, one in writing and the other orally,[69] provide a rather loose definition of the content of this amorphous body of rabbinic tradition.[70] In fact, in as much as the textual and substantive limits of the Oral Torah remain undefined in the classical talmudic sources, any rabbinic tradition can tendentiously be subsumed under its authoritative wings. Any rabbinic tradition, be its source and origin as it may, can simply be integrated into the inchoate body of Oral Torah revealed at Sinai.[71] With the exception perhaps of a few talmudic statements,[72] the Oral Torah represented for the classical rabbis a dynamic and living tradition, not one that is textually and literarily demarcated and confined.[73]

By contrast, Sherira's innovative declaration (however exaggerated or overstated) regarding the Mishnah's exclusive status as the textual-statutory embodiment of the Oral Torah,[74] underwritten by the theological assertion that God himself guided and ordained the Mishnah's composition, has far-reaching ramifications on the theoretical perception of the law. Indeed, the idea that the law is textually confined is consistent with legal formalism and the (formal) principles of legality, both of which are largely uncharacteristic of the talmudic worldview. The epistle, moreover, does not simply assert the jurisprudential status of the Mishnah (and Talmud) as the ultimate and complete embodiment of God's law, but also represents an attempt to articulate the historiographic, mythical, and theological underpinnings of this stance.

While the Mishnah's perceived stylistic, linguistic, and organizational "perfection" might be regarded as more conducive to Sherira's presentation of it as a binding and canonical legal "code" containing the ultimate articulation of God's Oral Torah,[75] the Talmud is another story altogether. While the Talmud

69 For rabbinic controversy over the doctrine of the Oral Torah, see, e.g., *Sifra*, Behuqotai, 8:12 (ed. Weiss, 112b).

70 See, e.g., *Sifre Deuteronomy* 351 (ed. Finkelstein, 408) and *b. Git.* 60b. The ambiguity surrounding the actual content of the oral revelation at Sinai is highlighted in the famous story recorded in *b. Menah.* 29b.

71 See, e.g., *b. Yoma* 28b (cf. *m. Qid.* 4:14; *t. Qid.* 5:17).

72 See esp. *b. Ber.* 5a. See also Gerald Blidstein, *Oral Law as Institution in Maimonides*, in The Thought of Moses Maimonides 167, 175 (Ira Robinson et al. eds., 1990); Berakhyahu Lifschitz, *Minhag 'u-meqomo be-midrag ha-normot shel torah she-be-'al-peh*, 24 Shenaton ha-Mishpaṭ ha-Ivri 123, 213 (2006–07); Sommer, Revelation and Authority, *supra* note 35, at 253–54. For the fascinating textual history of this tradition see Roni Shweka, *The Tablets of Stone, the Law, and the Commandment*, 81 Tarbiz 343 [2013]).

73 See Halivni, The *Breaking of the Tablets*, *supra* note 27.

74 See also Sa'adya's claims at the beginning of the second part of his *Kitāb Tahsīl al-Sharā'i' al-Sam'iyya* ("Book on Attaining the Revealed Commandments"), according to which "This essay establishes the tradition known from the Mishnah and Talmud." See David E. Sklare, Samuel ben Hofni Gaon and His Cultural World: Texts and Studies 160 (1996).

75 As I mentioned, however, Sherira's claim constitutes a stretch even for the Mishnah, given the presence of numerous contradictions, duplications, and inconsistencies.

was, more or less, textually fixed by the time of Rav Sherira (that is, in terms of its content, sequence, and general order, notwithstanding ongoing lexical fluidity),[76] it hardly resembles a legal "code" in any meaningful sense.[77] And yet, Sherira (in line with other late Geonic authorities) portrayed the Talmud – alongside the Mishnah – (however rhetorically) as a canonical and binding statutory "code" and the ultimate source of Jewish law. Indeed, not unlike the textual-statutory demarcation of the Oral Torah in the text of the Mishnah, "They (=the Geonim) did battle not merely on behalf of an amorphous body of tradition, but also on behalf of a specific literary crystallization, the Babylonian Talmud, which serves as the flagship of that tradition ... the Talmud served as the source of authority, from which almost all legal decisions were to be derived."[78]

76 Jacob Nahum Epstein has argued that the Geonim preserved, at times, alternative "editions," which predate "our edition" of the Talmud. See, e.g., JACOB NAHUM EPSTEIN, STUDIES IN TALMUDIC LITERATURE AND SEMITIC LANGUAGES 2:378 (3 vols., Melamed ed., 1983–91). See, more recently, Yoav Rosenthal, *On the Early Form of Bavli Mo'ed Qatan 7b-8a*, 77(1) TARBIZ 45–70 (2007). Others maintain that significant textual variants preserved by the Geonim stem neither from earlier stages of the Talmud's consolidation and redaction nor from the later history of the Talmud's textual transmission, but rather from an intermediate stage of development in which the Talmud's content and order were largely determined, but its language and phraseology remained fluid. See, e.g., Eliezer S. Rosenthal, *The History of the Text and Problems of Redaction in the Study of the Babylonian Talmud*, 57 TARBIZ 1 (1988); Eliezer S. Rosenthal, *'iyunim be-toledot Ha-nosakh shel hatalmud ha-bavli*, in JUBILEE BOOK IN HONOR OF RABBI MORDECHAI BREUER 2:571 (2 vols.; Moshe Bar Asher ed., 1992); Robert Brody, *Geonic Literature and the Talmudic Text*, in MEHQERE TALMUD 1: 237, 275 (Yaakov Sussman & David Rosenthal eds., 1990). Still others have argued that even the more "significant" textual variants generally reflect later developments in the history of the Talmud's textual transmission, stemming from "creative transmission" and deliberate interventions in an attempt to improve the text. See, e.g., Shamma Friedman, *On the Formation of Textual Variation in the Bavli*, 7 SIDRA 67, 73–74 (1991). For a recent summary and reevaluation of this matter see FUCHS, THE GEONIC TALMUD, *supra* note 47, at 28–29, 53.

77 See, e.g., FISHMAN, PEOPLE OF THE TALMUD, *supra* note. 57, at 1 ("When considered from certain vantage points, the Talmud's role as a guide to Jewish life is bewildering. Though construed as a legal reference work, a significant proportion of the Talmud's content does not pertain to law, and the legal traditions themselves are presented in the form of pending disputes (critical scholars have determined that the resolved disputes are actually late interpolations into the talmudic text). In other words, there is no evidence that the sages whose teachings are preserved in the Talmud, Babylonian amoraim of the third through sixth centuries C.E. intended to produce a prescriptive guide to applied Jewish law"); BRODY, GEONIM OF BABYLONIA, *supra* note 43, at 161 ("The Talmud is an extremely complex literary work, comprising legal and other materials, which evolved over several centuries. Even in its legal portions, many discussions are wholly or partly of an academic nature, and many disputes on practical issues remain unresolved. Furthermore, the material is not organized systematically, in the style of a legal code; a single issue may figure in a variety of contexts, and the relationship (if any) between the various discussions, as well as the weight to be assigned to them in deriving legal conclusions, is rarely self-evident. We have no way of knowing to what extent, if at all, the 'editors' of the Talmud – as distinct from the authors of the legal dicta embedded within it – intended to create a normative legal work rather than an academic or literary corpus").

78 BRODY, GEONIM OF BABYLONIA, *supra* note 43, at 161–62.

As in the case of the Mishnah, Sherira provides us with a theological, mythical, and narrative framework for the unique canonical status of the Talmud. In this context, the epistle maintains a structural and thematic equivalence between the historical processes and conditions that led to the composition of the Mishnah by Rabbi and those which led to the redaction of the Talmud by Ravina and Rav Ashi. Sherira emphasizes, moreover, that, much like Rabbi, Rav Ashi enjoyed the undivided subservience of his colleagues, employing the very same phraseology to portray the two monumental projects. There is even a hint at divine providence, which ostensibly accompanied and guided the redaction of the Talmud by Ravina and Rav Ashi:

> During all those years from after (the time of) Rav Papa, Rav Ashi was Gaon at Sura and he had come to Mata Mehasya … and his Torah and authority were affluent and abundant. And Huna bar Nathan, who was the exilarch during his days, and Maremar and Mar Zutra who came after him, were all subordinate to Rav Ashi … as we learned: "Rav Aha the son of Rava said: we too may say that from the days of Rabbi until Rav Ashi, we have not found Torah and authority combined in one person (lit. 'in one and the same place')".[79]

Sherira further asserts that, just like Rabbi's codification project, the canonization and closure associated with Ravina and Rav Ashi's redactorial project were predestined and revealed in the Book of Adam. Indeed, after Ravina and Rav Ashi legislative instruction ceased, while only interpretation and analogical-inductive reasoning based on the canonical sources remained within the purview of legitimate juristic activity.

> In this manner, (rabbinic) instruction accumulated generation after generation until Ravina at whose time it ceased. As Samuel, the astronomer, had seen written in the Book of Adam[80]: Ashi and Ravina are the conclusion of instruction. And after (this), although there was no instruction, there were interpretations and logical inferences, which are close to instruction, and those rabbis were called *rabbanan sabora'e* (lit. "the rabbis who conduct logical inferences").[81]

The epistle thus stresses the normative and theological equivalence between the canonical status of the Mishnah and that of the Talmud. By asserting that the composition and redaction of the Talmud was divinely guided, predestined, and socially ratified, Sherira lays the foundation for the unique jurisprudential status of the Talmud, alongside the Mishnah, as the ultimate source of Jewish law and the exclusive and complete textual articulation of God's Oral Torah.

79 IGGERET, *supra* note 43, at 90–91 (based on *b. Git.* 59a). Compare Sherira's assertion above, according to which "from the time of Moses until the time of Rabbi we did not find Torah and authority in one and the same place."

80 See David, *Book of Adam*, *supra* note 43, and the discussion above.

81 IGGERET, *supra* note 43, at 69 (French recension).

III SHĀFIʿĪ AND THE TEXTUAL-STATUTORY DEMARCATION OF ISLAMIC LAW

Shāfiʿī is often credited in the literature as the "architect" of Islamic jurisprudence and the promulgator of the "four-sources" theory of Islamic law – that is, the idea that Islamic law is based on four "roots": Quran, Hadith, consensus (*ijmāʿ*), and analogy (*qiyās*).[82] It has correctly been noted, however, that, since consensus and analogy are in fact viewed by him as subordinate to, and dependent on, the textual sources and not as independent sources of law from which new directives can be derived, they should not be regarded as "official" sources of Islamic law, certainly not on a par with the Quran and Hadith.[83]

Joseph Lowry has argued in this regard that the various combinations of Quran and Hadith indicated by the concept of *bayān* lies at the heart of the jurisprudential theory presented in Shāfiʿī's epistle.[84] According to this theory, the entirety of the law resides in the complementarity of Quran and Hadith, while all legal norms are necessarily and by definition manifested through one of five possible combinations of these sources: (1) Quran alone; (2) Quran and Hadith together, each expressing

[82] For the "four-sources" theory of Islamic law and Shāfiʿī's epistle, see, e.g., Joseph Schacht, An Introduction to Islamic Law 59–60 (1964).

[83] Joseph Lowry, *Does Shāfiʿī Have a Theory of 'Four Sources' of Law?* in Studies in Islamic Legal Theory 23 (Bernard Weiss ed., 2002). Compare also Hallaq, Islamic Legal Theories, *supra* note 14, at 29 ("It is no wonder then that the bulk of the treatise [=Shāfiʿī's epistle] is devoted to a discussion of the Sunna, its types, interpretation, and its function in elaborating the Sharīʿa. Nearly everything else seems tangential, discussed to a greater or lesser extent in order to shed light on, or expound, the Sunna. In insisting on Prophetic Sunna as the only binding textual authority next to the Quran, Shāfiʿī was arguing for a law that would be exclusively divine in its origin, and this required that he explain the manner in which non-textual sources – i.e., consensus and *qiyās* – may be utilized while maintaining the fundamental proposition that law derives from the Divine will.")

[84] See Lowry, Early Islamic Legal Theory, *supra* note 28, at 23–24; Joseph Lowry, *Some Preliminary Observations on al-Šāfiʿī and Later* Uṣūl al-Fiqh: *The Case of the Term* Bayān, 55(5–6) Arabica 505 (2008). The idea that the Quran and Hadith are the only binding and authoritative legal sources articulating the totality of God's revelation can also be seen as an argument for the very authority of Prophetic Hadith alongside the Quran. See, e.g., Hallaq, Islamic Legal Theories, *supra* note 14, at 29; Lowry, Early Islamic Legal Theory, *id.*, at 165 ("It also seems clear from the structure of the law as portrayed in the Risalā and from some of Shāfiʿī's remarks therein that Shāfiʿī considered the prophetic Hadith to be revelation, on a par in that respect with the Quran"); Shāfiī, Risāla, *supra* note 60, at 101 [translation, at 150]. ("Moreover, He paired the wisdom [understood as the practice of God's Emissary] imparted by Prophetic Practice with His Book, and made it to follow the Book") See also Shāfiī, Risāla, *supra* note 60, at 98 [translation, at 39]. ("Al-Shāfiʿī said: God put his Emissary in a position relative to His religion, His obligations, and His Book, in a way that clarified that He had made him a signpost of His religion. He did this by imposing the obligation to obey him and making disobedience to him unlawful. God also provided a clear statement about his excellence by pairing together faith in his Emissary and faith in Him"); and Shāfiī, Risāla, *supra* note 60, at 285–86 [translation, at 103].("I said to him: If it were permissible to abandon a Prophetic practice – because of the conclusions arrived at by some, out of ignorance of the position of such practices relative to the Book (=the Quran) – then one could abandon what we have mentioned above ... Whoever holds such an opinion invalidates the totality of the practices of God's Emissary, and that opinion is a sign of the ignorance of the one who holds it").

the same rule; (3) Quran and Hadith together, whereby the Hadith elaborates that which is only briefly mentioned in the Quran; (4) Hadith alone; (5) and, finally, in case the law is not manifest in either the Quran or the Hadith, one is authorized to engage in *ijtihād* (legal reasoning) and *qiyās* (analogical-inductive reasoning) based on strict inferences from the Quran and Hadith. Thus, according to Shāfiʿī, only the textual-statutory sources (i.e., the Quran and Hadith) should be regarded as binding legal sources.

Shāfiʿī's legal theory – namely, the idea that the Quran and Hadith enjoy an exclusive position as the primary sources of Islamic law, while consensus and legal reasoning are subordinate to the authority of the textual-statutory sources – was developed against the foil of competing theories, which recognized other legal sources as independent sources of law on a par with the Quran and Hadith. At the risk of oversimplification, early Islamic legal theory can be described as divided along the lines of legal "rationalists" (*ahl al-ra'y*), who used reason in addition to textual sources to determine the law, and legal "traditionalists" (*ahl al-ḥadīth*), who relied exclusively on the textual sources, the Quran and Hadith, to determine the law. The camps of legal "traditionalists" and "rationalists" represent in fact two extremes, while most jurists occupied a range of attitudes situated in between the two poles.[85] The followers of al-Ẓāhirī were regarded as the most extreme "traditionalists," insofar as they relied exclusively on the manifest meaning of the Quran and rejected, not only the use of independent reasoning/discretion (*ra'y*), but also more restricted forms of logic included under the rubric of *qiyās*.[86] Close by were the followers of Ibn Ḥanbal.[87] The early Ḥanafīs were situated on the opposite end of the

85 For surveys see, e.g., Joseph Schacht, The Origins of Muhammadan Jurisprudence, 98–132, 311–28 (1982); Aron Zysow, The Economy of Certainty: An Introduction to the Typology of Islamic Legal Theory 159–258 (2013); Hallaq, Islamic Legal Theories, *supra* note 14, at 82–124.

86 For Ẓāhirī "scripturalism" and the rejection of reason and logic see, e.g., Ignaz Goldziher, The Ẓāhirīs: Their Doctrine and Their History 11–18 (trans. W. Behn, 1971); Zysow, Economy of Certainty, *supra* note 85, at 167–87; David Vishanoff, The Formation of Islamic Hermeneutics: How Sunni Legal Theorists Imagined a Revealed Law 78–88 (2011); Robert Gleave, Islam and Literalism: Literal Meaning and Interpretation in Islamic Legal Theory 147–50 (2013). On the Ẓāhirī madhhab in general see Amr Osman, The Ẓāhirī Madhhab (3rd/9th–10th/16th Century): A Textualist Theory of Islamic Law 11–47 (2014); Devin Stewart, *Muḥammad b. Dawūd al-Ẓāhirī's Manual of Jurisprudence, al-Wuṣūl ilā Ma'rifat al-Uṣūl*, in Studies in Islamic Legal Theory 99–158 (Bernard Weiss ed, 2002); Abū Ḥanīfa Numān ibn Muḥammad (al-Qāḍī al-Numān), The Disagreements of the Jurists: A Manual of Islamic Legal Theory 212–67 (Devin Stewart ed., 2015). On Ibn Ḥazm's rejection of *qiyās* see George F. Hourani, Reason and Tradition in Islamic Ethics 167–89 (1985); F. I. Abdallah, *Notes on Ibn Ḥazm's Rejection of Analogy (Qiyās) in Matters of Religious Law*, 2 American Journal of Islamic Social Sciences 207–224 (1985); J. P. Montada, *Reason and Reasoning in Ibn Ḥazm of Cordova*, 92 Studia Islamica 165–85 (2001). On Ibn Ḥazm's connections with the Ẓāhirīs see Camilla Adang, *The Beginnings of the Ẓāhirī Madhhab in al-Andalus*, in The Islamic School of Law: Evolution, Devolution, and Progress 117–25 (Peri J. Bearman et al. eds., 2005).

87 See, e.g., Goldziher, The Ẓāhirīs, *supra* note 86, at 81–84; Schacht, Origins, *supra* note 85, at 128–32; Hourani, Reason and Tradition, *supra* note 86, at 273–74. On Ibn Ḥanbal's legal theory see in general Christopher Melchert, Ahmad Ibn Hanbal (2006); Saud Al Sarhan, *The Responsa of Aḥmad Ibn Ḥanbal and the Formation of Ḥanbalism*, 22 Islamic Law and Society 18 (2015).

spectrum, as they tended to embrace a relatively wide range of legal practices associated with reason and discretion, which extended far beyond the strict use of analogical-inductive reasoning (*qiyās*).[88] Shāfiʿī, who launched a systematic critique of the early Ḥanafī use of arbitrary forms of reason, offered a "compromise," rejecting those dimensions of *ra'y* that were associated with subjective and independent reasoning, while accepting the doctrine of *qiyās* in the sense of strict analogical-inductive reasoning based on the textual sources. Thus, he asserts:

> No one may express an opinion except on the basis of analogy (قياس) ... "Do you yourself," he continued, "permit someone to say: I employ preference without analogy" (استحسن بغير قياس)? "In my view," I replied, that is not permissible for anyone – though God knows best. Only scholars should express any such opinions at all, not others, and they should express opinions that are related to a report (الخبر) by following such a report, and in situations in which there is no report, by analogizing from a report (بالقياس على الخبر). If it were permissible to invalidate an analogy, then it would be permissible for the rationalists (لاهل العقول), who are not scholars of religious knowledge (اهل العلم), to express opinions, concerning matters for which there is no report according to whatever answer they happen to have at hand based on preference (من الاستحسان). Opinions given on the basis of anything other than a report or analogy are impermissible (وإن القول بغير خبر ولا قياس لَغير جائز).[89]

Shāfiʿī also rejected Ibn ʿUlayya's (d. 834) view of consensus (*ijmāʿ*) as an independent legal source and insisted, in contrast to the view of Ibn Ḥanbal and others who accepted a broad definition of Hadith, that only authentic Prophetic Hadith should be deemed authoritative and binding.[90] In the present context, it is particularly instructive to examine Shāfiʿī's jurisprudential theory against the backdrop of the ideas espoused by his former master, Mālik b. Anas (d. 796), according to whom the ongoing communal practice and collective tradition of Medina, the city of the Prophet, vouchsafed and preserved by the Medinan scholars and those who received from them, should be regarded as a jurisprudential source of law and an independent site of revelation, alongside the Quran and Hadith.[91] The authority vested in the Medinan

88 See Hallaq, Islamic Legal Theories, *supra* note 14, at 107–08; Rumee Ahmed, Narratives of Islamic Legal Theory 113–47 (2012); El-Shamsy, The Canonization of Islamic Law, *supra* note 17, at 22–28. After the ninth century, to be sure, Ḥanafī jurists "took steps to disassociate themselves from the reputation of being arbitrary reasoners." (Hallaq, Islamic Legal Theories, *id.*, at 108. See also Ahmed, Narratives of Islamic Legal Theory, *id.*, at 114).

89 Shāfiʿī, Risāla, *supra* note 60, at 613 [translation, at 213], from a chapter on subjective reasoning/preference (باب الاستحسان). Compare also Shāfiʿī, Risāla *supra* note 60, at 616 [translation, at 214: "If that is so, then scholars should not express any opinions in such cases except on the basis of religious knowledge – and the source of religious knowledge is a binding report – by means of an analogy from the indications of what is correct"].

90 Ibn Ḥanbal purportedly accepted the authority of nonprophetic hadith reports. See, e.g., Al Sarhan, *The Responsa of Aḥmad Ibn Ḥanbal*, *supra* note 87, at 38–39.

91 For discussions of Shāfiʿī's text-based jurisprudence as opposed to Mālik's custom-based jurisprudence see, e.g., Brannon Wheeler, Applying the Canon in Islam: The Authorization and Maintenance of Interpretive Reasoning in Ḥanafī Scholarship 43–45 (1996); Yasin Dutton, The Origins of Islamic Law: The Qur'an, the Muwatta and Madinan Amal 4–5 (1999); El-Shamsy, The

tradition can be described as customary, bottom-up, communal, memetic (*taqlīd*-based), and deontic, in contrast to the textual, top-down, hermeneutic (*ijtihād*–based), and epistemic nature of legal authority in Shāfiʿī's jurisprudence.[92] While the early theory of legal authority espoused by Mālik is largely consistent with the perception of legal authority found in the Talmud,[93] Shāfiʿī's construction of legal authority is more compatible with the rhetorical assertions of the late Geonim, most notably those of Saʿadya and Sherira.

In opposition to Mālik's reliance on bottom-up communal practice (*'amal*) as an independent source of law and carrier of revelation, Shāfiʿī sought to ground the entirety of Islamic law in the textual and revelatory authority vested in the Quran and Prophetic Hadith. The mimetic following of Medinan tradition was viewed by him as a negative form of *taqlīd* (imitation), contrasted with *ijtihād* (legal reasoning), which he understood as "the acceptance of a position without (textual-hermeneutic) evidence" (*qabūl qawl bi-lā ḥujja*).[94]

While Mālik exerted some influence on Shāfiʿī in the earlier stages of his career, in his final years, Shāfiʿī's critique of Mālik's communitarian construction of Islamic law and the jurisprudential and revelatory significance attached to Medinan practice (*'amal ahl al-madīna*) matured into a comprehensive polemical treatise entitled *Ikhtilāf Mālik* ("Disagreement with Mālik"), which was integrated into the Umm

Canonization of Islamic Law, *supra* note 17, at 63–68. For Mālik's theory of *'amal* see also Faruq Abd-Allah, Mālik's Concept of Amal in Light of Mālikī Legal Theory (PhD dissertation; University of Chicago, 1978); El-Shamsy, The Canonization of Islamic Law, *id.*, at 38–43. According to El-Shamsy (The Canonization of Islamic Law, *id.*, at 42), this understanding of Medinan tradition can serve as a corrective to the view of Schacht (An Introduction to Islamic Law, *supra* note 82, at 28–29), who argued that the earliest form of what later became the Islamic "legal school" (*maddhab*) was of regional nature ("This does not mean that the proto-Maliki school consisted of a unitary doctrine propagated by all Medinan scholars. Rather, the terms "the Medinans" [*al-madaniyyūn*] and "people of Medina" [*ahl al-madīna*] refer to scholars who claim to speak in the name of the Medinan tradition – irrespective of whether they form the majority or minority in Medina, or even whether they live in Medina at all. The early legal schools were regional in the sense that they were justified in regional terms"). See also the critique in Wael Hallaq, *From Regional to Personal Schools of Law? A Reevaluation*, 8 Islamic Law and Society 1 (2001).

92 For the Islamic notions of *taqlīd* (imitation) and *ijtihād* (legal reasoning) see, in general, Hallaq, History of Islamic Legal Theories, *supra* note 14, at 121–23.

93 See Kiel, *Authority of the Sages*, *supra* note 32; and Kiel, *Filial Piety*, *supra* note 31. To exemplify the notion of mimetic, interpersonal, and deontic authority characteristic of the Babylonian Talmud consider the anecdote in *b. Ber.* 62a (cf. *b. Hag.* 5b). The story rhetorically pushes the mimetic aspects of legal authority to its limits. While the student is reproached by his master for hiding under the bed, so as to obtain knowledge of proper sexual etiquette, the redactors give the final word to the student, who artfully justifies his actions by his need to learn Torah. This anecdote represents a Babylonian rabbinic reworking of a Palestinian rabbinic story concerning tannaitic authorities who followed their masters into the privy (*y. Ber.* 9:5 14c). For the relationship between the Palestinian and Babylonian versions, see Shamma Friedman, *A Good Story Deserves Retelling: The Unfolding of the Akiva Legend*, 3 *JSIJ* 73–76 (2004); Jeffrey Rubenstein, Stories of the Babylonian Talmud 211–14 (2010).

94 See Ahmed El-Shamsy, *Rethinking* Taqlīd *in the Early Shāfiʿī school*, 128 Journal of the American Oriental Society 1 (2008); El-Shamsy, The Canonization of Islamic Law, *supra* note 17, at 65–66.

(8:513–778).[95] In a passage contained in this work, Shāfiʿī points out the tendentious, amorphous and ambiguous employment of *'amal* by his Mālikī interlocutors:

> So, I cannot comprehend what you mean when you say *'amal*, nor do you seem to know it yourself according to what you have told me, nor could I find clarification with any one of you about what *'amal* or consensus (*ijmā'*) are. I am forced to conclude, then, that you simply call your own opinions *'amal* and consensus (*ijmā'*).[96]

In another passage, Shāfiʿī writes:

> I used to hold this opinion with this justification, but I stopped doing so, and may God grant me what is best; because I found some of them [the Medinans] claiming it as tradition (*sunna*), but then I did not find their claimed tradition to reach back to the prophet.[97]

This assertion highlights the significance Shāfiʿī attached to the textual basis of received tradition. Not unlike Sherira who stressed the reciprocal relationship of the textual-statutory sources and the established rabbinic tradition vouchsafed in the official custom of the two Geonic academies and courts, Shāfiʿī insisted on the reciprocity of received tradition and its textual-statutory embodiment in the form of reliable hadith-reports, in which context tradition is sifted through text and the textual reports are, in turn, validated and confirmed through an unbroken chain of tradition (*isnad*).

Ahmed El-Shamsy[98] argued that Shāfiʿī's epistle on legal theory represents a watershed in Islamic jurisprudence, insofar as the locus of legal authority is transferred in it from the living practice of the Muslim community to an increasingly demarcated canon of textual sources. Prior to Shāfiʿī, the Quran and *sunna* represented the "raw material" of religious law, vouchsafed in a vague notion of revelation, but, in no way, were regarded as the sole canonical embodiment of God's revelation. In this context,

95 El-Shamsy, The Canonization of Islamic Law, *id.*, at 63–64 (suggesting three gradual stages in the maturation of Shāfiʿī's position. In his earlier debate with the Ḥanafīs, "he still paid lip service to the Medinan legal tradition" [Umm 8:66, 84, 90]. In the debate with Ibn ʿUlayya "he declared local traditions to be unstable and equivocal" [Umm 9:25–26]. Only in the debate with Mālik he "would finally abandon the concept of a local legal tradition entirely").

96 Umm 8:739; El-Shamsy, The Canonization of Islamic Law, *supra* note 94, at 65. According to El-Shamsy, Shāfiʿī points out in this passage that "the anonymous '*'amal* of Medina' cannot in fact produce a single coherent result: it contains multiple contradictory voices but does not offer any systematic method for adjudicating among them … The reasons why certain sources – prophetic reports, scholars' opinions, and so on—were accepted as normative while others were not could not be deduced from an examination of the sources themselves, but only by reference to their reception, that is, whether or not they were followed by the community. This opacity rendered Mālik's *'amal* a 'black box.' One could not trace the reasoning that led to a particular ruling; one could only follow it blindly." For *'amal* as an early form of consensus see Lowry, Early Islamic Legal Theory, *supra* note 28, at 321–22; Dutton, The Origins of Islamic Law, *supra* note 91, at 35.

97 Umm 9:105; El-Shamsy, The Canonization of Islamic Law, *supra* note 17, at 67.

98 El-Shamsy, The Canonization of Islamic Law, *supra* note 94, at 3–4.

the Quran and *sunna* were continuously sifted through the filters of communal practice, local custom, and judicial discretion. Shāfiʿī's project of legal and theological canonization of the Quran and Hadith[99] validated their authority as the very fountain of Islamic normativity and embodiment of God's revelation.

Shāfiʿī's theory of the textual confinement of God's law and the elevation of the Quran and Hadith to canonical status as the exclusive sources of Islamic law and ultimate embodiment of divine revelation can shed light on Sherira's rhetoric surrounding the textual-statutory confinement of God's law in the text of the Mishnah-cum-Talmud. Both Sherira and Shāfiʿī voiced a clear formalist and legalistic rhetoric connected with the textual-statutory demarcation of the law and its perception as exhaustive, comprehensive, and self-sufficient. Both authors further manifested a discursive shift from communitarian, interpersonal, mimetic, customary, and deontic legal authority to textual, impersonal, hermeneutic, and epistemic legal authority focused on the exclusivity of the textual-statutory sources.

IV THE TEXTUAL-STATUTORY DEMARCATION OF ZOROASTRIAN LAW

Not unlike their Jewish and Islamic contemporaries, Zoroastrian jurists in the early Abbasid period similarly engaged in a "positivist" enterprise aimed at identifying the authoritative sources of Zoroastrian law. In this context, a formalist and legalistic rhetoric, confining the official sources of the law to a textual-statutory corpus, came to dominate "mainstream" Pahlavi literature. The Zoroastrian jurists sought to establish the normative and theological canonicity (and the textual contours) of the Avesta and Zand as the exclusive and complete articulation of Ohrmazd's[100] revelation of his law (Pahlavi *dād*; Avestan and Old Persian *dāta-*)[101] and tradition (Pahlavi *dēn*; Avestan *daēnā*)[102] to Zarathustra.[103] While the Zand itself goes back to the Sasanian period and probably earlier,[104] the ninth- and tenth-century Zoroastrian authors elevated the Zand to canonical and "official" status, both

99 Note the shift from the amorphous *sunna* to a corpus of Hadith.

100 Ohrmazd is the Pahlavi form of the name of the supreme Zoroastrian God, Ahura Mazdā (Avestan)/Ahuramazdā (Old Persian).

101 Kiel, *Reinventing Mosaic Torah*, *supra* note 23, at 339–47.

102 Skjærvø, *The Zoroastrian Oral Tradition*, *supra* note 29, at 20–25; Shaki, *Dēn*, *supra* note 29, at 279–81.

103 Certain scholars have attempted to marginalize the role of revelation in Zoroastrianism in comparison with Judaism and Islam. See, e.g., Janos Jany, Judging in the Islamic, Jewish and Zoroastrian Legal Traditions: A Comparison of Theory and Practice 45–50 (2012). See, however, the critique of this position in Kiel, *Authority of the Sages*, *supra* note 32, at 155–56 and Kiel, *Reinventing Mosaic Torah*, *id.*, at 339–47.

104 For a reconstruction of an Old Persian Zand from the Achaemenid period, see Prods Oktor Skjærvø, *Avestan Quotations in Old Persian? Literary Sources of the Old Persian Inscriptions*, *in* 4 Irano-Judaica 1 (Shaul Shaked & Amnon Netzer eds., 1999). See also Prods Oktor Skjærvø, *The Achaemenids and the Avesta*, in Birth of the Persian Empire, vol. 1: of The Idea of Iran 52 (Vesta Sarkhosh Curtis & Sarah Stewart eds., 2005).

normatively and theologically, and demarcated its substantive boundaries alongside the Avesta.

According to several accounts preserved in the *Dēnkard*, the Zand was revealed to Zarathustra in its entirety together with the Avesta, much like the rabbinic attempt to trace both the Written and Oral Torah back to Sinai and Shāfiʿī's argument that the revelation of the Book and Wisdom means the Quran and Prophetic Sunna (concretized in the Hadith). In a manner quite similar to Sherira's portrayal of Rabbi's endeavor to recover and retrieve the dispersed content of the Oral Torah revealed to Moses at Sinai (and Ravina and Rav Ashi's attempt to retrieve the underlying reasons of the Mishnah's rulings), the *Dēnkard* portrays a multigenerational project of rediscovery and retrieval of the lost/contaminated contents of the Avesta and Zand undertaken by a series of Iranian kings and sages, highlighting significant moments in this process:[105]

> Dārāy, son of Dārāy, having committed to writing the entire Avesta and Zand as it had been received by Zarathustra from Ohrmazd, commanded two copies to be made – one to be kept in the gubernatorial treasury and one in the Fortress of Books.
>
> Walaxš, son of Aškān, commanded a memorandum to be made and sent to the various provinces with orders for the safekeeping of the Avesta and Zand as it had come down in unadulterated form, as well as the teachings – to the extent each had escaped the harm and chaos caused by Alexander and the pillaging and robbing by the Romans and were now scattered throughout Ērānšahr – They remained with the sages in writing, but also in oral transmission.[106]
>
> His majesty Ardashir, king of kings, son of Pābag, guided on the straight path by Tansar, asked that all those scattered teachings be brought to the court. Tansar took charge: some he received, and some he left out of the "canon." And he issued the following order: As far as we are concerned, any exposition that differs from that in the Mazdayasnian Tradition, but which provides awareness and knowledge, is not inferior.
>
> Shapur (I), king of kings, son of Ardashir, brought back together the writings outside the Tradition on medicine, astrology and astronomy, time and place, nature and accident, becoming and decaying, transformation, logic and the many other

105 Dēnkard 4.15–21 (ed. Dresden, at 321–22). For the translation, see Shai Secunda, *The Talmudic Bei Abedan and the Sasanian Attempt to 'Recover' the Lost Avesta*, 18 Jewish Studies Quarterly 343 (2011); Shai Secunda, The Iranian Talmud: Reading the Bavli in its Sasanian Context 59 (2013). See also Mansour Shaki, *The Denkard Account of the History of the Zoroastrian Scriptures*, 49 Archiv Orientální 114 (1981); Shlomo Pines, *A Parallel between Two Iranian and Jewish Themes*, 2 Irano-Judaica 41 (1990); Carlo Cereti, La Letteratura Pahlavi: Introduzione ai testi con riferimenti alla storia degli studi ed alla tradizione manoscritta 59–61 (2001); Cantera, Studien, *supra* note 12, at 106–13; Kevin T. Van Bladel, The Arabic Hermes: From Pagan Sage to Prophet of Science 30–39 (2009).

106 The notion that the Avesta and Zand "remained with the sages in writing, but also in oral transmission," while attributed to a much earlier period, is reflective of the situation at the time of the text's redaction, i.e., the Abbasid period, in which the Zoroastrian tradition was well on its way of being committed to writing, but remained pervasively oral nonetheless. This was also the situation on the Jewish and Islamic side.

crafts and skills that were scattered in India, Rome, and other lands. He compared them with the Avesta and ordered any blemish-free copy to be given to the gubernatorial treasury. And he put up for discussion whether to place with the Mazdayasnian tradition all those that were not contaminated . . .

Shapur (II), king of kings, son of Ohrmazd, brought everything that was said up for discussion and examination in the dispute with all of the countrymen regarding what constitutes contamination of the waters. After Adurbād escaped unharmed by the word of the ordeal, he said this too (in dispute) with both those (regular) heretics and Nask-studying heretics. And he also said: "Now, we have seen in this world, unless a person leaves his evil Tradition, we shall work on him diligently (to see that he does)." And, so he did.

The present majesty, Xusrō, king of kings, son of Kawād, it is told, when he had overcome heresies and false doctrines by fully opposing them, he increased greatly, according to what was manifest in the Tradition, in every heresy the awareness and detailed examination of the four branches (priests, soldiers, farmers, artisans).

Scholars have previously noted the motif of lost/scattered Iranian wisdom recovered by a series of figures, a trope attested in numerous accounts in Middle Persian, New Persian, and Arabic,[107] while also stressing the affinity between the Iranian trope and similar Jewish traditions concerning the retrieval of the lost wisdom of the Hebrews.[108] In the present context, I note that the *Dēnkard*'s emphasis on the process of retrieving the scattered contents of the Avesta and Zand,[109] which were "stenographically" recorded by Zarathustra from the mouth of Ohrmazd and handed down "in unadulterated form" from generation to generation, is reminiscent of Sherira's portrayal of the multigenerational transmission/retrieval of the Oral Torah and particularly the involvement of Rabbi, and Ravina and Rav Ashi, in this process. The emphasis on fighting off heresy and false doctrine[110] (and particularly disbelief in the authoritativeness of the Zand itself)[111] is similarly reminiscent of the Karaite challenge to rabbinic tradition, which seems to underlie (at least in part) Sherira's agenda in composing his epistle.[112]

107 Van Bladel, The Arabic Hermes, *supra* note 105, at 30–39.

108 Pines, *Two Iranian and Jewish Themes*, *supra* note 105, at 41–51.

109 Notably, according to the text, the lost Avesta and Zand are not identical to the scattered wisdom, although the kings and sages were involved in the collection and retrieval of both. While the scattered wisdom is purportedly contained at present in the *Dēnkard*, it would seem that the eighth book of the *Dēnkard* in particular constitutes an attempt to textually demarcate and delineate the contours of the Avesta and Zand, by classifying the contents of its twenty-one *nasks* ("books"). Cf. Stausberg, *The Invention of a Canon*, *supra* note 12, at 264–66 ("the twenty-one *nasks* of the *dēn* catalogued in *Dēnkard* book 8 are an attempt at classifying the entire religious tradition and not specifically the Avestan corpus as has been commonly assumed by the previous generation of scholars").

110 Cf. Secunda, Iranian Talmud, supra note 105, at 58–63 (contextualizing the reference in this passage to heretics with the talmudic *be abedan* (בי אבידן).

111 "Nask-studying heretics" (Pahlavi *nask-ōšmurdārān ī jud-ristagānēn*).

112 For the extent of the anti-Karaite undertones in Sherira's epistle, see, e.g., Sklare, Samuel ben Hofni, *supra* note 74, at 90; Gafni, *On Talmudic Historiography*, *supra* note 43, at 293; Blidstein, *Oral Torah*, *supra* note 43, at 74. See, however, the assessment in Brody, Geonim, *supra* note 43, at 20n. 5 ("A number of scholars have suggested that these questions were motivated by a need to defend the

The *Dēnkard*'s account clearly reflects a "retrieval" model of legal transmission and a "stenographic" theory of revelation, according to which the extant Zoroastrian Tradition is the result of retrieval and preservation of that which has already been received in complete form by Zarathustra (*hamāg abestāg ud zand čiyōn zarduxšt az ohrmazd padīrift*; "the entire Avesta and Zand, as it had been received by Zarathustra from Ohrmazd").

This perspective, to be sure, is novel.[113] The structure of the surviving works of Zand[114] (redacted circa the late Sasanian period) generally reflects a "cumulative" model of legal transmission (which may be connected with a "participatory" paradigm of revelatory theology), according to which each generation adds another layer of tradition and participates in an ongoing effort to "constitute" the revelatory content. In that sense, even the insights of later jurists are introduced in the Zand with the formula *pad abestāg paydāg* ("in the Avesta it is manifest").[115] According to the pre-Abbasid scheme, the jurists were perceived as legislators partaking in the creation of Zoroastrian law.[116] The *Dēnkard*'s account, by contrast, echoes a legal-theological shift in Zoroastrian thought towards a stenographic-retrieval model of legal revelation, one which is likely informed by the legal and theological shifts that took place in the Islamic and Jewish legal cultures of the time, as reflected, in the thought of Sherira and Shāfiʿī.

Several Pahlavi texts describe a council/convention headed by the Sasanian king Xusrō that is said to have taken place in the sixth century. An illuminating version of this event, found in the letters of Mānuščihr, maintains that Xusrō and his council of jurists were essentially responsible for the canonization of the corpus of Avesta and Zand and the demarcation of its literary contours and legal contents:[117]

integrity of rabbinic tradition against Karaite criticism, but it now appears that they are representative of some of the sorts of questions which occupied the Rabbanite intellectuals of Qayrawan in this period"). See also the explicit reference in Iggeret, *supra* note 43, at 107 (French recension): "And in those days after him Anan [b. David] came forth" (ובאותן הימים בתריה נפק ענן).

113 For contesting views of revelation in Zoroastrianism see, e.g., Shaul Shaked, *Esoteric Trends in Zoroastrianism*, 3 Proceedings of the Israel Academy of Sciences and Humanities 188–89 (1969); Yaakov Elman, *Scripture Versus Contemporary Needs: A Sasanian/Zoroastrian Example*, 28(1) Cardozo Law Review 154–56 (2006).

114 E.g., the Pahlavi translations and commentaries to the *Videvdad*, *Hērbedestān* and *Nērangestān*.

115 Traditionally, the term *paydāg* was translated "revealed," which highlights its theological undertones, but "visible, manifest" is more accurate. I would like to thank Prods Oktor Skjærvø for pointing this out to me.

116 See Kiel, *Authority of the Sages*, *supra* note 32, at 158–59.

117 An alternative reconstruction of Xusrō's council focuses on the "fighting off of heresy" and grapples with disbelief in the authoritativeness of the Zand. In addition to the *Dēnkard* passage above, see also Zand ī Wahman Yasn 2.1–4 ("In the Zand of the Wahman Yasn and Hordād Yasn and Aštād Yasn it is manifest that, one time, the accursed Mazdak son of Bām-Dād, the adversary of the religious Tradition (*dēn petyārag*), appeared. And they (i.e. his followers) brought adversity to the religious Tradition of the gods. And Xusrō of immortal soul summoned before him Xusrō son of Māh-Dād, Weh-Šāpūr, Dād-Ohrmazd the dastwar of Azerbaijan, and Ādurfarnbay the deceit-less, and Ādurbād, Ādur-Mihr and Baxt-Āfrīd. And he requested a pact of them: Do not keep these Yasnas in concealment, yet do not teach the Zand outside your offspring. They made a pact with Xusrō"). See The

> It was like when Weh-šābuhr showed in the assembly of Xusrō of immortal soul, king of kings, son of Kawād, the twenty-one divisions (of the Avesta and Zand)[118] so that the "sages" (lit. "magi") abided by it. And they sealed a document (*nibišt āwišt*) [119] so that it was the way the "sages" (lit. "magi") (agreed) with it and as it had been decided. And, afterwards, the "sages" (lit. "magi") agreed with all the decisions he showed them and they were unanimous (*ham-dādestān*): to regard (them) as something special, as being on the level of certainty,[120] and in firm usage.[121]

In line with Sherira's account of the canonization of the Mishnah by Rabbi and that of the Talmud by Ravina and Rav Ashi, Mānuščihr envisions the canonization of the Avesta and Zand by Weh-šābuhr, a Zoroastrian jurist and high-priest (*mowbedān mowbed*) who lived during the sixth century,[122] as a "constitutional" moment in legal and revelatory history. Much like the authorization of the Mishnah's codification by Antoninus, Mānuščihr stresses that the canonization of the Avesta and Zand took

Zand ī Wahman Yasn: A Zoroastrian Apocalypse 134 [transcription], 150 [translation] (Carlo G. Cereti ed., 1995); Cereti, La Letteratura Pahlavi, *supra* note 105, at 59–61; Cantera, Studien, *supra* note 12, at 106–13; Van Bladel, The Arabic Hermes, *supra* note 105, at 30–39. On the question of the historicity of this council see Philippe Gignoux, *Sur l'inexistence d'un Bahman Yasht avestique*, 32 Journal of Asian and African Studies 53, 54–57 (1986), but cf. Secunda, *On the Age*, *supra* note 12, at 321–24.

118 For the twenty-one *nasks* of the Avesta and Zand, see Vevaina, *Enumerating the Dēn*, *supra* note 29.

119 Although the "sealing" of a document indicates some sort of contract/agreement between the attendant jurists, it may also refer to the canonical "sealing" of the Avesta and Zand. It is noteworthy that the Aramaeogram for Pahlavi *āwištan* ("to seal") is HTYMWN, the same verb used by the Geonim to indicate the canonization and sealing of the Mishnah and Talmud. See, e.g., Iggeret, *supra* note 43, at 7 (French recension): "Until Rabbi came and sealed it (=the Mishnah)" (עד שבא רבי וחתמה). Sherira also uses the synonymous root סתם in this context. See Iggeret, *id.*, at 97: "And the Talmud was sealed" (ואיסתתים תלמודא). For the terminology and conceptualization of canonical "sealing" in the rabbinic tradition see Shlomo Z. Havlin, *On Literary Sealing as the Basis for Periodization in Halakha*, in Studies in Talmudic Literature 148, 154–62 (1983). Compare also the Islamic doctrine perceiving Muhammed as the "seal of prophets" (*khātam al-nabiyyīn*) first mentioned in Q. 33:40. The literature on the precise meaning of the Quranic phrase (finality, closure, confirmation?) and the history of the doctrine is vast. See the recent discussions in Uri Rubin, *The Seal of the Prophets and the Finality of Prophecy*, 164(1) Zeitschrift der Deutschen Morgenländischen Gesellschaft 65 (2014); David Powers, *Finality of Prophecy*, in The Oxford Handbook of the Abrahamic Religions 254 (A. Silverstein & G. Stroumsa eds., 2015). Also compare the notion of "closure of the gates of *ijtihād*" (*insidād bāb al-ijtihād*) in the Islamic tradition, for which see the classical study of Wael Hallaq, *Was the Gate of Ijtihad Closed?* 16(1) International Journal of Middle East Studies 3 (1984).

120 Compare the parallel interest in epistemological certainty in Islamic jurisprudence, for which see Zysow, The Economy of Certainty, *supra* note 85, at 1–4. For the Geonic context, see Sklare, Samuel ben Hofni Gaon, *supra* note 74, at 159 ("Islamic legal theory is epistemological is nature. The central question is which of the sources of law (scripture, tradition, analogy or consensus) provides certain knowledge of legal rules and which furnish only probable opinion. The authority or legitimacy of a source is determined by its epistemological status. The Geonim and their contemporaries largely adopted this conceptual structure.")

121 Mānuščihr, Nāmagīhā, 1.4.17–18 (trans. Prods Oktor Skjærvø [unpublished]). Cf. Maneck Fardunji Kanga, *Epistle 1, Ch. 4, of Mānuščihr ī Juwān-jamān: A Critical Study*, 27 Indian Linguistics 46, 56–57 (1966).

122 On this figure see Secunda, *On the Age*, *supra* note 12, at 323–25.

place at a council summoned by the Sasanian King Xusrō and was thus authorized by his majesty.[123] Mānuščihr further emphasizes the unique legal and theological status of the Avesta and Zand, which were (now) believed to contain the binding and complete articulation of God's revelation, pointing out that the jurists agreed "to regard (them) as something special, as being on the level of certainty, and in firm usage." Sherira and Mānuščihr similarly stress the submission of Weh-šābuhr's, and Rabbi's (and Ravina and Rav Ashi's), colleagues and their yielding to the canonization project; both stress the idea of finality and closure connected with the "sealing" of the canonized works; and, finally, both authors emphasize the consensus and unanimity of the jurists.

The legal and theological canonicity accorded by Mānuščihr to the Avesta and Zand and that accorded by Sherira to the Mishnah-cum-Talmud are similar in many ways to the claims made by Shāfiʿī regarding the status of the Quran and Hadith. All three authors seem to participate in the elevation of their respective sacred works to canonical status in a normative and theological sense, while attempting to demarcate and confine God's law to a textual corpus. They share a formalist and legalistic rhetoric, connected with the textual-statutory confinement of the law, its comprehensiveness, and self-sufficiency. They similarly advocate a strong "authorial" interpretation of the law's divinity, and display a "retrieval" model of legal transmission in which the jurists are entrusted merely with unearthing and discovering that which has already been revealed by God. The "councils" surrounding the canonization projects similarly serve the purpose of grounding the formalist and legalistic jurisprudential rhetoric of these authors, connected with the textual-statutory confinement of God's law, in a founding myth.

In his letters, Mānuščihr launched a scathing attack directed at his brother Zādspram, himself a jurist and high-priest, for seeking to relax the requirements of the *baršnūm* ceremony – an Avestan purification ritual lasting nine days and nights prescribed for the removal of severe contamination (especially corpse impurity)[124] – utilizing in its stead a much simpler ceremony (*pixag*) consisting merely of fifteen ablutions, which was initially prescribed for lighter forms of ritual impurity.[125]

[123] This can be further compared with the Islamic legend concerning the council commissioned by the third caliph ʿUthmān ibn ʿAffān, which produced the canonical and authoritative Uthmanic codex of the Quran. I would like to thank Ahmed El-Shamsy and David Flatto for (independently) calling my attention to this comparison.

[124] A detailed description of the *baršnūm* ceremony performed when a person becomes polluted by dead matter is given in *Videvdad* chs. 8 and 9. See Mary Boyce, *Barašnom* in Encyclopædia Iranica, 3:756–57 (available online at www.iranicaonline.org/articles/barasnom). For the grades of ritual impurity associated with the *baršnūm* and *pixag* purification rituals, see, e.g., J. K. Choksy, Purity and Pollution in Zoroastrianism: Triumph over Evil 23–52 (1989); Yishai Kiel, *Shaking Impurity: Exegesis and Innovative Traditions in the Babylonian Talmud and Pahlavi Literature*, in Encounters by the Rivers of Babylon: Scholarly Conversations Between Jews, Iranians and Babylonians in Antiquity 413–34 (Uri Gabai & Shai Secunda eds., 2014).

[125] Mānuščihr, Nāmagīhā, *supra* note 121, 3.1–2: "It has come to my, Mānuščihr son of Juwān-jam, *rad* of Pārs and Kirmān, attention that, in some areas of the land of the Iranians, those who have made

Among other things, Mānuščihr criticizes his brother Zādspram for relying on subjective and independent reasoning ("for he [=Zādspram] spoke his own view as it seemed to him" [*čē-š wēnišn xwēš čiyōn-iš sahist guft*])[126] that is not backed up by the textual-statutory sources. Mānuščihr further asserts: "The other things he [=Zādspram] wrote in connection with this – except for those (decisions) which are 'manifest' to him to be the words of Abarg and (contained) in (at least) one teaching (*čāštag*) among them – he adjudicated as it seemed to him and as he deemed (fit) (*sahist ī čiyōn-iš wizīrēnīd*)."[127] Mānuščihr seems to be accusing his brother Zādspram of issuing legal decisions on the basis of his own subjective reasoning and what seems to him (*sahist*) – rather than on the basis of the textual-statutory sources (the Avesta and Zand) – at least insofar as those decisions in which he does not rely on the teachings of Abarg and the other teachers of old recorded in the Zand.[128]

Read in the light of contemporaneous debates among Muslim and Jewish jurists regarding the jurisprudential and juridical status of reason, logic, and discretion, it would seem that the disagreement between Mānuščihr and Zādspram, two of the foremost jurists of the Zoroastrian community of Iran in the ninth-century, should be understood along similar lines. Mānuščihr, in line with the mainstream of legal "traditionalists," argues that the law is based on the textual-statutory sources, whereas Zādspram seems to have recognized independent reasoning based on subjective discretion as a legitimate source of adjudication. It is, admittedly, somewhat difficult to reconstruct the actual position of Zādspram, whose part of the correspondence (and other legal writings) did not survive.[129] But even to the extent that Mānuščihr might have misrepresented his brother's actual position, using him perhaps as a straw man

decisions that pollution from corpses and other pollution are in the category of other (pollution), that should be washed with the *pixag*, they are (now) washing fifteen times with *gōmēz* (bull's urine) and once with water and (then) regard their bodies as clean. And, when they approach the water, fire, and ritually clean *barsom* (twigs) they do so in the measure of what (they regard as) ritually clean. They say: 'Zādspram son of Juwān-jam ordered the priests to give this kind of washing,' which seemed to me quite terrible and burdensome and, to my feeling, grasp, and liking, quite backward."
Cf. M. F. Kanga, *Life and Letters of Manushchihr Goshnjam*, *in* PROF. POURE DAVOUD MEMORIAL 2:189, 198–99 (2 vols., 1951).

126 MĀNUŠČIHR, NĀMAGĪHĀ, *supra* note 121, at 1.6.5. Cf. Manek F. Kanga, *A Critical Study of Epistle I Ch. 6 and 7 of Manuščihr Gošnjaman*, in MEMORIAL J. DE MENASCE 251, 255 (Philippe Gignoux & Ahmad Tafazzoli eds., 1974).

127 MĀNUŠČIHR, NĀMAGĪHĀ, *supra* note 121, at 1.6.1. Cf. Kanga, *Epistle I* Ch. 6 *and* 7, *supra* note 126, at 254.

128 On the ancient sages recorded in the Zand see Philip Gignoux, *La controverse dans le mazdéisme tardif*, *in* LA CONTROVERSE RELIGIEUSE ET SES FORMES 127 (A. Le Boulluec ed., 1995); CANTERA, *supra* note 12 164–239; Secunda, *On the Age*, *supra* note 12. On the legal "teaching" (*čāštag*) [as opposed to the "practice" (*kardag*) of the courts] in Zoroastrian law see Janos Jany, *The Four Sources of Law in Zoroastrian and Islamic Jurisprudence*, 12(3) ISLAMIC LAW AND SOCIETY 291, 298–302 (2005). See also Shai Secunda, *The Sasanian "Stam": Orality and the Composition of Babylonian Rabbinic and Zoroastrian Legal Literature*, in THE TALMUD IN ITS IRANIAN CONTEXT 140, 154–57 (Carol Bakhos & Rahim Shayegan eds., 2010); Secunda, *On the Age*, *id.*, at 337–38. And see ŠĀYIST NĒ ŠĀYIST 1.3–4 [ŠĀYAST NĒ ŠĀYAST : A PAHLAVI TEXT ON RELIGIOUS CUSTOMS 28–29 (Jehangir C. Tavadia ed. and trans., 1930)].

129 Other (nonlegal) texts by Zādspram survived, namely the SELECTIONS OF ZĀDSPRAM (WIZĪDAGĪHĀ Ī ZĀDSPRAM), for which see ANTHOLOGIE DE ZADSPRAM : EDITION CRITIQUE DU TEXTE PEHLEVI TRADUIT ET

(not unlike certain Shāfiʿī attacks on Ḥanafī doctrine), the letters of Mānuščihr provide an indispensable glimpse into the legal theoretical discourse and concerns of Zoroastrian jurists in the ninth century. As such, Mānuščihr's juxtaposition of two competing theories of jurisprudence and adjudication, corresponding with the contemporaneous camps of legal "traditionalists" and "rationalists," however inaccurately attributed to individual jurists, constitutes an invaluable source for the reconstruction and contextualization of Zoroastrian legal theory within the broader legal theoretical "landscape" that pervaded the Islamicate Near East in the early Abbasid period.[130]

V CONCLUSION

In this article, I hope to have contributed to the unsettling of the Western bifurcation inherent in the "law and religion" paradigm, by examining the overlapping functions of the two categories as two sides of the same coin – law as religion, religion as law – in Jewish, Islamic, and Zoroastrian discussions of legality and revelation in the early Abbasid period. In this context, we saw that "religious" or "revelatory" rhetoric work in tandem to reflect a coherent jurisprudential view. In all three systems, we traced a process of theologization of the law (i.e., advocacy of strong "authorial" models of revelation and "retrieval" models of legal transmission, while minimizing in the process the role of human agency in effecting the content of revelation), on the one hand, and a process of textual demarcation and confinement (giving rise in embryonic fashion to the principle of "legality" entailing the law's prospectiveness and stability), on the other hand.

We saw that Sherira, Shāfiʿī, and Mānuščihr played a particularly significant role in framing and articulating the stakes of the normative and theological canonization of their respective religious traditions, by insisting on the textual confinement of God's revelation – as pronounced at the initial revelatory moment in unadulterated form – in the Mishnah-cum-Talmud, Hadith, and Zand, corpora which soon enough came to be regarded as the exclusive,

COMMENTÉ (Philippe Gignoux & Ahmad Tafazzoli eds., 1993). He is also reported to have written "The Book of the Enumeration of Races" (*nibēg ī tōhmag-ošmārišnīh*), a treatise which has not survived but must have contained a description of animal species. See Philippe Gignoux, *Zādspram*, in ENCYCLOPÆDIA IRANICA (online edition, available at www.iranicaonline.org/articles/zadspram).

130 Although Mānuščihr essentially belonged to the camp of legal "traditionalists," as opposed to that of legal "rationalists," he was clearly far-removed from the more extreme "traditionalist" (or rather "scripturalist") tendencies of Ẓāhirī and certain Ḥanbalī jurists, who relied exclusively on the manifest meaning of the textual sources. Beyond his affirmation of the living Zoroastrian tradition vouchsafed in the doctrines of judicial practice (*kardag*) and legal consensus (*ham-dādestānīh*), Mānuščihr was acutely aware of the ambiguity inherent in the Avesta and Zand and the fact that varying textual accounts – either Avestan verses or legal teachings recorded in the Zand – occasionally support contradictory legal positions. Although Mānuščihr does not address *qiyās* (or its equivalent) explicitly, it would seem that some form or another of analogical-inductive logic based on the textual sources is inherent in his recognition of the ambiguity characterizing the revealed sources. In that sense, Mānuščihr's legal theory seems to resemble that of Sherira and Shāfiʿī, insofar as all three authors shared an aversion to subjective legal reasoning, while making a limited concession to the employment of analogical-inductive logic strictly based on the textual sources.

complete, and authoritative articulations of the law (alongside the Torah, Quran, and Avesta). Indeed, the parallel diachronic shifts in each of these religious traditions point to a broader legal-theological turn in the Islamicate culture of the early Abbasid period, which has major implications for mapping the history of the dynamics of law and religion.

www.ingramcontent.com/pod-product-compliance
Lightning Source LLC
LaVergne TN
LVHW052026200926
848481LV00005B/1594
* 9 7 8 1 1 0 8 7 0 7 9 2 3 *